The
Riau Islands

The **ISEAS – Yusof Ishak Institute** (formerly Institute of Southeast Asian Studies) is an autonomous organization established in 1968. It is a regional centre dedicated to the study of socio-political, security, and economic trends and developments in Southeast Asia and its wider geostrategic and economic environment. The Institute's research programmes are grouped under Regional Economic Studies (RES), Regional Strategic and Political Studies (RSPS), and Regional Social and Cultural Studies (RSCS). The Institute is also home to the ASEAN Studies Centre (ASC), the Singapore APEC Study Centre and the Temasek History Research Centre (THRC).

ISEAS Publishing, an established academic press, has issued more than 2,000 books and journals. It is the largest scholarly publisher of research about Southeast Asia from within the region. ISEAS Publishing works with many other academic and trade publishers and distributors to disseminate important research and analyses from and about Southeast Asia to the rest of the world.

The SIJORI Series

The
Riau Islands
Setting Sail

Edited By
Francis E. Hutchinson
&
Siwage Dharma Negara

ISEAS YUSOF ISHAK INSTITUTE

First published in Singapore in 2021 by
ISEAS Publishing
30 Heng Mui Keng Terrace
Singapore 119614
E-mail: publish@iseas.edu.sg
Website: http://bookshop.iseas.edu.sg

The responsibility for facts and opinions in this publication rests exclusively with the authors and their interpretations do not necessarily reflect the views or the policy of the publisher or its supporters.

This publication is made possible with the support of Konrad-Adenauer-Stiftung.

KONRAD
ADENAUER
STIFTUNG

ISEAS Library Cataloguing-in-Publication Data

Name(s): Hutchinson, Francis E., editor. | Negara, Siwage Dharma, editor.
Title: The Riau Islands : setting sail / edited by Francis E. Hutchinson and Siwage Dharma Negara.
Description: Singapore : ISEAS – Yusof Ishak Institute, 2021. | The SIJORI series; volume 3. | Includes bibliographical references and index.
Identifiers: ISBN 9789814951050 (soft cover) | ISBN 9789814951067 (pdf) | ISBN 9789814951074 (epub)
Subjects: LCSH: Kepulauan Riau (Indonesia)—Economic conditions. | Kepulauan Riau (Indonesia)—Politics and government. | Kepulauan Riau (Indonesia)—Social conditions.
Classification: LCC HC448 R4R486

Typeset by Superskill Graphics Pte Ltd
Printed in Singapore by Mainland Press Pte Ltd

CONTENTS

LIST OF MAPS

Conclusion

LIST OF TABLES

LIST OF FIGURES

FOREWORD

In 2012, the ISEAS – Yusof Ishak Institute embarked on an ambitious research project to understand the cross-border regions of Southeast Asia. Aptly designated "Floating Frontiers", the project focused not on the land borders, but the maritime areas. It has long been recognized that the countries of maritime Southeast Asia—Indonesia, Malaysia, Singapore and the Philippines—share a history of rich connectivity in centuries past through movements of its seafaring peoples and development of strong networks of economic, cultural and social ties.

There have been three attempts in maritime Southeast Asia to create subregional projects. SIJORI (Singapore-Johor-Riau Islands) is the first and the most developed. BIMP-EAGA (Brunei-Indonesia-Malaysia-the Philippines-East ASEAN Growth Area) is the second, and the Indonesia-Malaysia-Thailand Growth Triangle (IMT-GT) the third.

Regarding SIJORI, in the 1970s and 1980s, Singapore and Malaysia saw deep and mutually beneficial engagement in cross-border investment and trade. The contemporary interest of Singapore in the Riau Islands began later in the late 1980s with Batam. That soon gained momentum, moving beyond Batam to Bintan and Karimun. Since the governments of Singapore, Malaysia and Indonesia decided to promote SIJORI, the growth triangle has seen the three territories register population and palpable economic growth.

This research project has produced its first fruit, a SIJORI trilogy. The *SIJORI Cross-Border Region: Transnational Politics, Economics, and Culture* was the first volume. Then came *Johor: Abode of Development?* The third book *The Riau Islands: Setting Sail* is the final volume in the trilogy. Together, the three volumes provide a textured and qualitative understanding of subregional architectures and the resulting dynamics. We hope the analyses, the body of knowledge and data can be of use by highlighting the necessary refinements and adjustments that officials and investors may wish to make to the existing framework in light of changing developments.

The Riau Islands documents and analyses what is happening on the ground and the potential of the islands. It covers a large area and the spillover of dynamism arising from its location at the fortuitous nexus of Indonesia, Singapore and Malaysia.

In the thirty years since SIJORI was launched, the Riau Islands has emerged as the richest province in Indonesia, second only to Jakarta.

What lies ahead? The volume examines the province's economic dimensions and prospects by drilling down in the different sectors of manufacturing, tourism and the digital economy. The volume covers the political, social, cultural and ethnic dimensions as well as the urbanization and environmental trends taking shape. Without fear of contradiction, we can claim this book is the most comprehensive review of current developments in the Riau Islands.

With the volume as the backdrop, some key questions that emerge are the following: with the many layers of development, how can the original impetus of SIJORI be maintained; how will it change; how can it still be configured to address the interest of all partners and what are the shifting dynamics?

Going forward, external trends may play a bigger role in creating opportunities as well as limitations on future developments in this subregion. For instance, the global economic recession of 2009 and 2010 led to a recession in shipping worldwide, causing the shipbuilding industry to dry up in the Riau Islands. More recently, with intensifying tensions between the United States and China resulting in higher tariffs and sanctions placed by the former on the latter, some supply chains from China have been diverted to the region. Many American, Japanese, and even Chinese companies have sought to continue their production lines in some ASEAN countries—Malaysia and Indonesia among them. The redirection of supply chains can help to enhance the relevance of the Riau Islands and the growth triangle if the parties all agree it is in their interests. SIJORI should also think through how it can maximize on the Regional Comprehensive Economic Partnership (RCEP) or the Comprehensive and Progressive Agreement for Trans-Pacific Partnership (CPTPP) opportunities, with the two regional trade pacts coming into existence in 2019 and 2020. Finally, it should be pointed out that the COVID-19 pandemic has further affected supply chains, providing new opportunities for SIJORI. In the past, companies were strategically planning for *just in time* production. Today they are planning for *just in case* production and the subregion can capitalize on its capabilities and location.

The next phase of development may be unfolding for the Riau Islands and for SIJORI.

Chan Heng Chee
Ambassador-at-Large and Chairman, ISEAS – Yusof Ishak Institute

ACKNOWLEDGEMENTS

The idea for this project came from then Deputy Director of ISEAS – Yusof Ishak Institute, Ooi Kee Beng, who put forward the idea of studying Southeast Asia's "Floating Frontiers" in 2013. Focusing on border regions between Indonesia, Malaysia, the Philippines, and Singapore, the emphasis was, rather than on land borders, to be on connections between countries across the sea. Seen from a historical perspective, this is consistent with Southeast Asia's precolonial maritime focus, which was characterized by intense linkages. Consequently, the three sites of this project were: the Singapore and Johor Straits; the Sulawesi Sea; and the Andaman Sea.

This led to the work on the first volume of this series, *The SIJORI Cross-Border Region: Transnational Politics, Economics, and Culture*, which looked at the interaction between Singapore, the Malaysian state of Johor, and the Riau Islands in Indonesia. Following the publication of this volume, the then Director of the ISEAS – Yusof Ishak Institute, Mr Tan Chin Tiong suggested building on this work with stand-alone projects on Johor and the Riau Islands, respectively.

The second volume *Johor: Abode of Development?* was published in 2020. This volume on the Riau Islands is the third and final in this series. As with the first and second volumes, we have collaborated with the Professorship of Architecture and Territorial Planning of ETH Zurich to cartographically depict important dynamics. In-depth conceptual and empirical discussions with Hans Hortig and Karoline Kostka were extremely fruitful, and their work on the maps that accompany the chapters has provided a valuable visualization of many of the relationships explored in this book.

Heartfelt thanks go to Tan Juen and Benjamin Hu for developing the figures used and referred to in the various chapters. Juen also provided exemplary assistance in helping finalize the manuscript. Thanks are also given to the National Archive of the Netherlands for their permission to publish Map 3.1 from their holdings.

This project was supported by the ISEAS – Yusof Ishak Institute, under the support of then Director, Mr Tan Chin Tiong and now under Mr Choi Shing Kwok. We would like to convey our appreciation to them. We also thank Ooi Kee Beng for developing the Floating Frontiers concept. Ng Kok Kiong and Rahilah Yusuf of ISEAS Publishing helped edit and publish this volume in record time. We are grateful for the support from our friends at BP Batam, in particular Gloria Tan and Riatna Jeo, and at EDB, Jayashree Sadan and Boon Soon Bing, for linking us with key policymakers in Batam.

We would also like to express our gratitude to the contributors to this volume for their extensive work on their chapters.

This publication is made possible with the support of the Konrad Adenauer Stiftung.

Francis E. Hutchinson and Siwage Dharma Negara

CONTRIBUTORS

Mulya Amri is a public policy specialist focusing on urban and regional economic development issues. He is currently a senior consultant with the World Bank Indonesia and programme director at the Jakarta Property Institute, and previously a research fellow at the Asia Competitiveness Institute, Lee Kuan Yew School of Public Policy, Singapore. Mulya has co-written fourteen books and numerous articles on topics related to subnational economic development and governance in Asia, focusing on Indonesia. He has a PhD in Public Policy from the National University of Singapore and a Master's in Urban Planning from the University of California, Los Angeles.

Barbara Watson Andaya is Professor of Asian Studies at the University of Hawai'i and a former President of the American Association of Asian Studies. Her specific area of expertise is the western Malay-Indonesia archipelago, but her research and teaching interests encompass all Southeast Asia. Her publications include *The Flaming Womb: Repositioning Women in Early Modern Southeast Asia* (2006) and (with Leonard Y. Andaya) *A History of Early Modern Southeast Asia* (2015) and *A History of Malaysia* (2017).

Raymond Atje is a Senior Fellow with the Department of Economics, Centre for Strategic and International Studies, Jakarta. His research interests include economic growth and financial development. He has a PhD in Economics from New York University.

Andrew M. Carruthers is Assistant Professor of Anthropology at the University of Pennsylvania, where he specializes in the linguistic and socio-cultural anthropology of Malay-speaking maritime Southeast Asia. He studies the relation between language, mobilities, and infrastructures as a source of insight into the ways people navigate shifting and potentially hazardous terrains in their everyday lives.

Ulla Fionna is an independent scholar who has worked with the ISEAS – Yusof Ishak Institute and INSEAD. She has published extensively on parties and local politics in Indonesia, and her sole-authored book is entitled *The Institutionalisation of Political Parties in Post-authoritarian Indonesia: From the Grass-roots Up* (Amsterdam University Press).

Hans Hortig studied landscape architecture at the Technical University Berlin, the ETH Zurich and the School of Design, Mysore. In 2013, he joined the Architecture of Territory project under Professor Topalovic at the Future Cities Laboratory, Singapore and at the ETH Zurich where he taught design and research studios, organized lecture series and guided numerous student works. Since 2015, he has been running the cartographic studio *maps&more* with Karoline Kostka and recently started his PhD research on processes of extended urbanization in Southeast Asian palm oil plantation landscapes.

Francis E. Hutchinson is a Senior Fellow at the ISEAS – Yusof Ishak Institute and the Managing Editor of the *Journal of Southeast Asian Economies*. His research interests include: local economic development, industrialization, innovation, federalism and decentralization. He is the author of *Mirror Images in Different Frames? Johor, the Riau Islands, and Competition for Investment from Singapore* (ISEAS, 2015); and co-editor of the *SIJORI Cross-Border Region: Transnational Politics, Economics, and Culture* (ISEAS, 2016) and *Johor: Abode of Development?* (ISEAS, 2020).

Karoline Kostka studied landscape planning and architecture at TU Berlin, ETH Zurich and the School of Design Mysore and graduated in 2013 in Landscape Architecture and Open Space Planning. From 2013 to 2015 Karoline worked as a researcher at the ETH Future Cities Laboratory in Singapore. Currently, she teaches design and research studios at ETH Zurich, Architecture and Territorial Planning with Professor Topalovic. Since 2015, she has been running the cartographic studio *maps&more* with Hans Hortig. Their work has been published and exhibited in Villa Renata Basel (2017), Landesmuseum Zurich (2019) and Kunstmuseum Luzern (2019).

Max Lane is Senior Visiting Fellow with the Indonesia Studies Programme at the ISEAS – Yusof Ishak Institute, Singapore, and Visiting Lecturer at the Faculty of Social and Political Sciences, Gajah Mada University, Yogjakarta.

Lee Poh Onn is Senior Fellow and member of the Regional Economic Studies Programme at the ISEAS – Yusof Ishak Institute. He works on economic development issues in East Malaysia and also on natural resource management and cooperation in Southeast Asia.

Ady Muzwardi is an Assistant Professor with the Department of International Relations of the Faculty of International Relations at Universitas Maritim Raja Ali Haji in Tanjungpinang, and a consultant on tourism-related issues for the Riau Islands provincial government. His research interests include: special economic zones, port economics, and tourism—with a special focus on Indonesia's border regions.

Siwage Dharma Negara is Senior Fellow, Co-Coordinator of the Indonesia Studies Programme, and Coordinator of the Singapore APEC Study Centre at the ISEAS – Yusof Ishak Institute. He is Co-Editor of the *Journal of Southeast Asian Economies*. His research interests include: macroeconomic and development issues, connectivity, industrial and trade policies with special focus on Indonesia. He is the co-editor of the *Indonesian Economy in Transition: Policy Challenges in the Jokowi Era and Beyond* (ISEAS, 2019); and co-editor of *Aspirations with Limitations: Indonesia's Foreign Affairs under Susilo Bambang Yudhoyono* (ISEAS, 2018).

Faizal Rianto is a Lecturer at the Institute of Population and Environmental Policy, and Secretary of the ASEAN Studies Centre at the Raja Haji College of Social and Political Science in Tanjungpinang. Faizal holds a Master's in Public Policy from the Lee Kuan Yew School of Public Policy at the National University of Singapore. His main interests are development issues, community empowerment, public policy and administration, and local governance in Indonesia.

Sita Rohana is a researcher and anthropologist working at the Cultural Values Conservation Centre of the Indonesian Ministry of Education and Culture in Tanjungpinang. Her research interests include: urban culture, indigenous people and oral tradition in Riau, the Riau Islands, Jambi and Bangka-Belitung.

Norshahril Saat is Senior Fellow at the ISEAS – Yusof Ishak Institute. In 2018, he published *The State, Ulama, and Islam in Malaysia and Indonesia* (Amsterdam University Press), *Tradition and Islamic Learning: Singapore Students in the Al-Azhar University* (ISEAS), and edited *Islam in Southeast Asia: Negotiating Modernity* (ISEAS). Norshahril's articles have recently been published in journals such as *Asian Journal of Social Science, Contemporary Islam: Dynamics of Muslim Life, Review of Indonesian and Malaysian Affairs,* and *Studia Islamika.*

Wilmar Salim is an Associate Professor in Regional and City Planning Program and Head of Research Center for Infrastructure and Regional Development at Institut Teknologi Bandung. His research interests include: plan and policy implementation and evaluation; decentralization and urbanization; local and metropolitan governance; regional disparity and poverty; and political economy of climate change adaptation. He has published articles and book chapters on Indonesia's urban and regional studies.

Deasy Simandjuntak is political anthropologist and Associate Fellow at the ISEAS – Yusof Ishak Institute, Singapore. A recipient of the Taiwan Fellowship, Deasy is also a Research Fellow at the Center for Asia Pacific Area Studies, Academia Sinica, Taiwan. She completed her PhD in 2010 at the University of Amsterdam on the topic of "patronage democracy in Indonesia". Her main interests are Indonesian democracy, national and local politics and decentralization, and she has published in *Inside Indonesia*, the *European Journal of East Asian Studies*, and the *Asian Journal of Law and Society*.

Leo Suryadinata is currently Visiting Senior Fellow at the ISEAS – Yusof Ishak Institute and Adjunct Professor at the S. Rajaratnam School of International Studies, Nanyang Technological University (NTU). He served as Director of the Chinese Heritage Centre at NTU and was a Professor in the Department of Political Science, National University of Singapore before that. His latest books are *The Making of Southeast Asian Nations* (2015); *The Rise of China and the Chinese Overseas: Beijing's Policy in Southeast Asia and Beyond* (ISEAS, 2017).

Columbanus Teto is a Business Analyst for Commercial & SME Banking at PT Bank Central Asia Tbk (BCA). Prior to joining BCA in 2020, he was a Research Intern at the Center for Strategic and International Studies (CSIS), in Jakarta. His research interests include industrialization, banking, macroeconomics and public policy. He has a Bachelor's Degree in Economics from the University of Indonesia.

ABBREVIATIONS

AMDAL	*Analisis Mengenai Dampak Lingkungan*; Environmental Impact Assessment
APEC	Asia-Pacific Economic Cooperation
ASITA	Association of the Indonesian Tours and Travel Agencies
BAPEDAL	Badan Pengendalian Dampak Lingkungan; Environmental Impact Management Agency
Bappenas	Badan Perencanaan Pembangunan Nasional; National Development Planning Agency
BBK	Batam, Bintan, and Karimun
BI	Bank Indonesia; Central Bank
BIDA	Batam Industrial Development Authority
BIFZA	Batam Indonesia Free Zone Authority
BIG	Badan Informasi Geospasial; Geospatial Information Agency
BILIK	Bina Lingkungan Hidup Batam; Batam Environmental Development
BKPM	Badan Koordinasi Penanaman Modal; Investment Coordinating Board
BKSPK	Badan Kerja Sama Provinsi Kepulauan; Archipelagic Province Cooperation Agency
BP Batam	Badan Pengusahaan Batam; Batam Management Agency
BP3KP	Badan Pekerja Pembentukan Provinsi Kepulauan Riau; Agency for the Establishment of the Riau Islands Province
BPS	Badan Pusat Statistik; Central Bureau of Statistics or Statistics Indonesia
BUMDES	Badan Usaha Milik Desa; Village-Owned Enterprise
bupati	regent/district head
CBR	Cross-Border Region
CBT	community-based tourism
CDM	Clean Development Mechanism
DDI	domestic direct investment

DE	digital economy
DPD	Dewan Perwakilan Daerah; Regional Representative Council
DPOD	Dewan Pertimbangan Otonomi Daerah; Regional Autonomy Advisory Council
DPR	Dewan Perwakilan Rakyat; (National) People's Representative Council
DPRD	Dewan Perwakilan Rakyat Daerah; Regional People's Representative Council
DPUD	Destinasi Pariwisata Unggulan Daerah; Regional Leading Tourism Destinations
DPW	Dewan Perwakilan Wilayah; Regional Representative Council
E&E	electrical and electronics
EEZ	Exclusive Economic Zone
EIA	Environmental Impact Assessment
EKPPD	Evaluasi Kinerja Penyelenggaraan Pemerintahan Daerah; Evaluation of the Performance of Local Government Administration
FBSI	Federasi Buruh Seluruh Indonesia; All Indonesia Labour Federation
FCL	Future Cities Laboratory
FDI	foreign direct investment
FGD	focus group discussion
FSPMI	Federasi Serikat Pekerja Metal Indonesia; Federation of Indonesian Metal Workers' Unions
GDP	gross domestic product
Gerindra	Partai Gerakan Indonesia Raya; Pan-Indonesian Movement Party
GRDP	gross regional domestic product
Hanura	Partai Hati Nurani Rakyat; People's Conscience Party
HDI	Human Development Index
HKBP	Huria Kristen Batak Protestan; Batak Christian Protestant Church
ICT	information and communication technology
IDI	Indonesia Democracy Index
IDR	Indonesian rupiah
IKTK	Ikatan Keluarga Tapanuli Kepri; Riau Islands Tapanuli Family Association
IoT	Internet of Things
ISIS	Islamic State of Iraq and Syria
IT	information technology
kabupaten	district
KADIN	Kamar Dagang Indonesia; Indonesian Chamber of Commerce
kecamatan	subdistrict
KEK	Kawasan Ekonomi Khusus; Special Economic Zone

kelurahan	A village that is headed by a civil servant (*lurah*)
KKSS	Kerukunan Keluarga Sulawesi Selatan; South Sulawesi Family Association
kota	municipality
KPK	Komisi Pemberantasan Korupsi; Corruption Eradication Commission
KPU	Komisi Pemilihan Umum; General Election Commission
KSBSI	Konfederasi Serikat Buruh Sejahtera Indonesia; Confederation of Prosperous Worker Trade Unions
KSPI	Konfederasi Serikat Pekerja Indonesia; Confederation of Trade Unions of Indonesia
KSPSI	Konfederasi Serikat Pekerja Seluruh Indonesia; Confederation of All Indonesian Trade Unions
MICE	meetings, incentives, conferences and events
MNC	multinational corporation
MNE	multinational enterprise
MRO	maintenance, repair and overhaul
MUI	Majelis Ulama Indonesia; Indonesia Ulema Council
NDP	Nongsa Digital Park
NTT	Nusa Tenggara Timur
NU	Nahdlatul Ulama; a traditionalist Sunni Islam movement in Indonesia
O&G	oil and gas
OSM	Open Street Map
PAN	Partai Amanat Nasional; National Mandate Party
PBI	Partai Bhinneka Tunggal Ika; Unity in Diversity Party
PD	Partai Demokrat; Democratic Party
PDI-P	Partai Demokrat Perjuangan Indonesia; Indonesian Democratic Party of Struggle
pemekaran	blossoming or the proliferation of administrative units
Perhimpunan INTI	Perhimpunan Indonesia-Tionghoa; Indonesian-Chinese Association
PITI	Persatuan Islam Tionghoa Indonesia; Chinese Muslim Union of Indonesia
PKB	Partai Kebangkitan Bangsa; National Awakening Party
PKS	Partai Keadilan Sejahtera; Prosperous Justice Party
PLT	*pelaksana tugas*; acting administrative officer
pokdarwis	*kelompok sadar wisata*; tourism awareness group
PP	Peraturan Pemerintah; Government Regulation
PPBM	Persatuan Pemuda Bugis Makassar; Bugis Youth Assembly of Makassar
PPIB	Partai Perhimpunan Indonesia Baru; New Indonesia Alliance Party
PPP	Partai Persatuan Pembangunan; United Development Party

PRI	Province of the Riau Islands
PRRI	Pemerintah Revolusioner Republik Indonesia; Revolutionary Government of the Republic of Indonesia
PSMTI	Paguyuban Sosial Marga Tionghoa Indonesia; Indonesian of Chinese Descent Social Association
PT	*perseroan terbatas*; limited liability company
R&D	research and development
Reformasi	political movement to overthrow President Soeharto in 1998
Riau daratan	mainland aspect of Riau
Riau kepulauan	archipelagic aspect of Riau
RPJMD	Rencana Pembangunan Jangka Menengah Daerah; Regional Medium-Term Development Plan
RTRW	Rencana Tata Ruang Wilayah; Regional Spatial Plans
rumah liar	squatter settlements
SBY	Susilo Bambang Yudhoyono
SEZ	Special Economic Zone
SIJORI	Singapore-Johor-Riau Islands
SME	small and medium enterprise
SPSI	Serikat Pekerja Seluruh Indonesia; All Indonesia Workers Union
US$	United States dollar
VAT	Value Added Tax
VOC	volatile organic compounds
Walikota	City Mayor
WTE	Waste-to-Energy

Introduction

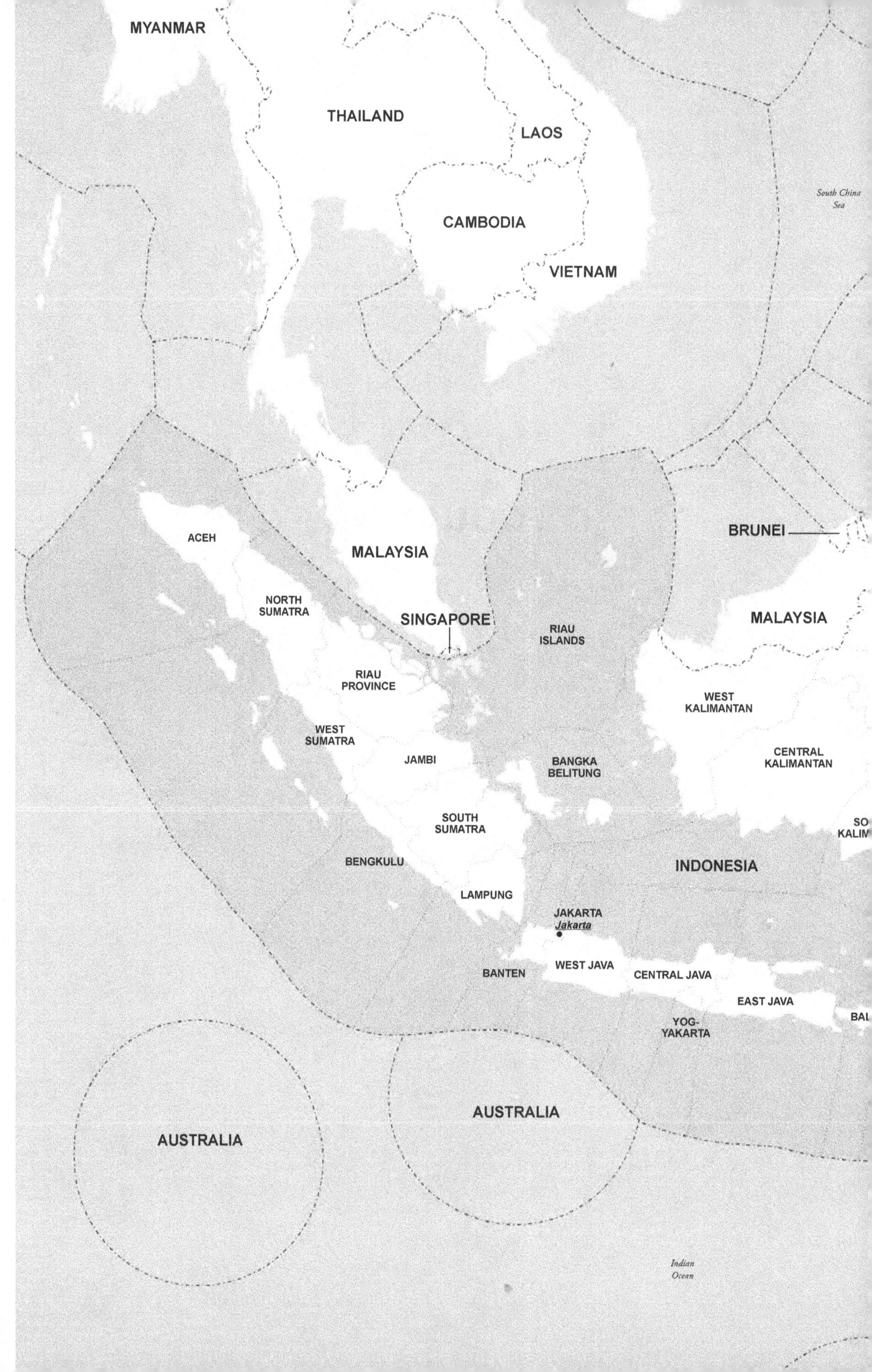
MYANMAR
THAILAND
LAOS
CAMBODIA
VIETNAM
South China Sea
MALAYSIA
BRUNEI
MALAYSIA
SINGAPORE
ACEH
NORTH SUMATRA
RIAU PROVINCE
RIAU ISLANDS
WEST SUMATRA
JAMBI
BANGKA BELITUNG
WEST KALIMANTAN
CENTRAL KALIMANTAN
SOUTH SUMATRA
BENGKULU
LAMPUNG
INDONESIA
JAKARTA
Jakarta
BANTEN
WEST JAVA
CENTRAL JAVA
EAST JAVA
YOG-YAKARTA
AUSTRALIA
AUSTRALIA
Indian Ocean

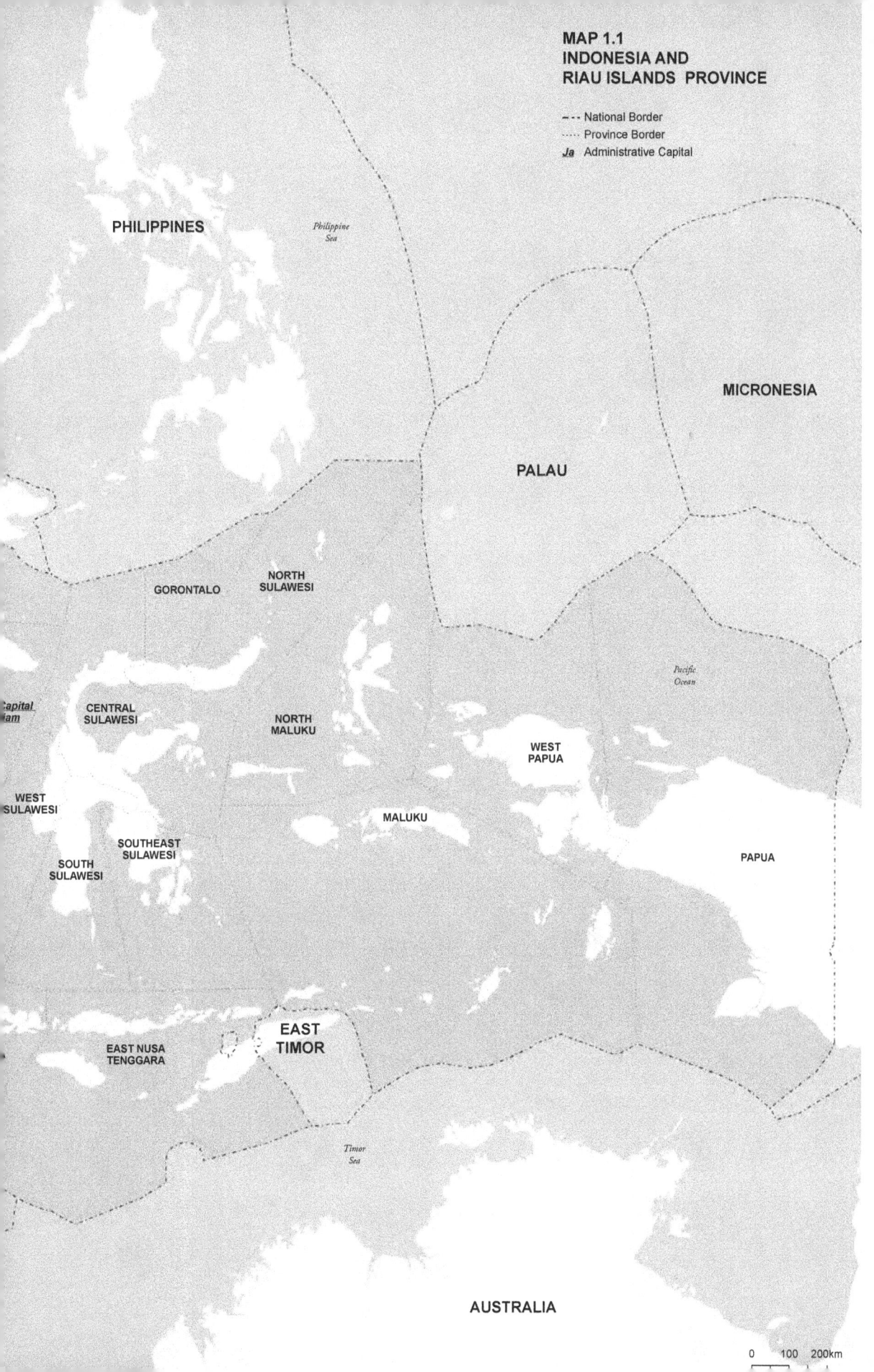

MAP 1.1
INDONESIA AND
RIAU ISLANDS PROVINCE

–‑‑ National Border
····· Province Border
Ja Administrative Capital

PHILIPPINES

Philippine Sea

MICRONESIA

PALAU

GORONTALO

NORTH SULAWESI

Pacific Ocean

Capital
iam

CENTRAL SULAWESI

NORTH MALUKU

WEST PAPUA

WEST SULAWESI

SOUTHEAST SULAWESI

MALUKU

PAPUA

SOUTH SULAWESI

EAST NUSA TENGGARA

EAST TIMOR

Timor Sea

AUSTRALIA

0   100   200km

1

SITUATING THE RIAU ISLANDS

Francis E. Hutchinson and Siwage Dharma Negara

INTRODUCTION

To Singapore's immediate south, the Province of the Riau Islands has a population of 2.2 million, and a land area of 8,200 square kilometres scattered across some 2,000 islands in 240,000 square kilometres of water. The better-known island groups include: Batam, the province's economic motor; Bintan, its cultural heartland and the site of the provincial capital, Tanjungpinang; and Karimun, a fishing and shipping hub near the Straits of Malacca. These island groups are more outwardly oriented and multiethnic, but the province also includes another three other island groups, namely Natuna, Anambas and Lingga, which are more isolated, rural, and homogeneous.

Within Indonesia, the Province of the Riau Islands[1] (PRI) is relatively small in demographic terms, and very remote from the centre of power. Logistics connections between PRI and major population centres in Java and Sumatra are underdeveloped and overpriced, effectively barring significant commercial and cultural exchange between the "centre" of the country and this far-off province. For much of the recent past, government services and communication were routed through Pekanbaru, the provincial capital of Riau Province, to which the Riau Islands used to belong.

Yet, the province is strategically located next to major shipping lanes and telecommunications infrastructure, making it one of the most connected areas in Indonesia. Furthermore, it is close to Singapore and, through the city-state, able to access global capital and expertise. The Riau Islands has also long sought to capture spillover from Singapore, with policymakers looking north to identify trends and commercial opportunities. Thus, the province is simultaneously affected by its marginality and centrality.

Despite its small size, the Riau Islands is an important site for manufacturing in Indonesia. In late 1989, spurred by considerable flows of foreign direct investment into Singapore and Johor, the Indonesian government liberalized the investment regulations for Batam, allowed more private sector participation, invested more resources in physical infrastructure and began to work with Singapore to develop its human resource base and market the island.

Enabled by these changes, and catalysed by a favourable international environment, manufacturing-related investment flowed into Batam, dramatically boosting incomes. Singapore and Singapore-based firms were important sources of investment, as well Japan, Hong Kong, Korea, and Taiwan. The bulk of investment was in the electrical and electronics sector, as well as supporting activities. Over time, manufacturing investment also began to spread to select locations in Bintan (Hutchinson 2015).

During the 1990–97 period, Batam's economy grew at or about 15 per cent per annum. The island's economy and the provincial economy more broadly underwent a structural transformation, away from primary sector activities such as fishing towards a deeper and more diversified industrial sector. Despite a small dip following the 1997/98 Asian Financial Crisis, this growth process continued during the early 2000s and in subsequent years.

Since its emergence in Batam, and subsequently Bintan in the 1990s, the export-oriented sector has changed the social fabric, urban centres, and daily life of its inhabitants. Beginning with electrical and electronics production, over the years the modern manufacturing sector has expanded to include shipbuilding and ship repair. Seeking formal sector employment, many people from across Indonesia have moved to the Riau Islands and, in the process, changed the face of the province.

As a result of this growth, living standards have improved dramatically in the province. Recent estimates show that per capita income of the Riau Islands has reached IDR117 million (US$8,550). This is the second-highest per capita income in Indonesia, surpassed only by the Jakarta capital region (BPS 2017).

This dramatic change in economic structure and living standards has been accompanied by several other far-reaching processes.

First, from around 500,000 people in the Riau Islands in 1990, the area is now home to more than 2 million people. Much of this expansion has taken place in Batam, whose population is now about 1.37 million (*Batampos*, 8 July 2019). Natural population increase has only played a minor role in this process, with the constant arrival of migrants from all across the country a major driver of growth. The pace and scale of this expansion has placed considerable stress on urban areas and the provision of public services. Moreover, the large-scale influx of people and the province's manufacturing-reliant model of growth also has important environmental implications.

Second, following the end of the New Order, and the decentralization process put in motion in 2001, the Riau Islands sought to secede from the larger Riau province.

There were various drivers for this process, including the territory's: different economic model; ethnic composition; self-perception as a discrete political entity; and grievances related to the turnaround time for decisions to be routed through the Riau capital, Pekanbaru.

In 2002, the establishment of the Province of the Riau Islands was announced and operationalized in 2004. In Bintan, a new provincial capital is emerging, with white administrative buildings being constructed on a small island ringed by mangrove trees. The young provincial civil service is still finding its feet, and is reaching out to the more remote parts of the province to foster a common identity.

Third, this increase in population has also changed the Riau Islands' demographic and political complexion. Long a region open to trade and commerce, the islands have absorbed diverse communities over the past centuries. Nonetheless, the rapidity and scale of the recent increase in population has given rise to an influential ethno-nationalist sentiment in the local political context. This has caused the Riau Islands to episodically change policy frameworks, away from manufacturing-related growth towards traditional activities such as fishing and farming (Hutchinson 2015).

Furthermore, despite the long run of rapid economic growth, there are indications that the Riau Islands may need to revisit its economic model. First, the growth of the manufacturing sector could be reaching its limit. Electronics production has gone through several rounds of contraction, with notable episodes in 2004 and 2010. The shipyard sector has also been hit by a global slump in prices. Thus, in parts of Batam, there are empty warehouses and shipyards sitting idle. And, in sharp contrast to the earlier breakneck pace of growth, in 2017 the province grew at a mere 2 per cent—well under the national average.

The economy also seems to be moving in new directions, with the services sector offering interesting possibilities. The tourism sector is growing consistently, with increasing numbers of domestic as well as international travellers. The number and range of ancillary services is expanding, generating demand for additional services-based jobs in the process. And, in the northeastern part of Batam, a cluster of digital economy firms is emerging. Young programmers from the Riau Islands and beyond are working in areas such as fin-tech, animation and website design. As with many of its other economic sectors, the island's digital economy is deeply intertwined with Singaporean firms, but also showing interesting potential for tapping the domestic market.

This volume is part of a trilogy that looks at the interactions between Singapore, the Malaysian state of Johor, and the Riau Islands. This book, *The Riau Islands: Setting Sail*, takes the early 1990s and the emergence and consolidation of PRI's manufacturing sector as a point of departure. It looks at the political, social, and environmental effects of this economic transformation within the Riau Islands, including the creation of the new province. It then explores the sustainability of this development process, including whether the province needs to revisit its manufacture-for-export model.

To this end, after this introduction, the second section locates the Riau Islands within the Indonesian context. The third one sets out its relationship with its neighbouring territories of Singapore and the Malaysian state of Johor. The final section sets out the aims and structure of this book.

THE RIAU ISLANDS IN INDONESIA

Despite the Dutch claiming formal sovereignty over the Riau Islands from the 1800s, their presence on the ground was limited until the early twentieth century. In 1911, the Dutch established a Residency (*Residentie*), with a capital in Tanjungpinang on Bintan Island. The Residency consisted of two aspects, namely the Indragiri Division which encompassed part of Sumatra, and the Tanjungpinang Division, which covered the Riau Islands. For its part, the Tanjungpinang Division was subdivided into four areas: Lingga, Karimun, Tanjungpinang and Pulau Tujuh.

During the Second World War, the Japanese divided the mainland and island aspects of Riau, with the first administered as part of Sumatra, and the second grouped with Singapore and Malaya (Andaya 1997). Following the Second World War, the incorporation of Riau into the emerging Republic of Indonesia was not a straightforward process. From 1945 to 1950, it was the site of contest between a group of elite Riau Malays, who wanted to re-establish the precolonial political entity of the sultanate, rather than joining the nationalist and unitary republic. It was only in April of 1950, that Riau was finally incorporated in the new nation as one of the last "recovered regions" (Wee 2016).

During the early 1950s, the mainland and island aspects of Riau were brought together again as part of the province of Central Sumatra. In 1958, the Province of Riau was established, which largely mirrored the contours of the Residency established during the Dutch period. Consisting of the two aspects of Riau, its capital was initially in Tanjungpinang. However, recognizing the economic importance of the oil-rich mainland portion of Riau, the provincial capital was subsequently moved to Pekanbaru in mainland Sumatra later that year.

Under the New Order, provincial governments were subsumed under the central government, which had exclusive control over a wide range of state functions, from fiscal policy to land management. This was particularly the case for issues pertaining to industrialization, science and technology, and regional policy. Provincial governments, for their part, were responsible for regulating business, urban services, and providing financing for regional development. However, the operational division of responsibilities differed across the country's provinces (Shah et al. 1994).

Beyond oversight of administrative issues, the central government was very influential over the political leadership of Indonesia's provinces, particularly in Riau. From the late 1970s onwards, the governors nominated to the province were Javanese military officers, who were personally known to Soeharto. This was met with resistance in Riau, where in keeping with tradition, elites preferred a locally born Malay to head the province. Nonetheless, central preferences prevailed. Given the mechanisms of selection, and the incentive structures within which these leaders operated, they were seen to prioritize central government issues rather than provincial ones (Malley 1999).

During the 1970s, the Riau Islands—and Batam in particular—acquired particular salience as part of Indonesia's strategy to develop its oil and gas sector. Much of the petroleum obtained in the mainland aspect of Riau was sent to Singapore for refining. Seeking to break into this higher value-added sector, the central government targeted Batam as a site for petroleum refining in the early 1970s (Nur 2000). To this end, the Batam Industrial Development Authority (BIDA) was created, with a mandate to attract capital and liaise with investors (BIDA 1980). This agency was funded by the central government and even had its headquarters, not in Batam, but in Jakarta (BIDA 1980).

In the late 1970s, under the stewardship of BJ Habibie, the Minister for Research and Technology, the priority for Batam shifted towards manufacturing. To this end, Batam was made a bonded zone in 1978, which enabled the duty-free import of inputs and subsequent export of finished goods. The central government also moved to upgrade the island's infrastructure, such as telecommunications, power, and air and seaports (*Far Eastern Economic Review*, 2 February 1985).

Despite central government attention, investment and the provision of incentives, this was insufficient to kick-start Batam's industrialization process. Of key concern was an overly restrictive foreign investment regime that required the divestment of a majority stake within a fifteen year period. Other issues included a shortage of industrial property, as well as water and electricity outages. Consequently, a mere thirteen foreign-owned firms were in operation in 1988 (Smith 1996).

Spurred by the realization that manufacturing-related investment was flowing into Singapore and Johor, the central government changed tack. In 1989, it enacted a number of liberalization measures, including allowing the private sector to own and operate industrial parks and dramatically watering down the divestment criteria (Pangestu 1991). A bilateral agreement was also signed with Singapore, covering the joint development and marketing of Riau Province. And, in 1992, Batam, along with its neighbouring islands of Rempang and Galang, were joined via a network of bridges, and collectively designated as bonded zones (Wong and Ng 2009).

As before, the central government continued to exercise control and influence over the Riau Islands. Referring to the growing links between Batam and Bintan to Singapore and Singapore-based firms, Habibie famously declared "don't consider SIJORI as owned by Riau, because Riau does not have the funds and the skills" (*Antara*, 28 October 1991).

As the islands began to grow, disputes between the central and provincial governments arose over the sharing of revenue arising from the sale of sand to Singapore, as well as the provision of infrastructure and services in Batam. Seeing the development potential offered by Bintan and Karimun, other central government agencies such as Home Affairs and Industry also sought to exercise influence over policy decisions (Smith 1996). As both Batam and Bintan began to develop, Jakarta-based conglomerates also established a presence on the two islands. This included the Salim Group, active in real estate and agri-business, as well as Soeharto's family members (Smith 1996; Wee 2016).

This top-down dynamic was upended in 2001, with the implementation of Indonesia's sweeping decentralization reforms. With the exception of a limited number of prerogatives, a wide selection of responsibilities were devolved to the provincial and particularly the local level. Elections for subnational office were established, and specific mechanisms for the transfer of resources from the centre downwards were formulated (Crouch 2010).

In the run-up to these reforms, political elites in the Riau Islands began to push for the establishment of a separate province. One key aspect of this drive was the development of the gas sector in Natuna, which would provide the financial wherewithal for the fledgling province. Other aspects of this argument were cultural, citing the historical specificity of the Riau Islands and its unique identity. This were complemented with grievances pertaining to the low number of Riau Islanders in the provincial administration, as well as the focus of the Pekanbaru-based government on palm oil and petroleum, rather than manufacturing (Hutchinson 2015).[2]

Legislated in 2002 and implemented in 2004, the Province of the Riau Islands was carved out of the larger Riau entity. Ismeth Abdullah, the former head of BIDA, was named as the governor of the caretaker administration, charged with establishing the provincial government and organizing the first gubernatorial elections (*Jakarta Post*, 26 June 2004).

In the subsequent years, the Riau Islands has established itself as a discrete political entity, with a new provincial government administration, and three rounds of gubernatorial elections. Under Indonesia's decentralized framework, the province now has a significantly bigger budget, as well as a more extensive range of responsibilities, not least supervising the budgets of a growing number of local governments.

Nonetheless, legacy issues of the early period remain, and these pose important questions for the relationship with the central government.

The first pending issue concerns the stewardship of the renamed Batam Industrial Development Authority, the Batam Indonesia Free Zone Authority (BIFZA).[3] In 2008, the agency's assets and employees were transferred from the central government to the provincial government, which also assumed responsibility for naming its Chairman (*Jakarta Post*, 13 October 2008). In 2016, following unhappiness over Batam's lagging economic growth, President Joko Widodo reasserted central authority over key appointments in the organization (*Straits Times*, 2 November 2017).

The second issue concerns the functional overlap between BIFZA and the Batam municipal government. In other parts of Indonesia, responsibilities pertaining to business licensing, investment liaison, and local infrastructure are carried out by the relevant local governments. However, due to its unique development and degree of central government control, these responsibilities have been carried out by BIDA/BIFZA. This has generated a great deal of tension between the two agencies, and added to investor uncertainties. Various organizational restructuring exercises have been proposed, with the latest decision being to subsume BIDA/BIFZA under the Batam municipal government (*Batampos*, 16 September 2019).

The third issue pertains to the legal status of Batam, Bintan and Karimun, and how these can be reconciled with the central government's move towards setting up a network of special economic zones. These islands have long received unique legal status under various guises, such as bonded zones or free trade zones (FTZ). This status, while enabling the duty-free import and export of goods, can also raise issues for firms present on the island who want to cater to the domestic market. In addition, this special customs status raises the complexity of procuring staples and daily foodstuffs, which much leave the domestic market and enter the free trade zone. Last, as Indonesia establishes a new generation of special economic zones, it is not clear how and whether this can be reconciled with Batam, Bintan and Karimun's current FTZ status (Negara and Hutchinson 2020).

The Riau Islands is a part, albeit small, of the sprawling Indonesian nation. As a province in a decentralized political structure, it has a degree of independence on issues such as investment policy and infrastructure investment. The province's geographic position is fixed as are its factor endowments, but there have been certain policy choices that have undeniably shaped the province's direction and the policy choices it faces today. However, despite this, the Riau Islands is still negotiating key aspects of its relationship with the central government. Thus, developments in the province are an amalgam of national policy frameworks, locally taken decisions and local dynamics.

THE RIAU ISLANDS AS PART OF SIJORI

When many look at the Riau Islands and its relationship with Singapore and Johor, they ground the relationship in 1990. This date is associated with the launch of the Singapore, Johor and Riau (SIJORI) Growth Triangle. This concept was supported by the governments of Singapore, Malaysia and Indonesia as a way to market the three territories with their differing factor endowments as one integrated whole.

It was this cross-border construct, and the potential benefits that it offered that catalysed the relationship between Batam, Bintan and eventually Karimun with its neighbours to the north. However, while an important date, this is not the beginning of the interactions between these three territories. Indeed, their interactions are much more complex, wide-ranging and rooted in history.

From the early 1700s until 1824, the areas along the Johor River and its close connections with the Riau Archipelago were the core of the Johor-Riau Kingdom. The kingdom was a sultanate—the prevailing political entity in archipelagic Southeast Asia at the time. This sultanate was in a strategic location, at the crossroads of two important maritime trading routes—the first running east and west, linking India and China; and the second north and south, connecting Java and the islands east of it with the South China Sea (Wee 2016).

The contours of the Johor-Riau Kingdom changed over time but, at its height, encompassed what are now: the states of Johor and Pahang in Malaysia; Singapore; and part of the Sumatran coast as well as the Riau Archipelago in Indonesia (Wee 2016). During this period, the capital city moved back and forth between Johor and Bintan (Carruthers 2018).

The Kingdom existed as a cohesive political entity up until 1824, when the Treaty of London was signed by the British and the Dutch. The agreement divided the area into a British-controlled northern aspect, comprising Singapore and the Malayan Peninsula, and a Dutch-controlled south. At that point in time, the political capital of the Johor-Riau Kingdom was in Tanjungpinang. The sultanate persisted as a political entity until 1911 at which point, rather than formally yielding control to the Dutch who sought to establish a direct presence there, the last Sultan of Riau renounced his position and moved to Singapore (Wee 2016).

Despite the formal separation of these territories, many ties persisted. The long maritime coastline between the territories as well as the different economic models imposed by the British and Dutch gave rise to a long-running and lively smuggling trade. In particular, the Dutch preference for awarding monopolies and the British preference for free trade gave rise to a lively flow of goods, drugs, weapons, and people between the two territories, which lasted well into the twentieth century (Tagliacozzo 2005).

Indeed, the Riau Islands retained close economic links with Singapore and Malaysia up until the 1960s, when travel between the countries for business or social purposes was possible without passports (Dedees 2015). However, in 1963, the tensions between Indonesia on one hand, and the newly constituted Malaysia on the other disrupted trade links behind tariff barriers and customs walls (Hutchinson 2016). It was these obstacles to trade that the Growth Triangle sought to reduce some thirty years later.

Beyond networks of electronics manufacture linking the Riau Islands with Singapore, trade linkages are deep and diverse, ranging from the provision of fresh fish to the export of live pork to the city-state. Furthermore, tourism is becoming an important nexus between the three territories. Singapore and Johor are major sources of visitors for the Riau Islands, most particularly Batam, Bintan and Karimun. In turn, growing numbers of residents from the Riau Islands are looking northwards, particularly towards Johor for healthcare services and higher education (Hutchinson 2020).

In addition, the Riau Islands has become an important gateway region for Indonesia, with migrants coming from across the country to the province before heading north into Johor and beyond. Many of these workers stay in Malaysia for the long term, but many others go back to Indonesia periodically to renew their visas, hence preferring to be based in the Riau Islands (Hutchinson 2020).

Beyond economic linkages, there are important cultural linkages binding the various territories. Given the movement of the Sultanate's capital between Johor and Bintan, there are important historic sites in and around Tanjungpinang. This includes the Grand Mosque of the Sultan of Riau, mausoleums of important sultans of the Johor-Riau Kingdom, as well as the grave of Raja Ali Haji, who is credited with codifying the Malay language (Carruthers 2018). Resun waterfall in Lingga is also an important site for religious pilgrimage for Malays from Singapore and Johor (Hutchinson 2020).

Thus, while the Riau Islands is undeniably a part of Indonesia, its proximity to both Singapore and Johor is also a fundamental part of its identity. Deep-rooted cultural and historical linkages bind the three territories. Economic ties run the gamut from electronics manufacture to the export of agricultural produce. And, people-to-people ties are also growing in size and complexity. It is exactly this duality that this book seeks to explore.

THE AIMS AND STRUCTURE OF THE BOOK

The first volume in the series, *The SIJORI Cross-Border Region: Transnational Politics, Economics, and Culture* was published in 2016. It arose out of a three-year project that brought together twenty-two specialists based in Singapore, Malaysia and Indonesia to explore cross-border dynamics between the three territories.

Collectively, the book's eighteen chapters explored two central questions: first, how have the component territories of the Cross-Border Region (CBR) evolved over the past twenty-five years as a result of deeper interactions; second, how will these territories look in the medium term, if some of the trends witnessed continue?

Seeking to widen the frame of analysis beyond the traditional Growth Triangle framework, the project referenced work on Cross-Border Regions, which are defined as territorial units from two or more nation-states (Perkmann and Sum 2002, p. 1). Consequently, the aggregate of the three territories—one national and two subnational, are taken as the unit of analysis.

In contrast to the Growth Triangle framework, which has varying geographical scales and privileges formal economic interactions, the CBR framework clearly specified the territorial extent of the entity under study, which allowed the centres of political power to be identified. Furthermore, rather than treating the border uniquely as a source of friction to trade between the components, the new framework incorporated it as a central element of Cross-Border Region's identity (Hutchinson and Chong 2016).

The application of the CBR framework enabled the analysis of formal and informal economic linkages between the territories, ranging from semiconductors to piracy and contraband. In addition, it also allowed us to appreciate the many directions the interactions took, from Singapore outward to these two territories, but also from Johor and the Riau Islands inwards to Singapore.

Nonetheless, due to its primacy in political and economic terms, the city-state loomed large in this work, almost always featuring as the central node in the relationship. The fieldwork carried out by the ISEAS – Yusof Ishak Institute team cast light on interesting dynamics taking place within both Johor and the Riau Islands, which, while often influenced by the trends taking place in the city-state, were also shaped by events taking place within their own respective countries.

Consequently, the second part of this project aims to complement this perspective through focusing more directly on the other two components of the Cross-Border Region. The second volume on Johor and this third volume on the Riau Islands seek to focus specifically on each of these subnational territories, with the aim of understanding their challenges as they navigate the gravitational pull towards their national capitals on one hand, and their linkages with Singapore and, through the city-state, international markets on the other.

To this end, the guiding questions for this volume are as follows:

- What have been the political, social, and environmental impacts on the Riau Islands of the rapid economic development seen since 1990?
- What can be said about the province's policy frameworks and the future of the manufacture-for-export economic model?
- How is the Riau Islands and its position within Indonesia evolving in response to these economic and political developments?

The project on the Riau Islands ran from 2016 to 2019, with the bulk of the fieldwork carried out in Indonesia in 2017 and 2018. There were sixteen researchers involved, with ten from ISEAS, and the remainder largely based in Indonesia.

In order to generate a shared framework for analysis, two conferences were held in ISEAS in 2017 and one in 2019. Following the conferences in 2017, some of the emerging findings were released as ISEAS publications. These publications have been compiled for inclusion into this book and updated where necessary. In addition, this volume has brought together additional research which has not been previously published.

As with its companion volume on Johor, the book is divided into three broad sections. The first section of the book takes the Riau Island's economic base as a starting point. It begins by reviewing Batam's manufacturing sector, long the key driver of the province's formal sector. This is complemented by analyses of two more dynamic sectors, namely tourism and the fledgling digital economy. The subsequent chapter revisits the crucial issue of Batam's special status as a free trade zone, and whether this can or should be altered in a significant way. The final chapter looks at ways of diversifying the province's economic base away from manufacturing as well as catalysing economic growth in its more remote regions.

The second section of the volume looks at the province's political context. It first places the creation of the Riau Islands Province in historical perspective, before looking at the processes inherent in establishing the new provincial government to administer and delivery public services. The section also analyses the conduct of political parties in the province, particularly how they operate at such a geographical remove from the national capital. Finally, it looks at industrial relations in Batam, which nicely exemplifies the interplay between formal sector employment generated via links with Singapore and political dynamics emanating from Java.

The third section looks at social and environmental issues, many of which have been directly affected by the province's rise in living standards and growing industrial base, as well as the sizeable influx of migrants from different parts of the country. This involves analysing urban and environmental challenges emerging from the rapid increase in population, as well as increasing religious diversity. And, the section also contains an analysis of four of the largest ethnic communities in the province, namely, Malay, Javanese, Batak and Chinese, and how they relate to each other.

The final section of the book sets out the main conclusions, highlighting the main themes raised in the chapters and returning to the central questions set out in the beginning. Having done this, it will identify areas to future research.

As with the first and second volumes in the series, this book is not just a theoretical or empirical enterprise, but it is also a cartographic one. Consequently, ISEAS researchers worked with the Professorial Chair of Territory and Urban Planning of ETH Zurich on a series of maps to accompany the book, and illustrate many of the interactions within the province as well as a selection of important sites. In addition to the Zurich team, two GIS specialists based at the ISEAS, Pearlyn Pang and Benjamin Hu, designed and produced the various maps within the chapters themselves.

Notes

1. In this book, the Province of the Riau Islands will also be referred to by its Indonesian name Provinsi Kepulauan Riau or Kepri for short.
2. For a fuller discussion of the negotiations between Riau Islands leaders and then President Megawati, consult Kimura (2013).
3. The entity is often referred to by its Indonesian name BP Batam, which stands for Badan Pengusahaan Batam.

References

Andaya, Barbara Watson. 1997. "Recreating a Vision: Daratan and Kepulauan in Historical Context". *Bijdragen tot de Taal-, Land- en Volkenkunde* 153, no. 4: 483–508.

BIDA. 1980. *The Batam Development Program*. Jakarta: Batam Industrial Development Authority.

BPS 2017 [Author to supply bibliographic information]

Brunet-Jailly, Emmanuel. 2005. "Theorizing Borders: An Interdisciplinary Perspective". *Geopolitics* 10: 633–49.

Crouch, Harold. 2010. *Political Reform in Indonesia After Suharto*. Singapore: Institute of Southeast Asian Studies.

Dedees, Adek Risma. 2015. "Imagining Malay in Border Communities: Konstruksi Identitas Nasionalisme Masyarakat Perbatasan di Kepuluan Batam". *Jurnal Ilmu Sosial dan Ilmu Politik* 19, no. 2: 215–32.

Huntington, Samuel P. 2006. *Political Order in Changing Societies*. New Haven and London: Yale University Press.

Hutchinson, Francis E. 2015. *Mirror Images in Different Frames? Johor, the Riau Islands, and Competition for Investment from Singapore*. Singapore: Institute of Southeast Asian Studies.

———. 2016. "The SIJORI Cross-Border Region: The Whole and Sum of Its Parts". In *The SIJORI Cross-Border Region: Transnational Politics, Economics, and Culture*, edited by F.E. Hutchinson and T. Chong. Singapore: ISEAS – Yusof Ishak Institute.

———. 2020. "In the Gateway's Shadow: Interactions between Singapore's Hinterlands". *Growth and Change*. https://doi.org/10.1111/grow.12359

———, and Terence Chong. 2016. *The SIJORI Cross-Border Region: Transnational Politics, Economics, and Culture*. Singapore: ISEAS – Yusof Ishak Institute.

———, and Serina Rahman. 2020. *Johor: Abode of Development?* Singapore: ISEAS – Yusof Ishak Institute.

Jessop, B. 2002. "The Political Economy of Scale". In *Globalization, Regionalization, and Cross-Border Regions*, edited by M. Perkmann and N. Sum. Basingstoke: Palgrave Macmillan.

Kimura, Ehito. 2013. *Political Change and Territoriality in Indonesia: Provincial Proliferation*. London: Routledge.

Malley, M. 1999. "Resource Distribution, State Coherence, and Political Centralization in Indonesia, 1950–1997". PhD dissertation, University of Wisconsin-Madison.

Negara, Siwage Dharma, and Francis E. Hutchinson 2020. "Batam: Life after the FTZ". *Bulletin of Indonesian Economic Studies*, https://doi.org/10.1080/00074918.2019.1648752

Nur, Yoslan. 2000. "L'ile de Batam a l'ombre de Singapore: Investissement singapourien et dependence de Batam". *Archipel* 59: 145–70.

Pangestu, Mari. 1991. "The Growth Triangle: An Indonesian Perspective". In *Growth Triangle: The Johor-Singapore-Riau Experience*, edited by Lee Tsao Yuan. Singapore: Institute of Southeast Asian Studies.

Perkmann, Markus, and Sum Ngai-Ling. 2002. "Globalization, Regionalization and Cross-Border Regions: Scales, Discourses and Governance". In *Globalization, Regionalization, and Cross-Border Regions*, edited by Markus Perkmann and Ngai-Ling Sum. Basingstoke: Palgrave Macmillan.

Phelps, N.A. 2004. "Triangular Diplomacy Writ Small: The Political Economy of the Indonesia-Malaysia-Singapore Growth Triangle". *Pacific Review* 17, no. 3: 341–68.

Shah, A., Z. Qureshi, A. Bagchi, B. Binder, and H.F. Zou. 1994. *Intergovernmental Fiscal Relations in Indonesia: Issues and Reform Options*. China Economics and Management Academy Working Papers No. 474. Beijing: Central University of Finance and Economics.

Smith, S.L.D. 1996. "Developing Batam: Indonesian Political Economy under the New Order". PhD dissertation, Research School of Pacific and Asian Studies, Australian National University.

Tagliacozzo, E. 2005. *Secret Trades, Porous Borders: Smuggling and States Along a Southeast Asian Frontier, 1865–1915*. New Haven, CT: Yale University Press.

Toh M.H., and Bo, J. 2016. "The SIJORI Cross-Border Region as an Economic Entity in 1990 and 2012, and Perspectives for 2030". In *The SIJORI Cross-Border Region: Transnational Politics, Economics, and Culture*, edited by F.E. Hutchinson and T. Chong. Singapore: ISEAS – Yusof Ishak Institute.

Wee, Vivienne. 2016. "The Significance of Riau in SIJORI". In *The SIJORI Cross-Border Region: Transnational Politics, Economics, and Culture*, edited by F.E. Hutchinson and T. Chong. Singapore: ISEAS – Yusof Ishak Institute.

Wong Poh Kam, and Ng Kwan Kee. 2009. "Batam, Bintan and Karimun: Past History and Current Development Towards Being A SEZ". Asia Competitiveness Institute, National University of Singapore.

Periodicals
Antara News
Batampos
Far Eastern Economic Review
Jakarta Post
Straits Times
Tempo

I
Economics

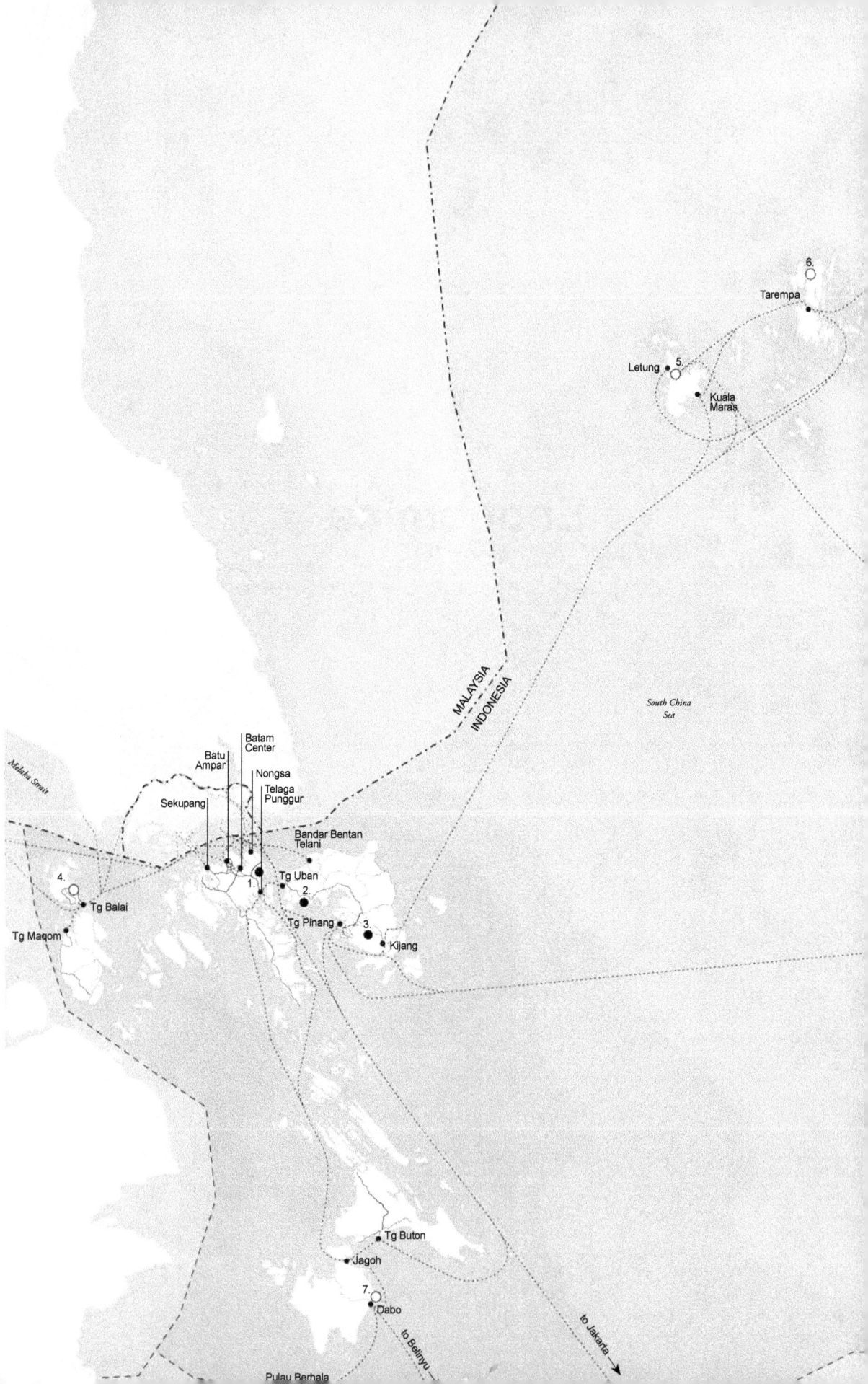

Batam
Center

Batu
Ampar

Nongsa

Sekupang

Telaga
Punggur

Bandar Bentan
Telani

MALAYSIA

INDONESIA

South China
Sea

Melaka Strait

6.

Tarempa

Letung 5.

Kuala
Maras

4.

Tg Balai

1.

Tg Uban

2.

Tg Magom

Tg Pinang

3.

Kijang

Tg Buton

Jagoh

7.

Dabo

to Belinyu

to Jakarta →

Pulau Berhala

MAP 2.1
MOBILITY AND TRANSPORT

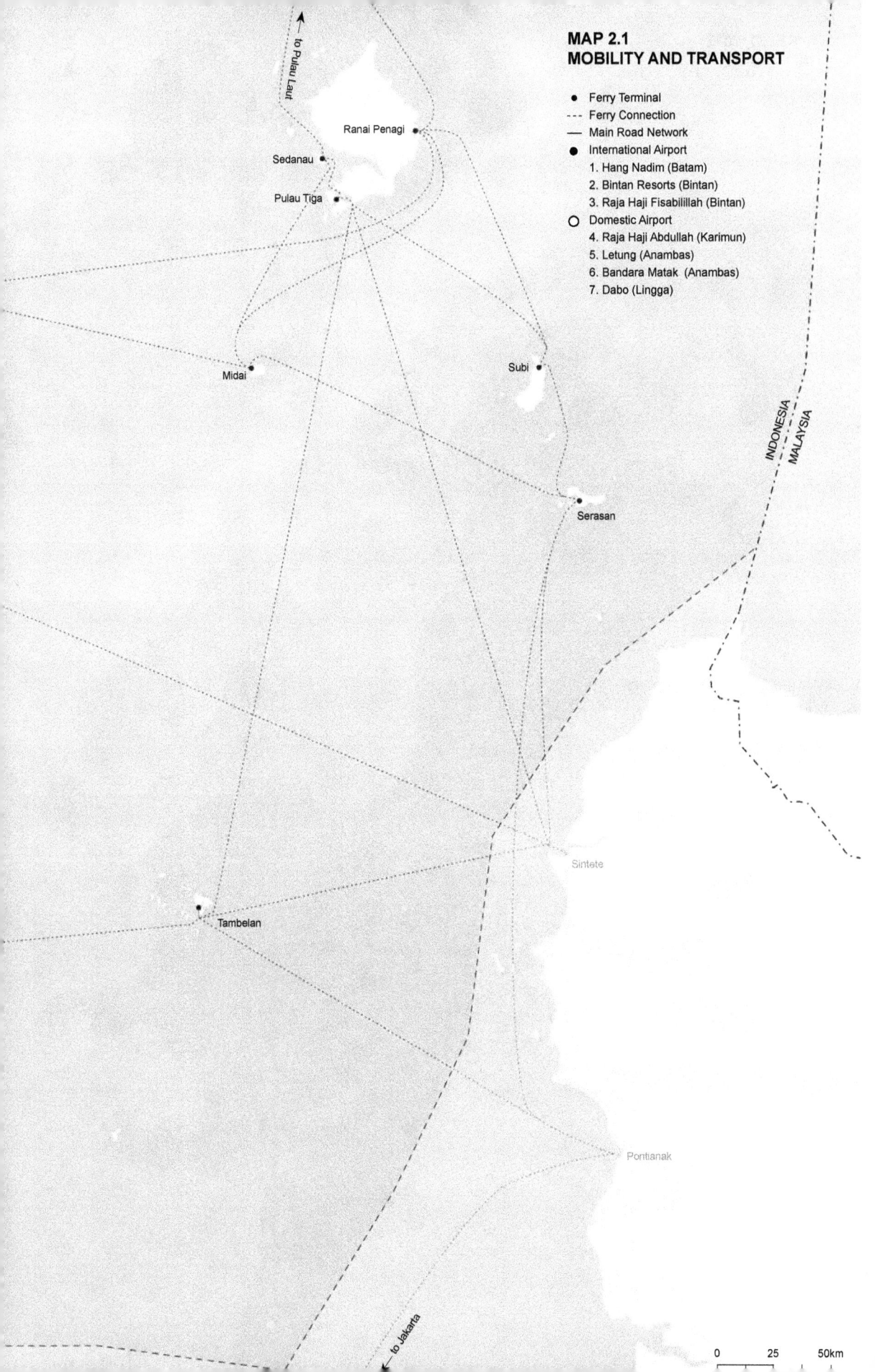

- Ferry Terminal
- - - Ferry Connection
— Main Road Network
- International Airport
  1. Hang Nadim (Batam)
  2. Bintan Resorts (Bintan)
  3. Raja Haji Fisabilillah (Bintan)
- Domestic Airport
  4. Raja Haji Abdullah (Karimun)
  5. Letung (Anambas)
  6. Bandara Matak (Anambas)
  7. Dabo (Lingga)

to Pulau Laut

Ranai Penagi

Sedanau

Pulau Tiga

Midai

Subi

Serasan

INDONESIA
MALAYSIA

Sintete

Tambelan

Pontianak

to Jakarta

0   25   50km

MAP 2.2
GINI RATIO, 2017

- 0.25— 0.30
- 0.30— 0.35

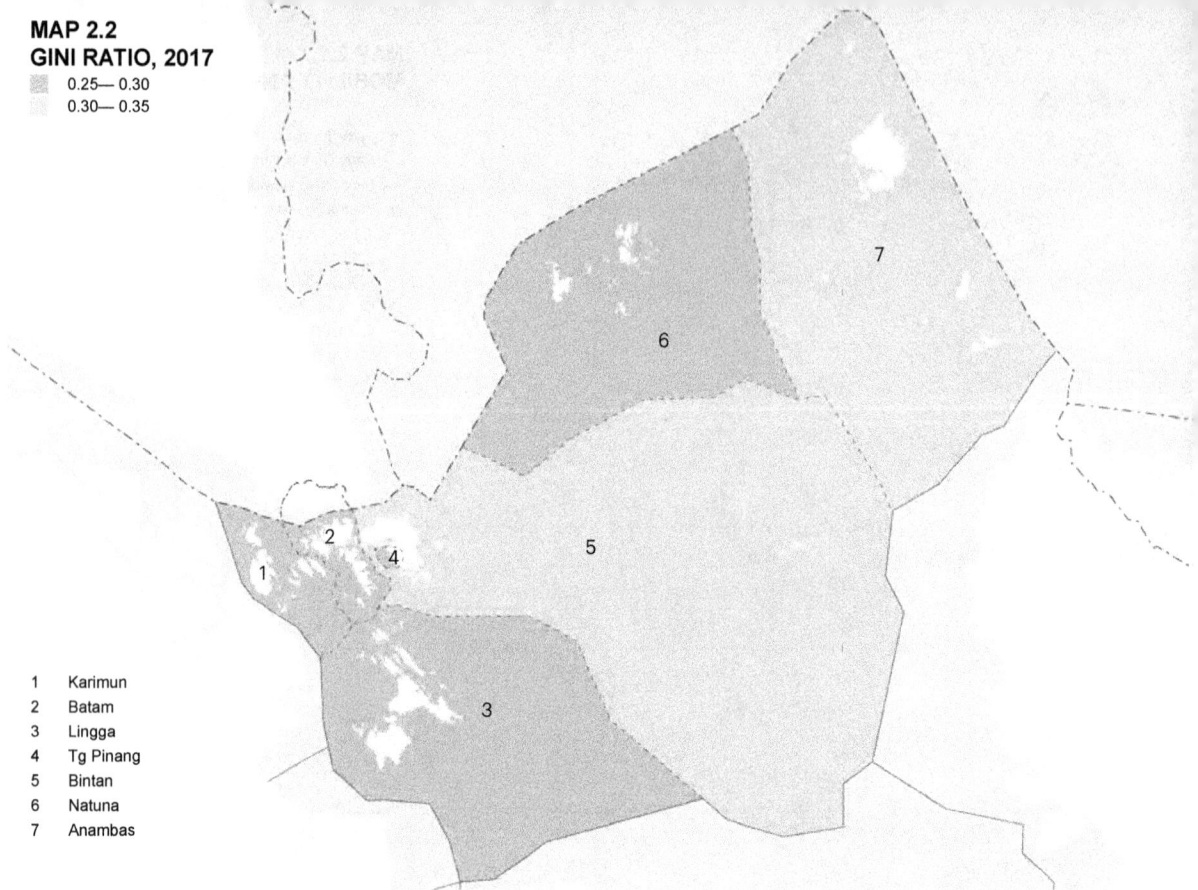

7

6

2
4

1

5

3

1   Karimun
2   Batam
3   Lingga
4   Tg Pinang
5   Bintan
6   Natuna
7   Anambas

MAP 2.3
HUMAN DEVELOPMENT INDEX, 2018

- 80— 85%
- 75— 80%
- 70— 75%
- 65— 70%
- 60— 65%

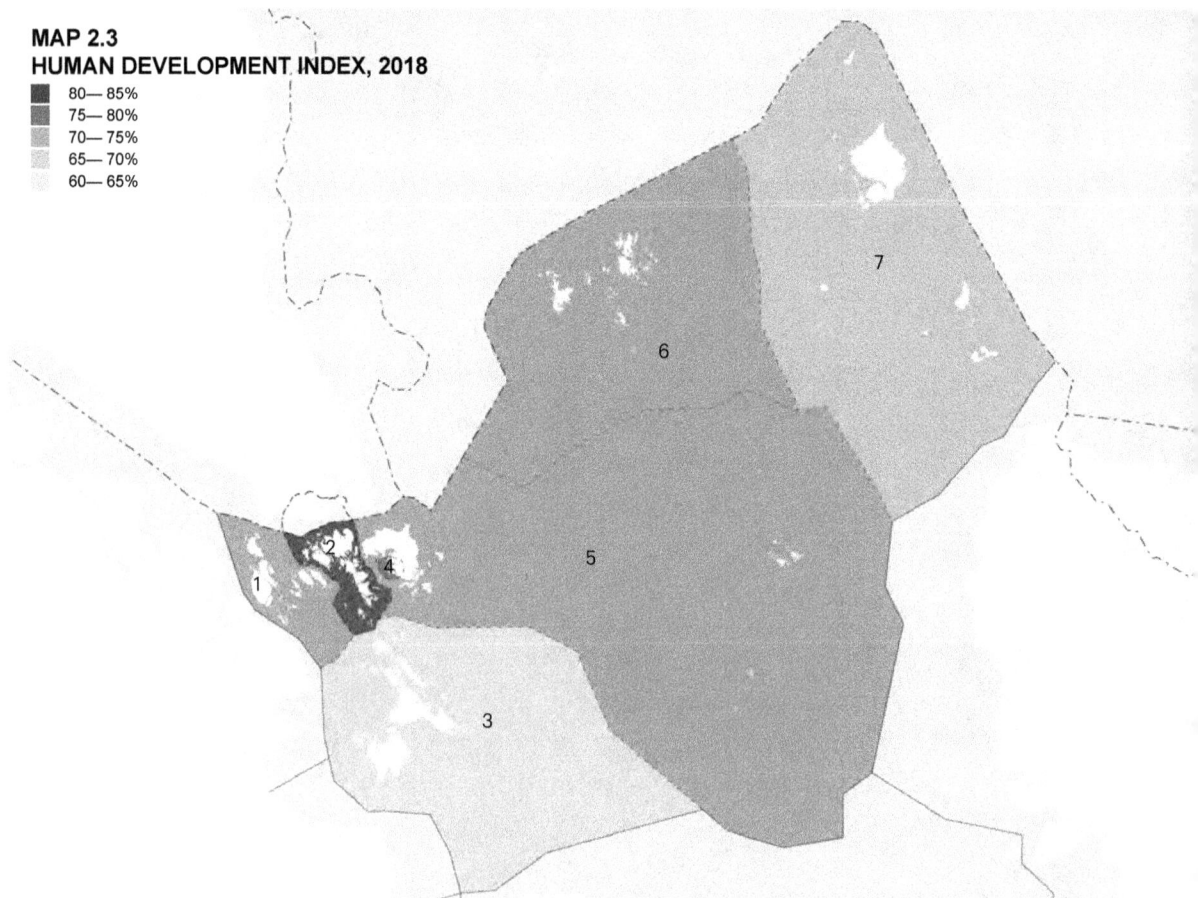

7

6

2
4

1

5

3

AP 2.4
POPULATION GROWTH RATE, 2017-18

3.0— 4.0
2.0— 3.0
1.0— 2.0
0.0— 1.0

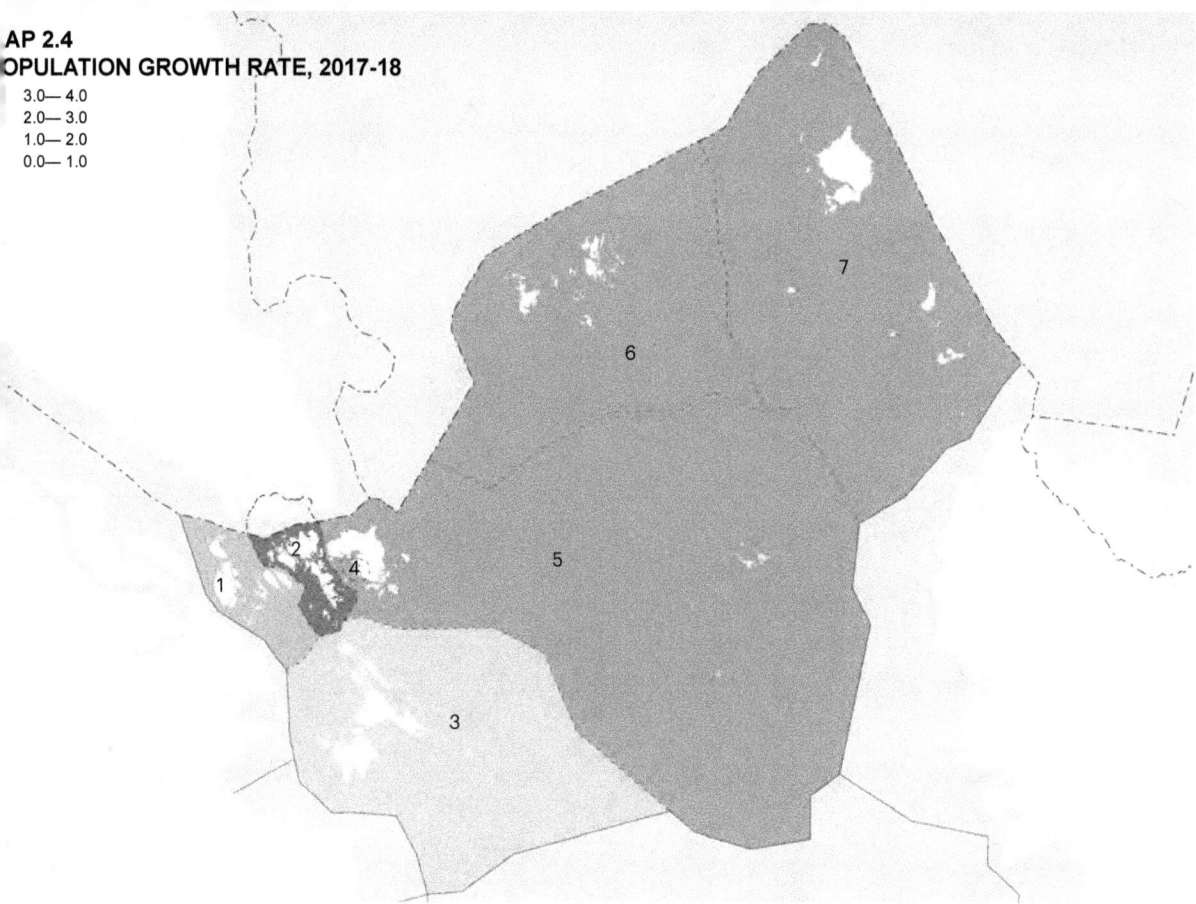

AP 2.5
UNEMPLOYMENT, 2018

8.0— 10.0
4.0— 6.0
2.0— 4.0

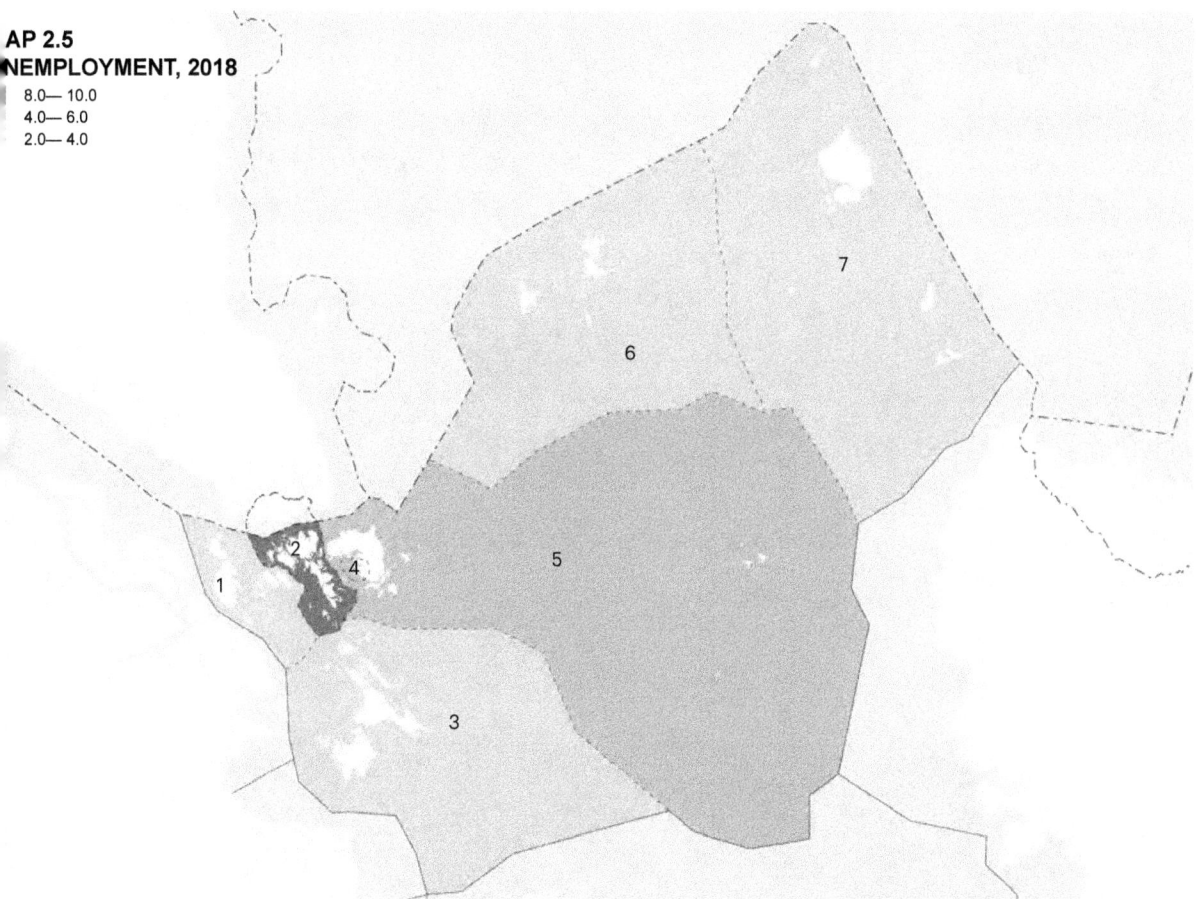

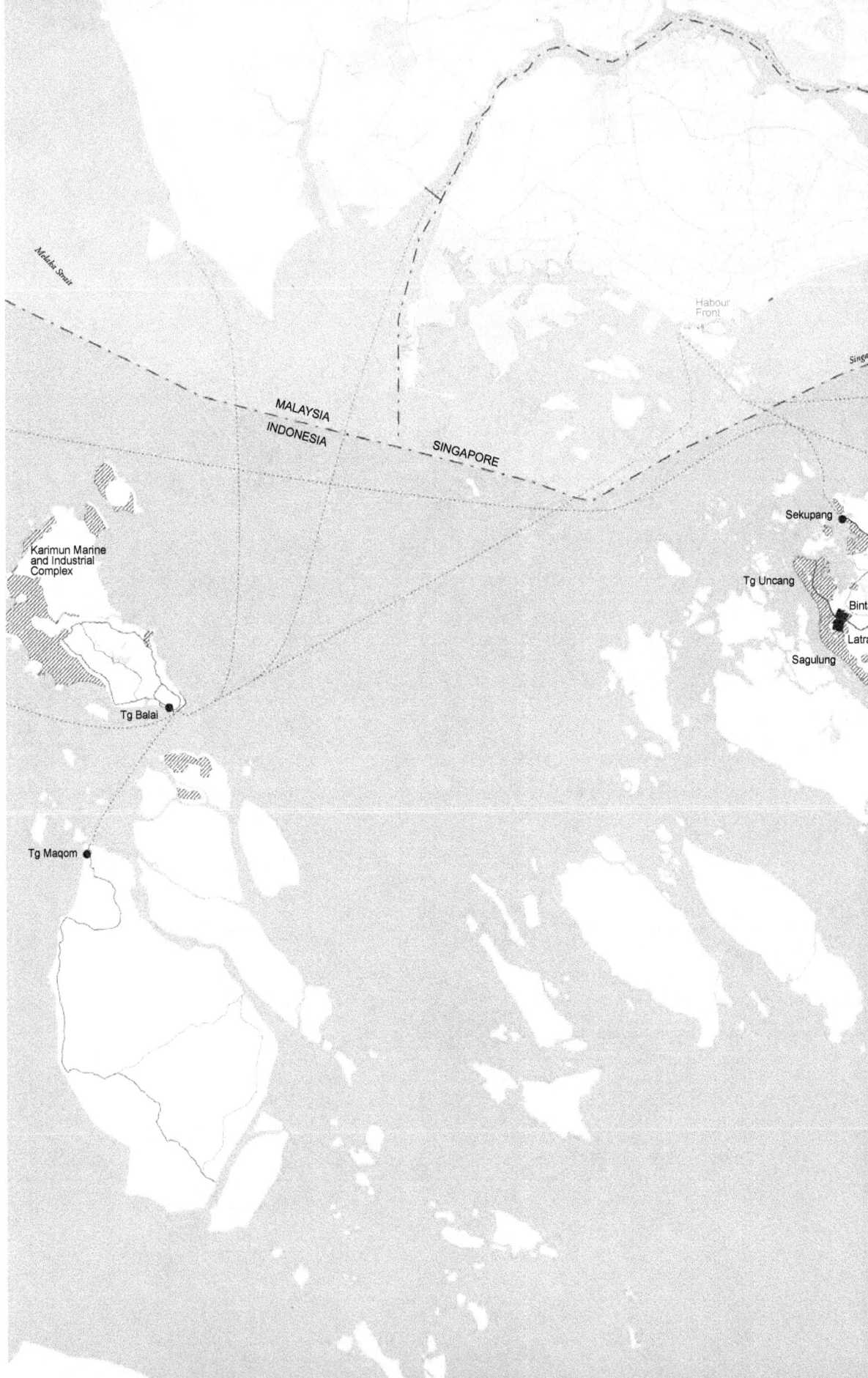

Melaka Strait

MALAYSIA

INDONESIA

SINGAPORE

Habour Front

Singapo

Sekupang

Tg Uncang

Binta

Karimun Marine
and Industrial
Complex

Latra

Sagulung

Tg Balai

Tg Maqom

MAP 2.6
MANUFACTURING SECTOR
IN BATAM, BINTAN AND KARIMUN

■ Industrial Park
▨ Industry and Logistic
-·-·- Ferry Connection
— Main Road Network

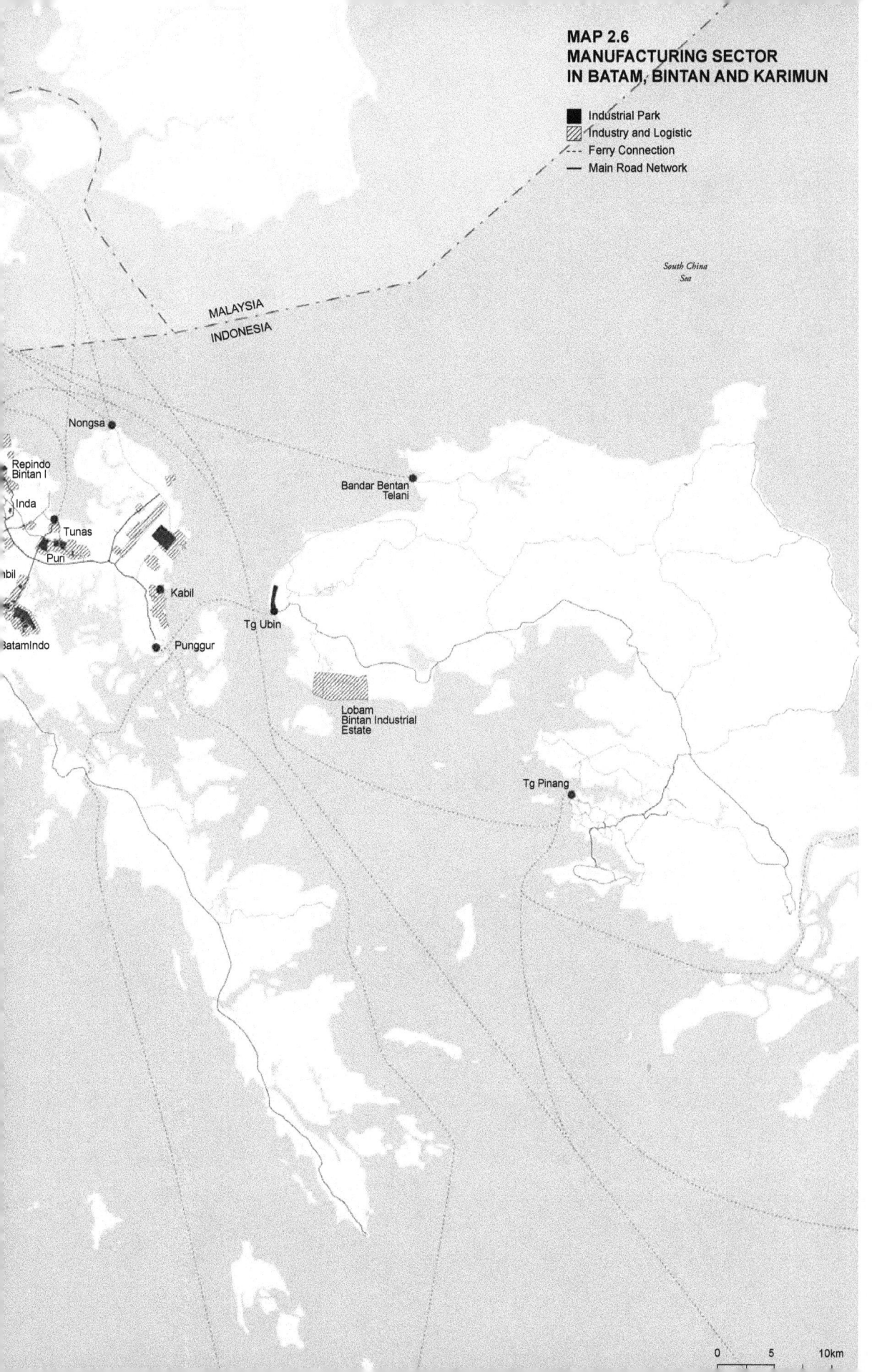

South China Sea

MALAYSIA

INDONESIA

Nongsa

Repindo
Bintan I

Inda

Tunas

Puri

bil

Kabil

BatamIndo

Punggur

Tg Ubin

Bandar Bentan
Telani

Lobam
Bintan Industrial
Estate

Tg Pinang

0   5   10km

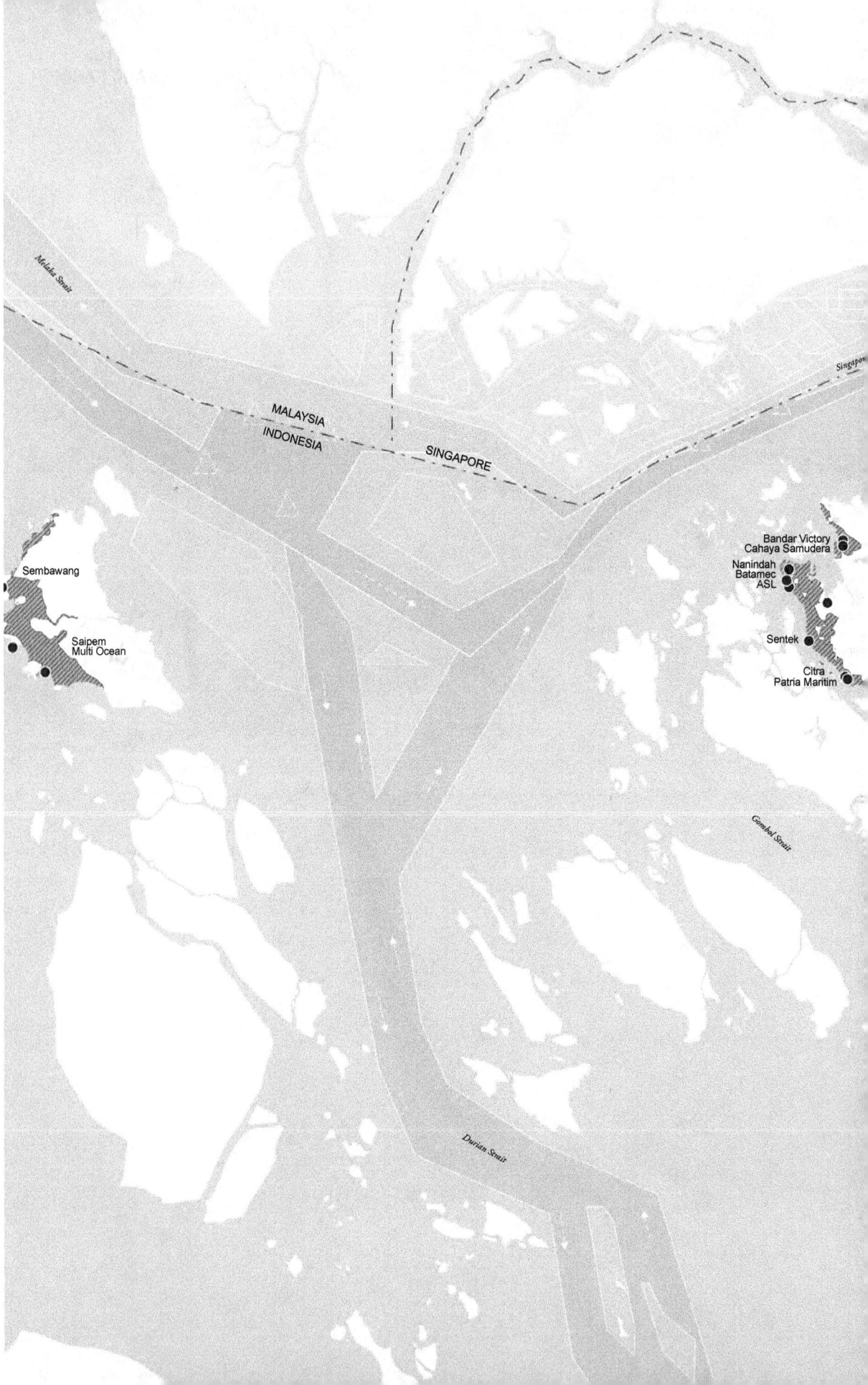

Melaka Strait

Singapore

MALAYSIA

INDONESIA

SINGAPORE

Sembawang

Saipem
Multi Ocean

Bandar Victory
Cahaya Samudera

Nanindah
Batamec
ASL

Sentek

Citra
Patria Maritim

Gombol Strait

Durian Strait

● Shipyard
▨ Main Shipbuilding Area
☐ Fairway

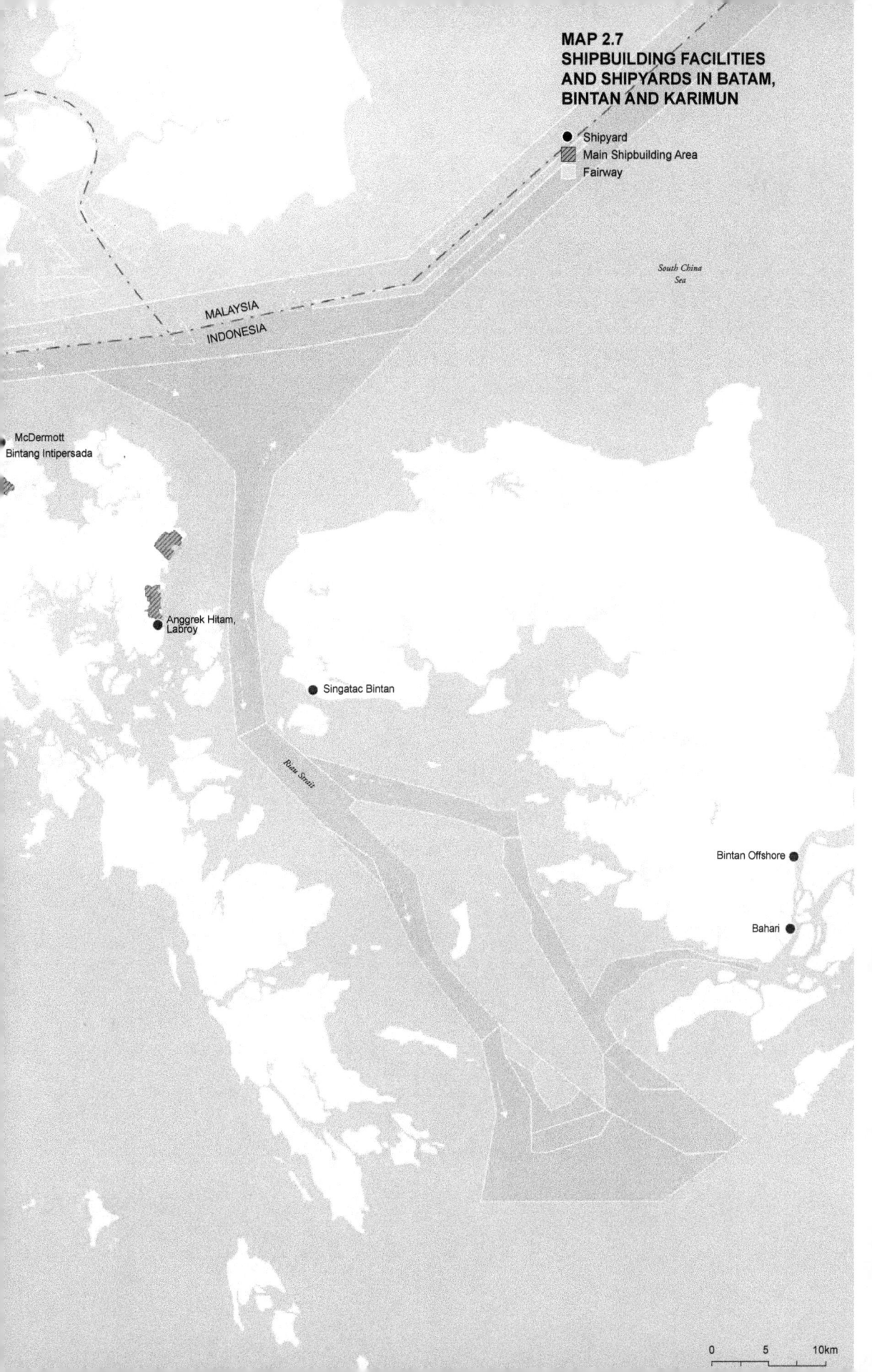

*South China
Sea*

MALAYSIA

INDONESIA

McDermott
Bintang Intipersada

Anggrek Hitam,
Labroy

● Singatac Bintan

Riau Strait

Bintan Offshore ●

Bahari ●

0   5   10km

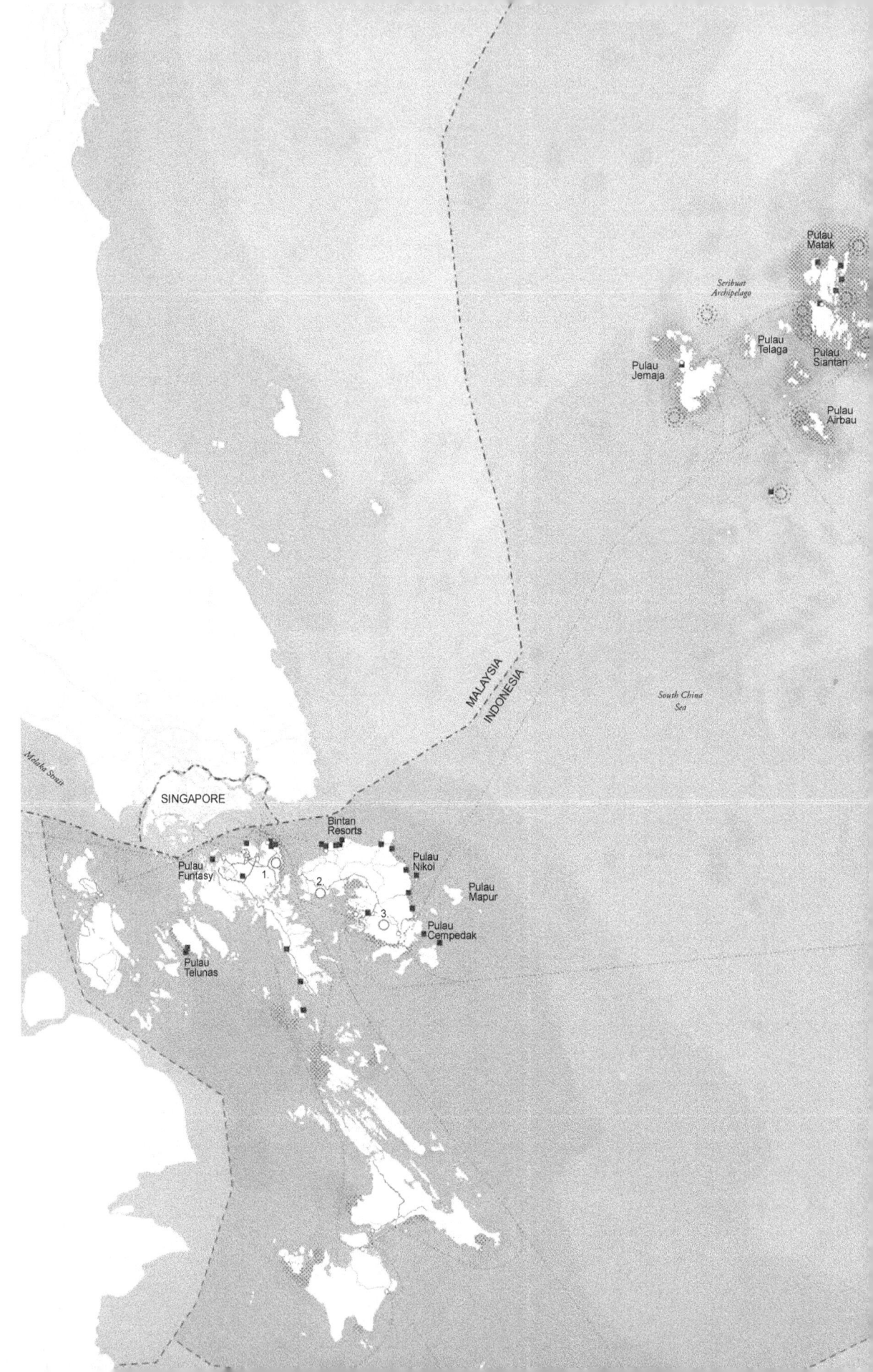

Pulau Matak

Seribuat
Archipelago

Pulau Telaga

Pulau Jemaja

Pulau Siantan

Pulau Airbau

MALAYSIA
INDONESIA

South China
Sea

Melaka Strait

SINGAPORE

Bintan
Resorts

Pulau Nikoi

Pulau Funtasy

1.

2.

Pulau Mapur

3.

Pulau Cempedak

Pulau Telunas

MAP 2.8
TOURISM

- ■ Resort
- ▦ Reef
- ◉ Diving Spot
- ◯ International Airport
  - 1. Hang Nadim (Batam)
  - 2. Bintan Resorts (Bintan)
  - 3. Raja Haji Fisabilillah (Bintan)
- ○ Ferry Terminal
- ---- Ferry Connection

Natuna

Pulau
Sedanau

Pulau
Batang

Pulau
Mida

Pulau
Subi Besar

Pulau
Serasan

INDONESIA

MALAYSIA

Sintete

Tambelan
Archipelago

Pulau
Tambelan
Besar

Pontianak

0   25   50km

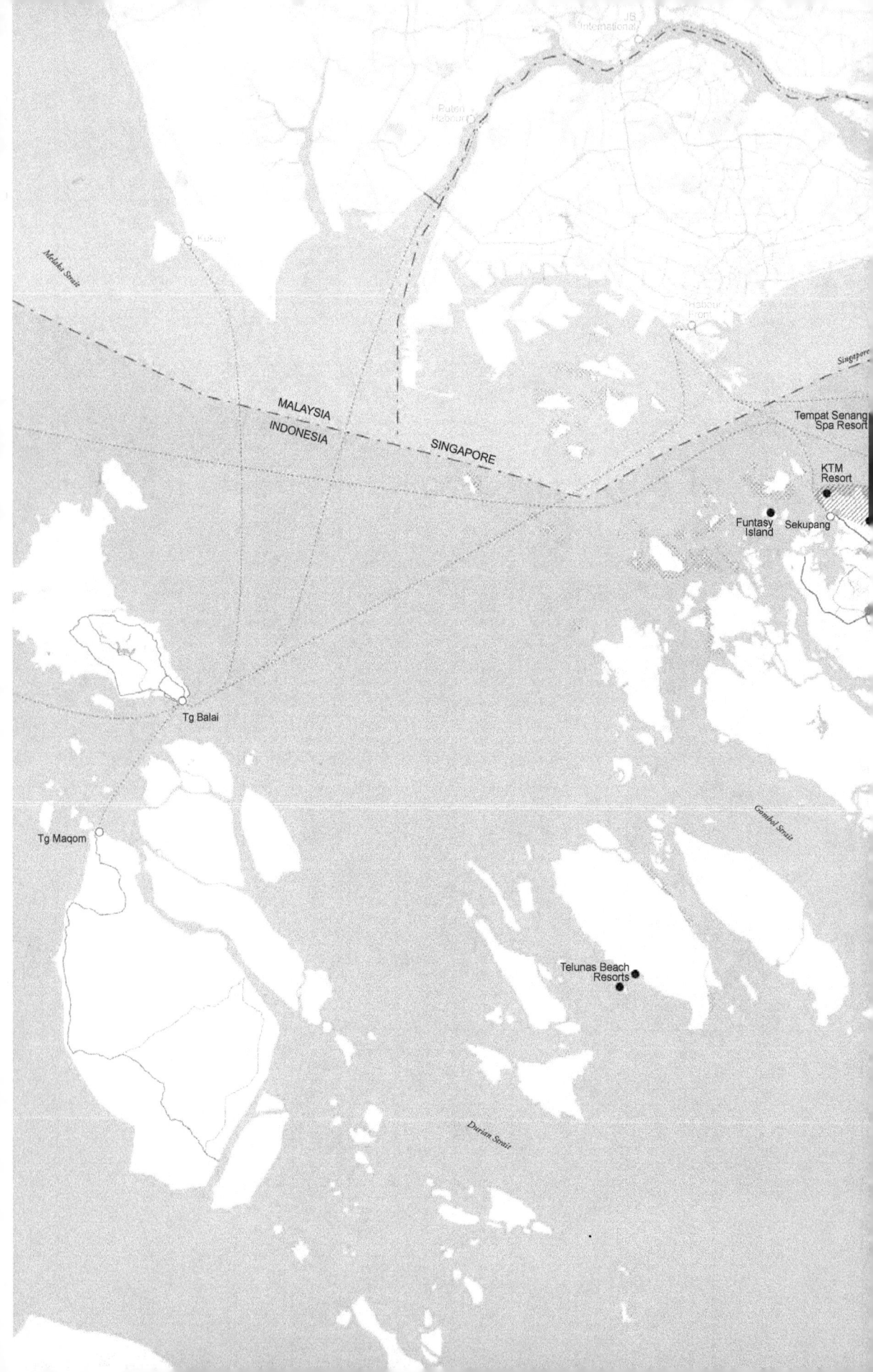

JB
International

Pulau
Habuur

Melaka Strait

MALAYSIA

INDONESIA

SINGAPORE

Habour
Front

Singapore

Tempat Senang
Spa Resort

KTM
Resort

Funtasy
Island

Sekupang

Tg Balai

Gombol Strait

Tg Maqom

Telunas Beach
Resorts

Durian Strait

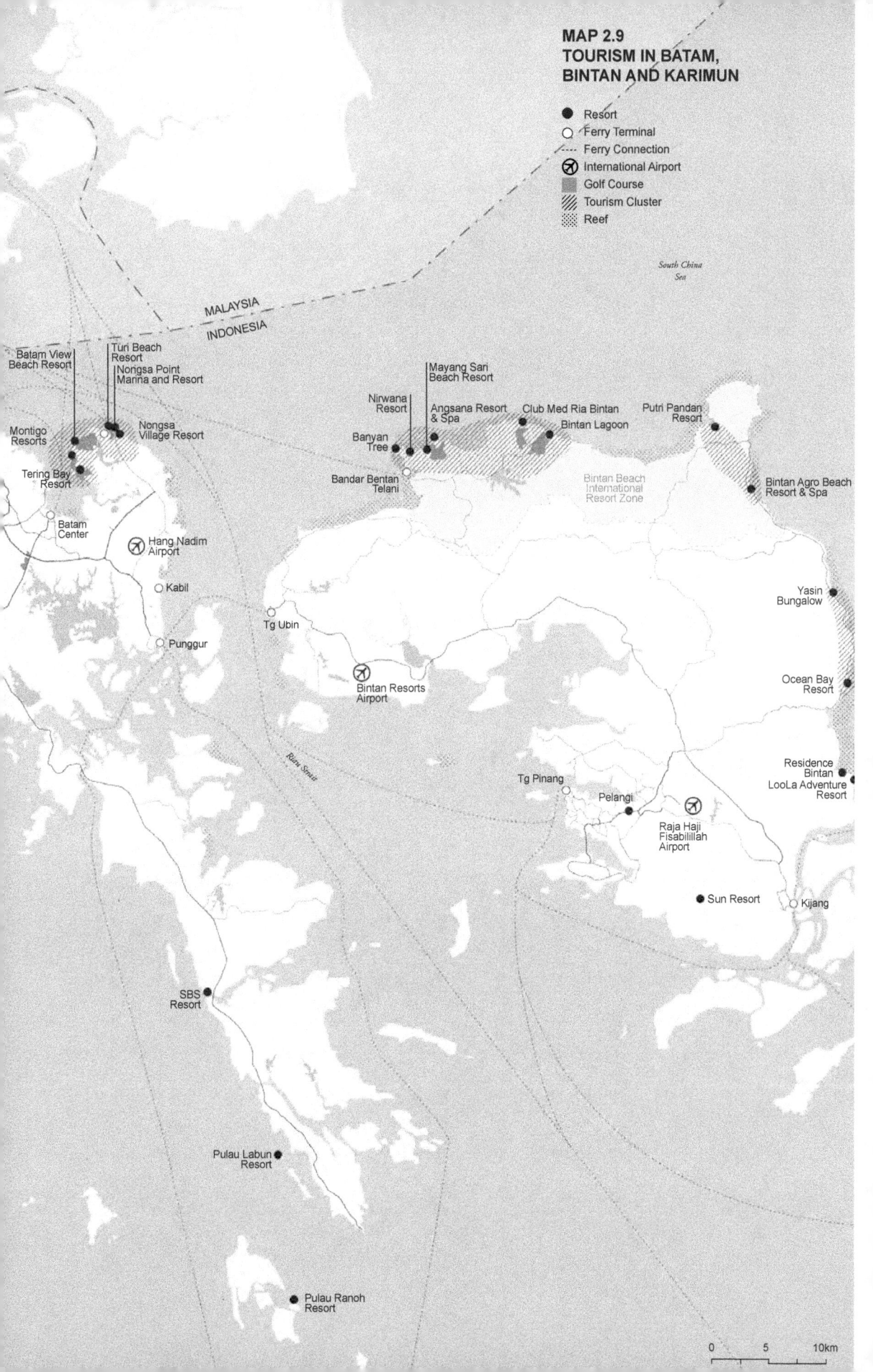

MAP 2.9
TOURISM IN BATAM,
BINTAN AND KARIMUN

- ● Resort
- ○ Ferry Terminal
- ---- Ferry Connection
- ✈ International Airport
- Golf Course
- Tourism Cluster
- Reef

South China
Sea

MALAYSIA
INDONESIA

Batam View
Beach Resort
Turi Beach
Resort
Nongsa Point
Marina and Resort
Nongsa
Village Resort
Montigo
Resorts
Tering Bay
Resort
Batam
Center
Hang Nadim
Airport
Kabil
Punggur
Tg Ubin

Mayang Sari
Beach Resort
Nirwana
Resort
Angsana Resort
& Spa
Club Med Ria Bintan
Bintan Lagoon
Putri Pandan
Resort
Banyan
Tree
Bandar Bentan
Telani
Bintan Beach
International
Resort Zone
Bintan Agro Beach
Resort & Spa

Yasin
Bungalow

Ocean Bay
Resort

Bintan Resorts
Airport

Riau Strait

Tg Pinang
Pelangi
Raja Haji
Fisabilillah
Airport

Residence
Bintan
LooLa Adventure
Resort

Sun Resort
Kijang

SBS
Resort

Pulau Labun
Resort

Pulau Ranoh
Resort

0   5   10km

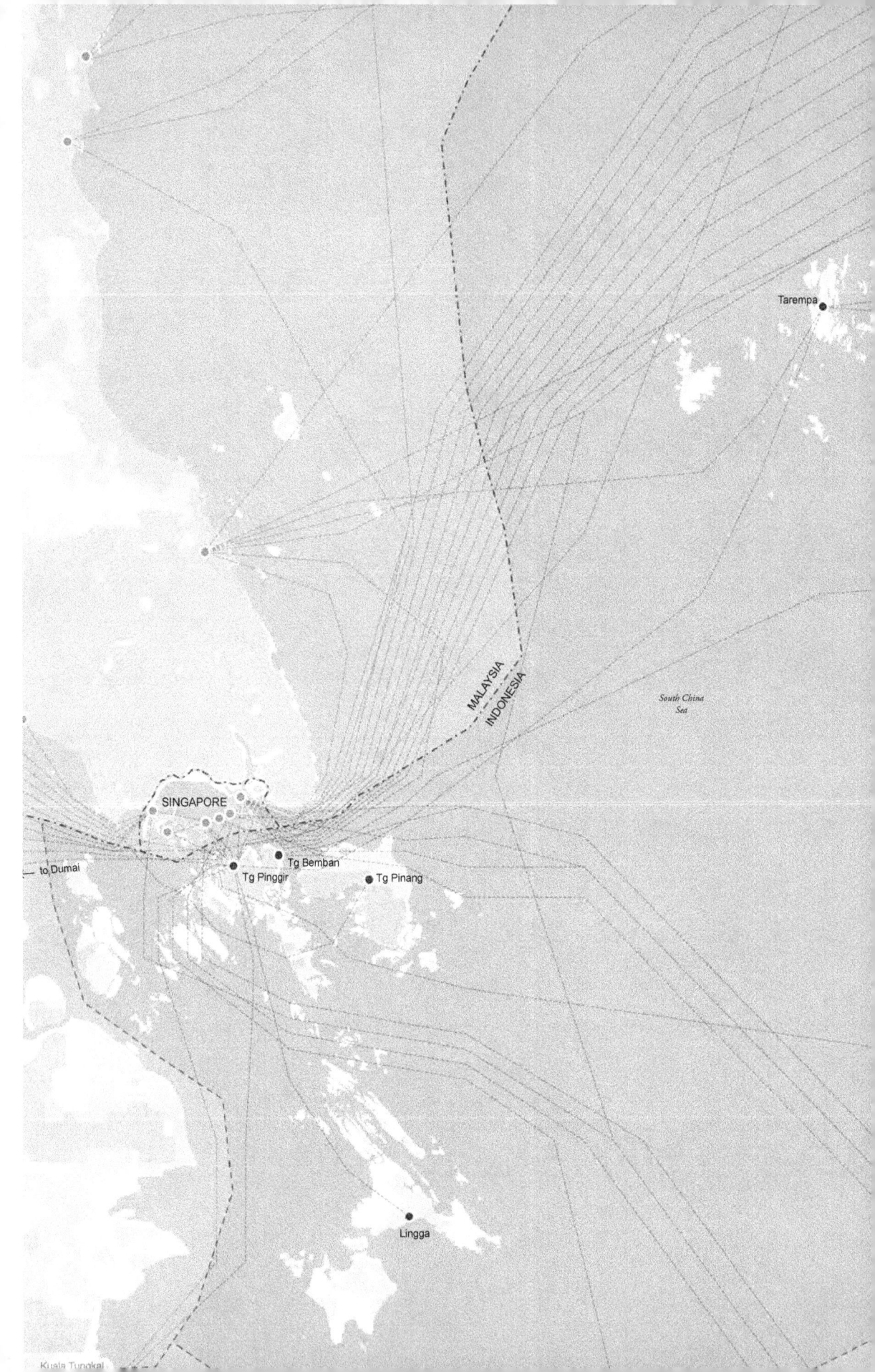

Tarempa

MALAYSIA
INDONESIA

South China
Sea

SINGAPORE

to Dumai

Tg Bemban

Tg Pinggir

Tg Pinang

Lingga

Kuala Tungkal

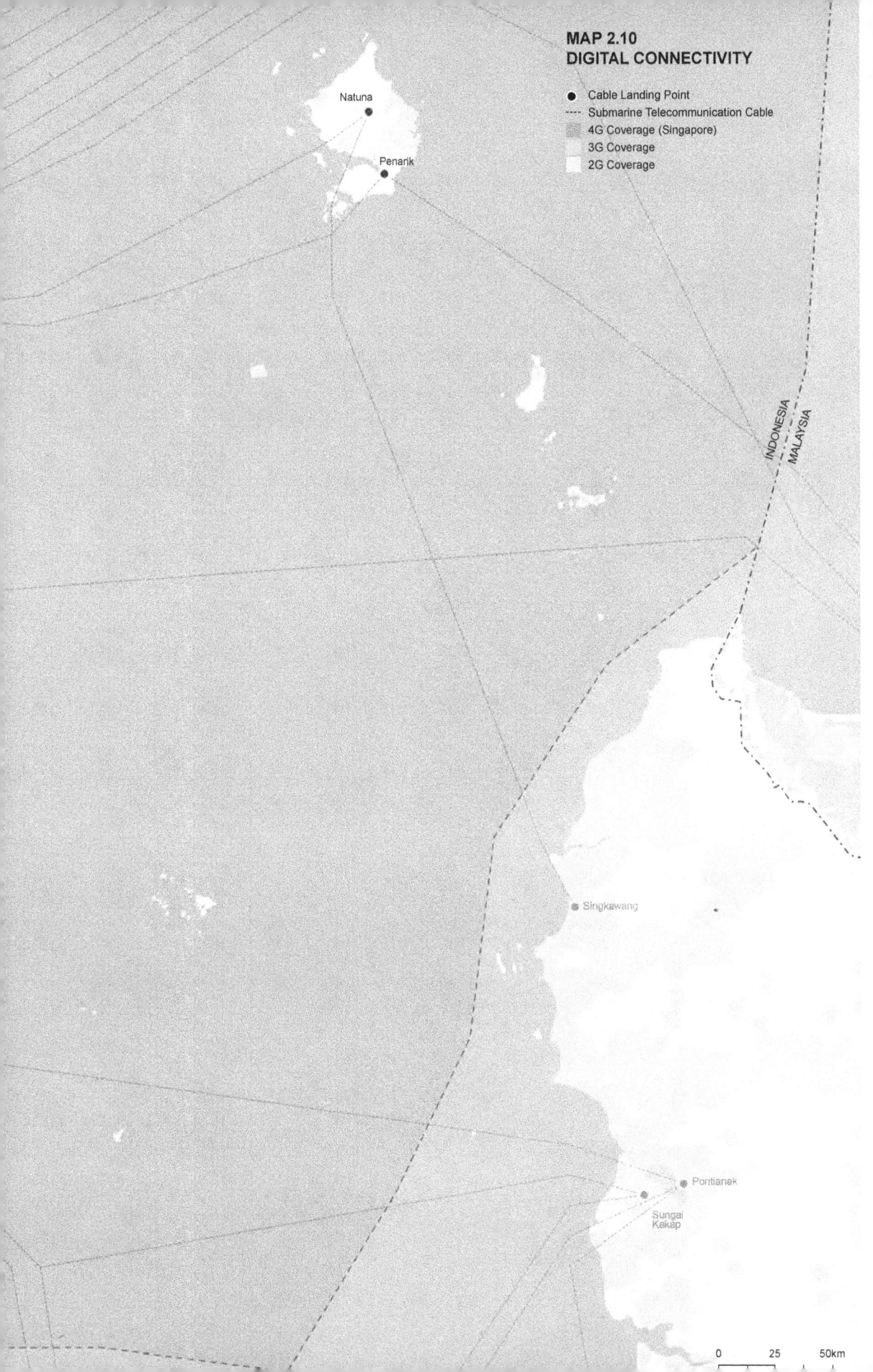

MAP 2.10
DIGITAL CONNECTIVITY

● Cable Landing Point
---- Submarine Telecommunication Cable
4G Coverage (Singapore)
3G Coverage
2G Coverage

Natuna

Penarik

INDONESIA
MALAYSIA

Singkawang

Pontianak

Sungai
Kakap

0   25   50km

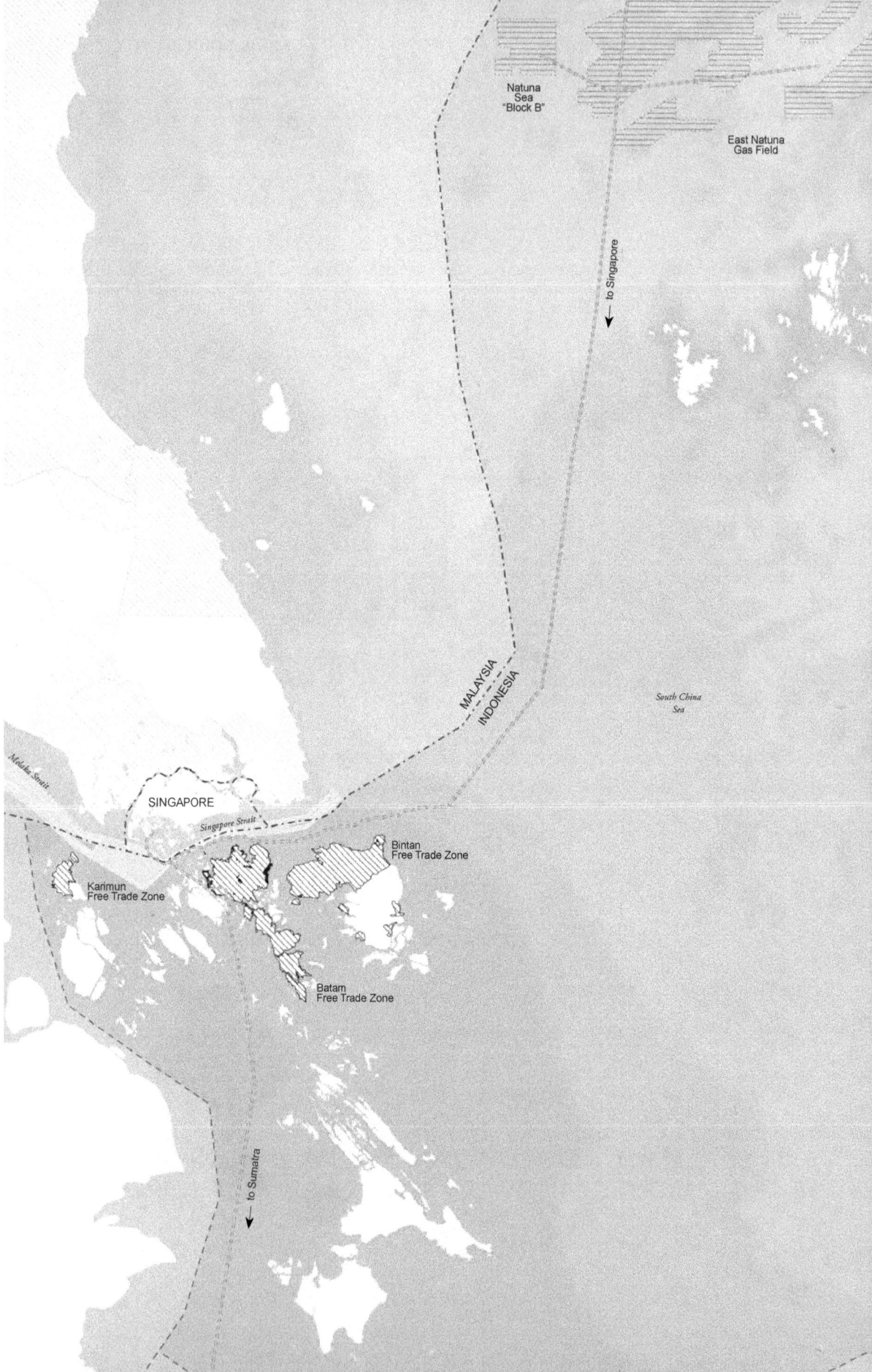

Natuna
Sea
"Block B"

East Natuna
Gas Field

to Singapore

MALAYSIA

INDONESIA

South China
Sea

Melaka Strait

SINGAPORE

Singapore Strait

Bintan
Free Trade Zone

Karimun
Free Trade Zone

Batam
Free Trade Zone

to Sumatra

MAP 2.11
ZONES AND TRADE REGIMES

Special Economic Zone
Gas Concession Zone
Oil / Gas Pipeline
Fairway
Industry and Logistic

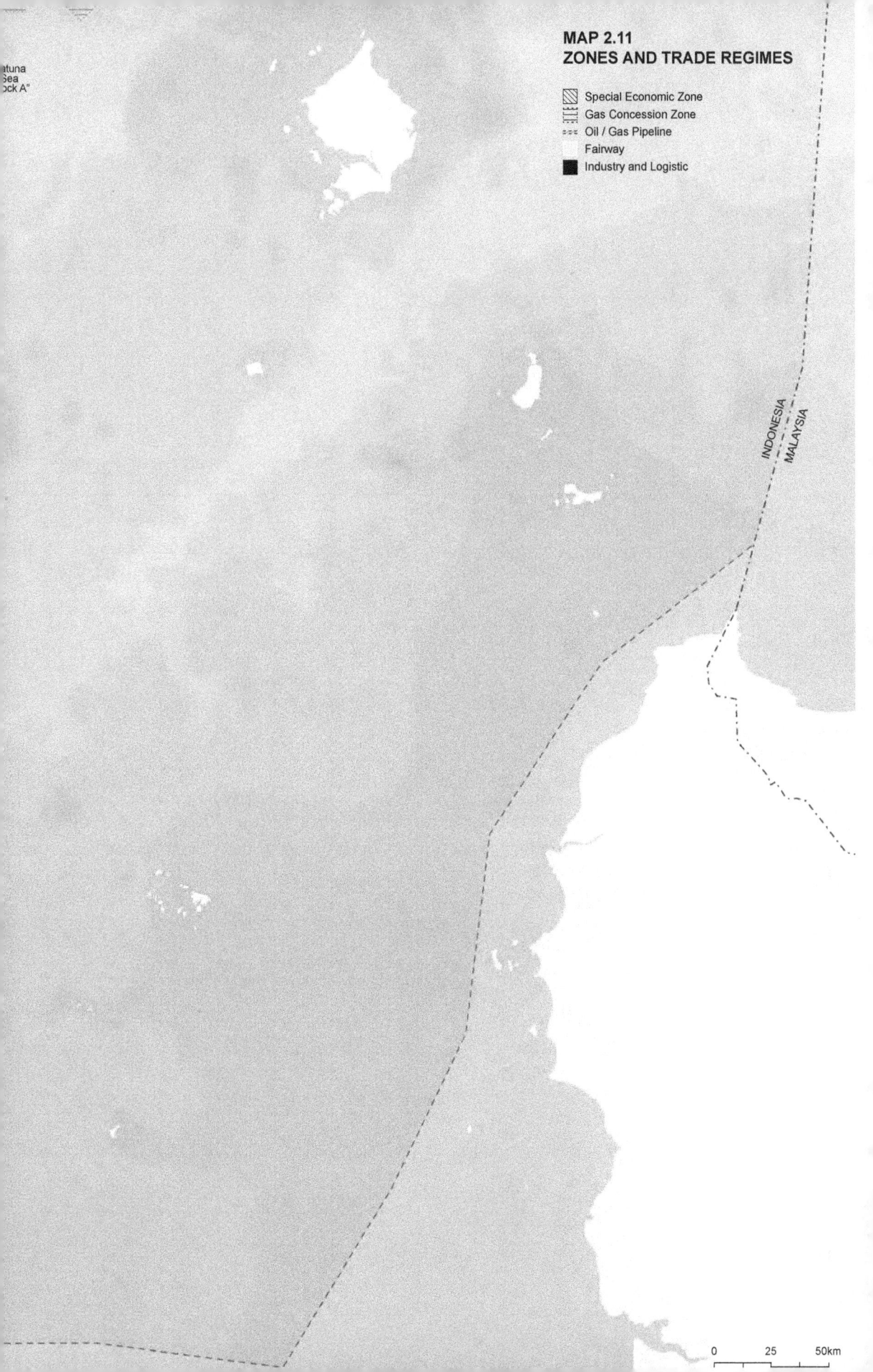

atuna
Sea
ock A"

INDONESIA
MALAYSIA

0   25   50km

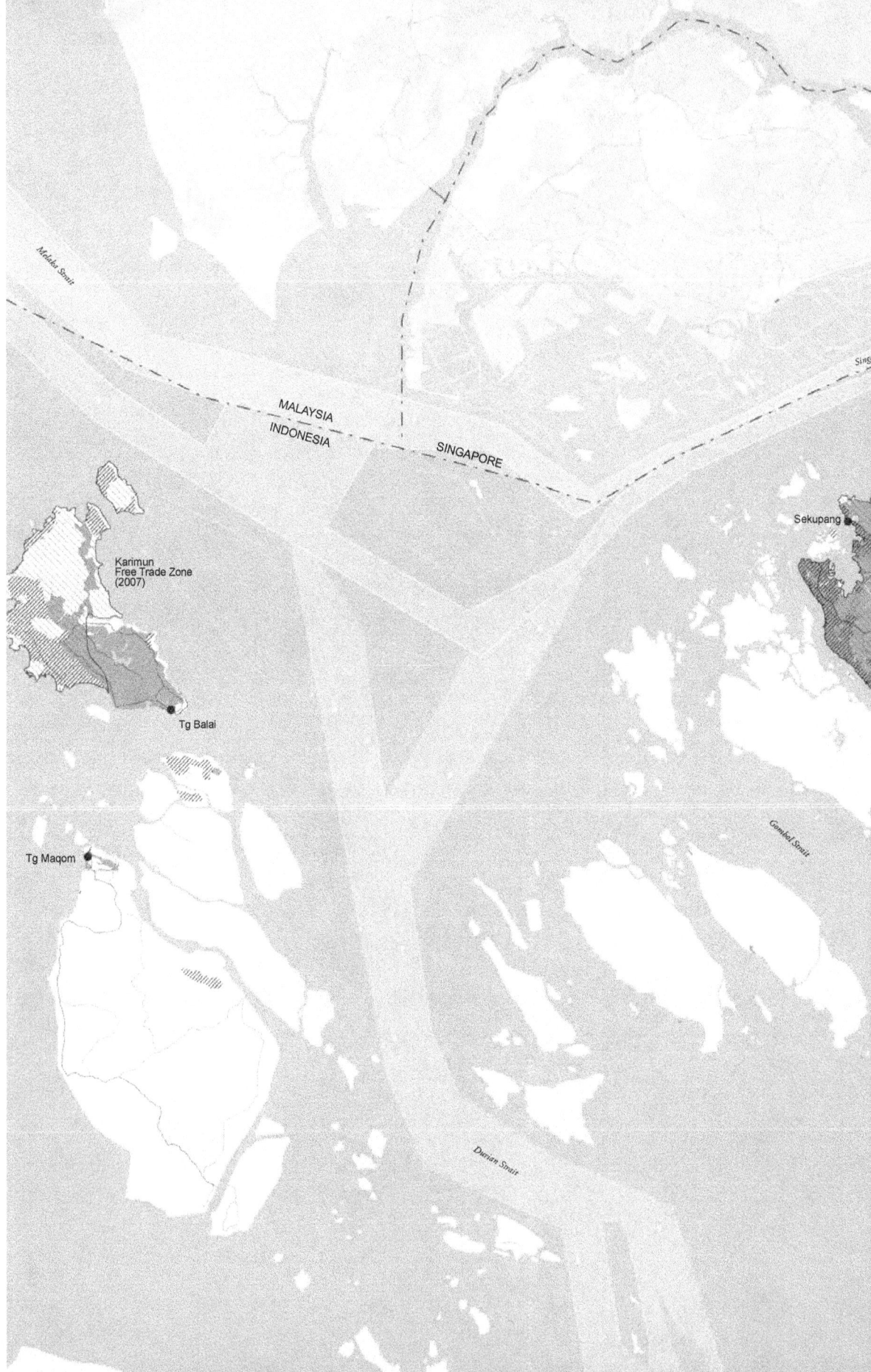

Melaka Strait

MALAYSIA

INDONESIA

SINGAPORE

Singapore

Karimun
Free Trade Zone
(2007)

Tg Balai

Sekupang

Tg Maqom

Gambol Strait

Durian Strait

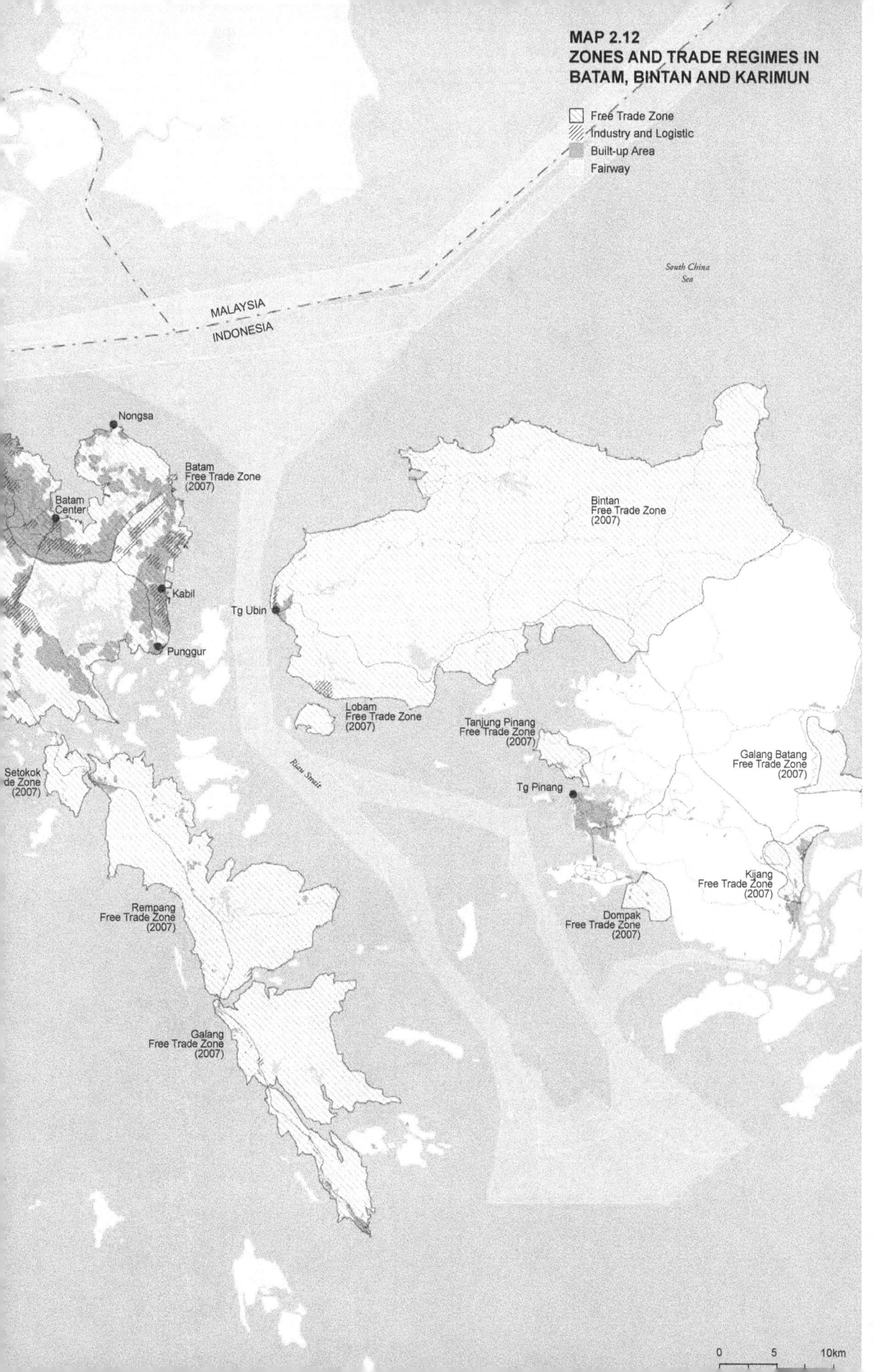

MAP 2.12
ZONES AND TRADE REGIMES IN
BATAM, BINTAN AND KARIMUN

Free Trade Zone
Industry and Logistic
Built-up Area
Fairway

South China
Sea

MALAYSIA
INDONESIA

Nongsa

Batam
Free Trade Zone
(2007)

Batam
Center

Kabil

Tg Ubin

Bintan
Free Trade Zone
(2007)

Punggur

Lobam
Free Trade Zone
(2007)

Tanjung Pinang
Free Trade Zone
(2007)

Galang Batang
Free Trade Zone
(2007)

Setokok
de Zone
(2007)

Riau Strait

Tg Pinang

Kijang
Free Trade Zone
(2007)

Rempang
Free Trade Zone
(2007)

Dompak
Free Trade Zone
(2007)

Galang
Free Trade Zone
(2007)

0   5   10km

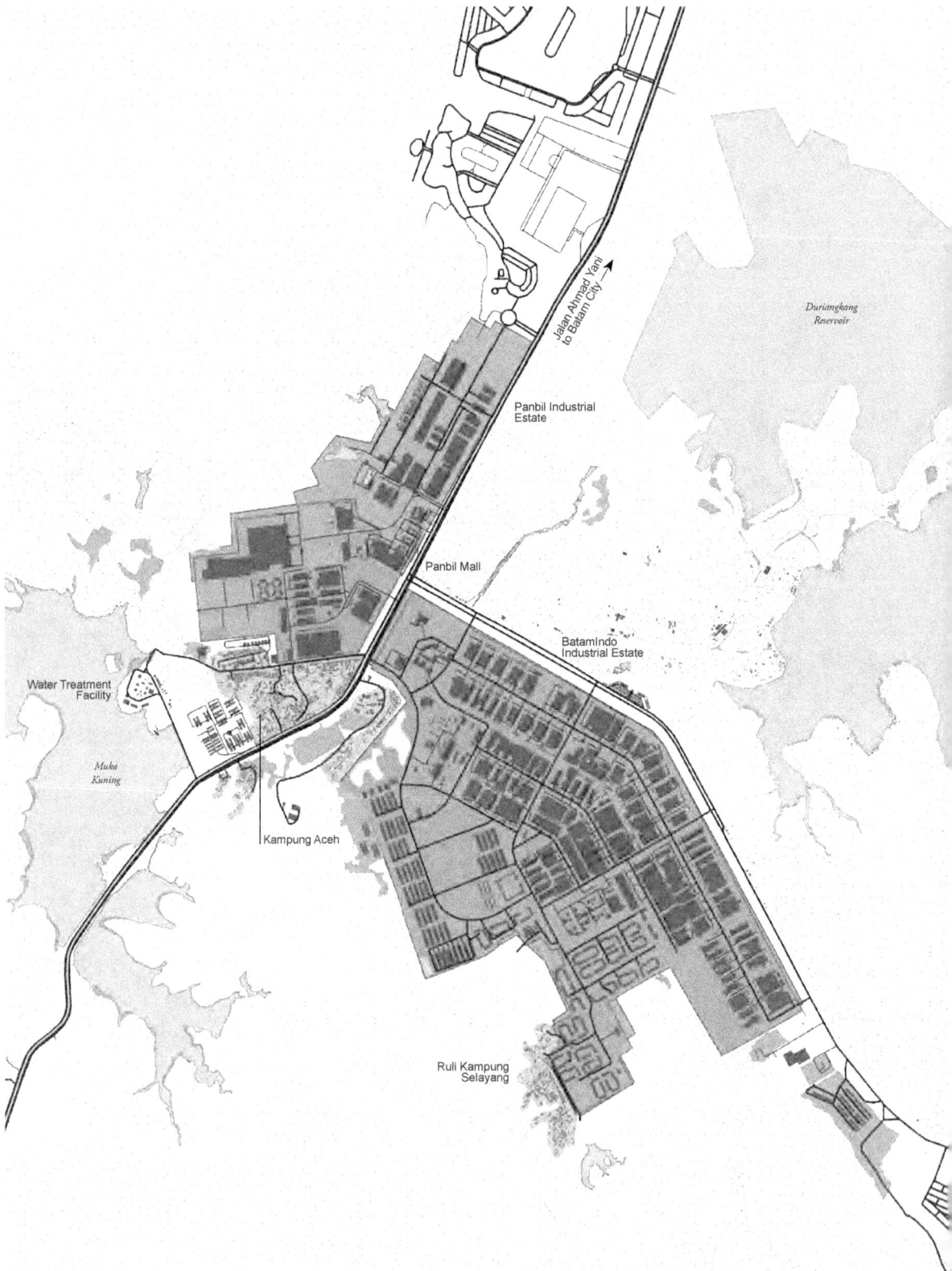

MAP 2.13
BATAMINDO INDUSTRIAL PARK, BATAM

Duriangkang Reservoir

Jalan Ahmad Yani to Batam City

Panbil Industrial Estate

Panbil Mall

BatamIndo Industrial Estate

Water Treatment Facility

Muka Kuning

Kampung Aceh

Ruli Kampung Selayang

0   250   5

MAP 2.14
BINTAN BEACH INTERNATIONAL
RESORT, BINTAN

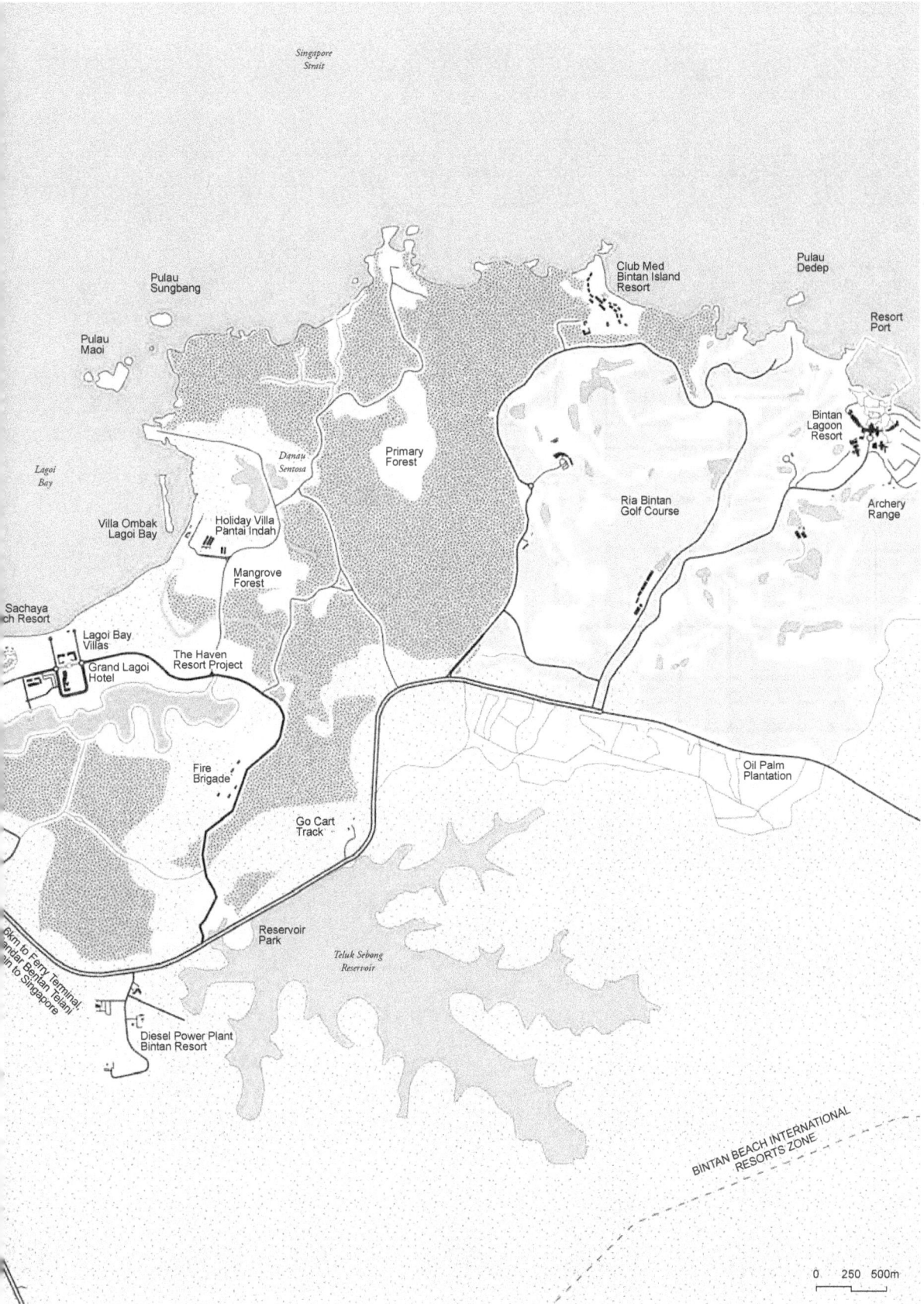

*Singapore
Strait*

Pulau
Sungbang

Pulau
Maoi

*Lagoi
Bay*

Villa Ombak
Lagoi Bay

*Danau
Sentosa*

Holiday Villa
Pantai Indah

Primary
Forest

Club Med
Bintan Island
Resort

Pulau
Dedep

Resort
Port

Bintan
Lagoon
Resort

Ria Bintan
Golf Course

Archery
Range

Mangrove
Forest

Sachaya
ch Resort

Lagoi Bay
Villas

Grand Lagoi
Hotel

The Haven
Resort Project

Fire
Brigade

Go Cart
Track

Oil Palm
Plantation

5km to Ferry Terminal.
andan Bintan Telani.
ain to Singapore

Reservoir
Park

*Teluk Sebong
Reservoir*

Diesel Power Plant
Bintan Resort

BINTAN BEACH INTERNATIONAL
RESORTS ZONE

0   250   500m

2

THE MANUFACTURING SECTOR IN BATAM
Viable or Just Desirable?

Siwage Dharma Negara and Francis E. Hutchinson

INTRODUCTION

Batam has an unbeatable business proposition. Situated a mere 20 kilometres from Singapore, linked by logistics networks, and possessing vastly cheaper land and labour, the Indonesian island is ideally placed to absorb investment from its wealthier neighbour. In theory, it should be teeming with investors and populated by factories and workers.

Indeed, this is just what happened during the 1990s and early 2000s. The liberalization of investment regulations, coupled with Batam's well-developed infrastructure and proximity to Singapore, made the island an attractive site for manufacturing operations seeking to escape the city-state's rising costs. During the 1990s, Batam's industrial base grew in size and sophistication, rapidly becoming one of the country's centres of electrical and electronics production. In the mid-2000s, the shipbuilding industry also began to develop on the island. Coupled with the older, more established tourism sector, Batam became a crucial source of foreign exchange for Indonesia. Through these three "motors", hundreds of thousands of formal sector jobs were created, and the island became one of the country's richest—with its economy often growing at more than 10 per cent per annum.

Over the last few years, the success of Batam's export-focused industrialization model has come under question. In 2017, the island's growth rate flatlined at 2 per cent per annum, very substantially below the national average. Indeed, exports have been decreasing since 2013, and unemployment has spiked over the last two years. The once-burgeoning ranks of semiconductor, hard-disk drive, and component manufacturers have atrophied since 2010, with few new arrivals and many more anchor firms closing their facilities. In 2013, the shipbuilding sector, once heralded as Batam's sunrise industry, also began to contract. At present, the majority of the island's shipyards sit idle, or have turned to lower-value repair jobs to cover costs. Unemployment is now above the national average.

This chapter attempts to understand the key trends within Batam's manufacturing sector, and whether the island's manufacturing for export model is still viable. To this end, the chapter is structured in the following fashion. First, it will provide background to the development of the manufacturing sector on the island. Second, it will analyse recent developments in the island's key industries, namely electrical and electronics (E&E) and shipbuilding and repair. Third, using data from Indonesia's largest and most comprehensive data source on manufacturing, it will compare Batam with other key manufacturing centres in the country to determine whether the island retains a comparative advantage in any of these sectors. The fourth and final section will analyse the implications for policy.

BACKGROUND[1]

In 1970, Batam was—to Jakarta-based policymakers—a remote and sparsely populated island. Seeking to leverage its proximity to Singapore, earn foreign exchange, and foster the development of the domestic manufacturing sector, the Indonesian government slated it for oil refining (Pertamina et al. 1972). To this end, the Batam Industrial Development Authority (BIDA) was established in 1971 by the central government and tasked with economic planning, building infrastructure, and handling investment applications for the island. Centrally funded and answerable to a board of presidential advisers, the Authority was headquartered in Jakarta for easier access to decision-makers.

In 1978, BJ Habibie, Indonesia's long-serving Minister for Research and Technology, became the agency's Chairman. Bringing his technical background in engineering to bear, Habibie wanted to use the island as a means of bypassing the regulatory and infrastructural issues plaguing Indonesia to attract investment in high technology industries. To this end, the island received extensive investments in infrastructure such as air and seaports, highways, power generation and telecommunications facilities (BIDA 1980).

Yet, despite its location and well-developed infrastructure, Batam's attractiveness was severely hampered by restrictive regulations on investment, equity and land ownership. In 1988, fifteen years after the agency's founding, the island housed a mere thirteen foreign firms (Smith 1996).

Spurred on by this middling performance and outshone by the Malaysian state of Johor, which had begun to attract growing numbers of electronics firms, the Indonesian government liberalized the island's regulatory framework in 1989.

Notably, foreign corporations were allowed to retain majority ownership of their facilities as well as operate industrial parks. Of key importance was the establishment of BatamIndo Industrial Park, a joint venture between two Singaporean government-linked corporations and three large Indonesian conglomerates. This 320-hectare facility offered multinational corporations high-quality infrastructure, notably reliable provision of utilities, as well as a helping hand in procuring licences and permits.

The results were immediate. Over the 1990–96 period, more than US$1.6 billion in foreign direct investment (FDI) flowed in (van Grunsven 1998). Batam's economy took off, growing at rates in the high teens during the same period. Of particular note were E&E firms, whose ranks expanded from four in 1990 to some sixty-two firms by 1997. These firms were largely Japanese, European, and US-owned firms expanding from their facilities in Singapore (van Grunsven and Hutchinson 2015). Batam's population also grew, from some 80,000 in 1990 to more than 250,000 in 1997 (Wong and Ng 2009).

While the Asian Financial Crisis and ensuing fallout deeply affected Indonesia's political context and economy, Batam was somewhat buffered. Indeed, the island grew at 3 per cent in 1998, while Indonesia's economy as a whole contracted by 13 per cent. And, from 1999 until 2004, Batam continued to grow positively and above the national average. In terms of FDI, the island and the Province of Riau, of which it was a part, continued to receive significant levels of new capital. While trailing Jakarta by a substantial margin, the province was on par with other industrial areas in the country such as East Java (BPSc, various years).

Over the next years, Batam benefited from a number of legal provisions that were, in principle, to bolster its business environment. First, in 2002, Batam and the neighbouring island of Bintan were included in the US-Singapore Free Trade Agreement, meaning that firms operating on these islands but routing their goods through Singapore had privileged access to the US market (*Business Times*, 15 July 2002). Second, in 2004, Batam, Bintan, Karimun and three other island groups opted to secede from Riau Province to establish a new political entity named the Riau Islands Province. In theory, this was to allow these islands to focus on their outward-looking and industrially based economic model. Finally, Batam's business environment was furthered supported by the decision of then President Yudhoyono to declare the island, as well as parts of neighbouring Bintan and Karimun, as Free Trade Zones in 2009. This status granted exemptions on import and export duties as well as expedited customs processes to firms operating on the islands. This status was new for Bintan and Karimun and clarified the situation for Batam-based investors who had previously enjoyed a number of frequently changing tax incentives (Juoro, Tan, and Tan 2013).

These years proved to be very beneficial for the Riau Islands in general and Batam in particular. From 2000 to 20009, both Batam and the economy of the Riau Islands grew between 7 and 8 per cent per annum, above the national rate of 5–6 per cent p.a. (Figure 2.1).

Notwithstanding a downturn in the electronics sector in 2004, the ranks of E&E firms in Batam subsequently grew. In addition, the island's industrial base

FIGURE 2.1
Economic Growth, 2000–18 (% year-on-year)

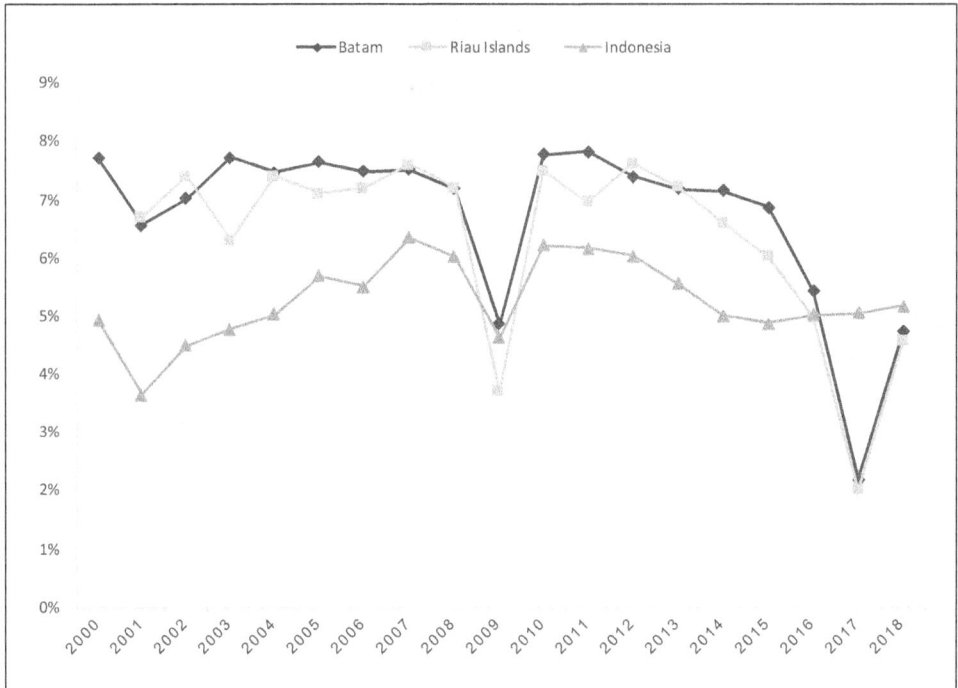

diversified with the consolidation of the shipbuilding industry. This was enabled by policy changes in Singapore and Indonesia. For its part, Singapore sought to offshore the sector's more labour-intensive components, and Indonesian cabotage regulations were amended in 2008—requiring all ships in the latter country's waters to be locally owned (Dick 2008). Consequently, the number of firms operating on the island increased dramatically.

In 2010, Batam and the wider Riau Islands were well-developed regions by Indonesian standards. The consistent flow of investment had fostered a large-scale shift away from fishing and agriculture towards manufacturing and other industrial activities, with the province deriving 58 per cent of GDP from this sector and another 36 per cent from services. In per capita terms, the Riau Islands were 60 per cent wealthier and Batam residents were twice as well-off as the national average (BPSc 2011; BPSd 2011). Batam had consolidated its status as the economic heart of the new province, generating 60 per cent of its GDP (BPSe 2016).

This situation continued until 2015, with both entities growing 1 to 2 per cent faster than the national average. Despite experiencing massive inflows of people from other parts of the country, economic growth has outpaced population increase, with the result that the Riau Islands is the wealthiest province in the country—Jakarta excepted (BPSd 2017).

However, the days of rapid growth may well be over. In 2016, the island and the province experienced lower growth rates, roughly at the national average. In 2017, the economies of Batam and the wider Riau Islands grew at a mere 2 per cent, substantially below Indonesia's aggregate growth of 5 per cent (Figure 2.1). Economic growth rates of Batam and the Riau Islands have improved in 2018, but they remain lower than the national growth rate.

These trends are also mirrored in flows of investment into Batam. FDI slowed down after the end of the commodity boom in 2012. In relative terms, the Riau Islands has lost ground to other provinces such as Central and West Java, which have begun to develop their industrial bases on the back of increasing levels of FDI (Figure 2.2a). Likewise, relative to other parts of Indonesia, Batam's small size and recent development means it lacks a large private sector with deep pockets to invest in local projects. Consequently, domestic direct investment (DDI) in Batam is dwarfed by the quantum of investment in other locations such as West, Central, and East Java (Figure 2.2b).

Exports from the Riau Islands fell year-on-year from US\$16.8 billion in 2013 down to US\$10.4 billion in 2016 (Figure 2.3). Since then, there has been a gradual export recovery reaching US\$13.4 billion in 2018, but its exports remain below the level of the booming period of 2013.

RECENT TRENDS IN BATAM'S MANUFACTURING SECTOR

As mentioned above, Batam's manufacturing sector has been waning in recent years. Table 2.1 shows the sector's growth has been declining from 7 per cent in 2011 to only around 2 per cent in 2017. Since more than 50 per cent of Batam's economy depends on the manufacturing sector, its middling performance has affected the island's overall economic growth rate. The table also shows that the manufacturing sector is not the only sector that has been dwindling. Sectors such as construction, trade, transportation, tourism, finance, and real estate have all experienced slower growth in recent years. Nevertheless, there are a few sectors with an increasing growth rate, i.e., information and communication; business services; and education services.

The declining role of the manufacturing sector in Batam can be clearly seen by looking at its contribution to GDP. In 2006, the manufacturing sector still contributed about 63 per cent of Batam's GDP. By 2018, its contribution to overall GDP had declined to 54 per cent. Conversely, the contribution of the services sector to Batam's GDP increased from 36 per cent in 2006 to 45 per cent in 2018 (see Figure 2.4).

Based on BPS' *Statistik Industri* (SI) data, it is interesting to note that the number of medium-large manufacturing firms in Batam has been relatively stable during the period of 2007 to 2014 (Figure 2.5). In 2015, there was a sudden jump in the number of manufacturing firms on the island. While the number of firms has increased gradually, the number of workers employed is stagnant or even declining in certain sectors. This indicates that manufacturing firms in Batam tend to be less labour-intensive in nature.

FIGURE 2.2
Realized Investment in Select Provinces

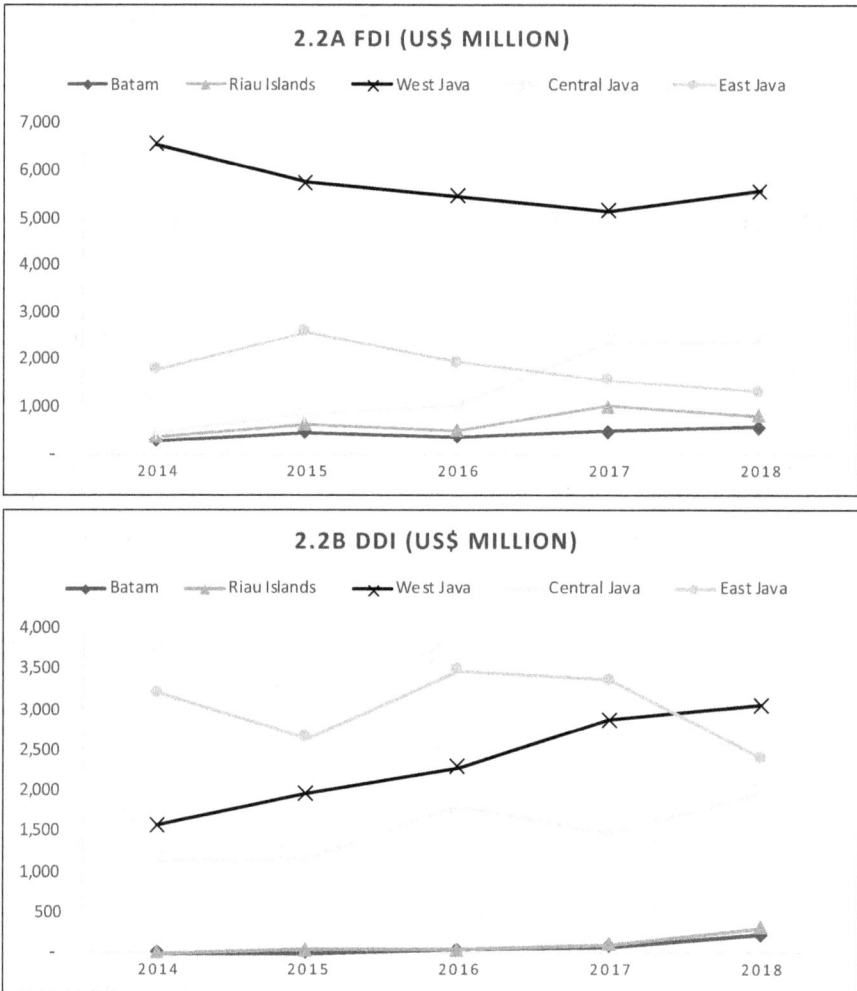

2.2A FDI (US$ MILLION)

2.2B DDI (US$ MILLION)

One of the reasons for Batam's declining levels of employment is its rapid increase in wages. Table 2.2 shows the base salary of Japanese companies in Jakarta and Batam. It illustrates that during the "golden era" of Batam's manufacturing sector in 2009 and 2010, the base salary of manufacturing workers on the island was higher than that of their counterparts in Jakarta. In 2013, there was a sudden jump in salary levels in Batam due to the booming commodity sector. From 2014 onwards, after the end of commodity boom, the base salary of manufacturing worker in Batam fell below that of their counterparts in Jakarta.

The following sections analyse trends in the E&E sector, before analysing the shipbuilding and ship repair sector.

FIGURE 2.3
Export-Import Value in Riau Islands Province (US$ million)

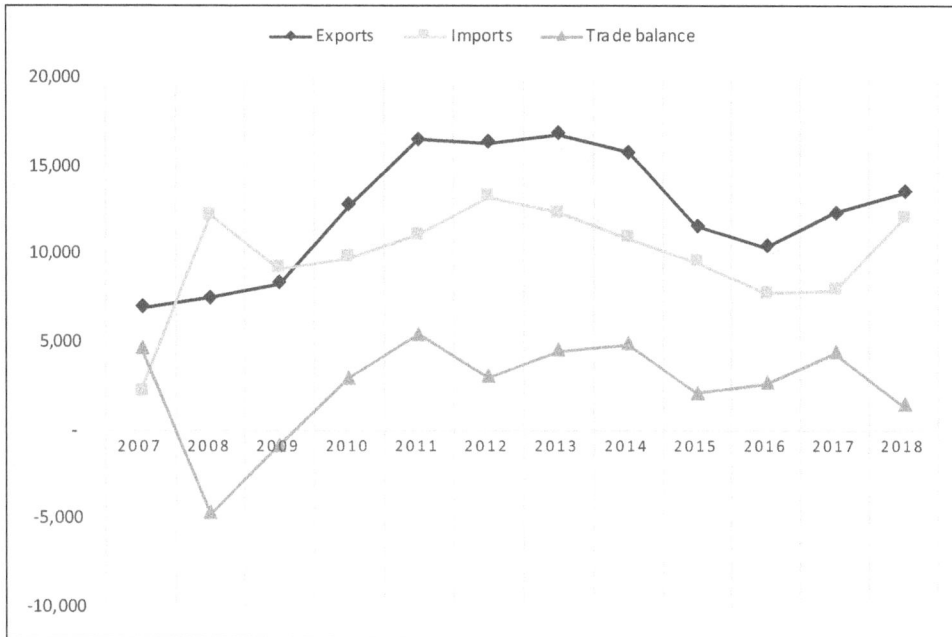

TABLE 2.1
Growth Rate of Selected Sectors in Batam, 2011–18

	2011	2012	2013	2014	2015	2016	2017	2018
Total GRDP	8%	7%	7%	7%	7%	5%	2%	5%
Manufacturing Industry	7%	7%	7%	7%	7%	5%	2%	4%
Construction	9%	8%	8%	9%	8%	7%	1%	8%
Wholesale, Retail & Repair	11%	12%	8%	7%	8%	7%	4%	5%
Transportation & Storage	8%	9%	8%	3%	6%	6%	4%	1%
Accommodation & F&B	9%	9%	8%	9%	6%	6%	6%	10%
Information & Communication	7%	16%	6%	9%	6%	7%	7%	13%
Financial & Insurance Activity	15%	6%	6%	6%	3%	7%	1%	6%
Real Estate	6%	7%	7%	7%	5%	5%	4%	–5%

Source: BPS via CEIC, authors' calculation.

Electrical and Electronics

The electrical and electronics industries have been one of the key pillars of the manufacturing sector in Batam. Using the BPS' manufacturing survey data, we can see a clear trend of declining employment in the sector, especially after 2010. However, in 2015, there was an increase in the number of E&E firms in Batam. This trends indicates that manufacturing firms in Batam are becoming less and less labour intensive. It is likely that firms in the E&E sector have been implementing

FIGURE 2.4
GDP Composition in Batam by Sector, 2006–18

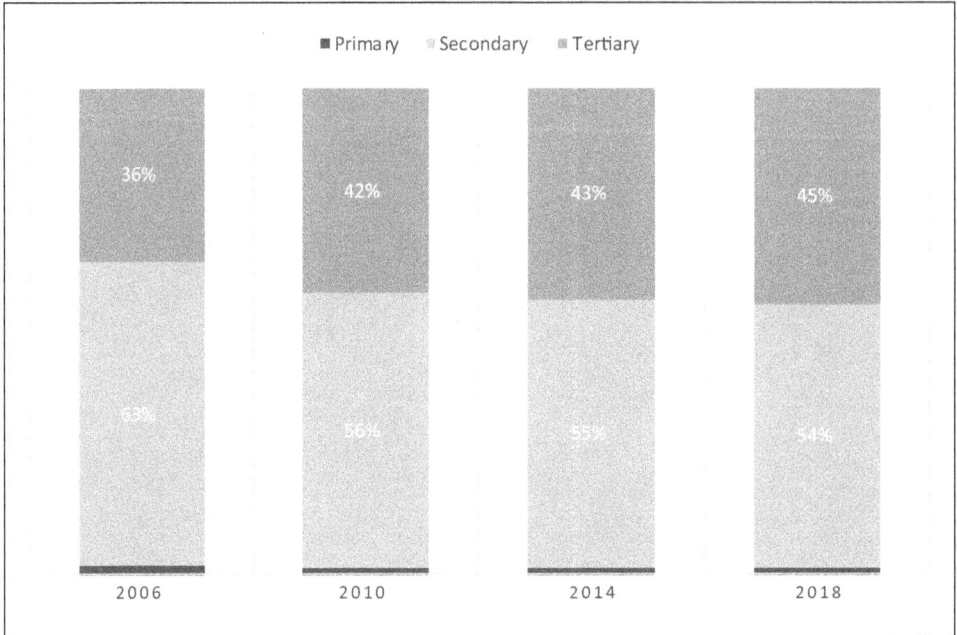

FIGURE 2.5
Total Number of Firms and Workers in the Manufacturing Sector in Batam, 2004–15

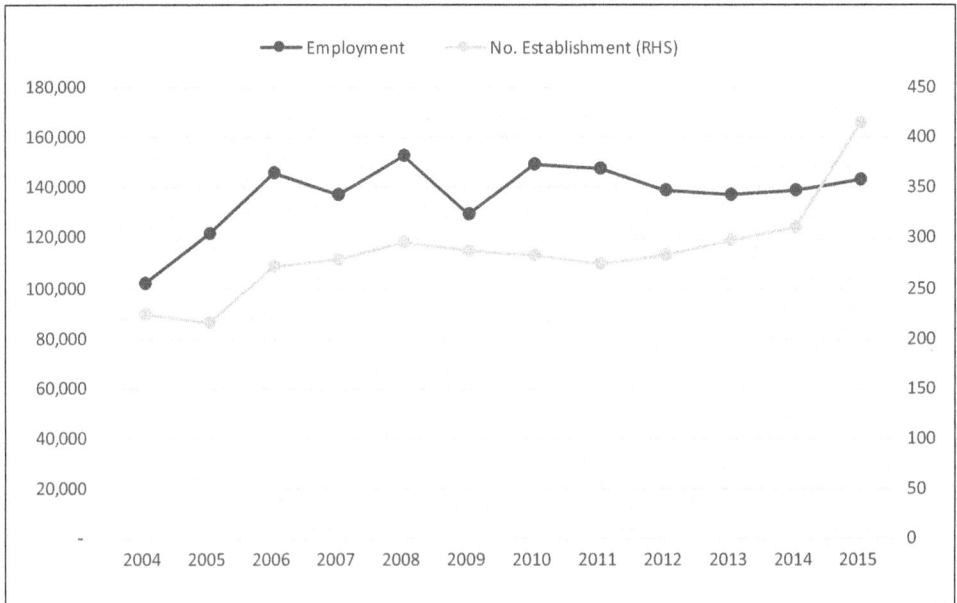

TABLE 2.2
Base Salary of Japanese Manufacturing Companies in Indonesia
(Average, Monthly, US$)

	Jakarta			Batam		
	Worker	Engineer	Manager	Worker	Engineer	Manager
1995	100–200	220–570	410–1,100	200	520–600	860–1,120
1996	94–160	210–530	300–2,050	170–200	280–860	860–2,800
1997	65–97	139–350	194–1,373	90	187	507
1998	56–66	107–340	261–1,229	61	191	491
1999	44–83	139–242	238–1,208	82	190	576
2000	30–214	33–322	39–847	51–62	119–232	422–649
2001	67	138	337	57–74	119–232	397–671
2002	108	205	540	68–97	125–386	461–946
2003	133	229	608	81–143	170–344	447–1,250
2004	130	252	619	95–112	391–559	335–1,117
2005	131	270	618	85–100	351–502	300–1,003
2006	177.7	311.37	548.25	96.2–129.1	248.7–348.3	506.4–999.3
2007	125–261	181–289	648–1,040	106–154	190–432	594–1,143
2008	131.3	257.4	705.50	NA	NA	NA
2009	147.7	294.4	811.58	162	375.8	632.2
2010	186	357	854	240	406	977
2011	209	414	995	NA	281	410
2012	239	433	1,057	177	313	1,355
2013	241	405	934	257	506	721
2014	263	425	1,015	239	405	807
2015	257	417	912	232	404	725
2016	310	472	1,035	287	387	876
2017	324	494	1,058	285	396	873

Note: We thank Honda Chizue and Hideki Fujie of the Japan External Trade Organization (JETRO) Singapore Office for providing this data.
Source: JETRO.

automation-related technology in response to a scarcity in qualified labour—a trend established by van Grunsven and Hutchinson (2014).

On one hand, the E&E sector has been stagnant since 2010, when a record thirty firms left in one year following a major industrial relations dispute (van Grunsven and Hutchinson 2015). Since then, the remaining base of E&E firms has further dwindled, with large factories such as Panasonic, NIDEC, and Sanyo closing down. New investments have been rare and have generated fewer jobs than in the past (Hutchinson 2017).

Recent data indicates that this trend has continued. Table 2.3 sets out the details of the entries and exits of E&E firms over the past five years. Closures have continued among the ranks of large, well-established MNCs, employing many hundreds of workers. This has not been offset by substantial new investments, with firm openings few and far between. In 2016, the Australian firm and consumer electronics producer, BlackMagic, invested US$3.8 million and will employ an estimated 150 people. The Chinese manufacturing giant Xiaomi opened a facility to make smartphones on the island in 2017.

FIGURE 2.6
Total Number of Firms and Workers in the Electrical and Electronics (E&E)
Industries in Batam, 2004–15

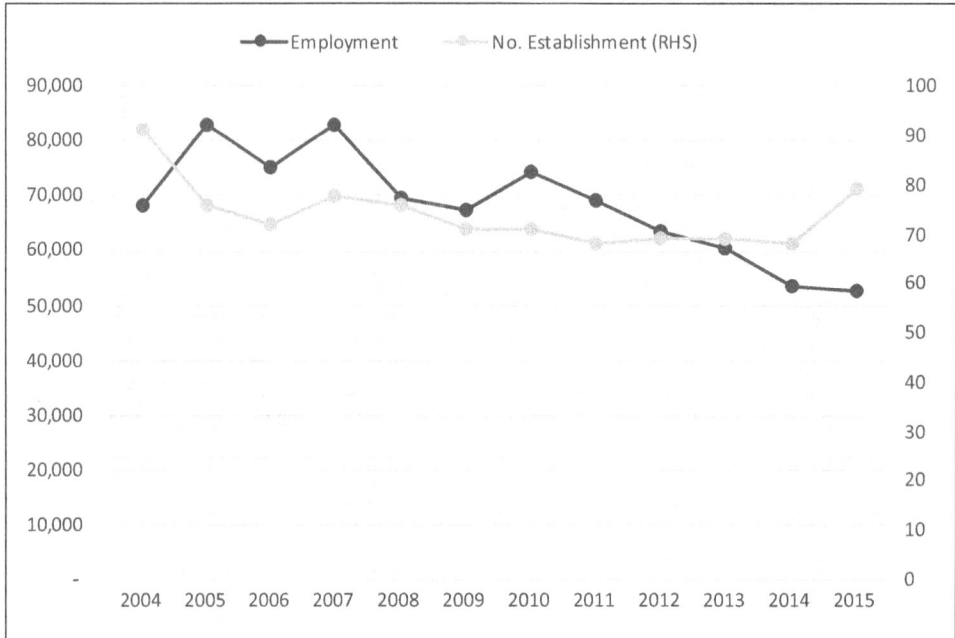

TABLE 2.3
Entries and Exits of Electrical and Electronics Firms in Batam

Name	Branch	Entry : Exit	Workers
NIDEC Seimitsu Batam/ PT Sanyo Precision	Electrical devices	1993 : 2013	500
PT Shin-Etsu	Data storage	1990 : 2013	600
PT Sun Creation	Electrical devices	2000 : 2013	1,000
PT Sanyo Energy	Batteries	1992 : 2013	684
PT Panasonic Shikoku	Data storage	2009 : 2011/12	1,200
Blackmagic	Consumer Electronics	2016	150
Xiaomi	Smartphones	2017	1,000–1,500

Sources: Author's own data and; F. Pangestu, "Increasing Wages Driving Investors Out of Batam Island", *Jakarta Post*, 15 July 2014; F. Pangestu, "Sanyo Subsidiary Closes Down Batam Unit Amid Soaring Labour Costs", *Jakarta Post*, 1 November 2016; F. Pangestu, "Closures Lead to Rise in Batam Jobless Rate", *Jakarta Post*, 26 August 2016.

Shipbuilding and Repair

The shipbuilding and repair sector is another important component of the manufacturing sector in Batam. Based on the BPS survey, the number of medium to large shipyards and ship repair firms in Batam has been increasing since 2011 (Figure 2.7). In 2013 and 2015, there were sudden increases in the number of shipyards in Batam, driven by increased demand in the offshore sector and derived demand

FIGURE 2.7
Total Number of Firms and Workers in the Shipbuilding & Repair Sector in Batam, 2004–15

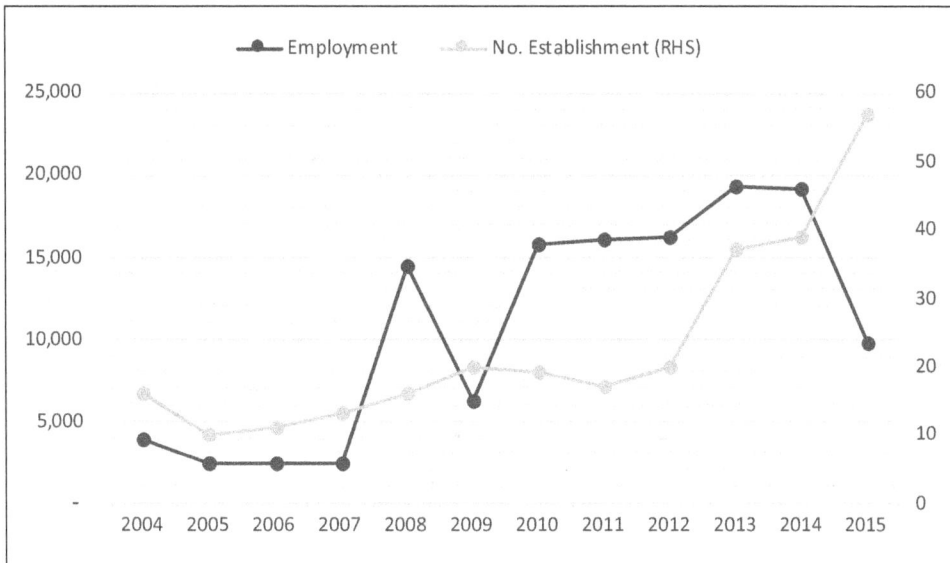

due to the commodity boom. However, in 2015, despite a sizeable increase in the number of shipyards, there was a substantial decline in the number of workers.

According to the Batam Shipyard and Offshore Association (BSOA), Batam had around 115 shipyards during its boom years in 2011–12.[2] They employed some 250,000 formal sector workers, produced 200 tugboats and 700 barges per year. However, in recent years there has been a cyclical downturn in the sector. Factors such as excess capacity, a sharp drop in oil prices, and domestic regulatory changes (such as the ban on raw mineral exports) have affected the sector's performance. As a result, the sector contracted sharply and, by 2015, less than 10,000 workers were employed in Batam's shipyards.

The downturn in the shipyard sector has spread to other parts of the manufacturing sector in Batam. According to Batam's Manpower Agency, more than 110 firms closed operations in 2015–16 (*Straits Times*, 2 November 2017). This trend has continued unabated, with fifty-three firms closing in the first half of 2017. As is to be expected, this has had an impact on unemployment levels. In 2015 and 2016, unemployment in the Riau Islands was 9 per cent, substantially above the national average of 6 per cent (BPSb 2016).

BATAM'S COMPARATIVE ADVANTAGE

In this section, we use SI from the Badan Pusat Statistik[3] (BPS) to examine the comparative advantage of firms based in Batam. The SI data provides establishment-level information on all large and medium manufacturing firms in the country on an annual basis. The SI questionnaire asks each firm information about its: overall production; exports; imports; employment; wages; capital; and foreign ownership, *inter alia*.

On average, some 24,000 firms are covered annually by the survey. However, it does not cover micro or small enterprises—defined as establishments with fewer than twenty employees. That said, data from the survey can still capture key dynamics in Indonesia's manufacturing sector since large and medium firms account for around 60 per cent of the country's GDP (Amiti and Davis 2011, p. 9).

For this exercise, data pertaining to the 2004–15 period is evaluated. This period covers the period after Batam and six other island groups in the Riau Archipelago seceded from the Province of Riau to become the Province of the Riau Islands (PRI) in 2004. The period also captures prevailing trends before and after 2009 when the island was first declared a Free Trade Zone (FTZ). The recent-available survey data is only until 2015. This means we are not able to capture the trough of the industrial decline in Batam, i.e. 2016–17. Nevertheless, we can still analyse the trends in some key sectors, which indicate an early decline compared to the overall manufacturing sector in Batam. The BPS changed industrial classification codes in 2010, consequently the time series before and after has been homogenized to ensure comparability.[4]

In the subsequent paragraphs, we compare firms in Batam with their counterparts in Java and Sumatra. Following a comparison of the number of firms, the number of workers employed, and the proportion of females employed and their evolution over time in each of the three locations, we then compare the performance of firms in terms of: average output; exports and imports; and productivity. For ease of analysis, we focus on the three manufacturing activities that are of vital importance for Batam: electronics; electrical goods; and the shipbuilding and ship repair industry.

Based on the survey's main findings, some 21,460 (or 83 per cent) of the 24,000 firms surveyed are located in provinces on Java and 2,785 (or 8.8 per cent) on Sumatra. With only 494 firms, the PRI accounts for only around 1.5 per cent of the total firm population. Within PRI, 84 per cent of firms (415) are based in Batam, the most industrialized part of the province.

Table 2.4 depicts the relative importance of these three sectors in each location in 2015 by firm number. As can be seen, while these firms are more numerous in the other two locations, they are proportionately more important for Batam's firm base.

Table 2.5 sets out the proportion of firms exporting and importing over the 2008–15 period in the three locations. With regards to international linkages, approximately 18 per cent of firms nationwide reported that they export some portion of their outputs and 20 per cent reported that they import some portion of their inputs. Batam is clearly more integrated in international production networks, as the proportion of firms engaged in international trade, be it exporting or importing, is noticeably higher than in Java and Sumatra. This could indicate that FTZ status has contributed to Batam's high export-import intensity.

TABLE 2.4
Sectors of Interest, 2015

Sectors	Batam	Java	Sumatra	Indonesia
Electronics	59 (14.2%)	248 (1.2%)	31 (1.1%)	317 (1.2%)
Shipbuilding	57 (13.7%)	62 (0.3%)	96 (3.4%)	200 (0.76%)
Electrical goods	20 (4.8%)	312 (1.5%)	69 (2.5%)	345 (1.31%)
Total	415	21,460	2,785	26,322

Source: Authors' calculation based on Statistik Industri.

TABLE 2.5
Proportion of Firms Exporting/Importing to Total Establishments

	Batam		Java		Sumatra		Indonesia	
	Export	Import	Export	Import	Export	Import	Export	Import
2008	37.3%	59.7%	13.2%	17.5%	20.8%	18.9%	14.7%	17.2%
2009	40.4%	57.1%	14.2%	17.3%	24.5%	18.9%	16.0%	16.9%
2010	48.4%	54.1%	16.2%	18.5%	29.7%	17.7%	18.8%	17.8%
2011	51.8%	60.9%	17.3%	19.2%	30.2%	19.1%	19.6%	18.5%
2012	49.5%	59.0%	17.5%	21.3%	30.3%	20.0%	19.6%	20.8%
2013	46.8%	59.9%	17.9%	24.5%	31.5%	20.3%	20.1%	23.3%
2014	45.3%	61.4%	16.0%	24.7%	24.8%	19.8%	17.6%	23.4%
2015	32.3%	67.7%	15.0%	25.9%	19.0%	22.8%	15.9%	25.1%

Source: Statistik Industri, authors' calculation.

As regards exports versus imports, in Batam the proportion of firms importing keeps increasing, but the proportion of firms exporting has been declining since 2011 (Table 2.5). This suggests that, despite its export orientation, the domestic market is increasingly important for a growing proportion of firms in Batam. Firms in Java demonstrate a similar trend of increasing imports and decreasing exports. Conversely, more firms in Sumatra export rather than import over the period under study, with the exception of 2015.

Table 2.6 shows the number of firms in the three industries in Batam, Java and Sumatra. It can be seen that Java has the largest number of firms in both the electrical goods and electronics sectors. Meanwhile, Sumatra has more firms in its shipbuilding sector than Batam or Java.

Turning to employment levels, Table 2.7 illustrates the number of manufacturing workers in the three locations during 2008–15. It shows that employment levels have been relatively stagnant in Batam over this period, at around 140,000–150,000 workers. In contrast, employment levels in Java have been growing steadily from around 3.6 million in 2008 to 4.4 million in 2015. Manufacturing employment in Sumatra has also been growing steadily, climbing from 497,000 in 2009 to 565,000 in 2015.

Batam has a high concentration of female workers. Due to the island's early development of the E&E sector, the island has been a reputed centre of employment

TABLE 2.6
Total Number of Firms in Key Industries in Batam, Java and Sumatra, 2008–15

	Electrical Goods			Electronics			Shipbuilding and Repair		
	Batam	Java	Sumatra	Batam	Java	Sumatra	Batam	Java	Sumatra
2008	14	242	24	62	136	78	16	53	44
2009	16	222	25	55	160	65	20	50	44
2010	13	274	23	58	189	71	19	45	43
2011	17	276	26	51	187	63	17	50	43
2012	18	279	26	51	191	64	20	49	48
2013	17	305	27	52	232	64	37	49	63
2014	20	306	29	48	230	58	39	53	69
2015	20	312	31	59	248	69	57	62	96

Source: *Statistik Industri*, authors' calculation.

TABLE 2.7
**Total Number of Manufacturing Employees and Female Workers in
Batam, Java and Sumatra, 2008–15**

	Batam			Java			Sumatra		
	Female	%	Total	Female	%	Total	Female	%	Total
2008	90,504	59.3%	152,538	1,800,670	49.1%	3,664,190	203,356	37.5%	541,903
2009	77,983	60.0%	129,985	1,797,510	49.6%	3,622,195	180,894	36.4%	497,503
2010	81,078	54.2%	149,682	1,820,425	48.3%	3,768,500	178,888	34.2%	522,806
2011	81,193	55.0%	147,593	1,864,075	48.4%	3,850,595	185,105	32.7%	565,529
2012	74,257	53.3%	139,297	2,007,482	48.8%	4,115,023	184,779	33.4%	553,984
2013	69,404	50.6%	137,277	2,051,371	48.9%	4,194,992	178,686	32.1%	556,325
2014	69,766	50.1%	139,337	2,118,672	48.8%	4,342,849	179,190	32.2%	555,711
2015	72,832	50.9%	143,057	2,185,583	49.7%	4,393,566	175,501	31.0%	565,551

Source: *Statistik Industri*, authors' calculation.

for women. However, Table 2.7 also shows that the share of female workers to total employment in Batam declined from around 60 per cent in 2008 to 50 per cent in 2015, converging to almost the same level as Java. Meanwhile, the share of female workers to total employment in Sumatra has been continuously declining from around 38 per cent in 2008 to around 30 per cent by 2015.

With regard to average employment per establishment, Figure 2.8 shows that firms in Batam on average employ considerably more workers than their counterparts in Java and Sumatra. However, in all three sectors of interest, this trend is narrowing, indicating that over time firms in Batam are employing fewer workers. The decline in employment level in Batam was started in the electronics industry around 2011, then followed by the shipbuilding and repair industry in 2012. Meanwhile, the employment level in the electrical industry experienced a big decline only around 2015.

As mentioned above, firms in Batam have a relatively high concentration of female workers. In particular, Figure 2.9 shows that in the electronics and electrical goods industries, firms in Batam on average employ more female workers than their

FIGURE 2.8
Employment Trends in Selected Industries, 2004–15

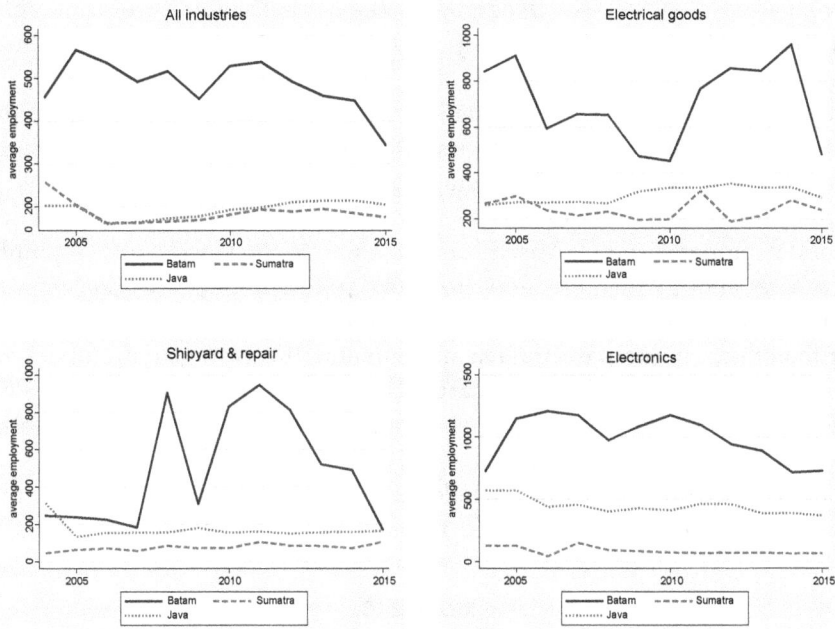

Source: *Statistik Industri*, authors' calculation

FIGURE 2.9
Share of Female Employment in Select Industries, 2004–15

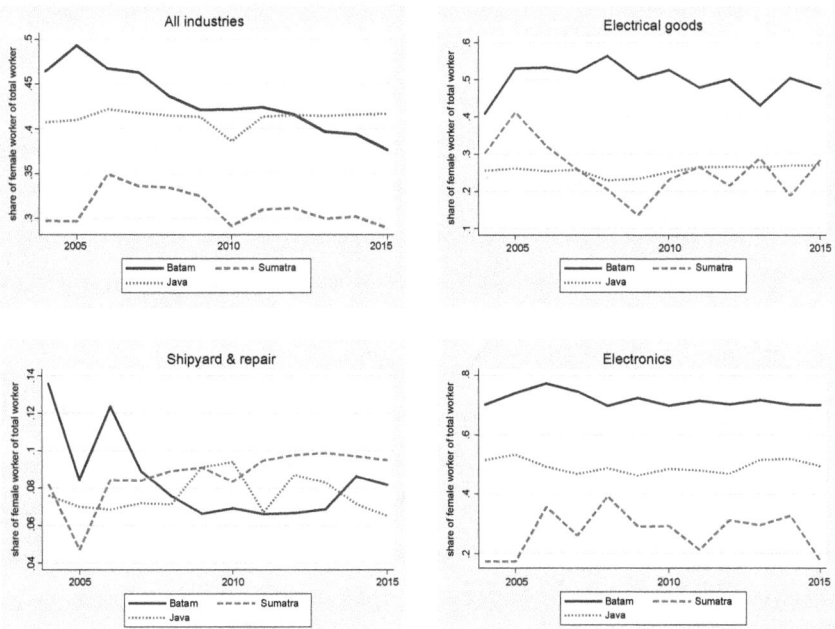

Source: *Statistik Industri*, authors' calculation.

counterparts in Java and Sumatra. However, this is not the case in the shipbuilding industry, where all three locations demonstrate low levels of female participation (below 1 per cent). When seen in aggregate, the overall share of women employed in the three sectors has progressively declined in Batam and Sumatra, but has remained stable in Java.

Turning now to output per worker, Figure 2.10 compares the trends of output per worker (in logarithmic) between firms in the three sectors in Batam, Sumatra and Java. The data shows that, on average, firms in Batam have a comparable level of output per worker with Sumatra-based firms but they have higher level of output per worker compared to Java-based firms. Turning to the key sectors, shipbuilding and electrical goods firms in Batam produced more output per worker than firms in Java and Sumatra. However, in the shipbuilding and repair industry, while still higher than their counterparts in Java and Sumatra, the average output per worker of Batam-based firms has declined, particularly since 2014. In contrast, Java-based shipbuilding firms are showing increasing levels of output per worker, possibly due to the growth of the domestic market.

Looking at manufacturing as a whole, firms in Sumatra have a relatively higher level of export per worker compared to both Batam and Java-based firms. This

FIGURE 2.10
Trends in Output per Worker in Select Industries, 2004–15

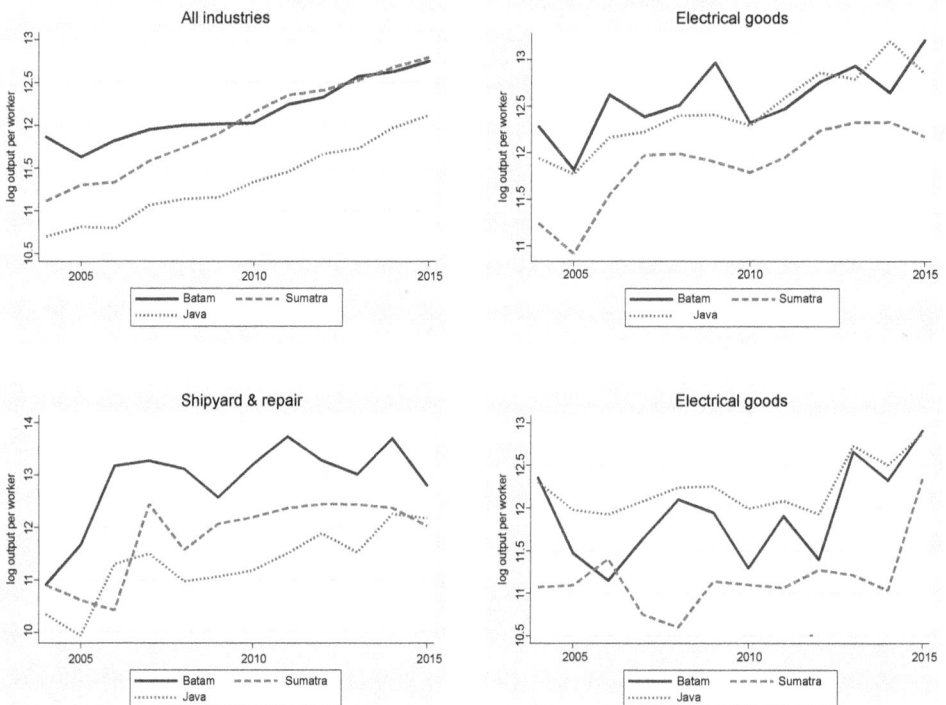

Source: *Statistik Industri*, authors' calculation.

trend is mainly driven by the commodity boom, which has particularly benefited Sumatra due to its palm oil and coal resources. Nevertheless, Batam-based firms have a relatively higher level of export per worker compared to their counterparts in Java. Regarding the specific sectors, Figure 2.11 shows that for the electronics and electrical goods sectors, firms in Batam perform relatively well in terms of export per worker compared to their counterparts in Java. In the shipbuilding industry, in line with declining output, the average export per worker of firms in Batam has declined since 2014 (see Figure 2.11, bottom left). It is noteworthy that even though the exports of Java's shipyards have declined sharply since 2012, their output has been increasing since 2013 (Figure 2.10, bottom left). This is because, unlike Batam, the shipbuilding industry in Java mostly caters to the domestic market, which has been experiencing increased demand due to the government's maritime projects and cabotage rules.[5]

Another interesting fact about manufacturing firms in Batam is the high import content of their production inputs. Figure 2.12 shows that, on average, firms in Batam imported around 50 per cent of their total inputs. This is much higher compared with firms in Java and Sumatra, at around 10 and 4 per cent, respectively.

FIGURE 2.11
Trends in Export per Worker in Select Industries, 2004–15

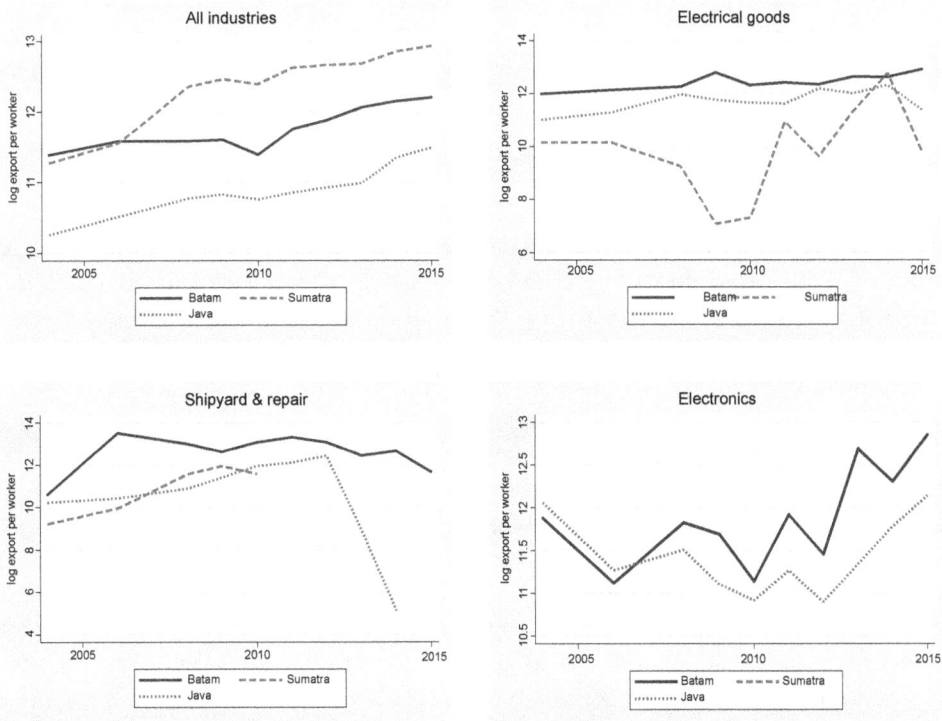

Source: *Statistik Industri*, authors' calculation.

FIGURE 2.12
Share of Imported Inputs in Production in Select Industries, 2004–15

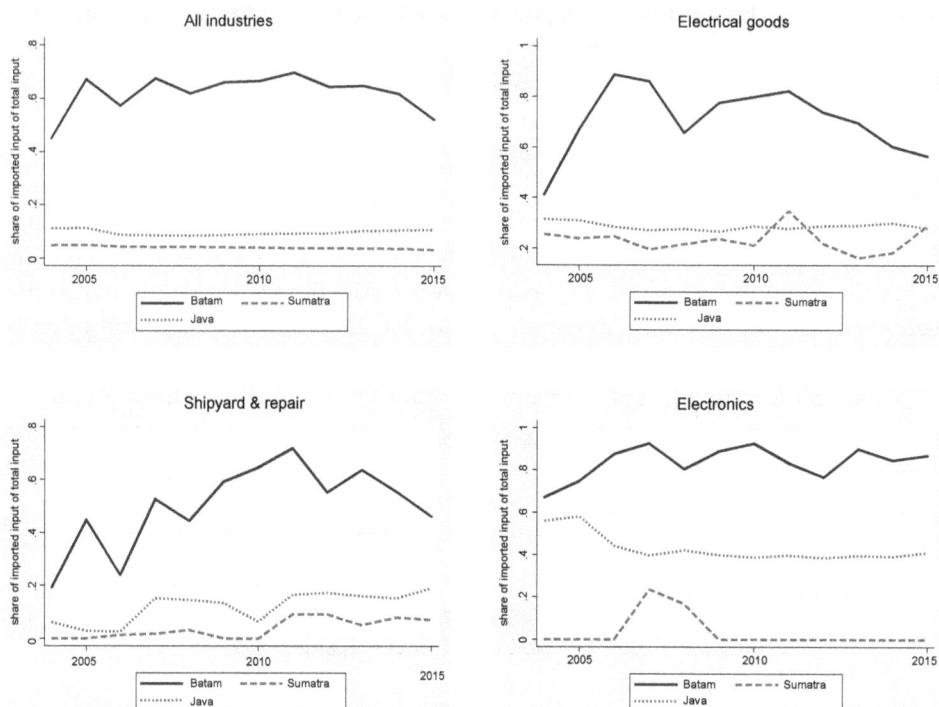

Source: *Statistik Industri*, authors' calculation.

Particularly for electronics firms in Batam, their dependence on imported components is very high, approaching 90 per cent of total inputs and this trend is relatively stable. In contrast, if we look at the levels of imports of components for the electrical goods and shipbuilding industries, they are lower at around 60 per cent and the trend is declining.

As mentioned above, one factor that may account for the decline of Batam's manufacturing sector is the island's rapid increase in labour wages. Figure 2.13 shows that firms in Batam on average pay relatively higher wages than their counterparts in Java and Sumatra—particularly the electronics and shipbuilding sectors. A rapid increase in nominal wages combined with slower external demand have placed high pressure on firms' profit levels, pushing firms to reduce headcount.

Finally, we use unit labour cost (ULC)—derived using the ratio of total labour compensation to labour productivity—to measure price competitiveness (Aswicahyono, Hill and Narjoko 2010, p. 1095). In this case, if nominal wages in one region rise faster than labour productivity, ULC increases, thus decreasing regional price competitiveness. Figure 2.14 shows that firms in Batam, on average, face lower ULC than their counterparts in Java and Sumatra—meaning that Batam has a significant price advantage in general and for the three key sectors in particular.

FIGURE 2.13
Average Wage per Worker in Select Industries, 2004–15

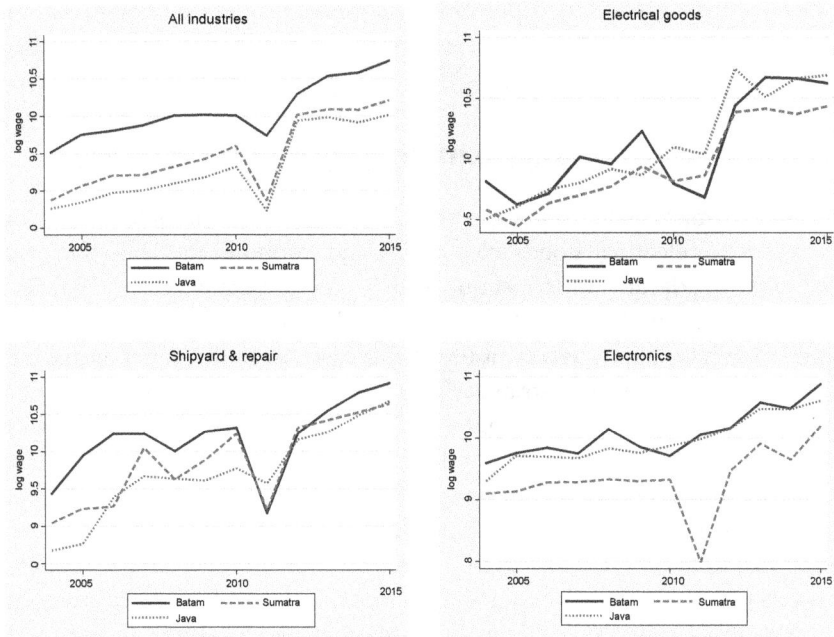

Source: *Statistik Industri*, authors' calculation.

FIGURE 2.14
Unit Labour Cost Trends, 2004–15

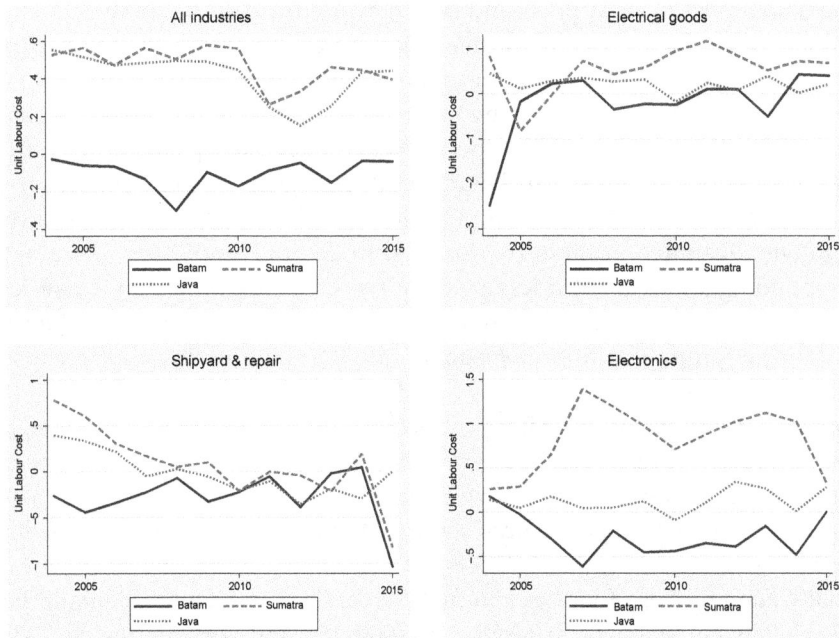

Source: *Statistik Industri*, authors' calculation.

How can we explain this trend? Despite its relatively higher nominal wage level, the trends in productivity levels in Batam show that the city remains competitive. Possibly due to their greater incorporation into global production networks, Batam-based firms employ greater number of workers and have higher output and export levels.

CONCLUSION AND IMPLICATIONS FOR POLICY

Since 2010, investment, firm numbers, and employment levels in Batam have dipped in key areas such as electrical goods, electronics, and shipbuilding. This state of affairs has prompted considerable introspection with regard to Batam's future, particularly which economic sectors to promote.

This chapter has sought to contribute to this discussion through comparing and contrasting Batam's overall industrial performance with that of Java and Sumatra. This has been complemented by an in-depth analysis of three specific sectors: electrical goods; electronics; and shipbuilding and repair.

These operations have revealed several findings. First, while relatively small in number, firms in Batam in the electrical goods, electronics, and shipbuilding and repair sectors employ more workers per capita and have higher levels of output, as well as a greater proportion of exports and imports relative to their counterparts in Java and Sumatra. Compared to firms in these other two locations, in general firms in Batam show considerably higher levels of output per worker.

Second, despite more firms being established in Batam of late, the proportion of firms exporting has been declining and the proportion of firms importing has been increasing. This suggests that more and more firms in Batam outsource their intermediate inputs from imports and sell their products on the domestic market. A similar pattern can be seen for firms in Java and Sumatra, in which a growing proportion of firms sell on the domestic market as opposed to overseas. This indicates that, over time, the domestic economy is more important for firms based in Batam.

Third, with regards to the three specific sectors studied, firms in the electronics and electrical goods industries in Batam produce higher output per worker than their counterparts in Java and Sumatra. Consequently, the island still has a strong comparative advantage in these two sectors. In contrast, indicators pertaining to the shipbuilding sector paint a less positive story. Looking forward, these results indicate that the first two sectors should remain central to strategies for the island, but that further promotion of or investment into the shipbuilding and repair sector may need to be re-evaluated.

Fourth, the growth of workers' productivity in Batam seems to outweigh the growth of nominal wage levels. This indicates that, despite rapid wage growth on the island, it still remains a competitive location for manufacturing overall. Batam's greater incorporation into global production networks due to its FTZ status may be a contributing factor.

Finally, the number of workers in medium and large establishments in Batam has been relatively stagnant at around 140,000–150,000 workers during 2008–15.

In contrast, employment levels in Java and Sumatra have been growing. Given an increase in firm numbers in Batam, it is possible that manufacturing is becoming more capital intensive and less labour intensive. In addition, the share of female workers is declining in Batam, converging to almost the same level as in Java. This suggests that either existing firms are altering their worker demographic, or that the new activities on the island are distinct.

Notes

1. This section draws on Hutchinson (2017) and Negara (2017).
2. Focus group discussion with Batam Shipyard and Offshore Association (BSOA) members, 4 June 2016.
3. Central Statistics Authority.
4. For the period before 2010, BPS uses industrial classification or ISIC rev 3 (KBLI 15-37). From 2010 onwards, it uses ISIC rev 4 (KBLI 10-33).
5. Cabotage rules regulate shipping activities which takes place within a country's waters and particularly restrict the activities of foreign vessels. The Indonesian government has implemented its Cabotage rules through the Maritime Law No. 17 of 2008, which aims to limit the number of foreign vessels operating in Indonesian waters and to give greater market share to local operators. The law requires companies to establish and licence themselves as "Indonesian Sea Carriage companies". It must be incorporated in Indonesia and must observe the 49 per cent foreign ownership limit.

References

Amiti, Mary, and Donald R. Davis. 2011. "Trade, Firms, and Wages: Theory and Evidence". *Review of Economic Studies* 79: 1–36.

Aswicahyono, H., H. Hill, and D. Narjoko. 2010. "Industrialisation after a Deep Economic Crisis: Indonesia". *Journal of Development Studies* 46, no. 6: 1084–108.

Batam Industrial Development Authority (BIDA). 1980. *The Batam Development Program*. Jakarta: Batam Industrial Development Authority.

BPSa. (Statistics Indonesia). Various years. *Indikator Ekonomi*. Jakarta: BPS.

BPSb. (Statistics Indonesia). Various years. *Indikator Utama Kepulauan Riau*. Tanjungpinang: BPS Kepulauan Riau.

BPSc. (Statistics Indonesia). Various years. *Produk Domestik Regional Bruto Kabupaten/Kota di Indonesia Menurut Lapangan Usaha*. Jakarta: BPS.

BPSd. (Statistics Indonesia). Various years. *Produk Domestik Regional Bruto Propinsi-Propinsi di Indonesia Menurut Lapangan Usaha*. Jakarta: BPS.

BPSe. (Statistics Indonesia). 2016. *Provinsi Kepulauan dalam Angka 2016*. Tanjungpinang: Badan Pusat Statistik – Provinsi Kepulauan Riau.

Dick, Howard. 2008. "The 2008 Shipping Law: Deregulation or Re-regulation?". *Bulletin of Indonesian Economic Studies* 44, issue 3: 383–406.

Hutchinson, Francis E. 2017. *Rowing Against the Tide? Batam's Economic Fortunes in Today's Indonesia*. Trends in Southeast Asia no. 8/2017. Singapore: ISEAS – Yusof Ishak Institute.

Japan External Trade Research Organisation (JETRO). 2016. *JETRO Survey on Business Conditions of Japanese Companies in Asia and Oceania*. Tokyo: Japan External Trade Research Organisation.

Juoro, U., Tan Khee Giap, and Tan K.Y. 2013. "Joint Expert Study on Competitiveness in Batam-Bintan-Karimun". Jakarta and Singapore: Komite Ekonomi Nasional/National University of Singapore.

Negara, Siwage Dharma. 2017. "Can the Decline of Batam's Shipbuilding Industry be Reversed?". *ISEAS Perspective* No. 2017/10, 16 February 2017.

Pertamina, Nishho-Iwai, and Pacific Bechtel. 1972. *Masterplan Batam: Industrial Development*. Jakarta: Pertamina.

Smith, S.L.D. 1996. "Developing Batam: Indonesian Political Economy under the New Order". PhD dissertation, Australian National University.

van Grunsven L. 1998. "The Sustainability of Urban Development in the SIJORI Growth Triangle: A Social Perspective". *Third World Planning Review* 20, no. 2.

———, and F.E. Hutchinson. 2014. "The Evolution of the Electronics Industry in the SIJORI Cross-Border Region". ISEAS Economics Working Paper no. 2/2014. Singapore: Institute of Southeast Asian Studies.

———, and F.E. Hutchinson. 2015. "The Evolution of the Electronics Industry on Batam Island (Riau Islands Province, Indonesia): An Evolutionary Trajectory Contributing to Regional Resilience?". *Geojournal* 82, no. 3: 475–92.

Wong P.K., and Ng K.K. 2009. *Batam, Bintan, and Karimun: Past History and Current Development Towards Being a SEZ*. Singapore: Asia Competitiveness Institute, National University of Singapore.

3

TOURISM IN THE RIAU ISLANDS PROVINCE
The Sunrise Sector

Ady Muzwardi and Siwage Dharma Negara

INTRODUCTION

Natural and cultural wealth are important components of tourism in Indonesia which, with more than 17,500 islands, is the world's largest archipelagic country. Leveraging on these assets, this sector has become a key driver of Indonesia's economy. Based on data from the country's Central Statistics Agency (BPS), in 2018, tourism outperformed other key foreign exchange earning sectors such as oil and gas, as well as coal and palm oil, contributing US$19.3 billion (BPS 2019a). The sector is also growing quickly, jumping 13 per cent in 2018 to reach 15.8 million visitors (Soenarso 2019).

Based on BPS data, in 2018 some 59 per cent of tourists visited Indonesia for holiday purposes, while 38 per cent did so for business (BPS 2019). From the ASEAN region, Malaysia and Singapore are the two biggest sources of tourists coming to Indonesia. From elsewhere in Asia, Chinese tourists came first, followed by Japan, South Korea, Taiwan and India. The highest number of tourist arrivals from the European region came from the United Kingdom, followed by the Netherlands, Germany, and France.

Tourism has also become one of the key sectors of the Riau Islands' economy. The Riau Islands is a province with some 2,000 islands (BPS Provinsi Kepulauan Riau 2018) located in the western part of Indonesia, bordered by Singapore and Malaysia.

Due to its many coastal areas and vast expanses of sea, the province has a variety of tourist attractions and offers some world-class accommodation and leisure facilities.

In July 2004, the Riau Islands seceded from Riau to form a separate province. The young province includes six main island groups, including Batam, Bintan, Karimun, Singkep-Lingga, Anambas, and Natuna. The capital city is Tanjungpinang on the island of Bintan. However, the largest and the most industrialized city in the province is Batam.

In recent years, the tourism sector has become increasingly important for the Riau Islands, due to its dynamic growth as well as a downturn in other areas of the economy such as the electrical and electronics as well as ship-building sectors (Hutchinson 2017; Negara 2017). Table 3.1 shows how tourism (represented by "Accommodation and Food & Beverages") has become a growth motor for the province.

Weak exports of manufactures have affected the growth of the industrial sector, as seen by the decline in the sector's contribution to gross regional domestic product (GRDP) since 2015. The number of layoffs in the manufacturing sector has been rising, as seen in the increase in the number of unemployed people from 2012 to 2017 (Figure 3.1). A significant increase occurred in 2016, when the number of unemployed people jumped 29.5 per cent from the previous year (Hutchinson 2017 and Negara 2017).

Figure 3.2 indicates that occupations related to tourism (i.e., trade, accommodation and restaurants) remain the main source of employment in the province. Furthermore, there is anecdotal evidence that many workers, who were laid off from the manufacturing sector, subsequently moved to tourism-related occupations. Therefore, the tourism sector has helped to cushion the impact of the economic recession. Figure 3.2 shows that, in 2016, the tourism sector together with social services absorbed the big employment decline in manufacturing. In the subsequent year, tourism became the largest employer for the residents of the Riau Islands, overtaking the manufacturing sector and other business sectors.

TABLE 3.1
Annual GRDP Growth in the Riau Islands Province by Sector, 2011–18

(%)	2011	2012	2013	2014	2015	2016	2017	2018
Agriculture, Forestry & Fisheries	4	2	4	8	6	6	−1	−3
Mining & Quarrying	3	5	3	5	9	6	−5	2
Manufacturing Industry	8	8	8	6	6	3	2	4
Construction	8	11	10	9	4	4	3	8
Wholesales & Retail Trade	7	7	10	9	9	10	6	6
Transportation & Storage	9	7	8	6	6	6	5	1
Accommodation, F&B Activity	9	9	8	7	6	5	12	11
Information & Communication	10	7	6	7	5	7	8	11
Real Estate	7	5	6	6	4	4	4	0
GRDP total	7	8	7	7	6	5	2	5

Note: Figures are in 2010 constant prices.
Source: Central Bureau of Statistics (BPS) via CEIC, 2019.

FIGURE 3.1
Number of Unemployed in the Riau Islands Province, 2012–18

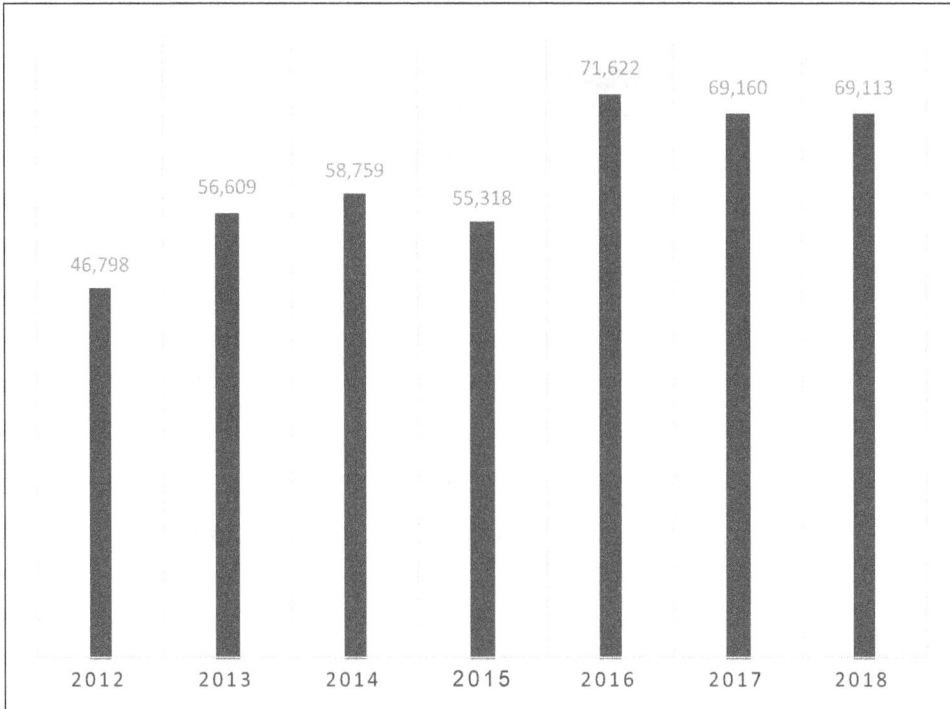

Source: Central Bureau of Statistics (BPS), 2013–19.

The Riau Islands' tourism sector has experienced ups and downs over time. In the era of President Soeharto, the growth of tourist visits increased quite rapidly. Specifically, the number of tourists visiting Lagoi in the Bintan Regency, increased from 114,000 in 1996 to 168,864 in 1997. Then, there was a significant decline in tourist visits during the Susilo Bambang Yudhoyono (SBY) presidency. The number of tourist visits decreased by 53 per cent in 2010, amid the global economic crisis. Subsequently in 2012, still in the SBY era, the number of tourist visits increased significantly by 149 per cent. In the Joko Widodo era, the number of tourist arrivals to the Riau Islands continued its upward trend. Even though there was a slight decline in 2016, on average the number of tourist arrivals increased by 8 per cent during the Joko Widodo era from 2014 to 2018. Looking at this trend, one might argue that the performance of the Riau Islands' tourism sector is strongly influenced by the global economic dynamism.

Interestingly, the weakening of the manufacturing sector is not linked to the tourism sector, as indicated by the number of tourist visits to the province (Figure 3.3). Even in 2017, when the Riau Islands' economic growth fell to 2 per cent, the number of tourists still increased by 11 per cent. Figure 3.4 indicates the increase in the number of tourists visiting three main tourist destinations in the province, which

FIGURE 3.2
Number of Employed Residents in Key Sectors in the Riau Islands Province, 2012–17

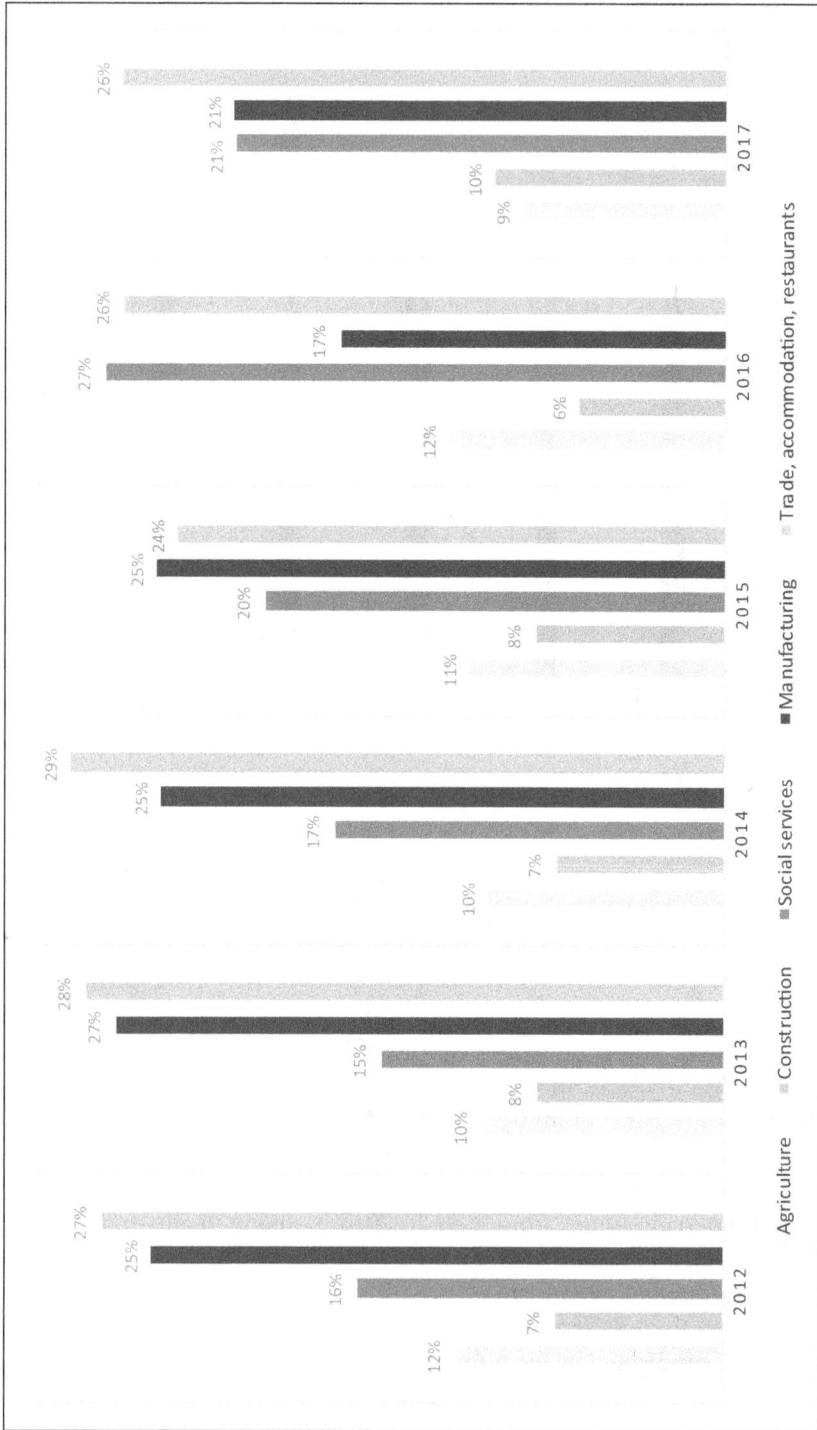

Source: Central Bureau of Statistics (BPS), 2013–18.

FIGURE 3.3
Inbound Tourist Arrivals and Economic Growth in the Riau Islands Province, 2004–18
(in thousands)

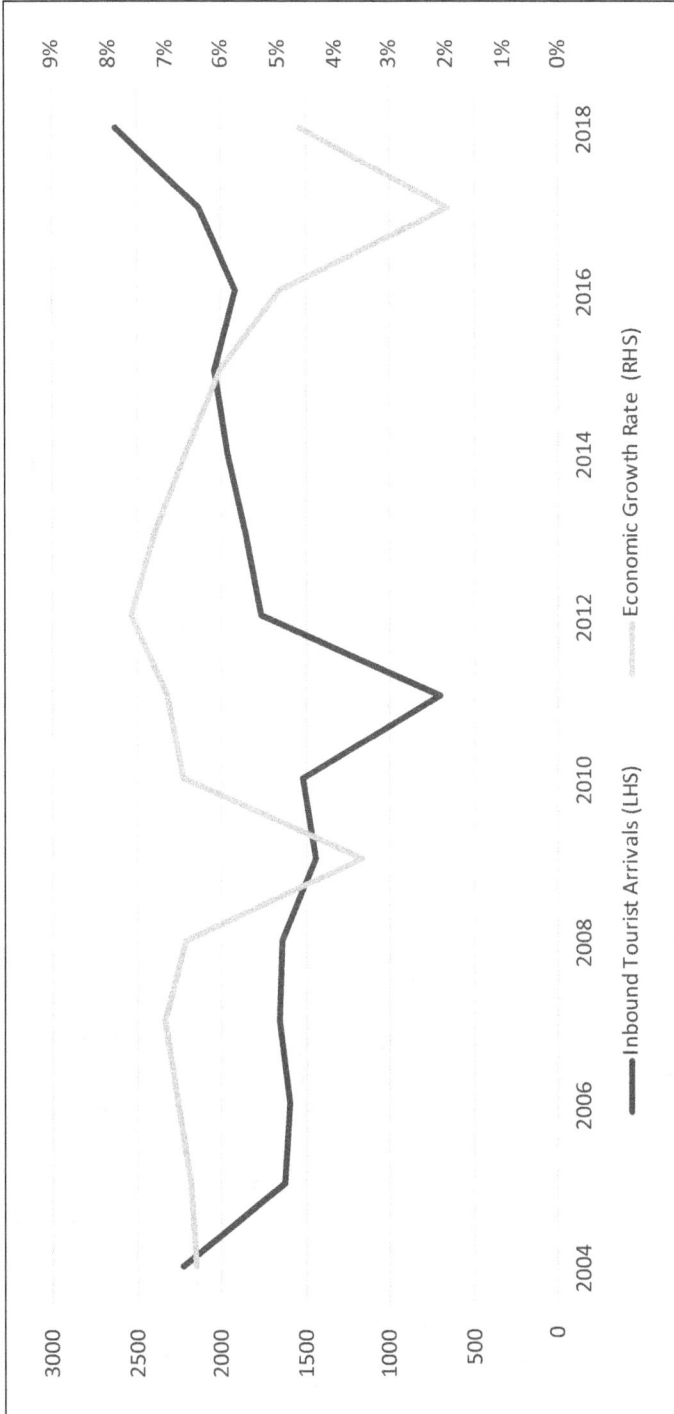

Source: Central Bureau of Statistics (BPS), 2005–19.

FIGURE 3.4
Number of Visitors to Batam, Bintan and Tanjungpinang, 2013–18
(in thousands)

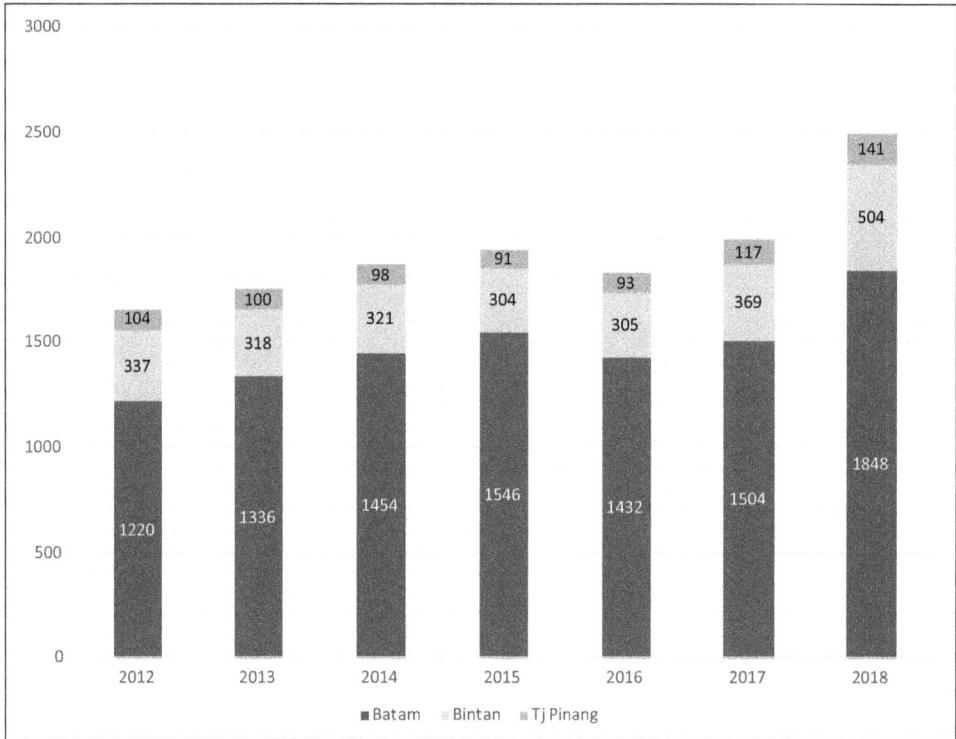

Source: Tourism Office, Riau Islands Province, 2019.

are Batam City, Bintan Regency, and Tanjungpinang City. Batam, in particular, has been the most popular site for tourists.

In 2018, the province received 2.6 million foreign tourists, a 23 per cent jump from the previous year (Figure 3.4). Most foreign tourists coming into the Riau Islands are from Singapore (53 per cent) and Malaysia (12 per cent). For Singaporean and Malaysian visitors, Batam and Bintan have become their popular low-cost weekend getaways due to their proximity and convenient connectivity—a 45 minutes ferry ride from Singapore or Johor Bahru. Moreover, in recent years, there is a growing number of Chinese tourists visiting the province, but overall this remains relatively small compared with Singaporeans and Malaysian visitors. It is important to note that domestic tourism is much bigger compared with the number of foreign tourists, reaching 4.2 million in 2018. Domestic tourists who visit the Riau Islands mostly come from nearby provinces, such as Lampung, South Sumatra, and Riau.

Beyond creating jobs, the tourism sector is also the main contributor to locally generated revenue for local governments, especially for Bintan. As can be seen from Table 3.2, 62 per cent of its locally generated revenue in 2018 stems from the tourism sector.

TABLE 3.2
The Share of Tourism in Local Government Revenue, Batam and Bintan, 2015–18

	Batam		Bintan		Tanjungpinang	
	Total Own-Revenue (in IDR billion)	Share of Revenue from Tourism (%)	Total Own-Revenue (in IDR billion)	Share of Revenue From Tourism (%)	Total Own-Revenue (in IDR billion)	Share of Revenue from Tourism (%)
2015	825	18	156	67	73	20
2016	892	18	187	56	72	23
2017	651	26	198	57	82	25
2018	1.069	20	221	62	84	30

Sources: (1) Tourism Office, Batam City; (2) Regional Revenue and Financial Management Office, Batam City, Bintan Regency and Tanjungpinang City, 2019.

Given the above backdrop and the importance of the tourism sector in the Riau Islands Province, this chapter examines how the central and local governments are seeking to develop the sector, particularly their promotion strategies and key challenges. The next section discusses the early period of tourism development in the Riau Islands. The subsequent section analyses the main actors and their respective plans. Then, the concluding section looks at the challenges and prospects facing the sector.

THE DEVELOPMENT OF THE TOURISM SECTOR

This section will look at the development of tourism in the Riau Islands Province through identifying and analysing events in three key areas in the sector.

Batam: The Entertainment City

Batam is the largest city in the province and a key hub for manufacturing activity. It has been a popular destination for travellers from Singapore and Malaysia for many years. However, more visitors from other countries in Asia, such as China, India and South Korea, as well as Europe have begun to visit the island recently, which is renowned for its duty-free shops, spas, golf courses, resorts and water sports.

Frequent ferry services connect Singapore's Tanah Merah port and Johor Bahru in Malaysia with Batam. The island has six ferry terminals located in Sekupang, Waterfront City, Batam Centre, Harbour Bay, Nongsapura, and Telaga Punggur. The journey from Singapore takes around 40 minutes, while from Johor Bahru it is around 90 minutes.

In the late 1980s, Batam started to develop its tourism area in Nongsa, on the northeast part of the Island. It was more well known for its gambling and prostitution (Vltchek and Indira 2018). As the number of foreign workers increased, the entertainment sector in the island thrived. Batam became popular for its nightlife, particularly karaoke, discos, and massage parlours. There are two famous gambling locations in Batam, namely the Red Zone and the Green Zone. The Red Zone, which includes Nagoya and Jodoh, is more down-market, while the Green Zone caters to more affluent tourists. One of the famous gambling areas is Marina City. During the 1990s boom period, the area was filled with expatriates and travellers from Jakarta. In the 2000s, the gambling industry in Batam reached a new level, with the establishment of casinos.

In 2004, the Indonesian government through the National Police Chief, General Sutanto, decided to prohibit all gambling activities in the country. As a result, all casinos and gambling sites were closed down and the industry in Batam came to an end. This change in policy hit the island's economy badly. Coupled with a global economic downturn, the 2004–8 period was difficult for Batam's tourism industry, which was reduced to depending on shopping and the area's nightlife to attract visitors.

In 2009, Batam, Bintan and Karimun were granted Free Trade Zone (FTZ) status by the central government, which provided an opportunity for Batam to revive its tourism industry. On one hand, the special tax regime entailed duty-free shopping for a range of goods, which gave a boost to the area's retail sector. On the other, the new incentives attracted new investment in a large facility in Nongsa, Montigo Resorts. The luxurious resort was opened in 2012 and managed by KOP Limited, a Singapore holding company with business interests in real estate development, hospitality, and entertainment. Currently, there are more than 100 villas available and some are offered for investors.

In addition, Sinarmas Land and KOP Ltd also have another development project, through their subsidiaries, in some parts of Nongsa. The project is designed for landed houses, low-rise condominiums, as well as other mixed-use commercial and hospitality developments. The first phase of development of the 228-hectare Nuvasa Bay project is estimated to cost about US$300 million (Huang 2016).

Another significant project is the Meisterstadt, a nine-hectare mega-superblock in Batam. This project is a joint venture led by the family of former President Habibie under the name Pollux Habibie International (Wareza 2019). The development of this area requires an investment fund of US$1 billion to develop an integrated residential-business-hospitality complex in Batam's central business area.

These developments have raised Batam's reputation and made it more upmarket, away from massage parlours towards other sectors, such as beauty parlours and wellness facilities, as well as activities centring on the island's natural attractions (Fadli 2019b). It is important to note that Singapore's role in drawing crowds through its international marketing network is critical for the progress of tourism promotion in the province. One example, the Singapore Cruise Centre and PT Nongsa Terminal Bahari have signed a marketing collaboration agreement in September 2017 to promote tourism in the Riau Islands (Chai 2017). The marketing partnership is aimed to pull in younger tourists and to prompt improvements in cruising facilities in both countries. Moreover, to boost tourism in Batam and the Riau Islands, Singapore and Indonesia have agreed to collaborate to promote high-end service activities in the Nongsa area such as Infinite Studios and Nongsa Digital Park, among others (Arlina Arshad 2018).

Bintan: The Resort Island

Bintan is the largest island in the Riau Islands Province and a key component of its tourism sector. It is well known for its high-end resorts, world-class golf courses, and its panoramic coastal attractions. The island is located just a ferry ride away from Singapore and Johor Bahru, Malaysia. There are frequent services from Tanah Merah Terminal in Singapore to Sri Bintan Pura Terminal in Tanjungpinang and Bandar Bentan Telani Terminal at Bintan Resorts. From Johor Bahru Ferry Terminal there are regular ferry services to Sri Bintan Pura Terminal in Tanjungpinang. However, Raja Haji Fisabilillah Airport in Bintan only caters to domestic flights.

The sector began to develop in the early 1990s with the construction of Bintan Resorts in Lagoi, on the northern coast of Bintan island. The project was part of an economic cooperation agreement between Indonesia and Singapore. This tourist resort area covers 23,000 hectares of land and is managed by PT Bintan Resorts Cakrawala, an operational arm of Bintan Resorts International Pte Ltd. Both companies are subsidiaries of Gallant Venture Ltd, an investment holding company listed on the Singapore Stock Exchange.

In March 1991, Radius Prawiro, Indonesian Coordinating Minister for Trade and Industry and Singapore's Deputy Prime Minister, Lee Hsien Loong, attended the facility's ground-breaking ceremony. Then, in mid-July 1996, the Bintan Resorts was officially opened by President Soeharto and Prime Minister Goh Chok Tong. This development started a new era of tourism investment. Since then, thirteen independent beach resorts and four golf courses have been constructed in the area, along with an ever-expanding range of recreational facilities and attractions.[1]

Together with Batam, in March 2009, Bintan Resorts was granted FTZ status. This entails special exemptions on import taxes as well as a less cumbersome business licensing process.[2] In turn, the Bintan local government has issued regulations making Bintan Resorts a priority development area (Muzwardi 2017).

To date, Lagoi has an array of accommodation in the form of hotel rooms (1,484 units), villas (253 units), chalets (51 units), lodge (31 units), hostels (40 units) and apartments (21 units).[3] According to the Manpower Office of the Bintan Regency, there are currently about 3,100 employees working in various resorts in Lagoi, in which about 64 per cent are employed in accommodation services.[4]

The popularity of Bintan resorts has risen due to its hosting of annual international sports events such as marathons, triathlons, extreme sports, and golf competitions. One key event is the Bintan Triathlon, held every year for the past fifteen years. Another high-profile race is the Tour de Bintan (an international cycling competition), which has also been held for ten years. In 2018, it had around 2,000 participants and attracted some 6,000 tourists.[5]

The number of tourists visiting the resort area continues to increase each year, with an average of 550,000 visits per year for the past ten years. In 2018, tourist arrivals in Bintan reached over 1 million people (BPS, Bintan Regency, 2019), which partially helped offset the economic recession facing the Riau Islands' economy. Due to its ever-expanding number of visitors, Bintan Resorts have become a significant contributor to the local government's revenue. In 2018, Lagoi contributed about 54 per cent of the Bintan Regency's regional income, which reached IDR206.5 billion. The contribution comes from the hotel, restaurant, and entertainment taxes, with a total value of IDR112.6 billion.[6] But overall, the tourism sector generates 60–70 per cent of the Bintan Regency's revenue.[7]

The trend seems positive as the private sector has been aggressively constructing high-end residential complexes and building infrastructure to improve access to the island. One key new facility is the construction of Bintan International Airport in the Busung area by PT BRC Lagoi in collaboration with Gallant Venture Ltd. The 3-km-runway airport is built to serve direct routes to China and Korea, and the investment value for this project is S$100 million. The construction of Cassia Apartments and several other new complexes in Lagoi, as well as those in the Trikora area, indicates a high expectation in the industry that the number of travellers to the island will continue to grow.

Tanjungpinang: The Historic Capital

Located on the southwestern coast of Bintan Island, Tanjungpinang is the capital city and second-largest city in the Riau Islands Province. It is a diverse city with multiple ethnic communities, including Malay, Javanese, Chinese, Minangkabau, Batak and Buginese. There are mosques, churches, as well as Hindu and Buddhist temples along its main roads. The Sri Bintan Pura ferry terminal is the main passenger port and is used by all domestic and international services from or to the city, with frequent connections to Singapore and southern Malaysia. There are also several domestic flights to Tanjungpinang from Jakarta.

Tanjungpinang has traditionally been a popular destination for shopping tourism, dating back to the Dutch colonial era. Historically, it was a market with regional reach located in the Strait of Malacca, which catered to trade from Europe to India and China. Thus, during the colonial period, many Singaporeans and Malaysians travelled to shop at Merdeka Market in Tanjungpinang. During that time, the transactions used the Malayan-Singapore dollar as local currency. This period ended with the confrontation between Indonesia and Malaysia in 1963–66. In October 1963, Jakarta officially stopped using the dollar and replaced it with the rupiah. Following this, Tanjungpinang declined as a site for tourism for visitors from Malaysia and Singapore.

The situation began to change in the 1990s with the opening of Bintan Resorts, as many international visitors transited through Tanjungpinang on their way there. In addition to shopping, tourists visited Penyengat Island, which was once the centre of the Johor-Riau Kingdom. Reachable by boat from Tanjungpinang, the island has historic monuments, including tombs and the graveyards of national cultural icons such as Raja Jaafar and Raja Ali Haji.[8]

Another well-known landmark on this island is the Sultan of Riau Grand Mosque, which commemorates the glory of the Riau Sultanate. The Sultan's palace, which exemplifies Malay architecture, remains even though it has been abandoned for more than eight decades.[9]

However, in the 2000s, the number of visitors again dropped dramatically as more tourists preferred to take a ferry directly from Singapore to Lagoi. As a result, there was a significant decline in the number of tourist arrivals through the Sri Bintan Pura port. In 2003, Air Asia, a low-cost airline, began operating several direct flights from Singapore and Malaysia to cities in Indonesia. This caused a further decline in the number of tourists to the city, as Singaporeans and Malaysians who used to visit Tanjungpinang were then diverted to visit other regions in Indonesia.[10]

Nowadays, Tanjungpinang's trademark as a shopping destination has faded, marked by the closing down of 120 shops in the Old Town (Kota Lama) in the Merdeka market. The area's main tourism activities are now reduced to those centring around Penyengat Island.

It is interesting to note that one local businessman and politician, Bobby Jayanto, has led a project to establish a religious monument.[11] As a chairman of a Chinese community association in Tanjungpinang, he managed to collect donations and build a temple named Vihara Ksitigarbha Bodhisattva, near Tanjungpinang. The temple was built in 2004 and officially opened in 2017 by the Riau Islands Governor, Nurdin Basirun (Limahekin 2017). It is open to the public and expected to attract more tourists, particularly from China.

Other regions such as Anambas, Karimun, Natuna and Lingga began to develop their tourism sector later, following the formation of the Riau Islands Province in 2004. Tourism activities in these islands are expected to be enhanced by the enactment of Law No. 27/2007, concerning the management of coastal areas and small islands. The law grants permission to private investors to manage small islands. As such, foreign investors can lease and use the allocated islands as exclusive tourism locations, which will hopefully catalyse investment.

POTENTIAL AREAS FOR DEVELOPMENT

The Riau Islands Province consists of 95 per cent sea and 5 per cent land. With many small islands and vast territorial waters, the province has significant marine tourism potential. Some of the small islands have white sandy beaches with beautiful landscapes. One in this province, Bawah in the Anambas island group, was named by CNN as one of the most beautiful islands in Asia (Figure 3.5) (Springer 2019).

Following the recent legislative changes, some islands are currently managed by private investors. At the time of writing, there are about fourteen islands managed by the private sector, and which have been turned into exclusive resorts, such as: Bawah, Nikoi, Joyo, Pangkil and Telunas. Bawah, for instance, was developed by a Singaporean shipping tycoon, Tim Hartnoll, who built a 35-room resort in the six-island cluster (Springer 2019). Roughly 95 per cent of the hotel's staff members are from Indonesia, with 32 per cent coming from the local community. Nikoi in Bintan won an award as the best private island in 2016 in the category of sustainable

FIGURE 3.5
Prospective Islands for Tourism Development in the Riau Islands Province

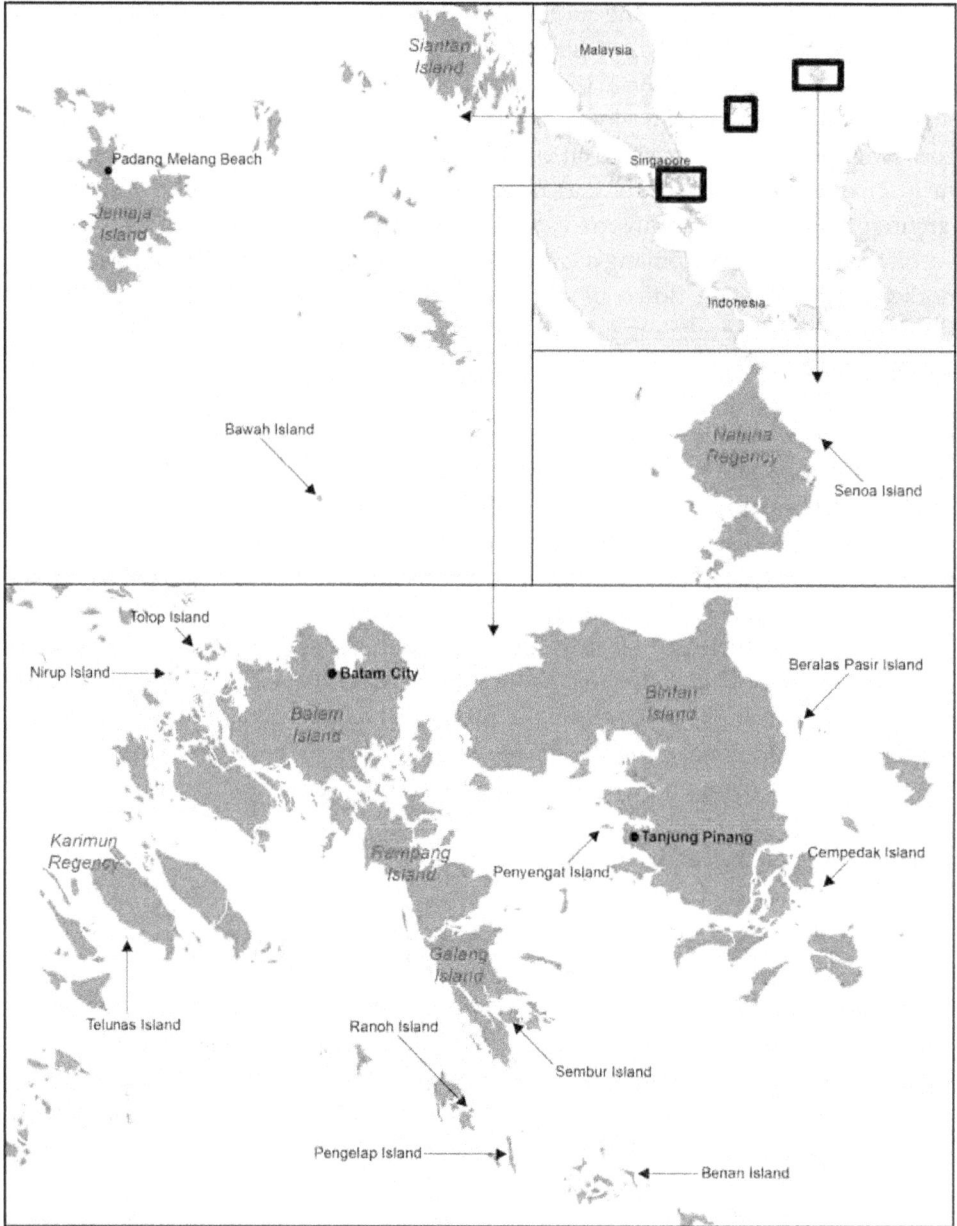

Source: Interview with Syamsul Bahrum, Secretary of SEZ council, Riau Islands Province, Riau Islands, 6 November 2018, on proposal for submission of special economic zones.

development and eco-tourism, given by the leading Conde Nast Traveller magazine (Ramadhanny 2016).

The development of these private islands into exclusive resorts has increased the number of high-end travellers. Moreover, it also contributes revenue to the local government as the investor must pay property tax (*pajak bumi dan bangunan*) as well as hotel and restaurant or entertainment taxes if applicable.[12]

The development of private islands in the Riau Islands is a high-cost investment endeavour, but is expected to support the livelihood of the surrounding community. This is because there is an obligation to hire local people and buy local community products, such as seafood from nearby areas and local crafts. To protect the environment, the developers of the private islands are required to build semi-permanent structures made of wood or bamboo.[13]

In addition to its natural potential, the Riau Islands Province also has a rich traditional and religious culture. These aspects are, however, still not fully developed.

Based on information from the Riau Islands provincial tourism board, there are many potential tourist destinations which have not been fully explored in the archipelagic province. These potential areas offer different types of tourist experiences ranging from nature tourism, agro-tourism, and eco-tourism (Table 3.3).

Meanwhile, outside Bintan, there are still untapped tourism possibilities, including Senoa Island in Natuna. Senoa Island has potential to be developed as a marine resort, site for water recreation including diving and snorkelling, as well as a geo-park. The local government has tried to build the port and road to provide access to the island. However, these projects cannot be completed due to lack of funding. At the time of writing, there is no investor interested in developing this island.[14] One industry player argues the need to establish a Natuna Development Agency (Badan Otoritas) similar to BP Batam, which focuses on tourism promotion and infrastructure development on that island.[15]

In addition to its natural and cultural potential, the Riau Islands also has another promising sector, which is its cuisine—especially seafood. Seafood exports are the fourth-largest source of revenue for the province reaching US$84.2 million in 2016 (BPS 2017). Nevertheless, to reap the benefits of the sector's full potential, the industry needs to attract more domestic and international investors. For this reason, the Riau Islands provincial government has been trying to promote its tourism investment opportunities to local, national, and international investors. In recent years, it has carried out the following measures: (a) built up a database of untapped tourism opportunities; and (b) provided investment support facilities, such as project profiles, an updated Regional Spatial Plan, as well as a more *detailed Spatial Plan (Rencana Detail Tata Ruang*, or RDTR) concerning tourism development areas; and provided funds to start new tourism projects. One example of the latter can be seen in Bukit Manuk Tanjungpinang, where the local government has built roads, set up telecommunications infrastructure, and supplied electrical power to attract investors.[16]

TABLE 3.3
Potential Tourist Attractions in the Riau Islands

Tourist Attraction(s)	Type	Characteristic(s)	Investment Prospects
Tanjung Siambang beach (Tanjungpinang)	Nature tourism	An exotic beach with plenty of coconut trees.	Accommodation, water tourism
Bukit Manuk (Tanjungpinang)	Agro-tourism	Land is suitable for fruit plantations	Agro-industry, forestry, outbound activities
Bukit Kucing (Tanjungpinang)	Eco-tourism	A protected forest area, which can be used for eco-tourism	Agro-industry, forestry, outbound activities
China Town Senggarang (Tanjungpinang)	Historical tourism	A 450 year Chinese temple Gambir house Vihara Dharma Sasana temple	Accommodation
Kuala Sempang forest (Bintan)	Eco-tourism	A 195-hectare mangrove forest	Accommodation, agro-industry, forestry, fish-farming
Lancang Kuning Village (Bintan)	Agro-tourism	A protected forest area, which can be used for eco-tourism and community based tourism	Beekeeping, agriculture
Duyung island (Lingga)	Nature tourism	White-sandy beach near Batam	Accommodation, water tourism
Senoa island (Natuna)	Nature tourism	White-sandy beach Rich coral reefs A geopark area	Accommodation, snorkelling, water recreation

Source: Authors' compilation from fieldwork research.

The Strategy

Promoting tourism has become one of the national development priorities under President Joko Widodo's administration. The President has stressed that the tourism sector could be the driving force of the economy amid the global economic turmoil (Asmara 2019). At the national level, the government wants to promote ten "New Balis" to develop new areas of the country, including: Toba Lake, North Sumatra; Mandalika, West Nusa Tenggara; Labuan Bajo, East Nusa Tenggara; and Borobudur, Yogyakarta.

The Riau Islands has not been included as part of this programme. However, the Ministry of Tourism has set up an initiative, called the "Hot Deals" project, which aims to develop the tourism sector in the Riau Islands. The project is an online marketing service which offers travel package deals. The service was initiated in 2017 by the Ministry of Tourism with support from ferry companies, hotels and restaurant chains, as well as service providers such as golf resorts and spas (Maulana 2018). Essentially, it provides discounted travel packages to attract tourists, particularly those who are stopping over in Singapore to visit Batam and Bintan. According to the Ministry of Tourism, the programme has been a success. In 2017 it sold 103,000 packages, in 2018 this rose to 700,000, and in 2019 is projected to have 1 million packages (*Tribunnews*, 17 July 2019). The Ministry is optimistic that such a programme can increase the number of visitors by taking advantage of its proximity to Singapore, a global tourist hub (Petriella 2019).

Another national programme that may have an impact on the province's tourism growth is the halal tourism programme. It is one of the main programmes under the National Shariah Economy Masterplan 2019–24, which aims to promote tourism among the region's growing middle-class Muslim community (Muhammad 2019). One out of the ten designated tourist destinations for the halal tourism programme is Tanjungpinang, particularly Penyengat Island. Currently, the programme is still in the planning stage, as the provincial government and relevant stakeholders are preparing the implementation guidelines. The initiative seeks to target travellers from southern Malaysia, Singapore and Brunei.[17] The plan has received a positive response from a majority of the city's Muslim residents, and tourism associations such as the Association of Tours and Travel Agencies (ASITA) strongly support the initiative.[18]

In the 2018 Regional Medium-Term Development Plan, the provincial government has set a target of reaching 4 million tourists by 2020. This target seems quite ambitious given that the number of tourists visiting the province only reached 2.6 million in 2018 and the global economic situation has not been improving of late (IMF 2019).[19] Furthermore, what is more difficult is to increase the length of the average visit. The target is to increase from 1.8 days per person in 2018 to 2.2 days per person by 2020. It is important to note that most visitors in the Riau Islands come during the weekend. Meanwhile, on a weekday, the average hotel occupancy rate is relatively low, under 30 per cent (*Tribunnews*, 17 July 2019).

To promote the growth of the tourism sector, the provincial government has formulated several strategies, which divide sector-related activities into three categories: (1) nature (marine tourism, eco-tourism, adventure); (2) culture (heritage and pilgrim tourism, culinary and shopping, and city and village); and (3) events (MICE and sport events) (Table 3.4).

The provincial tourism office has also set out measures to further boost the sector's performance, which include: optimizing the potential of existing tourist destinations; boosting accessibility; increasing synergy with tourism stakeholders in organizing tourism events; ramping up promotion; engaging local stakeholders in cooperation with international event organizers to convene various international events; developing inclusive tourist destinations through community-based tourism; encouraging halal tourism; disseminating and socializing local regulations regarding the promotion of Malay culture; and improving the quality of tourism human resources through training and professional certification (Figure 3.6).[20] Also, it has identified a number of programmes to develop the sector including: improving tourist attractions; increasing marketing; and institutional strengthening of key agencies. The creative economy is a key focus, including: development and promotion of local cuisine; socialization of intellectual property rights; and preparation of action plans.

Currently, the Riau Islands provincial government has identified seventeen regional leading tourist destinations (Destinasi Pariwisata Unggulan Daerah, or DPUD), spread over seven districts and municipalities (Table 3.5).

Moreover, the provincial government has also initiated some programmes to promote human resources in the tourism sector. One case in point is a coaching programme that is initiated by the local government in cooperation with the Indonesian Tourist Guide Association (ASITA) and the Indonesian Hotel and Restaurant Association. The programme aims to improve the standard of human resources concerning tourism services and the travel industry.

In 2018, the Riau Islands government proposed to the central government that it convert several of the province's islands into Special Economic Tourism Zones. The streamlined investment licensing and tax incentives are expected to bring in more investments. Moreover, the Riau Islands, together with other archipelagic provincial governments across Indonesia, have been proposing a new law concerning archipelagic provinces.[21] The rationale is that a special law is needed to provide more resources and a legal basis for local governments to promote their marine tourism.

To a certain extent, the efforts have shown some positive results, as the number of tourists to the Riau Islands has been increasing over time. This is partly due to a growing number of events, including races and tournaments, held in some of the islands. Currently, around 70 per cent of sport tourism events are carried out in Bintan. Learning from the success of those sport tourism events, the local government has been planning to hold more such events, which blend the island's attractive natural landscape with popular national and international sports events.

Based on fieldwork observation, most local governments in the Riau Islands Province have their respective tourism development strategies and programmes. The strategies often are relatively similar, such as promoting cultural attractions, optimizing existing tourist attractions by increasing accessibility, and increasing

TABLE 3.4
Cultural Attractions in the Riau Islands Province

Heritage and Pilgrim Tourism	City and Village Tourism	Culinary and Shopping Tourism
Penyengat Island, Tanjungpinang	Penyengat Island, Tanjungpinang	Nagoya Hill, Batam
Senggarang temple, Tanjungpinang	Nong Isa Village, Batam	BCS Batam
Damnah palace site, Lingga	Benan Island, Lingga	Lucky Plaza, Batam
Badang cemetary, Karimun	Downtown Nagoya, Batam	Seafood culinary Harbour Front Batam
Bukit Batu cemetary, Bintan	Engku Putri area, Batam	Seafood Tanjungpiayu, Batam
Linggam Cahaya museum, Lingga	Elang Laut Belakang Padang, Batam	Akau Potong Lembu, Tanjungpinang
Sulaiman Badrul Alamsyah Museum, Tanjungpinang	Kawal fishing village, Bintan	Coastal area, Karimun
Nong Isa cemetery, Batam	Mangrove forest, Gunung Kijang Village, Bintan	
Galang Refugee memorial, Batam	Padang Lamun Teluk Bakau Village, Bintan	
Kwan Im Statue, Batam		

Source: Tourism Office, Riau Islands Province, 2018.

FIGURE 3.6
The Riau Islands Province Tourism Development Strategy

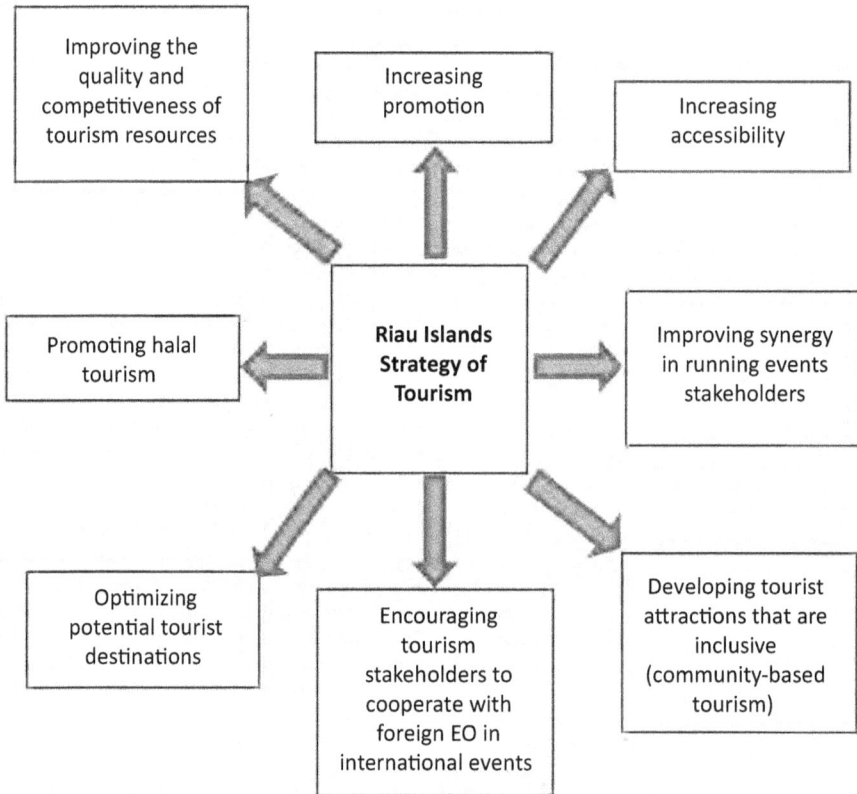

```
┌──────────────────┐    ┌──────────────┐         ┌──────────────┐
│ Improving the    │    │ Increasing   │         │ Increasing   │
│ quality and      │    │ promotion    │         │ accessibility│
│ competitiveness of│   │              │         │              │
│ tourism resources│    └──────────────┘         └──────────────┘
└──────────────────┘                ↑        ↗
          ↖                         │
                        ┌──────────────────┐
┌──────────────┐        │  Riau Islands    │        ┌──────────────┐
│ Promoting halal│  ⇐   │  Strategy of     │   ⇒    │ Improving synergy│
│ tourism       │       │  Tourism         │        │ in running events│
│              │        │                  │        │ stakeholders │
└──────────────┘        └──────────────────┘        └──────────────┘
          ↙              ↓          ↘
┌──────────────┐  ┌──────────────────┐  ┌──────────────────┐
│ Optimizing   │  │ Encouraging      │  │ Developing tourist│
│ potential tourist│ tourism         │  │ attractions that are│
│ destinations │  │ stakeholders to  │  │ inclusive        │
│              │  │ cooperate with   │  │ (community-based │
│              │  │ foreign EO in    │  │ tourism)         │
│              │  │ international events│ │                  │
└──────────────┘  └──────────────────┘  └──────────────────┘
```

Source: Riau Islands Province Tourism Office, Batam City Tourism Office.

synergy with stakeholders. For instance, the Bintan regency government has initiated some collaboration with village-owned enterprises (Badan Usaha Milik Desa or BUMDES) for the development of tourism villages under a community-based tourism model in Mapur and Lancang Kuning. With the enactment of the government regulation (PP) No. 8/2016 on Village Funds, it provides opportunities for the villages to purchase and manage assets as well as improve infrastructure. For example, Mapur village used the village funds from the central government to buy diving equipment as well as assets for homestays.

Moreover, the local government has set up an awareness group (Kelompok Sadar Pariwisata, or Pokdarwis) to promote several tourist destinations. These groups play an important role as an extension of the local government to manage tourist destinations. To date, there are forty-seven Pokdarwis in the Riau Islands Province, including: twelve in Batam; eighteen in Tanjungpinang; five in Bintan; four in Karimun; one in Lingga; five in Natuna; and two in Anambas Islands. However, not all Pokdarwis are currently active; among the few that are active, for example, Benan Lingga Island's Pokdarwis manages the Benan Island tourism

TABLE 3.5
Regional Leading Tourist Destinations in the Riau Islands Province

No.	Regency/City	Locations	Uniqueness/Potential
1	Batam	• Rempang and Galang zone • Nagoya	• white sandy beach, cottages, water sport, snorkeling, diving, fishing sport, fishing village • shopping
2	Bintan	• Trikora zone • Lepah River • Bintan Mountain • Lagoi	• white sandy beach, cottages, water sports, snorkeling, diving, fishing sport, fishing village
3	Tanjungpinang	• Penyengat Island • Hulu Riau old town zone	• A national heritage area with 46 cultural heritage sites • former royal palace of the Sultan of the Riau-Johor Kingdom
4	Karimun	• Buru Island • Pelawan beach	• natural hot spring, mosque of Raja Haji Abdul Ghani • trekking, swimming
5	Anambas	• Padang Melang beach • Temburun Waterfall	• white sandy beach, cottages, waters sport, snorkeling, diving, fishing sport, fishing village • a 250-metre waterfall with seven levels of falls
6	Lingga	• Benan Village • Mepar Village • Damnah Village	• white sandy beach, cottages, water sports, snorkeling, diving, fishing, fishing village • royal historical site of the Riau-Lingga Sultanate • Damnah Palace site
7	Natuna	• Senoa Island • Depih Bay	• white sandy beach, cottages, water sports, snorkelling, diving, fishing, fishing village

Source: Tourism Office, Riau Islands Province, 2018.

area in Lingga Regency and the Anambas' Pokdarwis manages the Padang Melang beach tourism area. But most of the tourism awareness groups have not yet begun to manage their assets. The problems are complex, including: lack of experience in managing and promoting tourism; scarcity of operational funds; and internal conflicts in the group.

Based on our fieldwork interviews, both provincial and local governments have been trying to provide supporting regulations to attract private investment and encourage community participation.[22] Eventually, the prospect of the tourism sector in the Riau Islands Province depends significantly on private sector investment. The latter is highly dependent on how the challenges listed below can be addressed effectively.

CHALLENGES

One of the main challenges in developing the tourism sector in the Riau Islands Province lies in unclear and overlapping regulations and policies. For instance, the masterplan from the central government has not been translated into clear and cohesive programmes at both the provincial and the local government levels. The provincial government has been facing difficulty in reconciling its development plan with local governments, who have developed their respective sectoral development plans without consulting others.

In addition, unclear/conflicting spatial plans trigger many land conflicts, which are constraining tourism development. For instance, when juxtaposed with resort development, the implementation of the Tourism Law (Law No. 10/2009) is often in conflict with the existing Forestry Law (Law No. 41/1999) on the use of forest area and the Maritime and Fisheries Law (Law No. 1 and No. 32/2014) on coastal zones, small islands and marine development. In one case, a reclamation for tourism development cannot be done in specific areas allocated for protected forest and marine conservation. To proceed with the reclamation, the government must first change its spatial planning document. One of the big issues occurs where the regional spatial plans (Rencana Tata Ruang dan Wilayah, or RTRW) at the provincial and regency level are in contradiction with the national spatial plan of the Ministry.

There are several cases of land conflicts concerning the development of tourism in the province.[23] One of the cases involves the construction of an integrated tourism city project in the Batu Licin area of Bintan Regency. It covers 1,200 hectares development of apartments, shopping centre, hotels, offices, and conservation sites. The project is projected to cost around US$30 billion. The developer, PT SUN Resort, has formed a consortium with a Chinese company. The project began in 2012, however, its progress is hampered due to land use regulations. The local government has not granted its recommendation for the use of land as a tourism site. According to the Bintan Regency's regulation No. 2/2012 on regional spatial planning, the area is not included as a tourism area. Therefore, the current resort development is considered a violation of the existing regulations. Interestingly, PT SUN Resort has carried out land acquisition and infrastructure development, supported by the previous local government administration.[24] Overcoming this land use issue requires a revision of the local spatial planning document. Besides, the legality of SUN Resort licensing needs a cross-ministerial joint decree, involving approval from the Ministry of Agrarian and Spatial Planning, Ministry of National Development Planning, and Ministry of Public Works and Public Housing.[25]

Another example can be found in Lancang Kuning Village, Bintan Regency, which is located in a protected forest area. Its village head has requested a permit from the Governor of the Riau Islands Province for the community to use 62 hectares of land in a protected forest area for agro-tourism development, such as bee-keeping, plantations for sunflowers, as well as snake fruit, dragon fruit and bananas. However, after almost a year the permit has yet to be approved by the Ministry of Environment and Forestry.

The problem of land conflicts was also mentioned by tourism awareness groups in several regions, such as East Tanjungpinang and Tanjungpinang City. Large tracts of land in those areas are owned by private companies, some of which are local and others are controlled by foreigners (Table 3.6).

On one hand, the large number of land assets whose management is controlled by foreigners is welcome as a sign of foreign investment. On the other, it reduces the availability of land for the development of community-based tourism. As a result, there is a local grievance that the size of resources available for the local community programmes has been shrinking.

TABLE 3.6
Foreign-Owned Land in Bintan Regency

No.	Company	Land Area (Hectare)	Business Area	Country
1.	PT. Bintan Resort Cakrawala	3,000	Accommodation, recreation and entertainment	Singapore
2.	PT. Pelangi Bintan Indah	338	Development and management of tourism areas	Singapore
3.	PT. Bintan Hotels	244	Hospitality	Singapore
4.	PT. Bintan Lagoon Resort	229	Accommodation, hotel and recreation services	Singapore
5.	PT. Ria Bintan	216	Accommodation, recreation services, and golf course	Singapore
6.	PT. Hanno Bali	144	Integrated tourism (accommodation, recreation and restaurants)	Canada
7.	PT. Bintan Land Resort	80	Accommodation services (cottage)	Singapore, British Virgin Island
8.	PT. Bintan Vista	75	Hospitality/cottage	Singapore
9.	PT. Libra Kharisma Alam	50	Accommodation, recreation services	Singapore
10.	PT. Hang Huo Investment	50	Four Star Hotel and Cottage	British Virgin Island
11.	PT. Berakit Resort	43	Accommodation services/ cottage	Singapore, British Virgin Island
12.	PT. Eresindo Bintan Adhika	40	Accommodation services and water tourism	Singapore
13.	PT. Kult Motorsports	30	Other entertainment and recreation activities	Singapore
14.	PT. The Haven International	28	Accommodation and real estate services that are owned or rented	Singapore, UK

Source: Tourism office, Bintan Regency, 2018.

As can be seen from Table 3.6, more than 4,500 hectares from a total of 22,300 hectares, or around 20 per cent of total land allocated for tourism under the Bintan Regency's Regional Spatial Plan is currently controlled by foreign companies. As of now, thirty-seven foreign companies have been granted real estate operational permits in the regency.

A different type of land issue has arisen in Natuna Regency. In this case, the conflict is caused by overlapping land rights. The local government cannot use the land intended for tourism development as the area belongs to the local community. This is a case of poor land use planning.[26]

Looking at the case of land conflicts that occur in Natuna, Bintan and Tanjungpinang, one can see that they involve conflicting interests among local governments, foreign companies and individual ownership. This conflict is likely to continue as long as the land use policy and spatial planning process in the Riau Islands Province remain unclear.

The lack of benefits to the local community was also raised by the regional tourism association. In Bintan Regency, local communities perceive that, beyond an increase in local government revenue, foreign investment does not contribute significantly to the local economy.

One case in point is related to the growing number of Chinese tourists coming to Bintan. These Chinese tourists came with chartered flights from China to Tanjungpinang. Most, if not all, Chinese tourists stayed in Bintan Pearl Beach Resort, Bintan Agro Resort, and Sahid Raya Bintan Beach Resort. Chinese travel agents handled the whole tour package from flight-bookings, departure pick-up, consumption, lodging, souvenir shopping, and attractions. They determined the tourist sites to be visited by Chinese tourists, including sites in Lagoi (Treasure Bay, Lagoi Bay), Busung (Telaga Biru), Mapur and Kawal (mangrove tours). The tour guides are also provided by Chinese travel agents. Given that all the economic activities are controlled by the travel agent, there are few benefits for the local economy and the people.

Another problem concerning the development of tourism in the Riau Islands is the shortage of infrastructure to support tourism development. Lack of good road access to other parts of the islands and poor quality of public transport infrastructure, in particular, makes transportation costs in the region more expensive compared to other destinations in Indonesia. This, in turn, prevents tourists from exploring the islands. Even in Bintan, travellers must rent their own transport, as there are no metered taxis and the bus system is underdeveloped.[28] Currently, Batam, Bintan or Karimun need significant investment in infrastructure such as highways, airports, bus terminals and ports.

The problem of basic infrastructure is more serious in Natuna, Anambas and Lingga. Particularly, Anambas and Natuna are two isolated island groups located 400–500 kilometres from Tanjungpinang. According to the Head of Tourism Development Department of the provincial government, there are many prospective tourist destinations in those island groups that badly need roads, electricity, Internet networks, banks, hospitals and other public amenities.[29]

While hard or physical infrastructure is important, soft infrastructure is also critical. Institutional and human resource capacity to manage tourism issues is often very weak. For example, there are many beaches in Batam that are left untapped due to mismanagement. They are often overcrowded and uncomfortable for foreign tourists to visit, such as Tanjung Pinggir Melayu beach.

Beyond overlapping regulations and lack of infrastructure, weak coordination and poor communication among stakeholders is another problem. Developing the province's numerous destinations requires the involvement of various stakeholders, including the government, private sectors, as well as the community. Alas, there is no well-established or systematic coordination to ensure greater stakeholder participation in promoting tourism in the region. Each of them works individually and is limited to a specific one-shot event without considering the potential of collaborative networking. As mentioned by ASITA, the coordination between tourism service entrepreneurs and the government or the community has not been fully optimized. Better coordination is important to ensure that development planning and implementation run in synergy. Currently, the coordination among stakeholders, which is mostly initiated by the local government is still not optimal. In addition, not every island is as popular as Batam, Bintan or Karimun. Anambas and Natuna have many attractive locations but are hard to access.

Finally, environmental degradation also plays a part in shaping the tourism sector in the Riau Islands. The province lies alongside one of the world's busiest shipping lanes, and over the years, oil pollution has become common and widely dispersed (Peachey, Perry and Carl Grundy-Warr 1998). In April 2019, there was a report about tourists checking out early from their resorts in Batam after oil was found on the beach. This oil allegedly originated from tanker ships in the Strait of Malacca, which had dumped their waste into the sea (Fadli 2019a).

Beyond oil pollution, some of the islands are extensively mined. For example, bauxite mines in Bintan have been active for more than eighty years. While production has been declining due to depleting reserves and a reorganization of Bintan's land use (Peachey, Perry and Grundy-Warr 1998), the effects are long-lasting. So far, there has been no initiative to stop bauxite mining activities or efforts to rehabilitate the landscape for economic use by local people and government (Panama 2019). Going forward, if environmental degradation continues unchecked, this may lead to a downturn in visitor numbers.

CONCLUSION

The Riau Islands' tourism sector has considerable potential due to the province's natural landscapes and rich cultural heritage. Yet, not many investors are coming to explore the possibilities. Regulatory uncertainties are one of the most common complaints made by the private sector. Addressing this issue, then requires good coordination, both among levels of government, as well as between agencies. Specifically, in the case of the Riau Islands Province, it is important to synergize the tourism development plans at the local government level with national-level policies. The existing regional development plans are often in contradiction with the national-level masterplan. As such, the provincial government should play a role in synergizing regional development plans with their national equivalents. In addition, efforts to promote community participation in the development of tourism should be encouraged.

Furthermore, tourism development in the Riau Islands also requires infrastructure investment. Currently, government budgets at the provincial and local levels are in deficit, which makes them less able to accelerate infrastructure development. Given this, budget support from the central government is critical, especially to improve roads, airports, seaports and other basic infrastructure. This can be linked with existing efforts by the provincial government to get central government endorsement of the new law concerning the governance of archipelagic provinces.[30]

Finally, to overcome chronic coordination problems, there is a need to promote the role of management authorities (Badan Pengusahaan, or BP). These agencies should be given more authority and resources to effectively regulate licensing and to enhance coordination among various stakeholders, including the local government, private sectors, and the community. Beyond promotion and marketing, BPs should also be more proactive to solve issues related to tourism, including environmental issues. To strengthen promotion and marketing innovation, the roles of other relevant stakeholders such as tour and travel associations and community groups are needed. An equally important element in the promotion and marketing innovation is the role of local communities.

Notes

1. Interview with Abdul Wahab, General Manager of Bintan Resort Cakrawala, Lagoi, Bintan, 29 November 2018.
2. Interview with Wan Rudy Iskandar, Head of the Tourism Office, Bintan Regency, Tanjungpinang, 15 September 2019.
3. Ibid.
4. This information is given during an interview with the Manpower Office of Bintan Regency, 5 November 2019.
5. Interview with Hasan, Secretary of Tourism and Culture Office, Bintan Regency, 21 September 2018.
6. Interview with the Regional Revenue and Financial Management Office Bintan Regency, 5 November 2019.
7. Interview with Wan Rudy Iskandar.
8. Raja Jaafar's ruling period (1805–32) marked the start of a new era of the Riau-Lingga Sultanate. Meanwhile, Raja Ali Haji was a nineteenth-century Bugis-Malay historian, poet, and scholar. In 2004, he was promoted to the status of the National Hero of Indonesia. Widely regarded as the father of the Indonesian Malay language, he wrote the famous poem Gurindam Dua Belas.
9. Interview with Azqrul Ienom, Head of Public Relations in Tanjungpinang Branch Leadership Council (DPC) the Indonesian Tourism Association (HPI), 29 September 2019.

10. Interview with Raja Fahrul, Chairman of Tanjungpinang Branch Leadership Council (DPC) the Indonesian Tourism Association (HPI), Tanjungpinang, 28 March 2019.

11. This is explored more fully in Chapter 17 of this volume.

12. Interview with Hasan, Secretary of Tourism and Culture Office, Bintan Regency, Bintan, 2 October 2018.

13. Ibid.

14. Interview with Irlizar, Head of Tourism Sector, Natuna Regency Tourism and Culture Office, 16 September 2019.

15. Interview with Edi Rusman Surbakti, Vice Chairman of Tourism Sector in Riau Islands Regional Chamber of Commerce and Industry (the period 2016–2019) and Vice Chairman of Regional Executive Boards (BPD) Indonesian Hotel and Restaurant Association (PHRI) period 2017–Incumbent, Tanjungpinang, 25 September 2019.

16. Interview with Mochammad Armandi, Head of Investment Promotion Development Planning, Tanjungpinang City One-Stop Integrated Service and Investment Services (DPMPTSP), 18 September 2019.

17. Interview with Surjadi, Head of the Tourism Office, Tanjungpinang City, Tanjungpinang, 28 November 2019.

18. Interview with Sapril Sembiring, Chairman of ASITA Tanjungpinang, 18 November 2019.

19. IMF (2019) world economic outlook projected a slowing down of economic growth in many developed countries for 2019 and 2020, including Singapore and Malaysia, the two largest sources of tourists for the Riau Islands.

20. Interview with Syamsul Rahman, Head of Destination Development and Tourism Industry Department, Riau Islands Province Tourism Office, 13 September 2018.

21. In 2008, seven provinces, i.e., Riau Islands, Maluku, North Maluku, East Nusa Tenggara, West Nusa Tenggara, North Sulawesi, and Bangka-Belitung, agreed to form a Cooperation Agency for Islands Provinces to push for the enactment of Islands Province Law (Undang Undang Provinsi Kepulauan). The latter asked for the revision of the general allocation fund (DAU) by considering the size of sea areas and the number of islands in the islands province.

22. Interview with Syamsul Rahman, Head of Destination Development and Tourism Industry, Riau Islands Province Tourism Office, 13 September 2018.

23. Ibid.

24. Interview with Wan Rudy Iskandar, former Head of Bappeda, Bintan Regency, 19 November 2019.

25. Interview with Suherry, Expert Staff of Bappeda, Bintan Regency, 27 November 2019.

26. Interview with Toni Yulifandri, Head of Section Tourism Marketing, Natuna Regency Tourism and Culture Office, 8 Maret 2019.

27. Interview with Azqrul Ienom, Head of Public Relations in Tanjungpinang Branch Leadership Council (DPC), the Indonesian Tourism Association (HPI), 29 September 2019.

28. Quoted from Amran, owner of Madu Tiga Beach and Resort, in Kadin Bintan FGD, Bintan Villa, Bintan Regency, 20 February 2019.

29. Interview with Syamsul Rahman, Head of Sector – Destination Development and Tourism Industry, the Riau Islands Province, 27 November 2018.

30. Interview with Raja Zakiah, Tourism Office, Riau Islands Province, 16 September 2019.

References

Anwar, Dewi Fortuna. 1994. "Sijori: ASEAN's Southern Growth Triangle; Problems and Prospects". *Indonesian Quarterly* 22, no. 1: 22–33.

Arlina Arshad. 2018. "Tech Park in Batam Opens, Aims to be 'Digital Bridge' between Singapore and Indonesia". *Straits Times*, 20 March 2018. https://www.straitstimes.com/asia/se-asia/tech-park-in-batam-opens-aims-to-be-digital-bridge-between-singapore-and-indonesia (accessed 13 October 2019).

Asmara, Chandra Gian. 2019. "Global Bergejolak, Jokowi Ingin Pariwisata Jadi 'Penyelamat' ". *CNBC Indonesia*, 30 August 2019. https://www.cnbcindonesia.com/news/20190830103518-4-95883/global-bergejolak-jokowi-ingin-pariwisata-jadi-penyelamat (accessed 16 October 2019).

Batam Indonesia Free Zone Authority. 2018. *Development Progress of Batam*.

BPS website. 2019. "Luas Daerah dan Jumlah Pulau Menurut Provinsi, 2002–2016". https://www.bps.go.id/statictable/2014/09/05/1366/luas-daerah-dan-jumlah-pulau-menurut-provinsi-2002-2016.html

———. 2019a. "Jumlah Devisa Sektor Pariwisata, 2015–2018". https://www.bps.go.id/dynamictable/2018/05/22%2000:00:00/1357/jumlah-devisa-sektor-pariwisata-2015-2018.html

BPS. 2017. "Ekspor Ekonomi Kreatif 2010–2016". Jakarta: BPS Indonesia.

———. 2019. "Perkembangan Pariwisata dan Transportasi Nasional Disember 2018". *Berita Resmi Statistik*, No. 12/02/Th.XXII, 1 February 2019.

———. Various years. *Indikator Utama Kepulauan Riau*. Tanjungpinang: BPS Kepulauan Riau.

Chai Hung Yin. 2017. "Singapore Cruise Centre Partners PT Nongsa Terminal Bahari to Promote Riau Islands Tourism". *Business Times*, 8 September 2017. https://www.businesstimes.com.sg/consumer/singapore-cruise-centre-partners-pt-nongsa-terminal-bahari-to-promote-riau-islands-tourism (accessed 16 October 2019).

Fadli. 2019a. "Tourists Check Out Early from Batam Resorts after Oil Found on Beaches". *Jakarta Post*, 10 April 2019. https://www.thejakartapost.com/news/2019/04/10/tourists-check-out-early-from-batam-resorts-after-oil-found-on-beaches.html (accessed 16 October 2019).

———. 2019b. "Batam Now Nail Care Haven for Singaporean Tourists". *Jakarta Post/Asia News Network*, 10 July 2019. https://www.asiaone.com/lifestyle/batam-now-nail-care-haven-singaporean-tourists (accessed 13 October 2019).

Grundy-Warr, Carl, Karen Peachey, and Martin Perry. 2002. "Fragmented Integration in the Singapore-Indonesian Border Zone: Southeast Asia's 'Growth Triangle' Against the Global Economy". *International Journal of Urban and Regional Research*: 304–28.

Huang, Claire. 2016. "Sinarmas Land and KOP to Develop Nuvasa Bay Areas in Batam". *Business Times*, 31 July 2016. https://www.businesstimes.com.sg/real-estate/sinarmas-land-and-kop-to-develop-nuvasa-bay-areas-in-batam (accessed 16 October 2019).

Hutchinson, Francis E. 2015. *Mirror Images in Different Frames? Johor, the Riau Islands, and Competition for Investment from Singapore*. Singapore: ISEAS – Yusof Ishak Institute.

———. 2017. *Rowing Against the Tide? Batam's Economic Fortunes in Today's Indonesia*. Trends in Southeast Asia, no. 8/2017. Singapore: ISEAS – Yusof Ishak Institute.

International Monetary Fund. 2019. *World Economic Outlook: Global Manufacturing Downturn, Rising Trade Barriers*. October 2019.

Limahekin, Thom. 2017. "Gubernur Resmikan Vihara Patung Seribu. Ini Pesan Nurdin Basirun dan Wali Kota Tanjungpinang". *Batam.Tribunnews*, 10 February 2017. https://batam. tribunnews.com/2017/02/10/gubernur-resmikan-vihara-patung-seribu-ini-pesan-nurdin-basirun-dan-wali-kota-tanjungpinang (accessed 26 October 2019).

Maulana, Hadi. 2018. "Gaet Wisman, Programme Hot Deals Kepri 2018 Diluncurkan". *Kompas*, 21 April 2018. https://travel.kompas.com/read/2018/04/21/113700327/gaet-wisman-programme-hot-deals-kepri-2018-diluncurkan (accessed 16 October 2019).

Muhammad, Fikri. 2019. "Diluncurkan Jokowi, Ini 4 Fokus Masterplan Ekonomi Syariah RI". *CNBC Indonesia*, 14 May 2019. https://www.cnbcindonesia.com/syariah/20190514155317-29-72406/diluncurkan-jokowi-ini-4-fokus-masterplan-ekonomi-syariah-ri (accessed 10 November 2019).

Muzwardi, Ady. 2017. *Free Trade Zone Menuju Kawasan Ekonomi Khusus di Batam, Bintan dan Karimun*. Yogyakarta: Expert.

Negara, Siwage Dharma. 2017. "Can the Decline of Batam's Shipbuilding Industry be Reversed?". *ISEAS Perspective* No. 2017/10, 16 February 2017.

———, and Hutchinson, Francis E. 2021. "The Manufacturing Sector in Batam: Back to the Future". In *The Riau Islands Province: Setting Sail*, edited by Francis E. Hutchinson and Siwage Dharma Negara. Singapore: ISEAS – Yusof Ishak Institute.

Panama, Nikolas. 2019. "Ketika Tambang Bauksit di Bintan Tidak Terhentikan". *Antaranews. com*. 22 March 2019. https://www.antaranews.com/berita/813922/ketika-tambang-bauksit-di-bintan-tidak-terhentikan (accessed 16 October 2019).

Peachey, Karen, Martin Perry, and Carl Grundy-Warr. 1998. "The Riau Islands and Economic Cooperation in the Singapore-Indonesian Border Zone". *Boundary and Territory Briefing*, Vol. 2. No. 3. International Boundaries Research Unit, University of Durham, UK.

Petriella, Yunita. 2019. "Evaluasi Programme Hot Deals: Sukseskah Mengerek Kunjungan Wisman?". *Bisnis.com*, 12 August 2019. https://ekonomi.bisnis.com/read/20190812/12/1135360/evaluasi-programme-hot-deals-sukseskah-mengerek-kunjungan-wisman. (accessed 16 October 2019).

Ramadhanny, Fitraya. 2016. "Pulau Nikoi Menang The Best Private Island 2016, Menpar Ucapkan Selamat". *Detik Travel*, 13 July 2016. https://travel.detik.com/travel-news/d-3252417/pulau-nikoi-menang-the-best-private-island-2016-menpar-ucapkan-selamat (accessed 16 October 2019).

Smith, Shannon. L.D. 1996. "Developing Batam: Indonesian Political Economy under the New Order". PhD dissertation, Research School of Pacific and Asian Studies, Australian National University.

Soenarso, Sugeng Adji. 2019. "BPS Mencatat Kunjungan Wisatawan Mancanegara 2018 Tumbuh 12,58%". *Kontan.co.id*, 3 February 2019. https://industri.kontan.co.id/news/bps-mencatat-kunjungan-wisatawan-mancanegara-2018-tumbuh-1258 (accessed 25 October 2019).

Springer, Kate. 2019. "Meet the Millionaires (and Billionaires) Behind Indonesia's Best Island Hotels". *CNN Travel*, 15 April 2019. https://edition.cnn.com/travel/article/indonesia-islands-millionaires/index.html (accessed 13 October 2019).

Tribunnews. 2019. "Hot Deals dan Tourism Hub Hidupkan Pariwisata Batam Bintan". 17 July 2019. https://www.tribunnews.com/kilas-kementerian/2019/07/17/hot-deals-dan-tourism-hub-hidupkan-pariwisata-batam-bintan (accessed 16 October 2019).

Vltchek, Andre, and Rossie Indira. 2018. "Batam Island—Indonesia's Pathetic Attempt to Create a Second Singapore". *Investig'action*, 17 July 2018. https://www.investigaction.net/en/batam-island-indonesias-pathetic-attempt-to-create-a-second-singapore/ (accessed 25 October 2019).

Wareza, Monica. 2019. "Gaet Habibie & Ilham Bangun Gedung Tinggi, Ini Proyek Pollux". *CNBC Indonesia*, 10 September 2019. https://www.cnbcindonesia.com/market/20190910133903-17-98320/gaet-habibie-ilham-bangun-gedung-tinggi-ini-proyek-pollux (accessed 16 October 2019).

Wong Poh Kam, and Ng Kwan Kee. 2009. "Batam, Bintan, and Karimun—Past History and Current Development towards Being A SEZ". Singapore: Asia Competitiveness Institute, National University of Singapore.

4

BATAM'S EMERGING DIGITAL ECONOMY
Back to the Future[1]

Francis E. Hutchinson and Siwage Dharma Negara

INTRODUCTION

Beyond well-known areas such as Batamindo Industrial Park, Kabil Port and the shipyards around Batu Ampar, investors have a new destination in Batam. It is Nongsa Digital Park, located on the island's northeast corner; and now receiving firm-owners, managers and talent scouts from Singapore.

Inaugurated in March 2018, the park contains several smallish buildings grouped around a lake where about 300 people work for some 50 firms. These IT professionals are engaged in tasks such as coding, application development, data analytics as well as web design for Singapore-based firms in various sectors including logistics, education, travel, fintech, and insurance.

Rather than using separate offices, these people gather in large shared spaces consisting of long tables with individual work stations. When necessary, they use separate rooms for in-depth discussions and, in other cases, teams working on specific projects occupy purpose-built and fitted rooms. The atmosphere is young and dynamic, with stencilled patterns on the walls, table football in the corner, and most people dressed in black.

Despite the informal vibe, these programmers and web designers work intently and are closely integrated into projects being done in their respective client firms in Singapore. Beyond being wired into headquarters, these professionals often travel to the city-state for training and, in other cases, supervisors come to Batam to induct or supervise new hires. Output, motivation and career development are monitored closely on-site.

Despite its small base, the number of firms and workers in the park have increased steadily since its launch. The first three office blocks are full and three new buildings have been completed. There are plans for a much larger development, with leisure facilities and residential areas nearby. There are also promising investments in the pipeline by other investors, including a large Indonesian conglomerate as well as an industry major.

While still small in size, the Digital Economy (DE) sector has many structural similarities with the export-for-manufacture model that underpinned Batam's rapid economic development in the 1990s and early 2000s. However, rather than leveraging Indonesia's abundant ranks of lower-cost unskilled labour, this new sector is entirely premised on utilizing skilled workers. Beyond helping to diversify the island's economic base, this sector also supports national plans and initiatives to develop the digital economy. However, as with its predecessor, there are a number of policy imperatives that decision-makers need to get right for this new sector to fully develop.

This chapter looks at the development of Batam's digital economy sector through: tracing how it developed; analysing its comparative advantage; relating it to national plans and priorities; and comparing it with the export-oriented manufacturing sector to identify challenges and choke-points going forward.

THE DIGITAL ECONOMY IN BATAM

The incipience of the digital economy in Batam can be traced to the Citramas group, an Indonesian conglomerate active in the real estate, tourism, infrastructure as well as oil and gas sectors. Long present in Batam, Citramas owns or has interests in diverse sectors on the island, such as: Kabil Port and an adjacent industrial estate; tourism facilities such as Nongsa Point Marine and Resort; and Infinite Studios, a media and creative services company.

In March 2018, Citramas launched the Nongsa Digital Park (NDP), which is being built in several phases. A hundred hectares have been set aside for the park as well as an accompanying international data centre (see Figure 4.1). Leveraging off existing infrastructure such as a dedicated customs and immigration terminal as well as existing ferry connections to Nongsa in Batam's northeast, the conglomerate plans to invest up to S$700 million in the facility (Arlina Arshad 2017). To date, three buildings with a capacity for 400 IT workers have been built, three more have been completed and another three buildings are in the pipeline.[2]

As of late 2019, there were some 50 firms using the Park, employing some 300 IT professionals between them—up from 40 firms and 150 workers 11 months previously. The majority of the clients of the Park are based in Singapore, and can be grouped into the following subsectors: logistics, insurance, web development, travel, data analytics, fintech, and e-learning (Table 4.1).

Many tenants are start-ups. One example is Energy Eco Chain, which was established in 2017 and specializes in accounting and application development for

FIGURE 4.1
Nongsa Digital Park

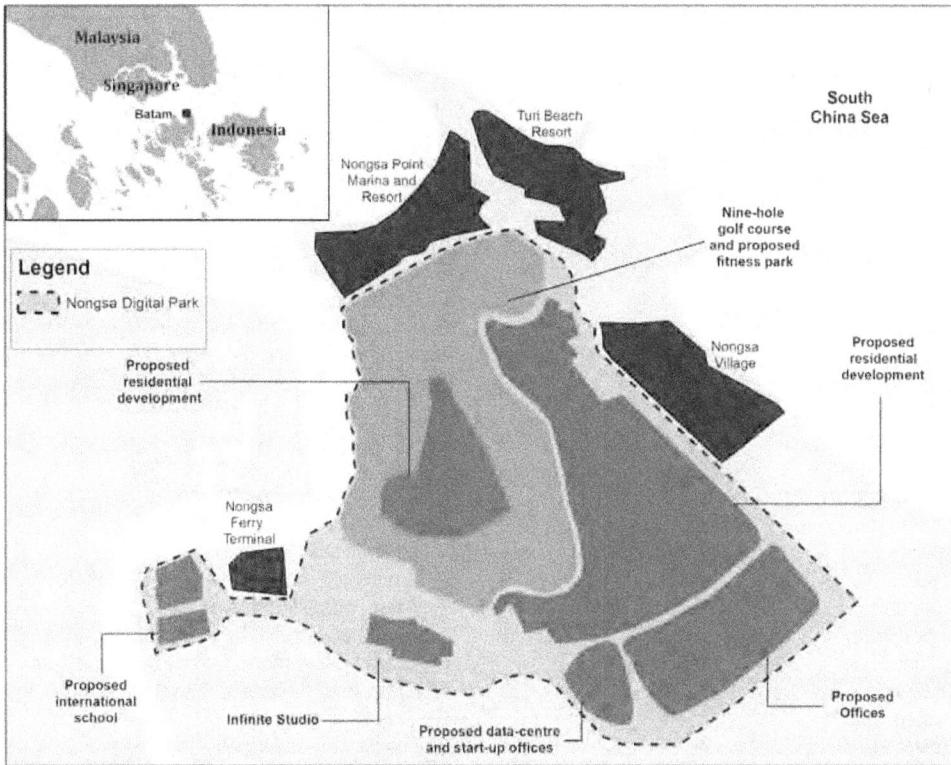

Source: Map provided by ISEAS – Yusof Ishak Institute © (2019).

energy systems. However, there are also established firms, such as the insurance giant AIA, which employs a substantial proportion of workers in NDP. Other firms are closely linked with key sectors in Singapore such as logistics, and are developing software to maximize the management of transport fleets and containers. Others are in areas with wider applicability, such as website design and development, software development, and customer service interface. And, there are some firms in more traditional sectors, such as such as Nanyang Inc., which rents tents and related shelters for outdoor events.

These firms do not hire their workers directly, but rather go through an intermediary, Glints. Glints is a talent recruiter and developer established in Singapore in 2013, which subsequently set up an affiliate in Indonesia in 2015. This firm identifies, recruits, and then deploys workers from across Indonesia to the digital park, after putting them through an eight-week training programme. While the workers in NDP collaborate with and respond to their Singapore-based firms, all human resource related issues are handled by Glints.[3]

An estimated 30 per cent of personnel in the park come from the Riau Islands, with the remainder coming from other parts of the country. Workers in NDP

TABLE 4.1
Indicative List of Firms in Nongsa Digital Park

Firm	Sector(s)
Haulio	Logistics
Versafleet	Transport management software
Nanyang Inc	Logistics rental for outdoor events
AIA	Insurance
FWD Insurance	Insurance
Liquidpay	Cashless payment solutions
Energy Eco Chain	Payment solutions for the energy sector
xfers	E-payment solutions
Futureflow	Financial management for entrepreneurs
Jublia	Business matching technology
Xexcide	Business consulting for SMEs
NEUENTITY	Web development, branding and design
Web Imp	Web design and development
Quark Spark	Web design and development
LDR Technology	Mobile technology and E-learning
Smarter Me	Online education for children
Data strategy	Marketing and analytics
Haste	Retail analytics
nexG	Enterprise, cloud, mobile, and IoT Service
Stendard	Workflow process management
HRnetGroup	Professional recruitment and staffing
bridge5asia	Integrated asset management for real estate
gleematic	AI with robotics process automation
Trusted Source	IT services and solutions
Prospace	B2B technology company
Suzerin	Software development
Vouch	Customer service interface
anywhr	Tour and travel firm
Infinite Studios	Media and creative services

Source: Site visit and company websites.

have degrees from Indonesia's leading universities, such as Bandung Institute of Technology, University of Indonesia, and Gadjah Mada University (Fadli 2019).[4]

The Nongsa area is rather far from downtown Batam, and the personnel in the park live off-site and commute individually or on buses provided by the local government. However, there are plans to further develop the park to include residential areas and a business incubator (Arlina Arshad 2017). Citramas has also signed a joint venture agreement with another local conglomerate, Sinar Mas Land, to develop an international digital business and services city, as well as additional residential areas on an 8-hectare swathe of land adjacent to the NDP (Faizal 2019). The architecture and urban planning firm Surbana has been engaged to develop a master plan for a digital economy hub, which would encompass the facilities being developed by both Citramas and Sinar Mas Land (*Straits Times*, 20 July 2019).

There is an ecosystem of firms and service providers developing—which bodes well for the establishment of this new sector. Infinite Studios, a media and creative services firm, is also located within the park, where it currently employs 350–400 animators and programmers. Beyond being a tenant in NDP itself, the studio is also a source of demand for skilled workers, thus helping to deepen the labour force. The area's skill base is gradually building up, enabled through work by Singapore-based institutions such as the Temasek Foundation International and Singapore Polytechnic in conjunction with local education providers such as Batam Polytechnic for IT literacy (Soeriaatmadja 2017). An affiliate of Infinite Studios, Infinite Learning, also provides vocational education in relevant areas.[5]

In what has been a resounding endorsement of NDP, Apple is building a Developer Academy within the Park's premises. In order to satisfy local content requirements in return for market access, Apple has committed to building three facilities to train IT workers in Indonesia. Jakarta, Surabaya and Batam are the three chosen sites (*South China Morning Post*, 2 April 2017). The Batam-based facility began operations in August 2019, and has two training programmes. The first course lasts two months and is being taught in conjunction with a local university, ITEBA. The second course lasts ten months. Upon graduation, it is hoped that graduates will feed into the local labour force.[6]

The possibilities offered by this new sector have caught the attention of national policymakers. During a visit to Singapore in late 2017, President Joko Widodo stated that Batam could act as a "digital bridge" between the city-state and many Indonesian cities (Leong 2017). Following this, in March 2018, the NDP was officially launched by the foreign ministers of Indonesia and Singapore (Arlina Arshad 2018).

BATAM'S COMPARATIVE ADVANTAGE

Why have these Singapore-based firms, many of which are small and capital-scarce, opted to source skilled labour from Batam?

Singapore has many advantages for firms in the digital economy. The population is extremely technologically savvy, and the city-state has many of the necessary attributes to foster firms in this sector. Its ease of doing business, low start-up costs, and well-developed venture capital ecosystem mean that Singapore is able to foster a high number of start-ups (McKinsey 2018).

Despite these attributes, however, the city-state is facing a pronounced labour crunch, with more vacancies than job applicants. This is due, in large part, to a shrinking workforce—a result of population ageing and increasingly tightening foreign worker quotas—as well as mismatches in the supply and demand of skills (Seow 2019; Leow 2019).

While not immediately obvious, the Riau Islands contains Indonesia's most digitally literate work-force outside of Jakarta (McKinsey 2018). And, as manufacturing firms found out in the 1990s, the island offers labour at a substantially lower rate than what is available in Singapore. For instance, the cost of hiring an IT employee in Batam is around S$500–S$2,000 per month, while the cost in Singapore for a similarly qualified worker is in the S$3,600–S$10,000 range (Table 4.2).

TABLE 4.2
Salary Rates for IT Workers in Singapore and Batam

Level	Singapore	Batam
Fresh IT graduate	S$3,600 p.m.	S$500 p.m.
Intermediate	S$5,000–S$7,000 p.m.	S$1,000 p.m.
Experienced	S$10,000 p.m.	S$2,000 p.m.

Source: Fadli (2019).

In addition, Singapore faces issues with the availability and cost of land due to the city-state's size and zoning restrictions (Danganan 2019). While IT operations are not land-hungry, Batam's rental costs are attractive, which can be important for small start-ups. Thus, in NDP, companies only rent work-stations and meeting-rooms on an as-needed basis.

The well-developed transport connections between Singapore and Batam are also key assets. Travel between the city-state and Nongsa in Batam takes a mere 40 minutes and is served by a variety of ferry companies. Thus, transport costs are low and return trips on the same day are possible.

This proximity and accessibility allow interactions between workers in the two locations, which are vital for establishing trust, team-building, and enabling creativity. This aspect is a key differentiator for Batam as compared to the Philippines or India, which also have deep ranks of digital workers. In addition, this proximity means that firms in Batam can piggy-back on Singapore's well-developed venture capital community for finance and mentoring.

And, perhaps most importantly, Batam is equipped with good connectivity. Just three locations in Indonesia—Jakarta, Dumai, and Batam—have 40 per cent of all connections in the country (McKinsey 2018).

At present, Batam is hooked up to the Batam-Dumai-Melaka cable system, a 400-km intra-Asia regional submarine link-up between Malaysia and Indonesia. The cable system has two routes—Melaka-Batam and Melaka-Dumai—and consists of two fibre pairs, with a design capacity up to 1.28 terabytes per second (Figure 4.2). Completed in 2011, the cable system was developed by a consortium of three telecom companies—Telekom Malaysia Berhad, Mora Telematika and XL Axiata.

Batam is also connected to Singapore through a submarine cable system linking Batam Centre station to Telin station in the city-state. The total length of the Batam-Singapore Cable System is around 73 km, connecting the landing sites through six fibre pair cables. To further increase the reliability of the system, two separate land routes are utilized to transmit four 10-gigabytes-per-second channels.

This high number of connections means that Batam is the most connected part of Indonesia. Further bolstered by its proximity, pings from Singapore to Batam take an estimated 3 milliseconds, compared to 2 milliseconds from the eastern part of the city-state to its west. In comparison, a ping from Singapore to Jakarta takes 35–70 milliseconds.[7]

FIGURE 4.2
The Batam-Dumai-Melaka Cable System

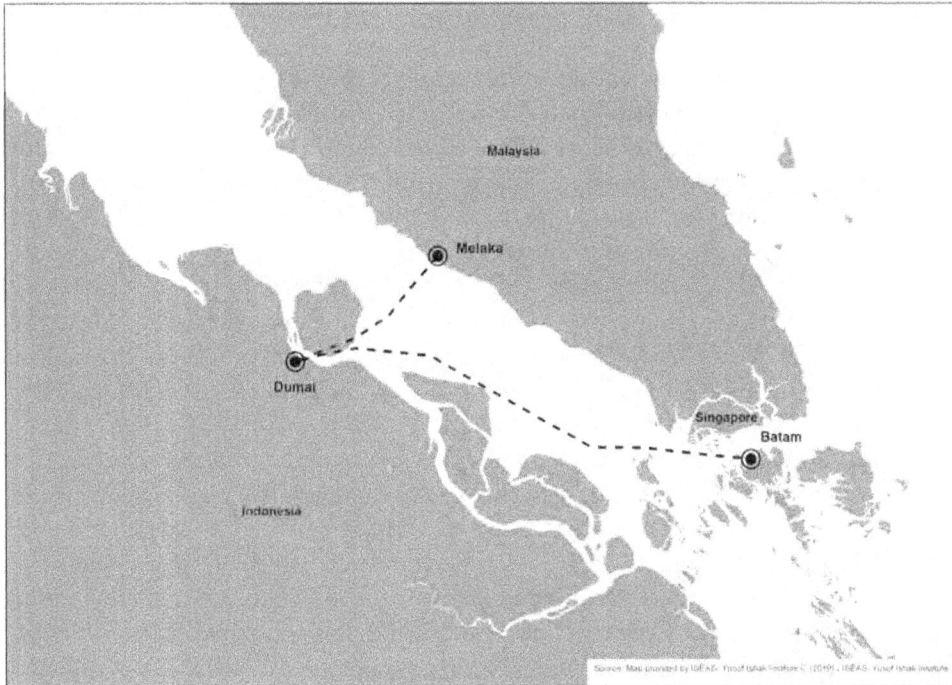

Source: Map provided by ISEAS – Yusof Ishak Institute © (2019).

NATIONAL PLANS AND PRIORITIES

A study conducted by Google, Temasek and Bain & Company predicts Indonesia's digital economy will dominate Southeast Asia in the future. The sector's value is expected to triple from US$40 billion in 2019 to US$130 billion by 2025. This will be driven by the rapid growth of its "consuming class", which is expected to more than double from 80 million in 2019 to around 170 million by 2030 (McKinsey 2012).

In 2019, Indonesia received more than US$4 billion in investment in the digital economy sector. This was led by some of Indonesia's unicorns—those start-ups with a value of over US$1 billion—like Bukalapak, Gojek, Tokopedia and Traveloka. Singapore-based Grab has also announced a multibillion-dollar commitment to investing in the country over the next few years (Google, Temasek and Bain & Company 2019).

President Joko Widodo has set a target of establishing 1,000 digital start-ups worth US$10 billion by 2020. The 1,000 start-ups programme is designed to foster the digital ecosystem in the country and to promote more local Unicorns (Nistanto 2016).

Anticipating the sector's growth, the government has invested significantly in infrastructure to promote faster and more reliable Internet access within the country. In October 2019, President Jokowi launched the Palapa Ring network, a 36,000-km-long broadband fibre-optic network worth approximately US$1.6 billion that connects the capitals of 514 districts and cities (Asmara 2019).

Likewise, Bank Indonesia (BI) has unveiled the Indonesia Payment System Blueprint 2025, which aims to integrate the digital economy and financial system to guarantee effective money creation and circulation, monetary policy transmission, stability of the financial system as well as economic and financial inclusion (Bank Indonesia 2019). Moreover, BI has set policies to continue to: foster the digitalization of the banking industry; promote its interlinkages with fintech; support the development of regional and national start-ups; as well as the evolution of fast, efficient and reliable payment system infrastructures.

In the public sector, Indonesia has launched the 100 Smart Cities Movement (Davy 2019). The concept focuses on how urban development can safely and effectively combine information and communications technology (ICT) and the Internet of Things (IoT) to manage public assets and services, including waste management, transportation systems, and law enforcement.

On soft infrastructure, the government has issued a regulation (No. 71/2019) on the implementation of electronic systems and transactions. The regulation includes some important provisions, such as: public and private electronic system operators; data localization requirements for public electronic system operators; deletion of electronic data; electronic certificates and electronic reliability certificates; electronic certification services; and data privacy, among others. Arguably, this regulation provides a legal base for the government to control and monitor data flows. Moreover, the regulation is needed to provide legal certainty for digital business operations in the country.

Specifically, the regulation stipulates that all digital companies, foreign or local, must have integrated data centres in the country. As a consequence, tech-giant companies like Google and Facebook must set up their data centres in Indonesia (*Jakarta Post*, 6 December 2019).

However, one of the biggest challenges for the sector is the shortage of trained professionals, such as developers, engineers, computing, and data analysts (McKinsey 2018). A World Bank study estimates that between 2015 and 2030, there will be a shortage of 9 million skilled and semi-skilled ICT workers in Indonesia (World Bank 2018). The consulting firm Korn Ferry Indonesia also reports that the country has been facing a serious gap in highly skilled workers in the digital technology sector. The skilled labour deficit will stand at 1.3 million by 2020 and grow to 3.8 million by 2030. This imminent tech talent deficit can hamper the growth of the digital industry in Indonesia (Korn Ferry 2018).

Meanwhile, the digital economy has created new jobs that did not exist some years back (McKinsey 2019). Conventional sectors like healthcare, manufacturing, mining, consumer goods, and travel will require new types of skills. By 2030, there will be 10 million jobs in new occupations that do not exist today. A projected 27 million to 40 million new jobs will be created in the same period if Indonesians learn new skills. This is higher than 23 million jobs that could be displaced by digitalization (McKinsey 2019).

Concerned about human capital issues, President Jokowi named Nadiem Makarim, the founder of Gojek as the Minister of Education and Culture at the start of his second administration, with the hope that he would bring the needed reform in the education sector. Nadiem believes that several subjects, including coding and programming, should become compulsory in the secondary and tertiary education curriculum (Soegiono 2019). While the Ministry of Education is still preparing changes in the curriculum, other ministries have initiated various ICT training programmes. For instance, the ICT Ministry has allocated US$7.9 million to train 20,000 digital workers (*Tempo Bisnis*, 17 January 2019). Similar programmes are being conducted by the Ministries of Industry, Research and Technology, and even Foreign Affairs (Pinandita 2019).

Private companies have actively joined forces in the effort to upskill and reskill local talent. Tech companies such as Google, Facebook, Apple, Amazon, Alibaba and Huawei, in various degrees, have been involved in digital training programmes. For example, since 2015, Google Indonesia has launched an initiative called Grow with Google, as part of its training programme for small and medium enterprises (SMEs), job seekers and developers (*Jakarta Post*, 7 December 2018). Amazon's cloud computing arm AWS and Alibaba Cloud have offered their respective cloud technology courses. Huawei has been working with the Ministry of Manpower to provide a transceiver station and microwave vocational training programme for 1,000 participants in Bekasi, West Java (Iswara 2019).

Facebook has provided training for SMEs, communities, and students in fifteen cities since 2018 to help them utilize the company's platforms (Mufti 2018). Apple has started its training centre for app developers in BSD City, Banten, West Java (in collaboration with BINUS University) since 2018 (Hutapea 2018). Since then, it has opened training centres in Surabaya (in collaboration with Ciputra University) and in Batam (in collaboration with Nongsa Digital Park).

Gojek, a local start-up, launched its training programme named GoAcademy in 2018. GoAcademy offers: an onboarding programme, called Engineering Bootcamp; an internship programme, known as GoSquads, which will expose college students to world-class engineers; and a boot camp for college students (*Jakarta Post*, 18 October 2019). To date, the programme has coached more than 200 promising college students. In addition, Gojek has collaborated with other companies, such as the start-up accelerator Digitaraya, to enhance human resources with digital skills. The programme, named Gojek Xcelerate, provides six-month training for twenty selected start-ups. It involves Google's start-up acceleration programme Google Developers Launchpad, McKinsey & Company and Swiss UBS.

Beyond the emergence of numerous tech companies, Indonesia's digital economy still faces considerable challenges. Some of these are related to: limited physical infrastructure capabilities (especially outside Java); a relatively small number of start-ups; and relatively few venture capitalists and tech incubators (McKinsey 2018). The national government is definitely aware of those challenges and has promised to improve the regulatory framework related to Indonesia's digital economy, particularly on e-commerce, data protection and a tax office regulation on e-commerce tax, as it aspires to become Southeast Asia's digital hub in the next five years (Aisyah 2019).

BACK TO THE FUTURE?

The digital economy sector clearly offers much potential. Like the manufacturing sector did in the 1990s and 2000s, it has the possibility of bringing in investment and spurring job creation. And, crucially for Batam, this new sector can generate demand for skilled workers, which was one of the criticisms aimed in the past at labour-intensive industries such as electronics and shipbuilding. However, it should not be forgotten that much of the groundwork underpinning the digital economy was laid by these less glamourous activities.

To this end, the paragraphs ahead will look at how the foundations of the DE sector were laid by the export-oriented manufacturing sector, and in doing so will see what lessons learned are applicable to its future potential and trajectory.

First, as with the birth of the electronics and shipbuilding sectors, the emergence of this sector needs to be seen as one part of the overall drive to revitalize the island's economy. Thus, beyond the needs of each sector, policymakers still need to address systemic issues such as Indonesia's low levels of productivity, and the underdeveloped logistics connections between Batam and other parts of the country (Damuri, Christian, and Atje 2015).

Second, policymakers cannot simply rely on Batam's comparative advantage to draw in investment. The scant progress made during the 1980s in bringing in labour-intensive manufacturing is a case in point. Despite the island's proximity and cost-proposition, businesses were unwilling to commit. Local investors were not attracted by Batam's small market and distance from major population centres. Foreign investors were daunted by requirements to divest majority control within fifteen years, as well as faulty infrastructure (Smith 1996). It was only in 1989 that key liberalization measures were enacted to dramatically reduce the divestment requirements and allow the private ownership and operation of industrial estates. Following this, FDI began to flow in and the manufacturing sector took off (Hutchinson 2015).

The establishment of Nongsa Digital Park was made possible by these changes in legislation. However, the nature of the digital economy requires a number of further changes to investment regulations for it to develop fully. Of key importance is the current stipulation that foreign firms operating in Indonesia need to invest US$250,000 to acquire a temporary licence and US$1 million to obtain a permanent licence.[8] While well suited to capital- and labour-intensive shipyards and electronics plants, these regulations are prohibitive for skill-intensive, yet low-capital operations, like web design and fintech.

Indeed, this provision explains why so few DE firms from Singapore have established affiliates in Indonesia. In order to be able to operate, they need to go through an intermediary that has invested sufficient capital to acquire a licence—

which in this case, is Glints. It also explains why the emerging cluster is led by large Indonesian conglomerates, rather than a variety of start-ups and firms from diverse backgrounds. Other areas of attention include developing incentives to promote the export of services, something that neighbouring countries such as Malaysia have begun to do.[9]

Third, the development and subsequent decline of the electronics sector has shown that Batam's skill base is limited. The inability of firms on the island to source qualified professionals meant that managers of multinational corporations (MNCs) were unable to justify locating more complex tasks on the island. Indeed, interviews carried out with a sample of long-present MNCs found evidence of automation—not to take advantage of increasing skills and competence among local workers—but rather due to the absence of a suitably qualified work-force (van Grunsven and Hutchinson 2016).

Similar comments have emerged from firms in the DE sector, where sourcing labour is a perennial issue. There is anecdotal evidence that even established firms in Jakarta need to offshore part of their operations to other IT hubs such as India and the Philippines (Bohang 2016). This problem is more acute in the Riau Islands, due to its smaller population base. In addition, considerable effort needs to be placed on getting workers ready for the needs of the workplace, as seen by the efforts made by Glints and other players in NDP to train personnel. The English language, in particular, has emerged as a source of concern (Arlina Arshad 2017). This issue is further exacerbated by the difficulty in acquiring work permits for skilled personnel from overseas, which is needed, at least initially in areas such as data science, IoT solutions architecture, machine learning, user experience design, and digital marketing.[10]

Fourth, the digital economy and its spillovers need to generate tangible benefits for local residents. The formal sector jobs generated by the manufacturing and tourist sectors have been a boon for the island and the Riau Islands Province more widely. However, while economically beneficial, these developments have not gone without controversy. Issues of pollution from shipyards, perceived unfair compensation for land, and the perception that people from other parts of the country have benefited disproportionately have been common (Lee, this volume; Wee 2016; Hutchinson 2015). Consequently, every effort needs to be made to ensure local people participate in and benefit from this new sector.

The months ahead will be crucial for the sector. Policymakers at the central and local level need to engage with firms present on the island to address regulatory bottlenecks and other issues. Linkages between education providers and NDP tenants need to be strengthened to ensure that the sector's demands for human capital are met. And local communities also need to be engaged, to ensure that benefits from the new sector are spread more widely. If these needs can be met in significant measure, Batam will be on the way to diversifying its economy, and generating highly skilled jobs that can retain local graduates.

Notes

1. This chapter draws on Francis E. Hutchinson and Siwage Dharma Negara, "Batam's Emerging Digital Economy: Prospects and Challenges", *ISEAS Perspective*, no. 2019/25, 10 April 2019.
2. Interviews with NDP management, Nongsa, Batam, 28 November 2018 and 30 October 2019.
3. Interviews with Glints management, Nongsa, Batam, 28 November 2018 and NDP management, 30 October 2019.
4. Interviews with NDP management, Nongsa, Batam, 28 November 2018 and 30 October 2019.
5. Interview with Marco Bardelli, Senior Director, Nongsa Digital Park, Singapore, 14 November 2019.
6. Ibid.
7. Ibid.
8. Correspondence with Mr Bin Boon Song, Head of International Policy, Singapore Economic Development Board, 30 October 2017.
9. Interview with BP Batam, 30 October 2019.
10. Interview with Marco Bardelli, Senior Director, Nongsa Digital Park, Singapore, 14 November 2019.

References

Aisyah, Rachmadea. 2019. "Indonesia Aims to Be Regional Digital Technology Hub in 2020". *Jakarta Post*, 20 February 2019. https://www.thejakartapost.com/news/2019/02/20/indonesia-aims-to-be-regional-digital-technology-hub-in-2020.html

Arlina Arshad. 2017. "Building up Batam as a Work-and-Play Digital Hub", *Straits Times*, 26 April 2017.

———. 2018. "Tech Park in Batam Opens, Aims to Be 'Digital Bridge' between Singapore and Indonesia". *Straits Times*, 21 March 2018.

Asmara, Chandra Gian. 2019. "Tol Langit Palapa Ring Diresmikan Jokowi, Untuk Apa?". CNBC Indonesia, 15 October 2019. https://www.cnbcindonesia.com/tech/20191015105114-37-107046/tol-langit-palapa-ring-diresmikan-jokowi-untuk-apa

Bank Indonesia. 2019. "Synergy, Transformation, and Innovation: Toward an Advanced Indonesia". Speech of the Governor of Bank Indonesia at Bank Indonesia's Annual Meeting, Jakarta, 28 November 2019.

BPS. (Statistics Indonesia). Various years. *Indikator Utama Kepulauan Riau*. Tanjungpinang: BPS Kepulauan Riau.

Bohang, Fatimah Kartini. 2016. "CEO Go-Jek Ungkap Alasan Lebih Banyak Pekerjakan 'Engineer' Asal India". *Kompas.com*, 17 November 2016. https://tekno.kompas.com/read/2016/11/17/12433967/ceo.go-jek.ungkap.alasan.lebih.banyak.pekerjakan.engineer.asal.india

Damuri, Yose Rizal, David Christian, and Raymond Atje. 2015. *Kawasan Ekonomi Khusus dan Strategis Indonesia: Tinjauan Atas Peluang dan Permasalahan*. Jakarta: Center for Strategic and International Studies.

Danganan, Arianna. 2019. "Data Centre Operators Turn West Amidst Tian Seng Space Crunch". *Singapore Business Review*, 18 February 2019.

Davy, Jonathan. 2019. "What Lies Ahead of Indonesia's 100 Smart Cities Movement?". *Jakarta Post*, 5 December 2019. https://www.thejakartapost.com/life/2019/12/05/what-lies-ahead-of-indonesias-100-smart-cities-movement.html

Fadli. 2019. "Young Indonesian Talents Sharpen IT Skills to Work for Singaporean Firms". *Jakarta Post*, 1 February 2019.

Faizal, Mohammad. 2019. "Sinar Mas Land-Citramas Group Garap Area Ekonomi Digital di Nongsa Batam". *SindoNews.com*, 26 February 2019. https://ekbis.sindonews.com/read/1382251/34/sinar-mas-land-citramas-group-garap-area-ekonomi-digital-di-nongsa-batam-1551190417

Google, Temasek, and Bain & Company. 2019. "e-Conomy SEA 2019: Swipe Up and to the Right: Southeast Asia's $100 billion Internet Economy, 2019. https://www.blog.google/documents/47/SEA_Internet_Economy_Report_2019.pdf

Hutapea, Erwin. 2018. "Senilai Rp615 Miliar, Apple Academy Pertama Asia Dibuka di BSD City". *Kompas*, 7 May 2018. https://properti.kompas.com/read/2018/05/07/131133721/senilai-rp-615-miliar-apple-academy-pertama-asia-dibuka-di-bsd-city

Hutchinson, Francis E. 2015. *Mirror Images in Different Frames: Johor, the Riau Islands, and Competition for Investment from Singapore*. Singapore: ISEAS – Yusof Ishak Institute.

———. 2017. *Rowing Against the Tide? Batam's Economic Fortunes in Today's Indonesia*. Trends in Southeast Asia, no. 8/2017. Singapore: ISEAS – Yusof Ishak Institute.

Iswara, Made Anthony. 2019. "Tech Giants Train Indonesians to Tap Into Latent Potential". *Jakarta Post*, 19 July 2019. https://www.thejakartapost.com/news/2019/07/19/tech-giants-train-indonesians-to-tap-into-latent-potential.html

Jakarta Post. 2018. "Google Eyes Another Million SMEs for Digital Upskilling". 7 December 2018. https://www.thejakartapost.com/news/2018/12/07/google-eyes-another-million-smes-digital-upskilling.html

———. 2019a. "GoAcademy: Gojek's Answer to Tech Talent Gap in Indonesia". 18 October 2019. https://www.thejakartapost.com/adv-longform/2019/10/18/goacademy-gojeks-answer-to-tech-talent-gap-in-indonesia.html

———. 2019b. "Google, Facebook to Set up Data Centers in Indonesia: Minister". 6 December 2019. https://www.thejakartapost.com/news/2019/12/06/google-facebook-to-set-up-data-centers-in-indonesia-minister.html

Korn Ferry. 2018. *The Global Talent Crunch 2018*. https://dsqapj1lakrkc.cloudfront.net/media/sidebar_downloads/FOWTalentCrunchFinal_Spring2018.pdf

Leong, Grace. 2017. "Batam Could Serve as 'Digital Bridge' between Singapore and Cities across Indonesia, Says President Joko Widodo". *Straits Times*, 7 September 2017.

Leow, Annabeth. 2019. "Labour Crunch Takes Centre Stage in the House". *Business Times*, 27 February 2019.

McKinsey and Company. 2012. *The Archipelago Economy: Unleashing Indonesia's Potential*. September 2012.

———. 2016. *Unlocking Indonesia's Digital Opportunity*. Jakarta: McKinsey Indonesia Office.

———. 2018. *The Digital Archipelago: How Online Commerce Is Driving Indonesia's Economic Development*. Jakarta: McKinsey Indonesia Office.

———. 2019. *Automation and the Future of Work in Indonesia: Jobs Lost, Jobs Gained, Jobs Changed*. Jakarta, 2019. https://www.mckinsey.com/~/media/McKinsey/Featured%20Insights/Asia%20Pacific/Automation%20and%20the%20future%20of%20work%20in%20Indonesia/Automation-and-the-future-of-work-in-Indonesia-vF.ashx

Mufti, Riza Roidila. 2018. "Facebook Launches Program to Boost Digital Skills of MSMEs".

Jakarta Post, 15 August 2018. https://www.thejakartapost.com/news/2018/08/15/facebook-launches-program-to-boost-digital-skills-of-msmes.html

Negara, Siwage Dharma. 2017. "Can the Decline of Batam's Shipbuilding Industry be Reversed?". *ISEAS Perspective* No. 2017/10, 16 February 2017.

———, and Hutchinson, Francis E. 2021. "The Manufacturing Sector in Batam: Back to the Future". In *The Riau Islands Province: Setting Sail*, edited by Francis E. Hutchinson and Siwage Dharma Negara. Singapore: ISEAS – Yusof Ishak Institute.

Nistanto, Reska K. 2016. "Gerakan 1.000 Startup Dicanangkan Hari Ini". *Kompas*, 17 June 2016. https://sains.kompas.com/read/2016/06/17/17151127/gerakan.1.000.startup.dicanangkan.hari.ini

Pinandita, Apriza. 2019. "Foreign Ministry Calls for Indonesian Startups to Go International". *Jakarta Post*, 25 November 2019. https://www.thejakartapost.com/news/2019/11/25/foreign-ministry-calls-for-indonesian-startups-to-go-international.html

Seow Bei Yi. 2019. "Singapore's Labour Crunch Issue: Why It's Happening and What More Can Be Done". *Straits Times*, 13 January 2019.

Smith, S.L.D. 1996. "Developing Batam: Indonesian Political Economy under the New Order". PhD dissertation, Research School of Pacific and Asian Studies, Australian National University.

Soegiono, Agie Nugroho. 2019. "Nadiem: Driving Education Reform Through Technology". *Jakarta Post*, 28 October 2019. https://www.thejakartapost.com/academia/2019/10/28/nadiem-driving-education-reform-through-technology.html

Soeriaatmadja, Wahyudi, 2017. "Singapore Start-ups See Opportunity in Indonesia's Digital Economy". *Straits Times*, 8 September 2017.

Straits Times. 2019. "Surbana to Plan Batam Digital Hub". 20 July 2019.

Tempo.Bisnis.com. 2019. "Kominfo Siapkan Rp109 M untuk Pelatihan 20 Ribu Digital Talent". 17 January 2019. https://bisnis.tempo.co/read/1165740/kominfo-siapkan-rp-109-m-untuk-pelatihan-20-ribu-digital-talent/full&view=ok

van Grunsven, Leo, and Francis E. Hutchinson. 2016. "Revisiting Industrial Dynamics in the SIJORI Cross-Border Region: The Electronics Industry Twenty Years On". In *The SIJORI Cross-Border Region: Transnational Politics, Economics, and Culture*, edited by Francis E. Hutchinson and Terence Chong. Singapore: ISEAS – Yusof Ishak Institute.

Wee, Vivienne. 2016. "The Significance of Riau in SIJORI". In *The SIJORI Cross-Border Region: Transnational Politics, Economics, and Culture*, edited by Francis E. Hutchinson and Terence Chong. Singapore: ISEAS – Yusof Ishak Institute.

Wong P.K., and Ng K.K. 2009. *Batam, Bintan, and Karimun: Past History and Current Development Towards Being A SEZ*. Singapore: Asia Competitiveness Institute, National University of Singapore.

World Bank. 2018. "Preparing ICT Skills for Digital Economy: Indonesia within the ASEAN Context". Presentation materials, 8 March 2018. https://blogs.worldbank.org/sites/default/files/preparing_ict_skills_for_digital_economy-revised_7mar2018.pdf

Yuniar, Resty Woro. 2017. "Going Local: How Apple Got Back into Indonesia's Smartphone Game". *South China Morning Post*, 2 April 2017.

5

BATAM'S SPECIAL ECONOMIC STATUS
A Mixed Blessing?

Raymond Atje

INTRODUCTION

Batam's development process has been quite unique among medium-size cities in Indonesia, as it has developed virtually from scratch. In the late 1960s, there were 6,000 people on the island, essentially fishermen and their families. Since then, Batam's population has been growing by leaps and bounds, and the number reached approximately 1.37 million people by 2019 (BPS 2019).

Over the decades, due to its proximity to Singapore and, through it, international capital, Batam has always been accorded one or another form of special status with certain privileges. Beginning in 1971, the government promulgated a series of regulations that were pivotal to the subsequent development of Batam. Then, it was merely an outpost station of the national oil company, PN Pertamina, which provided logistics and operational support to its offshore exploration activities. In 1972, Nisho-Iwai, a Japanese consultancy firm and Bechtel Corporation of the United Sates prepared a master plan for the development of Batam (Pertamina, Nisho-Iwai, and Pacific Bechtel 1972).

In 1973, the central government passed the Presidential Decree No. 41 which declared all of Batam island as an industrial zone (BIDA 1980). One important provision of the decree was the establishment of Batam Industrial Development Authority (BIDA) as the sole entity responsible for the island's economic development. BIDA was endowed with an extensive range of responsibilities to, among other things: develop and manage Batam as an industrial area; handle transshipment activities; plan and manage the island's infrastructure development; and expedite business licensing processes. B.J. Habibie, the Minister for Research and Technology, became BIDA Chairman in 1978 and took a direct interest in the island. He saw it as a means of concentrating scarce resources in a given location and bypassing many of the infrastructural problems facing other parts of the country. This support also allowed BIDA to deal with the relevant local governments within Riau Province effectively and, hence, enabled it to roll out infrastructure and promote business development on the island (Hutchinson 2017).

In 1978, the government designated all of Batam island as a bonded warehouse zone. Often referred to simply as a bonded zone, this is an area where dutiable goods may be stored, processed, or manufactured without paying duty. In 1992, the government decided to extent the zone to two adjacent islands, namely, Rempang and Galang. This area was thereafter known as the Barelang (Batam, Rempang and Galang) bonded zone (Wong and Ng 2009).

In 1999, the municipal government of Batam was granted autonomous status, implying that it had greater authority to manage the city, including its economy. In 2002, following the decentralization process launched in 2001, the Riau Islands was declared a separate province, and an interim governor was named in 2004. As will be discussed below, this process was to have some unintended ramifications for Batam's subsequent development.

In 2002, Batam became a bonded zone plus.[1] With this status, investors were entitled to additional incentives such as tariff and value added tax (VAT) exemptions on raw materials for export products as well as streamlined customs administration procedures. Then, in 2007, the government changed the status of Batam and that of Bintan and Karimun yet again (Wong and Ng 2009). Since then, the three islands have become part of the Batam-Bintan-Karimun Free Trade Zone (BBK FTZ), whose legal status is to remain in force for seventy years. Companies located in the FTZ would receive, among other things, exemptions from: import tariffs; VAT; luxury tax; as well as duties on goods entering and exiting the FTZ. In 2008, BIDA was renamed BP Batam (Batam Development Board), but is also referred to as Batam Indonesia Free Zone Trade Authority (BIFZA).[2]

SPECIAL ECONOMIC ZONE

A special economic zone (SEZ) has some specific features, including a geographically defined area, which is often: physically secured; under a single management entity; eligible for benefits based upon location within the zone; a separate customs area (duty-free benefits); and possessing streamlined procedures (FIAS 2008). In other words, it is an area with special privileges aimed at enhancing economic growth by way of attracting investment and promoting exports. According to this logic, FTZs can be classified as one form of SEZ.

Over the years, Indonesian government has been experimenting with various types of SEZ, with the aim of boosting exports. The most widespread form of export processing zone in Indonesia is bonded zone. As noted above, a bonded zone is an area where dutiable goods may be stored, processed or manufactured without payment of duties. In addition, the goods in question are also exempted from VAT and luxury goods tax, especially such inputs as raw materials, intermediate inputs and capital goods used to produce goods for export. As of 2012, there were about 1350 bonded zones in Indonesia (Damuri, Christian, and Atje 2015).

Prior to 2007, Batam was the largest bonded zone in Indonesia outside of Java. As discussed above, that year the central government decided to turn Batam and the adjacent Rempang and Galang, part of Bintan, and Karimun Island into a free trade zone, known as BBK FTZ.[3] Following the establishment of this FTZ, all bonded zones in Batam ceased to exist (Damuri, Christian, and Atje 2015).

In 2018, the government floated a proposal to turn Batam into an SEZ. In strictly legal terms, it should be noted that this would entail the island prematurely forfeiting its current FTZ status—which is meant to last seventy years. Indeed, in this particular case, the term special economic zone (*kawasan ekonomi khusus*, or KEK), has a specific definition, as specified in the relevant legislation, and is to be distinguished from other forms of economic zones such as FTZs or bonded zones.[4] Article 3 of Law no. 39, 2009 concerning Special Economic Zone stipulates: "An SEZ shall be made up of one or several zones dedicated for export processing; logistics; manufacturing; technology development; tourism; energy; and/or other economic activities."

According to this definition, an SEZ is essentially a designated growth area with certain facilities and incentives for companies operating within it. In particular, companies operating within the zone may eligible for income tax and property tax incentives. In addition, the importation of goods and merchandise into the zone may also enjoy: postponement of import duties; exemption from excise tax on raw materials or intermediate goods; exemption from VAT and luxury sales tax on taxable goods; and exemption from income tax (Articles 30–32).

As of January 2020, eleven SEZs are in operation. These zones concentrate on two main activities, namely, industry (manufacture) and tourism. The industrial zones include: Sei Mangkei in North Sumatra; Palu in Central Sulawesi; Galang Batang, Riau Islands Province; Arun Lhokseumawe in Aceh; Bitung in North Sulawesi; Maloy Batuta Trans Kalimantan in East Kalimantan; and Sorong in West Papua. Furthermore, different zones focus on different industries, depending on their respective comparative advantage. The primary objective of Sei Mangkei SEZ, for instance, is to become a centre for palm oil-related and rubber-related industries.

In addition, there are four tourism zones, namely: Tanjung Lesung in West Java; Mandalika in West Nusatenggara; Tanjung Kalayang in Bangka Belitung; and Morotai in North Maluku.[5]

Meanwhile there are four zones which are still under construction, namely: Tanjung Api-Api in South Sumatra and Kendal in Central Java for industry; and Singhasari in East Java and Likupang in North Sulawesi for tourism.[6]

It is important to note that an SEZ which has been declared as in operation, simply implies that it is ready to welcome companies that want to invest in the zone. There is no guarantee that companies will indeed invest there or that it is viable in the long run. The development of Morotai SEZ, for example, has been slow; as of October 2019, only 1.4 per cent of its total area of approximately 1,102 hectares has been developed (*Bisnis.com*, 18 February 2020).

It is not immediately clear why the central government has sought to turn Batam into an SEZ. One commonly cited reason has been the need to revitalize the island's economy, which has experienced a slow-down in recent years. Thus, recent leadership changes in Batam's economic agencies have always been accompanied by statements detailing desired levels of economic growth and a change in the island's legal status.

Since the Batam Municipality was made autonomous in 1999, there has been an overlap in government between BIDA and the municipal government, with disputes over their respective responsibilities. There have been efforts to resolve the issue. For instance, in 2006 the two came to an agreement whereby the authority for economic- and investment-related issues would be held by BIDA, and the municipal government would be responsible for social and environment issues. In the end, the agreement was short-lived, and has resulted in some unintended consequences. In particular, it has slowed down investment activities, since, in many instances, investors have to get approvals from both organizations (Hutchinson 2017).

It is perhaps to resolve the above-mentioned issue that the central government has recently appointed the Mayor of Batam as the ex-officio head of BIDA, which previously had always been held by a central government official.[7] There is, however, a lingering doubt that this appointment will resolve the above-mentioned coordination failure. In addition, one cannot rule out at the outset the possibility of conflict of interests. Note that as the head of BIDA, the Mayor is representing the central government to manage the agency's assets and revenues; yet, he is also the head of the municipal government, which contends that it has the right to the same endowments.

Be that as it may, one can nevertheless argue that merely changing the island's legal status without addressing the causes of its weakening economic performance may not be sufficient. Some of the issues that have been identified in the literature regarding Batam are: high labour costs; periodic strikes; coordination failures among different relevant authorities; and inadequate infrastructure (Hutchinson 2017; Tan et al. 2016). Some of these are arguably simply consequences of institutional changes both at the local and at the central government levels following the Asian Financial Crisis and political reform in Indonesia.

Moreover, it is impossible to turn the whole Batam Island into an SEZ since it contains residential areas which, by default, must lie outside such a zone. This is why the central government is considering carving out a number of enclaves in Batam and redesignating them as SEZs.[8] However, this raises questions as to which areas will qualify for this status, and how the transport of goods between these non-contiguous areas will be treated. In addition, there are no less than twenty-two industrial parks on the island that have been in operation for many years. Thus far, these parks have been able to attract investment, foreign as well as domestic, presumably because of the island's FTZ status and, prior to that, its bonded zone status. It is not clear whether these areas will also qualify for SEZ status.

In short, before changing Batam's status yet again, it is incumbent on policymakers to conduct a study on the potential economic implications of such a move. In particular, the change should take place only if the study clearly finds that the benefit of changing Batam's status significantly exceeds the status quo.

THE BATAM-BINTAN-KARIMUN FREE TRADE ZONE

A free trade zone is a geographic area where goods may be landed, stored, handled, manufactured or reconfigured and re-exported under a different customs regime from that of the rest of the country in which the zone is located. In other words, an FTZ is a duty-free area offering warehousing, storage and distribution facilities for trade, transshipment, and re-export operations (FIAS 2008, p. 10). When goods are moved from the zone to consumers within the country in question, they become subject to the prevailing customs duties.

The rationale for the establishment of BBK FTZ is spelled out in Law no. 44/2007. The law argues, implicitly, that BBK should be integrated into the global economy so as to stimulate economic growth by way of increasing export, investment and country's overall economic competitiveness.

The full implementation of BBK FTZ took place amid Batam's economic slowdown. As discussed elsewhere in this book, the sign of the island's economic slowdown emerged after the 1997/98 Asian Financial Crisis and became even more conspicuous following the 2008/9 Global Financial Crisis.[9] As it is, there seems little, if any, connection between the slowdown and the island's status as an FTZ.

It should be stated at the outset that the implementation of the BBK FTZ has been marred by problems almost immediately following its commencement. The zone has three zone councils, one each for Batam, Bintan and Karimun. The government settled on the structure of the zone councils only after four revisions. To the surprise of many investors and contrary to what the government implied, the councils did not include significant private sector representation. The chairman of the councils was the Governor of Riau Islands with the Mayor and the District Heads serving as Vice-Chairmen. Members of each council included the heads of regional customs office, tax office and land agency, as well as the city or district police chief, district attorney, regional military commanders and the regional FTZ administration agency head (Wong and Ng 2009).

More recently, in October 2017, the government replaced the entire management team of BP Batam with a group of Java-based senior civil servants, a move that implied a serious loss of confidence in the agency (*Straits Times*, 2 November 2017). At the same time, a proposal to rescind Batam's FTZ status and turn it into a special economic zone began to circulate. All of this preceded the above-mentioned appointment of the Mayor of Batam as the head of the agency.

Amid the slowdown, some industries might have hoped that their products would be able to enter the domestic market without subjecting them to the prevailing customs duties. One such industry is the shipbuilding. Batam's shipbuilding industry is the largest in Indonesia, with approximately 115 shipyards or around 46 per cent of all the country's shipyards. Yet, because of the island's FTZ status, its shipbuilding industry has not been able to benefit from the government's plan to promote maritime connectivity through a sea toll programme. While this programme is likely to increase the demand for ships, it will benefit those producing vessels for the domestic market. Those shipyards in operation in Batam are effectively precluded from benefiting from this initiative, as they are treated as foreign entities due to their geographical location within the FTZ (Negara 2017).

Meanwhile, Batam's economy began to pick up the pace again in 2017, driven primarily by a significant increase in domestic investment. At this juncture, it may be instructive to highlight two developments, which, because of their size, arguably indicate investors' confidence in the island's future prospects. The first is the establishment of a new industrial park, Nongsa Digital Park, to house digital companies. Citramas Group, the owner of the 100-hectare park, is aiming to generate up to 10,000 new jobs in the digital sector. As of late 2019, there were already some forty-five firms operating in the park, employing about 300 IT professionals between them (Hutchinson and Negara, this volume).

The second development is the plan to build an aircraft maintenance, repair and overhaul (MRO) facility in Batam. The endeavour is a joint venture between PT Batam Aero Technic, a subsidiary of Lion Air and GMF AeroAsia, a subsidiary of Garuda. If realized, the facility will significantly increase Indonesia's MRO capacity. However, it should be noted that in order to attract aviation companies, foreign ones in particular, the facility must first secure European Aviation Safety Agency and Federal Aviation Agency certification.

Finally, the manufacturing sector—the mainstay of the island's economy—is robust and becoming more diversified. The island currently has 22 industrial parks, with a total number of 950 tenants in 2017. See Appendix 5.1.

PREFERENTIAL TARIFF ARRANGEMENTS BETWEEN BBK FTZ AND THE INDONESIAN MARKET

When goods are moved from the BBK FTZ to customers in the rest of Indonesia, they become subject to the prevailing customs duties levied in the country and vice versa. As such, the BBK FTZ is essentially a separate customs area.

As noted, some producers in the BBK FTZ, such as the Batam shipbuilding sector, hoped to be able to sell their products in the domestic market without subjecting them to the prevailing customs duties. Yet, the different legal status of these firms has precluded selling on the domestic market.

However, there may be a way for firms to avoid the "firewalling" effect of the BBK FTZ and allow preferential treatment for certain products produced within the zone that enter the domestic market. While examples of such a practice may not be plenty, there are nevertheless models whereby two different customs territories of the same country agree to have a preferential tariff agreement between them. One example of direct interest is the 2003 China–Hong Kong Closer Economic

Partnership Agreement. Note that, while Hong Kong is part of China, it is actually a separate entity for customs purposes.[10] It is for the same reason that Hong Kong could become a member of APEC. The same applies for Taiwan's membership in APEC as Chinese Taipei.

The same idea may be applied to the BBK FTZ, whereby selected goods from the zone are subjected to tariffs at a preferential rate when they enter the rest of the country. The tariff rates should be such that they level the playing field between domestic producers and producers in the zone of goods in question. In other words, the tariff rates should consider the benefits that producers in the zone receive from the FTZ status but not available to domestic producers. The idea is that neither domestic producers nor producers in the zone will have advantage over each other. The goods that enter the basket are those that have excess domestic demand.

Consider, for example, a ship of a certain tonnage built in Batam. By itemizing its material inputs, e.g., ship engine, propulsion and blade, rudder, etc., one can calculate the amount of foregone tariffs that the manufacturer enjoys but domestic producers do not. The ship can then be sold in the domestic market simply by paying this amount to the government as well as taking into account any pecuniary benefits from the government that domestic producers may enjoy but producers in BBK FTZ do not.

CONCLUSION: WHICH WAY FORWARD FOR BATAM?

Despite some recent setbacks, Batam's economic prospects are arguably not as bleak as they may appear. Investment, foreign as well as domestic, continues to trickle in.

As noted, the government has proposed to transform Batam status from an FTZ to SEZ. It is not immediately clear as to what the government wants to achieve with this measure. If it is to address the island's economic problems, then it is doubtful that the proposed move would do the trick. Batam's existing economic problems have little, if any, to do with its current FTZ status. Moreover, the move will send a signal to investors that any government promise cannot be taken at its face value, given that the legislation prevailing under the BBK FTZ framework is to last seventy years.

The theoretical elimination of the dualism or overlapping authority between the Batam municipal government and BIFZA should be a positive development. However, there is much more that can be done. In particular, the municipal government should take advantage of the current economic downturn to push for further deregulation of the economy by, among other things, simplifying and streamlining investment procedures and regulations. The number of business licences and the time needed to start a business should be reduced to a bare minimum. In addition, there is also a need to improve the government's transparency and accountability. Furthermore, the government has to find ways to reduce the incidence of industrial relations problems that have inflicted significant costs on Batam's economy in the past. For instance, by creating a tripartite committee involving representatives from local governments, business organizations and labour unions to deal with industrial relations issues.

To conclude, over the decades Batam has enjoyed preferential treatment and exceptional incentives. Its economy has been able to develop at break-neck speed as a result. However, while tax incentives are an important part of any location's competitive advantage, they cannot, in and of themselves, constitute the sole attraction for investors. Rather than focusing on rolling out more and newer incentives, policymakers would be better off concentrating on improving the overall climate for business. And, given the size of Indonesia's economy today, it may be worth investigating fair ways of allowing firms in Batam to sell on the domestic market.

APPENDIX 5.1
Industrial Estates in Batam

Industrial estate development is an integral part of Batam's development, as they provide companies with necessary infrastructure and services. The number of industrial estates has not changed since 2005, with twenty-two estates that cover a total area of approximately 1,394 hectares. The size of the estates varies significantly. With the exception of Kabil Integrated Industrial Park (500 ha), Batamindo Industrial Estate (320 ha) and Panbil Industrial Estate (103 ha), all of the others are less than 100 ha. The smallest one, Malindo Cipta Perkasa Industrial Park, is only 2 ha in size, yet was home to thirty-seven companies in 2017. Tunas Industrial Estate houses 230 companies, or approximately 24 per cent of all tenants in the industrial estates listed in Table 5.A1.

TABLE 5.A1
Industrial Estates in Batam, 2017

	Year Opened	Area (ha)	Number of Tenants
Sekupang Makmur Abadi	1984	32	7
Batamindo Industrial Estate	1990	320	66
Taiwan International Industrial Estate	1990	54	11
Kabil Integrated Industrial Park	1991	500	34
Kara Industrial Park	1992	19	35
Lytech Industrial Park	1992	52	78
Citra Buana Centre Park I	1994	10	41
Mega Cipta Industrial Park	1994	5	59
Cammo Industrial Park	1995	18	29
Malindo Cipta Perkasa Industrial Park	1996	2	37
Indah Industrial Park	2000	16	9
Bintang Industrial Park II	2001	80	57
Latrade Industrial Park	2001	14	12
Panbil Industrial Estate	2001	103	26
Tunas Industrial Estate	2001	48	230
Citra Buana Centre Park II	2002	8	7
Citra Buana Centre Park III	2002	20	23
Hijrah Industrial Park	2002	6	21
Puri Industrial Park 2000	2002	24	36
Union Industrial Park	2003	23	57
Executive Industrial Park	2005	22	40
Sarana Industrial Point	2005	18	34
Total		1,394	949

Source: BIFZA (2019).

Notes

1. In 2005, the Bonded Zone Plus area was extended to the adjacent islands of Bintan and Karimun.
2. In this paper the terms BIDA, BP Batam and BIFZA are used interchangeably.
3. Established under Government Regulations nos. 46, 47 and 48, 2007.
4. Chapter II of the Law no. 39, 2009 concerning Special Economic Zones.
5. KEK official website: https://kek.go.id/peta-sebaran-kek
6. Ibid.
7. Government Regulation No. 62, 2019.
8. The government has recently suggested that it would establish two SEZs in Batam. See *Media Indonesia*, 29 September 2019, https://mediaindonesia.com/read/detail/262309-pemerintah-bangun-dua-kawasan-ekonomi-khusus-di-batam
9. Chapter 2 of this book explores the possible root causes of the slowdown.
10. The text of the agreement is available at https://investmentpolicy.unctad.org/international-investment-agreements/treaty-files/2657/download

References

Antara Kepri. 2019. "Investasi Baru Masuk ke Batam Rp691 Miliar". *Antara Kepri Online*, 22 April 2019. https://kepri.antaranews.com/berita/56007/investasi-baru-masuk-ke-batam-rp691-miliar (accessed 25 July 2019).

Batam Indonesia Free Zone Authority. 2019. *Development Progress of Batam Tahun 2018*, 2nd ed., vol. XXXIV.

BIDA. 1980. *The Batam Development Program*. Jakarta: Batam Industrial Development Authority.

Bisnis.com. 2017. "Pengembangan Hanggar, Lion Air Sudah Habiskan Rp600 Miliar". 12 October 2017. https://ekonomi.bisnis.com/read/20171012/98/698425/pengembangan-hanggar-lion-air-sudah-habiskan-rp600-miliar (accessed 25 July 2019).

———. 2019. "Nilai Komitmen Investasi di KEK Capai Rp85,3 Triliun". 10 October 2019. https://ekonomi.bisnis.com/read/20191010/9/1157587/nilai-komitmen-investasi-di-kek-capai-rp853-triliun (accessed 18 February 2020).

BKPM. 2019. *Perkembangan Investasi Berdasarkan Kabupaten Kota Per Sektor*. https://nswi.bkpm.go.id/data_statistik (accessed 25 July 2019).

BPS Batam. 2018. *Banyaknya Wisatawan Mancanegara (Jiwa) yang Datang Melalui Pintu Masuk Batam dan Pertumbuhannya (Persen) 2010–2017*. https://batamkota.bps.go.id/statictable/2018/11/07/69/banyaknya-wisman-jiwa-yang-datang-melalui-pintu-masuk-batam-dan-pertumbuhannya-persen-2010-2017.html (accessed 25 July 2019).

———. 2017a. *Nilai Ekspor dan Impor Kota Batam 2014–2018*. https://batamkota.bps.go.id/dynamictable/2017/10/03/25/nilai-ekspor-dan-impor-kota-batam-2014-2018.html (accessed 25 July 2019).

———. 2017b. *PDRB Kota Batam Atas Dasar Harga Konstan 2010 Menurut Lapangan Usaha 2010–2018*. https://batamkota.bps.go.id/dynamictable/2017/07/05/9/pdrb-kota-batam-atas-dasar-harga-konstan-2010-menurut-lapangan-usaha-2010-2018.html (accessed 25 July 2019).

BPS. Various years. *Indikator Utama Kepulauan Riau*. Tanjungpinang: BPS Kepulauan Riau.

———. Various years. *Statistik Industri Besar Sedang Manufaktur Indonesia Tahun 2011–2015*. Jakarta: BPS.

Coordinating Ministry for Economic Affairs. 2019. *Kembangkan Pusat Perawatan Pesawat di*

Batam, Pemerintah Dorong Sinergi Ciptakan Ekosistem Industri Penerbangan Berkelanjutan. https://www.ekon.go.id/berita/print/kembangkan-pusat-perawatan.4952.html (accessed 16 August 2019)

Damuri, Yose Rizal, David Christian, and Raymond Atje. 2015. *Kawasan Ekonomi Khusus dan Strategis Indonesia: Tinjauan Atas Peluang dan Permasalahan.* Jakarta: Center for Strategic and International Studies.

FIAS. 2008. *Special Economic Zones: Performance, Lessons Learned, and Implications for Zone Development.* Washington, DC: The World Bank Group.

Ford, M. 2013. "Violent Industrial Protests in Indonesia: Cultural Phenomenon or Legacy of Authoritarian Past?". In *New Forms and Expressions of Conflict at Work*, edited by Gregor Gall, pp. 171–90. Basingstoke: Palgrave Macmillan.

Government of Indonesia. 2009. "Undang-undang Republik Indonesia nomor 39, Tahun 2009 tentang Kawasn Ekonomi Khusus".

Hutchinson, F.E. 2017. *Rowing Against the Tide? Batam's Economic Fortunes in Today's Indonesia.* Trends in Southeast Asia, no. 8/2017. Singapore: ISEAS – Yusof Ishak Institute.

———, and Leo van Grunsven. 2017. "Industry Dynamics in Growth Triangles: The E&E Industry in SIJORI 25 Years On". ISEAS Economics Working Paper No. 2017-09. Singapore: ISEAS –Yusof Ishak Institute.

———, and S.D. Negara. 2019. "Batam's Emerging Digital Economy: Prospect and Challenges". *ISEAS Perspective*, no. 2019/25, 10 April 2019.

Jakarta Post. 2016. "BP Batam, Enerco Ink Deal on Rubber Oil Refinery". 20 September 2016. https://www.thejakartapost.com/seasia/2016/09/20/bp-batam-enerco-ink-deal-on-rubber-oil-refinery.html (accessed 25 July 2019).

MRO-Network. 2015. "Indonesia Lacks Certified MROs Despite Large, Growing Market". MRO-Network.com, 30 October 2015. https://www.mro-network.com/maintenance-repair-overhaul/indonesia-lacks-certified-mros-despite-large-growing-market (accessed 12 September 2019).

Negara, Siwage Dharma. 2017. "Can the Decline of Batam's Shipbuilding Industry be Reversed?". *ISEAS Perspective* No. 2017/10, 16 February 2017.

———, and F.E. Hutchinson. 2019. "Batam: Life after the FTZ?". *Bulletin of Indonesia Economic Studies* 55, no. 1.

Peachey, K., M. Perry, and C. Grundy-Warr. 1998. *The Riau Islands and Economics Cooperation in the Singapore Indonesia Border Zone.* Durham: International Boundaries Research Unit.

Pertamina, Nissho-Iwai, and Pacific Bechtel. 1972. *Masterplan Batam: Industrial Development.* Jakarta: Pertamina.

Tan K.G., Nurina Merdekawati, M. Amri, and Tan K.Y. 2016. *Agricultural Productivity: Decentralization and Competitiveness Analysis for Provinces and Regions of Indonesia.* Singapore: World Scientific.

Wong Poh Kam, and Ng Kwan Kee. 2009. *Batam, Bintan, and Karimun—Past History and Current Development towards Being A SEZ.* Singapore: Asia Competitiveness Institute, National University of Singapore.

World Bank. GDP growth (annual %). National Account Data. https://data.worldbank.org/indicator/NY.GDP.MKTP.Kd.zg (accessed 25 July 2019).

6

TOWARDS "BALANCED" DEVELOPMENT IN THE RIAU ISLANDS

Raymond Atje, Siwage Dharma Negara and
Columbanus Teto

INTRODUCTION

Regardless of their size or physical characteristics, all territories face formidable challenges in striving for equitable development. However, as an archipelagic province, whose 1,994 islands are scattered throughout some 427,600 km^2 of sea, this is particularly daunting for the Riau Islands.

Moreover, the Riau Islands' economy has slowed down in recent years, mainly driven by the recent slump in the manufacturing sector, mainly centred on Batam (Hutchinson and Negara in this volume). The province's dependency on this sector, which is largely concentrated in one part of its territory, indicates the success of the formerly named Batam Industrial Development Authority (BIDA) in pursuing the "Factory Asia" development model (Choi and Rhee 2014). Yet, on the other hand, it shows a structural vulnerability, as any shock to the manufacturing sector will certainly have a significant impact on the province's overall economic health. Consequently, the Riau Islands Province faces two key challenges: first, diversifying its economy to underpin sustainable growth going forward; and second, ensuring that the benefits of this growth are spread to a maximum within the province.

To this end, this chapter is comprised of five sections. Following this introduction, the second section sets out the basic characteristics of the Riau Islands' economy. The third provides a brief review of the province's economic development over the past few years. The fourth provides some ideas for addressing the economic imbalance in the province, and the fifth concludes.

THE RIAU ISLANDS' ECONOMY

The Riau Islands Province consists of: five districts, Bintan, Karimun, Anambas Islands, Natuna and Lingga; and two municipalities, namely, Batam and Tanjungpinang. In 2018, the province's population stood at 2.14 million, of which approximately 1.33 million or around 62 per cent lived in Batam. An additional 367,000 people lived in Bintan (including Tanjungpinang) and 231,000 in Karimun (BPS Provinsi Kepulauan Riau, 2019). Together, these three islands constitute about 90 per cent of the Riau Islands' population—indicating the province's economic and demographic centre of gravity.

The Riau Islands Province is rich in natural resources, such as minerals, oil, natural gas, and fisheries. The province's water, which constitutes around 97 per cent of its total area, contains large quantities of marine resources, in particular plentiful stocks of fish. In 2015, the agriculture, forestry and fishery sectors together contributed 3.6 per cent to the Riau Islands' gross regional domestic product (GRDP) or around IDR7.26 trillion (approx. US$498 million) in nominal terms. The fishery sector alone contributes two-thirds of the amount, or approximately 2.4 per cent of the province's GRDP, slightly below the national average of about 2.5 per cent of the country's GDP (BPS Kepri 2016).

Note that waters around the Natuna Islands also hold substantial natural gas reserves. According to one estimate, the reserves in East Natuna are about 46 trillion cubic feet (TCF), which constitute 35 per cent of total natural gas reserves in the country. While the reserves may be large, they also contain up to 72 per cent carbon dioxide and, hence, are much more expensive to extract (Karunia 2020).

Compared to other provinces in Indonesia, the Riau Islands has a relatively high GDP per capita, second only to Jakarta and above the level of its mother province, Riau (Figure 6.1). The province was able to achieve such a high living standard, arguably, due to its openness to international trade and investment. The rapid economic growth, especially, took place during the 1990s and early 2000s. Figure 6.1 shows, however, that after 2016 the growth of GDP per capita in the province has been relatively stagnant.

Likewise, rapid economic growth has contributed to lower unemployment and poverty in the province. The Riau Islands, in fact, has lower unemployment and poverty rates compared to other provinces in Indonesia (except Jakarta) (Figure 6.2 and Figure 6.3). Figure 6.2 shows that there was an increase in the unemployment rate between 2014 and 2015, which was caused by a massive contraction in the global offshore and marine industry. Those years, the offshore marine sector was grappling with worldwide oversupply and the massive fall in demand following the oil price collapse, from above US$100 to sub-US$50 by late 2014 (Tan 2015).

The province also has a lower poverty intensity (Figure 6.4). The poverty gap index estimates the depth of poverty by considering how far, on average, the poor

FIGURE 6.1
GDP per capita in Select Provinces, at Constant Prices (IDR million)

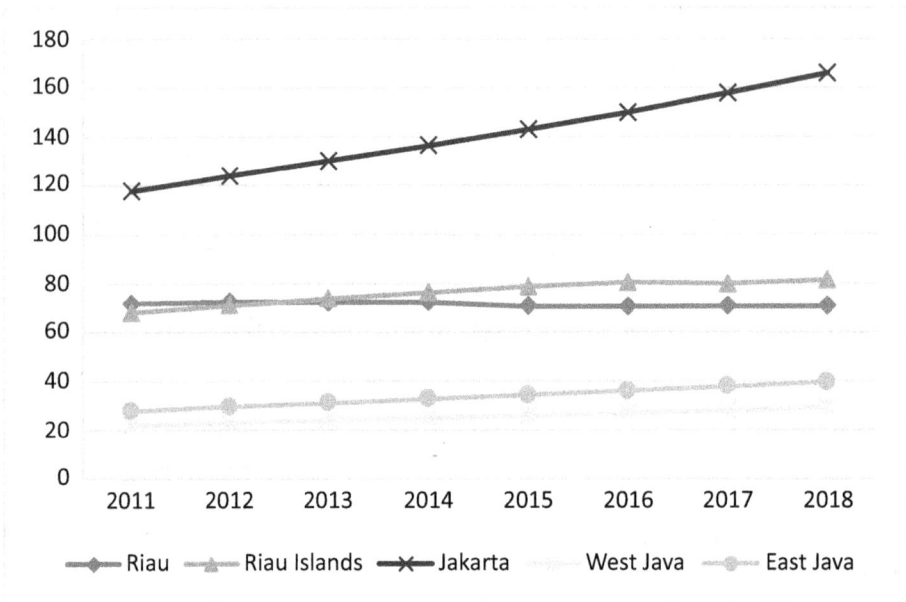

Source: BPS, via CEIC.

FIGURE 6.2
Unemployment Rates in Select Provinces (% p.a.)

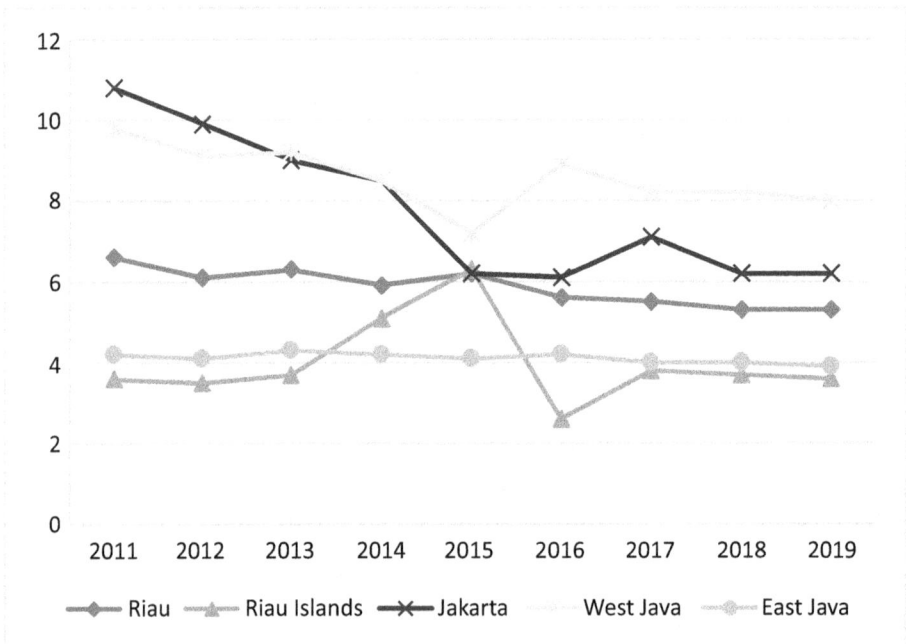

Note: This data is taken from CEIC, which uses BPS as the original source.
Source: BPS, via CEIC.

FIGURE 6.3
Poverty Rate in Select Provinces

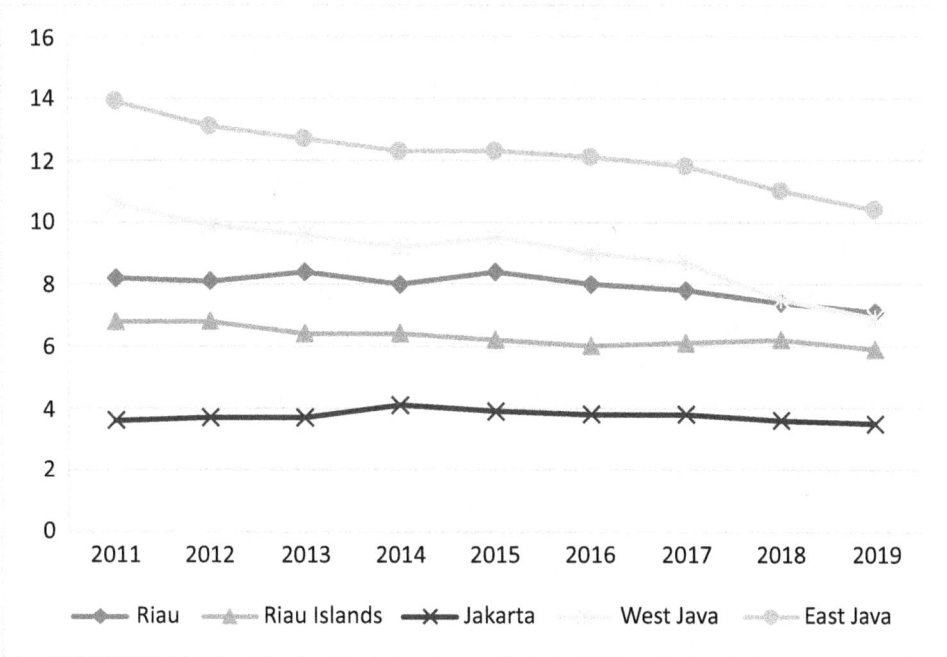

Source: BPS, via CEIC.

FIGURE 6.4
Poverty Gap Index in Select Provinces

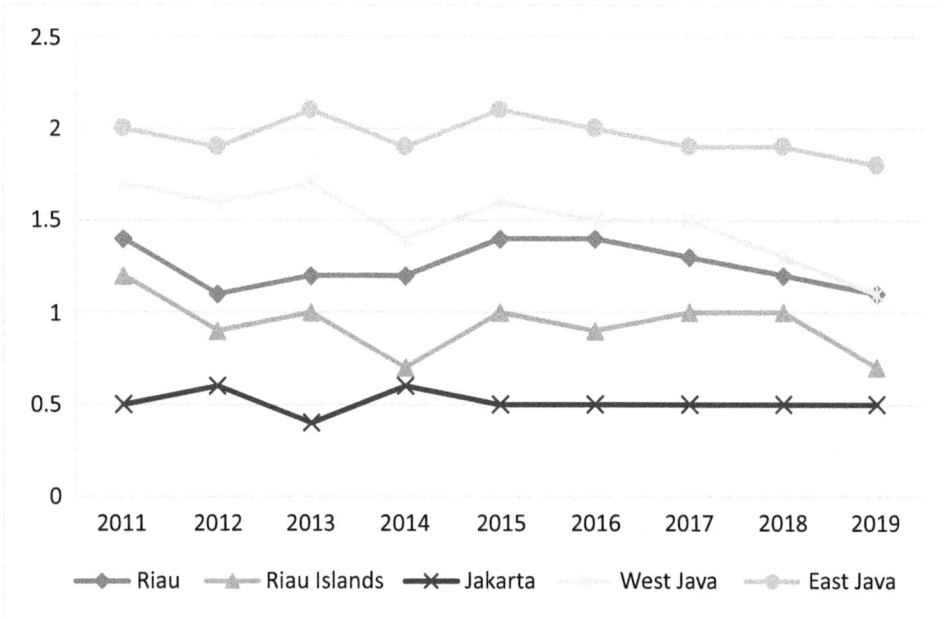

Source: BPS, via CEIC.

are from the poverty line. The Riau Islands' lower index means average poverty is relatively less severe compared to other provinces in the country.

The province also has a relatively high minimum wage rate. This is second only to Jakarta, slightly above the level of its mother province, Riau, and significantly higher than the provinces of West and East Java (Figure 6.5). The latter provinces have emerged in recent years as rivals for foreign direct investment in the manufacturing sector, and beyond their lower costs they have much bigger workforces.

Years of rapid economic growth have contributed to the province's respectable achievement in terms of human development. Figure 6.6 shows that, in 2019, the province obtained a relatively high score (75.5) in terms of its human development indicators. This is above its parent province, Riau, which obtained a score of 73. Moreover, relative to other archipelagic provinces in the country, such as Bangka Belitung, East Nusa Tenggara (NTT), Maluku or West Papua, the Riau Islands is far more competitive in regards to human development indicators.

Another interesting fact is that the province has a relatively higher literacy rate compared to the national average (Figure 6.7). In 2019, the Riau Islands scored 99 per cent in terms of literacy rate, far exceeding the national literacy average of 95.9 per cent. This indicates the workforce in the province, on average, is relatively better educated than that of the other provinces in the country.

While the Riau Islands Province seems more developed compared with other provinces in Indonesia, there is significant discrepancy in terms of economic

FIGURE 6.5
Monthly Minimum Wage (IDR thousand per month)

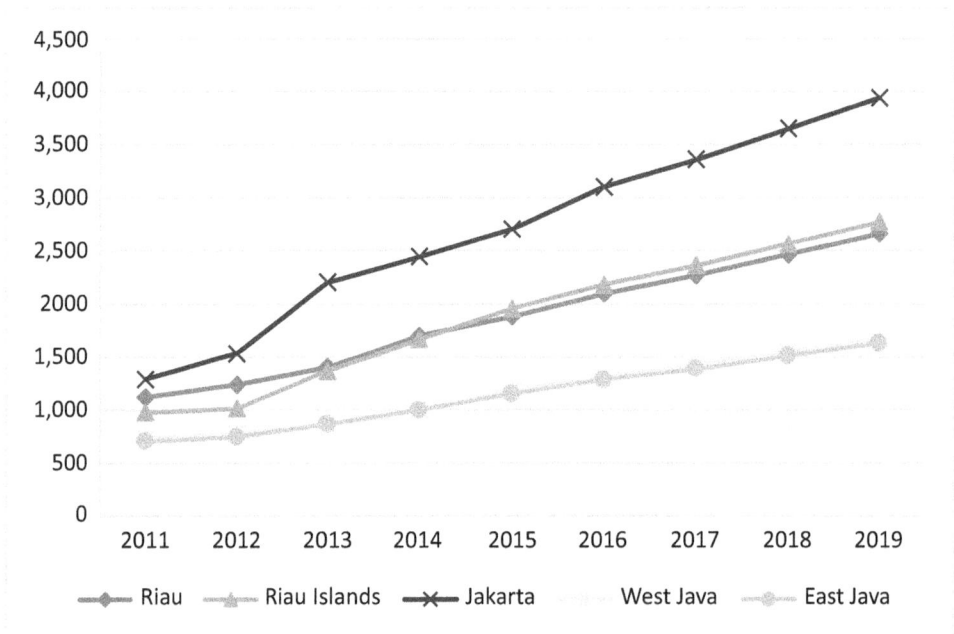

Source: BPS, via CEIC.

FIGURE 6.6
Human Development Index in Select Provinces

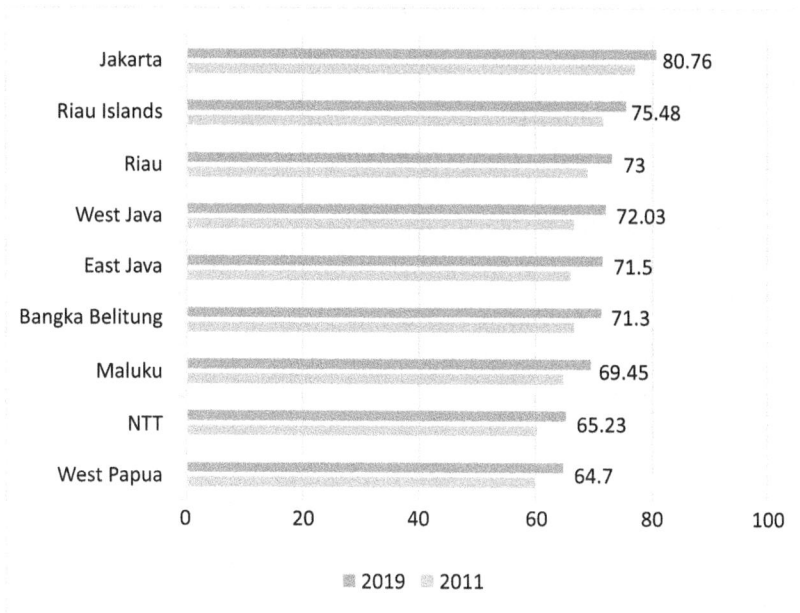

Jakarta	80.76
Riau Islands	75.48
Riau	73
West Java	72.03
East Java	71.5
Bangka Belitung	71.3
Maluku	69.45
NTT	65.23
West Papua	64.7

2019   2011

Source: BPS website, https://www.bps.go.id/dynamictable/2020/02/18/1772/indeks-pembangunan-manusia-menurut-provinsi-metode-baru-2010-2019.html

FIGURE 6.7
Literacy Rates in Select Provinces

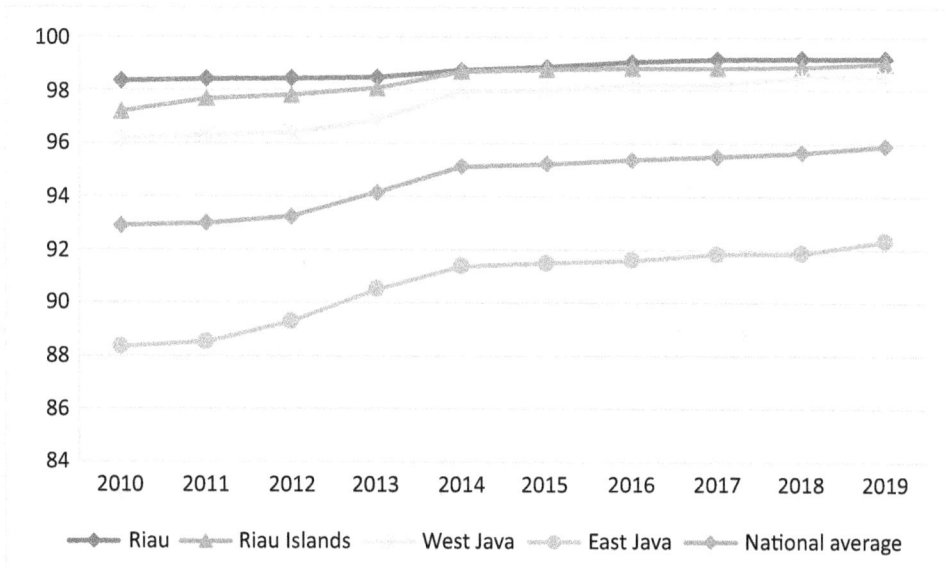

Riau — Riau Islands — West Java — East Java — National average

Source: BPS website, https://www.bps.go.id/dynamictable/2019/04/16/1618/rata-rata-lama-sekolah-menurut-provinsi-1996-2013.html and https://www.bps.go.id/dynamictable/2018/07/13/1536/persentase-angka-melek-huruf-amh-penduduk-usia-di-atas-15-tahun-menurut-provinsi-2015-2016.html development across its districts and municipalities. In 2018, the province's real GRDP was about IDR168.82 trillion (approx. US$11.5 billion in 2010 prices). Batam contributed 60.5 per cent of the province's total GRDP, i.e., around IDR102.1 trillion. Bintan (excluding Tanjungpinang) and Karimun contributed around IDR13.88 trillion (8.2 per cent) and IDR9.02 trillion (5.3 per cent), respectively, to the province's output. Tanjungpinang and the Natuna Islands contributed approximately IDR13.98 trillion (8.3 per cent) and IDR15.02 trillion (8.3 per cent), respectively, to the Riau Islands' GRDP.

Figure 6.8 shows the disparity with regard to the human development index in the province. While the province's average score was 75.5, Batam's HDI was 81.1, the highest in the province. Tanjungpinang came second, with 78.7. Other districts, however, scored below the province average. For instance, Lingga had a HDI score of 65, the lowest in the province. Anambas Islands had a score of 68.5 just above Lingga. Meanwhile, Natuna scored 72.6, which is also below the average score for the province (BPS 2019).[1]

Note that the variation in the districts' HDI scores is closely associated with the variation of the poverty gap index, within the province and between districts/municipalities. In terms of the poverty gap, Lingga Regency has the worst poverty intensity, followed by Tanjungpinang municipality. The latter is interesting, as while it has a high HDI, it also has a high poverty gap. The latter indicates that poverty in this municipality is relatively more severe compared to the average level poverty in the province. Yet, it has experienced a significant improvement between 2011 and 2019 (Figure 6.9). What is quite striking is that while the poverty gap has decreased in all

FIGURE 6.8
Human Development Index Scores within the Riau Islands Province

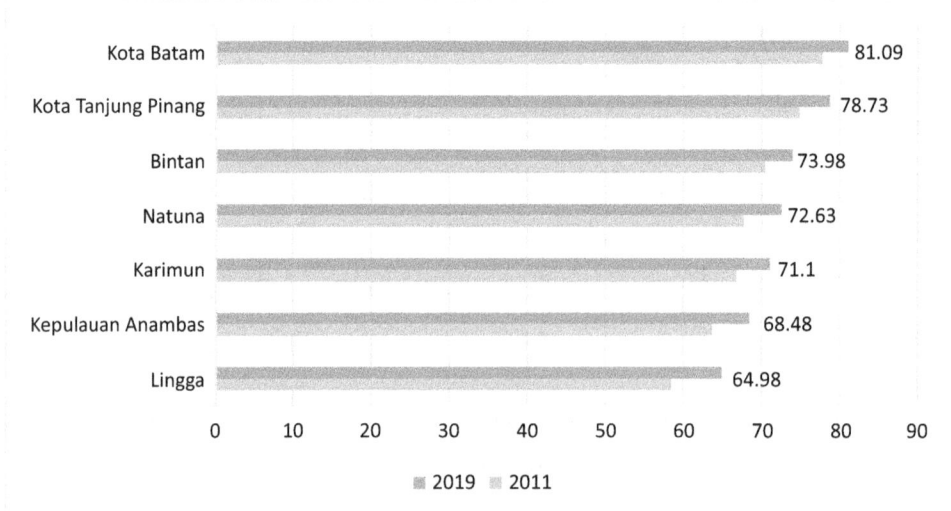

Kota Batam — 81.09
Kota Tanjung Pinang — 78.73
Bintan — 73.98
Natuna — 72.63
Karimun — 71.1
Kepulauan Anambas — 68.48
Lingga — 64.98

■ 2019   ■ 2011

Source: BPS website, https://www.bps.go.id/dynamictable/2020/02/17/1771/indeks-pembangunan-manusia-menurut-kabupaten-kota-metode-baru-2010-2019.html

FIGURE 6.9
Poverty Gap within the Riau Islands Province

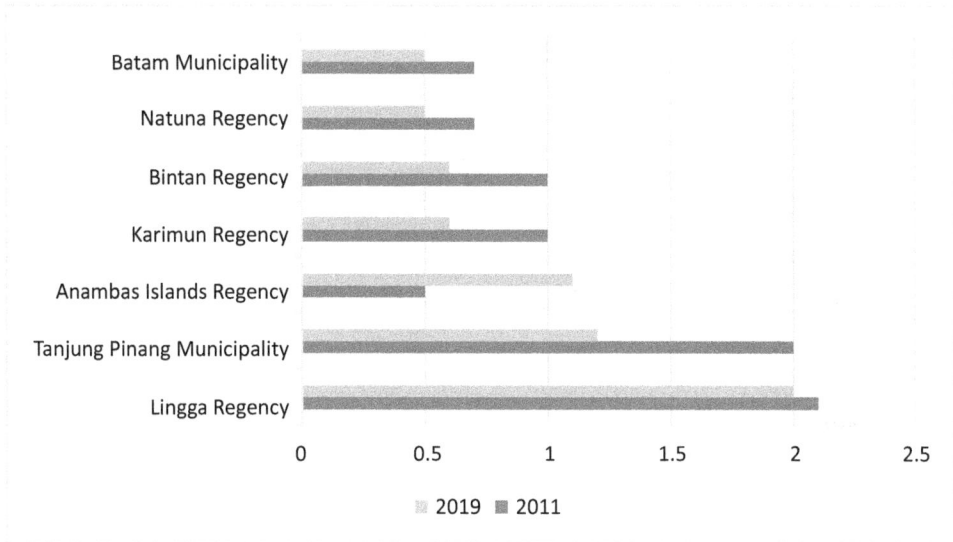

Source: BPS, via CEIC.

parts of the province, Anambas Islands, however, has experienced sharp increase in the poverty gap. This is in line with a dramatic economic contraction in the district, which contracted –8.2 per cent in 2018 (see Table 6.2).

Note that the economic structure might explain this wide variation in the HDI and poverty gap within the Riau Islands Province. Figure 6.10 provides a general mapping of the diversity of economic structure in the province. If we look at the GRDP composition of the districts and municipalities, we can see striking economic differences among them. Batam's economy is highly dominated by its manufacturing sector (Hutchinson and Negara, this volume). Bintan's is dominated by the services sector, especially tourism (Muzwardi and Negara, this volume). Karimun, for its part, has a relatively large primary sector, i.e., mining and quarrying. And, Tanjungpinang, the provincial capital, is mostly dominated by the services sector, i.e., government administration. Finally, the economy of Natuna, Lingga and the Anambas Islands all rely on the primary sector, e.g., fisheries, mining, as well as oil and gas.

Natuna needs a special mention as this remote district has a relatively low poverty gap, second only to Batam. The district has massive reserves of oil and natural gas. At present, there are thirteen oil and gas companies operating in the Natuna Sea: Conoco Philips Indonesia; Genting Oil Natuna; Indoreach Exploration; Lunding Oil & Gas BV; Peal Oil; Premier Oil Natuna Sea BV; Sayen Oil and Gas PTE LTD; Star Energy LTD; Titian Resources Indonesia LTD; West Natuna Exploration LTD; and Pertamina EP (Perkasa 2016).

In 2019, the oil and gas exploration company PetroChina showed its interest in joining Pertamina, a state-owned oil and gas company, to manage the East Natuna

FIGURE 6.10
GRDP Composition by Sector (Per cent of total GRDP of Respective District)

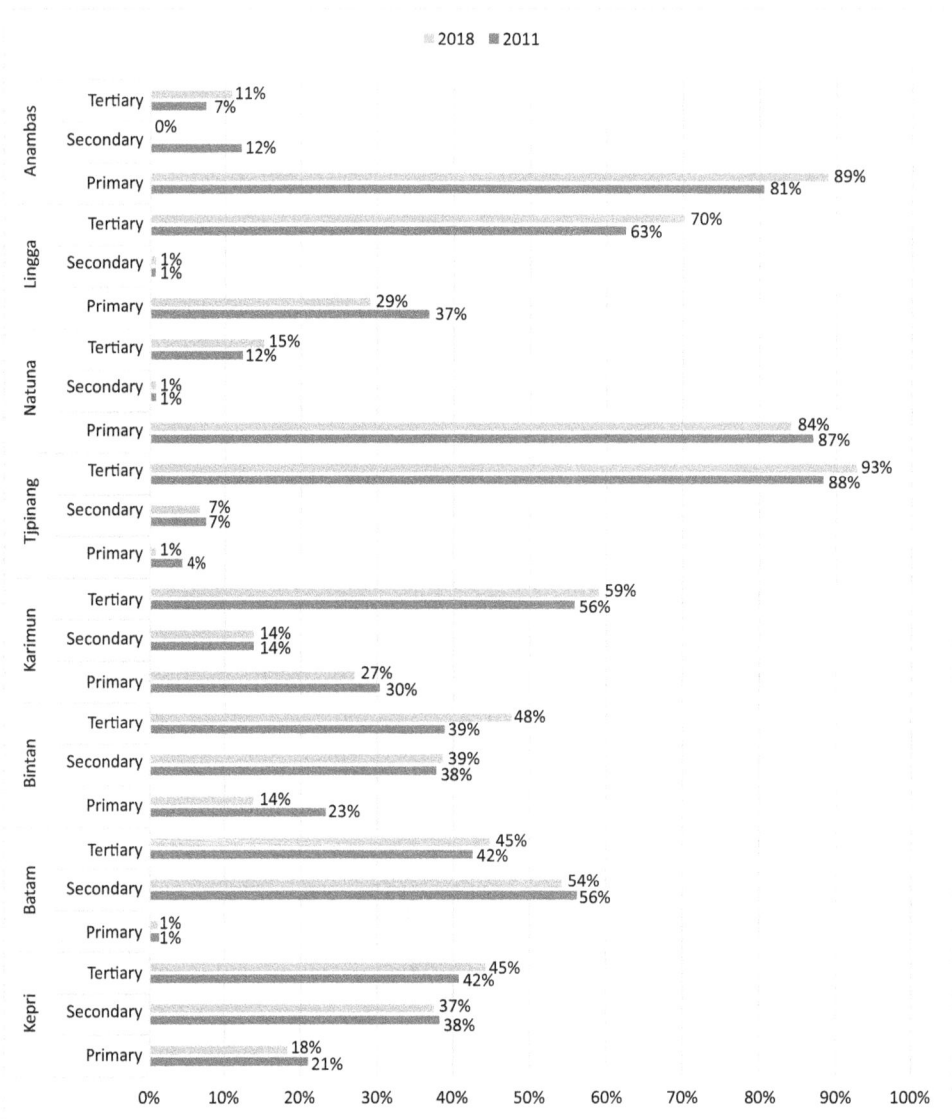

Source: BPS Kepri, via CEIC.

oil and gas block (*Tempo.co* 2020). Previously, in July 2017, Exxon Mobil had handed over the management of the block to PT Pertamina (Persero) (*Kompas*, 25 July 2017). Since then, Pertamina has been searching for investors who are willing to collaborate to develop the oil and gas industry in the area. If successful, the project will bring an investment of around US$40 billion (Wicaksono 2020). Nevertheless, oil and gas revenues are controlled by the central government. The province and district government, however, will receive the so-called revenue sharing fund (*Dana Bagi*

Hasil) from oil and gas revenues based on Law No. 33/2004. Much of the debate surrounding the sharing of finances derived from natural resources pertains to the perception of what is perceived as equitable. This issue has triggered discussions in Natuna about seceding from the Riau Islands to obtain a greater share of this revenue (see Andaya in this volume).

The wide variation in economic structure across the districts as shown in Figure 6.10 reflects clear socio-economic differentials within the province. Moreover, these differences reflect how districts specialize in the production of different goods and services. This is shaped by factors such as geographical location, demography, natural resources, institutional framework and consumption patterns.

Going forward, the main challenge for the province is how to boost the development of remote districts such as Anambas, Lingga and Natuna. These districts face significant geographical obstacles. Their remoteness, due to poor accessibility as well as poor infrastructure, has disconnected them from the growth centres in the province and Indonesia more widely. These three isolated districts rely on their natural resources, i.e., fisheries, minerals, oil and gas, and thus are highly dependent on primary sector growth.

RECENT TRENDS

The Riau Islands' economy has been experiencing a slowdown in recent years. In contrast to its breakneck growth in the 1990s and 2000s, the province's economy began to trend downwards after 2012. From a rate of 7.6 that year, it reached its lowest growth rate of 2 per cent in 2017—substantially under the national average for that year of 5 per cent. This was primarily due to a drop in the output growth of the Riau Islands' four main sectors namely: mining; manufacturing; construction; and trade and repair (car and motorcycle output). The mining sector's output growth fell from 5.8 per cent in 2016 to –4.6 per cent in 2017; the manufacturing sector also dropped from 3.4 per cent to 1.5 per cent; the construction sector decreased from 4.5 per cent to 3.5 per cent, and the trade and repair sector fell from 9.5 per cent to 6.3 per cent per annum. In 2018 these four sectors contributed 79 per cent to the province's GRDP (Table 6.1 and Figure 6.11).

The manufacturing sector is the mainstay of the province's economy. In 2018, there were 444 medium and large manufacturing companies in the province, of which some 390 were located in Batam, 19 in Bintan, 12 in Karimun and 16 in Tanjungpinang. Total employment in the industry was 139,241, of which Batam employed 120,239, Bintan 12,381, and Karimun 5,189 workers (BPS Provinsi Kepulauan Riau, 2019).

In 2017, the province's economic growth dropped to 2 per cent from 5 per cent per annum the previous year. At the same time, almost all the districts and municipalities experienced an economic slowdown. However, Anambas district was particularly hard hit and experienced a slight contraction that year and an ever greater one the following year (Table 6.2). Beyond its physical isolation, Anambas has the smallest population of all districts and municipalities in the Riau Islands. In 2018, the district's population was estimated to be around 42,000, or only about

TABLE 6.1
Economic Growth in the Riau Islands by Sector (% p.a.)

	2011	2012	2013	2014	2015	2016	2017	2018
Agriculture, Forestry and Fisheries	3.93	2.36	4.29	7.56	5.78	5.79	−1.21	−2.85
Mining	2.65	5.07	3.26	5.24	9.22	5.77	−4.59	1.55
Manufacturing	7.80	8.07	8.17	5.95	5.61	3.36	1.53	4.14
Electricity and Gas	10.33	7.20	7.24	9.68	5.60	8.75	6.47	−0.94
Water Supply, Waste Management and Recycling	8.16	5.11	4.02	2.03	2.85	5.26	9.54	1.60
Construction	8.32	11.31	9.98	9.04	3.53	4.47	3.45	7.93
Trade and Repair: Car and Motorcycle	7.12	6.91	9.79	8.51	8.66	9.54	6.27	6.28
Transportation and Warehouse	9.25	7.10	7.57	5.97	5.62	6.07	5.45	0.91
Accommodation and Food Beverage	8.83	8.67	7.72	6.64	5.63	5.20	11.93	11.00
Information and Communication	9.83	7.02	6.45	7.04	5.00	7.40	7.69	11.30
Finance and Insurance	14.95	6.56	6.07	5.79	3.47	5.59	3.03	6.03
Real Estate	7.30	4.94	5.67	6.39	4.24	4.40	4.33	−0.09
Company Services	11.73	9.31	7.36	2.02	2.77	6.18	7.25	7.40
Government Administration, Defense and Social Security	9.58	6.16	4.72	4.01	7.50	5.81	4.67	7.55
Education Services	1.69	12.39	3.07	4.27	6.15	8.85	9.88	1.69
Healthcare and Social Services	6.94	8.05	1.68	4.84	7.15	4.45	10.29	3.15
Other Services	−1.48	3.02	0.72	4.16	6.55	8.08	6.43	19.24
Riau Islands	*6.96*	*7.63*	*7.21*	*6.60*	*6.02*	*4.98*	*1.98*	*4.58*

Source: BPS Kepri, various years.

FIGURE 6.11
GRDP in the Riau Islands by Sector, 2018

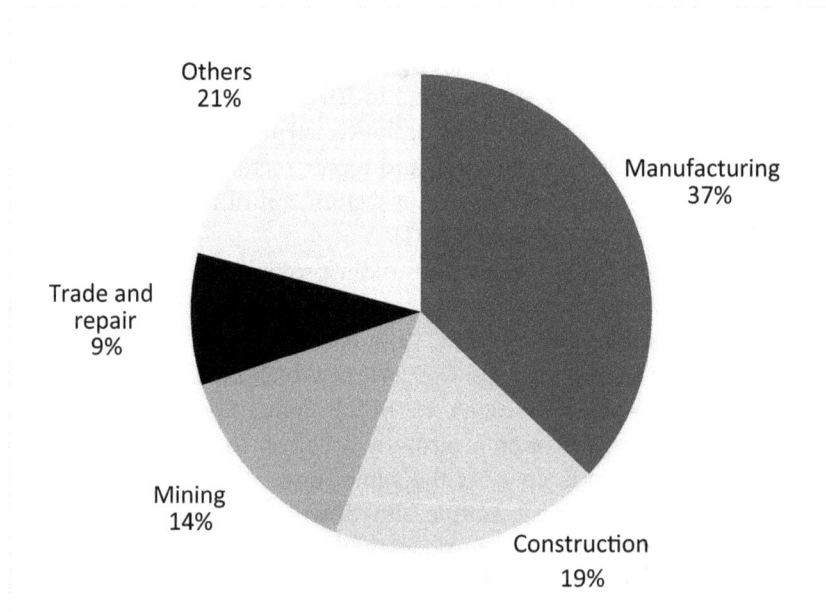

Source: BPS Kepri (2019).

TABLE 6.2
Economic Growth by Districts and Municipalities in the Riau Islands (% p.a.)

	2011	2012	2013	2014	2015	2016	2017	2018
Riau Islands	7.0	7.6	7.2	6.6	6.0	5.0	2.0	4.6
Karimun	7.0	7.2	7.1	6.9	6.5	6.2	5.3	5.0
Bintan	6.9	6.6	6.1	6.4	5.2	5.1	4.9	4.9
Natuna	2.6	7.8	4.6	4.4	3.9	3.0	0.9	2.4
Lingga	6.7	6.6	6.9	5.2	2.4	4.1	6.1	4.0
Anambas Islands	1.8	3.9	3.2	3.7	3.0	2.9	–0.1	–8.2
Batam	7.8	7.4	7.2	7.2	6.8	5.4	2.2	4.7
Tanjungpinang	7.0	7.1	7.8	5.3	5.7	5.0	2.7	3.2

Source: BPS Kepri, various years.

2 per cent of the province's total. Its economy depends heavily on the mining and quarrying sector, which contributed between 75 and 84 per cent of the district's GRDP (at current market price) during the 2015–19 period. Following the decline in global commodities prices, the sector's real growth has been adversely affected and recorded negative growth in recent years.

With regard to investment, the Riau Islands has been able to attract a significant amount of capital from foreign and domestic sources. Data from the Investment Coordinating Board (BKPM) reveal that, in 2019, the province received US$1.4 billion of FDI, up from approximately US$220 million in 2011. As Figure 6.12 shows, FDI that goes to the Riau Islands is relatively large compared to the total amount that goes to Sumatra. In 2019, the share of FDI that went to the Riau Islands was about 41 per cent of total that went to Sumatra, which comprises ten provinces. Note that Sumatra has been attracting declining amounts of FDI since 2016, as a result of low prices for commodities, such as coal and palm oil. Meanwhile, the volume of FDI that goes into the Riau Islands has been climbing. The industries that received a large amount of FDI (cumulative) in the manufacturing sector were: machinery and equipment; metal goods (excluding machinery and equipment); and chemicals and pharmaceuticals (Antara Kepri 2019).

Figure 6.13 compares the FDI that went to the Riau Islands with those that went to other main industrial areas, i.e., Jakarta, West Java, East Java, and Riau Province. The figure indicates that the Riau Islands remains an attractive location targeted by foreign investors. Note that investors that come to the Riau Islands are mainly export-oriented, while those that come to Java are mainly domestic-oriented ones.

Meanwhile, domestic investment has fluctuated even more than FDI over the same period. In 2011, the volume of domestic investment was IDR1.37 trillion (US$97 million) but subsequently dropped significantly to IDR43 billion (US$3 million) in 2012. In 2018, the volume of investment increased significantly to IDR4.39 trillion (US$307 million) from IDR1.4 trillion (US$97 million) the year before. In 2019, the figure increased further to reach IDR5.66 trillion (US$398 million) (Figure 6.14). A large fraction of domestic investment in 2018, around IDR3.18 trillion, went to Batam. In 2019, domestic investment in Batam reached IDR4.35 trillion (US$307 million)

FIGURE 6.12
Foreign Direct Investment in the Riau Islands, Riau and Sumatra (US$ billion)

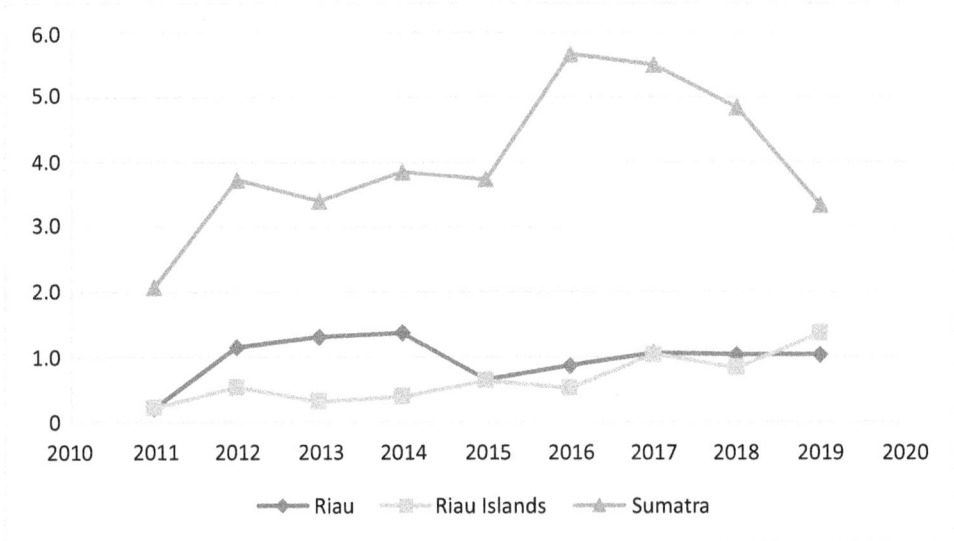

Source: BKPM, via CEIC.

FIGURE 6.13
Foreign Direct Investment in Select Provinces (US$ billion)

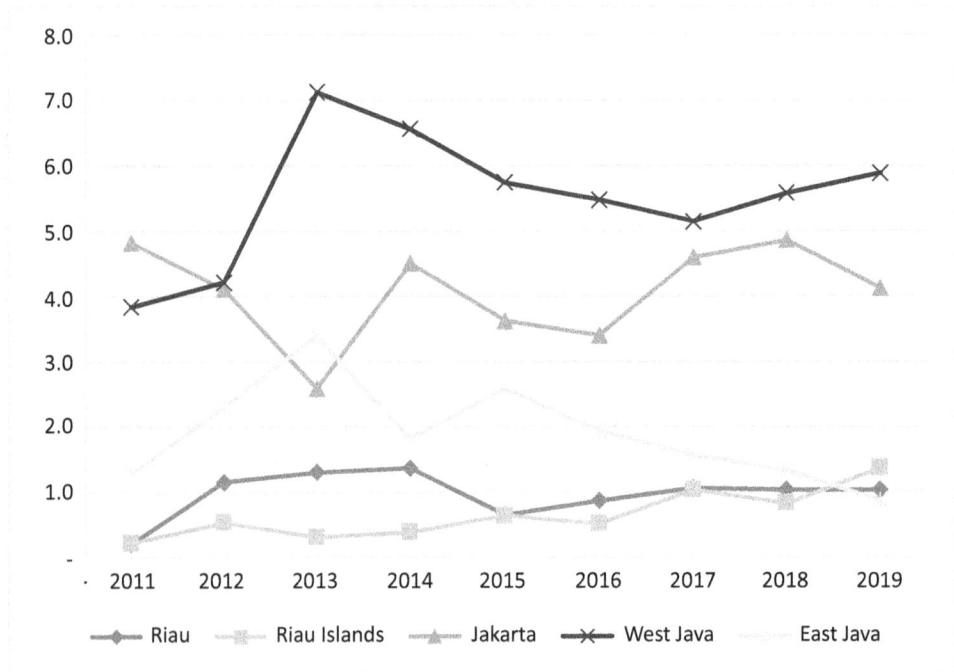

Source: BKPM, via CEIC.

FIGURE 6.14
Domestic Direct Investment in the Riau Islands, Riau and Sumatra (IDR trillion)

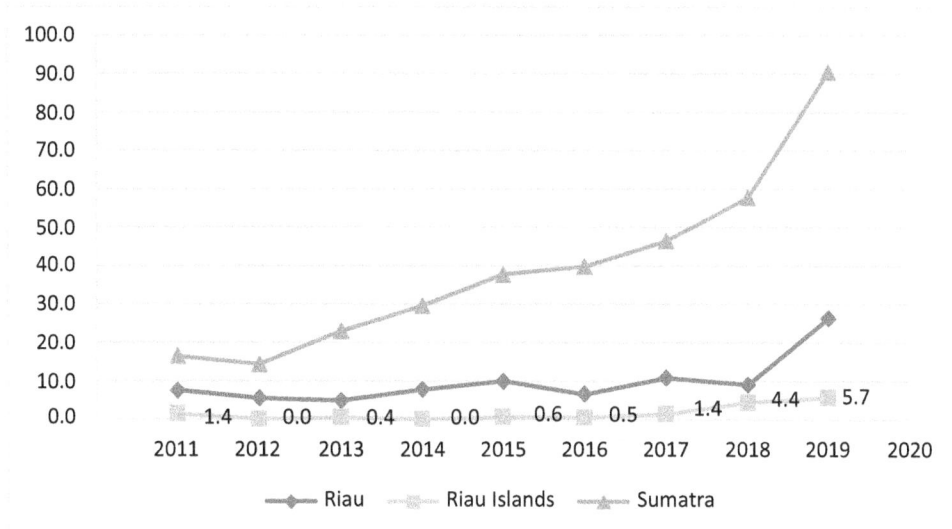

Source: BKPM, via CEIC.

(*TribunBatam.id* 2019). Note that unlike its relatively large share of FDI, the share of domestic investment that goes to the Riau Islands is relatively small compared to the total domestic investment in Sumatra, i.e., only around 6–7 per cent.

Figure 6.15 compares the DDI that went to the Riau Islands with those that went to other main industrial areas, such as Jakarta, West Java, East Java, and Riau Province. The figure indicates that, relative to those industrial areas in the country, the Riau Islands Province seems a less attractive location for domestic investors. Part of the reason is access to a large population base in the domestic market, which the Riau Islands has been lacking.

Nevertheless, the province is open to trade. In 2018, total foreign trade (export plus import value) reached US$25.3 billion. However, due to the US-China trade war, total foreign trade has declined to US$22.8 billion in 2019. Overall, the province's trade sector performs quite well. It continues to register a trade surplus, albeit it fluctuates from time to time (Figure 6.16). In 2011, its export amount to US$16.48 billion, while its import was about US$11.06 billion, implying a trade surplus of around US$5.42 billion. In 2018, its trade surplus dropped to approximately US$1.29 billion, with its export of around US$13.28 billion and an import of US$11.99 billion. Then in 2019, its trade surplus increased to approximately US$2.4 billion. This is because while export fall to around US$12.6 billion, import has fallen even further to around US$10.2 billion (Figure 6.16).

Beyond investment and trade, the Riau Islands is an important tourist destination. Indeed, it has attracted an increasing number of foreign tourists every year. According to a BPS report, it is ranked second as Indonesia's most-visited destination for

FIGURE 6.15
Domestic Direct Investment in Select Provinces (IDR trillion)

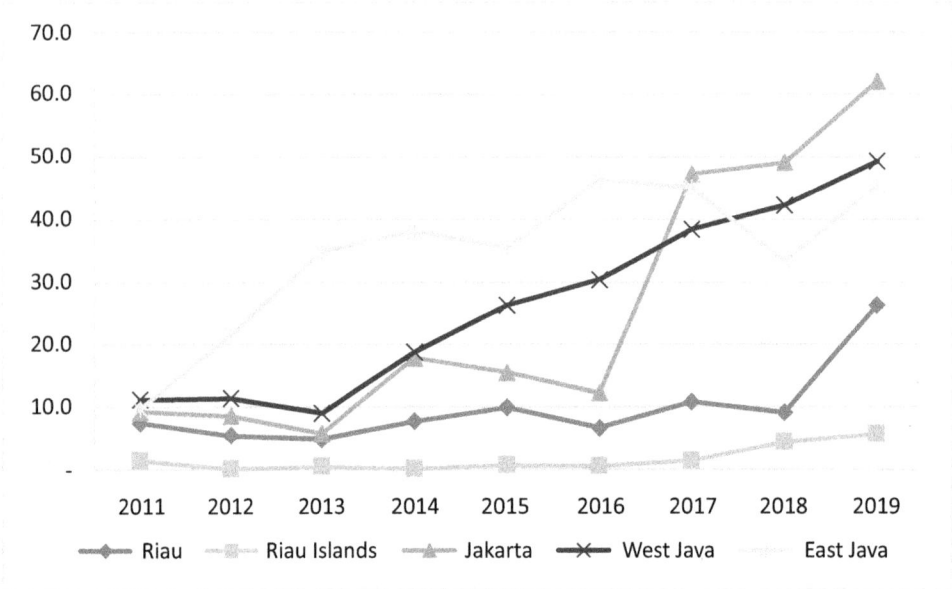

Source: BKPM, via CEIC.

FIGURE 6.16
Riau Islands Trade Performance (US$ million)

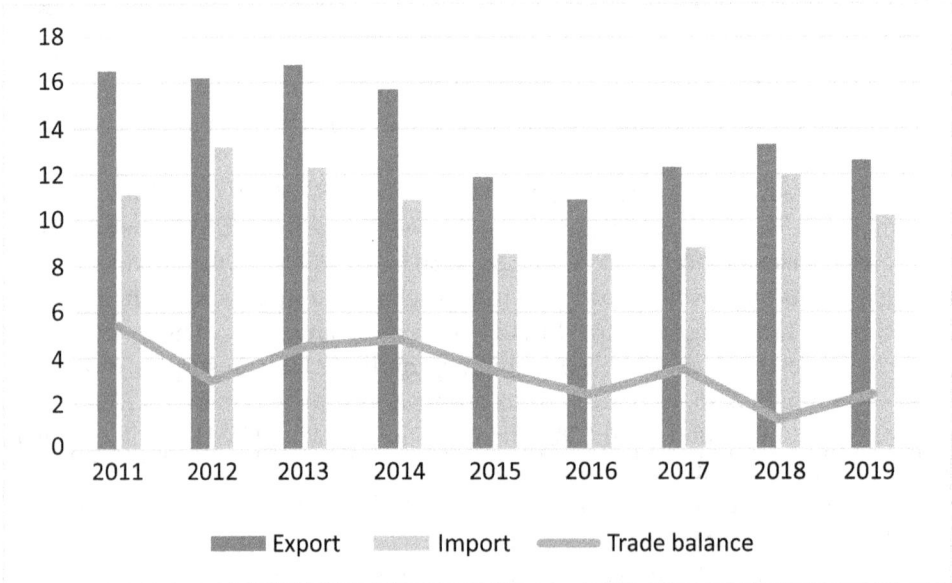

Note: 2019 figures are temporary figures. file:///C:/Users/User/Downloads/BRSbrsInd-20200115132605.pdf
Source: BPS Kepri 2020

foreign tourists after Bali (BPS Kepri 2020). These mostly consisted of visitors, from neighbouring Singapore and Malaysia (Muzwardi and Negara, this volume). In 2018 the number of foreign tourists visiting the Riau Islands was around 2.64 million, up from 1.72 million 2011 (BPS Kepri 2020; *Jakarta Post*, 16 January 2020).

Of the province's districts and municipalities, Batam occupies a prominent position, contributing around 60 per cent to the GRDP each year. Table 6.3 indicates how significant Batam's contribution is to the overall provincial output. This is not by chance, but rather is due to deliberate government policies implemented since 1970. Years of heavy infrastructure investment and strong political support from the central government have contributed to Batam's rapid growth. As a result, the city has developed from a small fishing village of 6,000 people in late 1960s to the mid-size city of over 1.3 million people currently (Hutchinson 2017).

Consequently, the province's economic development will continue to depend significantly on Batam's economic performance. In other words, the Riau Islands' future fortunes and misfortunes, to a large extent, will be directly attributable to those of Batam. In light of President Joko Widodo's policy to balance economic development between Java and outside Java, policymakers should use the same analogy for the Riau Islands Province. From a policy perspective, it is imperative to consider a suitable and innovative economic model for the Riau Islands' development.

IN SEARCH OF A NEW ECONOMIC MODEL

Since 2011 there has been active political lobbying from a group of island provinces (Maluku, North Maluku, West Nusa Tenggara, East Nusa Tenggara, Bangka Belitung, Riau Islands, North Sulawesi and Southeast Sulawesi) to push towards a stronger legal basis for them to govern their areas. A draft of the new bill concerning the management of archipelagic provinces was initiated by the national Parliament

TABLE 6.3
Batam's Contribution to the Riau Islands' Economy by Sector

	Contribution (%)
Electricity and Gas	89.4
Water Supply, Waste Management and Recycling	86.6
Manufacturing	*85.1*
Finance and Insurance	78.4
Information and Communication	71.8
Transportation and Warehouse	65.6
Accommodation and Food Beverage	64.9
Construction	63.9
Company Services	57.5
Real Estate	57.0
Other Services	50.3

Source: BPS Batam 2019 and BPS Kepri 2019, with authors' calculation.

(DPR) and was designed as an answer to the developmental policy bias experienced by archipelagic provinces.

At present, development policies implemented in archipelagic provinces are equated with those implemented on larger islands—even though they face very different logistical challenges. For provinces comprised of many small islands, high operational costs are required. However, the existing system of fiscal transfers from the central government to the provinces is calculated based on the size of their population. This fiscal structure is considered unfavourable to the eight island provinces as they have smaller, but more scattered populations and much higher logistical costs.

There are three main proposals in the draft bill concerning this group of provinces.

First, the expansion of these province's authority to manage marine natural resources from 0 to 12 miles from the coastline to the open sea, as measured from the outermost island under the authority of the province. Second, the provision of Special Allocation Fund (*Dana Alokasi Khusus*, or DAK) between 3 and 5 per cent of the national budget in addition to the general transfer funds (*Dana Alokasi Umum*, or DAU). This fund will support the development of the marine economic sector as well as infrastructure development in these provinces. Third, the synergy of the national policies in strategic areas, such as those concerning border management, sea and fisheries, and oil and gas sectors, should not undermine the interests of the archipelagic provinces. Many of the strategic policies in the above-mentioned areas are made in the absence of representatives from the archipelagic provinces.

The draft bill was first discussed in 2012, but was rejected by the Home Affairs Minister at that time, Gamawan Fauzi. This was because it was considered to potentially overlap with other laws (*Batamtoday.com*, 15 October 2012). Indeed, the draft law will affect several other existing laws and government regulations, including: Law No. 23 of 2014 which regulates the authority of the regional government, including those of the archipelagic provinces; Law No. 32 of 2014 concerning maritime affairs; Law No. 27 of 2007 concerning the management of coastal areas and small islands; and the Government Regulation No. 68 of 2014 concerning the arrangement of national defence areas.

While the demand for a new law concerning the archipelagic provinces has the support of parliament, however, the central government bureaucracy has a different viewpoint. The latter considers that a number of legislative items regarding the management of archipelagic provinces already exist. Indeed, these laws give privileges to the island provinces. For example, Law No. 23 of 2014 stated that these provinces are given special consideration in terms of the management of the marine resources in their respective jurisdictions. Therefore, there are no strong reasons for a new law. Rather, what is needed is to optimize the implementation of the existing regulations.

Notwithstanding, following Batam's remarkable development trajectory, one can see the importance of investment in infrastructure. The central government invested aggressively to provide basic infrastructure such as roads, ports, and power plants, in order to attract investment into the island. And, indeed, Batam has become a magnet for domestic and foreign investment (Damuri, Christian, and Atje 2015). If a similar strategy and political commitment are applied to the other islands in the province, this could help improve the Riau Islands' comparative advantage.

Looking at Batam's development model—whereby the central government was involved directly in managing and funding local economic development—one can argue that it is a thing of the past. It was made possible by the country's highly centralized government system which lasted until 1998. Following the end of the New Order in that year, and the introduction of the decentralization programme in 2001, district and municipal governments are given vastly more autonomy to administer their own economic, social and political affairs. This also minimizes intervention and control from the central government. On the one hand, the decentralized system allows more bottom-up aspirations to be accommodated by policymakers. On the other hand, it creates greater complications for balancing regional aspirations with the central government's agenda.

With regard to investment in infrastructure development such as road construction and maintenance, there is already a relatively clear division of labour between the central, provincial and local governments. A serious problem appears when it comes to the coordination of strategic infrastructure development—as national plans are not always in line or, even worse, are in conflict with the district governments' plans. A case in point is related to the plan to develop a bridge between Batam and Bintan (*Straits Times*, 12 July 2019). The 7-km bridge is estimated to cost as much as IDR4 trillion (US$265 million) and is expected to boost growth as well as trade with Singapore. The construction is set to start in 2020 and is scheduled to take three to four years to complete. With this bridge project, the central government wants to reposition Batam as an alternative shipping and manufacturing hub to Singapore with the potential to draw US$60 billion in new investment (*Straits Times*, 12 July 2019).

However, one may ask whether this bridge can also bring economic benefits to the other districts. For policymakers, the challenge is then to ensure that there will be economic spillovers from the investment, which is certainly not cheap, to the rest of the province. One relevant example is the Surabaya-Madura Bridge. Built in 2003 and fully operationalized in 2009, the bridge project did not create significant economic improvement for Madura, the lagging region. This indicates that infrastructure itself is not sufficient to accelerate growth in lagging regions, as this is dependent on the perception of investors. Thus, while infrastructure is important, it is also vital for policymakers to provide a conducive business climate and key assets such as a well-equipped labour force.

Batam's success story might be difficult to replicate, given that the political situation has changed especially after the 2001 decentralization reforms. In the current decentralized political system, the role of districts and municipal governments have become more influential in deciding development priorities for their respective regions. To balance regional development, the provincial government should play an active role to support infrastructure and human resource development in lagging areas.

In addition to Batam, two districts, namely Bintan and Karimun, as well as Tanjungpinang Municipality are also well placed to take advantage of their proximity to Singapore. Moreover, Bintan and Karimun are parts of the Batam-Bintan-Karimun Free Trade Zone (BBK FTZ), which was established in 2007. It is not immediately clear why Tanjungpinang, which is located on Bintan Island, was excluded from the BBK FTZ. But it, too, can benefit from its proximity to Singapore.

The same applies to Lingga District, which is located further south but is rather isolated and, hence, needs further opening up. Building access to the remote districts, like Lingga, Natuna and the Anambas Islands, should be the priority for current and future leaders of the province.

To be fair, the Indonesian government has been actively promoting the development of border areas as well as remote regions. Natuna and Anambas are Indonesia's outermost districts in the South China Sea. They are therefore eligible for obtaining the central government's special assistance for border regions as well as the Special Allocation Fund (*Dana Alokasi Khusus,* or DAK). The regional government, in turn, can use the funds to boost infrastructure development in their respective territories. Their location, which is in a conflicted area of the South China Sea, adds to the urgency to develop those remote districts. The government has been inviting several investors, from countries such as Japan and the US, to invest in Natuna (*Reuters* 2019). This is seen as a strategy to balance China's interest in exploring the oil and gas industry in the area (*Tempo.co* 2020).

This approach dovetails with national plans, as President Jokowi has reiterated his commitment to revitalize Indonesia's maritime potential. He has promised to resurrect the country's history as a maritime nation, in which development of its oceans, seas, straits, and bays are seen as a critical component of its identity (see Andaya in this volume).

CONCLUSION

While relatively a young province, however, the Riau Islands has performed relatively well compared to its "mother" province, Riau, in various socio-economic aspects. Some of the areas where the young province and the cities/regencies therein have generally excelled are in terms of subnational public sector performance, human development, and the poverty rate.

However, in terms of provincial competitiveness, Riau Islands faces a conflicted situation. On the one hand, its economy and quality of life have been improving. On the other hand, there is a lingering development imbalance between Batam and the other districts. Both the Riau Islands and Batam more specifically, are undergoing a transformation process where politically the local leaders and local Malay population are no longer keen on being dictated to by the central government (Amri and Rianto in this volume).

The foregoing discussion clearly shows that the Riau Islands' economy is too dependent on Batam's economy, particularly its manufacturing sector. Indeed, the manufacturing sector contributes around 37 per cent to the province's economy, of which Batam accounts for approximately 85 per cent (Table 6.3). Given this, the sustainability of Batam's manufacturing sector is important not only for its economy but for that of the province as a whole. The impressive development of the sector over the years has been due largely to its ability to attract foreign investment, especially from Singapore. The future of the sector, therefore, will depend on its ability to continue attracting FDI.

The province is blessed with plenty of natural resources, close access to the international community, and history of policy-induced industrial development in Batam, Bintan and Karimun. Nevertheless, to ensure its development sustainability, the Riau Islands Province must find a more innovative economic model to promote regional development, in particular in its remote districts.

What seems missing currently is policy synergy to tackle complex development challenges facing the archipelagic provinces. Particularly, the government and various stakeholders in the province should develop policy synergy in at least three areas, namely: fiscal, real, as well as the monetary and financial sectors. Concerning the fiscal aspect, two things need to be implemented, namely a productive and realistic budget followed by an effective budget execution. In the real sector, there must be policies to maintain and increase purchasing power and encourage investment. For this reason, fiscal incentives and economic policy packages are needed to promote investment climate in the province, thus boosting the performance of the real sector. Given that public finances are very limited, the government should encourage and make good use of private sector capital and expertise. Then in the monetary and financial fields, there must be monetary policies that support credit growth, especially for the SMEs and the digital economy, while maintaining financial sector stability.

Finally, as foreign investors are now more interested in capturing a larger share of the growing domestic market growing, it is important for the Riau Islands to also connect to the large domestic economy. The link can be through the manufacturing sector and/or agricultural as well as services sectors. Batam's economic prospects are certainly still promising. It will continue to play an important role in the province's economy. Investment, foreign as well as domestic, continues to trickle into the manufacturing sector, the mainstay of the island's economy. Nevertheless, in the future, flows of investment need to be diversified and spread out to locations across the province.

Notes

1. BPS has recently adopted a new methodology for measuring HDI, which is set out in the following link: https://www.bps.go.id/dynamictable/2020/02/17/1771/indeks-pembangunan-manusia-menurut-kabupaten-kota-metode-baru-2010-2019.html
2. Law 33 of 2004 concerning financial balance between the central and regional governments states that the revenue sharing fund (DBH) is sourced from the national budget (APBN) revenues that are collected from the regions and shared out based on certain percentages.

References

Antara Kepri. 2019. "Investasi Baru Masuk ke Batam Rp691 Miliar". 22 April 2019. https://kepri.antaranews.com/berita/56007/investasi-baru-masuk-ke-batam-rp691-miliar (accessed 25 July 2019).

Badan Pusat Statistik (BPS). *Statistik Industri Besar Sedang Manufaktur Indonesia 2011–2015.* Jakarta: BPS.

Badan Pusat Statistik (BPS) Batam. 2017. "Nilai Ekspor dan Impor Kota Batam 2014–2018". https://batamkota.bps.go.id/dynamictable/2017/10/03/25/nilai-ekspor-dan-impor-kota-batam-2014-2018.html (accessed 25 July 2019).

⸻. 2018. "Banyaknya Wisatawan Mancanegara (Jiwa) yang Datang Melalui Pintu Masuk Batam dan Pertumbuhannya (persen) 2010–2017". https://batamkota.bps.go.id/statictable/2018/11/07/69/banyaknya-wisman-jiwa-yang-datang-melalui-pintu-masuk-batam-dan-pertumbuhannya-persen-2010-2017.html (accessed 25 July 2019).

⸻. 2019. "Kota Batam Dalam Angka 2018".

⸻. "PDRB Kota Batam Atas Dasar Harga Konstan 2010 Menurut Lapangan Usaha 2010–2018". https://batamkota.bps.go.id/dynamictable/2017/07/05/9/pdrb-kota-batam-atas-dasar-harga-konstan-2010-menurut-lapangan-usaha-2010-2018.html (accessed 25 July 2019).

Badan Pusat Statistik (BPS) Kepri. 2016. "Potret Potensi Kelautan dan Perikanan Provinsi Kepulauan Riau". http://kepri.bps.go.id. (accessed 20 February 2020).

⸻. 2019. "Kepulauan Riau Dalam Angka Tahun 2018". Tanjungpinang, 2019. https://kepri.bps.go.id/publication/download.html?nrbvfeve=YmZmYjZmNTFhMDAyZjRkNGU0N2RkOTY2&xzmn=aHR0cHM6Ly9rZXByaS5icHMuZ28uaWQvcHVibGljYXRpb24vMjAxOS8wOC8xNi9iZmiNmY1MWEwMDJmNGQ0ZTQ3ZGQ5NjYvcHJvdmluc2kta2a2VwdWxhdWFuLXJpYXUtZGFsYW0tYW5na2EtMjAxOS5odG1s&twoadfnoarfeauf=MjAyMC0wMy0xNCAwODoxNTozOQ%3D%3D

⸻. 2019. "Nilai Export Menurut Bulan 2011–2020". https://kepri.bps.go.id/dynamictable/2019/03/15/362/nilai-ekspor-menurut-bulan-2019-us-.html (accessed 23 February 2020).

⸻. "Jumlah Wisatawan Mancanegara yang Datang (Jiwa) Per Bulan Tahun 2011-2019 https://kepri.bps.go.id/dynamictable/2019/03/03/358/jumlah-wisatawan-mancanegara-yang-datang-jiwa-per-bulan-tahun-2019.html

Batam Indonesia Free Zone Authority (BIFZA). 2019. *Development Progress of Batam 2018,* 2nd ed., vol. XXXIV.

Batamtoday.com. 2012. "Mendagri Tolak Bahas RUU Percepatan Pembangunan Daerah Kepulauan". 15 October 2012. https://batamtoday.com/home/read/20642/Mendagri-Tolak-Bahas-RUU-Percepatan-Pembangunan-Daerah-Kepulauan (accessed 23 March 2020).

Bisnis.com. 2017. "Pengembangan Hanggar, Lion Air Sudah Habiskan Rp600 Miliar". 12 October 2017. https://ekonomi.bisnis.com/read/20171012/98/698425/pengembangan-hanggar-lion-air-sudah-habiskan-rp600-miliar (accessed 25 July 2019).

BKPM. 2019. *Perkembangan Investasi Berdasarkan Kabupaten Kota per Sektor.* https://nswi.bkpm.go.id/data_statistik (accessed 25 July 2019).

Choi, Byung-il, and Changyong Rhee. 2014. *Future of Factory Asia.* Seoul: Korea Economic Research Institute.

Coordinating Ministry for Economic Affairs. 2019. *Kembangkan Pusat Perawatan Pesawat di Batam, Pemerintah Dorong Sinergi Ciptakan Ekosistem Industri Penerbangan Berkelanjutan.*

https://www.ekon.go.id/berita/print/kembangkan-pusat-perawatan.4952.html (accessed 16 August 2019).

Damuri, Yose Rizal, David Christian, and Raymond Atje. 2015. *Kawasan Ekonomi Khusus dan Strategis Indonesia: Tinjauan Atas Peluang dan Permasalahan*. Jakarta: Center for Strategic and International Studies.

Hutchinson, F.E. 2017. *Rowing Against the Tide? Batam's Economic Fortunes in Today's Indonesia*. Trends in Southeast Asia, no. 8/2017. Singapore: ISEAS – Yusof Ishak Institute.

————, and Leo van Grunsven. 2017. "Industry Dynamics in Growth Triangles: The E&E Industry in SIJORI 25 Years On". ISEAS Economics Working Paper No. 2017-09. Singaporea: ISEAS –Yusof Ishak Institute.

Jakarta Post. 2016. "BP Batam, Enerco Ink Deal on Rubber Oil Refinery". 20 September 2016 https://www.thejakartapost.com/seasia/2016/09/20/bp-batam-enerco-ink-deal-on-rubber-oil-refinery.html (accessed 25 July 2019).

————. 2020. "Riau Islands Province Ranks Second After Bali as Most-Visited Destination for Foreign Tourists". 16 January 2020. https://www.thejakartapost.com/travel/2020/01/16/riau-islands-province-ranks-second-after-bali-as-most-visited-destination-for-foreign-tourists.html (accessed 26 February 2020).

Karunia, Ade Miranti. 2020."Tahun Ini Pertamina Mulai Lakukan Pengeboran Minyak di Blok East Natuna" [This year, Pertamina Starts Drilling for Oil in the East Natuna Block]. *Kompas*, 9 January 2020. https://money.kompas.com/read/2020/01/09/155624826/tahun-ini-pertamina-mulai-lakukan-pengeboran-minyak-di-blok-east-natuna (accessed 23 March 2020).

Kompas. 2017. "Exxon Hengkang dari East Natuna, Pertamina Diuntungkan" [Exxon Outs from East Natuna, Pertamina Benefits]. 25 July 2017. https://ekonomi.kompas.com/read/2017/07/25/110425326/exxon-hengkang-dari-east-natuna-pertamina-diuntungkan?page=all (accessed 23 March 2020).

MRO-Network.com. 2015. "Indonesia Lacks Certified MROs Despite Large, Growing Market". 30 October 2015. https://www.mro-network.com/maintenance-repair-overhaul/indonesia-lacks-certified-mros-despite-large-growing-market (accessed 12 September 2019).

Negara, S.D., and F.E. Hutchinson. 2020. "Batam: Life after FTZ?". *Bulletin of Indonesia Economic Studies* 56, no. 1.

Peachey, K., M. Perry, and C. Grundy-Warr. 1998. *The Riau Islands and Economics Cooperation in the Singapore Indonesia Border Zone*. Durham: International Boundaries Research Unit.

Perkasa, Anugerah. 2016. "Laut Natuna Jadi Sumber Migas Asia" [Natuna Sea Is the Source of Asian Oil and Gas], *cnnIndonesia.com*, 23 June 2016. https://www.cnnindonesia.com/nasional/20160623134311-20-140387/laut-natuna-jadi-sumber-migas-asia (accessed 23 March 2020).

Reuters.com. 2020. "Indonesia Asks Japan to Invest in Islands Near Waters Disputed with China". 10 January 2020. https://www.reuters.com/article/us-indonesia-japan-southchinasea/indonesia-asks-japan-to-invest-in-islands-near-waters-disputed-with-china-idUSKBN1Z90IY. (accessed 13 March 2020).

Straits Times. 2019. "Bridge Linking Batam, Bintan in the Works". 12 July 2019. https://www.straitstimes.com/asia/se-asia/bridge-linking-batam-bintan-in-the-works (accessed 17 March 2020).

Tan Hwee. 2015. "New Normal Emerging in Offshore Marine". *Business Times*, 30 December 2015. https://www.businesstimes.com.sg/transport/review-outlook-2015/new-normal-emerging-in-offshore-marine (accessed 24 March 2020).

Tempo.co. 2020. "Diincar Cina, Natuna Simpan Cadangan Gas Bumi Terbesar". 6 January 2020. https://bisnis.tempo.co/read/1291637/diincar-cina-natuna-simpan-cadangan-gas-bumi-terbesar/full&view=ok (accessed 27 February 2020).

TribunBatam.id. 2020. "Kantor Perwakilan BI Kepri Akui PMDM Kepri Meningkat pada 2019". 2 January 2020. https://batam.tribunnews.com/2020/01/02/kantor-perwakilan-bi-kepri-akui-pmdn-kepri-meningkat-pada-2019 (accessed 10 March 2020).

Wicaksono, Pebrianto Eko. 2020. "Pemerintah Gencarkan Pencarian Minyak Bumi di Natuna" [The Government Intensified the Search for Petroleum in Natuna]. *Liputan6.com*. 7 January 2020. https://www.liputan6.com/bisnis/read/4150007/pemerintah-gencarkan-pencarian-minyak-bumi-di-natuna. (accessed 24 March 2020).

Wong P.K., and Ng K.K. 2009. *Batam, Bintan, and Karimun—Past History and Current Development towards Being A SEZ*. Singapore: Asia Competitiveness Institute, National University of Singapore.

II

Politics

STRAAT RIOU

onder directie van den

MET

Z. M. KORVET NEHALENNIA

BATTAM

BINTANG

GALLAT

Nota

MAP 3.1
STRAAT RIOUW 1840

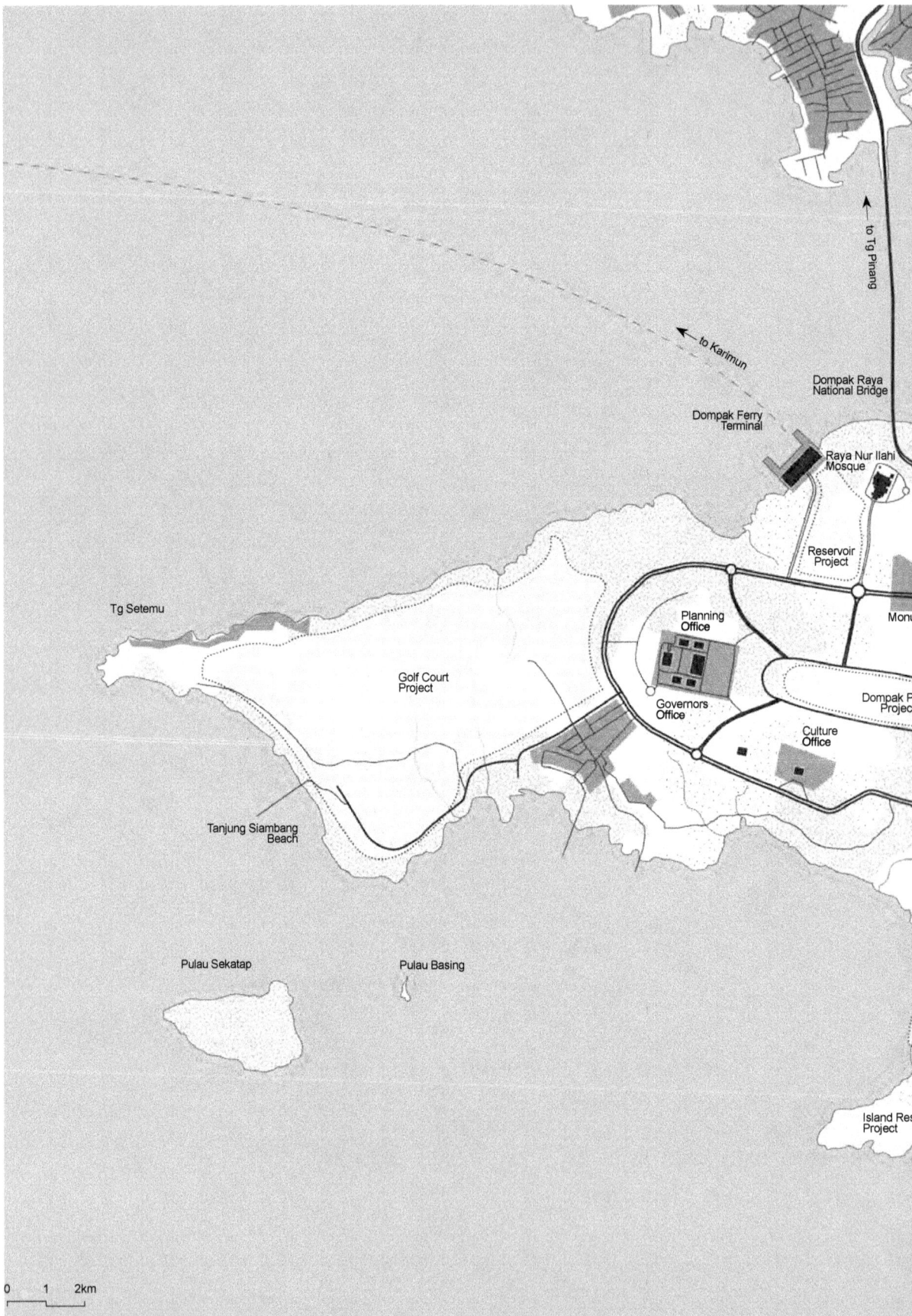

to Tg Pinang

to Karimun

Dompak Raya
National Bridge

Dompak Ferry
Terminal

Raya Nur Ilahi
Mosque

Reservoir
Project

Tg Setemu

Planning
Office

Monu

Golf Court
Project

Governors
Office

Dompak Pl
Project

Culture
Office

Tanjung Siambang
Beach

Pulau Sekatap

Pulau Basing

Island Reso
Project

0   1   2km

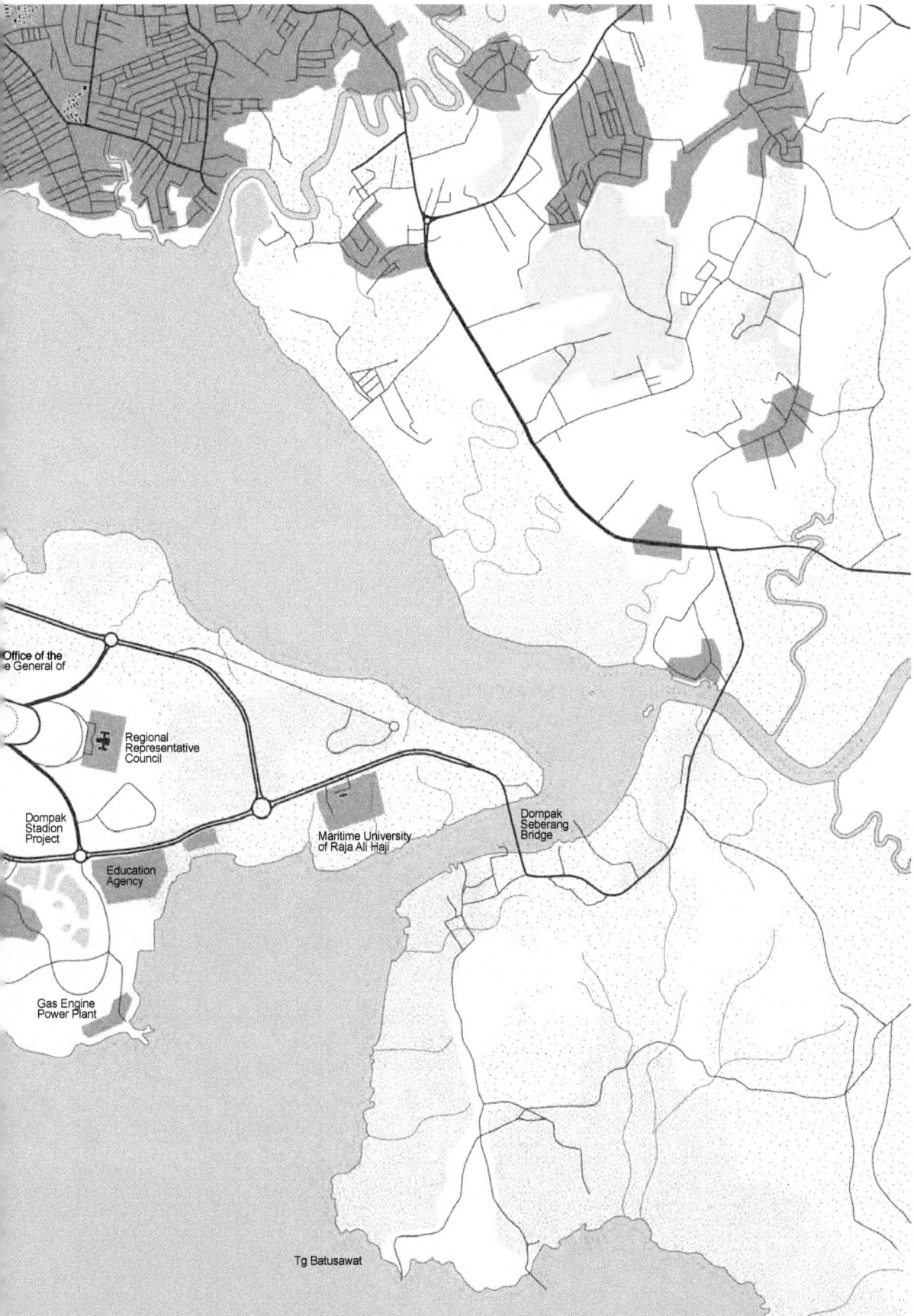

MAP 3.2
PULAU DOMPAK, CAPITAL OF RIAU
ISLANDS PROVINCE

Office of the
e General of

Regional
Representative
Council

Dompak
Stadion
Project

Education
Agency

Maritime University
of Raja Ali Haji

Dompak
Seberang
Bridge

Gas Engine
Power Plant

Tg Batusawat

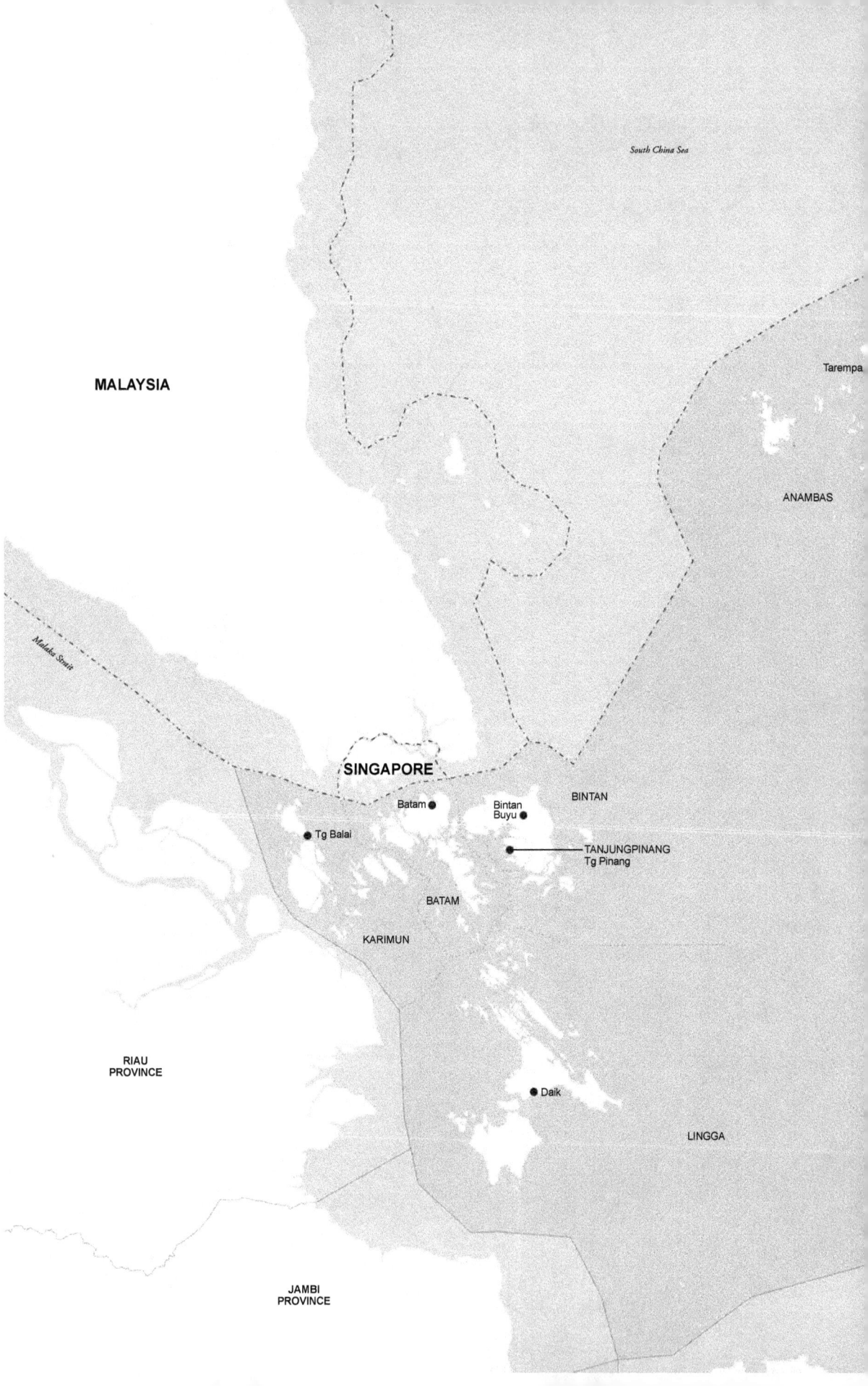

South China Sea

MALAYSIA

Tarempa

ANAMBAS

Malaka Strait

SINGAPORE

BINTAN

Batam ●

Bintan
Buyu ●

● Tg Balai

TANJUNGPINANG
Tg Pinang

BATAM

KARIMUN

RIAU
PROVINCE

● Daik

LINGGA

JAMBI
PROVINCE

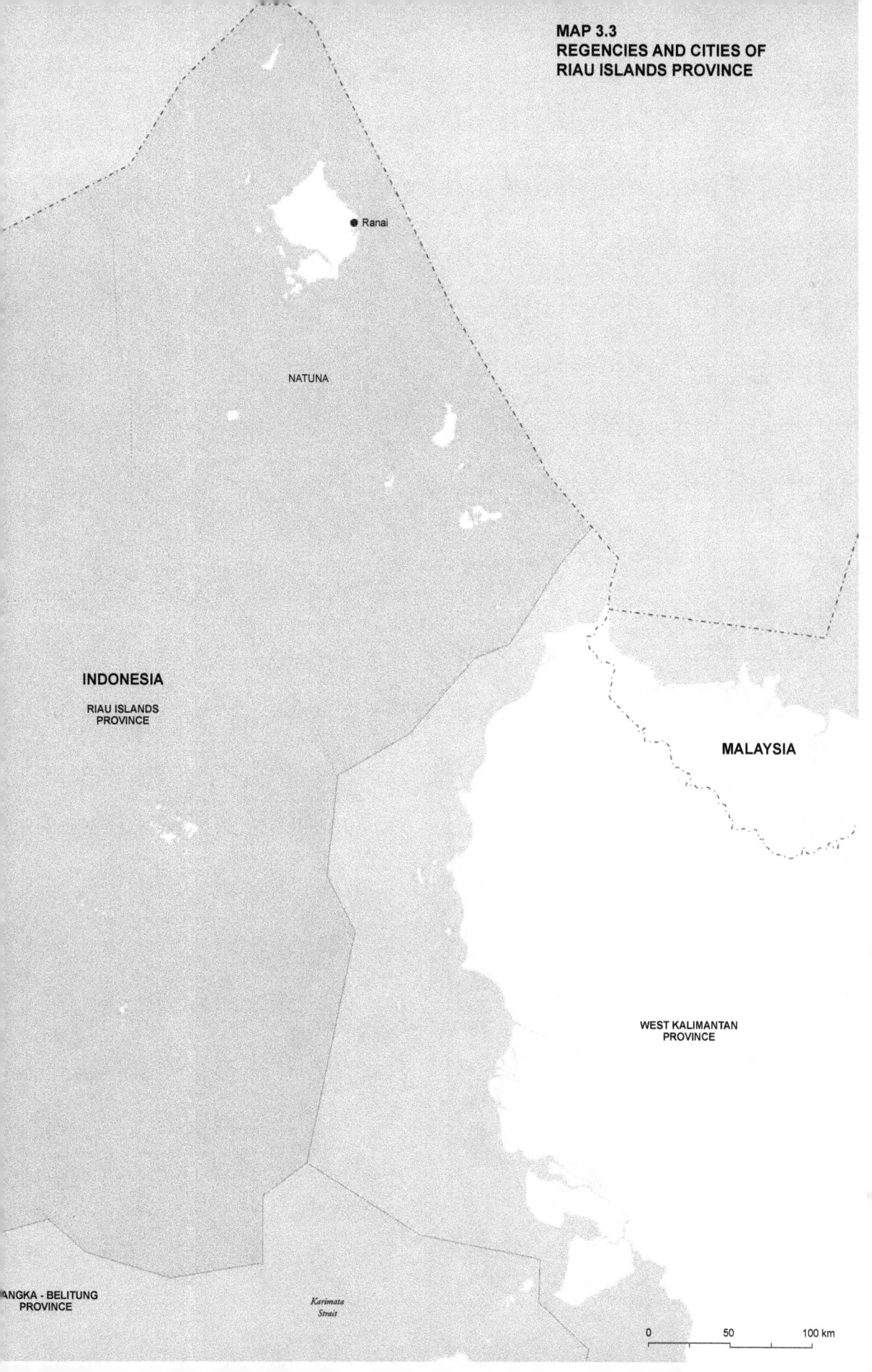

MAP 3.3
REGENCIES AND CITIES OF
RIAU ISLANDS PROVINCE

● Ranai

NATUNA

INDONESIA

RIAU ISLANDS
PROVINCE

MALAYSIA

WEST KALIMANTAN
PROVINCE

ANGKA - BELITUNG
PROVINCE

*Karimata
Strait*

0   50   100 km

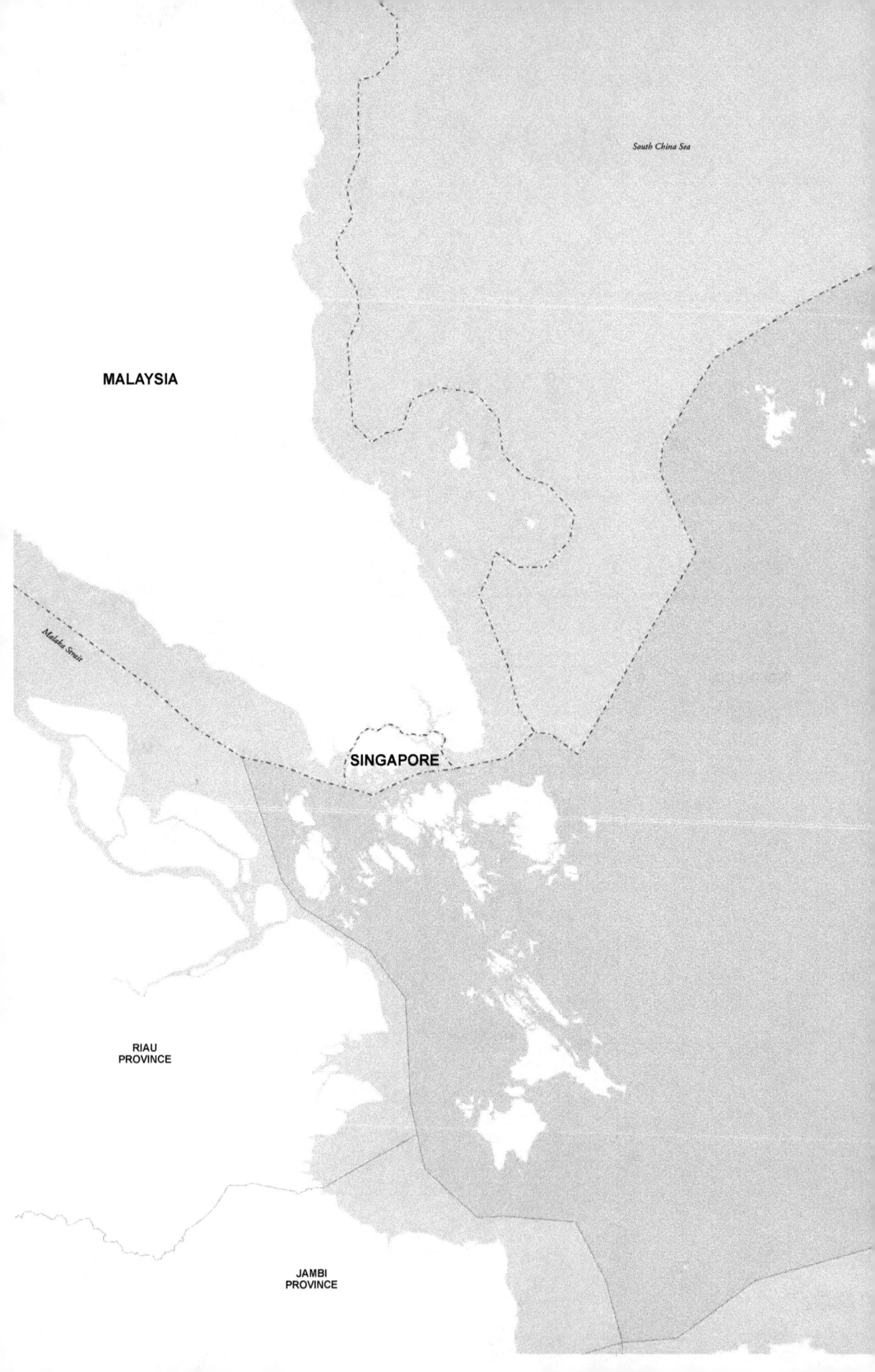

MALAYSIA

South China Sea

Malaka Strait

SINGAPORE

RIAU
PROVINCE

JAMBI
PROVINCE

Indonesian People's Representative Council
(Dewan Perwakilan Rakyat (DPR))
575 Parlamentarians
34 Provinces

■ 3 Parlamentarians
Riau Islands Province

INDONESIA

RIAU ISLANDS
PROVINCE

MALAYSIA

WEST KALIMANTAN
PROVINCE

NGKA - BELITUNG
PROVINCE

*Karimata
Strait*

0   50   100 km

South China Sea

MALAYSIA

Malaka Strait

ANAMBAS
(PPP)

SINGAPORE

BINTAN
(Demokrat)

TANJUNGPINANG
(PDIP)

BATAM
(PDIP)

KARIMUN
(Golkar)

RIAU
PROVINCE

LINGGA
(Nasdem)

JAMBI
PROVINCE

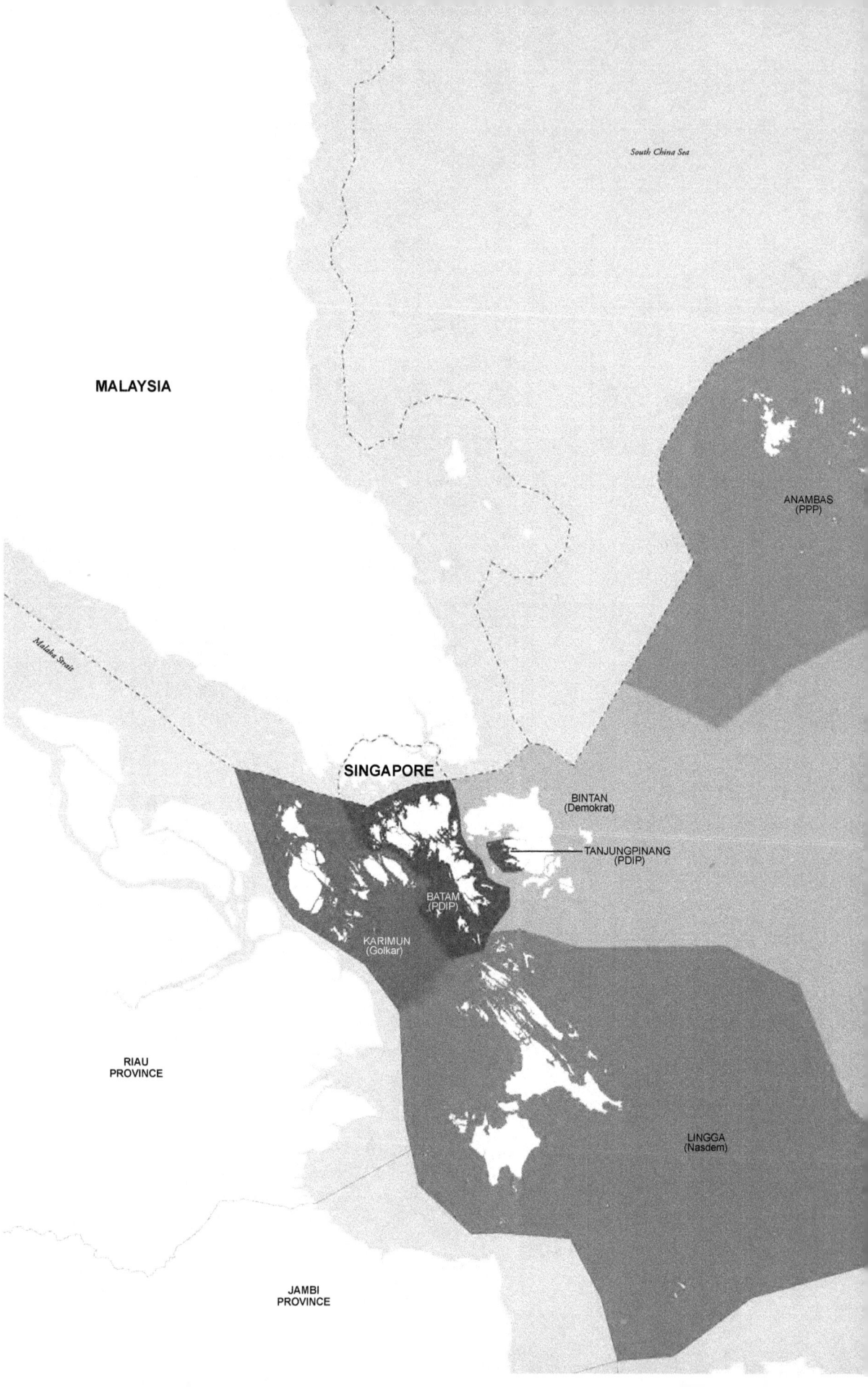

MAP 3.5
LEGISLATIVE ELECTIONS IN
RIAU ISLANDS PROVINCE, 2019

- PDIP
- Golkar
- Nasdem
- PPP
- PAN
- Demokrat

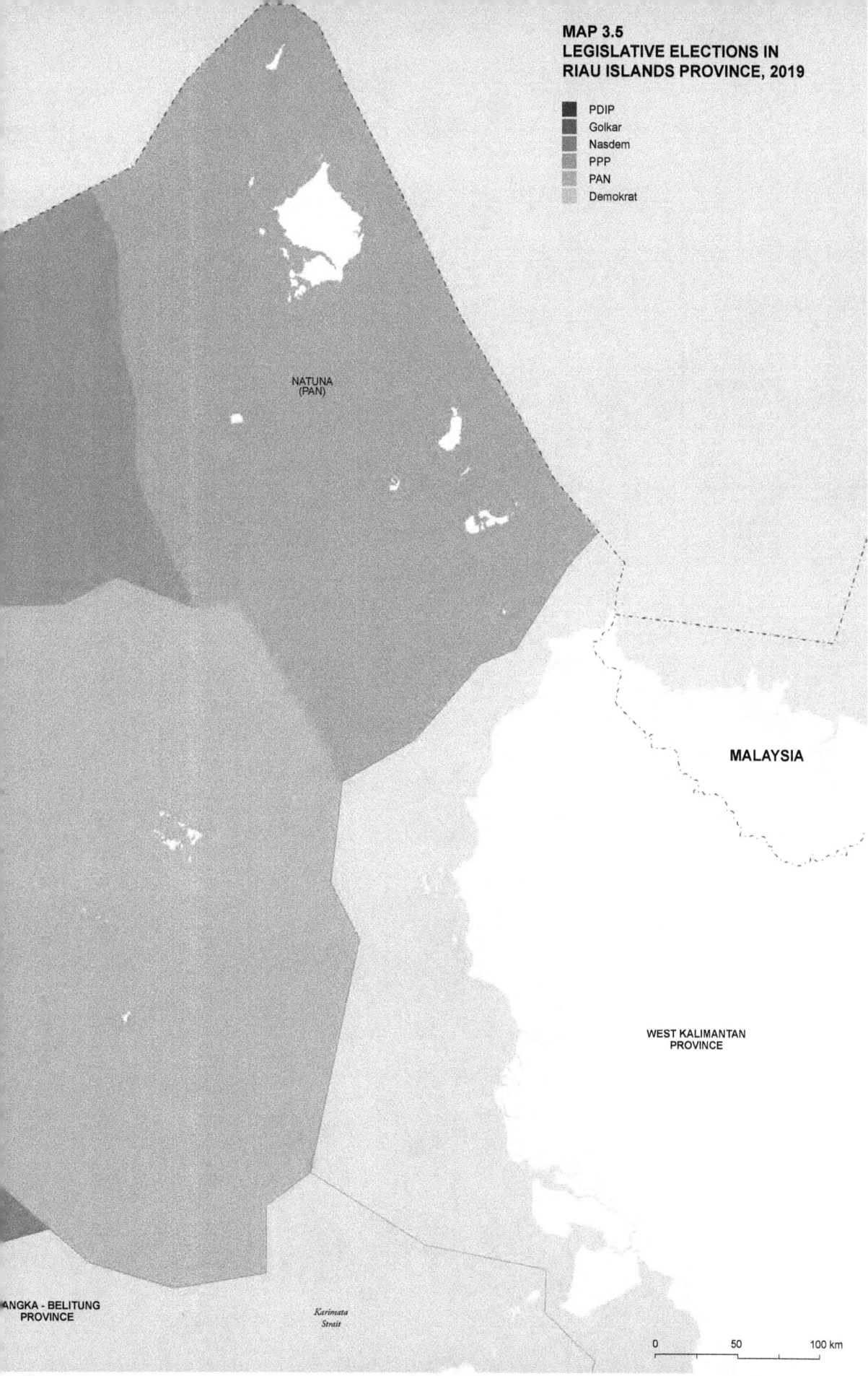

NATUNA
(PAN)

MALAYSIA

WEST KALIMANTAN
PROVINCE

BANGKA - BELITUNG
PROVINCE

Karimata
Strait

0   50   100 km

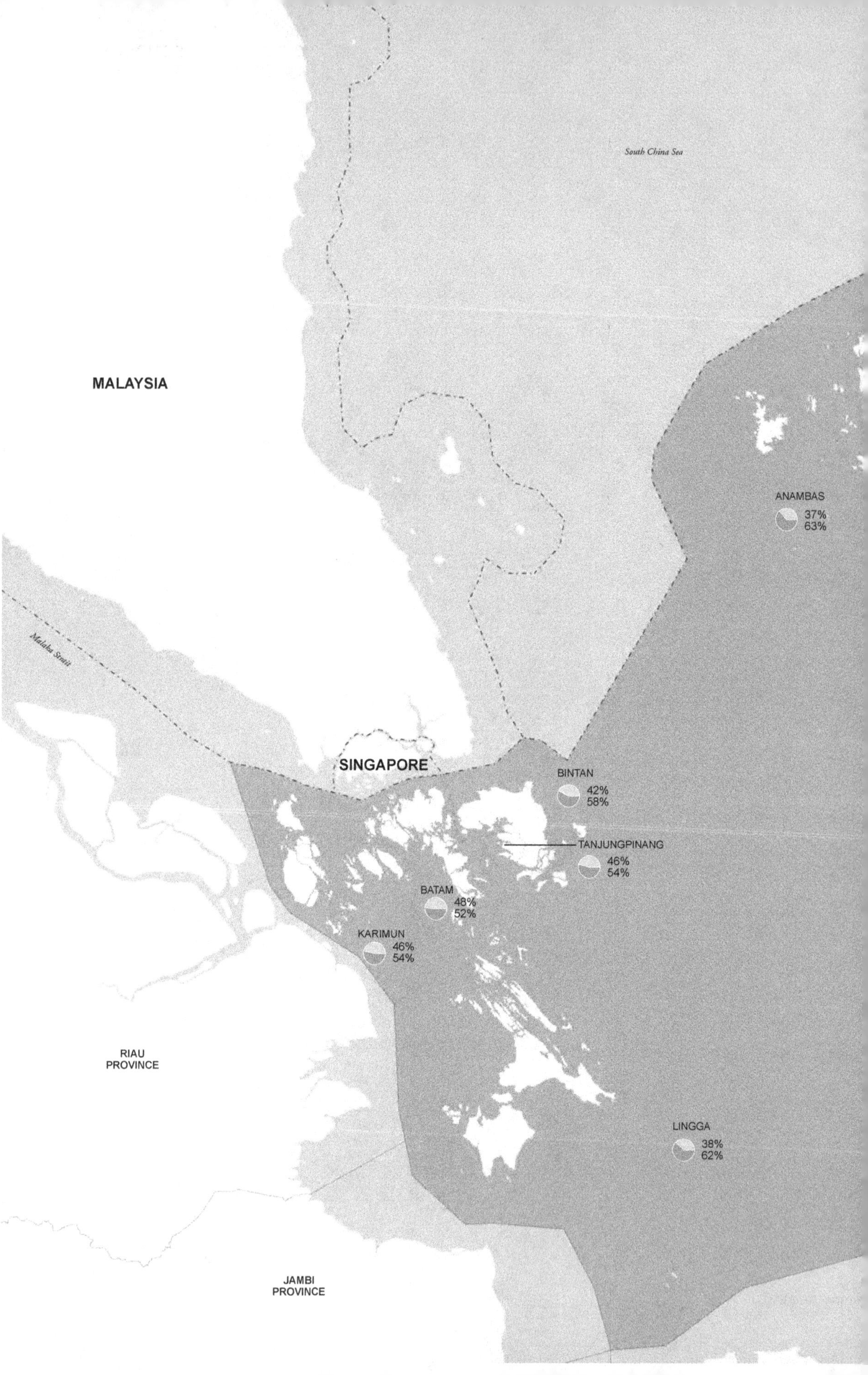

South China Sea

MALAYSIA

Malaka Strait

SINGAPORE

ANAMBAS
37%
63%

BINTAN
42%
58%

TANJUNGPINANG
46%
54%

BATAM
48%
52%

KARIMUN
46%
54%

RIAU
PROVINCE

LINGGA
38%
62%

JAMBI
PROVINCE

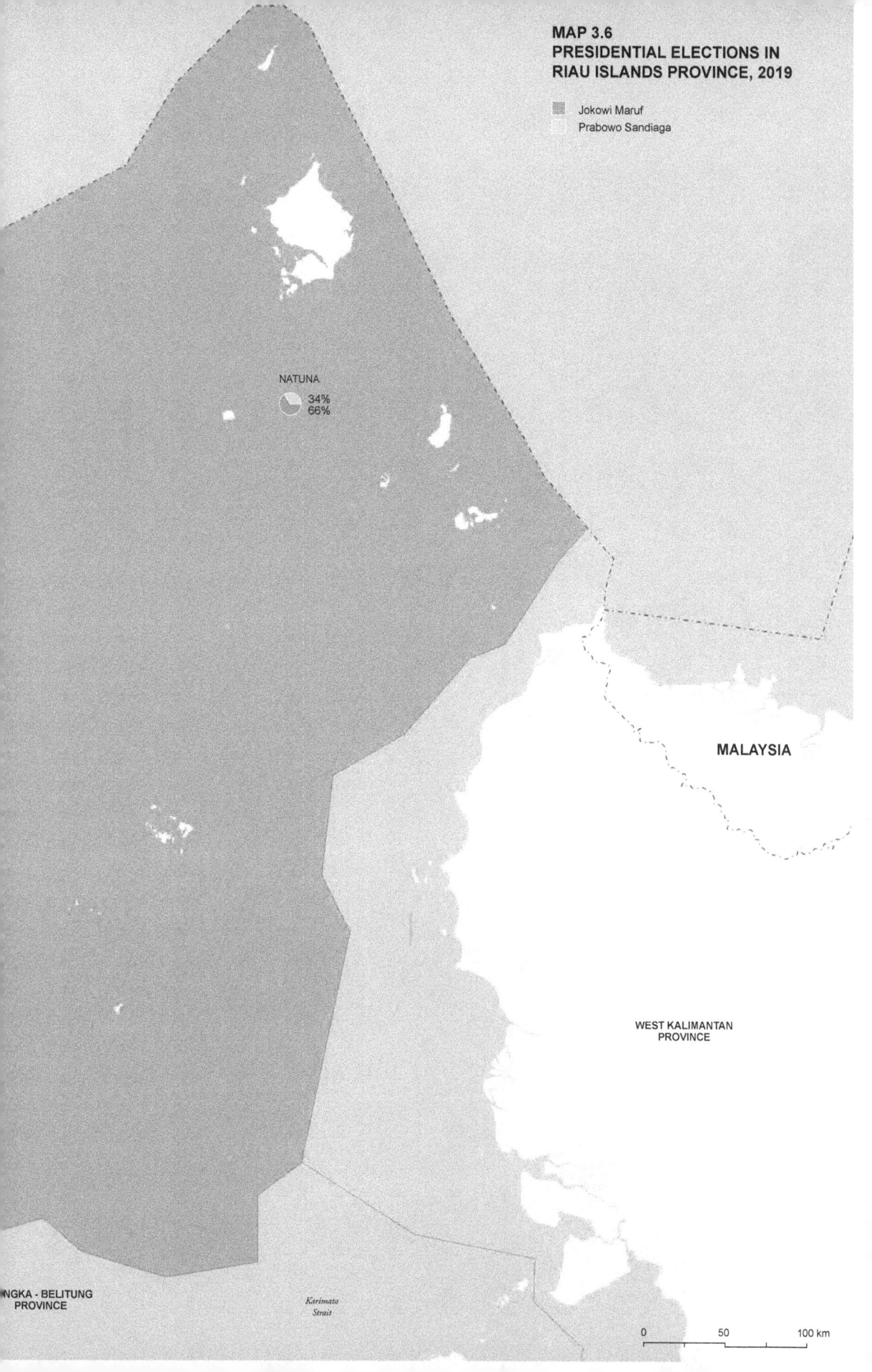

MAP 3.6
PRESIDENTIAL ELECTIONS IN
RIAU ISLANDS PROVINCE, 2019

Jokowi Maruf
Prabowo Sandiaga

NATUNA

34%
66%

MALAYSIA

WEST KALIMANTAN
PROVINCE

NGKA - BELITUNG
PROVINCE

*Karimata
Strait*

0   50   100 km

7

REVISITING KEPULAUAN RIAU
Shifting Relationships in a
Province of Islands

Barbara Watson Andaya

INTRODUCTION[1]

The winding path that led to the creation of Indonesia's modern province of Kepulauan Riau (Kepri) has deep historical roots, and the ramifications are still being played out. In 1997, more than twenty years ago, a collection of articles under the title of *Riau in Transition* was published in a special issue of the journal of the Royal Netherlands Institute of Southeast Asian and Caribbean Studies (Chou and Derks 1997). At that time Riau was the sixth largest of Indonesia's twenty-six provinces, extending from the foothills of Sumatra's Bukit Barisan to the Natuna islands in the South China Sea, with a land area covering 94,562 km² and a larger sea surface of around 235,000 km². It was further distinguished by its geographical separation. On the one hand was mainland Riau (*Riau daratan*) on the Sumatran side of the Melaka Straits, together with its offshore islands; on the other, insular Riau (*Riau kepulauan*), which included around 2,000 islands stretching from the Riau-Lingga archipelagos to the South China Sea. My contribution to this collection focused on the period from the sixteenth to the late twentieth century, giving particular attention to Riau-Johor, reconstituted after Melaka's conquest by the Portuguese in 1511, and its relationship with Malay areas along the east coast of Sumatra. Tracking the uneasiness that characterized the *daratan-kepulauan* association over nearly 500 years, I argued that despite the widespread perception of Riau as a Malay domain, the promotion of a sense of unity and commonality between mainland and island would be no easy task (Andaya 1997, p. 505). But when the final proofs went to press, there was no indication that the fall of the Soeharto regime and the subsequent demands for *reformasi* were around the corner. Nor could one then foresee the ripple effects of the regional autonomy law, which finally took effect in 2001, or that the rising tensions in the *daratan-kepulauan* marriage would reach such a point that divorce seemed the only solution. Under extreme pressure from island representatives, Jakarta eventually agreed to the creation of a new province of "island Riau". In 2002, only five years after *Riau in Transition* appeared, President Megawati Sukarnoputri signed the document that formally separated *kepulauan* Riau from the *daratan*. Despite some opposition, the new province was finally inaugurated in 2004.

This chapter revisits the history of Kepri in the light of developments over the last twenty years, taking as its departure point the Indonesian maxim that "the sea is the glue of the Indonesian archipelago" (*laut adalah perekat kepulauan Indonesia*) (Adhuri 2009, p. 134). Rarely questioned, this widely accepted assumption is open to debate when we consider the recent history of Kepulauan Riau. Even at the national level, where the connections between land (*tanah*) and water (*air*) have provided the terminology for "our homeland" (*tanah air kita*) so entrenched in nationalist rhetoric, the seas have only recently moved to the forefront of the government's agenda. In his inaugural address in 2014, President Joko Widodo was forthright: "We've turned our back on the seas, oceans, straits and bays for far too long. It is time for us to realize '*jalesveva jayamahe*' (in the ocean we triumph), a motto upheld by our ancestors in the past." Comparing himself to the captain of a ship only now unfurling its sails, he stressed that "oceans, seas, straits and bays are the future of our civilization" and urged all fellow-citizens to join him in resurrecting Indonesia's history as a maritime nation (*Jakarta Globe* 2014).

Nevertheless, ambitious plans to build an integrated marine system (*tol laut*) that will connect all Indonesia have faced major difficulties, many of which are due to poor coordination and inadequate consultation with local administrations (Wicaksana 2017). Communities whose livelihood depends on the ocean are still among the poorest in Indonesia, but they also face high costs of living because of the expense of inter-island shipping. Disappointment at the lack of progress have been expressed most keenly by Indonesia's eight archipelago provinces, where boundaries have been delimited by lines drawn across the sea bed rather than by visually evident markers (such as a "welcome to" entrance arch) and where many islands are only loosely connected to any administrative centre. Kepri has itself faced challenges from neighbouring provinces, most notably Jambi's long-standing claims to Pulau Berhala. In this case a compromise agreement in 2017 provided for Jambi-Kepri cooperation in developing tourism and the fishing industry, but elsewhere unresolved disputes between provinces regarding sea boundaries often surface (*Tribun Jambi* 2017; Adhuri 2009). In problematizing the notion of the sea as Indonesia's glue, this chapter argues that addressing political, social and economic inequities is more demanding for archipelagic provinces than for those joined by land, and that Kepri provides a revealing example of these inequities.

In setting the context, the first section discusses the role of the sea in the formation of Indonesia and the particular position of Kepri, where sections of the provincial maritime boundaries are national boundaries as well. The second considers the relationship between land and water in Kepri's predecessor, the kingdom of Johor-Riau, and how this relationship changed under the Dutch-controlled regency of "Riau and its dependencies". The third part reviews the creation of Kepri in 2004 in the light of post-1997 research, and the final section turns to the contemporary issues facing this archipelagic province where 96 per cent of its extensive surface area is water. Notwithstanding the historical connections between the Kepri heartland in the Riau-Lingga archipelagos and the many islands of the South China Sea, the realities of distance, economic disparities and cultural diversity pose a significant challenge for provincial cohesion. Despite calls for unity, these challenges will persist unless greater resources are invested to make Jakarta's promises of policies that will benefit all of Kepri's people a reality (Marsetio et al. 2017).

THE NATION, THE PROVINCE AND TERRITORIAL SEAS

The concept of a unity based on land-sea linkages was central to Indonesia's battle to obtain international acceptance as an archipelagic state. Although this principle was first articulated in 1957, the road towards recognition took many years because it involved a fundamental rethinking of existing maritime conventions. Butcher and Elson (2017) have tracked a historical narrative that stretches back into the nineteenth century, detailing the various measures taken to safeguard Dutch rights over the waters of the Netherlands Indies. However, a major step came in 1935 when the colonial government, fearing that Japanese fishing vessels were being used to gather military intelligence, clarified its definition of the Netherlands Indies "sea territory". While recognizing international rights of passage, Article 1 of the "territorial sea and maritime districts ordinance" (*territoriale zee en maritieme kringen ordonnantie*) stated that Dutch sovereignty extended 3 nautical miles from the low water line of islands or "parts of islands". The latter was interpreted to include rocks or reefs that were dry at low tide and were not more than 3 miles from any island belonging to the Netherlands Indies (Butcher 2009, p. 32; Butcher and Elson 2017, p. 36). In 1939, just before the outbreak of World War II, these provisions were reaffirmed in a second "territorial sea ordinance", which restricted the movement of foreign vessels (i.e., Japanese) within the colony's maritime territory but left Article 1 and the idea of "high seas" intact. This meant that the waters between the islands making up the Netherlands Indies continued to be open to international traffic (Syatauw 1961, pp. 170–72; Butcher 2009, p. 33; Butcher and Elson 2017, p. 41).

Inheriting this Ordinance, the government of the newly independent Indonesia could not legally object in 1957 when Dutch warships sailed through the Java Sea to what was then Dutch New Guinea. In December of that year Jakarta therefore took a radical step by unilaterally proclaiming sovereignty over "the water territory of the Republic of Indonesia". In clear and unequivocal language, the Djuanda Declaration (named for the then prime minister, Djuanda Kartawidjaja) stated that Indonesia was a unique "archipelagic state" composed of thousands of islands that "must be regarded as one total unit, regardless of the dimension or width of the waters connecting islands" (Butcher and Elson 2017, p. 73). The outcry from the world's maritime nations was immediate. The proposal to enclose the entire Indonesian archipelago though straight baselines connecting "the outermost points on the low water mark of the outermost islands" was regarded as a violation of international maritime law and even condemned as "the new piracy" (Butcher 2009, p. 41).

Indonesia, however, stood firm. Maintaining its stand that archipelagic states merited special consideration, the provisions of the Djuanda Declaration were legally enshrined in Act No. 4, "Concerning Indonesian Waters" (*Tentang Perairan Indonesia*), promulgated in February 1960. In revoking key provisions of the 1939 Ordinance, this Act formally stated that the Dutch application of maritime law had divided Indonesia into separate parts, with each island or group of islands having its own territorial sea (*karena membagi wilayah daratan Indonesia dalam bagian-bagian terpisah dengan terriorialnya sendiri*) (*Geographer* 1971, p. 2). Indonesia would now apply the concept of straight baselines as formulated in 1957. The width of the territorial sea would be extended from 3 to 12 nautical miles, encircling the entire archipelago and encompassing all the sea between its islands. Indonesia's maritime borders thus expanded to include an additional 254,000 km^2, so that the seas now made up around 56 per cent of the country's total area of 3,500,000 km^2 (Butcher and Elson 2017, pp. 112–13). To illustrate this new cartography, Indonesia presented the international community with a map showing for the first time the straight baselines that would nearly double the country's territorial size (Butcher 2009, pp. 41–42; see Figure 7.1).

This delineation of Indonesia's maritime borders, incorporating much of the South China Sea and the Java Sea, despite their previous status as international waters, was predictably greeted with further diplomatic protests. Eleven years later the American Bureau of Intelligence and Research remained adamant. "The Republic of Indonesia has established straight baselines based upon the so-called archipelago theory which is not recognized in international law." As a result, said the Bureau, "extensive areas" had been enclosed as "internal seas", overlapping with "many important straits of the region" (*Geographer* 1971, p. 2). For men like Malta's Ambassador Arvid Pardo, a passionate believer in the seas as the "common heritage of mankind", the Indonesian case was particularly disturbing. In 1973, contending that "archipelagos" were being arbitrarily created, he argued that Anambas and Natuna were "hundreds" of miles from the main Indonesian islands and could hardly be considered part of an archipelagic state. In a sharp response, the Indonesian delegation pointed out that these two island groups were only about 80 miles from Borneo, that in these waters there were many other Indonesian islands, and that in any event both the Anambas and Natuna groups were larger than Malta (Butcher and Elson 2017, pp. 112, 216).

International fears, however, were not laid to rest. There was as yet no general agreement regarding the construction of straight baselines in an archipelagic state, the status of waters inside those baselines and the treatment of foreign ships passing

FIGURE 7.1
Indonesian Waters According to Law No. 4 of 1960

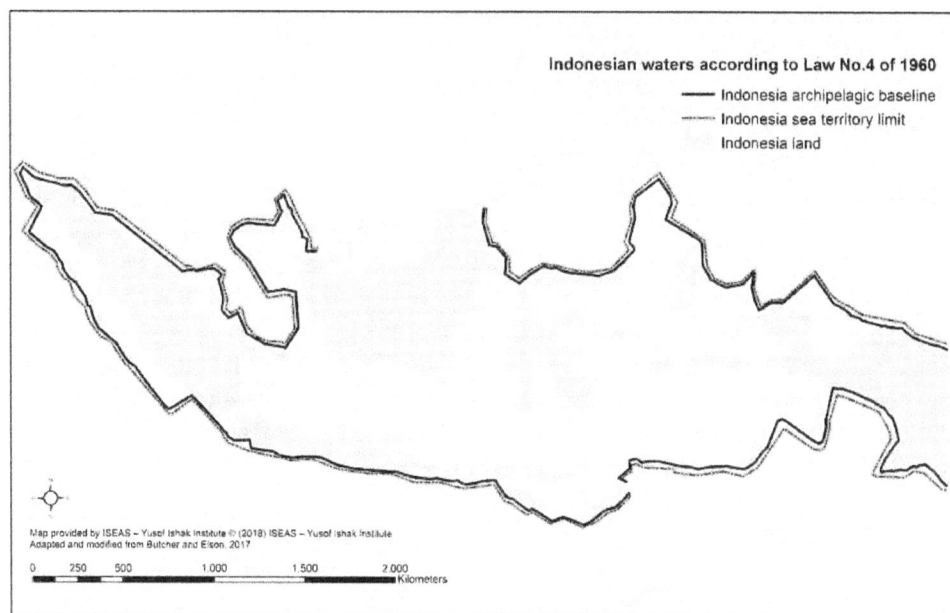

through such waters (Butcher and Elson 2017, p. 154). For several years these problems dominated the meetings of the United Nations' "Seabed Committee". It was not until December 1982, with the signing of the United Nations Convention of the Law of the Sea, that the position Indonesian had taken twenty-five years earlier was for the most part confirmed. Invoking the idea of *tanah air* and the idealized Djuanda vision of seas that had connected Indonesians as a people "since time immemorial", the Foreign Minister Mochtar Kusumaatmadja acclaimed the country's success in returning the waters between the islands "to their traditional unifying role" (Butcher and Elson 2017, p. 417; Rajan 1986, p. 141).

To this point there had been no serious discussion within Indonesia about the position of archipelagic provinces within an archipelagic state, although references to Riau sometimes surfaced in international meetings because sections of its maritime borders were also national borders (Arsana and Schofield 2013, p. 62). In 1960, Jakarta had been particularly sensitive to objections from Singapore and Malaya and therefore drew the baselines between the Malay Peninsula and Borneo so that the Natuna, Anambas and Tambelan groups were enclosed but much of the intervening waters were still left as high seas. Contentious issues such as fishing rights for Malaysian fishermen and Malaysian access to airspace above Indonesia's archipelagic waters were resolved in 1982, when Indonesia agreed to respect Malaysia's "existing rights and other legitimate interests". In subsequent years Indonesia sought to address the thorny issue of international rights of passage by designating three archipelagic north-south sea lanes, one of which passed through Riau waters in the South China

Sea. Though regarded by the International Maritime Organization as a "partial designation" because of the absence of an east-west passage through the Java Sea, Indonesia officially adopted these sea lanes in June 2002 (Djalil 2009).

During the 1970s, other disputes had developed with Vietnam, which believed its claims to the Spratly Islands were challenged by Indonesia's oil and gas exploration in the seas off Natuna. The potential for confrontation increased in March 1980, when Indonesia followed the example of several other coastal states and declared rights over an Exclusive Economic Zone (EEZ) that extended 200 nautical miles from the straight baselines of its territorial sea. Almost immediately Indonesia responded to Vietnamese objections by launching a large-scale military exercise in the Natuna area. The following year 350 Javanese families were relocated to the Natuna Islands as a "security belt", to be joined between 1982 and 1984 by another thousand families (Suryadinata and Izzudin 2017, p. 11; Tirtosudarmo 1990, p. 195). Over the next decade, however, tensions subsided and by 1996 the government was sufficiently confident to refer to the "Natuna Sea". In 2003 Vietnam accepted Indonesia's mapping of the seabed boundaries around Natuna, while Jakarta reaffirmed that it had no interest in the Spratly Islands (Suryadinata and Izzudin 2017, p. 12).

Despite settlements with Vietnam, Kepri's northern boundary continued to be a source of disputes because Indonesia's EEZ to the north of the Natunas overlaps with the "nine dash line" that has been used to justify Chinese claims in the South China Sea, but which Indonesia does not recognize (Arsana and Schofield 2013; Suryadinata and Izzudin 2017). In September 1996, in a show of defiance, *Indonesia's* military mounted an impressive demonstration of force in the Natuna region that involved nearly 20,000 troops, 40 aircraft and 50 naval vessels (Suryadinata and Izzudin 2017, pp. 11–14). Though relations with China subsequently improved, old antagonisms nonetheless resurfaced, leading President Jokowi to visit Natuna in June 2016. A year later, following repeated clashes between Chinese trawlers and patrol boats dispatched by the Indonesian Ministry of Maritime Affairs and Fisheries, Jakarta announced that the waters northeast of the Natuna Islands, which came under their claimed EEZ, would be renamed the "North Natuna Sea" (Laut Natuna Utara; see Figure 7.2). Regardless of vehement Chinese objections and a recurrence of tensions in 2019–20, Indonesia has not retracted its claim, which has been supported by the United States and Japan (Hunt 2016; Allard and Munthe 2017).

By contrast, the cross-border cooperation which underscores the economic links between Singapore, Malaysia and the main Kepri islands of Bintan, Batam and Karimun, has been largely successful (Hutchinson and Chong 2016; Simandjuntak 2018, p. 2). First conceptualized as SIJORI in 1989, this complex was re-envisaged and renamed the Indonesia-Malaysia-Singapore Growth Triangle in 1994. Here the maritime environment has in many ways fulfilled its anticipated role of reconnecting the Riau archipelago with Singapore and southern Malaysia. Singapore has invested heavily in Batam and Bintan, which are both favoured weekend destinations for Singaporeans, adding another dimension to the long-standing Chinese business network. Across the straits the crowds of Indonesians disembarking from ferries at Harbour Front attest the attraction of Singapore's urban modernity, and the close

FIGURE 7.2
Indonesia's North Natuna Sea

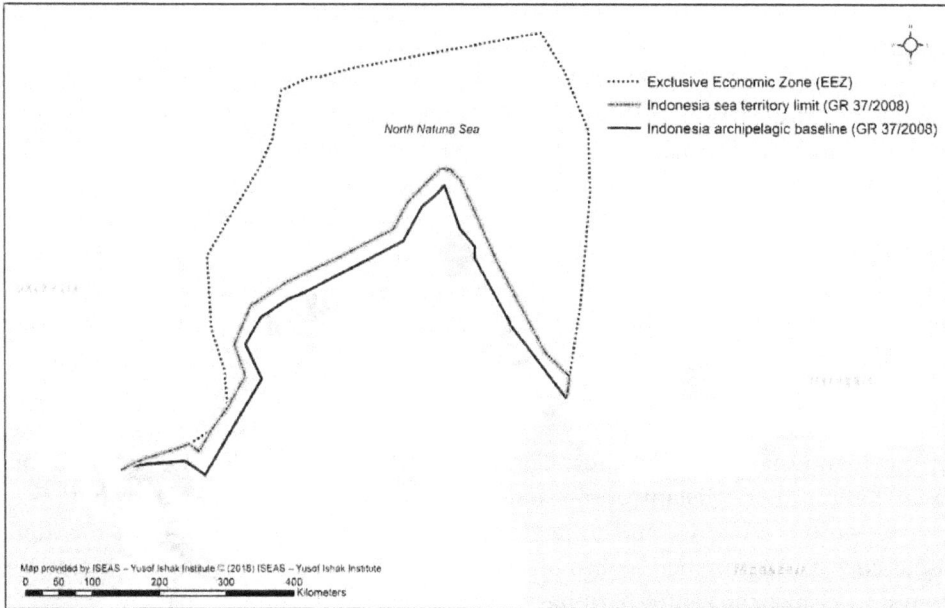

links between family and friends. It is worth noting that the wife of Kepri's former governor, Nurdin Basirun, is herself Singaporean. Yet ambivalences remain, since both local residents and recent migrants who have come to Batam in the hopes of obtaining lucrative work in Singapore or Malaysia often lack the documentation necessary to comply with immigration requirements. For such individuals, the seas serve as a telling reminder of frustrated dreams and of the boundary between lifestyles that the transnational cooperation between Singapore, Indonesia and Malaysia was touted to overcome (Ford and Lyons 2009, pp. 224–25; Lindquist 2009, pp. 2, 123–37; Long 2013, pp. 198–204; Lyons and Ford 2013, pp. 124–27).

Because Natuna is regarded as a "frontline island" (*pulau garis depan*) in Indonesia's relations with surrounding countries and because the Batam-Bintan-Karimun area is central to the "growth triangle" vision, Kepri leaders have some leverage in Jakarta. Indeed, Governor Nurdin specifically invoked Kepri's status as a province that "borders foreign countries" as a justification for increased funding. As the islands of the South China Sea assume greater importance in the wake of Jokowi's emphasis on maritime development, new questions have been raised about the special needs of Indonesia's eight archipelagic provinces, where the connecting seas comprise more than 75 per cent of their total size. Of these Kepri is the largest (96 per cent water), followed by Maluku (93 per cent), North Maluku (91 per cent), East Nusa Tenggara (88 per cent), West Nusa Tenggara (85 per cent), North Sulawesi (79 per cent), Bangka-Belitung (76 per cent) and Southeast Sulawesi (74 per cent). The unresolved problems faced by these provinces have shown all too clearly that the sea does not necessarily serve as the unifying ideal lauded by Mochtar Kusumaatmadja in 1982. Differences in ethnicity and culture, and the limitations on inter-island movement, mean that for most Indonesians the idea that water unifies provinces as well as the country itself remains "a process in the making rather than a statement of fact" (Ford and Lyons 2009, p. 222). Despite the implied parity of the *tanah-air* equation, archipelagic provinces must face the hard fact that landed enterprises associated with modernity and progress—plantations, mines, factories, shopping malls—have overwhelmed the sea in the national *imaginaire*.

Scholarly research since the publication of *Riau in Transition* has provided many nuanced accounts of the changes Kepri has experienced over the last twenty years. It is no longer neglected by Indonesian specialists, as was the case in 1997 (Chou and Derks 1997, p. 474). Yet this research has not been evenly distributed; analyses of Kepri's economy have focused on the core of the Indonesia-Malaysia-Singapore Growth Triangle, with an occasional nod towards the oil and gas of Natuna, and anthropological studies of identity and transborder mobility similarly concentrate on the Riau-Lingga archipelagos. The comparative lack of detailed information about Kepri's more distant possessions has been highlighted as the Natuna Sea assumes greater economic and strategic importance and as more voices are raised in discussions about provincial cohesion. Yet the islands of the South China Sea deserve attention because the centre-periphery tensions that contributed to national policies of decentralization and demands for greater autonomy are currently being played out at the local level. In this sense Kepri stands as an informative case study, for in February 2017 the Natuna and Anambas governments announced their intention of breaking away from Kepulauan Riau to form a separate province. The continuing restlessness at Kepri's margins sounds a warning call that al Azhar's contribution to *Riau in Transition* foresaw even before the new province came into being (Simandjuntak 2017b; Al Azhar 1997, p. 765).

RETHINKING SEA CONNECTIONS IN AN ARCHIPELAGIC PROVINCE

The current borders of Kepri are derived from Dutch maps that were based on precolonial ideas of maritime suzerainty when the sea was a key factor in linking outlying areas to the centre. The islands between the Malay Peninsula and Borneo, later regarded as "remote" and "neglected" were specifically identified by early Chinese and European cartographers because they were located on the sea route between China and the Melaka Straits.

Functioning as landmarks for navigators, these islands were also stapling points that provided good timber for broken masts and spars as well as access to fresh water. According to Malay texts, the most important island groups—Tambelan, Siantan, Jemaja, Bunguran, Serasan, Subi and Pulau Laut—had once been under the authority of the Javanese kingdom of Majapahit, but had been gifted to the Malay kingdom of Melaka in perpetuity (Jones 1997, pp. 130, 142; S. Ahmad 1979, p. 120; K. Ahmad 1975, p. 242; L. Andaya 2008, p. 186). The Portuguese captured Melaka in 1511, but the refugee dynasty, moving between the Johor River and the Riau Archipelago, continued to claim suzerainty over these distant domains. Connections became closer from the late seventeenth century as the settlement of Riau on the island of Bintan developed into a regional entrepôt, attracting shipping from Europe, China, India and the region more generally. In 1687, a Dutch envoy estimated that between 500 and 600 ships were anchored in the Riau River, specifically mentioning those from Johor-Riau's dependencies to the east—Jemaja, Siantan, Bunguran, Pulau Laut, Subi, Serasan and Tambelan—which came to be known as the "Pulau Tujuh", the seven islands (L. Andaya 1975, pp. 148–49) (see Figure 7.3).

These islands, like those in the Riau-Lingga archipelago, were primarily the domain of the sea peoples, the Orang Suku Laut, whose loyalty to the Melaka dynasty stretched back to the fifteenth century. Their navigational skills and knowledge of the often-perilous seas were unsurpassed, and it was they who guarded Riau's waterways and whose boats (*perahu*) comprised a substantial portion of its fleets. Their contribution to Riau's economy was equally important, for they delivered the rare ocean products, such as tortoiseshell, corals and sea slug (*teripang*) that were so valued in the international market (L. Andaya 1975, pp. 332–33; L. Andaya 2008, pp. 184–98). However, although Orang Laut leaders were rewarded with titles and

FIGURE 7.3
Islands between the Malay Peninsula and Borneo

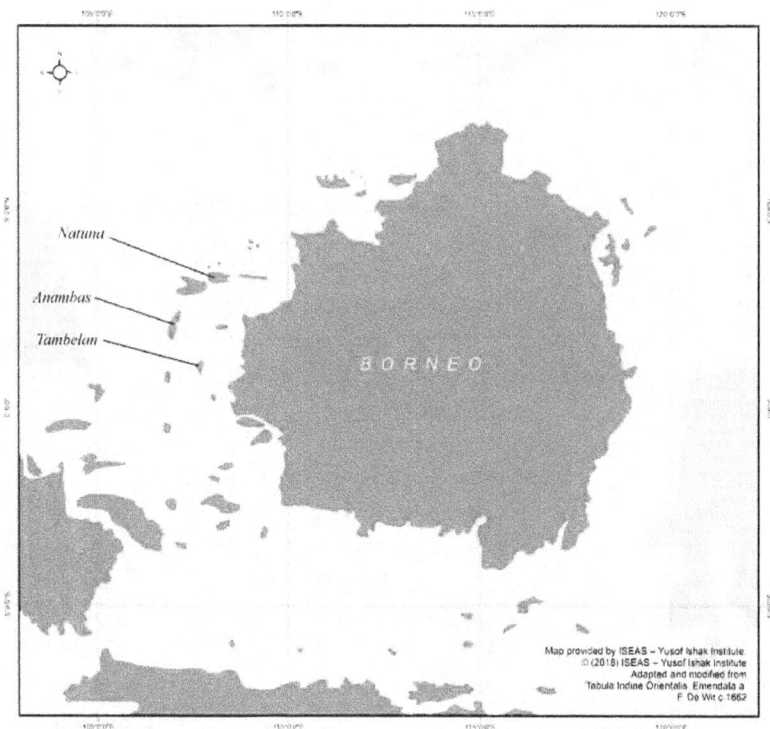

presented with gifts, Malay rulers never sought to restrict their nomadic traditions or incorporate them into a formal court-based structure, and their relationship was based on a long history of reciprocity and mutual benefit. There is no way, for instance, that Orang Laut from distant islands like Siantan could have been forced to render tribute to Riau-Lingga, and their willingness to die in its defence during the Dutch attack of 1784 attests a long history of beneficial interaction (Matheson and B. Andaya 1982, p. 170).

During the eighteenth century several developments combined to destabilize the foundations on which governance in Riau rested. In 1699 the murder of the Malay sultan brought the Melaka line to an end, but ushered in a period of conflict when loyalties were torn apart as Malays, Minangkabau from Sumatra and migrant Bugis competed for power (Andaya and Andaya 2017, pp. 84–121). The most far-reaching change, however, resulted from the arrogation of power by Bugis migrants who allied with the new Malay dynasty in the face of Minangkabau challenges. In 1728 the Bugis leader, now installed as viceroy or "junior king" (*Yang Dipertuan Muda*), assumed effective control of the Riau government. Despite the ritual oaths by which Bugis and Malays swore mutual allegiance, the Malay elite was relegated to a subservient role. The Bugis legacy of long-distance maritime trade and their renowned ability as fighters deprived the Orang Laut of their former duties, while their importance as collectors of sea products was overshadowed by Malay, Bugis and Chinese middlemen. In the meantime, hostilities with the Dutch, now in control of Melaka, steadily worsened and in 1784 Riau became a vassal state (*leenrijk*) of the Dutch East India Company. By the early nineteenth century the traditional ties between the Pulau Tujuh and the centre had been substantially weakened, enabling a number of individuals to use island bases to set themselves up as virtually independent rulers.

Meanwhile, the political and economic status of Riau had changed dramatically, for any possibility that it could once again assume its old role as a regional entrepôt ended with the founding of Singapore in 1819. In 1824 the Anglo-Dutch treaty permanently severed Riau from Singapore and Johor, now included in the British "sphere of influence" (*Surat-Surat* 1970, pp. 16, 61, 70; B. Andaya 1997, pp. 490–95). In 1830 the first article of a new treaty stated unequivocally that the kingdom of Lingga (residence of the sultan), Riau (residence of the viceroy) and its dependencies "by right of conquest" were now part of the Netherlands Indies (*Keradjaan Lingga dan Riau dan taluqnja ada suatu bahagian tanah Hindia Nederland sebab dialahkannja*) (*Surat-Surat* 1970, p. 92; see Figure 7.4).

Nonetheless, although successive contracts established Dutch prerogatives in the Riau-Lingga archipelago, the hundreds of island communities in the seas between the Malay Peninsula and Borneo received little attention. It was not until 1857 that Batavia formally moved to assert Riau's standing as overlord of this region, listing over 200 islands that included the Anambas, Natuna and Tambelan archipelagos in the South China Sea, "known to the natives as Pulau Tujuh" (See Map 5: Cribb 2000, p. 127; *Surat-Surat* 1970, pp. 117–26, 143, 175–80). Yet this did not mean that the borders of island Riau were universally accepted, and in 1886 Sultan Abu Bakar of Johor petitioned the British government to support his claim of sovereignty over

FIGURE 7.4
Administrative Divisions in Dutch Sumatra, 1824–37

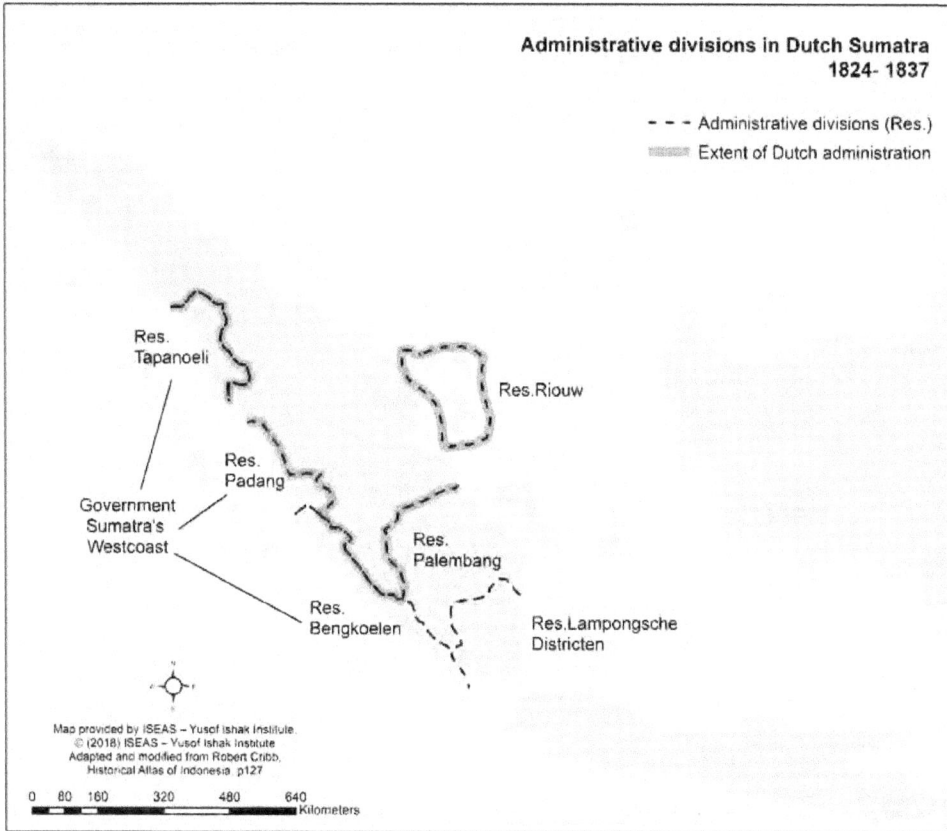

Administrative divisions in Dutch Sumatra
1824- 1837

- - - Administrative divisions (Res.)
▩▩▩ Extent of Dutch administration

Res.
Tapanoeli

Res.Riouw

Res.
Padang

Government
Sumatra's
Westcoast

Res.
Palembang

Res.
Bengkoelen

Res.Lampongsche
Districten

Map provided by ISEAS – Yusof Ishak Institute.
© (2018) ISEAS – Yusof Ishak Institute
Adapted and modified from Robert Cribb,
Historical Atlas of Indonesia p127

0   80   160   320   480   640
                                    Kilometers

the Natuna, Anambas and Tambelan groups. The British rejection of this request allayed Dutch concerns and questions of authority over Riau's islands in the South China Sea ceased to be a matter of concern or even interest. At the end of the nineteenth century the Dutch still relied on British sea charts, and inspection visits occurred only periodically. In 1896 when Resident A.L. van Hasselt prepared for a tour of the Pulau Tujuh, he could locate just two brief Dutch reports on the region, one published in 1868 and the other in 1875 (Van Hasselt and Schwartz 1898, p. 6; Netscher 1868; Kroesen 1875).

This Dutch neglect of the wider maritime environment in which Riau had traditionally operated meant that indigenous ideas of what Europeans considered "territorial waters" were hardly shaken. From the Malay perspective the seas belonging to any island extended from the shoreline to the horizon, so that in the treaty of 1820 Sultan Abdul Rahman could confidently refer to "our seas" (*kita punya laut*)—a phrase conveniently omitted from the Dutch translation (*Surat-Surat* 1970, p. 57). According to the Dutch resident, regardless of the numerous treaties detailing

FIGURE 7.5
Administrative Divisions in Dutch Sumatra, 1838–72

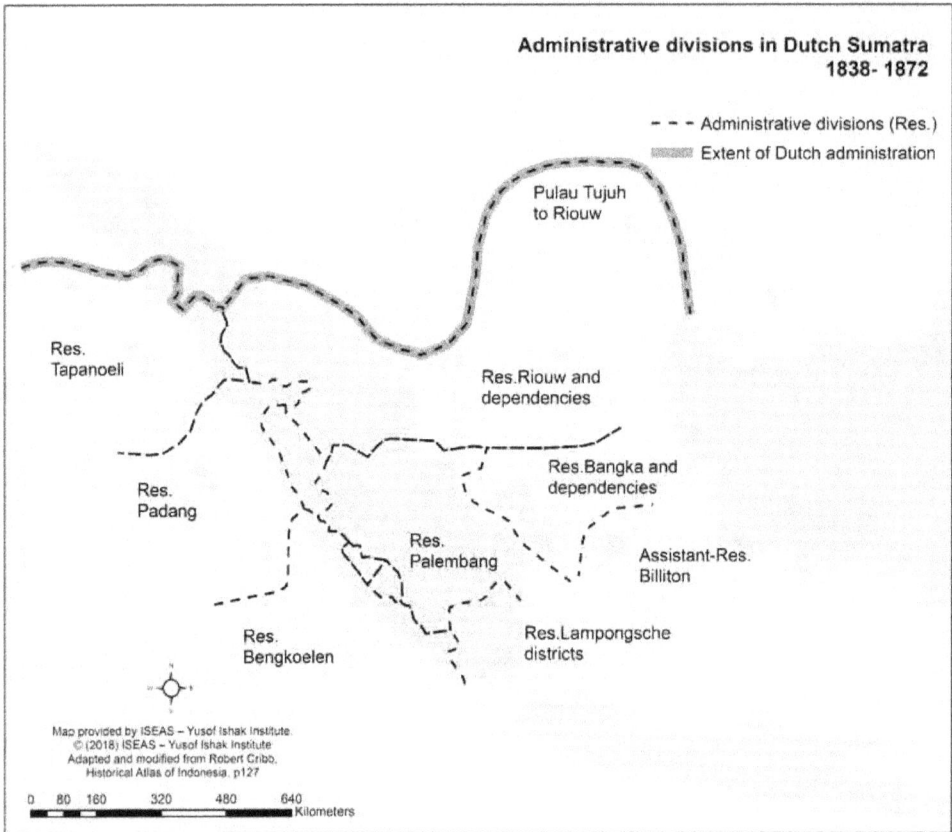

Administrative divisions in Dutch Sumatra
1838- 1872

- - - Administrative divisions (Res.)
▓▓▓ Extent of Dutch administration

Pulau Tujuh
to Riouw

Res.
Tapanoeli

Res.Riouw and
dependencies

Res.Bangka and
dependencies

Res.
Padang

Res.
Palembang

Assistant-Res.
Billiton

Res.
Bengkoelen

Res.Lampongsche
districts

Map provided by ISEAS – Yusof Ishak Institute.
© (2018) ISEAS – Yusof Ishak Institute.
Adapted and modified from Robert Cribb,
Historical Atlas of Indonesia. p127

0   80 160   320   480   640
Kilometers

colonial prerogatives regarding the collection of tolls, distribution of permits for the collection of sea products, and control of shipping, Sultan Abdul Rahman (1885–1911) "in fact conducts himself as if he exercises dominion (*heerschappij*) over the territorial sea" (Butcher and Elson 2017, p. 15). When Raja Ali Kelana, son of the last Bugis viceroy of Riau, accompanied resident Van Hasselt on the two-week inspection tour of the Pulau Tujuh, he repeatedly asserted the authority of Riau's religious court and affirmed Riau-Lingga's standing as arbiter of the Muslim religion and Malay custom (Ali 1986, pp. 20, 31, 34).

Unbeknownst to Riau's Malay-Bugis elite, colonial assertion of full maritime control was already in train as the Dutch moved towards closer surveillance of their territorial sea. Even though indigenous states were legally protectorates whose rulers supposedly retained many traditional rights, a 1902 decree placed the "territorial waters" of the Netherlands Indies under total Dutch authority, denying local suzerainty and expunging any idea of "our seas". In the kingdom of Riau-Lingga this process gathered pace as fears of foreign incursions intensified during the Russo-Japanese war, when a Russian warship in fact anchored at Anambas.

Japanese investment was a further matter of concern, and there were also reports that the Germans had plans to increase their economic and possibly military presence in Riau waters (Butcher and Elson 2017, p. 16; Campo 2002, p. 181).

In 1905, after six years of often acrimonious meetings, the Netherlands Indies government concluded a treaty with "Lingga, Riau and its dependencies" which made Dutch authority over Riau's seas explicit. The Sultan's flag could be flown on vessels within a three-mile limit from the shore, but "on the open sea they can only display the Dutch flag" (*Surat-Surat* 1970, p. 250). Three years later Dutch administrators were appointed in the main settlements of the Anambas and Natuna groups and on Pulau Serasan, while Tambelan was put directly under the Riau Resident in Tanjungpinang. In the meantime, rising resentment among the Malay-Bugis elite lent weight to the arguments of those who contended that the Dutch should assume direct control over Riau-Lingga. In 1910, successive clashes between the court and the colonial administration came to a head when Sultan Abdul Rahman, on the advice of his ministers, refused to sign a new political contract, claiming that it would deprive him of any real authority and reduce him to a "mere figurehead". His resistance provided the Dutch with sufficient cause for action, and in February of the following year he was formally deposed and he and his supporters "escaped" (*uitweken*) to Singapore. An appeal to Queen Wilhelmina brought no response, and efforts by the Malay-Bugis elite to restore the sultanate were similarly unsuccessful (Andaya 1977; Bruyn Kops 2019, p. 622; Abdur Rahman 1911, p. 9; Gordon 1999, p. 13).

Although the Dutch now had direct jurisdiction over the residency of Riau and its dependencies (*Riouw en Onderhoorigheden)*, the waters of the South China Sea still attracted only intermittent colonial attention (see Figure 7.6). An article in the *Bataviaasch Nieuwsblad*, one of the leading daily newspapers in the Dutch East Indies, even described the Pulau Tujuh as "stepchildren" of Riau, included only because they had once belonged to Melaka (*Bataviaasch Nieuwsblad* 1905). Reflecting the same attitude, the official *Atlas van Tropisch Nederland*, printed in 1938, does not supply a map of *"Riouw"* as a whole; rather, the Riau-Lingga archipelago and Anambas islands are included with Sumatra and the Malay Peninsula, while the Natuna and Tambelan archipelagos are depicted on the same pages as West Borneo (*Atlas* 1938, pp. 13, 26). This indifference persisted through much of the interwar period, although there were occasional reminders of legacies that had linked remote island communities to the Riau-Lingga heartlands. For example, royal graves on Tambelan recalled memories of a ruler who had fled to this Orang Laut stronghold in 1623, and it was at Tambelan that the various Amir (chiefs) of the Pulau Tujuh islands traditionally met before making their periodic trips to the royal palace on Lingga to affirm their loyalty. In the 1920s Tambelan people still remembered Pulau Tujuh assistance in the sultan's war against the Dutch in 1784 and spoke of "Daik" (meaning Lingga) with great respect (Vogelsang 1926, pp. 12, 16–17). It is revealing that during the campaign to restore the sultanate the greatest monetary contributions came from the Pulau Tujuh, where several Riau aristocrats had kinship connections and maintained business activities, including ownership of coconut plantations and shipping firms (Andaya 1997, p. 496; Anggraini 2014).

FIGURE 7.6
Administrative Divisions in Dutch Sumatra, 1906–32

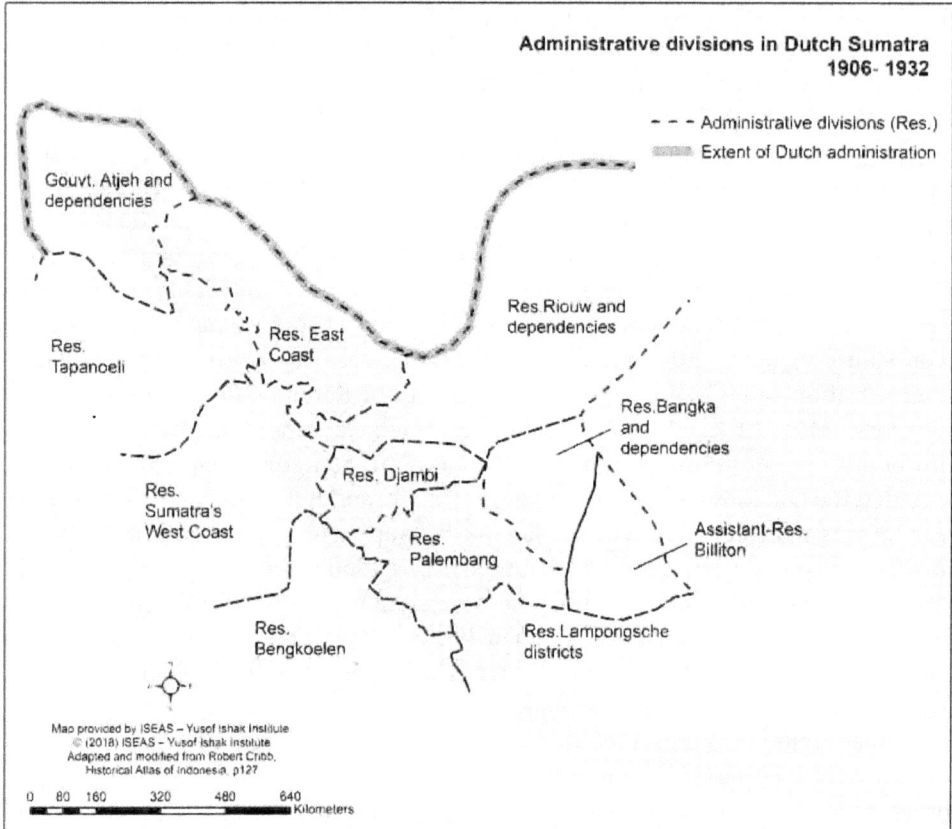

Administrative divisions in Dutch Sumatra
1906- 1932

- - - Administrative divisions (Res.)
▨▨▨ Extent of Dutch administration

Gouvt. Atjeh and
dependencies

Res.
Tapanoeli

Res. East
Coast

Res.Riouw and
dependencies

Res.Bangka
and
dependencies

Res. Djambi

Res.
Sumatra's
West Coast

Res.
Palembang

Assistant-Res.
Billiton

Res.
Bengkoelen

Res.Lampongsche
districts

Map provided by ISEAS – Yusof Ishak Institute
© (2018) ISEAS – Yusof Ishak Institute
Adapted and modified from Robert Cribb,
Historical Atlas of Indonesia, p127

0   80   160   320   480   640
                                               Kilometers

Despite the fact that fishing and the collection of marine products were still a significant source of income for most Riau islanders, the Dutch viewed the sea primarily as a transport surface rather than a source of potential wealth. Riau was certainly mentioned in overall reports of fishing activities, but the colonial government seemed more concerned about punishing Chinese fishermen from Singapore for stealing turtle eggs than protecting Malay and Orang Laut fishermen from foreign intrusion into their traditional fishing grounds. Little was done, for instance, to prevent Japanese boats from using driftnets and trolling inside the sea territory of the Netherlands Indies (Butcher and Elson 2017, p. 27; Butcher 2004, pp. 63, 148–49). Initiatives to encourage the motorization of indigenous fishing boats, which would substantially increase catches and thus the livelihood of fishing communities, were virtually absent. In Kepri the legacy of this was long-lasting; in 2001 only 38 per cent of the 2,274 fishing boats in the district (*kecamatan*) of Lingga were motorized (Butcher 2004, pp. 160–61, 209; *Dari Masa ke Masa*, p. 27). The profits from agriculture, plantations and mining ensured that the colonial gaze was always turned landwards. Even in the limited land area of the Riau islands government involvement was modest, and it was private enterprise that introduced rubber to Bintan in 1911 and developed bauxite and tin mining on the islands of Singkep and Karimun. By the same token, the coconut plantations in the Pulau Tujuh were usually financed by wealthy individuals in Singapore or Riau where the copra cargoes were directed. In 1906, three Penyengat rajas established a cooperative venture, the Sarikat Dagang Ahmadi, on the small island of Midai, in the Natuna group. At its height, the corporation's seventy-six members owned two-thirds of Midai's coconut plantations and maintained their own ship to transport copra to Singapore (Masykuri and Kutoyo 1982/83, pp. 37, 54). Despite the success of this initiative (recently inspiring local entrepreneurship awards that reflect the "spirit of Ahmadi"), Riau's overall economy in the colonial period was held together primarily by the wide-ranging Chinese network and its connections with Singapore (Anggraini 2014, pp. 74–75; Ng 1976). These connections were understandable in Tanjungpinang, which in 1930 was two-thirds Chinese (62.6 per cent), but the fact that the exiled Sultan and his family now lived in Singapore speaks to its wider appeal, and even Siantan Malays said they felt more at home in Singapore than in Natuna (Butcher 2004, pp. 63, 148; Ng 1976, p. 21; Haga 1920, p. 327).

From the colonial perspective, there was no need to invest time and resources in resuscitating older connections between the Pulau Tujuh and Riau, and there were no concerted efforts to improve sea transport. The Koninklijke Paketvaart-Maatschappij opened a fortnightly service in 1909, but for the most part it was Chinese boats (*tongkang*) and smaller *perahu* that carried cargo and passengers between islands. In Pulau Tujuh the absence of regular inter-island services also kept communities apart and limited interaction, especially during the northeast monsoon (November to March), when rough seas and strong winds kept shipping at home (Campo 2002, p. 181; Ali 1896, p. 33). In 1896 van Hasselt found that the Riau raja charged with collecting taxes from the entire Pulau Tujuh had not visited several key places, including Jemaja, Serasan, Subi and Tambelan, since he had been appointed four years earlier (Van Hasselt and Schwartz 1898, p. 55). There appeared to be little sense of a common destiny or shared interests; indeed, in 1909 the Dutch decided to place Tambelan under Tanjungpinang, precisely because they could see no obvious links to the Anambas and Natuna islands (Vogelsang 1926, p. 12; Campo 2002, p. 181). Even differences in Islamic practices contributed to the sense of localized identity. For instance, because of its close links to Singapore and the Malay Peninsula, Siantan had produced several *imam* known for their scholarly expertise; as Malays, they would have encountered a rather different environment in Tambelan, where it was customary to wear Javanese dress during Qur'an recitations (Mohd. Shaghir 2003, p. 343; Vogelsang 1926, p. 14).

Colonial attitudes towards the sea began to change from the mid-1930s, when apprehension about Japan's ambitions in Southeast Asia became a primary motivation for the passage of the 1935 Territorial Sea and Maritime Districts Ordinance and its 1939 successor (Butcher and Elson 2017, p. 41). Although Riau's territorial waters thereby garnered greater attention, the simultaneous decision to expand Riau *daratan* reflected Dutch preoccupation with administrative divisions on land. In December 1940 the department (*afdeeling*) of Bengkalis (including Siak, Pelalawan and Rokan and areas in the western portion of present-day Riau) was detached from East Coast Sumatra and incorporated into the Riau residency (O'Malley 1979, p. 241; Lufti et al., 1977, pp. 380–86).

It was this new formulation that greeted the Japanese, who captured Anambas on 26 January 1942 and Natuna shortly afterwards. However, the problems of administering such a vast area were soon recognized. A year after their landing in Tanjungpinang (February 1942), the Japanese separated the Riau-Lingga archipelago and the Pulau Tujuh from Sumatra and placed them under the administration of Singapore (Syonan-to). A new "Riau-syu" would include Siak, Kampar, Bengkalis and Inderagiri, and be administered by a military governor based at the oil-rich town of Pekanbaru.

Rather than uniting Riau communities, the war experience served to highlight ethnic and political differences among local populations, generating painful memories that are rarely discussed even today. The Chinese community, for instance, had been subject to direct Dutch authority since 1857, but had generally done well. They had therefore become the primary source of credit, and although many Malays could say, as did a Siantan man, that "I have a good *taukeh*" (*saya punya taukeh orang baik*), the resurrection of old resentments and even betrayal were always a possibility (Haga 1920, p. 326). On the eve of the invasion, Chinese-Indonesian shops in Tanjungpinang were looted, and the Japanese were able to capture a number of Singapore Chinese leaders who had escaped to Tanjungpinang. While the Chinese generally were staunchly anti-Japanese, they were divided by dialect and occupation and Japanese ruthlessness was a deterrent to any organized resistance.

Attitudes among Malays were also ambivalent. Viewing the Japanese as liberators, some were willing to wear Japanese uniforms and assist in maintaining order, at times helping to recruit labourers (*romusha*) for war projects like the infamous Thai-Burma railway. By contrast, older Malays still recall their experiences of injustice and cruelty, even at the hands of other Malays, while nomadic Orang Suku Laut speak of hard times and of the fear that their women might be violated (Massot 2003, pp. 64–66; Long 2013, pp. 87–93; Chou 2010, p. 79). It is revealing that in Kepri there is no tangible reminder of collective suffering, like that in mainland Riau, where a monument was erected in 1973 to the memory of around 80,000 *romusha* who died in horrifying circumstances while working on the Sumatran railroad (Hovinga 2010, pp. 132, 230, 357; Abdullah 2002).

THE CREATION OF KEPRI

Following the Japanese surrender in August 1945, Kepulauan Riau was quickly reclaimed by the returning Dutch, and was only transferred to the independent Indonesian state in December 1949. However, there was little understanding of what the new Indonesia would mean and loyalty to Jakarta had limited historical underpinnings (Long 2013, p. 49). Elite Malay pressure for a return to the sultanate invoked scant enthusiasm (Yong 2003, p. 97) and from 1950 to 1958 the former residency of Riau was organized into four *kabupaten*, namely Kampar, Bengkalis, Indragiri and Kepulauan Riau. Together with Jambi and West Sumatra, these areas were incorporated into Central Sumatra, with its centre at Bukittinggi. Almost immediately this amalgamation led to protests, notably among young Sumatran Malays who resented Minangkabau control of government, the privileging of Minangkabau culture and the fact that mining, oil production and forest extraction did not benefit Riau communities (Suryadi 2008, pp. 54–55). In January 1956 nearly 600 people attended the first Kongres Rakyat Riau (Congress of Riau People) in Pekanbaru to petition for the creation of a new province that would be limited to Kampar, Bengkalis, Indragiri, Kotapraja Pekanbaru and Kepulauan Riau. In July of the following year Jakarta gave its approval for this venture, the enactment only slightly set back by the outbreak of the separatist PRRI (Pemerintah Revolusioner Republik Indonesia) rebellion. Because of the unsettled situation in *daratan* Riau it was decided to designate Tanjungpinang as capital of the new province. To the delighted islanders it appeared as though Kepulauan Riau had regained something of its former status, but they were not to know that this was only a temporary measure. Just a few months later, in August 1958, the capital was transferred to Pekanbaru, a move that was bitterly resented by those who had foreseen a new era of prosperity and progress when the "Riau Islands" would stand proudly beside (or against) the *daratan* (Long 2013, p. 45; Ardi 2002, pp. 20, 70).

This resentment continued to fester after 1965 as the inauguration of the New Order government brought Riau under the ever-tightening grip of the central government. In mainland Riau antipathy towards Jakarta was strengthened by demographic shifts, for although migrants in hopes of economic opportunities had come from various parts of Indonesia, the greatest infusion was predictably from Minangkabau. Malays felt marginalized because top officials in the provincial administration were mostly ethnic Javanese or Minangkabau from the government GOLKAR party (Derks 1997, p. 705; Malley 1999, p. 88). From 1978 until 1998, the governors of Riau Province were Javanese military generals who were closely associated with the Soeharto regime. By 1981 around 65 per cent of Pekanbaru's population was from Minangkabau, and in 1989 a government team commented that "in every alley and lane one can hear people speaking Minangkabau .... Even non-Minangkabau use this language as a means of communication" (Andaya 1997, p. 503; Suparlan et al. 1989, pp. 89, 100, 117).

Minangkabau dominance was a cause of bitterness among Sumatran Malays, but in Kepulauan Riau the sense of estrangement was directed towards the *daratan* as a whole, often expressed through an implied comparison with Dutch colonial neglect (Ardi 2002, p. 70). In the early 1970s, for example, illiteracy in Kepulauan Riau was estimated at around 40 per cent, five times the equivalent figure in Pekanbaru (Esmara 1975, p. 48). Feelings of animosity were exacerbated because of Jakarta's apparent favouritism towards the *daratan*, symbolized in the struggle to gain recognition for provincial contributions to the independent Indonesian state. In 1995 a relatively minor figure from mainland Riau, Tuanku Tambusai, was elevated to the prestigious status of national hero, but despite extensive lobbying by Tanjungpinang officials, the same honour had not been extended to Raja Haji Fisabilillah, the Malay-Bugis leader who fought against the Dutch in 1784 (Barnard 1997).

The leaders of Kepulauan Riau felt this slight keenly, especially as they were beginning to realize the economic potential of the connections between Singapore and the Riau-Lingga archipelago. In the 1960s the island of Batam, with a population of around 3,500, had been primarily composed of fishing villages, but from 1970 its designation as a logistic and operational basis for oil and gas and as a future industrial region saw a substantial rise in investment and development. Batam was thought to exemplify a "new phenomenon" that could benefit by its proximity to Singapore and eventually become Indonesia's investment hub in the region. In 1971, the Batam Industrial Development Authority (BIDA) was established and although some economists were dubious about the future, the project soon began to yield profits. Declared a city in 1983, the free trading zone of Batam was now separated from the district of Kepulauan Riau, and the lines of political connections and economic profits were clearly drawn to Jakarta (Nur 2000, pp. 147–49; Faucher 2007, p. 145; Kimura 2013, p. 95).

In 1989, the creation of SIJORI and the inclusion of Karimun, Bintan and Batam as a special economic zone (*kawasan ekonomi khusus*) enabled a further flexing of Kepulauan Riau's economic muscle. In particular, Singapore investors could capitalize on land and labour as increasing numbers of Javanese and Batak migrants were attracted by the possibilities of employment. As one observer has remarked "you could almost forget that Batam was part of the Riau Province" (Suryadi 2008, p. 69). Expanded as the Indonesia-Malaysia-Singapore Growth Triangle, this initiative stimulated growth not just in Batam, but in neighbouring Karimun and Bintan. While Karimun was viewed as a site for the berthing of large cargo ships and industrial development, Bintan developed into a separate economic zone with tourism singled out for investment, which would come primarily from Singapore (Peachey, Perry and Grundy-Warr 1998, pp. 17–20).

A major development in Kepri's history has been the new attention given to the Natunas. In the early 1970s, long before there was any thought of a separate province, one observer noted the "special problem" posed by "the more isolated Riau islands". Because of the difficulty of sea travel during the northeast monsoon and the lack of air transport, as much as a year could elapse before a reply to any written communication between Natuna and Pekanbaru was received (Esmara 1975, pp. 44–45). Connections slowly began to improve after 1973, when a consortium of oil companies headed by the Italian company Agip discovered extensive gas fields about 225 km northeast of the Natuna islands, previously important only because they marked one of Indonesia's maritime boundaries. The economic value of the largest offshore natural gas deposits in the world was publicly registered in 1994 when the American giant Exxon announced ambitious plans for developments that would allow gas to travel by pipeline to a liquefied natural gas plant to be built on the main island of Natuna itself. The announcement also spoke of a marine terminal for supertankers to transport gas to markets like Japan and Korea, several thousand miles away (Pollack 1994). Little wonder that the Indonesian ambassador to Singapore suggested that the island areas of Riau could well become a separate province. Though quickly suppressed, this report aroused considerable debate in Riau (Derks 1997, p. 714). A new optimism about the future of Kepulauan Riau came in 1997, when Raja Haji Fisabilillah was finally declared a national hero. The following year a large statue of Raja Haji and four retainers was erected on the Tanjungpinang coastline (Long 2013, p. 69).[2]

It was at this point that *Riau in Transition* went to press. In the following twenty years Kepulauan Riau has attracted considerable scholarly attention because it became a prime example of what Indonesians termed regional blossoming (*pemekaran wilayah*) or the formation of new regions (*pembentukan daerah*). To a considerable degree, this "splitting and splitting" can be attributed to the fall of President Soeharto in 1998 and the impetus given to decentralization by *reformasi*, but the catalyst was President Habibie's promise of expanded regional autonomy (Booth 2011). While separatist movements and expressions of identity had been largely controlled under the New Order, there was now an ever-growing insistence that *reformasi* should also be felt at the provincial level. In *daratan* Riau, however, the demand for local autonomy was extended to a call for actual independence, with the invocation of independence for the area (*Riau merdeka*) endorsed by locally respected leaders, including Professor Tabrani Rab of the University of Riau. In early 2000, the Second Riau People's Congress (Kongres Rakyat Riau II) was organized in Pekanbaru to press for *Riau merdeka*, with Tabrani Rab assuming a prominent role (Colombijn 2003, pp. 351–58).

In island Riau the issues galvanizing public opinion were rather different. As elsewhere in Indonesia, the economic crisis that brought the end of the Soeharto regime propelled the issue of corruption into the public domain in a manner never before experienced. The collaboration between government officials at all levels and local business, so evident in Batam and Natuna, fuelled extreme anger that saw the burning of nightclubs, gambling houses and other places associated with corruption (Kimura 2013, p. 88; Aditjondro 2006, p. 332). For many Malays, resentful at the extent of migration and their exclusion from the new jobs now available, this was a time of reckoning. In 15 May 1999 a large meeting, terming itself the General Meeting of the Kepulauan Riau Community (Musyawarah Besar Masyarakat Kepri) brought together representatives from all over the islands. Though the governor and other provincial leaders hoped that the creation of new districts within the existing Riau could dispel public anger, the meeting jointly agreed that a new province was necessary in order to address the problems of poverty and to promote development for all. Soon afterwards a committee to prepare for the creation of Island Riau Province was formed (Badan Bersiapan Pembentukan Provinsi Kepulauan Riau), with leaders claiming that they were supported by all components in society (Kimura 2013, p. 89).

Subsequent events made it evident that Pulau Tujuh leaders were at best ambivalent about the idea of a separate province, but in the Riau heartlands most people accepted the idea that it would help minimize the bureaucracy, improve community services, resolve issues of cultural difference and detach the islands from the domination of Pekanbaru (Ford 2003, p. 142). Many of those who championed the idea of a new province were local aristocrats who could trace their links to the former sultanate and thought that a reshaping of Riau would be a means of purifying Malay culture. A second group, comprising more secular Malays and migrants, was simply alert to the political advantages that could be gained, especially since they considered that the Bugis-Malay elite and the Chinese had been the primary beneficiaries of New Order policies (Faucher 2005, p. 218). Through 2002 there were large demonstrations in favour of separation from mainland Riau, and effigies of opponents of the new province, notably the governor Saleh Djasit and the outspoken Tabrani Rab, were publicly burned. Various groups lent their support, and a committee for the Day of Kepri Community Pride (Hari Marwah Masyarakat Kepri), designated as 15 May to commemorate the 1999 meeting that marked the call for *kepulauan* separation. Delegations also brought pressure to bear in Jakarta, probably assisted by the intelligence agencies that saw the creation of Kepri as a means of undermining the separatist movement but also of guaranteeing national security. In addition, the military probably favoured the formation of new provinces because this increased the number of places where officers could be posted (Kimura 2013, p. 103). In October 2002 Megawati signed the official documents that brought Kepri into being.

Nonetheless, there was still some way to go before the presidential order was implemented. Leaders of the *daratan* continued to voice their opposition, and the local movement suffered a severe blow in 2003 when Huzrin Hood, a prominent spokesman for the Kepri movement, was convicted of misuse of public funds (Rab 2002; Faucher 2005, p. 135). The idea that some of the Kepri leaders were simply interested in furthering their own ambitions was reinforced when the regent (*bupati*) of Natuna, Daeng Rusnadi, initially refused to join, arguing that his *kabuputen* would thereby lose a substantial proportion of its oil and gas revenues. To circumvent these protests, Jakarta unilaterally approved the creation of Kepri before there was any agreement from the governor and the provincial legislature. Though this move was challenged, the Supreme Court decided that it was indeed within the rights of the national government (Kimura 2013, p. 104). On 1 July 2004, Ismeth Abdullah, a Javanese who had headed BIDA and thus had close connections with New Order investment in Batam, was installed as governor of Indonesia's thirty-second province, which would be divided into two cities (*kota* Tanjungpinang and *kota* Batam) and five *kabupaten* (Bintan, Anambas, Karimun, Lingga and Natuna). The following November, in apparent acknowledgement of Kepri's inauguration, the Bugis-Malay scholar Raja Ali Haji was incorporated into the pantheon of Indonesia's national heroes.

GOVERNING AN ARCHIPELAGIC PROVINCE

It is almost two decades since those heady days of early autonomy, and Kepri leaders are now confronting the realities of governing a province where over 96 per cent of the total area (252,601 km²) is water, and where the "land" comprises 1,994 islands, but only 30 per cent are inhabited (see Figure 7.7).

It is important to recognize, however, that Riau has long been conceptualized as a "maritime province". As early as 1958, long before the separation of *daratan* and *kepulauan* Riau, it was decided that a *perahu* should be at the centre of the provincial crest (*lambang*), surrounded by a forty-five-link chain (for the year of Indonesian independence) and riding on five waves (for Pancasila). The *lambang* adopted by Kepri in 2004 is very similar, although here the *perahu* sits atop seven waves, symbolizing July, the month that the new province was officially confirmed, while the number of links in the encircling chain invoke Kepri's status as Indonesia's thirty-second province.

Despite this visual assertion of Kepri's special status, it was soon evident that its leaders could present their needs more effectively if alliances were formed with other sea-oriented entities. In August 2005, shortly after Kepri formally took shape, a new organization was established to address issues common to archipelagic provinces, especially in relation to governance. Four years later it was renamed Agency for the Cooperation of Archipelago Provinces (Badan Kerja Sama Provinsi Kepulauan (BKSPK). In their joint statements, the eight BKSPK members have repeatedly reiterated the difficulties of administering areas connected by water rather than land, and stressed the need for more resources from the central government. A particular

FIGURE 7.7
Provinsi Kepulauan Riau

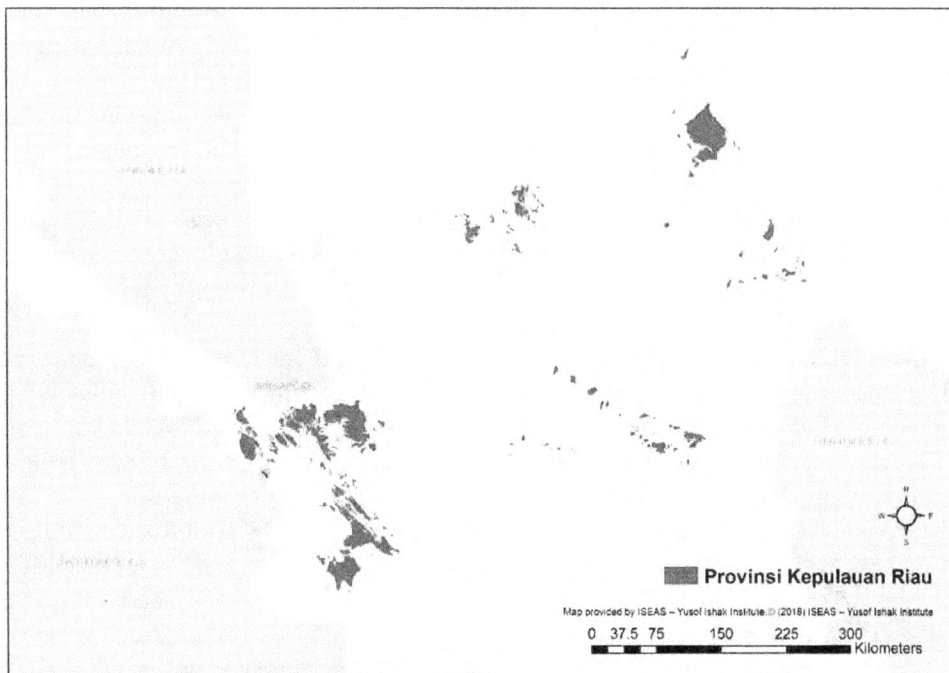

Map provided by ISEAS – Yusof Ishak Institute. © (2018) ISEAS – Yusof Ishak Institute

Provinsi Kepulauan Riau

0   37.5 75   150   225   300
                                         Kilometers

bone of contention has been the calculation of the general purpose grant, which provinces receive based on the land area and size of population. This obviously disadvantages archipelagic provinces, and the BKSPK meeting held in Bandung in September 2017 once more argued that the area covered by water should also be brought into financial calculations. Although the Republic of Indonesia had been in existence since 1945, they said, archipelagic provinces were still characterized by poverty, underdevelopment, ignorance and poor health. Because of their local knowledge, provincial authorities were best suited to address these problems. If more resources were available, *provinsi kepulauan* would be better equipped to deal with inequities in standards of living, communication, education, and access to medical facilities, while maintaining socio-culture traditions. A few months later, in January 2018, the "Batam declaration" restated the view that a special law was necessary to ensure that promises of regional autonomy were truly fulfilled (*Timor Express* 2017; *Antara News* 2018).

Although the issues outlined in these meetings are relevant to all archipelago provinces, they are particularly pronounced in Kepri because the water surface is so extensive and because the economic disparities so marked. The major islands of the Batam archipelago have been connected by the Barelang Bridge (named for Batam, Rempang and Galang), a series of six bridges initiated under former President Habibie. Since 2006 proposals have also been under consideration for a Batam-Bintan bridge, but although construction should begin in 2022, similar projects have not been planned for Kepri's other island groups. The Lingga archipelago, which consists of ten large islands and many smaller ones, is a case in point. The island of Singkep has a small airport, a heritage of former times when it was a centre for bauxite and tin mining, but otherwise inter-island communication is by water. Even a fast ferry can take 4 hours or more to cover the 120 km between Lingga and Tanjungpinang. Transportation issues are even more problematic in the Tambelan and Badas islands, where the trip by ferry to Tanjungpinang via Pontianak consumes almost an entire day and night. Since the Dutch reorganization of 1908 Tambelan has been administered from Bintan, but visits from officials are still rare and President Jokowi has himself stressed the urgent need for improved air connections. An airport was finally opened in 2020 after long delays caused by adverse weather and because all building materials had to be brought in from West Kalimantan (*Haluankepri.com* 2018).

Not surprisingly, the inequities created by distance are reflected in economic disparities. Kepri entered its new life with a strong economic base, and still enjoys the highest per capita income of the eight archipelago provinces. Nonetheless, the widening gap between centre and outlying islands (*pulau terluar*) has unsettled old ideas that all of Kepri would share in the economic rewards of autonomy. The Natunas, an archipelago of 154 islands, embodies in microcosm all the difficulties of making the *tanah-air* concept a reality. Only 40 miles long and 28 miles wide, Natuna Besar (officially Bunguran) is the centre of local government, and there are daily flights between Batam, Bintan and Singapore from the upgraded Ranai airport. Flight time is just a little over an hour, but the cheaper (and for ordinary people, the more affordable) alternative provided by the two state-owned PELNI ships can take two or three days. Transport between the twenty-seven inhabited islands is by small wooden motorboats (*pompon*) or small ferries, but may not be feasible during the high seas and strong winds that accompany the northeast monsoon. In the face of these realities the old adage that "the seas unite", so often invoked in defence of Indonesia's legal standing as an archipelagic state, breaks down (Puspitawati 2005, pp. 2–3).

The ramifications of geographical separation are considerable. A hundred years after Dutch officials noted the lack of medical facilities in the Natunas and the high incidence of beri-beri, access to good healthcare is still problematic, especially when serious cases can only be treated in Batam. Physical distance can also mean shortages of gas or even food, and in such cases the recourse is likely to be Malaysia, where canned goods are available at reasonable prices. According to one informant, the provincial government is often slow to respond to emergency situations "Our hearts are red and white (i.e., Indonesian), but our stomachs are Malaysian" (Afrida 2015). Household costs are extremely high because so many supplies have to be imported, but local incomes are low. Since fishermen have few technological skills and poor educational levels, the expansion of oil and gas exploration has not provided them with alternative sources of income when adverse weather keeps boats on shore. The apparent preference for Javanese and Sumatran migrants as workers has left many local people feeling aggrieved and resentful, comparing themselves to chickens dying in the middle of a rice barn (*ayam mati di lumbang padi*) (Marsetio et al. 2017, p. 79).

According to Law No. 23/2014 on regional government, which became effective in 2017, provincial governments are responsible for management of the seas within a zone of 12 nautical miles from individual islands, but surveillance beyond this zone rests with the national government. Natuna fishermen say that their small boats cannot deal with rough seas and that for years they have watched from the shoreline while large Thai, Chinese and Vietnamese ships harvested "tons of fish" in the surrounding waters. The inroads of Javanese ships are rarely mentioned but from the late 1980s they too were moving into Natuna seas, using the purse seine device, a long wall of netting that encloses not only a school of fish but other marine creatures as well (Butcher 2004, pp. 239, 264; Poitier, Petitgas and Petit 1997). Since 2014 the Indonesian government has taken a stronger stand against foreign fishing in Indonesian waters, and Susi Pudjiastuti, the popular former Minister of Maritime Affairs and Fisheries, was determined to clamp down on illegal fishing. Nonetheless, ten of the seventeen ships that were symbolically sunk in October 2017 were captured in the Natuna Sea (Marsetio et al. 2017, p. 76; *Jakarta Post*, 30 October 2017).

In short, in Natuna evidence that ordinary people are benefiting from a "trickle-down" of the prosperity associated with Batam and Bintan is notably absent. In 2015 it was estimated that 35 per cent of its population lived below the poverty line, with unemployment reaching 10.5 per cent, an increase from 7.6 per cent the previous year (Afrida 2015; Simandjuntak 2017b, p. 6). The marginalization of physical distance affects almost every facet of island life. In 2018 Indonesia was one of the world's largest online markets, but in Natuna Internet and mobile phone connections are slow or intermittent. The installation of a Kepri-wide fibre-optic network was scheduled for completion by 2019, but it will take many years before Internet penetration in the Pulau Tujuh will match that of Batam, Karimun and Bintan, where relatively higher ownership of computers and access to the Internet helped to rank Kepri fourth among thirty-three provinces in Indonesia's 2015 annual competitiveness analysis (Tan et al. 2016, p. 131).

Although officials are optimistic about the future of the oil and gas sectors in both Natuna and Anambas, fluctuating prices can affect revenues and here too distance may impose limitations. In 2017, for example, *ExxonMobil* announced that it "no longer wishes to continue further discussions or activity" in regard to the East Natuna gas field, citing issues of remoteness and economic feasibility (Asmarini 2017; Simandjuntak 2017a). Certainly one can point to other options that can stimulate the sea-oriented economy, especially given exhortations from former Minister Susi, who argued that "the sea has been ignored and has not been regarded as a source for the long-term prosperity of the Indonesian nation" (*TribunBisnis* 2017). Nonetheless, although Indonesia is the world's second-ranking producer of fish, crustaceans and aquatic plants, the weak surveillance of illegal fishing and harmful fishing methods as well as oversight of the marine environment more generally is a matter of record, both at the national and local level. In 2011, for example, it was reported that ocean health in the Tambelan region had been severely degraded by overfishing, and that the use of huge trawling nets had led to a sharp decline in fish stock as well as threatening several endangered species, including sea turtles. Fishing boats from outside the Tambelan islands have been blamed for the use of illegal fishing methods—explosives and poisons such as potassium cyanide—although corruption is rife and some local fishermen have been allegedly paid to direct outsiders to good fishing locations (*Jakarta Post*, 5 January 2011; Erlinda 2015; Waddell 2009).

Protection of the maritime environment is a matter of urgency because tourism has become a new focus of attention. Riau currently ranks third after Jakarta and Bali in terms of foreign visitors, but provincial officials are making efforts to draw tourists away from the bright lights of Batam and Bintan. The Anambas islands, for instance, became a *kabupaten* in 2008, and an airport was recently opened. An official investment guide highlights the marine ecology of its 255 islands, the diversity of coral reefs and fish, the attraction of diving and snorkelling, and the prospects of a designation as a marine conservation park. On the other hand, the same brochure also acknowledges that access to electricity, potable water and communication systems are limited, although improvements are in progress (*Kepulauan Anambas*, n.d.). Though visited by cruise ships, the Badas and Tambelan archipelagos are even more disadvantaged, and even a promotional website comments that reaching Tambelan is still "somewhat difficult". Until the completion of an airport in 2020 the most available connection with Tanjungpinang was the weekly car ferry (*Indonesia Tourism*, n.d.).

While the situation in the Pulau Tujuh underscores the tyranny of distance, economic disparities can also be found within the Riau-Lingga heartlands. For a number of years, the economic success of the Growth Triangle concept, and the positive effects on the Batam-Bintan-Karimun islands were unquestioned, despite the marked contrast between high-end shopping malls and Orang Suku Laut and transmigrant villages where the poverty level is high, educational levels low and faith in the government failing (Long 2016, p. 94 n. 7). For the most part it has been possible to overlook the extent to which this success was due to a cheap workforce largely dependent on incoming migrants. Nonetheless, there have been periodic labour disputes that have at times become violent, especially when poorly paid domestic employees have targeted outsiders as scapegoats (Negara 2017, p. 9). In 2013, a nationally generated labour strike pressing for higher wages paralysed around a thousand investment companies in Batam, and since then protests and demonstrations for improved working conditions have periodically occurred, prompting some companies to threaten a move to Vietnam or Malaysia (Fadli 2016). By June 2017 the economic situation had deteriorated to the extent that the Batam mayor was calling for government intervention. In that year alone seventy-eight companies closed down, 300,000 jobs were lost, and the growth rate was measured at only 2 per cent (Hutchinson 2017; Fadli 2017; *Batamcity* 2017).

Even if the old business model is reshaped, it is evident that development has come at a price, especially in Batam, which has become associated with a thriving sex industry, fuelled by male short-stay visitors and large numbers of male migrant workers. Women have been drawn into prostitution because of the high cost of living, the difficulty of finding work, and for migrant women, factory lay-offs, and the expectation that they should send money home (Peachey, Perry and Grundy-Warr 1998, p. 35; Ford and Lyons 2008; Lindquist 2009, pp. 138–41). In 2018 it was estimated that there were around 300 brothels in Batam, but a particularly serious issue is the rise in trafficking of children. The slow government response, which has effectively relinquished responsibility to civil society organizations, is probably due to the economic network that provides jobs not merely to sex workers but to hotel staff, hawkers, taxi drivers, and countless other service-industry occupations (*Global Indonesian Voices* 2016; Ong 2018). This consumer network, which extends deep into what Johan Lindquist has termed "the economy of the night", is also tied to the smuggling, sale and use of illegal drugs, notably Ecstasy which comes in via coastal ports but also through Batam's Hang Nadim airport (Lindquist 2009, pp. 71–97; Soeriaatmadja 2018).

Combined with location, the human mobility of this borderland area has opened the doors to other undesirable influences. Radical Muslims have seen Bintan and Batam as transit points for ISIS aspirants, and in 2016 six members of a shadowy Islamist group, Katibah Gonggong Rebus,[3] were arrested on charges of promoting terrorist activities and planning an attack on Singapore's Marina Bay resort (Ramakrishna 2017). Support for militants was said to come from the radicalized broadcasts of a local station, Hang Radio, although this has since been cleared by the Indonesian Broadcasting Commission (Chan 2017). Added security measures are now in place to monitor any suspected hardline Islamist organizations and prevent the spread of radical views, especially on university campuses (*Straits Times*, 9 May 2017).

The difficulties of inculcating a sense of regional cohesiveness bedevil all the archipelagic provinces, but are especially acute in Kepri because of the demographic differences between the two cities and the five *kabupaten*. From the outset the assumption that Malay culture would help unify the new Kepri was central to the movement for a new province, and in 2004 it thus seemed appropriate for each *kabupaten* to choose some art form with which it could be associated. Over the years, however, a number of scholars have questioned the extent to which Kepri can or should be considered a "Malay" province. In 2010, the Indonesian census revealed the discrepancies between the respective regions: while Lingga is 78.8 per cent Malay, Karimun 52.1 per cent, Anambas 87.2 per cent, and Natuna 87.5 per cent; the corresponding figures for Batam are 12.6 per cent, for Tanjungpinang 30.6 per cent and for Bintan 31.1 per cent. Overall, only 29.9 per cent of Kepri's total population self-identified as Malay (Long 2013, p. 43). In this context, the question of the degrees to which "Malayness" can generate a sense of Kepri unity has given rise to considerable academic discussion (Long 2013, pp. 11–16).

Over the last fifteen years innumerable festivals and conferences have been held to highlight Malay culture, most recently evident in the 2017 elevation of Sultan Mahmud as a third national hero (*pahlawan nasional*) because of his resistance to the Dutch in 1784. On the other hand, there has been little effort to embrace the idea of a more plural culture that might acknowledge the Javanese, Minangkabau and Batak presence or explore the long history of Chinese in Riau society. According to the 2010 census, individuals who defined themselves as Chinese comprised 7.7 per cent of Kepri's total population, with high concentrations in Karimun, Batam, which ranks tenth among Indonesia's cities in size of its Chinese population (61,883), and Tanjungpinang, third in the actual percentage of Chinese (14.2 per cent) (Arifin, Hasbullah and Pramono 2017, pp. 320–21). Most were born in the province and many can point to forbears who arrived three or four generations ago. For ten years (2002–12) the mayor of Tanjungpinang was a Chinese Muslim woman, Suryatati A. Manan (Lyons and Ford 2013, p. 121; Ananta et al. 2015, p. 217; Arifin, Hasbullah and Pramono 2017, p. 322). Despite the identification of "Malayness" as the foundation of Kepri identity, the process of selecting Malay symbols has caused fissures when certain choices are questioned, especially if professional rivalries are fed by competition for funding. Even the revival of a dying theatrical form like *mak yong*, most commonly associated with Kelantan in the Malay Peninsula, can give rise to acrimonious debates about different styles of performance, since not all of those involved concur with changes introduced to comply with current views about appropriate representations of Malay culture. Natuna's choice as its cultural icon was *mendu*, but in contemporary performances its animist and ritual associations have been laid aside in the interests of modernization and secularization (Pudentia 2010; Thomas 2016).

Against this background, the idea that Natuna and Anambas, or possibly the entire Pulau Tujuh, could disengage from Kepri is a telling example of the processes of "splitting, splitting and splitting again" that has gathered pace over the last decade (Booth 2011). In the case of Kepri, however, this process is complicated by the historical weakening of relationships between its component parts. Between 1787 and 1903 Lingga was the royal seat of the sultans of Riau-Lingga, but it was separated by several hours sailing from the Dutch administrative centre at Tanjungpinang and the residence of the Bugis Yamtuan Muda on Pulau Penyengat. To some degree, distance accounts for Lingga's exclusion from the Growth Triangle, and in turn explains the differing rate of development and the contrast in poverty levels. In 2010 this was 4.8 per cent in Batam but 15.8 per cent in Lingga, where the Orang Laut and transmigrant populations are still largely dependent on the poor returns from fishing and agriculture (Amri 2016, p. 173). Prior to the imposition of Dutch colonialism, the Pulau Tujuh were well integrated into the Riau-Lingga network because of their importance to maritime traffic and the value of their marine resources. Though these ties were still evident in the nineteenth century, they were already fading because of the economic attraction of Singapore, while any residual sense of loyalty to the centre dissipated following the abolition of the sultanate in 1911. This marginalization has been accentuated by the distinctiveness of dialects such as Natuna Malay and ambiguous attitudes from the centre that see Pulau Tujuh populations as "backward" and yet able to tap special powers that may infuse, for instance, an amulet with special protection (Kling 1976, p. 94). For communities in this neglected region, the formation of Kepri held out the promise that decades of neglect would now be redressed.

While there have been definite improvements over the last thirty years, progress has been frustratingly slow. Idris Zaini, legislative representative for Anambas, thus believes he is voicing the wishes of Pulau Tujuh people: "To this point development in the Riau islands has been dominated by Batam, Bintan, Tanjungpinang and Karimun areas, while there has been little change in Anambas, Natuna and Lingga" (*Garuda Nusantara* 2018). Posts and messages on social media have also been active in promoting the idea that Kepri development policies have always favoured the land (*daerah darat*) rather than the sea (Hida'at 2017). Memories of a time when these islands were recognized as a collective identity still survive in DPRD records, which recall the May 1950 division of Kepulauan Riau into four districts (*kewedanaan*), one of which was the Pulau Tujuh—significantly including Tambelan islands, although these were reallocated to Bintan in 1965 (*Dari Masa ke Masa* 2004, p. 3). Citing such records, supporters contend that the Pulau Tujuh was unified in the past, and should now be reintegrated as a separate province, which one advocate even suggested be renamed as *"Peripura"*—an English translation could be "Glorious Land" (*Koran Perbatasan* 2018).[4]

There is no guarantee, however, that the creation of a new province or a greater share of oil and gas revenues will resolve the problems of low incomes and unemployment, given the history of corruption among local leaders that saw the imprisonment of former Bupati Daeng Rusnadi. In 2016 a government amendment to electoral laws allowed individuals formerly convicted of crimes to stand for public office, and Daeng Rusnadi, enthusiastically welcomed following his return to Natuna in March 2018 after eight years imprisonment, said that he was happy to once again work for local development (*Lintas Kepri*, 20 March 2018). The ruling has also allowed the current *bupati*, Abdul Hamid Rizal, another prominent exponent of separation, to regain his position although in 2010 he too had spent three years in prison (*Jakarta Post*, 2 March 2016). His campaign took heart from the fact that Jakarta will allow the formation of ten more provinces from the current thirty-four, reaching a maximum of forty-four by 2025, and he openly expressed his view that the formation of a new Natuna-Anambas province was "very close". Meanwhile, leading figures in the Kepri DPR have predicted that the coming years will see the creation of Provinsi Khusus Batam and a second province, Provinsi Pulau Tujuh (Irawan 2016; *Lintas Kepri*, 14 March 2018). Kepri is thus set to become a test case for the feasibility of creating and sustaining a province where the unifying capacity of water is still debated and where geographically the reversed *air-tanah* imbalance is so marked.

CONCLUSION

In 1997, when *Riau in Transition* was published, few people could have foreseen the creation of a new province in which the overwhelming total of area covered was water. In thinking back over the pathways that led to the creation of Kepulauan Riau this chapter has drawn attention to the place of the sea in justifying Indonesia's international standing as an archipelagic state. It has been argued, however, that the seas have only recently been seriously considered as a national resource, and that the *tanah air* relationship that idealizes a sea-connected homeland intrinsic to Indonesia's identity has largely remained in the domain of rhetoric. Until 1998 there were only four provinces where the area covered by water was more extensive than land (Maluku, West and East Nusa Tenggara, and Sulawesi Utara). From 1999, following the passing of autonomy laws, this number has doubled with the addition of North Maluku (1999), Bangka Belitung (2000) and Southeast Sulawesi and Kepulauan Riau (2004). Though still very much a minority among Indonesia's thirty-four provinces, the *provinsi kepulauan* must have been heartened to hear President Jokowi's call for a refocus on the nation's "seas, oceans, straits and bays". At the same time, the pivot to the maritime environment offers new opportunities to explore the common belief that decentralization will improve the lives of ordinary people, even when island communities are separated by large stretches of sea that are not conducive to easy communication.

In focusing on the province of Kepulauan Riau, this chapter has argued that the precolonial island kingdoms of modern Indonesia, the *kerajaan kepulauan*, could hold together because there was an acknowledged centre that had sufficient economic resources and cultural capital to maintain a reciprocal relationship with far-flung but water-connected peripheries. In Kepulauan Riau these links were fundamentally weakened by the imposition of Dutch rule and colonial arrogation of control over the surrounding seas. From Batavia's viewpoint, the Pulau Tujuh of the South China Sea, which had been connected to the Riau-Lingga archipelago since the sixteenth century, were simply "stepchildren" of the Riau residency. Little thought was given to strategies for resurrecting even a semblance of old ties during the debates that preceded the final inauguration of Kepri in 2004, and it was hardly surprising that Natuna leaders were reluctant to join the new province or that they have renewed their calls for their own autonomy. Notwithstanding the historical connections between the Kepri heartland and the many islands of the Pulau Tujuh, the realities of distance, economic disparities and cultural diversity pose a significant challenge for provincial cohesion. Kepri's recent history provides an object lesson in the pitfalls that have accompanied the processes of regionalization, for here as elsewhere it has largely been local elites and specific sections of the population who have benefitted. The collusion between local officials and business interests, together with access to government and foreign contracts, has encouraged extensive corruption that has fed cynicism about the ideals expressed by so many leaders in their election campaigns. In the end, one can do no better than to cite Anne Booth's cogent summary, for in Kepri, as elsewhere, "the success of Indonesia's great experiment in decentralization will rest on the ability of provinces and districts to supply the services people need and in the extent to which local populations can control the behaviour of officials through public scrutiny of their decisions and through the electoral process" (Booth 2011, p. 54).

Notes

1. I would like to express my heartfelt gratitude to Francis Hutchinson, Siwage Dharma Negara, John Butcher and Nicholas Long for their comments and generous suggestions as I prepared this chapter. Any errors are of course my own responsibility.
2. In 2005 the statue was destroyed in a storm, and only the plinth remains.
3. Literally "Boiled Snails Cell".
4. I am most grateful to Nicholas Long for his suggestions regarding a translation of "peripura".

References

Abdullah, H.M. Syafei. 2002. *Tragedi Pembungunan Rel Keretapi Muarasijunjung-Pekanbaru (1943–1945)*. Pekanbaru: Unri Press.

Abdur Rahman bin Mahomed Eusope, Raja. 1911. "One Treaty Read, Another Offered for Signature". *Straits Times*, 15 February 1911, p. 9.

Adhuri, Dedi S. 2009. "Social Identity and Access to Natural Resources: Ethnicity and Regionalism from a Maritime Perspective". In *The Politics of the Periphery in Indonesia: Social and Geographical Perspectives*, edited by Minako Sakai, Glenn Banks and J.H. Walker, pp. 134–52. Singapore: NUS Press.

Aditjondro, George. 2006. *Korupsi Kepresidenan: Reproduksi Oligarki Berkaki Tiga: Istana, Tangsi, dan Partai Penguasa*. Jakarta: PT LKiS Pelangi Aksara.

Afrida, Nani. 2015. "Natuna, a Tale of Remote and Neglected Islands". *Jakarta Post*, 31 October

2015. http://www.thejakartapost.com/news/2015/10/13/natuna-a-tale-remote-and-neglected-islands.html (accessed 26 May 2018).

Ahmad, A. Samad, ed. 1979. *Sulalatus Salatin (Sejarah Melayu)*. Kuala Lumpur: Dewan Bahasa dan Pustaka.

Ahmad, Kassim. 1975. *Hikayat Hang Tuah*. Kuala Lumpur: Dewan Bahasa dan Pustaka.

Ali Kelana, Raja. 1986. *Pohon Perhimpunan: Kisah Perjalan Raja Ali Kelana ke Pulau Tujuh*. Jakarta. Departemen Pendidikan dan Kebudayaan.

Al Azhar. 1997. "Malayness in Riau; The Study and Revitalization of Identity". *Bijdragen tot de Taal-, Land en Volkenkunde* 153, no. 4: 764–73.

Allard, Tom, and Bernadette Christina Munthe. 2017. "Asserting Sovereignty, Indonesia renames part of South China Sea". Reuters, 14 July 2017. https://www.reuters.com/article/us-indonesia-politics-map/asserting-sovereignty-indonesia-renames-part-of-south-china-sea-idUSKBN19Z0YQ (accessed 25 May 2018).

Amri, Mulya. 2016. "A Periphery Serving Three Cores: Balancing Local, National and Cross-Border Interests in the Riau Islands". In *The SIJORI Cross-Border Region: Transnational Politics, Economics, and Culture*, edited by Francis E. Hutchinson and Terence Chong, pp. 154–80. Singapore: ISEAS – Yusof Ishak Institute.

Ananta, Aris, Evi Nurvidya Arifin, M. Sairi Hasbullah, Nur Budi Handayani, and Agus Pramono, ed. 2015. *Demography of Indonesia's Ethnicity*. Singapore: Singapore: ISEAS – Yusof Ishak Institute.

Andaya, Barbara Watson. 1977. "From Rum to Tokyo: Riau's Search for Anti-Colonial Allies, 1899–1914". *Indonesia* 24, no. 2 (October): 125–56.

———. 1997. "Recreating a Vision: Daratan and Kepulauan in Historical Context". *Bijdragen tot de Taal-, Land en Volkenkunde* 153, no. 4: 484–508.

———, and Leonard Y. Andaya. 2017. *A History of Malaysia*. 3rd ed. London: Palgrave Macmillan.

Andaya, Leonard Y. 1975. *The Kingdom of Johor 1641–1728: Economic and Political Developments*. Kuala Lumpur: Oxford University Press.

———. 2008. *Leaves of the Same Tree: Trade and Ethnicity in the Straits of Melaka*. Honolulu: University of Hawai'i Press.

Anggraini, Lisa, ed. 2014. *Spirit Entrepreneurship Bermula dari Midai, Natuna*. Batam: Batam Pos, Entrepreneur School.

Antara News. 2018. "Delapan Provinsi Kepulauan Sepakati Deklarasi Batam". 29 January 2018. https://www.antaranews.com/berita/681378/delapan-provinsi-kepulauan-sepakati-deklarasi-batam (accessed 3 June 2018).

Ardi, Sumantri. 2002. *Amuk Melayu dalam Tuntutan Provinsi Kepulauan Riau*. Pekanbaru: Unri Press.

Arifin, Evi Nurvidya, M. Sairi Hasbullah and Agus Pramono. 2017. "Chinese Indonesians: How Many, Who and Where?". *Asian Ethnicity* 18, no. 3: 310–29.

Arsana, I Made Andi, and Clive Schofield. 2013. "Indonesia's 'Invisible' Border with China". In *Beijing's Power and China's Borders: Twenty Neighbors in Asia*, edited by Bruce A. Elleman, Stephen Kotkin and Clive Schofield, pp. 61–80. Armonk, NY: M.E. Sharpe.

Asmarini, Wilda. 2017. "ExxonMobil Says Will Drop Discussions over Indonesia's East Natuna Gas Field". Reuters, 8 July 2017. https://www.reuters.com/article/us-indonesia-gas-exxon-mobil-idUSKBN1A30JB (accessed 8 June 2018).

Atlas van Tropisch Nederland. 1938. Batavia: Koninklijk Nederlandsch Aardrijkskundig Genootschap.

Barnard, Timothy. 1997. "Local Heroes and National Consciousness: The Politics of Historiography in Riau". *Bijdragen tot de Taal-, Land- en Volkenkunde* 153, no. 4: 509–26.

Batam City. 5 December 2017. https://batam-city.com/78-companies-went-bankrupt-in-batam-leaving-1286-people-left-unemployment/ (accessed 8 June 2018).

Batam Times. 2016. "Nurdin: Mari Bersama Ciptakan Kepri Aman dan Tenteram". 23 November 2016. http://www.batamtimes.co/2016/11/23/nurdin-mari-bersama-ciptakan-kepri-aman-dan-tenteram/ (accessed 10 May 2018).

Bataviaasch Nieuwsblad. 1905. "De Riouw-archipel. Indrukken eener Reis door den Riouw-archipel in begin 1905". 23 May 1905.

Booth, Anne. 2011. "Splitting, Splitting and Splitting again: A Brief History of the Development of Regional Government in Indonesia Since Independence". *Bijdragen tot de Taal-, Land en Volkenkunde* 153, no. 4 (1997): 473-82.167; 1 (2011): 31–59.

Bruyn Kops, G.F. de. 1919. "Riouw en Onderhoorigheden". In *Encyclopaedie van Nederlandsch-Indië*. 2nd ed. Vol. III, edited by D.G. Stibbe, pp. 605–26. The Hague: Nijhoff.

Butcher, John G. 2002."Getting into Trouble: The Diaspora of Thai Trawlers, 1975–2002". *International Journal of Maritime History*, 14, no. 2 (December): 85–121.

———. 2004. *The Closing of the Frontier: A History of the Marine Fisheries of Southeast Asia, C.1850–2000*. Singapore: Institute of Southeast Asian Studies.

———. 2009. "Becoming an Archipelagic State: The Juanda Declaration of 1957 and the 'Struggle' to Gain International Recognition of the Archipelagic Principle". In *Indonesia Beyond the Water's Edge: Managing an Archipelagic State*, edited by R.B. Cribb and Michele Ford, pp. 28–48. Singapore: Institute of Southeast Asian Studies.

———, and R.E. Elson. 2017. *Sovereignty and the Sea: How Indonesia Became an Archipelagic State*. Singapore: NUS Press.

Campo, J.N.F.M à. 2002. *Engines of Empire: Steamshipping and State Formation in Colonial Indonesia*. Hilversum: Verloren.

Chambert-Loir, Henri, and Siti Maryam R. Salahuddin. 1999. *Bo' Sangaji: Catatan Kerajaan Bima. Jakarta*: École française d›Extrême-Orient/Yayasan Obor Indonesia.

Chan, Francis. 2017. "Batam Radio Station Cleared of Allegation That It Spreads Radical Islamic Teachings". *Straits Times*, 3 November 2017. https://www.straitstimes.com/asia/se-asia/batam-radio-station-cleared-of-allegation-that-it-spreads-isis-propaganda (accessed 8 June 2018).

Chou, Cynthia. 2010. *The Orang Suku Laut of Riau, Indonesia: The Inalienable Gift of Territory*. London and New York: Routledge.

———, and Will Derks. 1997. "Introduction". *Bijdragen tot de Taal-, Land en Volkenkunde* 153, no. 4: 473–82.

Colombijn, Freek. 2003. "When There Is Nothing to Imagine: Nationalism in Riau". In *Framing Indonesian Realities: Essays in Symbolic Anthropology in Honour of Reimar Schefold*, edited by Pieter J.M. Nas, Gerard A. Persoon and Rivke Jaffe, pp. 333–70. Leiden: KITLV Press.

Cribb, Robert. 2000. *Historical Atlas of Indonesia*. Richmond, Surrey: Curzon.

Dari Masa ke Masa: DPRD Kepri dalam Angka. 2004. Dewan Perwakilan Rakyat Daerah, np.

Derks, W. 1997. "Malay Identity Work". *Bijdragen tot de Taal-, Land- en Volkenkunde* 153, no. 4: 699–716.

Djalil, Hasjim. 2009. "Indonesia's Archipelagic Sea Lanes". In *Indonesia Beyond the Water's Edge: Managing an Archipelagic State*, edited by R.B. Cribb and Michele Ford, pp. 59–69. Singapore: Institute of Southeast Asian Studies.

Erlinda. 2016. "Tambelan, Pulau yang 'Terabaikan' di Laut Cina Selatan". *Kompasiana*. 18 May 2016. https://www.kompasiana.com/evierlinda/tambelan-pulau-yang-terabaikan-di-laut-cina-selatan_560d2bb4127f61c8151f43eb (accessed 9 June 2018).

Esmara, Hendra. 1975. "An Economic Survey of Riau". *Bulletin of Indonesian Economic Studies* 11, no. 3 (November): 25–49.

Fadli. 2016. "Workers Strike, Block Apple Subcontractor Factory in Batam". *Jakarta Post*, 12 January 2016. http://www.thejakartapost.com/news/2016/01/12/workers-strike-block-apple-subcontractor-factory-batam.html (accessed 9 June 2018).

———. 2017. "Batam Economy in a State of Emergency". *Jakarta Post*, 16 June 2017. http://www.thejakartapost.com/news/2017/06/16/batam-economy-in-a-state-of-emergency-mayor-says.html (accessed 8 June 2018).

Faucher, Carole. 2005. "Regional Autonomy, Malayness and Power Hierarchy in the Riau Archipelago". In *Regionalism in Post-Suharto Indonesia*, edited by Maribeth Erb, Pryambudi Sulistiyanto and Carole Faucher. pp. 125–41. London: Routledge Curzon.

———. 2007. "Contesting Boundaries in the Riau Archipelago". In *Renegotiating Boundaries: Local Politics in Post-Suharto Indonesia*, edited by Henk Schulte Nordholt and Gerry van Klinken, pp. 443–58. Leiden: Brill.

Forbes, Vivian Louis. 2014. *Indonesia's Delimited Maritime Boundaries*. Heidelberg: Springer.

Ford, Michele. 2003, "Who are the Orang Riau? Negotiating Identity across Geographic and Ethnic Divides". In *Local Power and Politics in Indonesia: Decentralisation and Democratisation*, edited by Edward Aspinall and Greg Fealy, pp. 132–47. Singpore: Institute of Southeast Asian Studies.

———, and Lenore Lyons. 2006."The Borders Within: Mobility and Enclosure in the Riau Islands". *Asia Pacific Viewpoint* 47, no. 2 (2006): 257–71.

———, and Lenore Lyons. 2008. "Making the Best of What You've Got: Sex Work and Class Mobility in the Riau Islands". In *Women and Work in Indonesia*, edited by Michele Ford and Lenore Lyons, pp. 173–94. London: Routledge.

———, and Lenore Lyons, 2009. "Fluid Boundaries: Modernity, Nation and Identity in the Riau Islands". In *Indonesia Beyond the Water's Edge: Managing an Archipelagic State*, edited by R.B. Cribb and Michele Ford, pp. 221–37. Singapore: Institute of Southeast Asian Studies.

Garuda Nusantara Online. 2018. "Idris Zaini: Propinsi Natuna Anambas Harus, Karena Kepri Tak Perhatian". 30 March 2018. http://gardanusantaraonline.com/2018/03/30/idris-zaini-propinsi-natuna-anambas-harus-karena-kepri-tak-perhatian/ (accessed 8 June 2018).

Geographer. 1971. "International Boundary Studies Series A. Limits in the Sea. Straight Baselines: Indonesia". *Bureau of Intelligence and Research* no. 35, 20 July 1971.

Global Indonesian Voices. 2016. "Commercial Sex Industry in Batam". 18 October 2016. http://www.globalindonesianvoices.com/25057/commercial-sex-industry-in-batam/ (accessed 8 June 2018).

Gordon, Alijah ed. 1999. *The Real Cry of Syed Shaykh al-Hady*. Singapore: Malaysian Sociological Research Institute.

Haga, B.J. 1920. "De Klappercultuur en Coprahandel in de Poelau Toedjoeh (Riouw)". Koloniale *Studiën* 4, no. 2: 314–42.

Haluankepri.com. 2018. "2019, Bandara Tambelan Rampung". 23 April 2018. http://www.haluankepri.com/bintan/112114-2019-bandara-tambelan-rampung.html (accessed 8 June 2018).

Hida'at, R. Patria. 2017. "Menanti Provinsi Pulau Tujuh". *TanjungPinang Pos*, 30 January 2017 (accessed 4 August 2018).

Hovinga, Henk. 2010. *The Sumatran Railroad: Final Destination Pakan Baroe, 1943–1945*. Leiden: KITLV Press.

Hunt, Luke. 2016. "Indonesia's New North Natuna Sea: A Response to an Old China Problem". *The Diplomat*, 3 August 2016. https://thediplomat.com/2017/08/indonesia-new-north-natuna-sea-a-response-to-an-old-china-problem/ (accessed 23 May 2018).

Hutchinson, Francis E. 2017. *Rowing Against the Tide? Batam's Economic Fortunes in Today's Indonesia*. Trends in Southeast Asia, no. 8/2017. Singapore: ISEAS – Yusof Ishak Institute.

———, and Terence Chong, eds. 2016. *The SIJORI Cross-Border Region: Transnational Politics, Economics, and Culture*. Singapore: ISEAS – Yusof Ishak Institute.

Indonesia Tourism. N.d. www.indonesia-tourism.com/riau-archipelago/tambelan_archipelago.html (accessed 9 June 2018).

Irawan. 2016. "Sebelum 2025, Provinsi Kepri Bisa Dimekarkan Jadi Provinsi Khusus Batam dan Provinsi Pulau Tujuh". *Batam Today.com*, 25 May 2016. http://m.batamtoday.com/berita72325-Sebelum-2025,-Provinsi-Kepri-Bisa-Dimekarkan-Jadi-Provinsi-Khusus-Batam-dan-Provinsi--Pulau-Tujuh.html (accessed 28 May 2018).

Jakarta Globe. 2014. "Jokowi's Inaugural Speech as Nation's Seventh President". 20 October 2014. http://thejakartaglobe.beritasatu.com/news/jokowis-inaugural-speech-nations-seventh-president/ (accessed 6 June 2018).

Jakarta Post. 2011. "Overfishing Depleting Tambelan islands Maritime Resources". 5 January 2011. http://www.thejakartapost.com/news/2011/01/05/overfishing-depleting-tambelan-islands-maritime-resources.html (accessed 9 June 2018).

———. 2017. "Indonesia Sinks 17 More Fishing Ships". 30 October 2017. http://www.thejakartapost.com/news/2017/10/30/indonesia-sinks-17-more-fishing-ships.html (accessed 8 June 2018).

Jones, Russell, ed. 1997. *Hikayat Raja-Raja Pasai*. Shah Alam: Fajar Bakti.

Kepulauan Anambas Archipelago, Riau Islands Province: Invitation to Invest in Tourism-based Community Development. http://indonesia-tourism-investment.com/files/anambas.pdf. (accessed 4 June 2018).

Kimura, Ehito. 2013. *Political Change and Territoriality in Indonesia: Provincial Proliferation*. New York: Routledge.

Kling, Zainal. 1976. "Magical Practices in a Rural Malay Community in Sarawak". In *The Nescent (i.e. nascent) Malaysian Society: Developments, Trends, and Problems*, edited by H.M. Dahla,. pp. 71–97. Kuala Lumpur: Jabatan Antropologi dan Sosiologi, Universiti Kebangsaan Malaysia.

Koran Perbatasan. 2018. "'Peripura' Salah Satu Penamaan untuk Natuna Provinsi Khusus". 4 May 2018. https://koranperbatasan.com/peripura-salah-satu-penamaan-untuk-natuna-provinsi-khusus (accessed 4 August 2018).

Kroesen, R.C. 1875. "Aanteekeningen over de Anambas-, Natoena-, en Tambelan-Eilanden". *Tijdschrift voor Indische Taal-, Land- en Volkenkunde* 21: 235–47.

Lindquist, Johan A. 2009. *The Anxieties of Mobility: Migration and Tourism in the Indonesian Borderlands*. Honolulu: University of Hawai'i Press.

Lintas Kepri. 2018a. "Hamid Rizal: Besok Natuna Jadi Provinsi, Saya Siap Jadi Gubernurnya". 14 March 2018. https://lintaskepri.com/hamid-rizal-besok-natuna-jadi-provinsi-saya-siap-jadi-gubernurnya.html (accessed 28 May 2018).

———. 2018b. "Daeng Rusnadi: Kalau Rakyat Masih Menghendaki, Kenapa Tidak!!". 20 March 2018. https://lintaskepri.com/daeng-rusnadi-kalau-rakyat-masih-menghendaki-kenapa-tidak.html (accessed 9 June 2018).

Long, Nicholas J. 2013. *Being Malay in Indonesia: Histories, Hopes and Citizenship in the Riau Archipelago*. Singapore and Copenhagen: NUS Press and NIAS Press.

———. 2016. "Why Indonesians Turn against Democracy". In *The State We're In: Reflections on Democracy's Troubles*, edited by Joanna Cook, Nicholas J. Long and Henrietta L. Moore, pp. 71–96. Oxford and New York: Berghahn.

Lutfi, Muchtar et al. 1977. *Sejarah Daerah Riau*, Jakarta: Departemen Pendidikan dan Kebudayaan.

Lyons, Leonore and Michele Ford. 2014. "The Chinese of Karimun: Citizenship and Belonging at Indonesian's Margins". In *Chinese Indonesians Reassessed: History, Religion and Belonging*, edited by Siew-Min Sai and Chang-Yau Hoon, pp. 121–37. London: Routledge.

Malley, Michael. 1999, "Regions: Centralization and Resistance". In *Indonesia beyond Suharto: Polity, Ethnicity, Society, Transition*, pp. 71–108. Armonk, NY: M.E. Sharpe.

Marsetio et al. 2017. "The Construction of Marginality of Border Areas: A Case Study of Natuna Island in Indonesia". *International Journal of u- and e- Service, Science and Technology* 10, no. 9: 71–84.

Massot, Gilles. 2003. *Bintan: Phoenix of the Malay Archipelago*. Singapore: Gunung Bintan.

Masykuri and Sutrisno Kutoyo, ed. 1982/1983. *Sejarah Kebangkitan Nasional Daerah Riau*. Pekanbaru: Departemen Pendidikan dan Kebudayaan.

Matheson, Virginia and Barbara Watson Andaya, trans and ed. 1982. *Tuhfat al-*Nafis [The Precious Gift]. Kuala Lumpur: Oxford University Press.

Mohd Shaghir Abdullah, Hj. Wan. 2003. "Manuskrip Melayu Pattani: Hubungan Pattani, Natuna, Kelantan, Terengganu dan Kemboja". In *Peradaban Melayu Timur* Laut, edited by A. Aziz Deraman, pp. 341–54. Kuala Lumpur: Dewan Bahasa dan Pustaka.

Moser, Sarah and Alyssa Shamsa Wilbur. 2017. "Constructing Heritage through State Architecture in Indonesia's Riau Islands". *ABE Journal* (Online), 11.

Negara, Siwage Dharma. 2017. "Can the Decline of Batam's Shipbuilding Industry be Reversed?". *ISEAS Perspective* No. 2017/10, 16 February 2017.

Netscher, E. 1854. "Beschrijving van een Gedeelte der Residentie Riouw". *Tijdschrift voor Indische Taal-, Land- en Volkenkunde* 2: 108–270.

———. 1864. *"Togtjes in het gebied van Riouw en Onderhoorigheden"*. *Tijdschrift voor Indische Taal-, Land- en Volkenkunde* 12 (1862): 233–54; 14 (1864): 1–23, 340–51.

Ng Chin Keong. 1976. "The Chinese in Riau: A Community on an Unstable and Restrictive Frontier". Research Project Series no. 2, Institute of Humanities and Social Sciences College of Graduate Studies, Nanyang Technical University.

Nur, Yoslan. 2000. "L'île de Batam à l'ombre de Singapour: investissement singapourien et dépendance de Batam". *Archipel* 59: 145–70.

Ong, Justin. 2018. "'Don't Have Younger?' Battling Batam's Festering Issue of Youth and Child Sexual Exploitation". *Channel NewsAsia*. 27 May 2018. https://www.channelnewsasia.com/news/asia/batam-child-sex-prostitutes-exploitation-abuse-singapore-10244372 (accessed 8 June 2018).

Peachey, Karen, Martin Perry and Carl Grundy-Warr. 1998. *The Riau Islands and Economic Cooperation in the Singapore Indonesian Border Zone*. Durham: International Boundaries Research Unit, University of Durham.

Poitier, Michel, Pierre Petitgas, and Didier Petit. 1997. "Interaction between Fish and Fishing Vessels in the Javanese Purse Seine Fishery". *Aquatic Living Resources* 10: 149–56.

Pollack, Andrew. 1994. "Exxon Leads Signers of Indonesian Gas Deal". *New York Times*, 24 November 1994. https://www.nytimes.com/1994/11/17/business/company-news-exxon-leads-signers-of-indonesia-gas-deal.html (accessed 7 June 2018).

Pudentia Maria Puranti Srisunarti. 2010. "The Revitalization of Mak Yong in the Malay World". *Wacana* 12, no. 1 (April): 1–19.

Puspitawati, Dhiana. 2005. "The *East/West* Archipelagic *Sea Lanes* Passage through the Indonesian Archipelago". *Maritime Studies* (January–February): 1–13.

Rab, Tabrani. 2002. *Bersatulah Riau (Penolakan Propinsi Kepri)*. Pekanbaru: Riau Cultural Institute.

Rajan, H.P. 1986. "The Legal Regime of Archipelagos". *German Yearbook of International Law* 29: 137–53. Reprinted in *Law of the Sea*, edited by Hugo Camino, pp. 135–54. London: Routledge, 2017.

Ramakrishna, Kumar. 2017. "The Threat of Terrorism and Extremism: A Matter of When, and Not If". *Southeast Asian Affairs 2017*, edited by Daljit Singh and Malcolm Cook, pp. 335–50. Singapore: ISEAS – Yusof Ishak Institute.

Simandjuntak, Deasy. 2017a. "Natuna and Anambas Intend to Separate from Riau Islands Province". *ISEAS Commentaries* 2017/8, 6 February 2017. https://iseas.edu.sg/medias/ commentaries/item/4858-natuna-and-anambas-intend-to-separate-from-riau-islands-province-a-commentary-by-deasy-simandjuntak (accessed 23 May 2018).

———. 2017b. "Developing Poor Little Rich Natuna's Economy". *ISEAS Perspective*, no. 2017/43, 27 June 2017.

———. 2018. "A Special Law for Archipelagic Provinces: Is It Necessary for Kepri?". *ISEAS Perspective* 2018/10, 23 February 2018.

Soeriaatmadja, Wahyudi. 2018. "Batam Authorities Seize 66kg of Jakarta-bound Drugs, Officials Believe Singapore Was Possible Transit Point". *Straits Times*, 29 January 2018. https:// www.straitstimes.com/asia/se-asia/batam-authorities-make-big-drug-bust (accessed 24 July 2018).

Straits Times. 2017. "Police Take Steps to Prevent Spread of Radicalism". 9 May 2017. https:// www.straitstimes.com/asia/se-asia/riau-police-take-steps-to-prevent-spread-radicalism (accessed 8 June 2018).

Suparlan, Pusardi, et al. 1989. *Interaksi Antar Etnik di Beberapa Poprinsi di Indonesia*. Jakarta: Departemen Pendidikan dan Kebudayaan,

Surat-surat perdjandjian antara Kesultanan Riau dengan pemerintahan² V.O.C. dan Hindia Belanda 1784–1909. Jakarta: Arsip Negara, 1970.

Suryadi, Hery. 2008. *Gerakan Riau Merdeka: Menggugat Sentralisme Kekuasaan yang Berlebihan*. Yogyakarta: Pustaka Pelajar

Suryadinata, Leo and Mustafa Izzudin. *The Natunas: Territorial Integrity in the Forefront of Indonesia–China Relations*. ISEAS – Yusof Ishak Institute, 2017.

Syatauw, J.J.G. *Some Newly Established Asian States and the Development of International Law*. The Hague: Nijhoff, 1961.

Tan Khee Giap et al. *Annual Competitiveness Analysis and Development Strategies for Indonesian Provinces*. Singapore: World Scientific Publishing, 2016.

Thomas, Karen. 2016. "Theatrical change paralleling socio-political developments in Indonesia's Natuna archipelago in the South China Sea: The case for Malay *mendu* theatre performance". *Indonesia and the Malay World* 44, no. 130: 327–41.

Timor Express. 2017. "Problematika dan Solusi Provinsi Kepulauan atau Berciri Kepulauan". 17 October 2017. http://timorexpress.fajar.co.id/2017/10/17/problematika-dan-solusi-provinsi-kepulauan-atau-berciri-kepulauan/ (accessed 3 June 2018).

Tirtosudarmo, Riwanto. "Transmigration and its Centre-Regional Context: The Case of Riau and South Kalimantan Provinces/ Indonesia". Ph.D. Thesis. ANU 1990.

Tribun Jambi. 2017. "Pulau Berhala Dimiliki Kepri, Kini Jambi Kebagian Mengiklankan dan BangunInfrastruktur". 11 November 2017. https://jambi.tribunnews.com/2017/11/11/ pulau-berhala-dimiliki-kepri-kini-jambi-kebagian-mengiklankan-dan-bangun-infrastruktur/ (accessed 5 August 2018).

Tribunebisnis 2017. "Menteri Susi Sedih Sumber Daya Laut Lama Terlupakan". 30 October 2017. https://www.tribunnews.com/bisnis/2017/10/30/menteri-susi-sedih-sumber-daya-laut-lama-terlupakan/ (accessed 3 June 2018).

Van Hasselt, A.L. and Schwartz, H.J.E.F. *De Poelau Toedjoeh in het Zuidelijk Gedeelte der Chineesche Zee*. Leiden: E.J. Brill, 1898.

Vogelsang, A.W.L. 1926. "Gegevens betreffende den Tambelan- en den Watas-Archipel". *Adatrechbundels* 26: 12–21.

Waddell, Sarah. "Rising to the Challenge of Providing Legal Protection for the Indonesian Coastal and Marine Environment". In *Indonesia beyond the Water's Edge: Managing an Archipelagic State*, edited by R.B. Cribb and Michele Ford. Singapore: ISEAS – Yusof Ishak Institute, 2009, pp. 172–94.

Wicaksana, I Gede Wahyu. "Indonesia's Maritime Connectivity Development: Domestic and International Challenges". *Asian Journal of Political Science* 25, no. 2 (2017): 212–33.

8

STATE FORMATION AND STATE CAPACITY IN THE RIAU ISLANDS PROVINCE

Mulya Amri and Faizal Rianto[1]

INTRODUCTION

The formation of Riau Islands as Indonesia's thirty-second province in 2004 can be seen as part of a broader trend that saw the creation of new subnational government entities—seven provinces and 112 districts in total—throughout the country after the end of the New Order era (Tirtosudarmo 2008; Kimura 2013). This can be considered as a rational response from the peripheries against decades of centralization of wealth and power in Jakarta that culminated in the late 1990s (Emmerson 2000; Mietzner 2014; Malley 1999).

At the same time, the desire to form a separate Province of the Riau Islands (henceforth PRI) can also be understood through local cultural and historical circumstances that are unique to the region. These include a shared history of being torchbearers of the great Malay civilization and maritime empires that dominated the local seas before the arrival of European explorers and colonizers (Trocki 2007; Killingray, Lincoln and Rigby 2004; Long 2013).

This combination of both rational interests and cultural sentiments was argued to have motivated numerous subnational separatist movements in South Asia, such as in Assam, Kashmir, and Punjab (Mitra 1995). In Indonesia, some subnational movements were indeed separatist in nature, as in the cases of Aceh, Papua, (mainland) Riau, and East Timor.[2] In contrast to these, however, the goal of subnationalism in the Riau

Islands was not separatism, but broad autonomy in the context of decentralization. Still, in line with Mitra's (1995) thesis, this chapter argues that both rational interests and cultural sentiments were the main motivations for establishing PRI in 2002 and are still relevant for understanding much of the political dynamics taking place in the province in 2019.

This chapter describes state formation and capacity in the Riau Islands Province. We acknowledge the definition of the state as adopted by Ruggie (1993), namely an institution with legitimacy to exercise power over territorial space. But in this case, we also refer to the state as an autonomous government entity that may not be necessarily independent, such as a state in a federal country, or a province in decentralized Indonesia.

Following Costantini (2015, p. 24), this chapter defines state formation as "the process by which a state forms and evolves as a result of agents engaging in a struggle for power that leads to the creation and transformation of the sites of authority". As for state capacity, this chapter adopts the framework put forward by Besley and Persson (2009), covering a state's ability to achieve its stated goals by sustaining the market economy, taxing citizens, and achieving political equilibrium. The first part describes state formation, and the latter part describes state capacity.

In considering PRI as a subnational state, it is helpful to understand subnational movements, which are defined by Mitra (2012) as "collective efforts used to assert cultural nationalism in a territorial space that corresponds to a homeland that its advocates strongly believe to be legitimately theirs". He argued that subnational movements take a path that starts with build-up, followed by conflict, and if the movement is successful, culminates with banalization (Mitra 2012). Build-up of the movement starts with the establishment of a common identity, often defined by a common affinity towards a certain ethnicity, language, religion, or a collective sense of being oppressed. As the movement builds up, a conflict then takes place between proponents of the movement and the central state (or another higher-level authority seen as element of the central state). Finally, if the movement succeeds and an autonomous subnational entity is established, it becomes inducted into the day-to-day politics of running a government.

This chapter starts with an overview of Indonesia's abrupt and extensive adoption of the devolution of authority to the subnational level right after the fall of Soeharto's New Order regime in 1998. Subsequently, it explains the process of PRI's formation within the political context of central-eastern Sumatra, starting with the secession of Riau from Central Sumatra Province in 1958, until the secession of the Riau Islands from Riau Province in 2002.

In so doing, the chapter discusses the relevant motivations, actors, and actions related to such secession. Throughout this narrative, aside from the rational struggles over power and wealth, it finds the notion of "Malayness", or the unique sentiment of "Being Malay" (Long 2013), to play a prominent role in the formation of a cultural identity to support the formation of PRI. Next, the chapter explains the processes of institutional development and state capacity in PRI after the province was formed, including the development of government structure, manpower, budget and political dynamics. Finally, it ends with an overview of the PRI's progress with some key indicators of human development, and assessment of the extent to which the new province has lived up to its promise.

Ultimately, the chapter concludes that PRI's state formation is a natural process where cultural identities are being reasserted and local autonomies renegotiated in a large and diverse post-colonial country like Indonesia. Following Mietzner (2014), it argues that the formation is largely positive—despite the obvious hiccups—in achieving a balance between keeping the country intact while allowing local stakeholders to have enough authority to achieve the kind of development that they want.

RIAU ISLANDS IN THE CONTEXT OF DECENTRALIZATION

The formation of PRI through the separation from Riau Province in 2002, and its subsequent enactment in 2004 was not a unique phenomenon for Indonesia and was just one of the ways in which some of the country's internal territories changed in terms of physical boundaries and cultural identities (Kimura 2013). In fact, there were seven new provinces established within a five-year period following the end of the New Order in 1998. These include: North Maluku (formed in 1999, separated from Maluku); Gorontalo (2000, from North Sulawesi); Bangka Belitung Islands (2000, from South Sumatra); Banten (2000, from West Java); West Papua (2001, from Papua); West Sulawesi (2004, from South Sulawesi); and Riau Islands (2002, from Riau). Aside from these seven provinces, 112 new subprovincial districts (*kota* or *kabupaten*, also called regencies) were also formed.

Indonesia sees the formation of new subnational governments in both a positive and negative light. On one hand, subnationalism seemed to accommodate the demands of many local stakeholders. Indeed the process is formally called *pemekaran* (which translates positively as proliferation or blossoming). On the other hand, the process also seemed to have gotten out of hand, with increased cases of corruption, abuse of local power, and the rise of local leaders who acted as "little kings" (Hadiz 2003). Indonesia thus put a moratorium on the creation of new subnational governments between 2009 and 2012; after which the requirements for secession have become more difficult.

Not all attempts at creating new subnational entities were successful. Some proposed new provinces did not materialize, such as the cases of East Sulawesi (Tirtosudarmo 2008) and Central Papua (Brata 2008; Sumule 2003). In the case of East Sulawesi, Tirtosudarmo (2008) indicates that the movement was motivated largely by political and territorial claims, but without a strong enough cultural identity in ethnic or religious terms. This contrasts with the formation of Gorontalo province, whose population (largely Muslims and Gorontaloese) is distinct ethnically and religiously from the main province of North Sulawesi (largely Christians and Minahasans). The same goes for the separation of North Maluku (largely Muslim) from Maluku (largely Christian), of West Sulawesi (largely of the Mandar ethnic group) from South Sulawesi (largely Bugis), and of Banten (largely Bantenese) from West Java (largely Sundanese).

Seen within a longer timeframe of Indonesia's post-colonial trajectory, the formation of new subnational entities has been a common affair. When Indonesia first declared independence in 1945, the country had only eight provinces: Sumatra, Kalimantan, Sulawesi, the Lesser Sunda Islands, Maluku and three provinces in Java Island: West Java, Central Java and East Java. Sumatra was later divided into three provinces (North Sumatra, Central Sumatra and South Sumatra) in 1950, and Kalimantan was apportioned into West Kalimantan, East Kalimantan and South Kalimantan in 1956. Many of these new provinces were created based on subnational cultural sentiments or as part of a strategy to deal with separatist threats. By the end of the "Old Order" era in 1966, Indonesia had twenty-four provinces.

Under Soeharto, separatist movements were largely crushed and a common national identity and governing system—arguably based on Javanese values—were adopted. Subnational governments were an extension of the central government and formal local leaders and their annual budgets were very much decided in Jakarta—making Indonesia one of the most centralized states in Southeast Asia (Malley 1999). During this thirty-two-year era, only three new provinces were established: Bengkulu (1967), West Irian (1969, later renamed as Irian Jaya), and East Timor (annexed in 1976). The pent-up demand from various subnational regions to establish their cultural identities was bound to burst. Meanwhile, old separatist movements remained alive in some of Indonesia's most peripheral regions such as Aceh, Irian Jaya, and East Timor.

Demand for larger autonomy and fiscal resources (or even independence) finally found an outlet in 1998 (Kimura 2013). The fall of Soeharto provided space for Indonesia's subnational regions to demand more governing authority and self-determination over their territories, including a fairer share of the revenue from natural resources (Malley 1999). East Timor broke off from Indonesia in 1999 and became the independent nation of Timor-Leste. Threats of separatism from Irian Jaya and Aceh, and to a lesser degree from oil-rich provinces such as Riau and East Kalimantan, became more worrying than ever. To keep the country from disintegrating, Indonesia adopted a large-scale decentralization measure that devolved much of its governing authority to the district (subprovincial) level.[3] This was a strategic choice to give in to local demands but without allowing provinces to gain too much in strength. There was fear that stronger provinces could lead to stronger separatist movements (Emmerson 2000).

The provinces plagued by separatism were dealt with carefully. Irian Jaya was renamed Papua and obtained "special autonomy" where the bulk of natural resource revenue originating from the province was sent back to be used at their discretion.[4] Similarly, Aceh was allowed special autonomy, where it could apply shariah law and have local political parties.[5] Throughout the country, the new decentralization laws now allow localities to decide on their own development priorities and the central government distributes the financial resources for them to do so. In a positive light, this is viewed as "new regionalism" where local stakeholders are rediscovering their regional identities, redrawing the boundaries of their territories, and renegotiating their relationship with the central government (Tirtosudarmo 2008).

Decentralization in Indonesia was primarily driven by concerns of political and ethnic identity rather than economic rationality, much to the "disappointment" of many decentralization scholars (Malesky and Hutchinson 2016), and despite the increasing realization of the strategic roles that subnational governments can play in local economic development and industrialization (Hutchinson 2013; OECD 2013; Oates 1972). The inception of the Riau Islands as a separate province from Riau occurred largely in this context. But to understand the motivation for this movement, and why PRI was more likely to be approved by the central government (despite rejection from Riau Province), this chapter needs to explain the history of subnationalism in Riau and in the Riau Islands.

FORMATION OF RIAU ISLANDS PROVINCE

Riau's Malay Kingdoms

The history of the Riau Islands and its surrounding regions goes back hundreds of years to the Melaka sultanate, which served as an entrepôt connecting India, China and the eastern parts of Indonesia (Rab 2002). Melaka was not only a centre of trade but also a centre of Malay culture and the hub for Islam's spread in Southeast Asia. The fall of Melaka to European powers made the kingdom move its capital to Johor; and the sultan of Johor then held influence over several smaller kingdoms, including Riau and Lingga to the south of the Singapore Strait.

The conflict between Dutch and British colonial powers in Southeast Asia over territorial authority culminated in the Treaty of London, signed in 1824. Traditional territories of Johor kingdom were divided based on an imaginary line that stretched along the Melaka Strait, where those to the south and west of the line became areas of Dutch influence, while those to the north and east of the line became British. Consequently, Peninsular Malaysia, including Johor and Singapore became British, while Sumatra and the islands to the immediate south of the Singapore Strait— including the Riau Islands—became Dutch.

The treaty led to a weakening of local rulers. Sultan Husen (Hussein) of Johor sold Singapore to Raffles in 1824 for a lump sum payment and a monthly stipend for the rest of his life (Ardi 2002; Rab 2002). Meanwhile, on the other side of the border, Sultan Abdurrahman of the Riau-Lingga kingdom acknowledged Dutch rule in the region and allowed the European power to establish a residency (*Residentie Riow*) in Tanjungpinang in return for protection for himself and his descendants (Rab 2002).

By the end of the nineteenth century, the Riau region was receiving increased foreign investments. Initially, these went mainly into plantations (rubber, copra), forestry, and mining. In 1893, the Sultan of Lingga gave concessions to foreign businesses for tin mining in Singkep Island, employing 300 locals and 700 migrant workers, mostly from China (Ardi 2002). Such mining activities further expanded to Karimun and Kundur islands, attracting many migrants and affecting the local population, who were mostly Malays working as farmers, fishers, and gatherers of forest products. Other foreign economic activities included logging, where logs were shipped to build Singapore and served the marine and shipbuilding industries there (Ardi 2002). Exploration of oil and gas started in 1924 by SOCAL (later renamed as Caltex and now Chevron) and production began in 1952 in the Minas oil fields in the Siak District or Regency of Riau, mainland Sumatra (Potter and Badcock 2001; *Jakarta Post*, 21 May 2014).

Riau Province

The 1948 amalgamation of three former Dutch residencies (West Sumatra, Jambi, and Riau) into a larger province of Central Sumatra[6] under the new Republic of Indonesia left many in Riau disappointed (Ardi 2002). The provincial capital of Central Sumatra was in Bukittinggi, West Sumatra, while the capital of Riau Residency was in Tanjungpinang. From the very beginning, there were already demands from people in Riau to take the oil-producing region of Siak (then part of Bengkalis Regency) out of Central Sumatra and turn it into a new province-level special territory (Ardi 2002). At the same time, separatist forces under the banner of the Revolutionary Government of the Republic of Indonesia (PRRI) based in Central Sumatra increasingly became a concern for the Sukarno government.

Local sentiments pushing for Riau to be its own province gained traction, and ultimately a law was issued in 1958 to split Central Sumatra three ways into West Sumatra, Jambi, and Riau.[7] At the same time, several other provinces in Indonesia, such as Sulawesi and Lesser Sunda, were also further divided into smaller provincial territories.

The 1958 law identified Tanjungpinang (the original capital of *Residentie Riow*) as the provincial capital of Riau to enable the immediate functioning of the new province. This made sense as Tanjungpinang already had readily available office buildings and a workforce trained in public administration from the Dutch era. However, the law also stated that the capital could be moved elsewhere if needed. After just one year, in 1959, a committee established by the Minister of Home Affairs indeed decided to move the provincial capital to Pekanbaru in mainland Sumatra (Rab 2002), leaving Tanjungpinang in a reduced position as the capital of Riau Islands Regency. Moving the provincial capital to Pekanbaru allowed the central government to have a much closer presence to the oil-producing regency of Bengkalis and better deal with the separatist movement, PRRI, also based in mainland Sumatra.

The motivation for Riau's secession from Central Sumatra was cited officially in Law 61/1958 and described in detail by Halim (2001). Formally, the issues were geographic distance and communication problems between the provincial capital in Bukittinggi and the regency capitals, which led to subpar and unequal delivery of services across various regencies. It was also acknowledged that the regency governments would like to have direct communication with the central government in Jakarta.

Following Mitra's (1995) argument presented earlier, the reasons for Riau's 1958 secession from Central Sumatra were partly rational and partly cultural. Secessionists claimed that more development took place in West Sumatra compared to Riau, and natural resources were exploited largely for the interests of "outsiders" (*Riau Pos*, 8 August 2011). Culturally, the Riau people identified themselves as Malays while the people of West Sumatra were Minangs. Secession proponents argued that many provincial government posts were held by people from Jakarta or West Sumatra, but not from Riau (*Riau Pos* 2011).

These reasons remained relevant for the subsequent demands for Riau's independence in the late 1990s. Several books published during that era were clearly pro-independence and provocatively titled, such as *Why Must We Have Independence? Tears and Blood of Riau People in Fighting for Dignity* (Halim 2001), published by the University of Riau Press.[8] In general, there were three political camps in Riau: those who wanted independence, those who wanted a federal system, and those who wanted expanded autonomy (Heri 2002).

Materially, there was disappointment at how the exploitation of Riau's riches (i.e., mining of oil in Siak, natural gas in Natuna, tin in Singkep, and sand in Karimun), as well as unfair compensation of land grabs in Bintan and Batam Islands did not materialize into better living standards for the local, native Malays (Halim 2001; Rab 2002). In the late 1990s, Riau was one of the provinces that contributed the most foreign exchange to Indonesia but had amongst the highest poverty rates (Halim 2001). Even as late as in 2015, there was still disappointment over the fact that gas from Natuna was sent directly to Singapore through a subsea pipeline while many areas in the Riau Islands were still in dire need of power (Antara 2015).

Culturally, Rab (2002) argued how the governor of Riau was always appointed by the central government, despite the people's wish to be governed by a local figure. For example, in 1985, members of the Riau Provincial Assembly (DPRD) voted for Ismail Suko, a native of Riau, for governor. Suko was preferred over General Imam Munandar, an army office from East Java who was proposed by the central government. Suko won the election but Munandar was made governor, nevertheless. This is chronicled in detail in a book titled *Riau's Tragedy in Upholding Democracy: The 2 September 1985 Incident* (Asril 2002).[9] Ironically, less than three years after he became governor, Munandar passed away, and was replaced by Soeripto, another armed forces officer of Javanese origin appointed by the central government (Asril 2002).

Riau Islands Province

The escalation of demand for Riau Islands' separation from Riau Province in the early 2000s was motivated by material and cultural sentiments. This is similar to the motivations that drove the secession of Riau from Central Sumatra in 1958, and the pro-independence movement in Riau in the 1990s.

The shifting of Riau's provincial capital from Tanjungpinang to Pekanbaru in 1959 disappointed many people in the Riau Islands, especially those who saw their region as the centre of the original Riau-Lingga kingdom. Culturally, the people of the Riau Islands considered themselves as "archipelagic Malays" as opposed to "mainland Malays". As a maritime kingdom, their main economic activities were fishing, seafaring and trading, as opposed to mainland Sumatra, where most were engaged in farming. Currently, many people from the Riau Islands identify themselves as "Kepri people" (*orang Kepri*), where Kepri is short for Kepulauan Riau (Riau Islands), to distinguish themselves from mainland Riau people. A detailed account of "Malayness" as the primary cultural identity of "Kepri people" is presented in Long (2013).

In terms of rational interests, the site of the provincial capital was indeed a contentious issue. For example, the creation of Central Sulawesi province in 1964 heightened a local power struggle over whether the capital should be in Palu or Poso (Tirtosudarmo 2008). In the case of Riau, the shifting of the provincial capital from Tanjungpinang to Pekanbaru in 1959 was argued to be detrimental for development in Riau Islands, largely due to the distance from the capital and difficulty for residents to attract the attention of provincial leaders (Ardi 2002). Local figures in the Riau Islands testified that the archipelagic parts of Riau were falling behind their peers in mainland Sumatra in terms of their economic development (Alhajj 2012).

The Riau Islands had abundant natural resources, such as tin in Singkep and Kundur, bauxite in Kijang, granite in Karimun; but not much of the benefits of these resources were felt by locals (Ardi 2002). Similarly, industrial development in Batam and tourism activities in Bintan were claimed to be more beneficial to foreign investors and Jakarta-based elites than to locals, and attracted workers largely from outside the region (Alhajj 2012).

In the case of PRI's formation, the Malay ethnic group was said to be "angry" and "frustrated" at the neglect of development in the archipelagic areas of Riau. This was portrayed in the book entitled *Malay Anger in the Demand for Riau Islands Province* (Ardi 2002).[10] In this book, Ardi explained that anger (*amuk*) and sulking/resentment (*ajuk*) were two important facets of Malay culture. For example, Malays in Riau Islands have, for a long time, expressed *ajuk* towards development in Batam, which he argued was detrimental to the local people. *Amuk* was, therefore, a reaction to reclaim local authority due to pent-up emotions of accommodating foreign and Jakarta-based interests, as shown in this sentence: "with Malay anger, hopefully, we can play a role and be respected in our own territory" (Ardi 2002).[11]

Following the aforementioned build-up, an opportunity to escalate tensions into conflict came with the fall of the New Order regime and the start of Indonesia's reform movement (*reformasi*). Student protests in Jakarta played an important role in toppling Soeharto and provided inspiration for students in the Riau Islands. The discourse to establish a separate Riau Islands Province started during the Grand Conference of Riau Islands People (Musyawarah Besar Masyarakat Kepulauan Riau) on 15 May 1999 in Tanjungpinang. This was attended by the representatives of twenty-two subdistricts within Riau Islands Regency (Ardi 2002). The conference resulted in three demands (Alhajj 2012): first, to accelerate the equitable development of people's welfare through the establishment of a separate province; second, to apportion Riau Islands into the following regencies and/or cities: Tanjungpinang, Bintan, Karimun, Lingga Islands, and Pulau Tujuh (Natuna Islands); third, to convert Batam—at that time an administrative city—into an autonomous city within PRI.

To follow up on these demands, an executive team for the formation of PRI, commonly known as the "Team of Nine" was established, comprised of prominent Riau Islands leaders based in Tanjungpinang, Pekanbaru and Jakarta, led by Mr Huzrin Hood (Ardi 2002). At the time, Huzrin Hood was a member of the People's Representative Assembly of the Riau Islands Regency (DPRD Kabupaten Kepulauan Riau). In late 1999, he was again elected as DPRD member and became head of the assembly's Committee for the Establishment of PRI (Badan Pekerja Pembentukan Provinsi Kepulauan Riau, or BP3KP) (Alhajj 2012). In 2001, Hood was elected as Head (*bupati*) of the Riau Islands Regency. Many saw him as a symbol of resistance against Pekanbaru (Ardi 2002) and as someone who was willing to resign from his post if PRI formation failed (Rab 2002, p. 43). Some others saw this movement as one that was led by local elites (Rab 2002).

The movement to establish PRI faced major challenges, especially from the governor of Riau. The governor was concerned that the formation of PRI would lead to the secession of other areas in Riau, such as oil-rich Bengkalis (Azlaini 2001). Separation of Riau Islands would also lead to declining income for Riau, since the regency contributed substantially to Riau Province's income through industrial estates in Batam, tourist resorts in Bintan, as well as natural gas from Natuna.

One of the major opponents of PRI's formation was Tabrani Rab, professor at the University of Riau, who wrote the book *Riau, Let's Unite (Rejection of PRI)* (Rab 2002).[12] Through an analysis of the lineage of rulers in the area, he argued that the Malay kingdoms in Lingga, Kampar, Siak and Indragiri were part of one kingdom: Riau. Further, he stated that when Riau Province was established in 1958, there was no intention to create two separate provinces. He questioned: "Will our 500-year history be divided into two provinces, Maritime Riau and Mainland Riau? Let the people dividing Riau be damned by the spirits of Riau's Sultans" (Rab 2002, p. 7).[13]

Rab was a member of the Local Autonomy Advisory Board (Dewan Pertimbangan Otonomi Daerah, or DPOD), a central level decentralization forum that reports directly to the President.[14] DPOD rejected the formation of PRI on the following grounds: the process did not have the approval of Riau's governor and provincial assembly; moreover, there were also objections from the regent and the regency assembly of Natuna (Rab 2002). It was said that the reason for Natuna's rejection was because they were treated unfairly while being part of the Riau Islands Regency (Riau Mandiri, 30 March 2002, quoted in Rab 2002).

The DPOD report also stated that the Riau Islands did not have the human resource capacity to be a province. Rab (2002) argued that becoming a province would turn the local Malays into second-class citizens in their own territory, unable to compete against migrants, and under the influence of foreigners, Jakarta-based powers, and implicitly, local elites like Huzrin Hood. It was also argued that the domination of Chinese businesses (be they from Singapore, Hong Kong or Malaysia) in the Riau Islands would change Batam into "Hong Kong country" (Heri 2002, p. 45).[15]

Proponents of the new province rejected these claims, and they were particularly offended that the Governor of Riau and his supporters seemed to indicate that movement for PRI formation was driven by foreign, instead of local Malay interests. They countered with statements that PRI was the true home of Malay people and that the "Malayness" of Riau Islands should not be questioned as Malays are found everywhere, in contrast to Pekanbaru, where it was difficult to even hear Malay being spoken due to the large number of migrants (Ardi 2002, p. 75).

The movement to establish PRI used three major strategies (Ardi 2002): first, through a communicative approach to the provincial government in Riau, which failed; second, through mass movements (demonstrations) to prove that the demand was broad-based and not just reflective of elite interests, and; third, through lobbying to the central government and national congress. The third strategy was the most successful as the creation and abolition of subnational governments were within the authority of the congress.

PRI formation proponents understood very well the central government's concern to keep the country together amid threats of separatism. While some in Riau Province demanded independence, proponents of PRI firmly declared themselves part of the unitary state of Indonesia (Negara Kesatuan Republik Indonesia), and this allowed them to gain the support of the central government, which was trying to prevent Riau Province from seceding (Kimura 2013). Proponents of PRI formation demanded the central government acknowledge them as a province within Indonesia, but were not afraid to threaten separatism, as shown in this statement: "We have had enough of being lied to. As dignified Malay people, if we cannot have our own province, then why should we be afraid to 'shout independence'?" (Ardi 2002, p. xii).[16] They distinguished their movement from Riau separatism and even took a jab at Riau's claims of ethnicity: "Whereas the people of Mainland Riau wish to form their own country by separating from Indonesia, the people of Riau Islands are very wise to fight within the corridors of the unitary state of Indonesia. This is the difference between us Malays and non-Malays" (Ardi 2002, p. 46).[17]

Despite discouraging advice from the local autonomy advisory council (DPOD), the national congress (DPR RI) established a special committee (panitia khusus) to review the proposed formation of PRI, based on signatures of fifty DPR RI members who used their right to take the initiative (Heri 2002). Between 24 January and 4 February of 2002, allegedly 5,000 people gathered at the Hotel Indonesia Roundabout in Jakarta, a popular place to conduct mass rallies, to show that the province's formation was not an elite affair, as had been claimed by Pekanbaru (Ardi 2002). In May of 2002, to commemorate the three-year anniversary of the first public demand for the creation of PRI, mass demonstrations took place in Tanjungpinang, which involved dramatic events such as the burning of statues of prominent people who opposed PRI formation, ceremonial changing of civil servants' shirts, and the changing of nameplates in office buildings (Ardi 2002).

The government finally approved the formation of PRI through Law 25/2002, signed in October of 2002. The new province was to consist of five existing autonomous regencies and cities in Riau Province, namely: Karimun Regency; Natuna Regency (including areas which later became Anambas Regency); Riau Islands Regency (consisting of areas which later became Bintan Regency and Lingga Regency); Batam City; and Tanjungpinang City.

STATE CAPACITY IN RIAU ISLANDS PROVINCE

The second section of this chapter explores state capacity in PRI after its formation. Keeping with Mitra's (2012) framework, the following includes a description of the process of becoming a province in the administrative sense, or a "banalization" of the struggle for PRI. After the formal establishment of PRI in 2002, there was a "vacuum" period during which PRI was under the supervision of the Assistance Team (Tim Asistensi) of the Ministry of Home Affairs.[18] During this brief period, the team was tasked to find a suitable mode of governance for the province. Their suggestion was that PRI as a province would have no governor in its initial three years, and that the governor of the parent province (Riau) would govern both provinces jointly. The governor of Riau would also prepare and authorize PRI's budget, which would be in the form of financial assistance from Riau Province.[19] However, PRI proponents rejected the proposal and pushed to have their own democratically elected governor.

This demand was accommodated, and PRI conducted its first gubernatorial election in 2005—together with six other provinces and more than 200 cities and regencies nationwide that took part in Indonesia's first-ever direct local elections. In the meantime, to start the actual functioning of PRI as a province, the central government appointed Mr Ismeth Abdullah, chairman of the Batam Industrial Development Authority (BIDA), an institution that has played an important role in the development of Batam since the 1980s, as acting governor in 2004. Ismeth was originally appointed as BIDA chairman by President Habibie in 1998 to lead industrial development in Batam.[20] His tenure as BIDA chairman (1998–2004) was considered successful and he received prestigious government awards in 2000 (Satyalencana Pembangunan) and 2003 (Bintang Jasa Utama).

Between 2002 and 2008, there were several changes to the cities and regencies within PRI. In 2003, parts of Riau Islands Regency broke off and became a new regency called Lingga. This regency includes the Lingga and Singkep islands, where the old Lingga kingdom was based. Secondly, the remaining parts of Riau Islands Regency were renamed as Bintan Regency in 2006 because the area is now largely confined to Bintan Island and surrounding areas. Thirdly, in 2008, parts of Natuna Regency broke off and became the new Anambas Islands Regency (sometimes also known as Pulau Tujuh, based on old terminology used during the Dutch era).

Politics

Indonesia's post-1998 *reformasi* era was not only known for local autonomy but also for local democracy. Since its formation, PRI has had three direct gubernatorial elections;

in 2005, 2010 and 2015. PRI's first gubernatorial election in 2005 was depicted well by Choi (2007). Acting Governor Ismeth left his post in early 2005 and participated in the election as a gubernatorial candidate. His candidate for vice-governor was Mr Muhammad Sani, then regent of Karimun and a senior local Malay bureaucrat who had held various positions in the Riau Islands. Ismeth is not a Malay and did not originally come from the Riau Islands, so his partnership with Sani was considered politically required to win the votes of the local Malay community. The Ismeth-Sani pair won the election by a landslide, collecting more than 60 per cent of the votes (Choi 2007).

Interestingly, Huzrin Hood—often considered as one of the central figures in the formation of PRI—did not participate in the race for governor. He was convicted in 2003 for misappropriating funds in 2001–02, when he was head of Riau Islands Regency (*Tempo*, 8 March 2010). Huzrin was freed in 2006 after serving his sentence, just missing the 2005 election. A corruption case also saw the end of Ismeth Abdullah's tenure as governor in 2010. He was detained in February of that year for corruption in the procurement of fire engines that took place during his tenure as BIDA chairman (*Kompas*, 23 February 2010).

Being detained prevented Ismeth from his original plan to bid for re-election in May 2010. Ismeth was about to compete against his former vice governor, Sani, for the governorship. Sani partnered with Soerya Respationo as his vice-governor candidate. Soerya was the head of the PDI-P party in PRI, a party that has been traditionally very strong in Batam. Ultimately, the Sani-Soerya pair won the 2010 elections rather narrowly, by winning about 37 per cent of the votes, while the two other candidate pairs (one pair included Ismeth's wife) each collected 31 per cent of the votes (*Kompas*, 9 June 2010).

Whereas during the Ismeth-Sani administration of 2006–11, PRI's long-term development plan focused on improving human resources and infrastructure,[21] the Sani-Soerya administration changed priorities for the 2011–16 period. Optimizing the utilization of marine and fishery resources, as well as developing marine-based tourism were some of their targets,[22] and this was considered more in line with the demands of the local population.

By the time of the subsequent local elections in 2015, Sani and Soerya had parted ways and competed against each other for the governor position. This time, Sani partnered with Nurdin Basyirun, a senior Malay bureaucrat who served two periods as regent of Karimun in 2005–15. Previously, Sani and Nurdin had already worked closely as regent and vice-regent, respectively, of Karimun in 2001–5. The pair won the 2015 governor elections by a close margin, winning 53.2 per cent of the votes, while opponent Soerya and his vice-governor candidate secured the remaining 46.8 per cent (*Batamnews*, 14 December 2015).

The marine and fisheries sectors remained a strong focus of PRI for the Sani-Nurdin administration. But they also added more prioritized policies to develop PRI's manufacturing and shipyard sectors, as well as increase the role of the port authority (Badan Usaha Pelabuhan).[23]

Indeed, Sani and Nurdin were supposed to govern the province in 2016–21. However, Sani passed away in April 2016 due to sickness, one year after being re-elected. To take over his place, vice-governor Nurdin was inaugurated as governor in May 2016. In December 2017, Mr Isdianto, Sani's younger brother, was chosen as the new vice-governor. Nurdin's tenure as governor also did not last long. In July 2019, he was detained for corruption relating to the issuance of an unlawful permit for a land reclamation project (*Kompas*, 12 July 2019). Isdianto, Sani's brother, has immediately since then became the acting governor.[24]

Regardless of the leaders, local elections have been a vibrant and popular affair in Riau Islands, especially considering the diverse ethnic base of PRI's population. The Indonesia Democracy Index (IDI), published annually since 2009 by the National Development Planning Agency (Bappenas) and the Central Statistics Agency (BPS), identifies PRI as among Indonesia's better-performing provinces (ranked eighth out of thirty-four provinces, with an IDI score of 76.3 in 2017) in terms of democratic achievements. PRI's overall IDI score fluctuated mildly from 73.6 in 2009 to 65.6 in 2012 but has been steadily improving since then (see Figure 8.1). For six of the nine years between 2009 and 2017, PRI's IDI score has been higher than the average score for Sumatra provinces and for Indonesia. This seems to indicate that PRI's quality of democracy is not bad. However, many other Indonesian provinces have been improving in terms of their IDI score.

Going into the different aspects of the IDI, as seen in Figure 8.2, PRI performed relatively better in terms of Civil Liberty, despite showing a trend of deterioration in 2009–13 and improvement since then. The Civil Liberty aspect measures freedom of speech, religion, and assembly and suggests that PRI is quite a liberal place in terms of expressing political and religious viewpoints. Meanwhile, PRI's scores for the Political Rights aspect—which includes people's participation in politics and in the monitoring of governance processes—seemed to be its weakest until 2014 but has improved tremendously since then. Low scores for political rights in the earlier period seem to suggest that the people have not been participating actively in the day-to-day functioning of politics and governance and that these have remained largely an elite affair, although that is changing. PRI's performance in the Democratic Institutions aspect (i.e., having free and fair elections, an active role of the assembly) fluctuated over the years but remained fairly stable.

Public Management

Immediately after its formation, PRI faced challenges in its institutional development. It did not have functioning organizations or adequate personnel to run the bureaucracy.[25] Between 2002 and 2004, the number of civil servants working for the fledgling PRI government numbered around 100 personnel. Initially, civil servants from cities and regencies within PRI were requested to transfer to the provincial level. However, many were hesitant to answer the call, largely due to: a perceived career uncertainty; lack of sound personnel management system; and small budget

FIGURE 8.1
Indonesia Democracy Index with the Riau Islands Province in Perspective, 2009–15

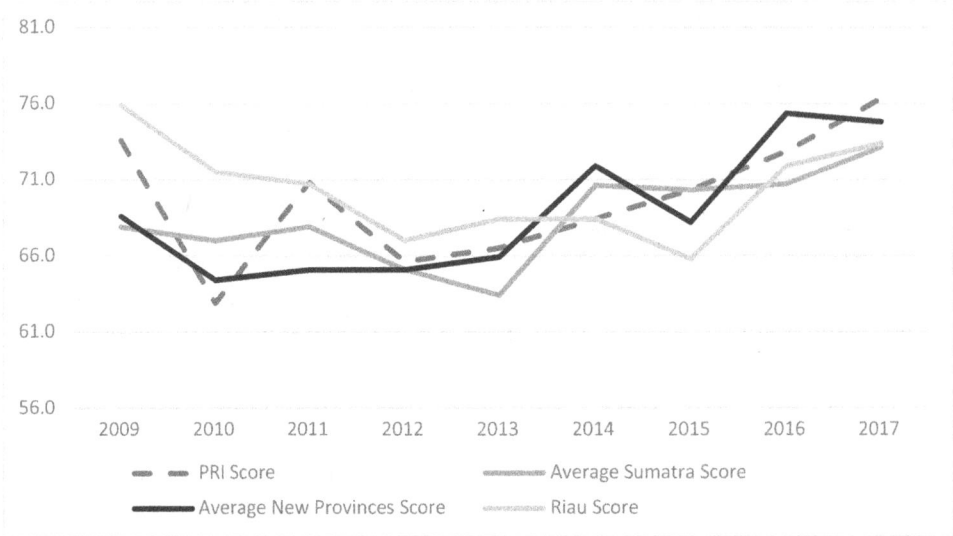

Legend:
- PRI Score
- Average Sumatra Score
- Average New Provinces Score
- Riau Score

Source: Authors based on data from the Central Statistics Agency (BPS).

FIGURE 8.2
Components of Indonesia Democracy Index for the Riau Islands, 2009–17

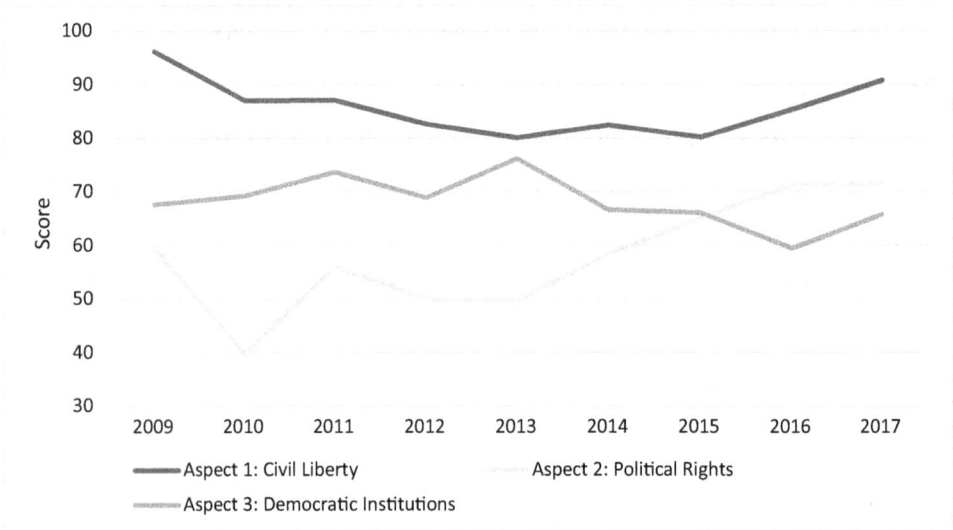

Legend:
- Aspect 1: Civil Liberty
- Aspect 2: Political Rights
- Aspect 3: Democratic Institutions

Source: Authors based on data from the Central Statistics Agency (BPS).

for the provincial organization. Many who already held comfortable positions in their respective regencies were reluctant to transfer to the PRI provincial government as they might not have been able to keep their positions at the province level, or they would have had to compete for promotion against more qualified people. Payment issues also contributed to the low number of personnel transfers. During that period, civil servants at the provincial level received fewer benefits than those in the regencies and cities. Consequently, PRI in its early years depended on unqualified personnel employed as auxiliaries (*pegawai tidak tetap*), mainly as clerks or administrators.

The provincial government started to offer more benefits and better performance incentives to civil servants in 2006. Subsequently, the provincial government started its own recruitment processes, both through transfers from cities and regencies as well as through open recruitment. Personnel transfers were mainly from Bintan Regency (previously called Riau Islands Regency), Tanjungpinang City, and Karimun Regency.

Over time, PRI attracted more qualified personnel and, as of 2016, there were 2,714 civil servants at the provincial level (not including those at the cities and regencies). This translates to a civil servant to population ratio of about 0.13, which is consistent with the proportion in Riau. The parent province had 7,969 civil servants at the provincial level and a population of 6,500,971 in 2016, leading to a civil servant to population ratio of 0.12 per cent. The ratio of provincial civil servants to the population in 2016 for other provinces varies from 0.08 per cent in Banten (with Banten being a relatively denser province) to 0.24 per cent in Bangka Belitung Islands (a new province in Sumatra).

Most civil servants in PRI (about 72 per cent) have a bachelor's degrees or higher, about 18 per cent have diplomas, and about 10 per cent are high school graduates or lower (see Figure 8.3). The proportion of bachelors' degree holders was highest in 2016 at 72 per cent, whereas in previous years it was: 68 per cent (2015), 71 per cent (2014), 69 per cent (2013), and 70 per cent (2012). Between 2010 and 2016, the number of PRI civil servants grew at an average rate of about 5.1 per cent per year. It was not possible to get personnel data for 2004–6 due to poor integration of the filing system in PRI, where data and other official files were kept by an individual either in a portable mass storage device or in a personal or office computer.[26] This highlights one of the growing pains in the life of a newly formed province, consistent with the narrative of "banalization" mentioned earlier.

According to the legal document on the formation of the Riau Islands Province,[27] Tanjungpinang was designated as the capital, but during the province's early years, the provisional centre of administration was Batam. This was done to ensure a smooth transition of government functions until the first elected governor was inaugurated. Batam was a much larger city than Tanjungpinang and had been the growth centre and industrial hub of the Riau Islands. Thus, the city had the infrastructure and capacity to support PRI's interim government functions.

Tanjungpinang formally became PRI's capital only in 2006, shortly after the inauguration of PRI's first elected governor, Ismeth Abdullah. However, due to a lack of office space for the growing provincial government, the latter had to make do with temporary space. Some of these temporary solutions were former offices of the

FIGURE 8.3
Number of Civil Servants in the Riau Islands Government by Education Level, 2010–16

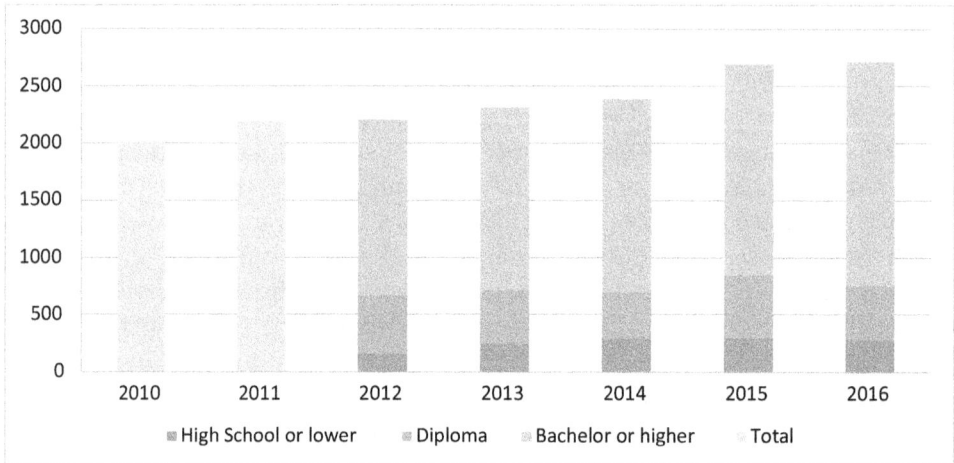

Source: Authors based on data from PRI annual statistical publication Kepulauan Riau Dalam Angka, 2012–2017.

Riau Islands Regency, and the PRI government was even said to have rented shop houses (*rumah toko*) in Tanjungpinang City, some of which were in "unrepresentative conditions" (Detiawati 2008). This led to the demand for a new, dedicated compound for PRI government offices. The location of this compound was later decided to be on the island of Dompak, off the coast but still within the limits of Tanjungpinang City (see Map 3.2).[28]

Technically, the main factor in determining Dompak Island as the location for the provincial government compound was geographical, with the zone not overlapping with or located in an existing town or a city. Another factor was land, with the zone not being located on productive land. Also, the site had to have enough vacant and affordable land available. Dompak Island fulfilled these requirements, including the government's budget (Detiawati 2008), despite its rather isolated location away from the Tanjungpinang city centre.

The master plan for the provincial government office compound in Dompak was completed in 2007, but has been revised twice—in 2012 and 2014. In each revision, the environmental management plan was amended due to a mismatch between plan and implementation, subpar economic and social development plans, and conflict of existing regulations (Amelia and Mussadun 2015).

Dompak was planned as a multiyear scheme, with several strategic developments, namely, the Gubernatorial Office Complex, Provincial Assembly Building, a mosque, a sports stadium, and Dompak Bridge (there were three bridges connecting Dompak with mainland Tanjungpinang: Dompak Bridge I, II and III). The cost of development was IDR1.6 trillion. However, the ambitious development plan was revised due to concerns about the financial capacity of the province. After the revision, the construction of the sports stadium was removed from the strategic plan (*Jawa Pos*, 20 November 2016).

Physical development in Dompak faced some issues. Dompak Bridge I, for example, a 1.5-km-long bridge that connects mainland Tanjungpinang and Dompak Island, collapsed in 2015, eight years after completion (*Tempo*, 4 October 2015). The provincial government also faced a lawsuit by one of its contractors for construction delays and was made to pay IDR42 billion out of the IDR92 billion demanded (*Tribunnews Batam*, 29 April 2013).

Aside from dealing with office space, a government agency needs to manage public revenue and expenditure. As seen in Figure 8.4, the provincial government budget (APBD) for PRI grew substantially from 2004 to 2015. In 2015, PRI's revenue and expenditure were about IDR3,227 billion and IDR3,670 billion, respectively (in current prices). In 2004, the corresponding figures were about IDR245 billion and IDR239 billion, respectively (in current prices). These translate to average increases of about 29 per cent per year for revenue and 33 per cent per year for expenditure.

In terms of expenditure on a per capita basis, PRI's provincial expenditure grew from IDR658,000 in 2006, to IDR1.06 million in 2010, and to IDR1.86 million in 2015, according to the annual financial statistics of the province government, published by BPS. As a comparison, the corresponding figures for Riau Province were IDR632,000 in 2006, IDR770,000 in 2010, and IDR1.68 million in 2015. Both PRI and Riau Province have markedly higher provincial government expenditure per capita than the average for Indonesia's provinces, which were IDR288,000 in 2006, IDR472,000 in 2010, and IDR1.09 million in 2015. In terms of the types of expenditure, PRI's direct expenditure has been consistently larger than its indirect expenditure, indicating that a good percentage of the budget has been used for rubrics that "directly" benefit the population, such as goods, services, and capital spending (see Figure 8.4).

Own-source revenue contributed to between 25 and 44 per cent of PRI's total revenue. This was relatively higher than in many other Indonesian provinces (see Figure 8.5). The larger part of PRI's revenue (an average of 61 per cent over the years) came from transfers from the central government, but out of these transfers, close to two-thirds came from the revenue-sharing component (*Dana Bagi Hasil*[29]) (see Figure 8.6). Only about one-third came from unconditional grants (*Dana Alokasi Umum*). The opposite is found in many other provinces, where revenue primarily comes from unconditional grants. Thus, it can be said that PRI is financially more independent than other provinces, primarily due to its higher level of locally-sourced income.

In terms of government performance, the Ministry of Home Affairs has been conducting an annual evaluation of the performance of regional governments (Evaluasi Kinerja Penyelenggaraan Pemerintahan Daerah, or EKPPD) since 2009. The evaluation was conducted for various roles and responsibilities that regional governments were tasked to do, and the source for evaluation was the respective regional governments' annual report. The evaluation was conducted for all subnational government entities (provinces, cities, and regencies) throughout the country, where each regional government was ranked against its peers. The evaluation rankings are shown in Table 8.1.

FIGURE 8.4
Government Revenue and Expenditure of the Riau Islands, 2004–15
(IDR million, current prices)

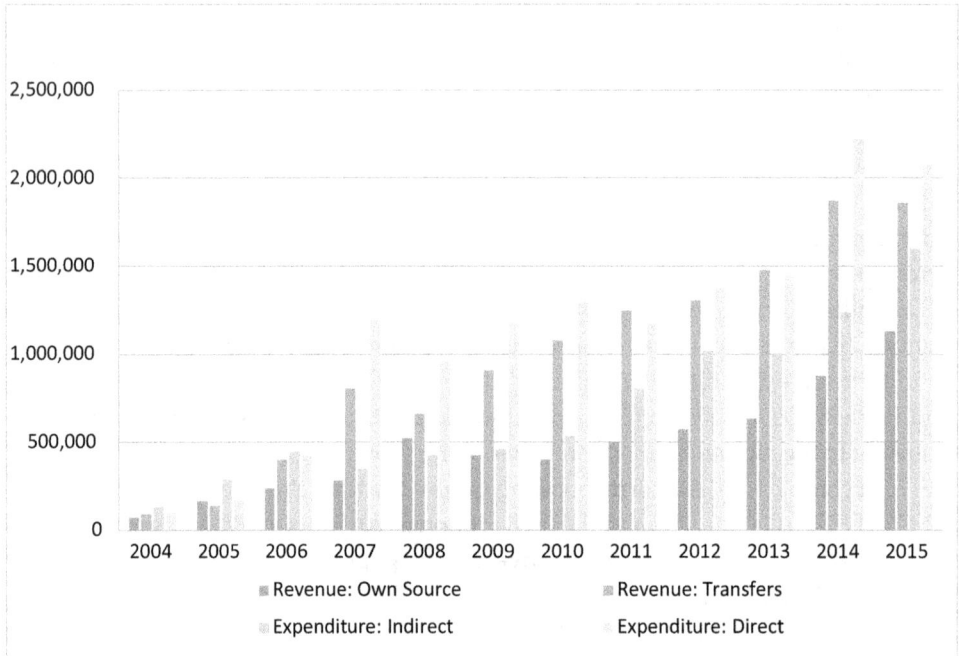

- Revenue: Own Source
- Revenue: Transfers
- Expenditure: Indirect
- Expenditure: Direct

Source: Authors based on data from Directorate General of Fiscal Balance, Ministry of Finance www.djpk.kemenkeu.
go.id

FIGURE 8.5
Own-source Revenue as Percentage of Provincial Revenue: Riau, PRI and
New Provinces, 2012–15

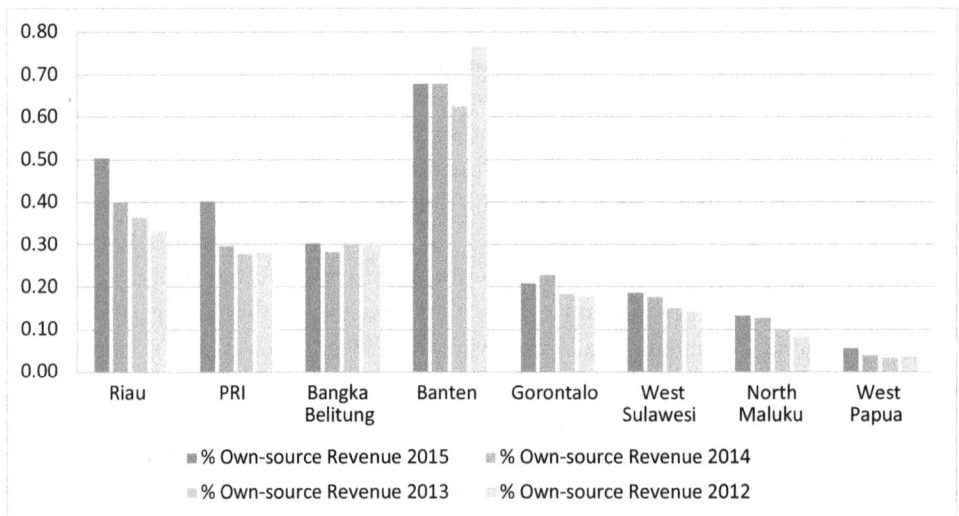

- % Own-source Revenue 2015
- % Own-source Revenue 2014
- % Own-source Revenue 2013
- % Own-source Revenue 2012

Source: Authors based on data from Directorate General of Fiscal Balance, Ministry of Finance.

FIGURE 8.6
Revenue-Sharing Transfers as Percentage of Provincial Revenue: Riau, PRI, and New Provinces, 2012–15

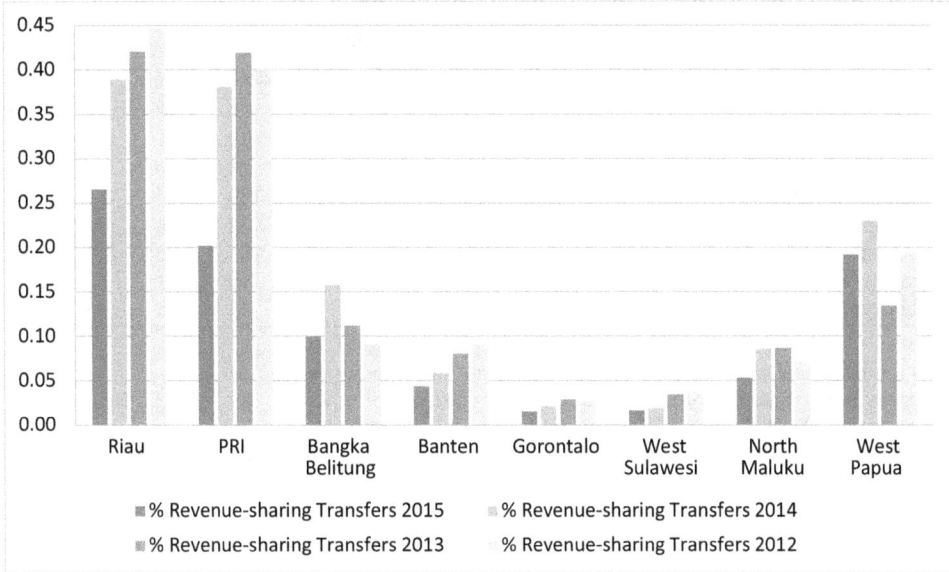

Source: Authors based on data from Directorate General of Fiscal Balance, Ministry of Finance.

Table 8.1 shows that PRI is ranked quite highly in terms of government performance, constantly within the top ten among thirty-three provinces since 2011 (see row 1). The province has consistently received scores of above 2.5 ("high" performance), except in 2010 when it received a "medium" score of 1.56. Within the local governments in PRI, two cities, namely Batam and Tanjungpinang, were ranked quite highly in 2013 (sixteenth and fourteenth respectively, out of ninety-one cities evaluated), but dropped in 2014 and 2015. PRI's regencies experienced the most improvement. For example, Bintan Regency was ranked tenth out of 395 regencies in 2014, which was encouraging considering the regency was ranked 255th of 344 regencies in 2009 (see row 3). Karimun, Natuna, and Lingga regencies similarly improved between 2009 and 2012, but then slipped due to a faster rate of improvement in other regencies.

The EKPPD scores reveal subnational government performance in general, namely related to their role in delivering public service for the local population. But more specifically in terms of the government's role in facilitating economic growth, PRI has not been doing very well. Figure 8.7 shows the PRI's provincial competitiveness ranking among Indonesia's thirty-three provinces, between 2013 and 2016, as described by the Asia Competitiveness Institute at the National University of Singapore (Tan et al. 2013, 2015, 2017; Tan, Amri and Ahmad 2017). Here, the "Overall Competitiveness" Index is divided into four sub-indices, namely: (1) Macroeconomic Stability, (2) Government and Institutional Setting, (3) Financial, Businesses and Manpower Conditions, and (4) Quality of Life and Infrastructure Development.

TABLE 8.1

Regional Government Performance Evaluation (EKPPD): Rank for PRI and Cities/Regencies
Therein, 2009–16

	EKPPD Rank							
	2009	2010	2011	2012	2013	2014	2015	2016
1. Riau Islands Province[a]	16	28	8	5	4	6	10	8
2. Karimun Regency[b]	283	278	133	38	78	61	178	73
3. Bintan Regency[b]	255	201	47	30	15	10	30	19
4. Natuna Regency[b]	303	262	197	124	139	150	175	222
5. Lingga Regency[b]	312	240	232	205	130	284	192	193
6. Anambas Regency[b]	n.a.	n.a.	n.a.	161	156	138	267	259
7. Batam City[c]	37	55	60	39	16	31	89	39
8. Tanjungpinang City[c]	19	57	44	32	14	25	41	51

Notes:

a. PRI was ranked out of 33 provinces throughout 2009–14, and 30 provinces in 2015–16;

b. Karimun, Bintan, Natuna, Lingga and Anambas were ranked out of 344, 346, 365, 373, 383, 395, 384, 397
   regencies in 2009, 2010, 2011, 2012, 2013, 2014, 2015, 2016 respectively

c. Batam and Tanjungpinang were ranked out of 86, 86, 90, 91, 91, 93, 91, 93 cities in 2009, 2010, 2011, 2012,
   2013, 2014, 2015, respectively.

Source: Authors based on data from Directorate General of Regional Autonomy, Ministry of Home Affairs http://
otda.kemendagri.go.id/

In terms of Overall Competitiveness, PRI has fared rather well in comparison
with Indonesia's thirty-three provinces, with a ranking that fluctuates mildly between
seventh and twelfth positions between 2013 and 2016 (Tan et al. 2013, 2015, 2017; Tan,
Amri and Ahmad 2017). Interestingly, of the four sub-indices measured, PRI did poorly
in Government and Institutional Setting, and ranked thirty-second out of thirty-three
provinces in 2016 despite being consistently in the top ten for the other three sub-
indices (see Figure 8.7). This shows that despite PRI's relative advantage in terms
of economic potential, business, and quality of life, there have been concerns about
how the government has managed the economy. Aspects which particularly scored
low in the perception surveys were those related to Institutions, Governance, and
Leadership (PRI was ranked third from the bottom in 2016), as well as Competition,
Regulatory Standards, and Rule of Law (PRI was ranked fourth from the bottom in
2016) (Tan, Amri and Ahmad 2018). Such concerns were primarily due to negative
business sentiments towards the governing of PRI's main industrial and population
centre, Batam, where tensions in industrial relations were frequent, and the scope
of responsibilities between the city government and the Batam Indonesia Free Zone
Authority (BIFZA) were unclear and overlapping.[30]

Governance and corruption issues continued to plague PRI. The alleged corruption
case of the International Port of Dompak, for example, also extended the controversy
on the development of Dompak Island as the provincial government office compound.
Port construction would have cost IDR121 billion, but it has not been completed and
is now in a neglected condition (Batamnews, 8 September 2017).

Other corruption cases involved IDR25 billion by the port authority (Badan Usaha
Pelabuhan), namely PT Pelabuhan Kepri, and alleged cases of corruption by the

FIGURE 8.7
PRI's Provincial Competitiveness Ranking by Environment, 2013–16

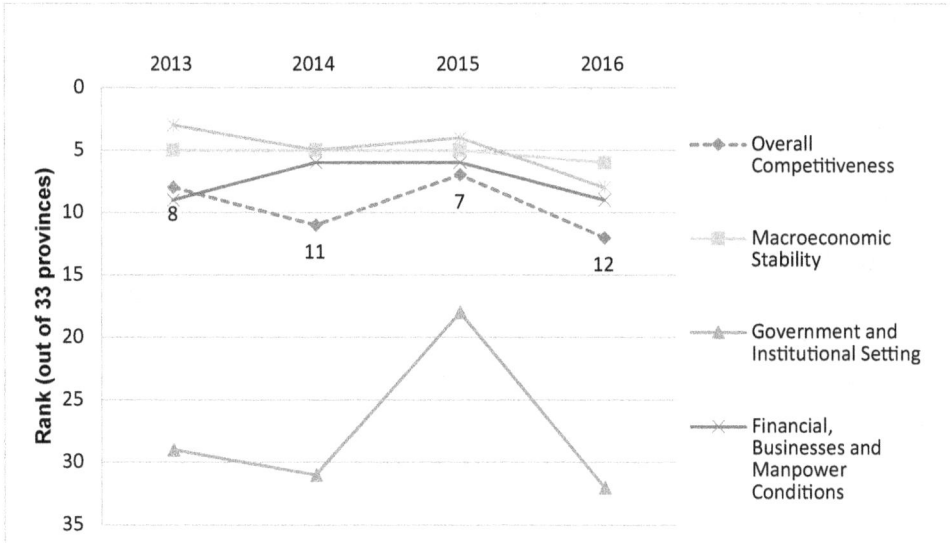

Source: Authors based on Tan et al. (2013; 2015; 2017), Tan, Amri and Ahmad (2017).

Provincial Department of Education and Sports (Dinas Pendidikan dan Olahraga) of Riau Province in 2015. Allegations of corruption in the 2015 budget (IDR2.8 billion) were related to the activities of Youth Pledge and Youth Jamboree in Tanjungpinang. These alleged cases of corruption are being investigated by Tanjungpinang City Police Department (*Tribunnews Batam*, 1 January 2018).

Furthermore, the PRI's prosecutor general (Kejaksaan Tinggi) is investigating alleged misappropriation of non-oil and gas revenue sharing funds that had not been paid by the PRI government to seven cities and regencies in 2014, 2015 and 2016, worth IDR785 billion. In this case, the prosecutor-general has questioned several provincial government officials, among them the Head of Revenue Office (Dinas Pendapatan Daerah), Head of Development Planning Agency (Badan Perencanaan Pembangunan Daerah), and Acting Head of Finance and Asset Management Board (Badan Pengelola Keuangan dan Aset Daerah (Haluan Kepri 2016).

Human Development

Aside from economic governance, PRI seems to be doing rather well in a number of other aspects, including human development. In 2002, when Riau Islands was a regency within Riau Province,[31] its Human Development Index (HDI) was 67.3. This placed it at a rather mediocre ranking of 135 of 341 cities and regencies throughout Indonesia. Natuna Regency's HDI was lower at 64.7, putting the regency at a ranking of 217. Both figures were below the provincial HDI for Riau (the parent province of PRI), which was 69.1 in 2002.

When statistics for PRI began to be collected in 2004, the province's HDI stood at 70.8. Batam's more advanced level of development and large population certainly helped improve the figure for PRI collectively. PRI's HDI at the time was below that of Riau Province (72.2), but still, it was the eighth highest out of Indonesia's thirty-three provinces. Over time, PRI's performance in HDI improved in absolute terms and relative to other Indonesian provinces. By 2007, PRI's HDI was the sixth highest nationwide. Starting in 2010, Indonesia adopted a change in the HDI calculation methodology, in line with global standards. Using the new methodology, PRI's HDI in 2018 was 74.8 (see Figure 8.8), the fourth highest out of thirty-four Indonesian provinces (behind only Jakarta, Yogyakarta and East Kalimantan). Meanwhile, using the new methodology, Riau's HDI was adjusted and became 72.44 in 2018, substantially below PRI's. From Figure 8.8, we can also see that HDI in PRI has been improving over time and is well above the level for Riau (the parent province), and above the average for Sumatra and the newly established provinces.

Despite improvements in HDI, the disparity of development within the province itself remains an issue. Lingga and Anambas were among PRI's regencies that received the lowest HDI in 2016, at 62.4 and 66.3 respectively—although they have also improved significantly over the past six years (see Figure 8.9). Lingga's and Anambas' low HDI stood in contrast with that of Batam and Tanjungpinang, which obtained a high of 79.8 and 77.8, respectively. Batam's HDI in 2016 was the highest for Indonesia, beating the capital, DKI Jakarta, which obtained a slightly lower HDI of 79.6. Meanwhile, Lingga's HDI was just slightly above that of West Papua province (62.2), which was among Indonesia's least developed provinces.

Specifically, on poverty rates (see Figure 8.10), we see that the level of poverty in the province was relatively low and remained on a declining trend. PRI's poverty rate was 6.2 per cent in 2015, which was below Riau's (8.4 per cent). Both PRI and Riau fared better in achieving a poverty rate that was lower than in other provinces, with the nationwide poverty rate standing at 11.2 per cent, the Sumatra average at 11.0 per cent, and the average for new provinces at 11.6 per cent in 2015.

Among the cities and regencies within PRI, most had a low poverty rate, except for Lingga Regency and, to some extent, Tanjungpinang City. The latter had the largest proportion of poor people in the province—15 per cent in 2015. Worryingly, the trend has been worsening for the past four years (see Figure 8.11). Interestingly, Tanjungpinang City, which obtained high HDI and EKPPD scores for government performance, had the second-highest poverty rate after Lingga, at close to 10 per cent in 2015. However, poverty was on a declining trend in Tanjungpinang considering the city had a 12.6 per cent poverty rate in 2010. Overall, except for the case of Lingga, the poverty rate in the local jurisdictions of PRI was favourably low.

CONCLUSION

In 2019, the Riau Islands Province celebrated its seventeenth birthday. It is a relatively new province, but its achievements have been commendable. Within a short period,

FIGURE 8.8
Human Development Index: PRI in Perspective, 2010–18

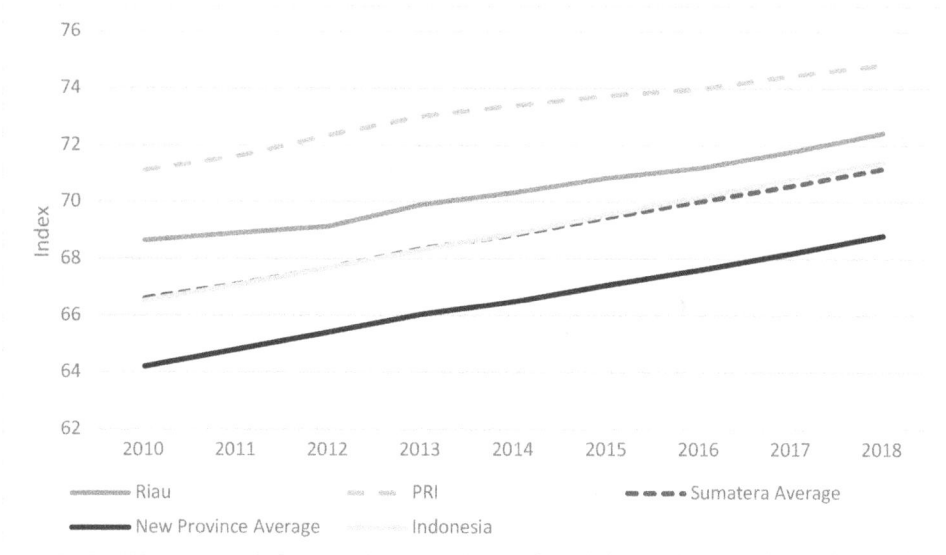

Source: BPS Website.

FIGURE 8.9
Human Development Index: PRI and Cities/Regencies Therein, 2010–16

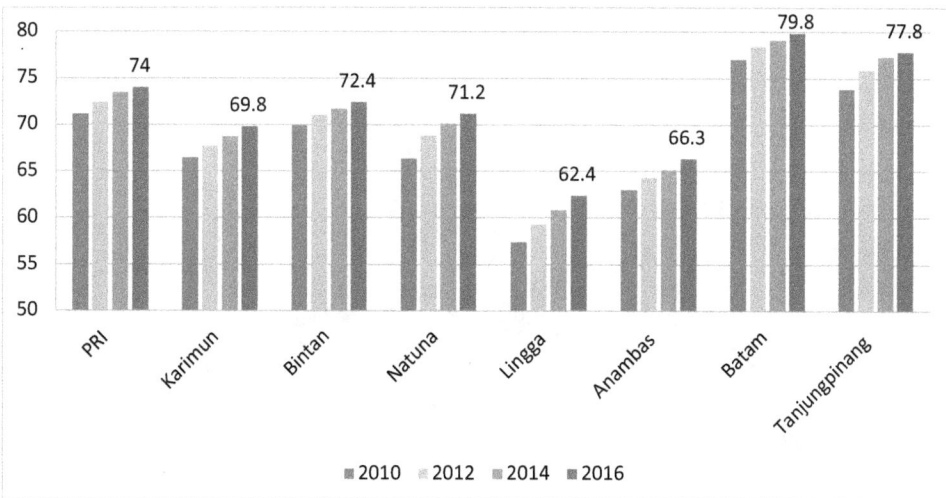

Source: BPS Kepulauan Riau website.

PRI has surpassed Riau, its "parent" province, in multiple aspects. Some of the areas where PRI and the cities/regencies therein have generally excelled are subnational public sector performance (EKPPD), human development (HDI), and poverty rate. In terms of democracy (IDI), PRI's scores have been relatively stable, although it is

FIGURE 8.10
Poverty Rate: PRI in Perspective, 2010–15

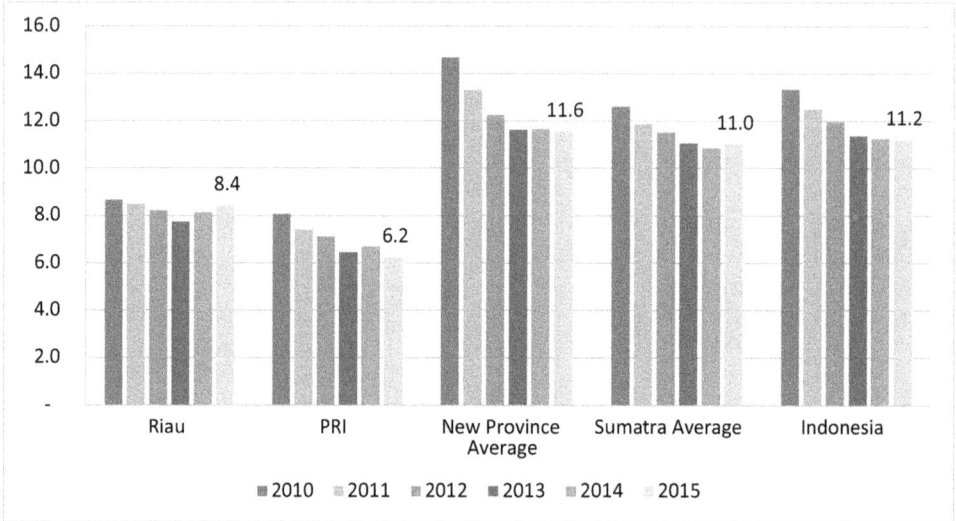

Source: BPS Website.

FIGURE 8.11
Poverty Rate: PRI and Cities/Regencies Therein, 2010–15

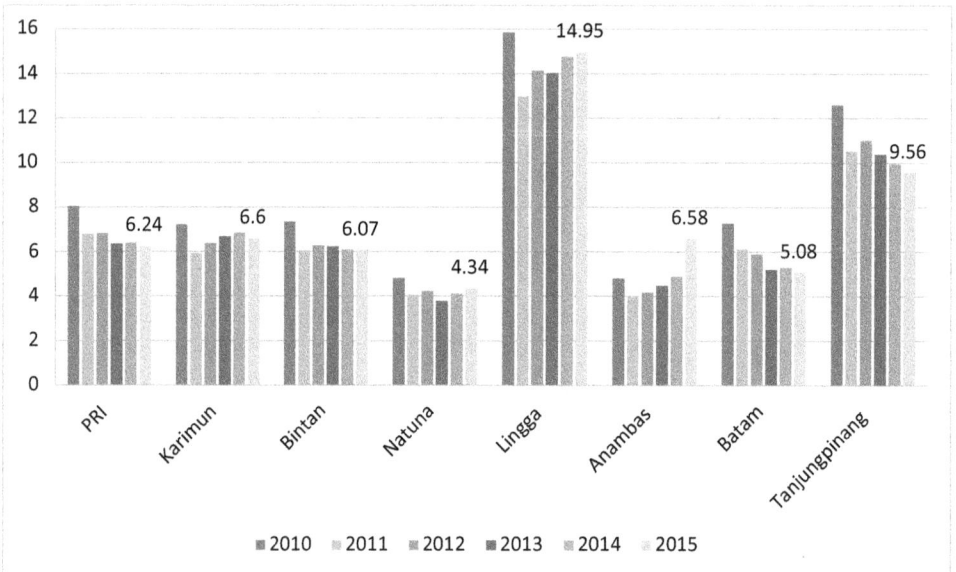

Source: BPS Kepulauan Riau website.

slipping down the ranks due to other provinces improving faster. PRI is doing rather well in Civil Liberty, but is still lagging in Political Rights—indicating that there is more room for regular people to be involved in the local political and governing processes.

In terms of provincial competitiveness, again PRI faces a conflicted situation where its economic and quality of life aspects have been laudable, but the way Batam's industrial areas have been governed left many investors wary. PRI, and more specifically Batam, is undergoing a transformation process where politically the local leaders and local Malay population are no longer keen on being a "periphery" and merely an economic development tool for Jakarta and Singapore (Amri 2016). Industrial development activities and foreign direct investment in 2017 may not be as substantial as it was twenty years ago, but that does not make Batam a less vibrant place now that it has become a full-blown city with more than 1 million population. The city is attracting more domestic investment nowadays, particularly in the consumption and tourism sectors, as well as investment in the digital economy.

The creation of new subnational government entities by way of secession has garnered much criticism as politically driven movements that do not have a real grassroots basis. And certainly, there are many newly created regencies in Indonesia whose operations are highly dependent on central government transfers. However, the need to acknowledge local identities and local interests throughout Indonesia is real, and it has pushed for decentralization and the creation of many smaller governing units with better reach into the population (Mietzner 2014).

Various indicators show that local conditions have improved since PRI's secession from Riau, in ways that the local population seems to prefer. The province may be lucky that it has plenty of natural resources, very close access to the international community, and a history of policy-induced industrial development in Batam, Bintan and Karimun. Thus, PRI is in no way a generic case that can be replicated easily elsewhere. Seventeen years after its establishment, despite various aspects that still need to be improved upon, the local population does not seem to be questioning whether the formation of PRI as a separate province from Riau was a good idea.

Notes

1. This chapter was first published as *State Formation in Riau Islands Province*, Trends in Southeast Asia Series, no. 15/2018 (Singapore: ISEAS – Yusof Ishak Institute, 2018).
2. East Timor separated from Indonesia and became an independent state in 2001.
3. Decentralization in Indonesia kicked off based on Law 22/1999 (regarding subnational governments) and Law 25/1999 (regarding fiscal balance between the central and subnational governments). Over time, the former has been revised as Law 32/2004 and further as Law 23/2014, while the latter has been revised as Law 33/2004 (currently under another revision process). The evolution of the decentralization laws has brought about a stronger governing role for the provinces as coordinator of local district governments.
4. Special autonomy for Papua (and later also for West Papua as a province that broke off from Papua) is governed by Law 21/2001.

5. Special autonomy for Aceh is governed by Law 18/2001 and further by Law 11/2006.
6. Formation of Central Sumatra Province was based on Law 10/1948.
7. Formation of West Sumatra, Jambi, and Riau Provinces was based on Law 61/1958.
8. The original title in Indonesian is *Mengapa Harus Merdeka? Tangis dan Darah Rakyat Riau dalam Memperjuangkan Sebuah Marwah*.
9. The original title in Indonesian is *Tragedi Riau Memperjuangkan Demokrasi: Peristiwa 2 September 1985*.
10. Original title is *Amuk Melayu dalam Tuntutan Provinsi Kepulauan Riau*.
11. Original sentence in Indonesian is: *"Dengan adanya Amuk Melayu mudah-mudahan kita dapat berperan dan dipandang di daerah sendiri."* (Ardi 2002, p. xii).
12. The original Indonesian title is *Bersatulah Riau (Penolakan Provinsi Kepri)* (Rab 2002).
13. The original sentence in Indonesian is: *"Adakah lintasan sejarah yang lebih dari 500 dan tahun ini akan dipecah menjadi Provinsi Riau Lautan dan Riau Daratan. Terkutuklah oleh para arwah Sultan Riau orang-orang yang memecah Riau."* (Rab 2002, p. 7).
14. The advisory board was established based on Government Regulation no. 129/2000.
15. The original sentence in Indonesian is: *"Besarnya gelombang etnis Cina masuk Kepri (dari Hongkong, Singapura, maupun Malaysia), dan negara-negara Asia Timur lainnya, menandakan masyarakat Kepri.... mengalami ketidaksiapan secara ekonomi dalam membendung gerakan ekonomi Cina ... Kepri sangat mungkin bahkan berpeluang besar menjadi 'negeri Hongkong'"* (Heri 2002, pp. 74–75).
16. The original statement in Indonesian is: *"Cukup sudah kita dibohongi sebagai bangsa Melayu yang bermarwah, kalau tidak bisa propinsi mengapa takut 'teriak merdeka'."* (Ardi 2002, p. xii)
17. The original sentence is Indonesian is: *"Dimana masyarakat Riau daratan berkeinginan membentuk Negara sendiri memisahkan diri dari NKRI, masyarakat Kepri dengan bijak berjuang dalam koridor Negara Kesatuan Republik Indonesia. Di situlah perbedaan orang Melayu dengan orang yang bukan Melayu"* (Ardi 2002, p. 46).
18. Interview with Said Jaafar, PRI's first provincial secretary (2004–5), conducted in May 2017.
19. The Governor of Riau would also prepare and authorize the provincial budget for PRI.
20. Since Batam was declared a Free Trade Zone in 2007, BIDA has been renamed BIFZA (Batam Indonesia Free Zone Authority) or Badan Pengusahaan Batam (BP Batam).
21. Medium-Term Development Plan (RPJMD) of Riau Islands Province 2010–15.
22. Ibid.
23. Medium-Term Development Plan (RPJMD) of Riau Islands Province 2016–21.
24. The detention of high-profile political figures for corruption is not an extraordinary phenomenon in Indonesia, especially since the country established an independent Corruption Eradication Commission (Komisi Pemberantasan Korupsi, or KPK) in 2002 (Schütte 2012). North Sumatra also has had two governors detained for corruption: Syamsul Arifin in 2011, and Gatot Pujo Nugroho in 2016. Meanwhile, PRI's neighbouring and former parent province, Riau, has had three of its governors detained for corruption: Saleh Djasit in 2008, Rusli Zainal in 2012, and Annas Maamun in 2014.
25. The following account is based on interviews with the former acting head of the PRI personnel office, Mr Hasbi, in November 2016.
26. In this case, the data was kept by an unidentified individual who was transferred to another institution in 2016, and since then the data files for these years have not been recovered, according to Mr Hasbi.
27. Law 25/2002 on the Formation of Riau Islands Province, Articles 7 and 15.

28. This decision was based on Governor of PRI Decree (Surat Keputusan) No. 308/2006 and Mayor of Tanjungpinang Decree No. 30/2007 on the office location of PRI government agencies (*Tanjung Pinang Pos*, 30 January 2011).
29. Revenue-sharing funds are funds that are shared back by the central government to the areas that produced those revenues in the first place.
30. Accounts of confusing and overlapping authority between the Batam City Government and BIFZA (previously BIDA) have been described in many documents (Hutchinson 2015; Amri 2016).
31. Riau Islands Regency in 2002 includes the current regencies and cities of Bintan, Tanjungpinang and Lingga. By this time, Karimun, Batam and Natuna were already established as regencies and cities in their own right, and thus were not included under Riau Islands Regency.

References

Alhajj, Effendy Asmawi. 2012. "Sejarah Pembentukan Provinsi Kepulauan Riau" [The History of the Formation of Riau Island Province]. *Effendy Asmawi Alhajj* (blog). 23 March 2012. http://effendyalhajj.blogspot.sg/2012/03/sejarah-pembentukan-provinsi-kepulauan.html

Amelia, Puteri Rizqi, and Mussadun. 2015. "Analisis Kesesuaian Rencana Pengembangan Wilayah Pulau Dompak Dengan Kondisi Eksisting Bangunan (Studi Kasus: Pulau Dompak, Kota Tanjungpinang, Provinsi Kepulauan Riau)". *Jurnal Pengembangan Kota* 3, no. 1: 26–39.

Amri, Mulya. 2016. "A Periphery Serving Three Cores: Balancing Local, National, and Cross-Border Interests in the Riau Islands". In *The SIJORI Cross-Border Region: Trans-National Politics, Economics, and Culture*, edited by Francis Hutchinson and Terence Chong. Singapore: ISEAS – Yusof Ishak Institute.

Antara. 2015. "Gubernur: Gas Natuna Dieksploitasi Untuk Kepentingan Singapura". *ANTARA*, 25 February 2015. https://kepri.antaranews.com/berita/32291/gubernur-gas-natuna-dieksploitasi-untuk-kepentingan-singapura

Ardi, Sumantri. 2002. *Amuk Melayu Dalam Tuntutan Provinsi Kepulauan Riau*. Pekanbaru, Riau: Unri Press.

Asril, Zaili. 2002. *Peristiwa 2 September 1985: Tragedi Riau Menegakkan Demokrasi*. Yogyakarta: Adicita Karya Nusa.

Azlaini, Agus. 2001. *Setahun Dewan Pakar Daerah Riau*. Pekanbaru, Riau: Unri Press.

Batamnews. 2015. "Ini Hasil Rekapitulasi Final KPU Pilkada Kepulauan Riau di Karimun dan Lingga". 14 December 2015. https://www.batamnews.co.id/berita-9422-ini-hasil-rekapitulasi-final-kpu-pilkada-kepulauan-riau-di-karimun-dan-lingga.html

———. 2017. "Penyelidikan Dugaan Korupsi Pelabuhan Dompak Belum Ada Kemajuan". 8 September 2017. http://batamnews.co.id/berita-25892--penyelidikan-dugaan-korupsi-pelabuhan-dompak-belum-ada-kemajuan.html

Besley, Timothy, and Torsten Persson. 2009. "The Origins of State Capacity: Property Rights, Taxation, and Politics". *American Economic Review* 99, no. 4: 1218–44.

Brata, Aloysius Gunadi. 2008. "Pemekaran Daerah Di Papua: Kesejahteraan Masyarakat vs. Kepentingan Elit". *Makalah Simposium Nasional Riset Dan Kebijakan Ekonomi: "Dampak Bencana Alam Dan Lingkungan Terhadap Pengelolaan Ekonomi Indonesia"*, Departemen Ilmu Ekonomi Fakultas Ekonomi, Universitas Airlangga, Surabaya, pp. 20–21.

Choi, Nankyung. 2007. "Local Elections and Democracy in Indonesia: The Riau Archipelago". *Journal of Contemporary Asia* 37, no. 3: 326–45.

Costantini, Irene. 2015. *Statebuilding versus State Formation: The Political Economy of Transition in Iraq and Libya*. Italy: University of Trento.

Detiawati, Venni Meitaria. 2008. "Penetapan Pulau Dompak Sebagai Lokasi Pusat Perkantoran Pemerintah Provinsi Kepuluan Riau". Yogyakarta: Gadjah Mada University. http://etd.repository.ugm.ac.id/index.php?mod=penelitian_detail&sub=Penelitian Detail&act=view&typ=html&buku_id=38513

Emmerson, Donald K. 2000. "Will Indonesia Survive?". *Foreign Affairs* 79: 95–106.

Hadiz, Vedi. 2003. "Reorganizing Political Power in Indonesia: A Reconsideration of so-Called 'Democratic Transitions'". *Pacific Review* 16, no. 4: 591–611. https://doi.org/10.1080/0951274032000132272

Halim, Edyanus Herman. 2001. *Mengapa Harus Merdeka: Tangis Dan Darah Rakyat Riau Dalam Memperjuangkan Sebuah Marwah*. Pekanbaru, Riau: Unri Press.

Haluan Kepri. 2016. "Kejati Diminta Serius Tuntaskan Kasus DBH Kepri". *Haluan Kepri*, 5 September 2016. http://haluankepri.com/tanjungpinang/94627-kejati-diminta-serius-tuntaskan-kasus-dbh-kepri.html

Heri, Zulfan. 2002. *Riau Beroposisi*. Pekanbaru, Riau: Unri Press.

Hutchinson, Francis E. 2013. *Architects of Growth? Sub-National Governments and Industrialization in Asia*. Institute of Southeast Asian Studies.

———. 2015. *Mirror Images in Different Frames? Johor, the Riau Islands, and Competition for Investment from Singapore*. Institute of Southeast Asian Studies.

Jakarta Post. 2014. "History Unveils Chevron's Great Contribution to Indonesia's Economy". *Jakarta Post*, 21 May 2014. https://www.pressreader.com/indonesia/the-jakarta-post/20140521/281633893272514

Jawa Pos. 2016. "Kemegahan Jembatan Dompak dan Pusat Pemerintahan Kepri". *Jawa Pos*, 20 November 2016. https://www.jawapos.com/read/2016/11/20/65510/kemegahan-jembatan-dompak-dan-pusat pemerintahan-kepri-1

Killingray, David, Margarette Lincoln, and Nigel Rigby, eds. 2004. *Maritime Empires: British Imperial Maritime Trade in the Nineteenth Century*. Suffolk: Boydell Press in association with the National Maritime Museum.

Kimura, Ehito. 2013. *Political Change and Territoriality in Indonesia: Provincial Proliferation*. Vol. 46. Milton Park, Abingdon, Oxon; New York; Routledge.

Kompas. 2010. "Ismeth Abdullah Ditahan KPK". *KOMPAS.com*, 23 February 2010. https://nasional.kompas.com/read/2010/02/23/03114063/Ismeth.Abdullah.Ditahan.KPK

———. 2010. "Sani-Soerya Menangi Pemilukada Kepri". *KOMPAS.com*, 9 June 2010. https://regional.kompas.com/read/2010/06/09/14221632/Sani.Soerya.Menangi.Pemilukada.Kepri

———. 2019. "KPK Tahan Gubernur Kepri Nurdin Basirun". *KOMPAS.com*, 12 July 2019. https://nasional.kompas.com/read/2019/07/12/06545821/kpk-tahan-gubernur-kepri-nurdin-basirun

Long, Nicholas J. 2013. *Being Malay in Indonesia: Histories, Hopes and Citizenship in the Riau Archipelago*. Asian Studies Association of Australia: Southeast Asian Publications Series and NUS Press. https://nuspress.nus.edu.sg/products/being-malay-in-indonesia

Malesky, Edmund J., and Francis E. Hutchinson. 2016. "Varieties of Disappointment: Why Has Decentralization Not Delivered on Its Promises in Southeast Asia?". *Journal of Southeast Asian Economies* 33, no. 2: 125–38. http://dx.doi.org.libproxy1.nus.edu.sg/10.1355/ae33-2a

Malley, Michael S. 1999. "Resource Distribution, State Coherence, and Political Centralization in Indonesia, 1950–1997". Madison: University of Wisconsin-Madison. https://search. library.wisc.edu/catalog/999933809002121

Mietzner, Marcus. 2014. "Indonesia's Decentralisation: The Rise of Local Identities and the Survival of the Nation-State". In *Regional Dynamics in a Decentralized Indonesia*, edited by Hal Hill. Singapore: Institute of Southeast Asian Studies.

Mitra, Subrata K. 1995. "The Rational Politics of Cultural Nationalism: Subnational Movements of South Asia in Comparative Perspective". *British Journal of Political Science* 25, no. 1: 57–77. https://doi.org/10.2307/194176

———. 2012. "Sub-National Movements, Cultural Flow, the Modern State, and the Malleability of Political Space: From Rational Choice to Transcultural Perspective and Back Again". *Transcultural Studies*, no. 2: 8–47.

Oates, Wallace E. 1972. *Fiscal Federalism*. New York: Harcourt Brace Jovanovich.

OECD. 2013. *Delivering Local Development*. Ireland: OECD Publishing.

Potter, Lesley, and Simon Badcock. 2001. *The Effects of Indonesia's Decentralisation on Forest and Estate Crops in Riau Province: Case Studies of the Original Districts of Kampar and Indragiri Hulu*. CIFOR.

Rab, Tabrani. 2002. *Bersatulah Riau (Penolakan Provinsi Kepri)*. Pekanbaru: Riau Cultural Institute.

Riau Pos. 2011. "Wawancara H Wan Ghalib Sempena HUT Ke-54 Provinsi Riau: Utamakan Program Akar Rumput". *Riaupos.co*, 8 August 2011. http://www.riaupos.co/1267-berita-utamakan-program-akar-rumput.html

Ruggie, John Gerard. 1993. "Territoriality and Beyond: Problematizing Modernity in International Relations". *International Organization* 47, no. 1: 139–74. https://doi.org/10.2307/2706885

Schütte, Sofie Arjon. 2012. "Against the Odds: Anti-corruption Reform in Indonesia". *Public Administration and Development* 32, no. 1: 38–48.

Sumule, Agus. 2003. *Mencari Jalan Tengah: Otonomi Khusus Provinsi Papua*. Gramedia Pustaka Utama.

Tan, Khee Giap, Mulya Amri, Linda Low, and Kong Yam Tan. 2013. *Competitiveness Analysis and Development Strategies for 33 Indonesian Provinces*. Singapore: World Scientific.

Tan, Khee Giap, Nurina Merdikawati, Mulya Amri, and Blake Harley Berger. 2015. *2014 Annual Competitiveness Analysis and Development Strategies for Indonesian Provinces*. Singapore: World Scientific.

Tan, Khee Giap, Mulya Amri, and Nursyahida Ahmad. 2017. *2016 Annual Competitiveness Analysis and Development Strategies for Indonesian Provinces*. Singapore: World Scientific.

Tan, Khee Giap, Mulya Amri, Nurina Merdikawati, and Nursyahida Ahmad. 2017. *2015 Annual Competitiveness Analysis and Development Strategies for Indonesian Provinces*. Singapore: World Scientific. http://www.worldscientific.com/worldscibooks/10.1142/10246

Tanjung Pinang Pos. 2011. "Ketika Dompak Bermetamorfosa". 30 January 2011. http://www.tanjungpinangpos.co.id/ketika-dompak-bermetamorfosa/

Tempo. 2010. "PAN Usung Huzrin Hood Sebagai Calon Gubernur Kepulauan Riau". *Tempo*, 8 March 2010. https://nasional.tempo.co/read/230909/pan-usung-huzrin-hood-sebagai-calon-gubernur-kepulauan-riau.

———. 2015. "Belum Selesai Dibangun, Jembatan Satu Dompak Roboh". 4 October 2015. https://nasional.tempo.co/read/706245/belum-selesai-dibangun-jembatan-satu-dompak-roboh

Tirtosudarmo, Riwanto. 2008. "State Formation, Decentralisation and East Sulawesi Province:

Conflict and the Politics of Transcending Boundaries in Eastern Indonesia". CRISE Working Paper No. 56. Oxford: CRISE.

Tribunnews Batam. 2013. "Pemprov Kepri Harus Bayar Rp 42 Miliar Ke Kontraktor Jembatan Dompak I". 29 April 2013. http://batam.tribunnews.com/2013/04/29/pemprov-harus-bayar-rp-42-miliar-ke-kontraktor-jembatan-dompak-i

———. 2018. "Tiga Kasus Korupsi Yang Ditangani Polres Tanjungpinang Mengendap. Ini Tanggapan Kapolres". 1 January 2018. http://batam.tribunnews.com/2018/01/01/tiga-kasus-korupsi-yang-ditangani-polres-tanjungpinang-mengendap-ini-tanggapan-kapolres

Trocki, Carl A. 2007. *Prince of Pirates: The Temenggongs and the Development of Johor and Singapore, 1784–1885*. Singapore: NUS Press.

9

PARTIES IN THE PERIPHERY
Organizational Dilemmas in Indonesia's Kepri Province[1]

Ulla Fionna

INTRODUCTION

This paper investigates political parties in Indonesia's Kepulauan Riau (Kepri) Province, as a case of local politics occurring in the country's periphery. As one of Indonesia's outermost provinces, Kepri's political dynamics are a significant indicator of how parties are faring in regions with typically limited infrastructure and little attention from central party offices.

Although case studies of local politics and elections in Indonesia have proliferated since the commencement of decentralization (e.g., Erb and Sulistiyanto 2009), the investigation of parties in this particular region has so far been limited mainly to Choi Nankyung's work (2007, 2009). In her study on the Batam municipal elections, she pointed to the weaknesses of the parties, particularly regarding recruitment and election management. This chapter examines the parties' overall organization at the provincial level, with particular attention being paid to how their activities are managed, and uses the 2015 gubernatorial election as a case study.

This chapter argues that the political and economic gaps between the provincial capital of Tanjungpinang and the commercial centre of Batam have created problems in organizational capacity for political parties in the province. While branches in Tanjungpinang coordinate the overall organization in Kepri, there is a strong need for the parties to focus their attention on the more populated and vibrant Batam. The provincial branches have consequently become largely inactive and undermanaged, and their activities infrequent and erratic. Local politics have thus come to be dominated by local figures who—although having party affiliations—gain popularity and public standing, first and foremost as individuals.

KEPRI PROVINCE: SMALL YET STRATEGIC

Kepri Province was established in 2004 as Indonesia's thirty-second province (under Law No. 25, 2002), following increasing demands for secession from Riau Province. The idea had strong opposition from the provincial government in Riau, which feared the loss of revenue from manufacturing, tourism, and natural resources (Amri 2016). Indeed, it was the combination of resentment caused by the inadequate size of revenues from local resources that were redistributed back to the region, dissatisfaction with the Riau provincial government in general, along with Malay cultural subnationalism, which inspired the idea to form a new province (Kimura 2010, p. 437).

Kepri Province consists of two cities (Batam and Tanjungpinang) and five rural regencies (Bintan, Karimun, Lingga, Anambas and Natuna). Although it only hosts 0.71 per cent of Indonesia's population and its area is only 0.43 per cent of the country's size (Badan Pusat Statistik Provinsi Kepulauan Riau 2018), its importance is due to several factors. Primarily, its strategic location has been beneficial to its economic profile. One of its main cities, Batam, is an industrial hub and the population centre of the province and it is located only 20 km from cosmopolitan Singapore. By comparison, it is almost 900 km from the Indonesian capital of Jakarta, and has attracted sizeable foreign investments which made it a significant destination for Indonesian job-seekers. The province was ranked the eighth most competitive province in Indonesia according to an index based on variables such as macroeconomic stability, government and institutional setting, financial, business and manpower conditions, and quality of life and infrastructure development (Tan et al. 2015).

Given its strategic location and economic potential, political parties in the province have tried to tap into local aspirations and to integrate themselves into local politics.[2] Parties have the function of linking voters to the state by bringing the interests of the former to the attention of the latter. In contrast, the absence of parties leads to a segregation between public aspirations and government policies which, left unmanaged, may create resentment and even unrest. The more votes parties receive, the greater the parties' say in local politics. The peripheral uniqueness of Kepri Province makes the party branches an appropriate study of how decentralization affects a local polity.

INVESTIGATING PARTY CAPACITY

Parties are crucial to democracies for several reasons. They are important means of political participation and free elections (de Tocqueville 1945; Dahl 1998; Huntington

1991), the main "mediators between the voters and their interests" (Gunther, Montero and Linz 2002, p. 58), as well as the "main agent of political representation" and "virtually the only actors with access to elected positions in democratic politics" (Mainwaring and Scully 1995, p. 2). While it is generally agreed that parties are compulsory for democracies, there are variants in measuring parties' success and capacity. Essentially, parties need to have a "presence at the local and national levels", "somewhat stable roots in society" (Mainwaring and Scully 1995), and remain active beyond election periods (Duverger 1964, p. xvi). As such, local branches are an accurate indicator of their capacity, as they manage daily grassroots operations and activities (Janda and Colman 1998), as well as campaigning for local elections. Ideally, parties' local branches should be staffed by professional administrators (Katz and Mair 1994; Szczerbiak 1999; Webb and Kolodny 2006) and have stable sources of funding (Webb 1995). Another key function for the branches is to serve as the first point of contact for potential members (Katz and Mair 1994, p. 14; Vanhanen 2000; Mair and van Biezen 2001). Recruiting members is important if the parties are to prove themselves "viable channels of political representation" (Katz and Mair 1994, pp. 14–15).

While these are the ideals, political parties in Indonesia have generally struggled to perform most of these functions, mainly because of their organizational limitations. Parties had organizational and ideological freedom following the 1945 independence period, but conditions as a newborn country were challenging for most of them in establishing a well-organized network of branches. This freedom proved short-lived, as the Sukarno and subsequently Soeharto governments began to severely curb the influence of political parties.[3] When Soeharto stepped down in 1998, parties (re)gained political freedom, but had no experience in building well-functioning branches. Worse still, decades of political repression had created parties adjusted to a patronage system and an electorate that was deeply disillusioned.[4]

Meanwhile, pressure for more governmental reforms mounted. Under Soeharto's New Order (1966–98), Indonesian development had been focused on the centre, and demands for better (re)distribution of revenue to the regions underlined the campaign for decentralization. The centre-periphery divide generated by the "centripetal power" (Malley 1999, p. 72) system was justified by the argument for national unity and integrity. Consequently, the championing of local interests was deemed threatening and generally discouraged and/or repressed (Walker, Banks and Sakai 2009, p. 2). In contrast, under decentralization, local identity and aspirations were given much more space to grow. At the same time, demands for greater transparency and attention to local interests quickly led to more scrutiny of local governments and local politics.

Political parties now had to build branches across the archipelago, and deal with local elections. Such tasks are no small feat in Indonesia. While the barrier of entry for new parties is low, the organizational requirements to compete in elections are increasingly arduous. To compete in the 1999 elections, parties had to have regional chapters in 50 per cent of all provinces and 50 per cent of districts/municipalities in the province. Those requirements have been increased in 2014. Parties now have chapters in 100 per cent of the provinces, 75 per cent of the districts/municipalities, and 50 per cent of sub-districts. Furthermore, many of these parties have limited resources and funding.[5]

Placing the requirements for solid organizations and the historical and institutional challenges that parties face side by side, this study identifies several indicators for party organizational capacity. These are by no means exhaustive. The focus of this study are the branch offices—primarily their organizational structure and processes, including: the physical buildings; general upkeep; staffing issues; and overall management. The range of activities carried out as well as how they are initiated and managed are also analysed. Most specifically, the 2015 gubernatorial elections are examined to provide detailed insights into these matters.

METHODOLOGY

Three fieldwork trips were conducted to observe the conditions of party branches in the province first-hand—to Tanjungpinang in November 2016 and March 2017 and to Batam in July 2017. Local party politicians (also from the major parties) and political observers were interviewed. The foci of the visits to party branches was finding out how they are administered in general, specifically in relation to office set-up, staffing and the overall condition of the branches. Interviews with local staff about meetings and activities were also used to gauge the financial situation of the specific branch—something that parties do not usually give information on voluntarily.

Other than these first-hand data, previous research on the organization of political parties in Indonesia, with specific attention on earlier works about Kepri Province, was consulted. Data on local politics and local elections were obtained from the Election Commission (Komisi Pemilihan Umum, KPU), previous reports and analyses and also from interviews with observers.

PARTY (DIS)ORGANIZATION IN KEPRI:
COMMERCIAL CENTRE VS PROVINCIAL CAPITAL

Except for those with solid financial management, parties rely a great deal on the loyalty of local cadres to man their branches. As these cadres often do not possess sufficient administrative skills, such arrangements translate into a direct lack of professionalism. They tend not to have any clear operational system, nor any filing and record-keeping mechanisms. The staff's minimal administrative skills also mean that their capacity in handling correspondence tends to be poor. These unpaid cadres have to manage daily operations, and some parties let them reside in the offices in lieu of compensation. Initiatives for activities are also often lacking as party officials usually prioritize their public positions (as members of the legislature or local heads) and thus rarely visit the branches. Instead, it is the individual cadres who wish to improve their popularity that would organize activities. It is only during election periods that there is a greater frequency of events, but at other times, the branches are inactive (Fionna 2013).

FIGURE 9.1
The Location of Tanjungpinang and Batam

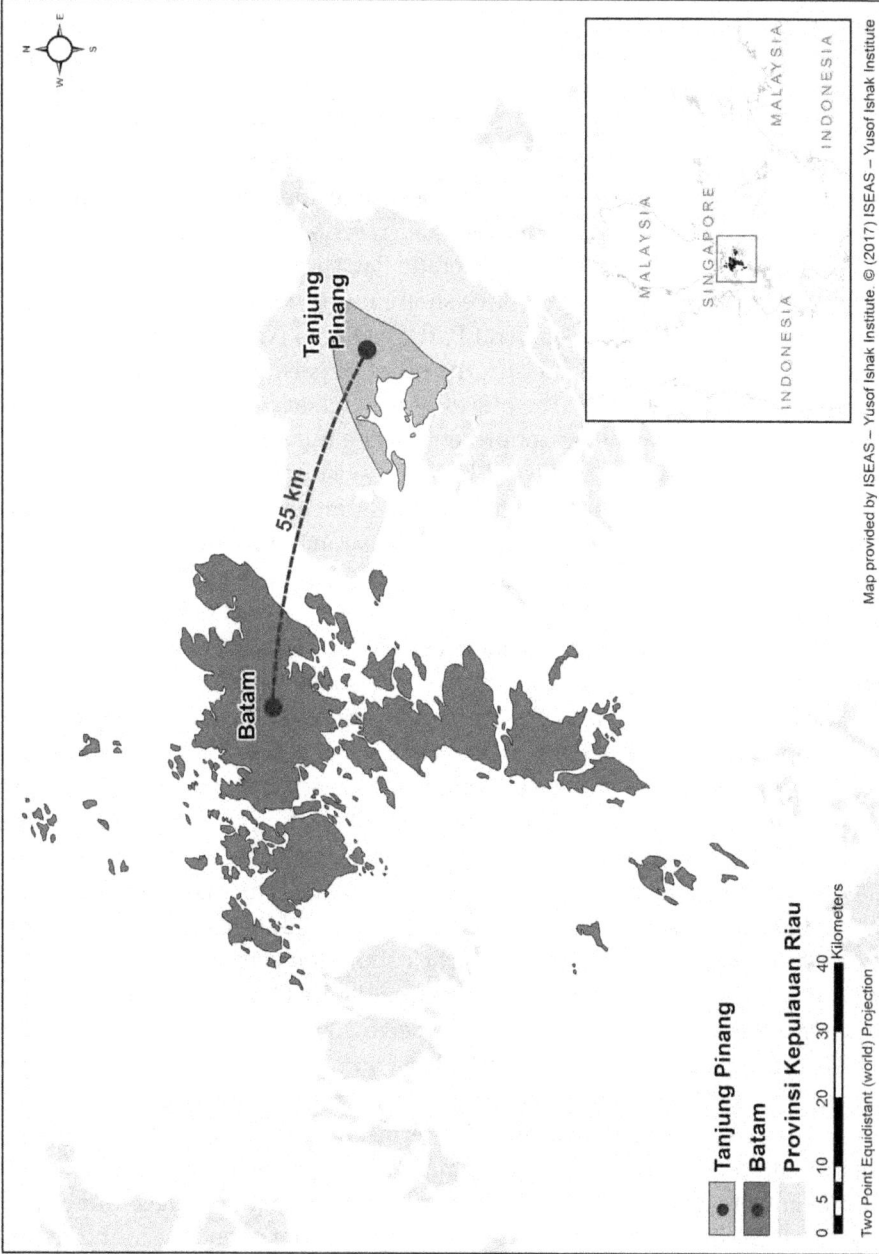

Map provided by ISEAS – Yusof Ishak Institute. © (2017) ISEAS – Yusof Ishak Institute

Locationwise, the branches in Kepri Province generally choose to be around the city centre of Tanjungpinang. They are usually either dormant or managed by cadre-volunteers without professional training. The handful of personnel who staff the offices seem to have few tasks to do, and they usually socialize with each other while manning the office. Furthermore, many have sporadic office hours and not all branches are open every day. Only the Golkar Party employed personnel with some professional skills, who would staff the branches and carry out administrative tasks. Overall, the offices have acceptable working conditions, with telephones and desktops, and they typically have designated rooms for meetings, as well as separate offices for branch leaders. In those cases where there is no full air-conditioning, it is the designated offices for leaders and meeting rooms that are provided with the facility. Golkar, Indonesian Democratic Party – Struggle (PDI-P) and Democrat Party (PD) are three parties that have shop houses serving as their branches, while Nasdem Party's (National Democrat Party, or Partai Nasdem) office is a residential house.[6] During the fieldwork visits, the office of Nasdem Party was closed and no one was manning the office. The offices of the Golkar Party, PD and PDI-P are open daily, but party officials were not present during our visits. Instead, it was the cadre volunteers who attended to the public and to visitors.

The disorganized nature of these party branches suggests, not only that it is hard for these parties to sustain an active appearance, but also that being non-active outside of election periods is normal and accepted. Office hours are kept to a bare minimum and on the rare occasions when activities are held, much typically depends on the initiative of a handful of leaders to function. These activities are normally not part of the yearly agenda, but are instead organized on an ad hoc basis.

The dependence on particular cadre(s) or leader(s) for these activities is usually quite apparent. Typically, banners put up for these events clearly carry the name of these people, who will normally make a speech during the event to boost their recognizability among voters.[7] This suggests that funding for these events comes from these candidates, who are hoping to improve their standing for coming elections, and that it is these figures in the parties and not the parties themselves as organizations, that initiate and organize these events. Rather than taking charge and utilizing these events to promote themselves, the parties allow the active individuals to promote themselves instead. This dependence on local figures leads easily to the domination of party branches by certain cadres and personalities.

There is a condition unique to Kepri that aggravates the lack of capacity at the party branch level. In most provinces in Indonesia, the capital would usually be the biggest city in both economic and demographic terms. In Kepri, although Tanjungpinang is the provincial capital, Batam is its primary city.[8] For one thing, Batam's population (approximately 1.2 million) is about five times that of Tanjungpinang's (approximately 200,000). Batam's economy also dwarves Tanjungpinang's,[9] and the former is also more prosperous in general than the latter.[10] In political terms, Batam also has more voters and proportionally takes up more than half the seats in the provincial parliament. As a matter of fact, Batam's number of voters is far higher than other regions, such that even with the lowest election turnout in the province, it still manages to register the highest number of votes (see Appendix Table 9.A2).

For these reasons, Batam makes a more attractive anchor point for political parties. Meanwhile, the Tanjungpinang branch offices—while formally the provincial coordinator of party activities—maintain minimal levels of organization and are generally inactive and disorganized. These discrepancies are clearly demonstrated by how the major parties in the province choose the sites for their events.

Partai Golkar has held various activities throughout the province in the past few years. As the New Order legacy party, it still conducts Safari Ramadhan, a series of trips aimed at exerting its presence and influence across the region. During the New Order period (1966–98) this strategy was effective in maintaining the party's popularity, intimidating voters into casting their votes for Golkar, particularly as the other two parties allowed (PPP and PDI) had to play by a much stricter set of rules when campaigning.[11] In Kepri, Partai Golkar has scheduled these trips across all the regencies and municipalities, with the provincial chairman Ansar Ahmad himself leading the scheduled trips.

While the safari trips covered the province, the party's other activities in Kepri were largely focused on Batam. For instance, in July 2016, the inauguration of party officials for Kepri Province was conducted in Batam. Although the provincial branch is located in the capital, Tanjungpinang, the election of the provincial chairman in 2015 was done in Batam, and so was the inauguration of the provincial office in 2016 when Setya Novanto, the party chairman himself, came to inaugurate the new staff line-up. The occasion was also utilized as an outreach event, as Novanto led a walk across the city together with around 30,000 Batam residents. Notably, it would be quite difficult to attract the same crowd in Tanjungpinang.

Similarly, Batam has a certain appeal as location for activities for PDI-P. Its previous provincial meeting for both Kepri and Riau province was held in Batam in 2015, clearly signifying Batam's strategic importance, which outweighs Tanjungpinang—despite the latters' status as provincial capital.

PD showed a more balanced approach in their latest major activity in the province. Fresh from his defeat in the Jakarta gubernatorial election, Agus Yudhoyono (son of former president Susilo Bambang Yudhoyono, PD's main patriarch) visited Kepri Province. The party organized various activities around his four-day visit, which were distributed equally between Tanjungpinang and Batam. Kepri Province holds a special place for PD because the party has been exceedingly successful there, winning the gubernatorial position, the Bintan regency and Batam mayor position (although mayor Rudi who was elected in 2015, then left for Nasdem Party). During his visit, the young Yudhoyono inaugurated the provincial office and the staff, launched a book, jogged with a crowd of supporters, and gave talks at various events.

During an interview, a Kepri PD official revealed that the defection to Nasdem Party of chairman Rudi, who is also mayor of Batam, has left the municipal branch office in the hands of a temporary chair or task officer (*pelaksana tugas,* or PLT). This seems to have destabilized the PD in Kepri, and even its municipal branch office has been taken over by Nasdem (*Batam News*, 6 September 2016). The reliance on local figures means that the branch will now have to find a replacement of equal stature. Organizationally, however, the official being interviewed insisted that Tanjungpinang has always been the coordinating centre and that there has been no major shift or disruption in party organization caused by the defection.[12]

Among the parties that were less successful in the last legislative elections, there is a clearer prioritizing of Batam over Tanjungpinang. Gerindra Party (Partai Gerakan Indonesia Raya, or Pan-Indonesian Movement Party), which gained three seats in 2014, held crowd-drawing activities but also low-key ones such as communal breaking of fast and a domino tournament, in Batam. Hanura Party (Partai Hati Nurani Rakyat, or People's Conscience Party), the winner of two seats in 2014, centred the commemoration of its tenth anniversary in 2016 in Batam. The party also set up a new provincial branch in Batam (Haryati 2017). A party official explained that although the party's office is in Tanjungpinang, they hold many (more) activities in Batam. With its new three-storey office, the party aims to "improve their work mobility" (mobilitas kerja), and the coordination of all provincial-level organizational matters. The PKS (Partai Keadilan Sejahtera, or Prosperous Justice Party) also held their provincial coordinating meeting (rapat koordinasi wilayah, or rakorwil) in Batam. Nasdem Party was another that swore in a new line-up of provincial staff in Batam, while also holding various activities celebrating its anniversary there.

Perindo, a new party founded in 2015 and led by media mogul Hary Tanoesoedibjo, conducted the inauguration of its staff in Batam, opened a clinic in a Batam mall and held a chess competition in the same city. Berkarya Party, established on the fame of former president Soeharto's son Tommy, lists a Batam address as its provincial branch and has chosen to hold its provincial coordination meeting in Batam. Notably, the last two parties mentioned have not competed in elections yet, but have already sidelined Tanjungpinang.[13]

Although the activities listed here are by no means exhaustive, there is an emerging pattern among the parties which strongly points to Batam as a worthy choice for activities. As a Partai Golkar official said, Tanjungpinang is not as attractive a site. There are obvious reasons behind Batam edging out Tanjungpinang for party events. With an airport that is bigger and has more frequent flights to Jakarta compared to Tanjungpinang's, inviting national leaders or figures to Batam is easier. Sharing the agenda of Partai Golkar's provincial office, this official listed three major events for the party this year—two of which were held in Batam, and one in Tanjungpinang. Batam is also a better location for crowd-intensive events such as long marches, staged entertainment and political rallies. Batam's image as a more rewarding site is so prevalent among parties that they disregard the fact that many Batam voters are temporary residents who may not cast their votes there during polling day.

As such, while coordination meetings (rapat koordinasi, or rakor) are at times still held in Tanjungpinang, activities that demand large crowds are likely to be held in Batam. Yet, national laws regarding political parties state that they must have a coordinating branch in the provincial capital. In this sense, Tanjungpinang's role as the location for coordinating offices will not be replaced. Since the Election Commission (Komisi Pemilihan Umum, or KPU) inspects these branches before every general election, parties have to ensure that the provincial branch remains active to some extent. The Commission also inspects branches to ensure that they are operational, which means that party officials and leaders will have to be present at the branches more often than was observed during the fieldwork visits done for this study. However, nothing is stated about verifying whether the provincial branch indeed coordinates activities across the relevant province. This means that the parties can keep juggling between the two important cities, and continue to have Tanjungpinang as the official provincial branch, while concentrating their activities to Batam instead.

THE 2015 GUBERNATORIAL ELECTION IN RIAU ISLANDS PROVINCE

This article thus far has pointed to the difficulties that political parties face in Kepri. Meanwhile, the introduction of direct local elections in 2005 has presented more challenges in the form of candidate management and campaigning. Yet, instead of focusing on their internal organization to improve recruitment, parties have generally been adopting ways to recruit individuals from outside to run as their candidates.[14]

The primacy of candidates in Indonesia's elections has been increasing. This was most notable in 2014. Article 214 of the 2008 Law No. 10 on Parliamentary Elections brought about further changes. In the closed system implemented in previous elections, parties had more authority in the placement of candidates on the ballot paper, and voters chose political parties. Under the said law which eliminated the party ranking list, only the number of votes determine the candidates' success in winning a seat. As such, each candidate only has themselves to rely on for votes, and the ranking in the ballot paper no longer matters.[15] While the 2009 elections only saw the initial consequences of these trends, the 2014 rounds experienced the full effect, with candidates even strategizing to compete against candidates from their own parties.

Law No. 8 of 2015 on local elections states that to nominate a candidate for local elections, a party or a coalition of parties needs to have at least 20 per cent of the seats in the provincial parliament (Dewan Perwakilan Rakyat Daerah, or DPRD) or 25 per cent of votes collectively. For a pair of candidates to win, the accumulation of votes needs to reach a majority.[16] As the electoral systems increasingly heighten the importance of candidates, the main focus of parties has been about finding the most electable figure. With provincial- and municipal-/regency-level direct elections, parties are now required to manage candidate nominations for 537 local elections.[17] The absence of recruitment processes means that parties have had to adjust strategies to manage the demand to nominate candidates as well as manage multiple local elections. The main strategy now boils down to courting the most electable candidate to join them and to form a coalition with other parties to get enough seats for the nomination ticket.[18] Beyond this, parties do very little.

A close look at the 2015 Kepri gubernatorial election shows that parties have assumed a passive role in local elections. While parties usually lay idle outside election periods, the nuances and consequences of parties' dysfunction is worthy of further investigation. As with many other *pilkada* cases, the 2015 gubernatorial election in Kepri showed that parties did little beyond providing political credentials for the candidates and acting as electoral vehicles.

Specifically, the interaction between parties' organizational weaknesses and the electoral system has resulted in two prominent trends. First, while elections are largely powered by candidates, parties remain the predominant avenue for nomination as independent nominations are hard to obtain and largely less successful than as campaigning with the backing of a political party.[19] Beyond the nomination process per se, it is the candidates who have to attract votes. As such, local elections are mostly about the popularity of candidates, and parties merely act as their logistical vehicles and providers of symbols.

Second, local elections perpetuate parties' lacklustre attempts at local recruitment. Parties find it easy to get away with their failures at internal recruitment by choosing external candidates whom they deem electable or popular. And, since the parties' electoral function has been largely taken over by candidates, their poor grassroots organization has no incentive to improve.

As can be seen in Kepri's 2015 gubernatorial elections, the candidates were local figures, though they were party politicians, who were better known for their success in building up personal influence and popularity outside of their party. And it was the candidates' team (more commonly known as *tim sukses* or success team) that managed the campaigns.

There were two pairs of candidates in the 2015 gubernatorial election in Kepri. The first consisted of Muhammad Sani and Nurdin Basirun. Sani was governor (2010–15) and vice-governor (2005–10, under former governor Ismeth Abdullah) of the province. Nurdin was former regent of Karimun and chair of the provincial branch (Dewan Perwakilan Wilayah or DPW) of Nasdem Party in Kepri. Other parties joining the coalition and declaring support for this pair were Democrat Party, Gerindra Party, National Awakening Party (PKB), United Development Party (PPP) and the Golkar party faction led by Agung Laksono.

The second pair comprised Soerya Respationo and Ansar Ahmad. Soerya, the candidate for governor, was vice-governor under Sani (2010–15) and chair of the provincial branch of PDI-P. Ansar was a former regent of Bintan and chair of the provincial branch of Golkar Party in Kepri. This pair also had the support of other members of the coalition: People's Conscience Party (Partai Hanura), Prosperous Justice Party (PKS), National Mandate Party (PAN) and the Golkar faction led by Aburizal Bakrie. Notably, as with most if not all local elections in Indonesia, the coalition was not based on any particular agenda other than backing the candidate(s) that it thought had the better chance of winning.

As further testament to the primacy of individual candidates in elections, even securing candidacies was mostly the effort of the individuals themselves. They lobbied for support within the parties as well as outside, particularly making use of their positions as bureaucrats and public figures. Interviews with party officials on candidacy procedures also indicated the parties' limited involvement in selecting and managing candidates. They indicated that parties were mostly passive in choosing candidates, and also confirmed the lack of rigour in recruitment procedures. A Democrat Party official clearly indicated that it is up to the candidates to approach the party and to "obey the wishes of the party".[20] While this may seem to mean that parties are demanding, it more probably highlights the fact that parties are the only vehicles available to potential candidates, rather than any organizational capacity these parties may have per se.

One Golkar Party official framed the mechanism for securing candidacy through emphasizing the active role of the candidates. Focusing on the process as a "two-way communication" where both parties and candidates have similar interests, this official referred to the candidacy of Soerya and Ansar. In his opinion, the decision of his party was based on the fact that these individuals had solid grassroots support and that their programmes were "realistic".[21]

The role of parties largely diminished after the candidates were chosen. And it was the head of the "success team" that designed and organized campaign activities for the candidates. Funding was similarly the candidate's and his team's responsibility. In the words of an observer, the role of the parties during the campaign was "zero".[22] While this remark may be an exaggeration, it is nevertheless a correct enough observation about the minimal role played by the parties during the campaign.

Much of the campaign dynamics also depended on the candidates' assets. The four individuals made strategic use of their own standings in the campaign. Sani had run in three separate elections either as governor or vice-governor, and his success (he was vice-governor to Ismeth Abdullah in 2005–10) clearly indicated his electability. He was immensely popular amongst the indigenous Malays as the Father of Malays *(Bapak Melayu)* who often referred to themselves as Pak Sani's children *(anak Pak Sani)*. His age was, however, considered a disadvantage.

Although he came from East Java, rather than Kepri, Soerya had been successful in creating a positive image as a hands-on and caring leader—acquiring the nickname "The Father of Small People/Commoners" *(Bapaknya Wong Cilik)*. However, he had also gained a reputation as a gangster *(preman)* and leader of a "self-help" organization often employed to intimidate labour organizations.[23]

In terms of programmes, the Sani-Nurdin pair (abbreviated as SANUR) ran a campaign that was formulated as an aspiration for "a prosperous Malay land that is noble in behaviour *(berakhlak mulia)*, environmentally friendly, and successful in maritime affairs" (Indopolitika 2015). Pair number two Soerya-Ansar Ahmad's (abbreviated as SAH) platform was "(for) Riau Islands that is safe, prosper, modern, noble *(berakhlak)* and cultured, built on the principles of unity and cooperation". An observer noted that SANUR's platform was more attractive and catchy, and had resonance with President Joko Widodo's own programme which also emphasized maritime development.[24] SANUR's programmes resonated better with the locals also because of greater attention paid to issues such as the free trade zone and inter-regional connectivity—both of which were sensitive issues for voters worried about their own economic progress. These tactics proved successful as the first pair secured a total of 53.2 per cent of the votes, against the second pair's 46.8 per cent.

Interviews with locals suggest that it would have been difficult for an outsider to win this election—a remark aimed at Soerya.[25] The first pair demonstrated their awareness of this sentiment and capitalized on it. A closer look at the results indicates that origin did matter. The fact that Sani and Nurdin are Karimun natives seemed to have been a factor in their victory there. In addition, Sani's track record as governor of Tanjungpinang may have contributed to his victory. Conversely, Ansar Ahmad is from Bintan. Aside from Bintan, Anambas is the only region in Kepri where SAH won (see Figure 9.2).

If voter turnout is any indication, Kepri voters seemed very interested in their gubernatorial elections. The voter turnout in 2005 was 52 per cent. In 2010, it had gone up to 53.2 per cent, and in 2015, it had further improved to 55.4 per cent. However, a study has indicated that there is still some disappointment among voters over the lack of vigour and options in Kepri's local politics. Specifically, the study noticed a growing antipathy among locals over the lack of choices and over the smear campaign deployed by the candidates.

What is clear from Kepri's gubernatorial election in 2015 is that candidates and their teams have overwhelmed the role of political parties. Our discussion suggests that, generally, there is only a small pool of possible and electable candidates for local elections. Being seventy-two years old at that time, Sani's age generated some resentment over the lack of alternative candidates, and his sudden death soon after inauguration did indeed leave the province without a vice-governor. In rather similar fashion, the exit of Mayor Rudi from PD to Nasdem Party was deeply felt by the first party, which now has to find a viable replacement to support in the next Batam mayoral election. Compounded by weak organizational capacity, excessive dependence on individual figures for electoral viability has reduced the role of parties to a search for popular candidates. What this also reveals is the fact that the recruitment function of parties is limited, and they now snub grassroots recruitment and internal training as electoral mechanisms.

CONCLUDING REMARKS

It is clear that the current framework of electoral law, organizational requirements and voting trends demands a lot in terms of the organizational capacity of political parties. These challenges are manifested in the unprofessional management found at the branch level, where offices suffer from minimal staffing, and activities are erratic and dependent on the initiative of individual cadres. Rather unique to the province, the demographic gap between the provincial capital and main commercial city has created another set of challenges. Consequently, these organizational restrictions and the developing electoral dynamics that predominantly evolve around the candidates have reduced the role parties play to one about finding the most electable figures. In turn, parties increasingly rely on the popularity and capacity of their chosen candidates to carry them through.

Although the ability of parties to sustain operations and to adjust to the realities of contemporary local politics should be noted, there have been negative

FIGURE 9.2
Votes for Candidates by Regencies and Cities in the 2015 Kepri Gubernatorial Election

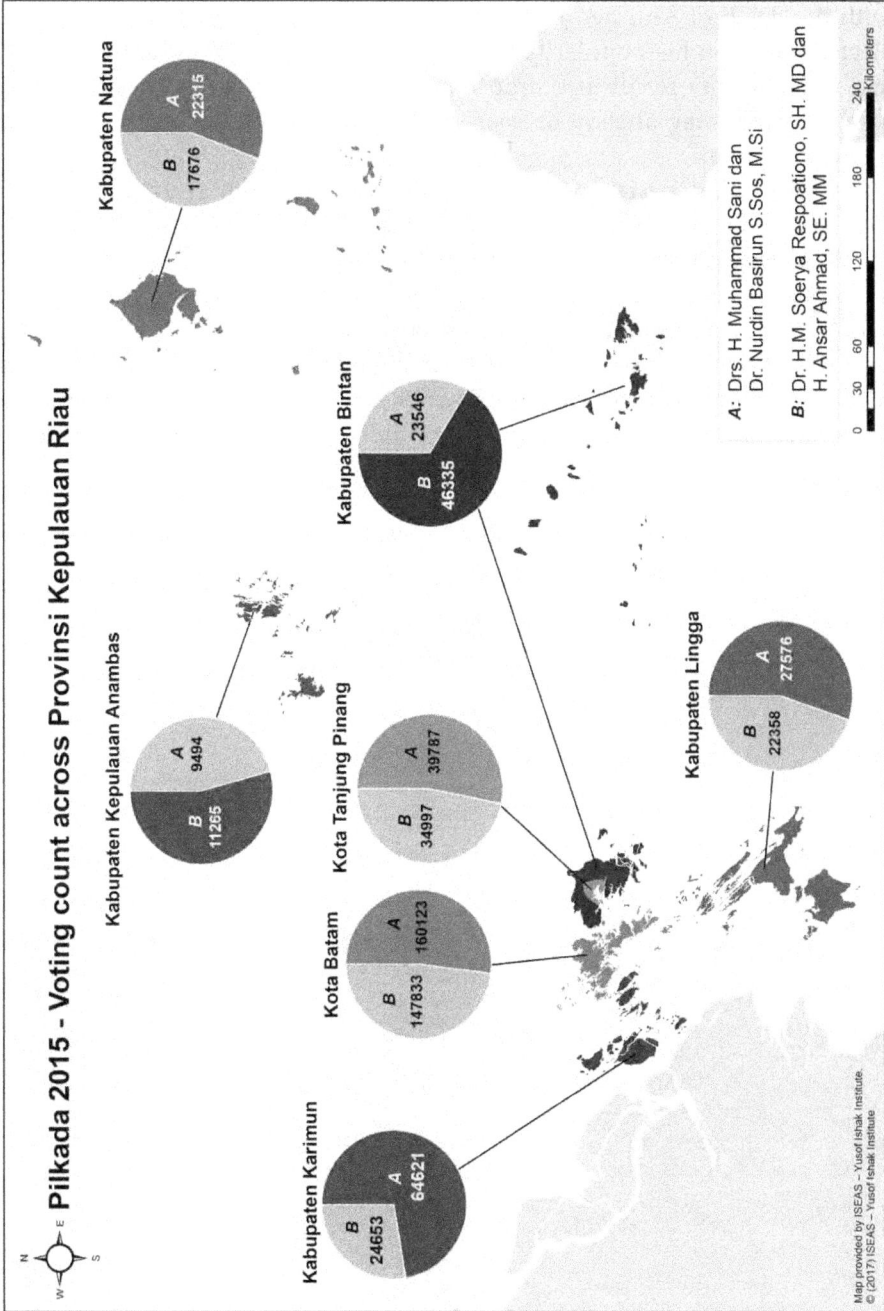

Pilkada 2015 - Voting count across Provinsi Kepulauan Riau

effects on Kepri's local politics that should not be downplayed. Individual leaders' administration and lifespan are usually shorter and less stable than those of well-institutionalized political organizations. Kepri Province experienced this first-hand with the death of Sani two months into his governorship. As governor Sani was elected based on his popularity, the implications of having a replacement who is less popular may result in a drop in the level of trust in the government. Such dissatisfaction may already be seen in the sense of disenfranchisement and low electoral turnout.

As one of Indonesia's peripheral provinces with a relatively small population, Kepri is not a priority for the central offices of national parties. With competition in much bigger electorates taking place closer to Jakarta, most prominently in Java, the central party offices would naturally not be inclined to focus their attention on smaller and more far-flung provinces such as Kepri.

Overall, with the sorry state of their organization at the moment, it is highly unlikely that political parties in Kepri will be a game changer, even in local politics. They have grown reliant on a handful of individual leaders and are getting away with neglecting the main aspects of political party work.

APPENDIX

TABLE 9.A1
Voting Results in the 2014 Legislative Election in the Riau Islands

Parties	Votes	Percentage
Nasdem Party	2,365	2.5
PKB	3,846	4.1
PKS	5,520	5.8
PDI-P	19,442	20.6
Golkar	19,465	20.6
Gerindra	5,881	6.2
Demokrat	7,984	8.4
PAN	2,992	3.2
PPP	7,940	8.4
Hanura	15,741	16.6
PBB	1,711	1.8
PKPI	1,742	1.8

TABLE 9.A2
Number of Registered Voters and Votes in the Riau Islands 2015 Gubernatorial Election

Municipality/Regency	Registered Voters	Votes	Turnout Percentage
Bintan	99,424	72,973	73.4
Karimun	174,990	95,435	54.5
Anambas Islands	30,574	21,641	70.8
Batam	641,015	320,055	49.9
Tanjungpinang	146,211	77,961	53.3
Lingga	69,588	53,340	76.7
Natuna	51,995	42,459	81.7

Source: Election Commission (Komisi Pemilihan Umum, KPU).

Notes

1. This chapter was first published as *Parties in the Periphery: Organizational Dilemmas in Indonesia's Kepri Province*, Trends in Southeast Asia Series, no. 17/2017 (Singapore: ISEAS – Yusof Ishak Institute, 2017).

2. Parties in Indonesia are notorious for corruption, primarily as party politicians act as brokers and decision-makers for projects which involve kickbacks for their personal benefit. For an extensive discussion on this matter, see, for example, Mietzner (2015).

3. For detailed discussion on these issues, see, for example, Feith (1962) and Reeve (1985).

4. For discussions on various aspects of democratic transition, see, for example, Samuel and Nordholt (2004); Mietzner (2009); Bunte and Ufen (2009).

5. As state funding is limited and membership dues and contribution are hard to enforce, parties have had to resort to unlawful and corrupt practices. See Mietzner (2013). For a discussion on the operational challenges of enforcing membership dues, see Fionna (2013).

6. Case studies in Malang suggest that while most parties (except Partai Golkar) rent their offices, the better organized parties are able to manage the constant moving and stay active, while the less organized ones may have a long hiatus of not having an office between the moves (Fionna 2013).

7. Author's observations in Tanjungpinang, January 2017.

8. To note, Batam was the temporary capital of Kepri Province when it was first established in 2004. See Hutchinson (2015, p. 103) for details. For full discussion on the history of the establishment of the province, see Amri (2016).

9. Revenues received by Batam in 2015 were about S$226,645,000 and Tanjungpinang's were S$85,885,000—making the former about 2.64 times bigger than the latter's. See Badan Pusat Statistik (2016b).

10. At 10.4 per cent in 2013, the prevalence of poverty in Tanjungpinang was double that of Batam at 5.2 per cent. See Badan Pusat Statistik (2015a).

11. For example, the other two parties had much shorter campaign periods and were allowed smaller funding.

12. Interview with Democrat Party's Kepri Province secretary, Husnizar Hood, July 2017.

13. The fact that two parties have successfully registered and have their organizational requirements verified by the Elections Commission to compete in the 2019 elections suggests that they may have ended up registering their Tanjungpinang Branch as the provincial branch for registration and verification purposes. See Pananrang (2017).

14. With some exceptions, as in the case of PKS, which has been more disciplined in regular internal recruitment. See Fionna (2013).

15. See Law no. 10 of 2008 (Presiden Republik Indonesia 2008).

16. See Law no. 8 of 2015 (Presiden Republik Indonesia 2015).

17. The Election Commission has scheduled the elections to gradually be synchronized for the first time across all 537 regions in 2027. See Setiawanto and Radja (2015).

18. As the numbers of elections and potential candidates have made it difficult for parties to identify these individuals, surveys have proliferated as a somewhat reliable method.

19. Independent candidates need to get the ID cards of 10 per cent of the constituency, and so far only less than 10 per cent of independent candidates have been successful.

20. Interview with PD official, November 2016.

21. Interview with Partai Golkar official, November 2016.

22. Interview with Ady Muzardy, lecturer at Universitas Maritim Raja Haji Ali, March 2017.
23. See Kompasiana (2015); also Kaskus (2013).
24. Interview with Ady Muzardy, March 2017.
25. Interview with Ady Muzardy, March 2017.

References

Amri, Mulya. 2016. "A Periphery Serving Three Cores: Balancing Local, National, and Cross-Border Interests in the Riau Islands". In *The SIJORI Cross-Border Region: Transnational Politics, Economics, and Culture*, edited by Francis E. Hutchinson and Terence Chong, pp. 154–80. Singapore: ISEAS – Yusof Ishak Institute.

Badan Pusat Statistik. 2015a. "Indikator Utama Kepulauan Riau 2015", p. 31. http://kepri.bps.go.id/website/pdf_publikasi/Indikator-Utama-Kepulauan-Riau-Semester-I-2015.pdf

———. 2015b. "Penduduk Indonesia per Provinsi Tahun 2010 (Sensus)". Informasipedia, 30 April 2015. http://informasipedia.com/kependudukan/penduduk-indonesia-sensus/penduduk-indonesia-per-provinsi-sensus/172-penduduk-indonesia-per-provinsi-tahun-2010-sensus.html (accessed 25 September 2017).

———. 2016a. "Luas Daerah dan Jumlah Pulau Menurut Provinsi, 2002–2015". https://www.bps.go.id/linkTabelStatis/view/id/1366 (accessed 26 September 2017).

———. 2016b. "Provinsi Kepulauan Riau Dalam Angka 2015". http://kepri.bps.go.id/website/pdf_publikasi/Provinsi-Kepulauan-Riau-Dalam-Angka-2016.pdf

Badan Pusat Statistik Kepulauan Riau. 2018. "Indikator Utama Kepulauan Riau 2018". Tanjungpinang: BPS Kepuluan Riau.

Batam News. "Penampakan Kantor Demokrat Batam Digusur DPW Nasdem Kepri". 6 September 2016. http://batamnews.co.id/berita-16054-penampakan-kantor-demokrat-batam-digusur-dpw-nasdem-kepri.html (accessed 2 August 2017).

Beintan Boeskh Cakra May Hendra Putra. 2016. "Partisipasi Politik Masyarakat Kepulauan Riau Pada Pemilihan Kepala Daerah Gubernur Periode 2015–2020". *Jurnal, Prodi Ilmu Administrasi Negara Fakulas Ilmu Sosial Dan Ilmu Politik, Universitas Maritim Raja Ali Haji*: 1–22.

Bunte, Marco, and Andreas Ufen, eds. 2009. *Democratization in Post-Suharto Indonesia*. London: Routledge.

Choi, Nankyung. 2007. "Elections, Parties and Elites in Indonesia's Local Politics". *South East Asia Research* 15, no. 3 (November): 325–54.

———. 2009. "Batam's 2006 Mayoral Election: Weakened Political Parties and Intensified Power Struggle in Local Indonesia". In *Deepening Democracy in Indonesia: Direct Elections for Local Leaders (Pilkada)*, edited by Maribeth Erb and Priyambudi Sulistiyanto. Singapore: Institute of Southeast Asian Studies.

Dahl, R.A. 1998. *On Democracy*. New Haven: Yale University Press.

de Tocqueville, A. 1945. *Democracy in America*. New York: A.A. Knopf.

Duverger, Maurice. 1964. *Political Parties: Their Organization and Activity in the Modern State*. London: Methuen.

Erb, Maribeth, and Priyambudi Sulistiyanto, eds. 2009. *Deepening Democracy in Indonesia: Direct Elections for Local Leaders (Pilkada)*. Singapore: Institute of Southeast Asian Studies.

Faucher, Carole. 2007. "Contesting Boundaries in the Riau Archipelago". In *Renegotiating Boundaries: Local Politics in post-Soeharto Indonesia*, edited by Henk Schulte Nordholt and Gerry van Klinken. Leiden: KITLV Press.

Feith, Herbert. 1962. *The Decline of Constitutional Democracy in Indonesia*. Ithaca: Cornell University Press.

Fionna, Ulla. 2013. *The Institutionalisation of Political Parties in Post-authoritarian Indonesia: From the Grass-roots Up*. Amsterdam: Amsterdam University Press.

Gunther, Richard, José Ramón Montero, and Juan J. Linz. 2002. *Political Parties: Old Concepts and New Challenges*. Oxford: Oxford University Press.

Haryati, Dewi. 2017. "Segera Diresmikan, Kantor DPD Hanura Kepri Bakal Dilengkapi Cafe". *Tribun Batam*, 2 March 2017. https://batam.tribunnews.com/2017/03/02/segera-diresmikan-kantor-dpd-hanura-kepri-bakal-dilengkapi-cafe (accessed 2 August 2017).

Huntington, Samuel. 1993. *The Third Wave: Democratization in the Late Twentieth Century*. Oklahoma: University of Oklahoma University Press.

Hutchinson, Francis E. 2015. *Mirror Images in Different Frames? Johor, the Riau Islands, and Competition for Investment from Singapore*. Singapore: Institute of Southeast Asian Studies.

Indopolitika. 2015. "Inilah Visi Dan Misi Muhammad Sani-Nurdin Basirun Di Pilgub Kepri". 3 September 2015. https://indopolitika.com/inilah-visi-dan-misi-muhammad-sani-nurdin-basirun-di-pilgub-kepri/ (accessed 27 March 2017).

Janda, Kenneth, and T. Colman. 1998. "Effects of Party Organization on Performance during the 'Golden Age' of Parties". In *Parties and Democracy: Party Structure and Party Performance in Old and New Democracies*, edited by Richard Hofferbert. Oxford: Blackwell.

Kaskus. 2013. "Warga Batam Siaga Kerusuhan". 23 October 2013. https://www.kaskus.co.id/thread/526726f4118b46200e000004/warga-batam-siaga-kerusuhan/ (accessed 2 November 2017).

Katz, R.S., and P. Mair. 1994. *How Parties Organize: Change and Adaptation in Party Organization in Western Democracies*. London: Sage.

Kimura, Ehito. 2010. "Proliferating Provinces: Territorial Politics in Post-Soeharto Indonesia". *South East Asia Research* 18, no. 3: 415–49.

Kompasiana. 2015. "Sani Versus Soerya: Pertarungan Putih versus Hitam (2)". 9 May 2015. https://www.kompasiana.com/oktavianalubis/555310a06523bd490c16ff14/sani-versus-soerya-pertarungan-putih-versus-hitam-2 (accessed 2 November 2017).

Mainwaring, Scott, and T.R. Scully. 1995. *Building Democratic Institutions: Party Systems in Latin America*. Stanford: Stanford University Press.

Mair, Peter, and Ingrid van Biezen. 2001. "Party Membership in Twenty European Democracies". *Party Politics* 7, no. 1: 5–21.

Malley, Michael. 1999. "Regions: Centralization and Resistance". In *Indonesia beyond Suharto: Policy, Economy, Society, Transition*, edited by D.K. Emmerson, pp. 71–105. Armonk, NY: M.E. Sharpe.

Mietzner, Marcus. 2009. *Military Politics, Islam and the State in Indonesia: From Turbulent Transition to Democratic Consolidation*. Singapore: Institute of Southeast Asian Studies.

———. 2013. "Party Financing in Post-Suharto Indonesia: Between State Subsidies and Political Corruption". *Contemporary Southeast Asia* 29, no. 2: 238–63.

———. 2015. "Dysfunction by Design: Political Finance and Corruption in Indonesia". *Critical Asian Studies* 47, no. 4: 587–610.

Pananrang, Aqsa Riyandi. 2017. "Ini 14 Parpol Calon Peserta Pemilu 2019, Rhoma Irama Gagal Lagi, 2 Partai Lama Gugur". *Tribun Timur*, 18 October 2017. https://makassar.tribunnews.com/2017/10/18/14-partai-fiks-calon-peserta-pemilu-2019-2-parpol-lama-tak-lolos-ini-daftar-lengkapnya (accessed 26 October 2017).

Presiden Republik Indonesia. 2008. "Undang-Undang Republik Indonesia Nomor 10 Tahun

2008". 31 March 2008. http://www.jdih.kemenkeu.go.id/fullText/2008/10TAHUN2008UU. htm (accessed 30 October 2017).

———. 2015. "Undang-Undang Republik Indonesia Nomor 8 Tahun 2015". 18 March 2015. http://www.dpr.go.id/dokjdih/document/uu/1627.pdf (accessed 10 October 2017).

Reeve, David. 1985. *Golkar of Indonesia: An Alternative to the Party System*. Oxford: Oxford University Press.

Samuel, Hanneman, and Henk-Schulte Nordholt. 2004. *Indonesia in Transition: Rethinking Civil Society, Region, and Crisis*. Yogyakarta: Pustaka Pelajar.

Setiawanto, Budi and Aditia Maruli Radja. 2015. "Tujuh Gelombang Pilkada Serentak 2015 Hingga 2027". *Antara News*. 17 February 2015. https://www.antaranews.com/ berita/480618/tujuh-gelombang-pilkada-serentak-2015-hingga-2027 (accessed 26 October 2017).

Szczerbiak, A. 1999. "Testing Party Models in East-Central Europe". *Party Politics* 5, no. 4: 525–37.

Tan, Khee Giap, Nurina Merdikawati, Mulya Amri, and Blake Harley Berger. 2015. *2014 Annual Competitiveness Analysis and Development Strategies for Indonesian Provinces*. Singapore: World Scientific Publishing.

Tomsa, Dirk. 2008. *Party Politics and Democratization in Indonesia: Golkar in the Post-Suharto Era*. London and New York: Routledge.

Vanhanen, T. 2000. "A New Dataset for Measuring Democracy, 1810–1998". *Journal of Peace Research* 37, no. 2: 251–65.

Walker, J.H., Glenn Banks, and Minako Sakai. 2009. *The Politics of the Periphery in Indonesia: Social and Geographical Perspectives*. Chicago: University of Chicago Press.

Webb, P.D. 1995. "Are British Political Parties in Decline?". *Party Politics* 1, no. 3: 299–322.

Webb, P. and R. Kolodny. 2006. "Professional Staff in Political Parties". In *Handbook of Party Politics*, edited by R.S. Katz and W. Crotty. London: Sage.

10

THE RISE AND DECLINE OF LABOUR MILITANCY IN BATAM[1]

Max Lane

INTRODUCTION

In providing an overview summary of trade union activity in Batam, this chapter analyses the region's political history over the last several years. This approach is employed because there appears to have been a strong surge in national trade union reorganization activity since the end of the New Order in 1998. Explaining the evolution of that history, and how it has manifested in Batam, has determined the framework for this chapter. It is structured as follows: the first section provides a basic outline of historical and social context, both of the trade union sector as well as of some other aspects of Batam; the following section describes the history of the emergence of industrial militancy nationally and in Batam; the third elaborates on the process that has led to a decline of that hostility; and, the conclusion sketches out the implications of this history of the rise and decline of such combat.

HISTORICAL AND SOCIAL CONTEXT

Batam is a unique site of development, consciously created to take advantage of its proximity to Singapore. It is therefore to some extent "artificial" in a sense that its sociology and economy have evolved as an enclave offshoot of Indonesia's economic connectivity with Southeast Asia. This is particularly reflected in its demography, both in terms of originating ethnicity, as well as political demography. It should be noted that in contemporary Indonesia, ethnic and political demography overlap with each other as most political parties represented in the national parliament have specific geographic areas where their support is strongest.[2]

Before delving deep into the trade union situation in Batam, it is pertinent to briefly discuss its demography. The central and salient feature here is the major immigrant population, which has come into being over an approximate fifteen-year period. The original indigenous population of Batam Malays now exists alongside Javanese, Batak, Minangkabau and other Malay Sumatran immigrants, which gives the Batam population and society the character of a frontier, or new society. By 2010, across the whole province of Riau, "Malays"—presumably local Malays—formed only 30 per cent of the population. This phenomenon is even more pronounced in the town of Batam itself. In 2000, the Malay population was already below 20 per cent of the population, with Javanese being the largest group, followed by Bataks and Minangkabau people from Sumatra. The migration of workers to Batam has given the island a population growth of 8 per cent, the highest in Indonesia.

An introduction to the history of trade unions in Indonesia is useful. There have been several phases in the country's history where unions had a very different character from what is observed today. Between 1950 and 1965, trade unions were fundamentally an extension of the organizational and mobilization activities of political parties. Almost every large party, irrespective of ideological outlook, had affiliated unions, or unions where they were dominant in the leadership. Moreover, union activity was integrated into party competition. After 1959, when elections were continuously postponed, party competition took the form of a competition over the scale of mobilization as a show of strength. Post 1962, this competition was used to show support for the government's orientation towards "socialism à la Indonesia". During this period, unions associated with the Indonesian Left, especially the Communist Party of Indonesia, grew the fastest and were the most active. The main issues were as often about wages and conditions as they were ideological.

From October 1965, when that section of the Army under the command of Major-General Soeharto took control of the country, the Indonesian Left, along with associated trade unions, was subjected to severe repression, including mass arrests and executions. Activities by all trade unions, including those sympathetic to the new regime, were also suspended. In the early 1970s, under international pressure, the New Order government established a trade union federation, the All Indonesia Labour Federation (Federasi Serikat Buruh SeIndonesia , or FBSI). This union, which underwent name and structural changes, was essentially an extension of the state in its efforts to control industrial unrest throughout the period until the fall of Soeharto in 1998. In fact, during the last decade of the New Order, the FBSI was known as the All Indonesia Workers Union (Serikat Pekerja Seluruh Indonesia, or SPSI). It carried out only the most minimal member-based activities. By the early 1990s, new initiatives began to challenge the dominance of this single state union. In most cases, the leaders of the new unions were jailed and their activities suppressed. Some of these unions revived after 1998, engaging in actual conventional union activities, such as campaigns around salaries and working conditions.

DEMOGRAPHY, PARTY POLITICS AND THE GENERAL CONTEXT FOR UNIONS

To understand the trade union situation in Batam, two interrelated issues need to be understood.

The *first* issue relates to *diversity in party identification*. Over the last ten years (in fact even since the 1920s), trade unions have been intimately connected with national political developments. Indonesian politics has been chiefly characterized by the ongoing evolution of a new scenario of more-or-less open electoral politics, with a proliferation of parties. Elections have taken place for local and national parliaments, as well as for various positions in the executive arms of government, such as president, governors, mayors, and regents.

Political party life has been characterized by competition between parties on the national level. With all parties enjoying bases of support in specific geographical areas, it is often the case that the locations of particular ethnic populations coincide with each other. These localized support groups have long histories, and similar patterns can be identified even in the 1955 general elections. Since 2013, almost all the large union confederations have aligned with existing political parties.

As discussed in the introductory section, Batam has a predominantly immigrant population. In what ways might the specific migrant demographics have relevance? The first fact to note is that as a result of this demography, the basis for any "natural" continuity of pre-existing traditional local support for particular political parties has been weakened. Batam has completely changed from the Malay fishing community that gave it its character in previous decades.

FIGURE 10.1
Population Growth in Batam up to 2015

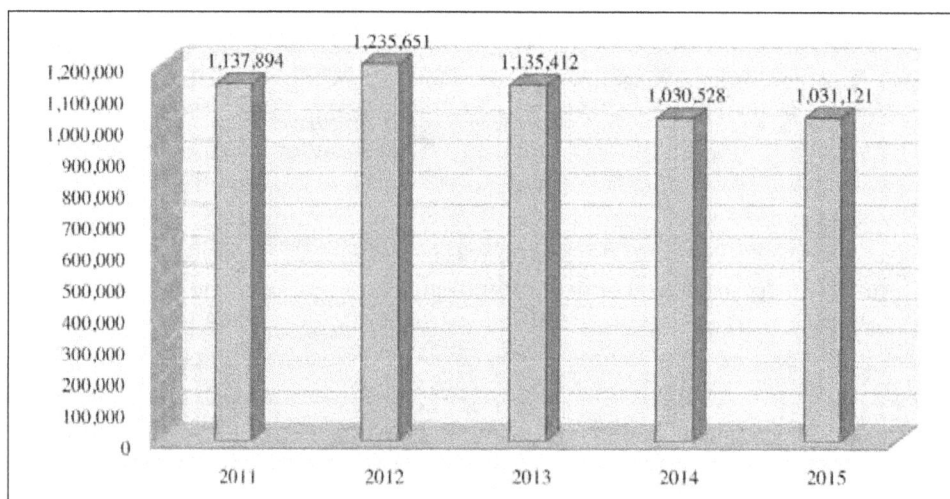

Source: https://www.bpbatam.go.id/eng/batamGuide/batam_figures.jsp

As of 2016, official statistics give a figure of 931,435 for the total workforce, 807,000 of which are classified as urban based.[3] It is not clear what portion of this workforce is employed on a sufficiently permanent basis at workplaces with a labour force of sufficient size to be suitable for unionization.[4]

Indeed, as a consequence of a majority migrant population, Batam has displayed one of the most diversified of electoral party allegiances. In the 2009 elections, usefully representative as occurring before the polarization effected by the Widodo-Subianto competition, many parties (thirty-eight) were able to stand candidates. Of these, twenty-one parties scored above one per cent and thirty-four parties secured over 1,000 votes. This is one of the clearest pictures of the politico-cultural diversity of party identification.

On the other hand, it should also be noted that in the same elections there was essentially no significant policy differentiation between the parties. These party identifications were most likely reflections of social networks resulting out of hometown contacts or familiarity with different individuals. The largest party was Susilo Bambang Yudhoyono's Partai Demokrat at 10 per cent followed by Golkar and the Partai Demokrasi Indonesia–Perjuangan (PDI-P) with 9.3 per cent each. While these were also the three leading parties nationally, no one party particularly dominated. A party that was later to become a major axis of affiliation for Indonesia's most active union confederation, Confederation of Trade Unions of Indonesia (Konfederasi Serikat Pekerja Indonesia, or KSPI), namely Prabowo Subianto's Gerindra was not yet active in Batam in 2009. Significantly, however, its partner from 2013, the Partai Keadilan Sejahtera (PKS) scored relatively high in 2009 with nine per cent. The current president of the KSPI, Said Iqbal, stood as a PKS candidate in Riau in 2009.

A *second* factor mirrors the political sociology of the section of the workforce employed in workplaces large enough to be unionized. This is the *newness of the workforce*. On Java, in the factory belt areas around Jakarta, for example, most workers are young and have been recruited into factories or other large workplaces since 2000–2 when the recovery after the 1997 financial crisis began. Many have less than ten years' experience as factory workers or as workers in any kind of large, technology-based workplace. Most come from a family background where their parents also had no, or very minimal, experience of urban formal sector employment—which also means no experience of trade union membership or activity.

This has also been the case for the vast majority of workers who came to Batam at a young age to escape unemployment in their home province. However, there does not seem to be any good data that can be used to elaborate on the kind of experience they brought with them. Discussions with informants, including workers, in Batam in 2017, indicate that very few have significant experience, except for a very small group that previously worked in shipyards on Java.

This has meant, on Batam, as well as in another parts of Indonesia, that no pre-existing strong loyalties exist for particular trade unions. Trade union memberships have only been built since the 2000s and remain relatively fluid, however "solid" they may appear at any one moment.

This demographic diversity reflected the diversity of electoral results nationally, giving Batam the profile of a mini Indonesia. By 2014, the election results in Batam also reflected a national trend of reducing the number of parties represented. There were members elected from ten parties, nine of which were also the major parties represented nationally. A feature of politics in Batam, including trade union politics, is the large extent to which it reflects national developments.[5] Perhaps one difference is that there was a slightly more even spread in the voting among the nine most important parties than in other single regions. As a matter of fact, in the presidential elections in 2014, there was a 56 per cent vote in favour of Joko Widodo, also similar to the national outcome (*Berita Satu* n.d.).

Batam vs. Jakarta

Although obvious differences remain, certain aspects of this demographic profile make Batam appear similar to Jakarta and the rest of Indonesia. The key similarities are, as pointed out before, the newness of the workforce, the lack of experience with unions, and the absence of entrenched union loyalties—with such loyalties also developing only recently. The demographic diversity also meant that the general "diversity" of trade unions prevalent around Indonesia also exists in Batam.

Another interesting similarity is the higher cost of living in Batam, which is similar to that in Jakarta. No doubt this is connected to the high level of imports for almost everything needed by the people on the island. In discussions with some factory workers, they also indicated that an additional financial pressure was the expectation that they could send money home. This has meant that trade unions in Batam have had a basis for demanding a large increase in wages.[6] The minimum wage in Batam remains almost on par with Jakarta. At the end of 2017, the minimum wage was increased from IDR3,241,125 to IDR3,523,427 (Maulana and Susanti 2017). This was the standard increase of 8.7 per cent that was announced for all of Indonesia (Sugianto 2017). Jakarta, Batam and Karawang have the highest minimum wages in the country.[7] In Central Java, in contrast, the minimum wage can be below IDR2 million.

At this point, it is also necessary to emphasize the key differences. Jakarta's economy and workforce operate on a totally different scale from that of Batam. Moreover, Jakarta's day-time population stands at approximately 15 million, compared to Batam's just over 1 million. The number of large-sized manufacturing enterprises in the Jakarta factory belt area is also much greater than in Batam.

TRADE UNION POLITICS: EARLY PERIOD

After the Habibie government ended the policy of a single state-authorized union in 1998, there was a process of fragmentation of the existing single union (Lambert 1993), as well as an evolution of dissident unions and a mushrooming of new enterprise organizations.[8] This occurred throughout Indonesia but concentrated in areas that were attracting manufacturing investment, including Batam. Batam, under the New Order government, had already been treated as a special investment site. The demographic basis for union consolidation was further enhanced after 2001–2, when investment started to return to Indonesia after the 1997 Asian Financial Crisis.

This period saw elements of an unplanned demographic shift to Batam, with some outbreaks of social unrest. In 2002, for example, there was widespread ethnic unrest between the Javanese and the Bataks over various perceived grievances. There had also been earlier clashes between people from Flores and Bataks. The clashes were serious, and newspapers reported that large shopping centres in Nagoya and Sekupang Seaport were deserted. Public transportation disappeared temporarily, too. A police official explained at the time that the situation was tense as 95 per cent of the population were migrants from other parts of Indonesia and that relations between the various newcomers had not settled (*Jakarta Post*, 7 February 2002).

Among other things, Batam has a sense of the harsh life of a frontier town comprised mostly of poor migrant labourers. For example, in May 2004, there were clashes between squatters in illegal housing and the police (*Straits Times*, 15 May 2004; *Jakarta Post*, 15 May 2004). In the same year, there were large demonstrations by union members for wage rises (*Detik.com*, 4 December 2004). This level of social unrest—with occasional outbursts and also worker demonstrations—appears to continue throughout the period until 2010.[9] Worker protest activity escalated after that, perhaps sociologically supported by the stabilization of the demographic situation.

The return growth was slow and gradual, but by 2007, there were 240,509 Indonesian citizens employed in Batam City, and 164,476 people (65 per cent of whom were female) worked in secondary industries (Ford 2014). By this time, most of the trade unions operating in Indonesia were also active in Batam. This is clearly revealed by the 2009 elections. Michele Ford (2014, pp. 353–54) documents members of the following unions as having stood as candidates under the banners of various parties:

- Federation of Indonesian Metal Workers' Unions (Federasi Serikat Pekerja Metal Indonesia, or FSPMI);
- Confederation of All Indonesian Trade Unions) (Konfederasi Serikat Pekerja Seluruh Indonesia or KSPSI); and
- Confederation of Prosperous Worker Trade Unions (Konfederasi Serikat Buruh Sejahtera Indonesia, or KSBSI).

The first two came out of the fragmentation and reformation process of the New Order era state-authorized union. The third, KSBSI, evolved out a dissident union established under the New Order, and also suppressed at that time. Although a dissident union opposed to New Order authoritarianism, it was not left-wing or radical, but was more aligned with moderate social democratic unionism.[10]

These are still the three main union formations in Batam today,[11] along with the FSPMI, having been the most politically active and having the greatest impact on union atmospherics, until at least 2013–14.

THE RISE OF MILITANCY: A NATIONAL TREND (2011–13)

Batam's industrial relations scene did attract attention before 2011, when there were some outbursts of worker anger, sometimes provoked by xenophobic or ethnic reactions. For instance, there had been rioting at the Dubai-owned Drydocks World Graha shipyards in 2010 when an Indian security guard allegedly insulted an Indonesian worker. Thousands of workers rioted against Indian personnel. In 2011, another shipyard riot broke out when security guards assaulted two workers. This incident did not seem to have an ethnic or racialist aspect (*Straits Times*, 21 September 2011). However, these have not been repeated after 2011.

Perhaps the most important point to note is that starting from 2011 until today, trade union activity in Batam has mirrored national trends. While Batam's economic experience over the past seven years has been different in its specifics, than, for example, the Jakarta region, trade union activity between 2010/11 and 2017 has been more or less similar. This reflects the fact that the existing national union confederations and federations seem to be highly centralized.[12] It will be a central element of the conclusion of this initial survey of unionism in Batam that developments there have been, are likely to remain, dependent on national trends. This is especially the case now since the initial teething period of unsettled ethnic relations resulting from the rapid demographic shift, has subsided.

Escalation of labour mobilization became very evident throughout 2011. It is difficult to determine the exact reasons for this, but it seems that by around 2010, most of the larger union federations and confederations had stabilized after more than a decade of fragmentation, re-formation, and, to a certain extent at the factory base level, renewal. This stabilization was buttressed by the relative revival of manufacturing growth over the previous period. By 2010, there was a larger and more stable workforce, with at least three union confederations with substantial dues paying membership, namely, the three cited previously, the KSPI (including the FSPMI), the KSPSI and the KSBSI.

In Jakarta, and in several other cities, there were also unions that grew out of, or were connected to, the more radical dissident political currents that had emerged in opposition to the New Order in the 1980s. While the KSBSI emerged from a union that had been part of the opposition and suppressed before 1998, it was not politically radical in its orientation. However, in Batam, none of these more radical unions were or are present.[13] This is also an important factor in understanding the dynamics of union politics over the last few years.

The escalated mobilizations were visible nationally, in Jakarta and in other provinces, including Batam. These were of a different character than either the ethnic, racial or unorganized or semi-organized outbursts that had occurred in Batam in the earlier years. The national escalation was framed around two time periods. The first was May Day and the second was the November–December period which, at least up until recently, was the period when increases in the official minimum wage were determined. May Day became the day when major unions, spearheaded by the KSPI/FSPMI, would announce their campaigns for wage increases, and also for an end to day labour hire (called "outsourcing"). In 2011, they announced that they planned a "national strike" at the end of the year to demand wage increase.

This pattern of announcing wage and other demands at large rallies in the month of May, leading to a national strike in October or November was a pattern every year from 2011 to 2013. Between May and November, many warm-up actions would be organized, including road blocks and motor-bike mobilizations by large numbers of workers. And then on set dates in either October or November, major demonstrations in the factory belt areas around Jakarta and other cities—including Batam—would take place.

Vanguard Agency

Between 2010 and 2013, the end-of-year national mobilizations were always called by an umbrella alliance of Union Confederations and Federations. The first was a coalition between the KSPSI and the KSPI. Other unions would also mobilize on the same dates, but separately. Later, after tensions between these two confederations prevented further grouping, another alliance emerged to organize these actions. This was a pact between the KSPI and various unions, most of which had emerged from the fragmentation and re-formation of the old New Order era state-sanctioned union structures.

On every occasion between 2011 and 2013, the FSPMI metalworkers union (mainly workers from assembly factories of cars, motorbikes, whitegoods and electronic goods) was the driving force of the mobilizations. FSPMI was the leading Federation in the KSPI confederation. Between 2010 and 2011, a formation known as the Garda Metal (Metal Battalion), was the spearhead of most demonstrations.[14] The Garda Metal was a well-drilled formation of union members recruited to play the leading role in such mobilizations. They were, in fact, also provided with a separate black-and-red para-military style uniform. The presence of several hundreds of these disciplined Garda Metal union members at the head of a demonstration gave the workers in the mobilization increased confidence.

An interesting observation here is that many Garda Metal members received advanced education in political and economic issues. During the 2010–12 period, thousands of members of the FSPMI, and Garda Metal in particular, attended so-called "Ekopol" (Political Economy) courses. Key educators in this programme were initially drawn from the activists who had been part of the more radical wing of the opposition to the New Order. This meant that the FSPMI had an educated and trained spearhead formation that was able to provide leadership at the factory level, across all plants that were covered by it. Some Ekopol-trained unionists also became de facto leaders at the individual company level, leading more militant actions, including actions by workers from one factory offering solidarity to workers in other facilities, who were on strike or in dispute with their employer.

The role of the FSPMI, the Garda Metal and the Ekopol political education was central in enabling escalation between 2010 and 2013.

Batam

The Garda Metal was also developed in Batam. Ekopol courses were regularly taught as well, and by the same educators as in the Jakarta area.

The FSPMI was already active and well organized early in the 2000s. By 2008, the electronics federation alone had 13,515 members, of whom 10,115 were women.[15] The members were spread across twenty-five companies, only two of which had more than 1,000 members. Their 2009 report to members listed numerous ongoing cases of individual disputes as well as a fairly comprehensive training programme for some members, especially in regard to legal aspects of industrial relations. Officials from national headquarters also made regular visits. Their list of cases indicated that they were taking many disputes to court. A list of Garda Metal members from 2011 provides the names of 298 members.[16] Most are listed as being part of delegations from mainly electronics firms, but some also from shipyards. Apart from visits from national officials, the Jakarta Ekopol educators also regularly visited Batam to give courses.[17] These included discussions on the tactics of mobilization.

This means that the FSPMI, even by 2009, had a large dues-paying membership in Batam, and a substantial Garda Metal force. Batam was thus equipped with the same vanguard structure as Jakarta. It is not surprising then that in 2011 and 2012, the worker mobilizations were large and militant. Apart from being a demographically pioneer settler society equipped with mobilization organizations such as Garda Metal, and a solid base in the FSPMI, and with other unions also present, Batam had already shown the potential for tensions to heat up considerably.

In 2011, after the Jakarta-based May Day declaration that there would be a campaign leading up to November mobilizations around wage demands and the demand to end outsourcing (day labour hire), meetings and actions took place in Batam. The most well-known ones took place in May 2011 and then climaxed in November 2011, and were very militant actions resulting in confrontations with the police (Setiawan 2011).[18] In November, the actions received wide national media coverage with reports of workers bearing government cards as they entered the compound of the mayor. The demonstrations were called by the KSPSI, KSPI, which includes the FSPMI and the FSBSI—the three main groups operating in Batam.

The November 2011 demonstrations took place over two days with all the major union federations demanding a new minimum wage of IDR1,760,000 (US$200 in 2011). The employers' association proposed IDR1,260,000, while the wage council suggested IDR1,360,000 (*Jakarta Post*, 24 November 2011; *Jakarta Globe*, 25 November 2011). The Mayor supported a figure closer to the wage council's proposal.[19] Police used tear gas and rubber bullets to disperse the mobilization which appeared to involve up to 10,000 workers (*Jakarta Post*, 26 November 2011). Batam town areas, including some government offices, were shut down for three days. These militant mobilizations, with the clashes with police, meant that Batam received extra prominence in the media (*detikNews*, 23 November 2011). For example, in 2011 in Jakarta, the workers' wage demands were more or less met, and extensions of their protests did not need to go ahead.

In 2012, the same pattern of activity took place with unions announcing on May Day in Jakarta that there would be a build-up to a national mobilization in October, which would again demand substantial wage rises and an end to outsourcing. With the experience of 2011 behind them, and a further year of training and education, primarily in the FSPMI and Garda Metal, the October 2012 mobilizations were probably the largest and best organized of any between 2011 and 2013 (the 2013 mobilizations were more effective in some respects, but less so in others). In the Jakarta factory belt area, the demonstrations were very large and were followed by several months of solidarity actions between unions. The Garda Metal presence was very evident in both the preceding warm-up actions, as well as during the demonstrations on 2 and 3 October 2012.

According to worker participant reports, the Batam mobilizations were also large and effective. This time, however, there were no serious clashes with the police, despite successful occupations by workers in some areas. The authorities announced that "thousands" of police and security personnel were being mobilized (Anjasfianto 2012; *Batamtoday*, 1 October 2012). It is worth reproducing one report from a participant:[20]

At 8 am, 3 October 2012, Batam city traffic was completely paralysed. This was the fastest the workers' movement had ever been able to close down an area in any part of the country in a national strike. This action did not face repression, as the wage action last year did when there were shootings [with rubber bullets]. The combined forces of the TNI and Polri were helpless against a wave of strikes.

By 6 am, a number of masses had located in four locations, namely Tumenggung stadium, Tanjung Uncang, Simpang Franky (Batam Centre) and Main (Batu Ampar). This movement was led by the Garda Metal Batam acting as field executor. The mass spread into groups: "sweeping" groups,[21] groups blocking roads and groups occupying strategic points, managing to break the combined security forces of the TNI and Polri.

At 7:30 am, as the sweeping masses went out of the factory, the force of the apparatus focused on the masses in the Tumenggung stadium, the masses blocking the street (at the Franky intersection) and the mass groups of KSPSI and the KSBSI going to the Mayor's Office. The apparatus could not move freely because they were surrounded by a mass of workers who had just come out of the factory at 7:30 am who came from various regions. Workers came from Tanjung Uncang-Sampang, Batu Ampar, Tunas Industries, Muka Kuning and Panbil, and Cammo areas, to Tumenggung stadium. The workers' movement successfully paralyzed the city of Batam in just three hours.

Workers succeeded in urging the Mayor of Batam, Speaker of DPRD and Kadisnaker, to meet workers at the Tumenggung stadium. The Mayor of Batam, Ahmad Dahlan and his entourage, who were on the way to the action site were besieged by the masses who came from the Muka Kuning area and the masses who came from the Tanjung Uncang area. Ahmad Dahlan promised to fulfil all the demands of the workers, including wage demands of IDR2,200,000 (non-sector), IDR2,500,000 (sector 1), IDR3,200,000 (sector 2) to be discussed in the Batam City Wage Council.

For the Batam labour movement, this is a great victory. It is not easy to exert force on Batam's Mayor, Ahmad Dahlan, who is famous for being arrogant to workers.

Moreover, the action process does not use the aid of command cars and sound devices, because the police/TNI officers blocked FSPMI access to rent cars and sound systems.

As indicated in the report above, the Garda Metal led the actions in the field that carried out sweepings, roadblocks and occupations of road intersections. The KSPSI and KSBSI mobilized their members at government offices. In Batam, the Garda Metal's spearhead role was even more real than in the Jakarta region, where it was their disciplined and uniformed show of force at the head of a mobilization that gave the workers confidence. The coordinator of the Batam Garda Metal, Suprapto, was quoted as saying that a total of 25,000 workers were involved in the day's mobilization (*Liputan6* 2012).

This report by a sympathizer captures the elated atmosphere among unions at the end of 2012. Throughout Indonesia, the unions won substantial wage increase. In Batam, the official wage rose from IDR1,320,000 to IDR2,040,000 and even higher in some sectors.[22] This is at least a 65 per cent rise.

DECLINE OF MILITANCY AND BEGINNING OF CO-OPTION (2013–17)

The momentum from the successful 2012 mobilizations carried through into 2013. There was another May Day call for a national action at the end of the year, when again there would be a round of discussions on raising the official minimum wage. In the Jakarta factory belt areas, there were frequent mobilizations and factory pickets throughout 2013. Sweeping actions were common, resulting in increased activity by new local organizations mobilizing people to take action—physical harassment—against picketing workers.[23] A worker organizing centre was also burned down. There were also an increasing number of employers presenting charges against workers to police for harassment or damaging property. While there are no comprehensive statistics on this, union activists confirm an intensification of harassment and pressure.

Despite this, the 2013 mobilizations still took place. However, the process appeared to be not as well organized and somewhat more chaotic than in 2012. Individual reports from workers in different factories seemed to indicate uncertainty on the part of the union leaderships supporting the actions as to what scale and what kind of action they wanted.[24]

Whatever the internal situation may have been inside the KSPSI during 2013, the wage outcome was less than desired. This contrasted greatly with the results from 2012. In Jakarta, there was a new Governor, Joko Widodo. He had agreed to the big wage increases in 2012, a situation he was faced with very soon after coming to office as Governor. In 2013, he agreed to a much lower wage increase (Dewi 2013).

Batam

In Batam, the 2013 mobilizations seemed to go well, although some actions failed. Media reports stated that activity was paralysed in around 1,000 foreign companies in Batam and that sweeping activities took place in twenty-six industrial areas. Significantly, they also reported that, as in the Jakarta area, employers also called in non-government militia groups such as Pemuda Pancasila, to provide physical security outside their factories. In Batam, the minimum wage rose from IDR2,040,000 to IDR2,422,092, going up to just over IDR2,600,000 in sector 1, which includes some of the heavier industries (Kho 2014).

The Scenario Changes

On 8 November 2013, in Bekasi, in the centre of the Jakarta factory belt, representatives of unions (including the KSPSI/FSPMI), employers, local government, the police and army signed the Bekasi Industrial Harmony Declaration. The declaration contained six points. Although they were all formulated in very general terminology, it was clear that it was a declaration against conflict and militancy. The final points emphasized the need to create a climate where enterprises could be productive and develop in a competitive environment. The emphasis was on consensus, cooperation and developing industrial relations where everyone benefited (Manumoyoso and Mulyadi 2012). Much of the language was reminiscent of New Order industrial relations language. It signified a major change in the KSPSI/FSPMI's orientation.

Connected to this development, the people who had been leading the Ekopol education were excommunicated from the union and those courses stopped. An instruction was issued stating that members should not have contact with them.[25]

Other changes also appeared during 2014. The KSPSI/FSPMI started to select members to stand for national and local parliament as the candidates of several different parties. There had been an orientation to gain parliamentary representation as far back as 2009. When the declaration of harmony took place, members were already selected to stand for election via these parties. In the 2014 parliamentary elections, none of the FSPMI members received a quota to be elected in their own right, although two were elected to district parliaments after receiving surplus votes from their respective parties. "Go Politics", as the union called it, was not something new. However, the presidential elections, also scheduled for 2014, did result in a new political orientation.

The 2014 elections were a contest between Joko Widodo, at that time Governor of Jakarta and nominated by the Indonesian Democratic Party of Struggle (PDI-P), and Prabowo Subianto, nominated by his own party Gerindra and supported by Partai Amanat Nasional (PAN) and Partai Kesejahteraan Sosial (PKS). The three major union groupings, KSPSI, KSPI and KSBSI—the three dominant on Batam—were divided on this question. KSPSI and KSBSI supported Widodo. KSPI/FSPMI, on the other hand, came out in strong support for Prabowo Subianto.

KSPI's support for Prabowo, articulated by its central leader, Said Iqbal, marked a new turn in union politics. The union, which had evolved the Garda Metal and had opted for working through various parties, now opted for a clear orientation to one political pole of attraction, Gerindra and PKS.[26] The implications of this new turn have been significant, especially given the increasingly polarized ideological contestation that has occurred in Indonesia since 2014. It has meant that the KSPI/FSPMI has supported many of the positions and tactics associated with the political pole represented by Gerindra, the PKS and their other allies. This has included actively supporting the candidacy of Anies Baswedan and Sandiago Uno, representing Gerindra and PKS, against that of the PDI-P candidate, Basuki Tjahaja Purnama (Ahok), a Chinese Christian. Their support included fusing the 2016 annual minimum wage union mobilization with the "Bela Islam" mobilizations against Ahok's candidacy.[27]

While KSPI member unions still have active disputes with individual employers, and carry out public campaigns in support of improvements in welfare provisions, there are two major visible changes resulting from the turns in industrial and political orientations noted above. First, the annual May–November push for major mobilizations to demand wages and conditions improvements has been de-emphasized. This was especially notable in 2015 when the Widodo government moved to end the annual consideration of the minimum wage based on assessment of minimum dignified living standard costs. The new system would allow that consideration only every five years. Instead, there would be an automatic wage increase based on a formula related to economic growth and inflation. All the unions opposed this. However despite its obvious threat to future wage rises, the 2015 end-of-year mobilizations echoed much less than ever in 2014.[28] In 2016, it appeared as if they had almost disappeared, being submerged in the anti-Ahok "Bela Islam" mobilizations, with that campaign's appeal to anti-Chinese and sectarian sentiment. Industrial campaigning became much more limited to enterprise-level disputes, and was not the subject of national campaigning.

The second change has been the integration of many KSPI/FSPMI activities into the political agenda of the Gerindra/PKS opposition to President Widodo.

These changes have been also reflected in Batam.[29] Since 2014, the same de-escalation of islandwide industrial campaigning has taken place. Protests have not disappeared but the previous dynamic of trying to make the mobilizations stronger and larger each year has vanished. The emphasis has returned to the handling of enterprise-by-enterprise disputes. Often, these are also not about wage rises, but rather delays in wage payments.[30] Among previously active workers, one hears the common refrain of disappointment at the de-escalation. On the other hand, there appears to be a consensus among all of the three union groupings in Batam that disputation must be kept to a modest level in order not to scare away investors. This seems to reflect the spirit of the 2013 Bekasi Declaration of Industrial Harmony.

While neither Gerindra nor PKS appear to be increasing their activity in Batam, this does not mean that the KSPI/FSPMI has not been carrying out activities consistent with their agendas. The KSPI/FSPMI statements now regularly combine their demands around wages and welfare with political demands consistent with the Gerindra/PKS agenda. It appears that one of the largest union mobilizations in Batam—although still only described to be in the hundreds—in 2017 has been one opposing the proposal for a 20 per cent threshold of members of the current parliament as a requirement to nominate candidates for the presidency in 2019.

This new provision, now passed into law, will make it more difficult for Gerindra to nominate Prabowo Subianto to stand as president. The threshold is supported by the PDI-P and most of the parties currently supporting the Widodo government. The eight-point manifesto for the protest action also indicated opposition to the Widodo government's new regulation allowing it to ban organizations opposed to non-Pancasila ideas. The first organization banned was the fundamentalist Moslem Hizbut Tahir Indonesia. Gerindra and PKS have also opposed the ban.[31] This protest, still led by the red and black uniformed Garda Metal, was in August 2017 and was part of a national KSPI mobilization (*Koran Perdjoeangan Suara Kaum Buruh*, 8 August 2017). The other six demands in the manifesto relate to wage and welfare issues.

The analysis here emphasizes the changes in the national political campaigning of the most active union confederation, the KSPI. There appeared to be little resistance to this from trade union leaderships in Batam, although there were protests from the most militant members, some of whom later left the unions or became less active.[32] Indeed, there appears to be a consensus among all unions in Batam now that the weakening economic conditions mean that strikes and other militant activities should be reduced. Likewise, disputes involving pickets and other actions are to be kept at a minimum. Discussions with some workers and officials indicate that such disputes are primarily about late payment of wages.[33]

CONCLUSION

Indonesia's general socio-economic conditions, with low wages compared to cost of living, and employment uncertainty, suggest that industrial disputation at the workplace will not go away. In the meantime, the new 2013–14 political orientation of the unions that had been the spearhead for three years of escalating national industrial campaigning has ended that escalation. It would also seem that efforts to improve industrial conditions for the workforce are being integrated into the politics of contestation among the existing parliamentary political parties. It seems likely to stay this way until a new forefront force emerges. Given the fluidity and newness of the Indonesian trade unions, there remains a possibility, although there are no visible signs at the moment.

The experience of trade unionism in Batam over the last decade indicates that dynamics there have reflected national patterns. This is a reflection of the organizational strength of the national union structures that have access to many more resources than what a single district could muster. There are no signs of major differences between developments in Batam and the rest of Indonesia. One partial exception is that there does not seem to be a basis for a serious or large anti-Chinese and sectarian fundamentalist politics in Batam. While this does not relate directly to unionism, it could be a subject for further research. It does mean that, unlike in Jakarta, the KSPI/FSPMI unions have not been dragged so close to such politics as they have been in Jakarta.

Batam's own economic ups and downs can expect to affect levels of workplace industrial disputation. However, repeats of the high and militant levels of mobilization experienced during 2010–13 are unlikely except as part of a new national developments. If economic decline does worsen workplace tensions, repeats of ethnic and racialist unrest as occurred before the recent nationally led mobilizations, could possibly erupt again—depending on whether socio-economic conditions exacerbate tensions.

Notes

1. This chapter was first published as *The Rise and Decline of Labour Militancy in Batam*, Trends in Southeast Asia Series, no. 8/2018 (Singapore: ISEAS – Yusof Ishak Institute, 2018).
2. This chapter is based on a perusal of news media reports of trade union activity in Indonesia and Batam for the period surveyed here. I also travelled to Batam for a one-week visit in February 2017. I was able to speak with several current and former trade union activists. These interviews helped provide some general background and context, but were most important in assisting in identifying additional documentation. Most interviews were carried out in an informal discussion format. Given the short duration of the visit, the interview and discussion activity were not with a "sample" that can be considered representative. Documentary materials have been used as the main key source. This also includes some media published by trade unions themselves.
3. This appears to be a figure for the potentially employable over the age of fifteen. See Badan Pusat Statistik Provinsi Kepulauan Riau. N.d.(a).
4. Authority (BIDA) reported in 2008, "the total number of SMEs in Batam during the last ten years attained 9,900 unit with at least 60,000 employees". If these figures are accurate, the average number of employees in these small to medium enterprises was only six! This would make these enterprises very unorganizable. However, are only 60,000 people out of 900,000 employed in such SMEs? See Hendrawan (2012).
5. See Marie (2014). The parties represented were: PDI-P 8 members; Golkar 7 members; Gerindra 6 members; Demokrat 5 members; PAN 5 members; Hanura 4 members; Nasdem 4 members; PKS 4 members; PKB 3 members; PPP 3 members; and PKPI 1 member.
6. The official Poverty Line for Batam up until 2016 was IDR525,425 per head, just over IDR2 million for a family of four. This is the second highest for any *kabupaten* in the Province of the Riau Islands. Indonesian official poverty lines are drawn, based on a very minimalist assessment of needs. Source: http://kepri.bps.go.id/linkTableDinamis/view/id/24.
7. Karawang has a minimum wage of IDR3.9 million. This is a result of the fact that the trade union campaign of 2010–12/13 were the most intense and effective in Karawang.
8. See Ford (2000, p. 67). Also, Duncan (2015, p. 87).
9. There are no clear collected statistics of this but surveys of news digests indicate regular, if small-scale activity.
10. For an overview on unions since the Reformasi period, see *IndoProgress* (2007).
11. There are no available studies that can provide more information on the sociology of the membership of these unions, nor reliable figures for their membership sizes in Batam. To obtain a serious picture of the sociology of membership extensive ethnographic work is needed on site among the workforce.
12. For further data on national trade union activity during this period, see Lane (2019).
13. It is not impossible that there are individual workers who have loyalties to one of these unions outside Batam, or small groups of such workers.
14. Information on the Garda Metal is primarily obtained from following their activities via social media, including Garda Metal (n.d.). Their presence at mobilizations is easily

identifiable because of their striking black and red uniforms and military style formations. There is also a Garda Metal Facebook Group where some information can be gleaned. I have also held discussions with former members of Garda Metal in Batam and in Jakarta.

15. "Laporan Pimpinan Cabang Spee FSPMI Kota Batam", March 2009.

16. Garda Metal Batam, Excel Data List. I have not been able to date this list for certainty, but it is either 2011 or 2012. Discussions with former members, February 2017.

17. These courses were very important in helping form core leadership groups. Discussions with former Ekopol students, Batam, February 2017.

18. See Setiawan (2011) for an example of the kind of confrontations taking place in Batam during this period, even as early as 2009. FSPMI banners are very prominent.

19. Official minimum wages are decided by local government, after hearing submissions from employers and workers, via a tripartite wages council, who also make a recommendation.

20. See the Indonesian version at Yunarko (2012).

21. "Sweeping" is the practice of groups of union members travelling around industrial areas and urging other workers in less unionized factories to join the action. This had been practised in the Jakarta factory belt area all through 2012. It grew out of the practice of inter-factory solidarity actions. Many of the leaders of these "actions-from-below" had also received Ekopol education.

22. In addition to an official minimum wage for each district, there are also official minimum wages for different industry sectors.

23. In fact, the escalation seemed to start after the 2012 mobilizations. See *Jakarta Globe*, 30 October 2012; *Berita Satu*, 29 October 2012).

24. It is difficult to get a fully clear picture of the situation leading up to the November 2013 actions. My impressions are based on communications with union members in the area but also the reports that have surfaced on a variety of union member Facebook groups.

25. For the official ex-communication Instruction, see "Email from Said Iqbal to FSPMI Branches No. 01835/Org/DPP FSPMI/VIII/2014 Hal: Instruksi organisasi", reproduced in Duncan (2015), p. 87.

26. Iqbal himself had stood as a PKS candidate in the electorate of Riau in 2009.

27. See also Charmila (2017).

28. In 2014 and 2015 demonstrations did still take place. However, it was clear that framework had been deprioritized.

29. FSPMI Batam's ongoing activities, both campaigns around economic and welfare issues, as well as more specifically political issues are very evident from their Facebook page (FSPMI Batam Island n.d.).

30. Interviews with SBSI union official, February 2017.

31. It should be noted here that most human rights organizations have opposed the ban.

32. Discussions with ex-members of FPSMI and other unions in Batam, February 2017.

33. Discussions with workers on factory sites and an official of the SBSI union confirmed this.

References

Anjasfianto, Zabur. 2012. "Aksi Buruh Blokir Jalan Sempat Ricuh Dengan Aparat". *TribunBatam.id*. Laporan Tribunnews Batam, 3 October 2012. http://batam.tribunnews. com/2012/10/03/aksi-buruh-blokir-jalan-sempat-ricuh-dengan-aparat

Badan Pusat Statistik Provinsi Kepulauan Riau. N.d.(a) "Penduduk 15+ angkatan kerja menurut golongan umur dan daerah tempat tinggal". https://kepri.bps.go.id/linkTableDinamis/view/id/121

———. N.d. "Official Poverty Line for Batam Table". https://kepri.bps.go.id/linkTableDinamis/view/id/24

Batamtoday. 2012 "Polda Kepri Turunkan Ribuan Personil Amankan Demo Buruh di Batam". 1 October 2012. https://www.indoleft.org/news/2004-12-04/thousands-of-batam-workers-demand-wage-increase.html

Berita Satu. 2012. "Labour Coordination Posts Attacked by Thugs, Workers Assaulted". *Indoleft,* 29 October 2012. https://www.indoleft.org/news/2012-10-29/labour-coordination-posts-attacked-by-thugs-workers-assaulted.html

———. 2014. "Jokowi-JK Menang 55,98% di Batam". 17 July 2014. https://www.beritasatu.com/pemilu2014-aktualitas/197506-jokowijk-menang-5598-di-batam.html

Charmila, Winda A. 2017. "Labor Protesters Burn Ahok-Djarot's Floral Tributes". *Jakarta Post.* 1 May 2017. https://www.thejakartapost.com/news/2017/05/01/labor-protesters-burn-ahok-djarots-floral-tributes.html

Detik.com. 2004. "Thousands of Batam Workers Demand Wage Increase". *Indoleft,* 4 December 2004. https://www.indoleft.org/news/2004-12-04/thousands-of-batam-workers-demand-wage-increase.html

detikNews. 2011. "Demo Buruh Di Batam Berakhir Ricuh, Belasan Mobil Dirusak". 23 November 2011. https://news.detik.com/berita/1774134/demo-buruh-di-batam-berakhir-ricuh-belasan-mobil-dirusak

Dewi, Sita W. 2013."Despite Workers' Boycott, Council Proposes Minimum Wage". *Jakarta Post,* 1 November 2013. https://www.thejakartapost.com/news/2013/11/01/despite-workers-boycott-council-proposes-minimum-wage.html

Duncan, David. 2015. "'Out of the Factory, Onto the Streets': The Indonesian Metalworkers Union Federation (FSPMI) as a Case of Union Revitalisation in Indonesia". BA Honours thesis, Australian National University.

Fadli and Andi Hajramurni. 2013. "Massive Strike Nearly Cripples Industries in Batam". *Jakarta Post,* 1 November 2013. https://www.thejakartapost.com/news/2013/11/01/massive-strike-nearly-cripples-industries-batam.html

Ford, Michele. 2000. "Continuity and Change in Indonesian Labour Relations in the Habibie Interregnum". *Asian Journal of Social Science* 28, no. 2: 59–88.

———. 2014. "Learning by Doing: Trade Unions and Electoral Politics in Batam, Indonesia, 2004–2009". *South East Asia Research* 22, no. 3: 341–57.

FSPMI Batam Island. N.d. Facebook. https://www.facebook.com/FSPMI-Batam-Island-158938780871750/

Garda Metal. N.d. FSPMI. http://fspmi.or.id/garda-metal

Hendrawan, Bambang. 2012. "The Small Medium-Sized Enterprises Characteristic in Batam Free Trade Zone That Able to Acquire Debt". *Procedia Economics and Finance* 4: 76–85.

IndoProgress. 2007. "Serikat Buruh/Serikat Pekerja Di Indonesia". 21 August 2007. https://indoprogress.com/2007/08/serikat-buruhserikat-pekerja-di-indonesia/

Jakarta Globe. 2011. "27 Arrests after Batam Riot Violence". 25 November 2011.

———. 2012. "Workers in Jababeka Area Attacked". 30 October 2012.

Jakarta Post. 2002. "Parts of Batam Deserted after Riots, Killing". 7 February 2002.

———. 2004. "Squatters Try to Hold Batam to Ransom". 15 May 2004.

———. 2011a. "Massive Worker Rally in Batam Erupts into Chaos, Six Injured". 24 November 2011.

———. 2011b. "Mayor Defies Workers' Higher Wage Demands". 26 November 2011. https://www.thejakartapost.com/amp/news/2011/11/26/mayor-defies-workers-higher-wage-demands.html

Kho, Dickson. 2014. "Upah Minimum Kota (UMK) Kota Batam Tahun 2014". Informasi tentang Karimun dan Batam (January 2014). http://karimunbatam.blogspot.com/2014/01/upah-minimum-kota-umk-ums-kota-batam-tahun-2014.html

Koran Perdjoeangan Suara Kaum Buruh."Di Batam, Meski Hujan Buruh Antusias Ikut Aksi". 8 August 2017. https://www.koranperdjoeangan.com/di-batam-meski-hujan-buruh-antusias-ikut-aksi/

Lambert, Rob. 1993. *Authoritarian State Unionism in New Order Indonesia.* Perth: Asia Research Centre, Murdoch University.

Lane, Max. 2019. *An Introduction to the Politics of the Indonesian Union Movement.* Singapore: ISEAS – Yusof Ishak Institute.

Liputan6. 2012. "Buruh Batam Blokir Sejumlah Akses Ke Kawasan Industri". 3 October 2012. http://news.liputan6.com/read/441756/buruh-batam-blokir-sejumlah-akses-ke-kawasan-industri

Manumoyoso, Ambrosius Harto, and Agus Mulyadi. 2012. "Harmoni Industri Bekasi Dideklarasikan". *KOMPAS.com* 8 November 2012. http://megapolitan.kompas.com/read/2012/11/08/17052399/Deklarasi.Harmoni.Industri.Bekasi.Didukung

Marie, Anne. 2014. "Inilah Daftar Lengkap Anggota DPRD Batam 2014-2019". *Tribun Batam,* 29 August 2014. https://batam.tribunnews.com/2014/08/29/siang-ini-pelantikan-dprd-batam-inilah-daftar-lengkapnya

Maulana, Hadi, and Reni Susanti. 2017. "UMK Batam Naik Di Tengah Lesunya Perekonomian". *Kompas.com,* 3 November 2017. http://regional.kompas.com/read/2017/11/03/14293341/umk-batam-naik-di-tengah-lesunya-perekonomian

Setiawan, Gagan. 2011. "Kerusuhan Demo Buruh Batam". YouTube, 30 May 2011. https://www.youtube.com/watch?v=gHDbPb7zjT8

Straits Times. 2004. "Parts of Batam Deserted after Riots, Killing". 15 May 2004.

———. 2011. "Security Guards, Soldier Beat Workers, Start Batam Riot: Witness". 21 September 2011.

Sugianto, Danang. 2017. "Ini Daftar Lengkap Upah Minimum Provinsi 2018". *detikFinance,* 6 November 2017. https://finance.detik.com/berita-ekonomi-bisnis/3715288/ini-daftar-lengkap-upah-minimum-provinsi-2018

Yunarko, Oleh Andry. 2012. "Reportase Monas Batam: Suatu Awal Kemenangan Baru". *Edukasi,* 3 October 2012. http://edukasiperburuhan.blogspot.com/2012/10/reportase-monas-batam-suatu-awal.html

III

Social and Environmental Issues

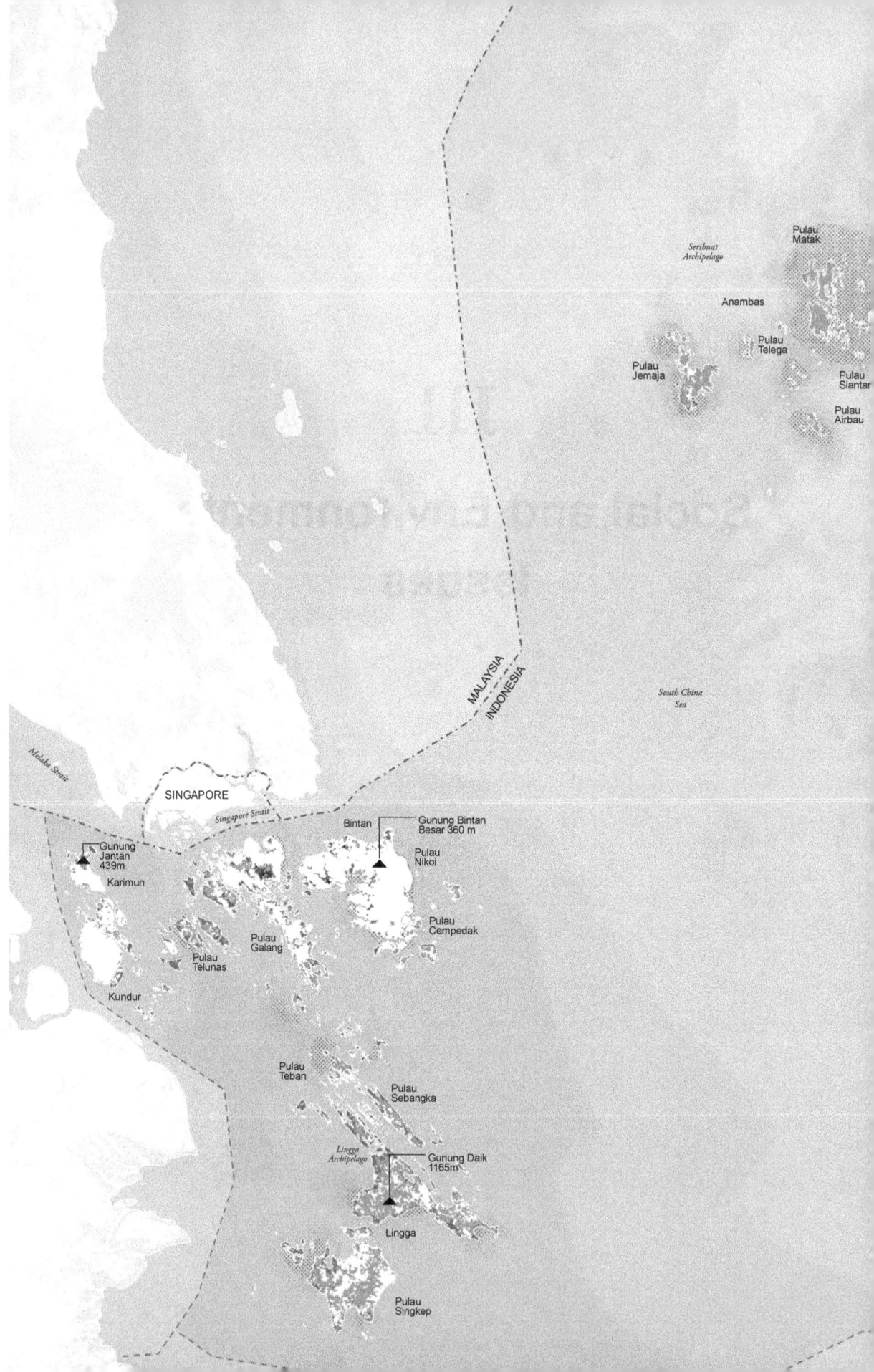

Pulau Matak

Seribuat Archipelago

Anambas

Pulau Telega

Pulau Jemaja

Pulau Siantar

Pulau Airbau

MALAYSIA

INDONESIA

South China Sea

Melaka Strait

SINGAPORE

Singapore Strait

Bintan

Gunung Bintan Besar 360 m

Gunung Jantan 439m

Pulau Nikoi

Karimun

Pulau Cempedak

Pulau Galang

Pulau Telunas

Kundur

Pulau Teban

Pulau Sebangka

Lingga Archipelago

Gunung Daik 1165m

Lingga

Pulau Singkep

MAP 4.1
NATURAL LANDSCAPE ELEMENTS

▲ Mountain Peak
■ Water Reservoir
■ Mangrove Forest
■ Forest
⦂ Reef

Gunung Ranai
1033m

Natuna

Pulau
Sedanau

Pulau
Batang

Pulau
Mida

Pulau
Subi Besar

Pulau
Serasan

INDONESIA
MALAYSIA

Tambelan
Archipelago

Pulau
Tambelan
Besar

0   25   50km

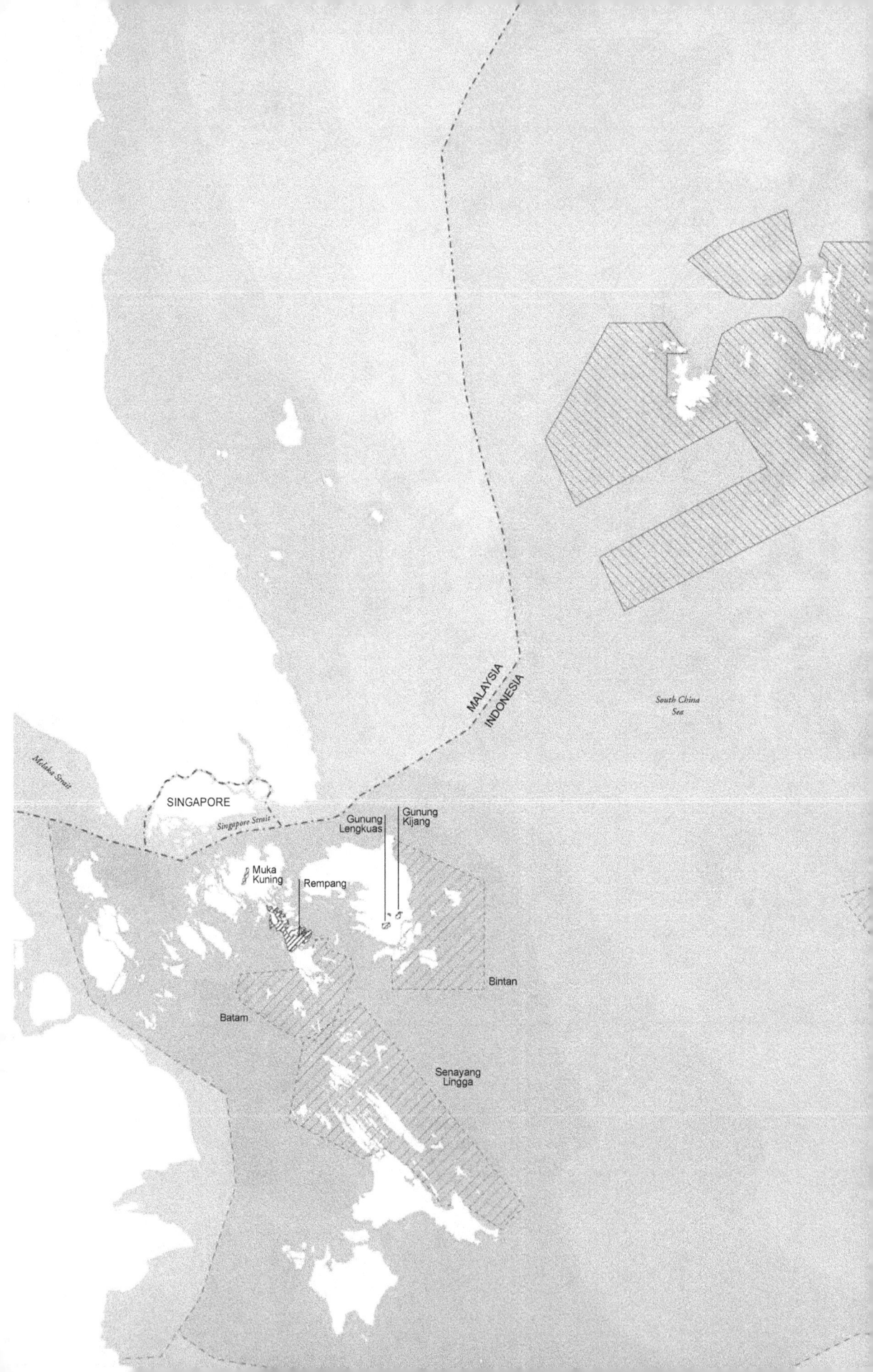

MALAYSIA

INDONESIA

South China
Sea

Melaka Strait

SINGAPORE

Singapore Strait

Gunung
Lengkuas

Gunung
Kijang

Muka
Kuning

Rempang

Bintan

Batam

Senayang
Lingga

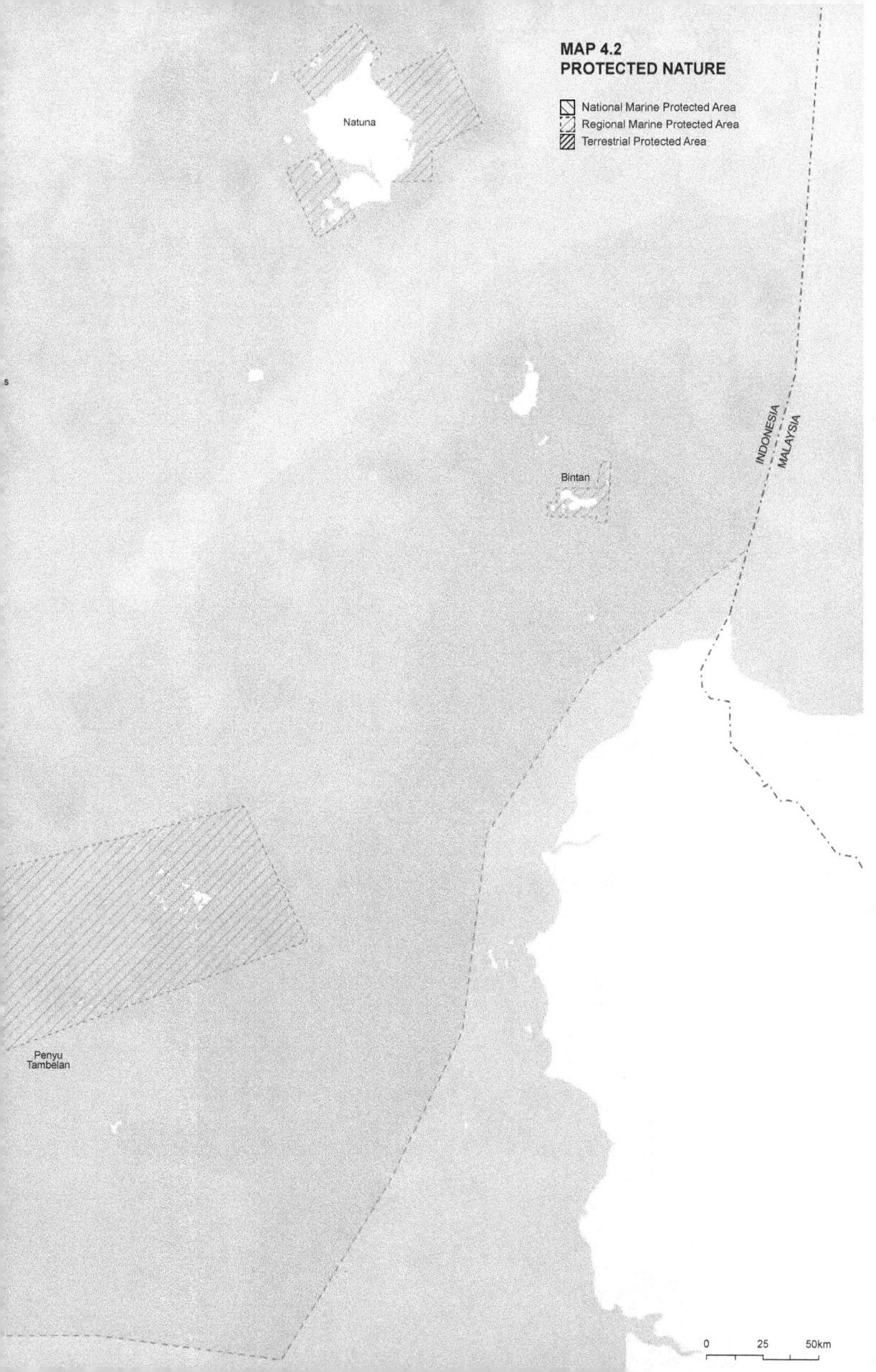

MAP 4.2
PROTECTED NATURE

National Marine Protected Area
Regional Marine Protected Area
Terrestrial Protected Area

Natuna

Bintan

INDONESIA

MALAYSIA

Penyu
Tambelan

0   25   50km

1950 - 1990

Teluk Mata Ikan

Batu Merah

Batu Besar

Belakangpadang

Batam Lestari

Tg Riau

Tg Kassem

Pulau Buloh

Tg Piayu

Bulan

Gembol Strait

Setokok

Rana Strait

Rempang

Galang

0   2.5   5km

MAP 4.3
TRANSFORMATION OF BATAM

1990 - 2011

Nongsa

Batu
Ampar

Tg Bemban

Belakangpadang

Batu Besar

Batam
Center

Sekunpang

Hang Nadim
Airport

Waterfront

Kabil

BatamIndo

Punggur

Bulan

Setokok

Gembol Strait

Riau Strait

Rempang

Galang

2.5   5km

Seribuat
Archipelago

Anambas

South China
Sea

MALAYSIA

INDONESIA

Melaka Strait

SINGAPORE

Singapore Strait

Batam

Bintan

Karimun

Lingga

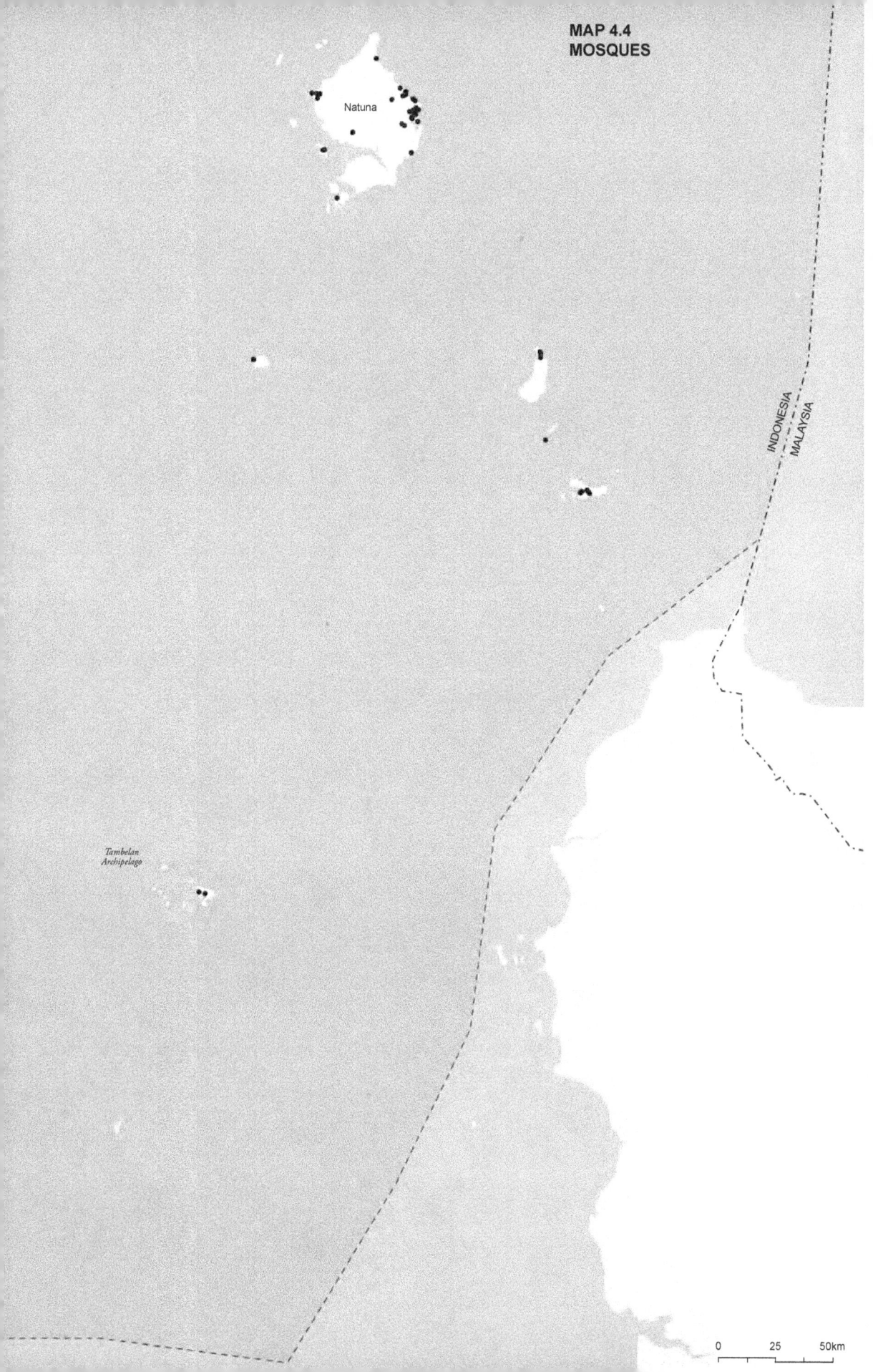

MAP 4.4
MOSQUES

Natuna

INDONESIA

MALAYSIA

Tambelan Archipelago

0   25   50km

Melaka Strait

MALAYSIA

INDONESIA

SINGAPORE

Singapore

Belakangpadang

Masjid Agung Karimun

Tg Balai

Masjid
Riaya

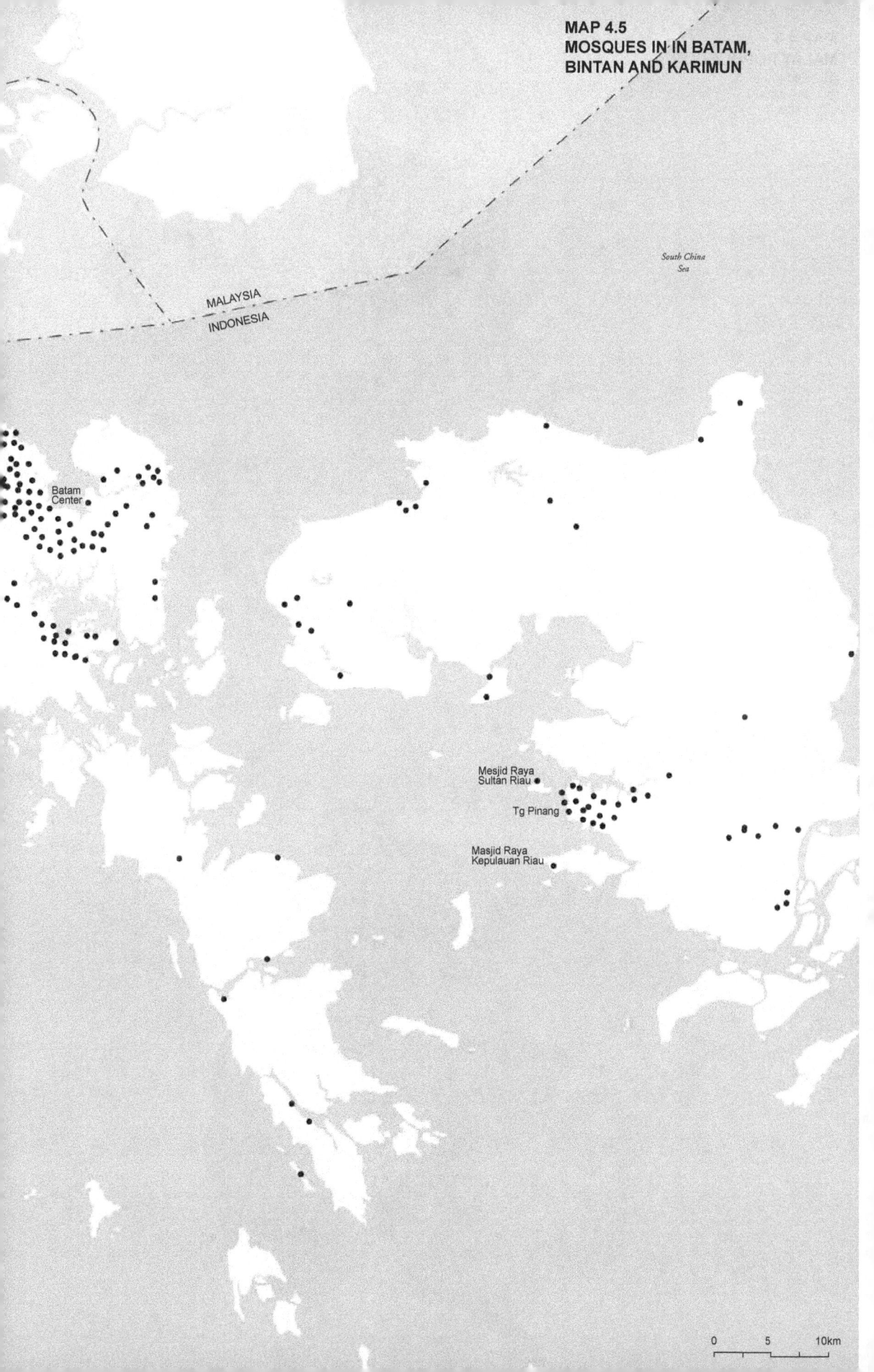

MAP 4.5
MOSQUES IN IN BATAM,
BINTAN AND KARIMUN

South China
Sea

MALAYSIA

INDONESIA

Batam
Center

Mesjid Raya
Sultan Riau

Tg Pinang

Masjid Raya
Kepulauan Riau

0   5   10km

**MAP 4.6
MALAY POPULATION**

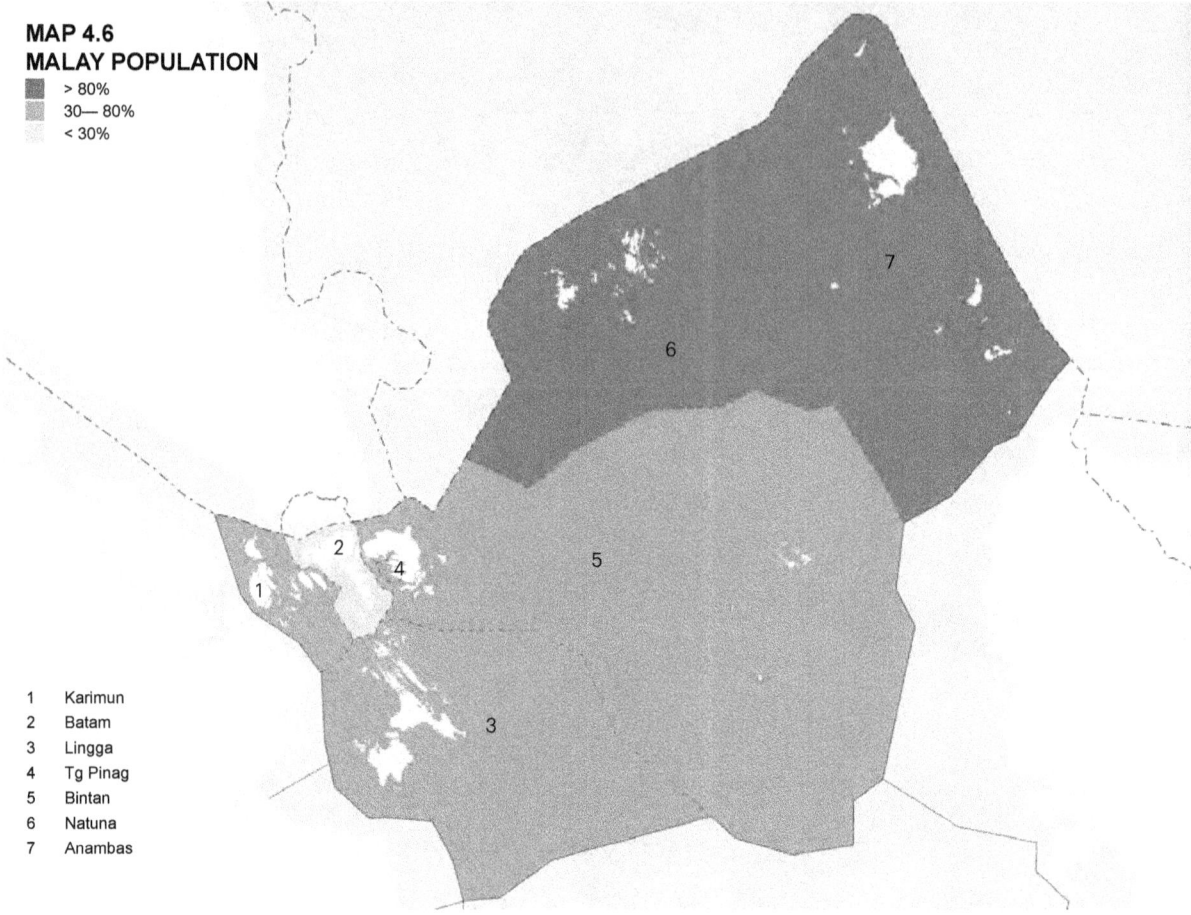

- > 80%
- 30— 80%
- < 30%

1 Karimun
2 Batam
3 Lingga
4 Tg Pinag
5 Bintan
6 Natuna
7 Anambas

**MAP 4.7
JAVANESE POPULATION**

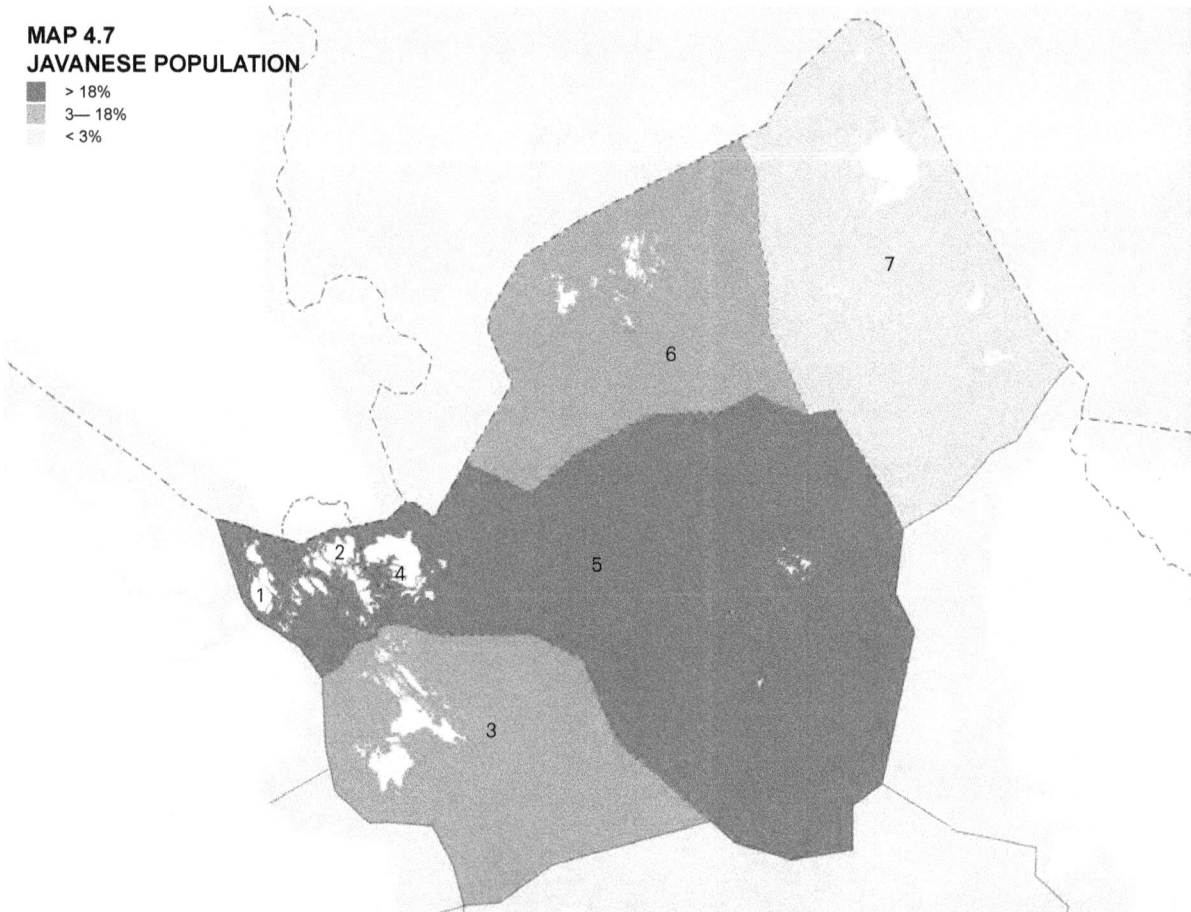

- > 18%
- 3— 18%
- < 3%

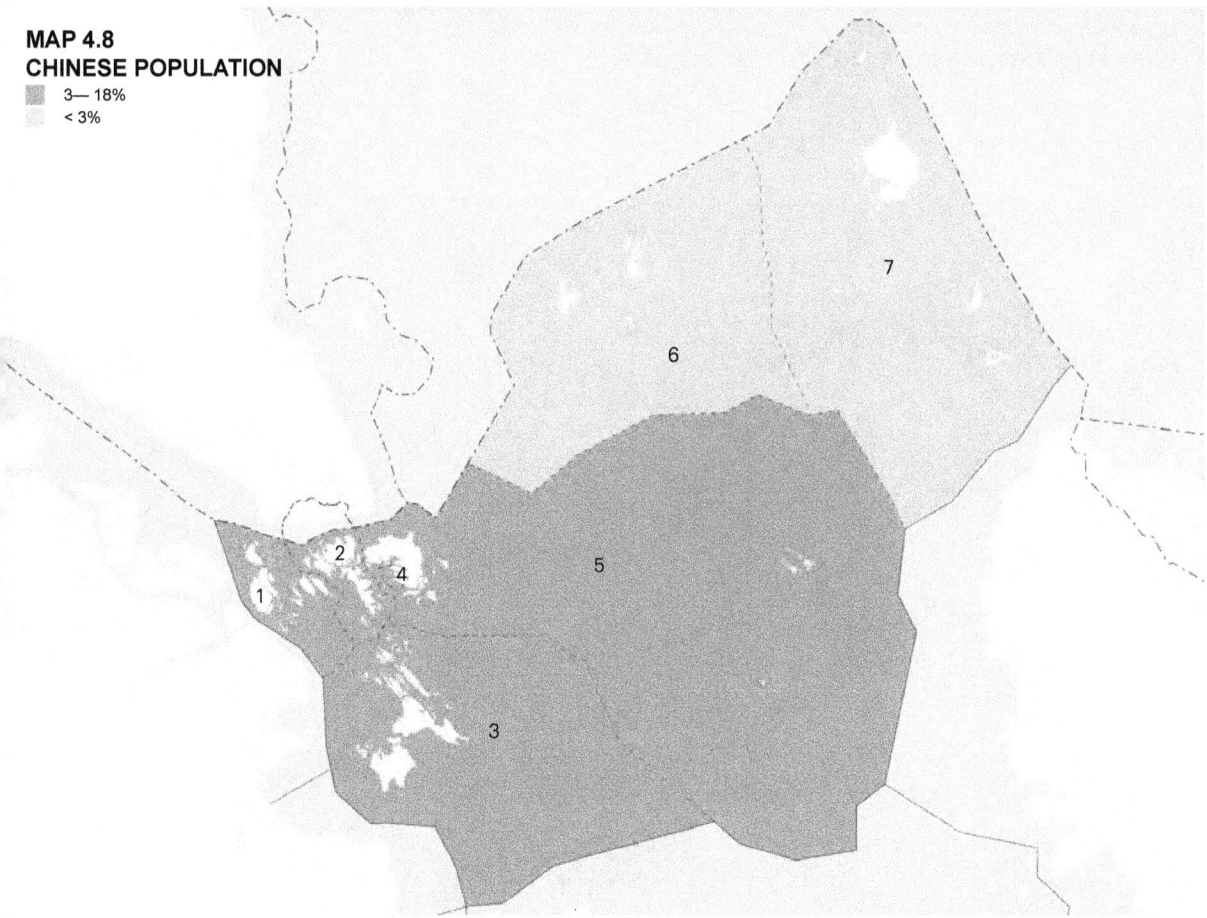

MAP 4.8
CHINESE POPULATION

- 3—18%
- < 3%

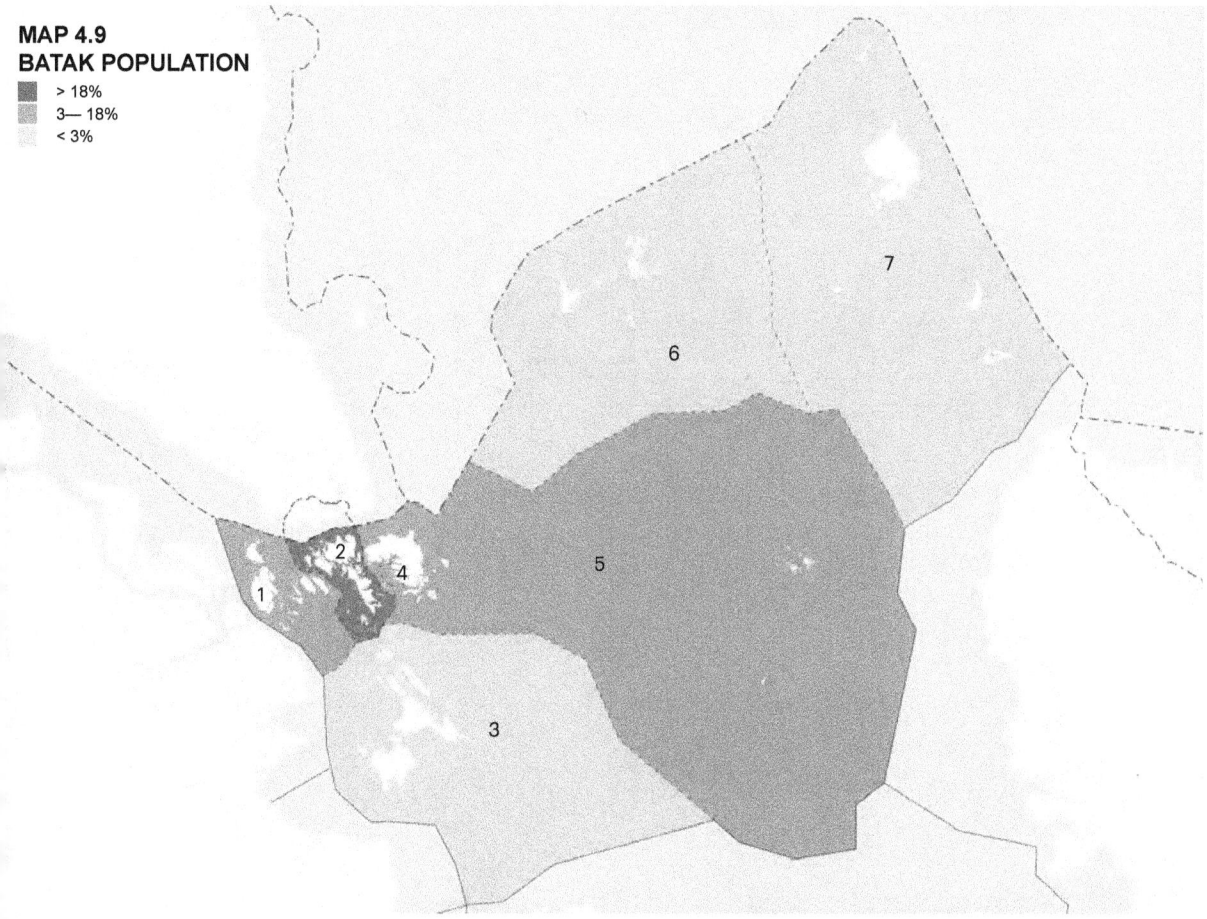

MAP 4.9
BATAK POPULATION

- > 18%
- 3—18%
- < 3%

MAP 4.10
BATAM WEST COAST. SHIPPING INDUSTRY

PT Multi Prima
Shipbuilder

Palma Prograss
Shipyard PT

*Sungai
Binti*

Sagulung
Batam City

Pulau Tengah

PT China
Communications
Construction Industry
Indonesia

Momentum
Shipyard

PT Cita Beton

Kelong
View Inn

to Sekupang, Batam

Kampung
Pulau
Buluh

to Palembang, Sumatra

Jami Nurul Iman
Mosque

PT Cita
Shipyard

Selat Bulan

KSB Ship

Pulau Bulan

Pulau Teluk

0   250   500

MAP 4.11
BINTAN EAST COAST. TRIKORA BEACH

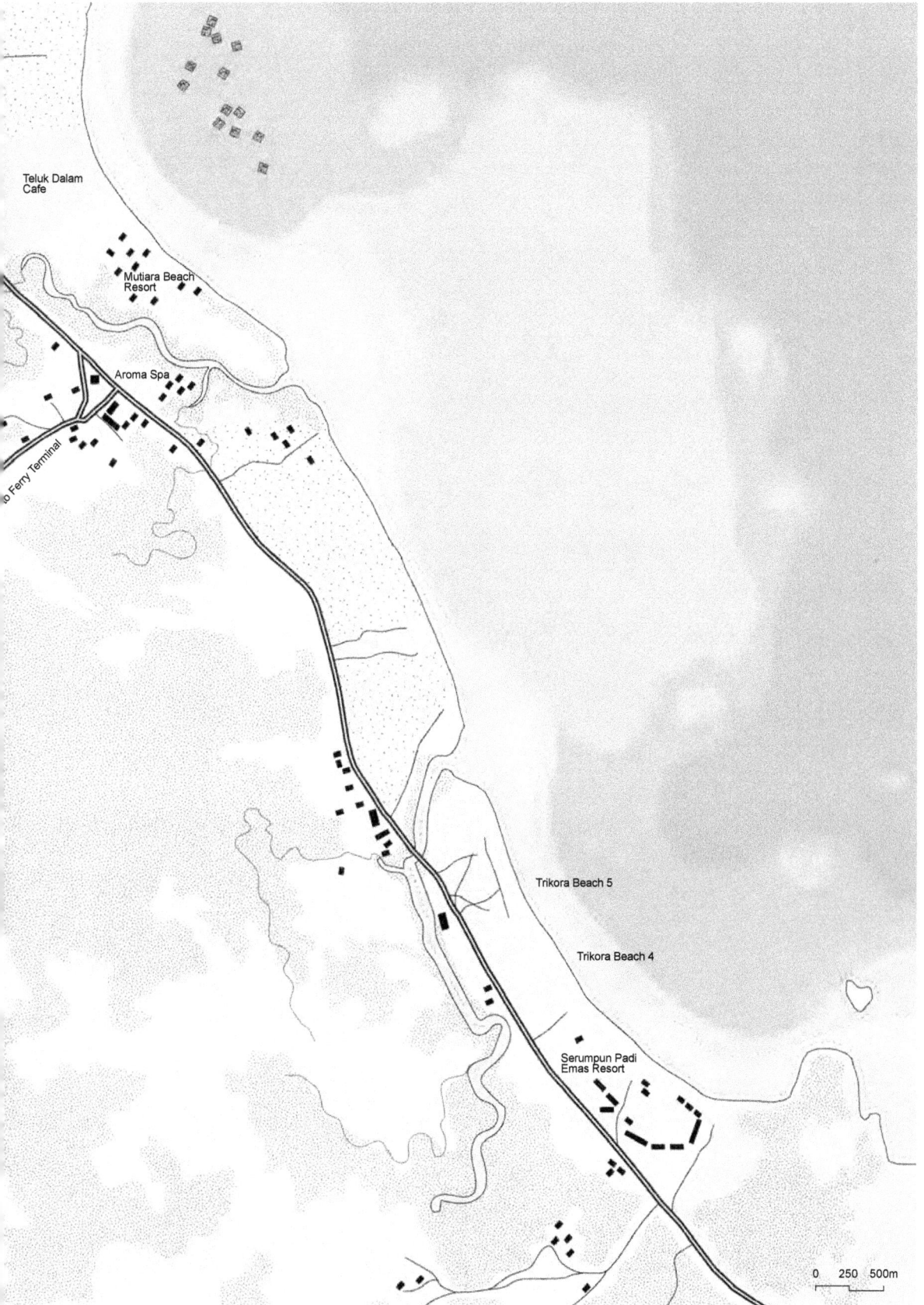

Teluk Dalam
Cafe

Mutiara Beach
Resort

Aroma Spa

o Ferry Terminal

Trikora Beach 5

Trikora Beach 4

Serumpun Padi
Emas Resort

0   250   500m

11

URBANIZATION TRENDS IN THE RIAU ISLANDS PROVINCE

Wilmar Salim[1]

INTRODUCTION

The Province of the Riau Islands (PRI) is one of the provinces in Indonesia created by Law No. 25 of 2002, and which entered into effect in 2004 (BPS Kepulauan Riau 2006). The new province was carved out of the larger Riau Province, following the decentralization reforms of 1999 that intended to bring the government closer to the people through empowering local and provincial governments (Firman 2009). The creation of PRI was one of eight such reform processes that occurred in Indonesia since the onset of *Reformasi* in 1998.

The separation of the Riau Islands from Riau Province was led by local elites and was motivated by a number of factors, including: long-standing identity tensions in the region; the island dwellers' feeling of being neglected by the mainland provincial government in Pekanbaru; and the opportunity to garner greater revenues from gas fields in the Natuna Islands (Hutchinson and Chong 2016; Fitriani, Hofman and Kaiser 2005).

In the extant literature on the region's development, Riau (Islands) is known as a site of cross-border development initiated by Singapore government in the 1980s with the creation of the Indonesia-Malaysia-Singapore Growth Triangle (IMS-GT), which includes Singapore, Johor in Malaysia, and Riau (abbreviated as SIJORI). The Singapore government's vision was to manage the "hinterlandization" of its economy by providing capital to its neighbours, while Johor and Riau provided land and labour (Bunnell et al. 2012).

This vision dovetailed with that of the Indonesian government, which began to develop Batam Island from the 1970s. The intention was to build Batam as a site of industrial activity to capture spill-over from Singapore. By 1991, the largest foreign direct investor in the island was Singapore—its main industries of interest being real estate, tourism, metal processing, drilling equipment and electronic component assembly (Toh and Low 1993). With a very high population growth rate from 1990 to 2000 resulting from a large influx of migrant workers from other regions in Indonesia, especially Java (Firman 2004), Batam became the Riau Islands main urban centre.

Batam is not the only site of development in the province. Bintan Island, the largest of the Riau Islands, also received substantial foreign direct investment, mainly for the development of high-end tourism facilities (Chang 2001). The principal urban centre of Bintan is Tanjungpinang, an old Malay town where the seat of Riau-Lingga Sultanate on Penyengat Island was located. There are also other settlement centres in the region such as in Karimun and Singkep, islands that have experienced considerable population growth—especially after the creation of PRI.

The objective of this chapter is to provide an overview of urbanization trends in the Riau Islands since the province's creation. The chapter analyses the process behind trends in urbanization and attempts to forecast potential growth in the future. To do so, it focuses on the demographic, physical and territorial aspects of urbanization. The demographic aspect of urbanization refers to the increasing urban population in an area due to natural growth and net migration. The physical aspect is characterized by the increasing size or expansion of built-up areas in one locality. Meanwhile, the territorial aspect of urbanization is defined by the official reclassification of rural into urban areas. This aspect can be associated with a pattern of *in situ* urbanization, which brings the city into the countryside (Friedmann 2013).

For the purpose of this research, several methods of data collection and analysis were employed. First, a desk study of government policy material and statistical data available online was carried out. Second, site visits to Batam and Tanjungpinang cities and Bintan Regency were carried out in 2017. During these field trips, interviews were conducted, including with government officials from PRI. Finally, the spatial analysis of statistics—on population data, village potential data (PODES) and land cover data–was used as the primary method of analysis. The available data period covered in this analysis is between 2007 and 2015.

This chapter is divided into several sections. An overview of urbanization in Riau Islands Province is provided in the next section, followed by analyses of population growth and distribution, growth of built-up areas, and urban status. The subsequent section discusses urban development processes and associated issues in three regions of interest: Batam, Tanjungpinang and Bintan. The chapter concludes with some ideas about the potential growth of urban areas in the province.

OVERVIEW OF URBANIZATION TRENDS IN THE
RIAU ISLANDS PROVINCE

The earliest population statistics on main settlement centres in Sumatra are recorded in a Dutch publication *Nederlandsch Oost-Indie* (Lith 1893 in Miksic 1989). The number of settlement centres in Sumatra at the time was limited to seven towns. These included: Palembang, Bengkulu, Medan, and Teluk Betung on mainland Sumatra; and Muntok, Tanjungpinang and Belitung in the outer islands (Miksic 1989). The statistics suggest that Tanjungpinang on Bintan Island was one of the earliest towns inhabited by Europeans.

When the Dutch arrived in the region in the early seventeenth century, the Johor-Riau Kingdom allied with them to counter the Portuguese and later negotiated an alliance that would extend Dutch control over Malacca, allowing the kingdom to control the Riau-Lingga islands (Andaya and Andaya 2001). Two centuries later, the Dutch signed the Anglo-Dutch Treaty in 1824, which divided the region into British and Dutch territories. The Malay Peninsula and Singapore came under the British, while Sumatra and Riau-Lingga Islands were under Dutch control (Gorlinski 2016). Henceforth, the Johor-Riau Kingdom was divided into two sultanates (Johor and Riau-Lingga), with the Dutch having stronger presence on the Riau-Lingga Islands. The capital of the Riau-Lingga Sultanate was in Daik on Lingga Island, while the Dutch built a fort in Tanjungpinang. Tanjungpinang's population in 1893 was 3,946, of which 125 people were Europeans (Miksic 1989). After the abdication of the last sultan and the dissolution of the Riau-Lingga Sultanate in 1911, the Dutch renamed the Riau-Lingga Islands as *Residentie Riouw en Onderhoorgheden* (Riau Residency and Dependencies) with its capital in Tanjungpinang (Wee 2016).

After Indonesia's independence, the Riau Residency became a part of Central Sumatra Province, which then was renamed as Riau Province in 1957. The capital was briefly in Tanjungpinang, until it was relocated to Pekanbaru in 1958. The relocation is considered a sign that the new province would be ruled under Indonesia, and not the revived neo-Malay sultanate (Kimura 2007). Later, Tanjungpinang became a less significant town in Riau Province—it was just the capital of the Riau Islands District, one of several in the Riau Province. When Riau Islands Province was established in 2002, the city was reinstated as the provincial capital.

At the time of its creation, the PRI only consisted of three districts (Riau Islands, Karimun and Natuna) and two municipalities (Batam and Tanjungpinang). Lingga District was carved out of Riau Islands District in 2003, while Kepulauan Anambas was created from Natuna District in 2008, adding more districts in PRI. Riau Islands District was renamed Bintan District in 2006—to distinguish the name of the district from the name of province (Presiden Republik Indonesia 2006).

There are almost 1,800 islands in this province, which together comprise only 4 per cent of the total area of 251,000 square kilometres in the province (Amri 2016). The first governor of Riau Islands Province was Ismeth Abdullah, the former Head of the Batam Industrial Development Authority (BIDA). The number of islands, subdistricts and villages in each district and municipality in PRI are summarized in the Table 11.1.

URBANIZATION TRENDS

In this section, several urbanization trends are analysed, including: the province's population growth and distribution; the expansion of built-up areas; as well as the status of its various subdistricts.

Trends in Population Growth and Distribution

The PRI's population grew from 0.5 million in 1990 to 1 million in 2000 (Ananta 2016), 1.3 million in 2007, finally reaching around 2 million people now. The largest share of this population lives in Batam City, home to more than a million people. The Figures 11.1 and 11.2 show the growth of population in the cities and districts in Riau Islands Province between 2007 and 2015.

In Figure 11.1, we can see that Batam experienced a steady increase all those years, especially between 2009 and 2010—when it witnessed the highest population growth rate of 22 per cent (own calculation). Meanwhile, the second and third largest portions of PRI's population reside in Karimun District and Tanjungpinang City, with 225,000 and 202,000 residents in 2015, respectively. Overall, the population growth rate of PRI follows the same pattern as the growth rate of Batam City.

As we can see in Figure 11.2, the population of Karimun and Lingga districts fluctuated between 2007 and 2009, then steadied at around 225,000 and 88,000 people, respectively. Meanwhile, the population of Natuna District dropped between 2007 and 2008, due to the creation of Kepulauan Anambas District out of Natuna District. Both districts then experienced steady population growth of around 73,000 and 39,000 individuals, respectively. Also, Bintan District experienced steady population growth since 2010, reaching close to 150,000 people. This suggests that Batam is the main driver of population growth in PRI, contributing significantly to its level of urbanization.

TABLE 11.1
Administrative Divisions in Riau Islands Province, 2015

District/City	No. of Islands	Number of Subdistricts	Number of Villages	Capital City (Subdistrict)
Karimun	251	12	71	Tanjung Balai (Karimun)
Bintan	240	10	51	Bandar Seri Bentan (Teluk Bintan)
Natuna	154	15	76	Ranai (Bunguran Timur)
Lingga	531	10	82	Daik (Lingga)
Kep. Anambas	238	7	54	Tarempa (Siantan)
Batam	373	12	64	(Batam Kota)
Tanjungpinang	9	4	18	(Tanjungpinang Kota)
Riau Islands Province	1,796	70	416	Tanjungpinang (Bukit Bestari)

Source: BPS Kepulauan Riau (2016).

FIGURE 11.1
Population Growth in Batam, Tanjungpinang and Riau Islands Province

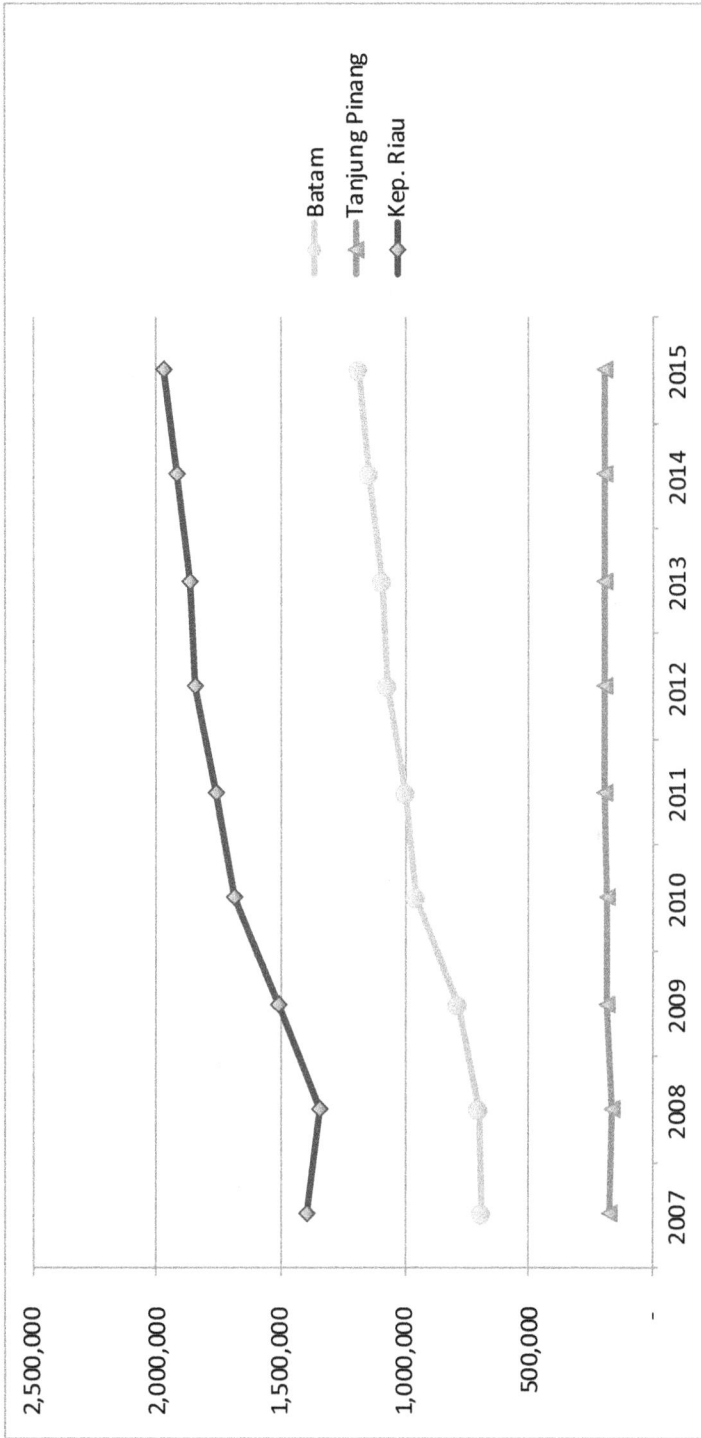

Source: Author's drawing based on statistical data from BPS Kepulauan Riau (2016).

FIGURE 11.2
Population Growth in Riau Islands Province by District

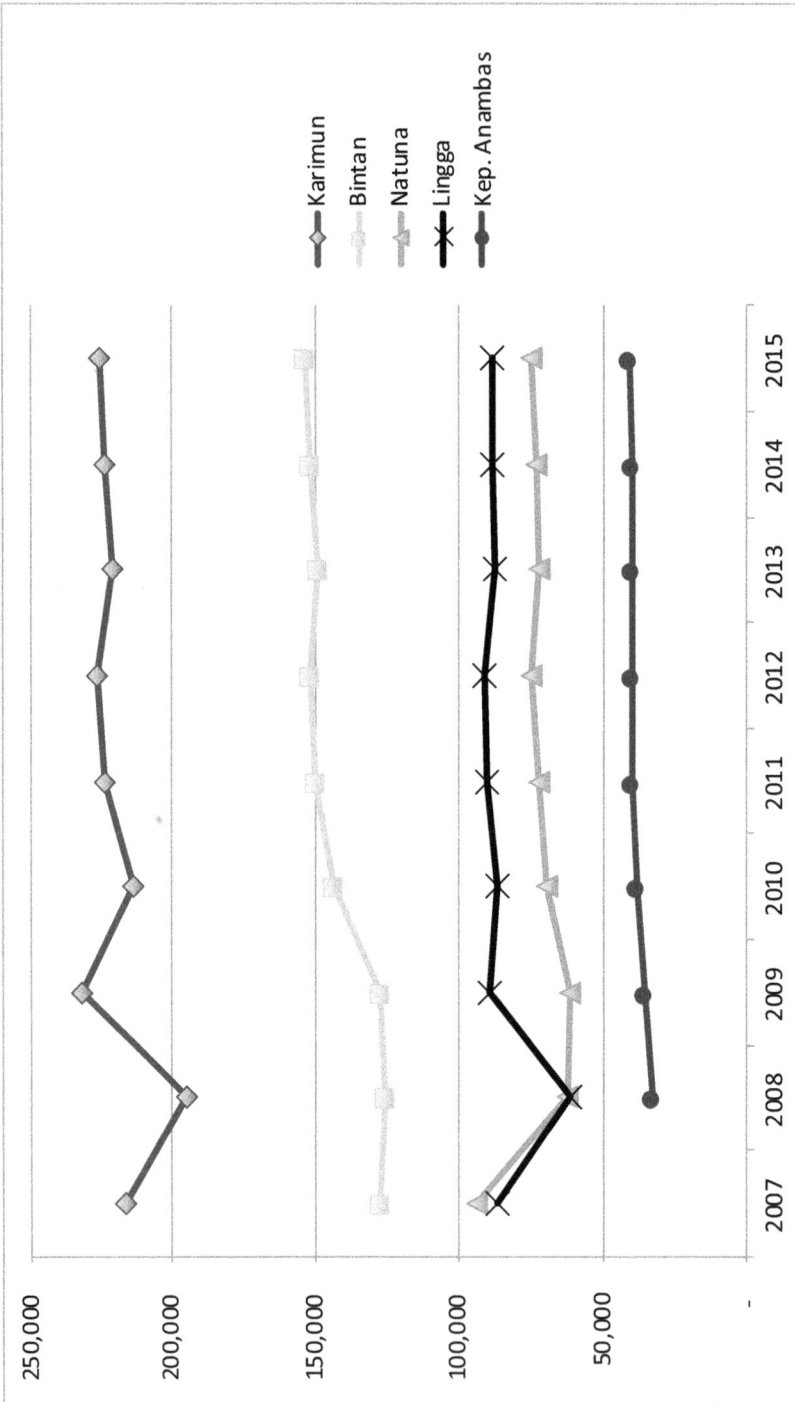

Source: Author's drawing based on statistical data from BPS Kepulauan Riau (2016).

In terms of the share of urban population, out of 1.7 million people in 2010, about 82.8 per cent (1.4 million) are considered to live in urban areas. They are highly concentrated in Batam City (around 66 per cent of the urban population), followed by Tanjungpinang City (12 per cent), Karimun District (9 per cent), and Bintan District (6 per cent). While almost all of the population of Batam and Tanjungpinang are urban (97 per cent and 94 per cent, respectively), the majority of the population in Karimun and Bintan districts are also urban (61 per cent and 60 per cent). Thus, outside of Batam and Tanjungpinang municipalities, Karimun and Bintan can also be considered as urban districts.

In order to analyse the distribution of the population in a district or a city, a different set of population data, the Village Potential (PODES) data, is used. The data available for this analysis is from 2008 to 2014. Using the subdistrict boundary map of each district and city in PRI, the distribution of population can be analysed as shown in Figures 11.3 and 11.4 (only for Batam, Bintan, Karimun and Tanjungpinang). The analysis consists of two aspects: the distribution of population of more than 50,000 and 100,000 by subdistrict; and the distribution of population density of more than 1,000 and 5,000 individuals per square kilometre.

Regarding the distribution of population by subdistrict in Riau Islands Province, we can observe the increasing number of subdistricts with more than 50,000 and 100,000 people between 2008 and 2014. The subdistricts with more than 50,000 people used to be concentrated only in Batam and Tanjungpinang City on Bintan Island, but now are also found in Karimun. There were only two subdistricts in Batam (Batam Kota and Sagulung) that had more than 100,000 people and five subdistricts in Batam (Batuaji, Bengkong, Lubuk Baja, Sekupang and Sungai Bedug), and one in Tanjungpinang (Tanjungpinang Timur) which had a population of between 50,000 and 100,000 in 2008.

However, in 2014, this grew to four subdistricts in Batam (Batam Kota, Sagulung, Batuaji, and Sekupang). Meanwhile, subdistricts with 50,000 to 100,000 people now increased to eight: four in Batam (Batu Ampar, Bengkong, Lubuk Baja and Sungai Bedug); three in Tanjungpinang (Tanjungpinang Timur, Tanjungpinang Barat and

TABLE 11.2
Urban Populations in Riau Islands Province

District/City	Population	% of Total	Urban Population	% of Urban	% of Total Urban
Karimun	212,561	12.7	130,443	61.4	9.4
Bintan	142,300	8.5	86,331	60.7	6.2
Natuna	69,003	4.1	30,836	44.7	2.2
Lingga	86,244	5.1	33,116	38.4	2.4
Kep. Anambas	37,411	2.2	14,667	39.2	1.1
Batam	944,285	56.2	917,998	97.2	66.0
Tanjungpinang	187,359	11.2	177,396	94.7	12.8
Riau Islands Province	1,679,163	100	1,390,787	82.8	100

Source: Modified from Population Census 2010 data (Badan Pusat Statistik Indonesia 2011).

FIGURE 11.3

Population Distribution in Bintan, Batam and Karimun by Subdistrict, 2008

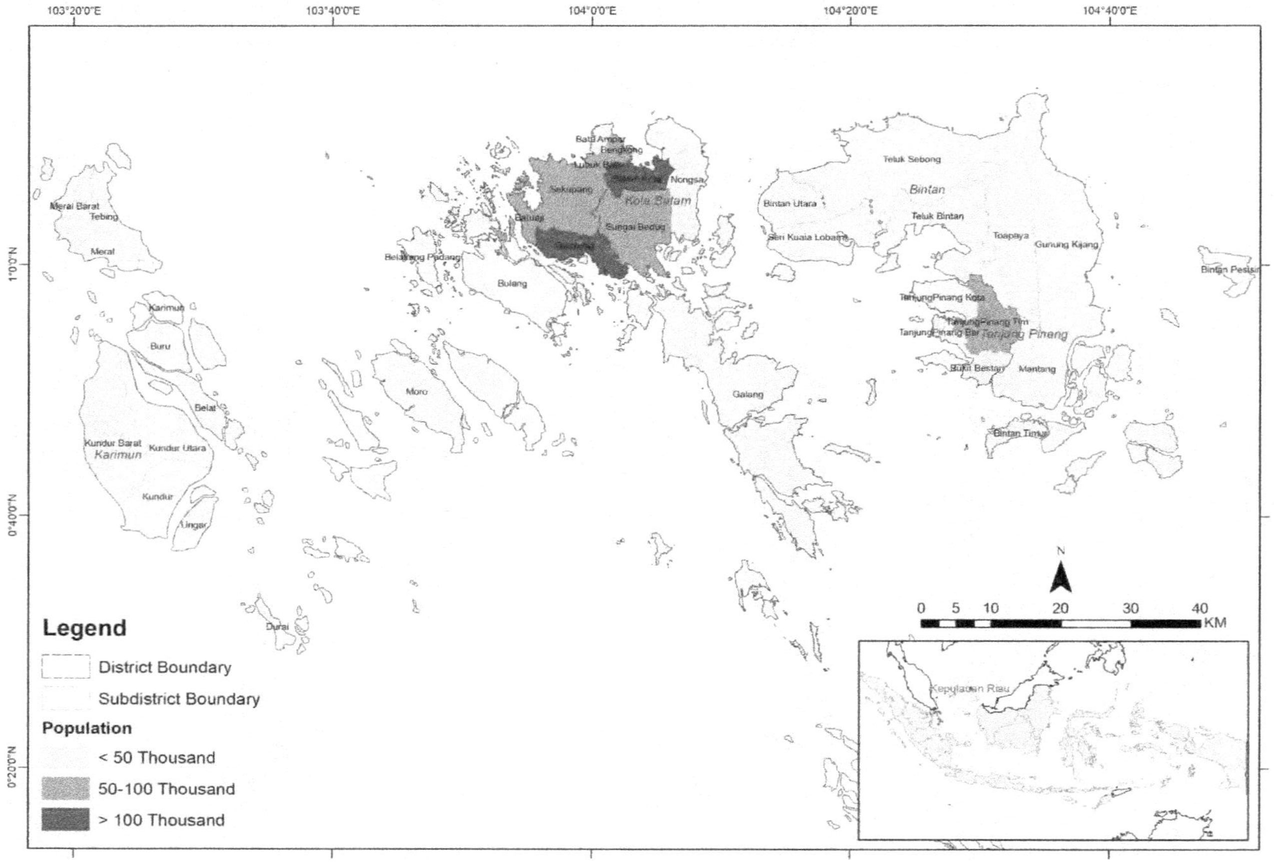

Source: Author's drawing based on Village Potential (2008) data.

FIGURE 11.4

Population Distribution in Bintan, Batam and Karimun by Subdistrict, 2014

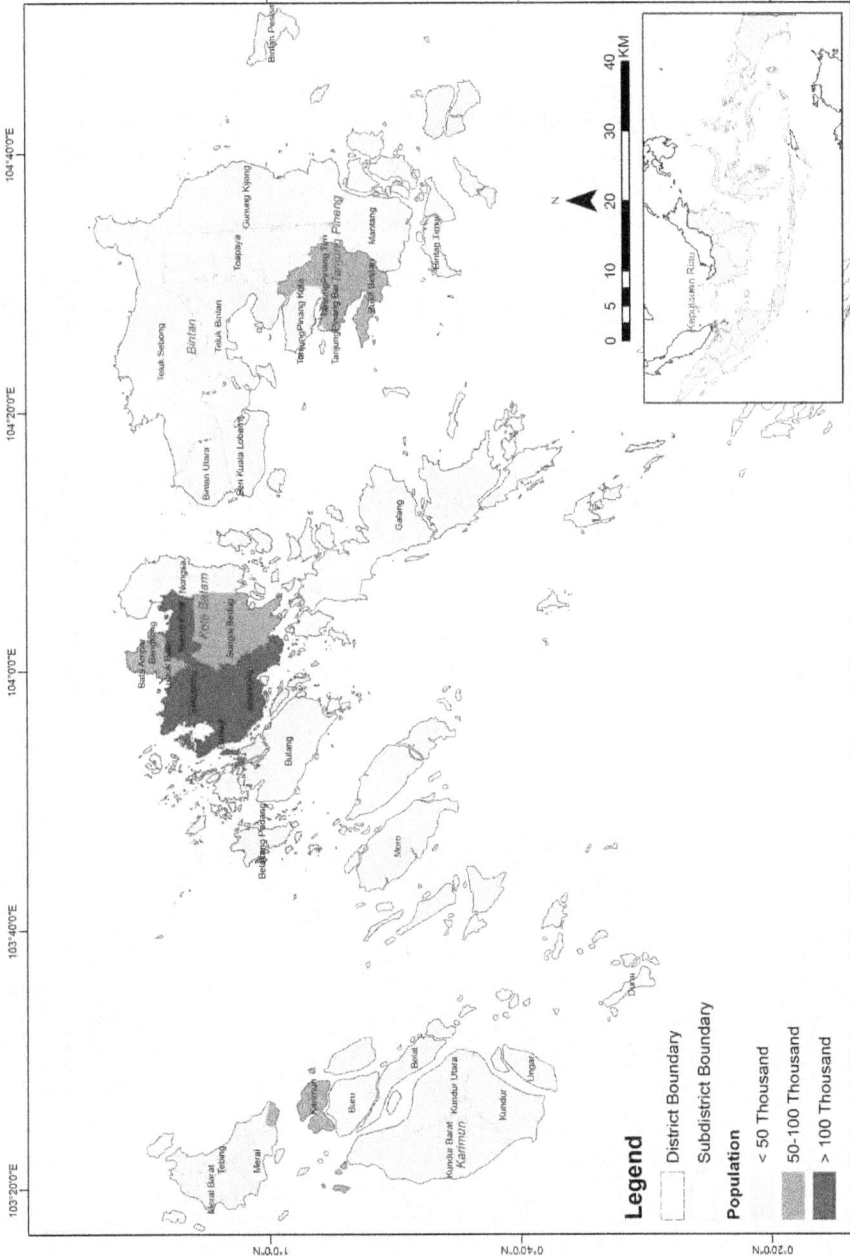

Source: Author's drawing based on Village Potential (2014) data.

Bukit Bestari); and one in Karimun District (Karimun Subdistrict). Thus, we can see how Batam's population is reflected in several subdistricts on the Northwest side of the island. Similarly, in Tanjungpinang and Karimun, an increasing share of the population is concentrated in the main subdistricts.

With regard to population density, we observe that, in 2008, two subdistricts in Batam (Lubuk Baja and Bengkong) had a population density of more than 5,000 people per square kilometre, and an additional five subdistricts in Batam, one in Tanjungpinang (Tanjungpinang Barat) and one in Karimun District (Meral), had a population density between 1,000 and 5,000 people per square kilometre.

Meanwhile, in 2014, the number of subdistricts with a population density of more than 5,000 people per square kilometre increased to three and they were all in Batam (Lubuk Baja, Bengkong and Batu Ampar). Also, subdistricts with a population density between 1,000 and 5,000 people per square kilometre were in Batam (four subdistricts), Tanjungpinang (one subdistrict, Tanjungpinang Barat), and Karimun (one subdistrict, Meral).

Thus, except for one subdistrict in Batam (Batu Ampar), there was no other subdistrict that was reclassified into different density class in 2014—despite the increasing population density in general for all districts and cities in PRI between 2008 and 2014. This illustrates how rapid Batam's population growth has been. In fact, the population density of Batu Ampar subdistrict in Batam has doubled from 4,135 people per square kilometre in 2008 to 8,498 people per square kilometre in 2014. See Figures 11.5 and 11.6.

The Growth of Built-up Areas

The growth of built-up area is analysed by using land cover data provided by the staff of the Regional Development Planning Agency (Bappeda) of PRI. The original data consists of a variety of land cover classes but, for the purpose of this analysis, we use only two categories: built-up areas and non-built-up areas. Based on land cover data, the total land area of Riau Islands Province is 7,753 square kilometres. In 2009, the built-up area of the province was only 272.57 square kilometres or 3.52 per cent of total land in the province, and by 2015 it had increased to 361 square kilometres or 4.7 per cent. The distribution of built-up areas among districts and cities in PRI is depicted in Table 11.3. The largest built-up area is in Batam City, followed by Bintan District and Tanjungpinang City. Meanwhile, the largest growth of built-up areas took place in Bintan District, followed by Tanjungpinang City and Lingga District. However, the fastest growth of built-up areas between 2009 and 2015 was recorded in Lingga District, then Bintan District and Tanjungpinang City.

If we look at the maps of the development of built-up areas in Karimun, Batam and Bintan Islands, we can see that built-up areas are visible in and around Tanjungpinang City, towards the East, in subdistrict of Mantang (Bintan District), as well on the northwest part of Bintan Island. From observations on the ground, the development of built-up areas in this region has been dominated by the construction of housing and commercial complexes, especially shophouses (*rumah toko*), similar

FIGURE 11.5

Population Density in Bintan, Batam and Karimun by Subdistrict, Riau Islands Province, 2008

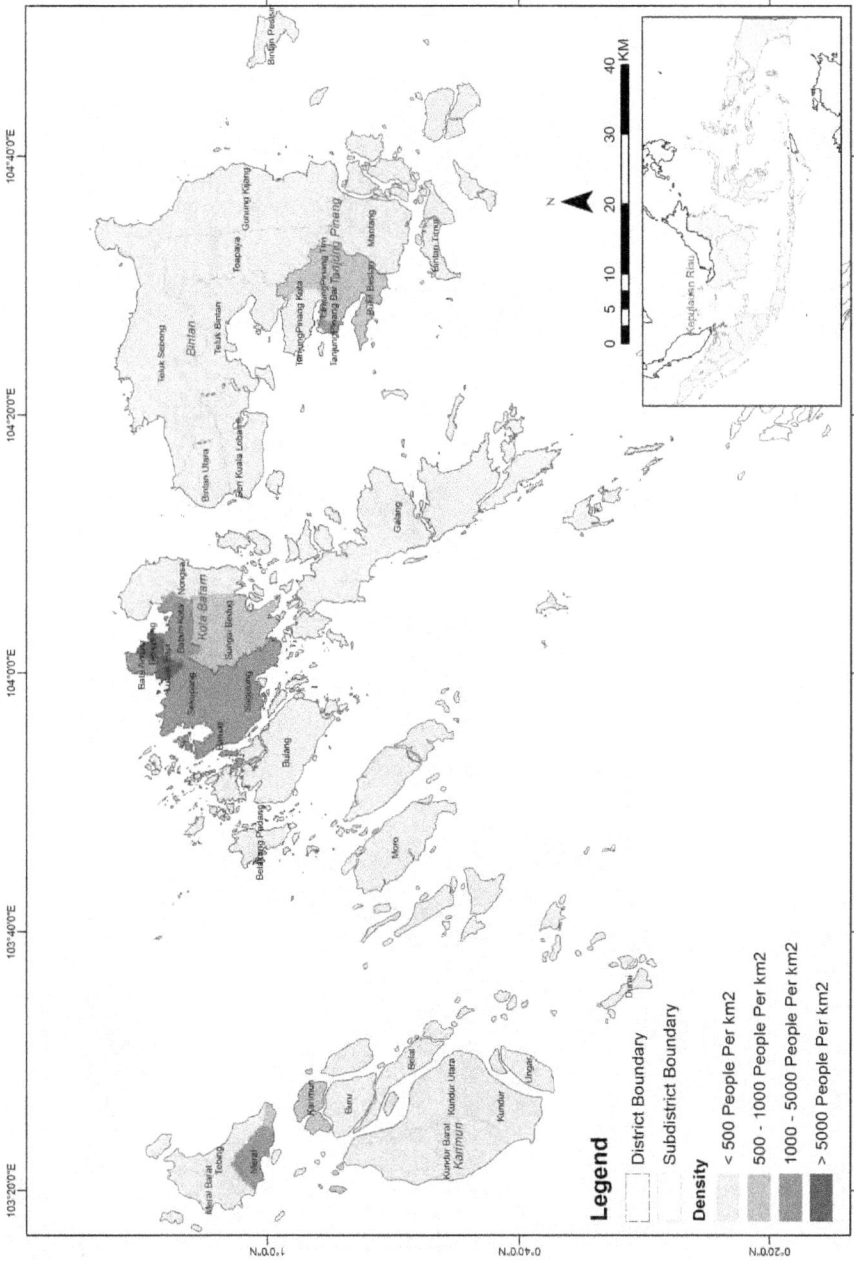

Source: Author's drawing based on Village Potential (2008) data.

FIGURE 11.6

Population Density in Bintan, Batam and Karimun by Subdistrict, Riau Islands Province, 2014

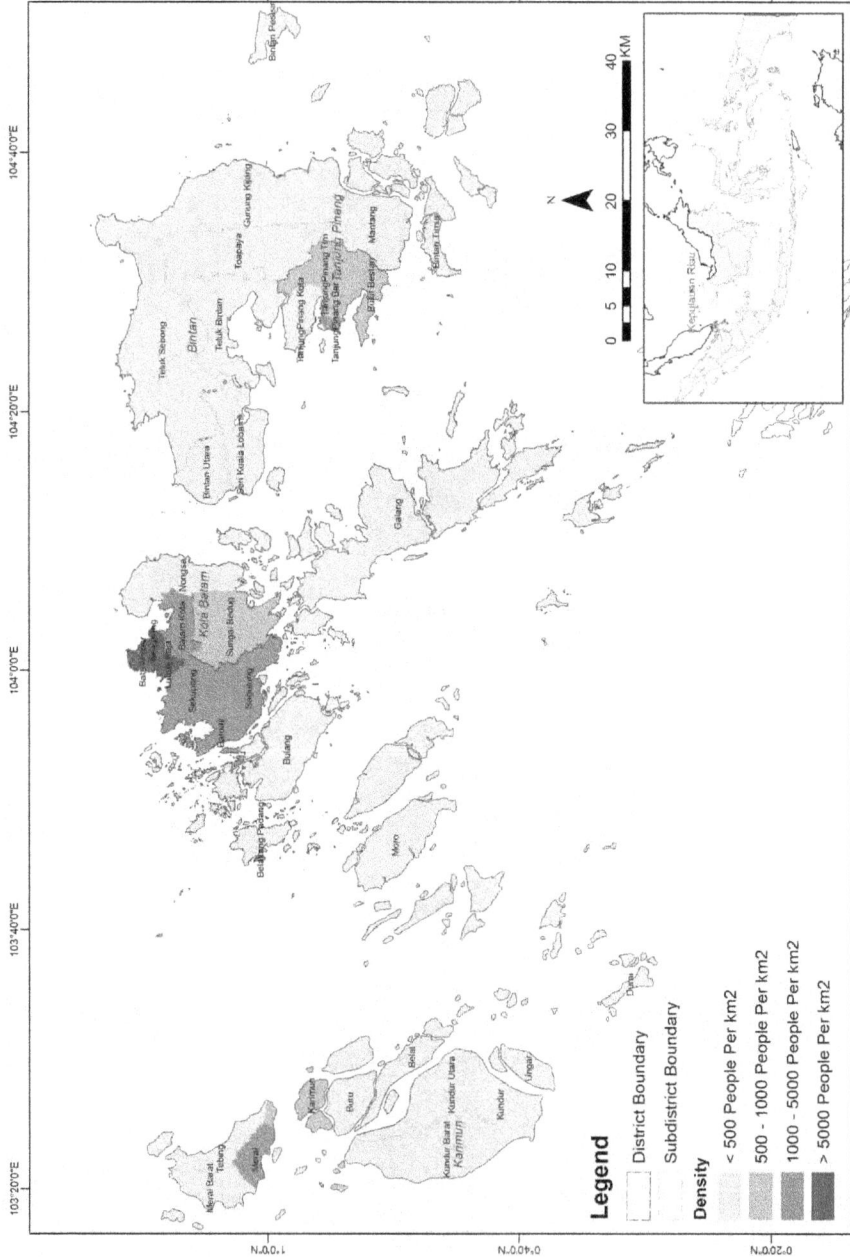

Legend

District Boundary

Subdistrict Boundary

Density

< 500 People Per km2

500 - 1000 People Per km2

1000 - 5000 People Per km2

> 5000 People Per km2

Source: Author's drawing based on Village Potential (2014) data.

TABLE 11.3
Built-up Areas in Riau Islands Province in 2009 and 2015

District/City	Built-up Area 2009		Built-up Area 2015		Growth
	Area (km²)	Percentage	Area (km²)	Percentage	Area (km²)
Karimun	19.7	2.4	25.8	3.1	6.1
Bintan	30.5	2.4	63.8	5	33.3
Natuna	20.9	1.1	23.7	1.2	2.9
Lingga	5.2	0.3	15.9	0.8	10.7
Kep. Anambas	0.7	0.1	1.3	0.2	0.7
Batam	172.1	17.4	181.8	18.4	9.8
Tanjungpinang	23.6	16.4	49	34	25.4
Riau Islands Province	272.6	3.5	361.3	4.7	88.8

Source: Regional Development Planning Agency (Bappeda) of Riau Islands Province.

to urban development in other parts of the country. The same development is also seen along the coast of Karimun Besar Island in Karimun District, which could be the result of growing industrial estates. Meanwhile, the development of built-up areas in Lingga District (not in the maps) is concentrated in Daik, following its development as the district capital, and in Singkep Island.

Urban Status

The last part of analysing the urbanization trends in PRI includes depicting the status of subdistrict in each district, i.e., whether they are considered as urban or rural subdistricts.[2] Based on this analysis, there are several subdistricts in districts other than Batam and the city of Tanjungpinang that can be classified as urban. These include: Karimun, Kundur, Meral and Tebing (in Karimun District); Bintan Utara, Seri Kuala Lobam, Bintan Timur and Toapaya (in Bintan District); Singkep in Lingga District; Bunguran Timur in Natuna District; and Siantan in Kepulauan Anambas District. Meanwhile, almost all subdistricts in Batam (except Bulang and Galang) and all subdistricts in Tanjungpinang City are classified as urban. Figure 11.9 visualizes the distribution of subdistricts with urban status in PRI in 2014.

SELECTED URBAN DEVELOPMENT AND CURRENT ISSUES

In this section we discuss three areas in the Riau Islands Province that have experienced significant urban development over the last ten years—Batam, Tanjungpinang and Bintan.

Batam City

Batam is an island, municipality and the largest city in the PRI. It is located approximately 20 kilometres south of Singapore, separated only by the Singapore Strait. The island's land area is approximately 415 square kilometres. As mentioned,

FIGURE 11.7
Built-up Areas in Bintan, Batam and Karimun, 2009

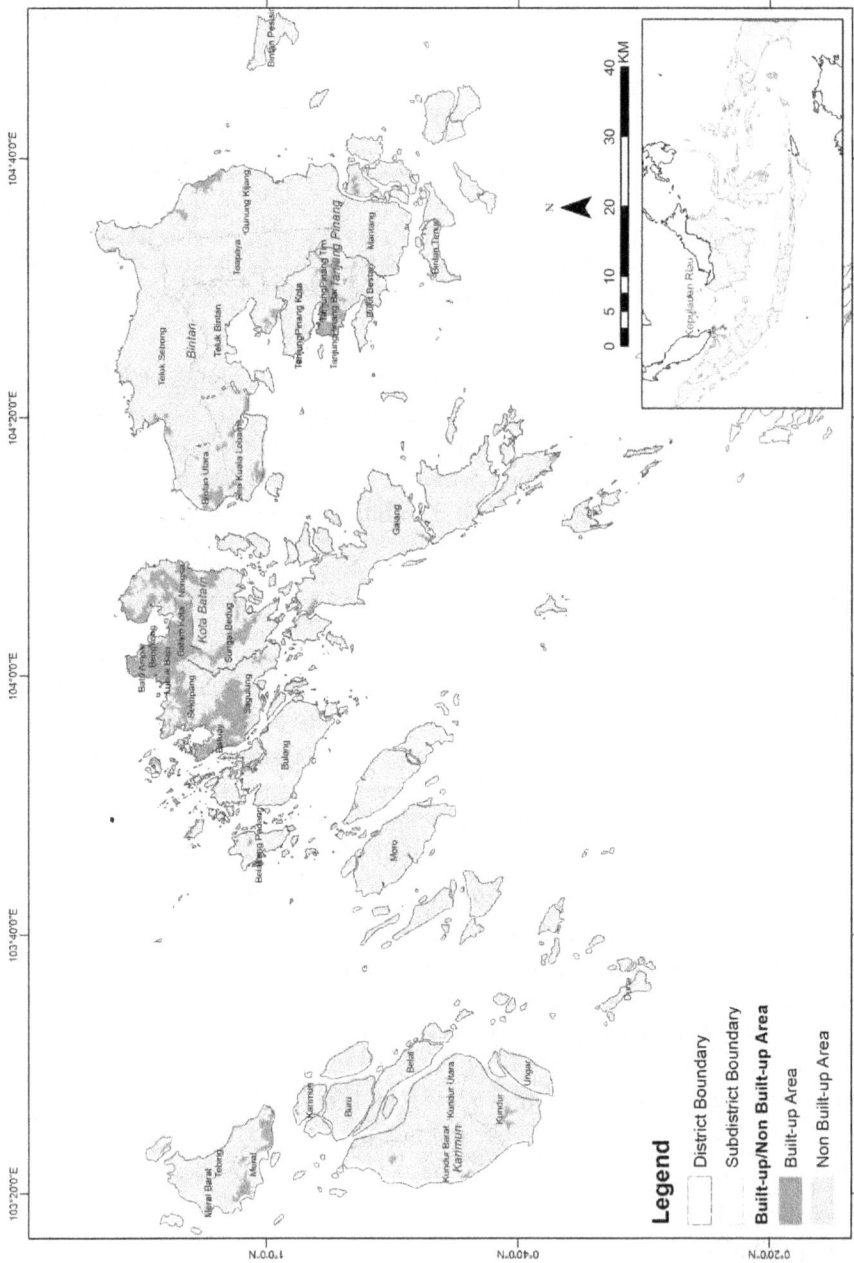

Source: Author's drawing based on land cover 2009 data.

FIGURE 11.8
Built-up Areas in Bintan, Batam and Karimun, 2015

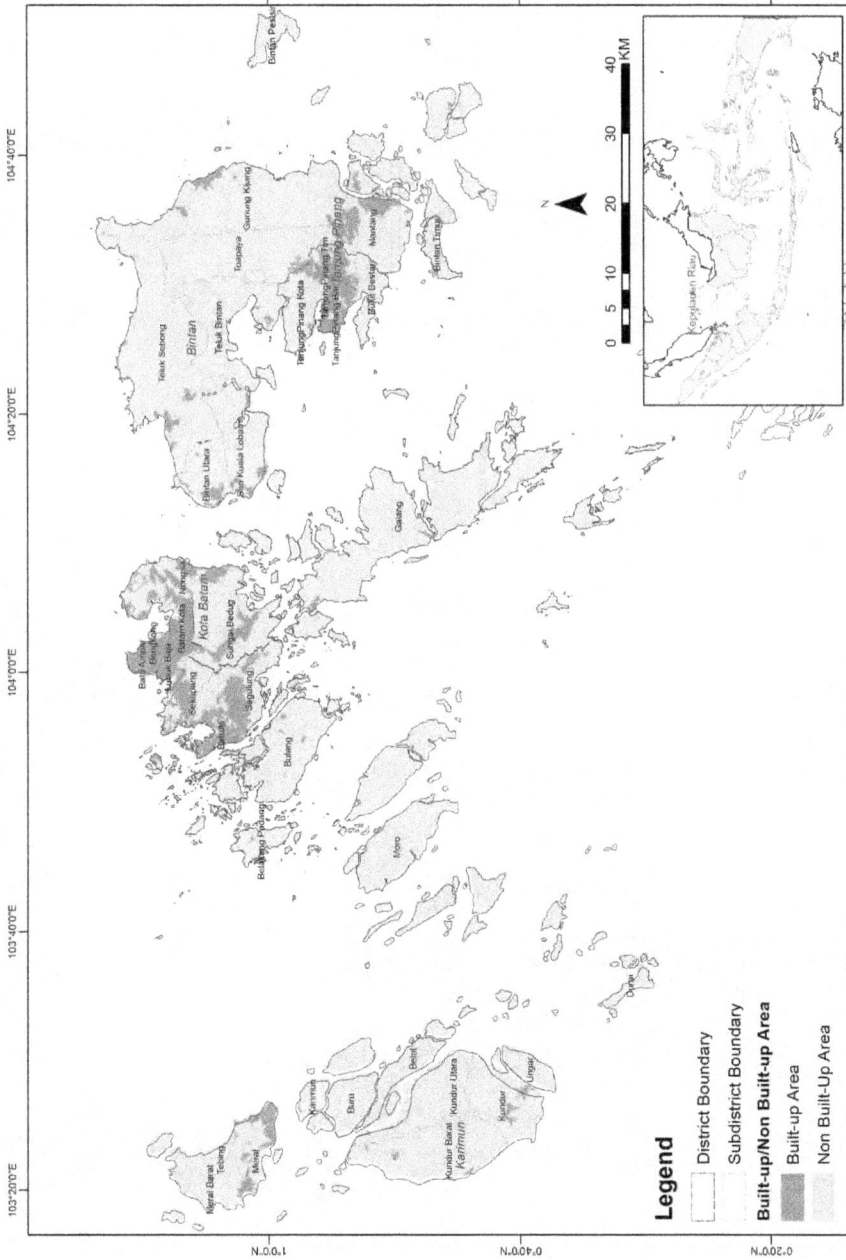

Source: Author's drawing based on land cover 2015 data.

FIGURE 11.9
Urban Subdistricts in Riau Islands Province, 2014

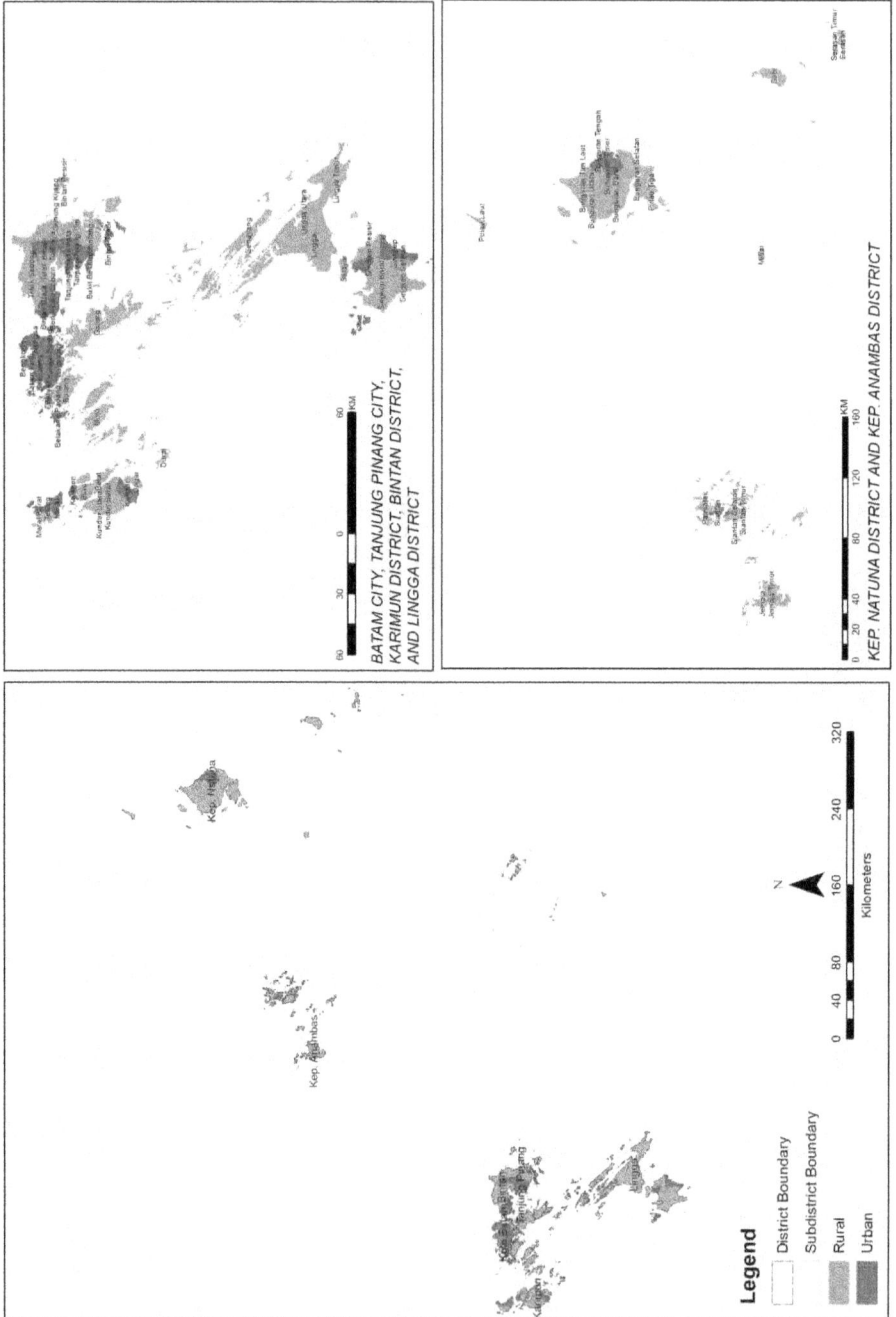

BATAM CITY, TANJUNG PINANG CITY, KARIMUN DISTRICT, BINTAN DISTRICT, AND LINGGA DISTRICT

KEP. NATUNA DISTRICT AND KEP. ANAMBAS DISTRICT

Legend

District Boundary
Subdistrict Boundary
Rural
Urban

Source: Author's drawing based on Village Potential 2014 data.

about 18 per cent of its land is built-up area. The island used to be run exclusively by a development authority established by the central government, namely the Batam Industrial Development Authority (BIDA). The island was established as an administrative city in 1983, as part of Riau Province. Once a bonded zone, and now a free trade zone, Batam enjoys significant foreign direct investment (FDI), especially from Singapore.

In 2005, there were more than 700 foreign companies from thirty-four countries with an accumulated FDI of more than US$3 billion in Batam (Toh 2006). Based on data from Batam Island Free Trade Zone Authority (BIFZA), by June 2015, accumulated investments reached US$19.83 billion, including: US$3.88 billion government investment; US$5.82 billion domestic private investment; and US$10.13 billion of FDI. Batam's economy is mainly based on manufacturing and tourism. Moreover, 1780 foreign companies are now operating in Batam (BIFZA 2016). Its economic growth has remained above 7 per cent over the past ten years, except in 2009 when it slipped to 4.7 per cent (BP Batam 2011) due to the impact of the Global Economic Crisis.

After decentralization in 1999, the island gained autonomy as a municipality with an elected mayor. Currently, Batam City comprises twelve subdistricts (*kecamatan*) and sixty-four wards (*kelurahan*) (Badan Pusat Statistik Batam 2016). Simultaneously, BIDA was restructured as the Batam Indonesia Free Zone Authority (BIFZA), or known as Badan Pengusahaan (BP) Batam. This situation disrupted the island's management due to overlapping spheres of authority.[3] Basically, BP Batam controls and manages all land in Batam, but according to the decentralization policy, most responsibilities—including land and spatial management—are devolved to the local (city and district) governments. The main issue that resulted from this is that the development and location permits are granted by the city government, without consultation from BP Batam.

Batam is served by the Hang Nadim International Airport, which connects it with other urban centres in Indonesia. Currently, there is only one international flight to Kuala Lumpur available. However, the airport has been used as the hub and aircraft maintenance facility for the Lion Air group, a company that set the world record for the largest single order of 230 aircrafts from Boeing several years ago. The city is also served by a number of ferry terminals, which connect it with other cities in Sumatra, as well Singapore and Malaysia. In 2015, more than 1.4 million international tourists visited Batam, of which, about 62 per cent were Singaporeans (Badan Pusat Statistik Batam 2016).

Batam also recently reported the highest annual population growth rate in Indonesia, and in the world. Its population, based on the Population Census of 1990, was only 106,000. It quadrupled to 434,000 in 2000 at an annual growth rate of 15.1 per cent. In 2010, the population was 944,000. With an annual growth rate of 8.1 per cent between 2000 and 2010, Batam was named as the city with the fastest-growing population in the world (Massy-Beresford 2015). The most recent population data based on citizen registration showed that Batam hit the million-population mark in 2012 (1.06 million), which made it the newest metropolitan city in Indonesia. Its population in 2015 was 1.19 million, the result of an annual growth rate of 4.6 per cent between 2010 and 2015. The high rate is largely driven by immigration instead of natural increase. About two-thirds of the population growth between 2000 and 2010 was contributed by migrants. With industrial development and investments, Batam has attracted many workers from other parts of Indonesia, especially Java (Firman 2004). As the city with the highest minimum wage in Indonesia, Batam was especially attractive for job seekers, although not all landed a formal sector job, with many working in the informal sector or becoming unemployed (Amri 2016).

The influx of migrant workers soon turned out to become the source of development problems in the island. A couple of decades ago, three issues related to unregulated flow of migrants into Batam were identified: the extensive squatter housing development; under- and unemployment; and rising crime rate (Grundy-Warr, Peachey, and Perry 1999). Little investment in low-income housing is the cause of squatter housing development (*rumah liar*), in Batam. Moreover, the lack of industrial experience and specific job skills made it hard for many migrants to obtain formal employment. Young women are more likely to be hired by companies than men, making it more common for men to enter the informal sector. To address the migrant issue, at one point, the Batam City government enacted a by-law to control the number of migrants by requiring them to have skills and qualifications to work, register, and pay a bond as assurance. Its implementation was messy as there were accusations of bribery and inadequate registration procedures. The by-law was then suspended, but discussion about its re-enactment appeared several years later (*Batam Pos*, 21 September 2015).

The problem of squatter settlements persists even today, as migrants continue to enter Batam at an unregulated rate, while the government struggles to build rental accommodations at an equal pace. Although it is claimed that around 27,000 such settlements have been cleared and that the residents were relocated to proper housing facilities, it is estimated there were still around 48,000 workers living in these areas (Amri 2016). Another issue identified recently from discussion with officers from Batam City Development Planning Agency is residential segregation. Apparently, high-class residential areas have developed in and around Batam Centre, the city central business district, while the middle-class residential areas are developed in Sekupang and Batu Aji. Lower income residential areas are sprawling in other subdistricts farther away from the city centre.

The problems of squatter settlements and residential segregation are not properly addressed by the authorities, as it is unclear who is responsible for dealing with this issue (Amri 2016). In the Batam City Spatial Plan that was formulated in early 2000 (Pemerintah Kota Batam 2004), the squatter issue is mentioned as something that needs prevention (from new development) and control of old ones, which means clearance. However, it is not mentioned how and where residents should be relocated. The section on housing and settlement in the Plan does not mention provision for low-income housing. It only states that vertical housing (such as apartments) should be built, without specific locations and classification. The spatial plan of Batam City has undergone revision for several years now, but there is no development guidance provided by the city government with regard to the informal settlement problem. Fortunately, the central government (via the Ministry of Public Works and Housing) initiated the "city without slums" programme (KOTAKU) in 2015. The objective of this programme is to eliminate slum areas in the cities by 2019. Although it sounds unrealistic to achieve, many cities are relying on this program, including Batam to deal with this issue.

Regardless of the mounting problems associated with the migrant population and squatter development that Batam has, in the proposed spatial planning document (RTRW), the city is planned to hold a population of up to 2.5 million. This is based on the estimate of freshwater availability from six existing reservoirs with two planned reservoirs as well as an additional 0.5 million people.[4] An increase in population density is expected in several settlement centres, such as Nongsa, Batu Ampar, Lubuk Baja, Sekupang and Sei Beduk, with the development of high-rise apartments.

The focus of development for Batam in the near future will still be on industrial estates, supported by infrastructure development such as a container port in Tanjung Sauh, a cargo port in Sekupang and Kabil, and land transportation projects (Batam Monorail, Batam Toll Road and Batam-Bintan Bridge). The Hang Nadim airport passenger terminal will also be revitalized and expanded (BIFZA 2015). It seems that the expectation is that, with the proposed expansion of industrial and urban activities, the migrants would be absorbed into the job market, and the informal settlement problem will gradually disappear with combined measures from both city and national governments.

Tanjungpinang City

As mentioned earlier, Tanjungpinang was one of few historical urban settlements in Sumatra in the late nineteenth century and was briefly the capital of the newly created Riau Province following Indonesia's independence. Tanjungpinang is located on the southern part of Bintan, the largest island of PRI, and consists of four subdistricts. Around 34 per cent of the land is built-up area. Tanjungpinang is also the seat of PRI's capital, which is built on Dompak Island in the south of the city.

The population of the city was about 86,000 in 1990 and increased to almost 135,000 in 2000 at an annual growth rate of 4.5 per cent. In 2001, Tanjungpinang was incorporated as an autonomous city. At the time, it consisted of two subdistricts, and was the capital of Riau Islands District. Based on the 2010 Population Census, its population was 187,400. Thus, the population growth rate decreased from the previous decade to around 3.3 per cent annually between 2000 and 2010. The current population estimate of Tanjungpinang is around 204,000 (BPS Kepulauan Riau 2016). It is estimated that Tanjungpinang received 2,400 immigrants every year, for five years before the last population census in 2010 (Badan Pusat Statistik Indonesia 2011)[5] and that migrants contributed to around two-fifths of population growth of the city between 2000 and 2010. This is a slightly lower contribution compared to migrants' contribution to Batam's population growth.

The bulk of Tanjungpinang's economy is in the tertiary sector, mainly trade, hotels and restaurants; followed by the secondary sector, mainly construction; and then the transportation and communication industry. The hotel and restaurant industry could be the most important sector due to the city's status as the provincial capital. In fact, the hotel occupancy rate in 2012 was estimated at 46 per cent (Badan Pusat Statistik Tanjungpinang 2013). This industry also has the highest level of employment compared to other industries. The government- and tourism-related sectors can also support other sectors, such as construction, transportation and communication, services and finance, as well as electricity and freshwater. Tanjungpinang is served by an airport, which serves domestic flights to other cities in Indonesia, and a harbour that provides ferry services to other cities in the province, as well as to Singapore and Malaysia.

However, as a growing small town, Tanjungpinang faces several issues, mainly regarding its infrastructure. One notorious problem is energy shortages. Blackouts occur for two to three hours on a daily basis. The city government has tried to increase the power supply by connecting the city grid to a power plant built for Lobam industrial park in Bintan District. The city spatial planning document (RTRW Kota Tanjungpinang 2014–2034) reveals the plan to build other energy sources for the city, including Diesel Power Plants in Air Raja and Suka Berenang; Coal Power Plants in Galang Batang and Sungai Lekop; as well as linking to the Batam-Bintan interconnection network.

The city also faces issues related to sanitation, especially among communities living on the coasts. It is a common practice for houses in fishing villages to flush into the sea, which causes environmental degradation. The city government has tried to encourage residents to use onsite sanitation, but has not been quite successful. The city planned to build a communal sanitation facility using vacuum technology, however it lacks the finance to implement the plan (personal communication with the staff of the city government). On top of that, the most recent development that has occurred in the city is coastal land reclamation. Due to a lack of private land available for development, there is a trend to reclaim coastal areas and incrementally build on them. However, the reclamation activity causes mangrove deforestation, which raises concerns from environmental activists and traditional fishermen (*Haluan Kepri*, 13 April 2017).

Another development taking place in Tanjungpinang is that the city government is relocating to a new government centre in Senggarang, away from the old town. Senggarang is located in the north part of the city and can be reached either by boats from the harbour in the old town, or by a radial road that is built to circumvent the bay and opens to the northern part of the city. The city government is planning to develop that area as the new urban centre for different functions, not only government facilities (the mayor's office and local parliament buildings have been built), but also as a centre for business, trade and services, and as a transportation hub. The new urban centre is then supported by three subcentres around the city, i.e. the old town, Batu Sembilan area and Simpang Km 14 area. Thus, while the provincial government is developing Dompak Island as its government centre in the south, the city government is building Senggarang area as a multifunction centre in the north. The city spatial plan (RTRW Kota Tanjungpinang 2014–2034) commits to developing some parts of Dompak and Air Raja areas as industrial zones. Surrounded by Batu Sembilan and Simpang Km 14 as subcentres, urban development in the east has occurred at a fast rate, as reflected by the growth of built-up areas.

Bintan District

With an area of 2,402 square kilometres, Bintan Island is the largest island in the Riau Islands Province. Since 2001, the island has been divided into two local governments: Tanjungpinang Municipality and Bintan District. The size of Bintan District's land area is around 1,946 square kilometres and includes ten subdistricts and fifty-one villages. The capital of Bintan District used to be in Tanjungpinang, but was relocated to Bandar Seri Bentan in Teluk Bintan subdistrict in 2004. The new government centre is located approximately 32 kilometres from Tanjungpinang City to the north.

As a direct outcome of the Singapore-Johor-Riau (SIJORI) growth triangle development, two flagship projects were built in Bintan: Bintan Industrial Estate located in Lobam and Bintan Beach International Resort located in Lagoi (Grundy-Warr, Peachey and Perry 1999; Bunnell et al. 2012). Lobam is located on the northwest side, while Lagoi is located on the north side of the island. Similar to Batam, Bintan has seen influx of capital from Singapore in industrial parks and high-end tourism facilities (Toh 2006). The Government of Indonesia also set up a master plan for the Batam-Bintan-Karimun special economic zone development, where Bintan is being developed for industrial parks, tourist resort and agricultural products.

The manufacturing industry has contributed the most to the Gross Regional Domestic Product (GRDP) of Bintan District in recent years. According to the Local Promotion and Investment Agency, the number of large companies increased from 70 in 2013 to 213 in 2014. This was accompanied by an increase of small and medium enterprises from 325 in 2013 to 552 in 2014 (Badan Pusat Statistik Kabupaten Bintan 2015). The mining sector is now the second largest contributor to the GRDP. Bintan Island used to be known as the major producer of bauxite for the country. Nowadays, its mining activities focus on granite and sand. However, in terms of employment, the agriculture sector has the largest share of employment in 2014 (25 per cent of workforce), followed by the services sector (21 per cent) and trade, restaurant and hotel sector (19 per cent). Thus, out of the three backbone sectors of Bintan Island, the manufacturing industry contributes most to the economy in terms of GRDP, while the agriculture sector contributes most in terms of jobs provision, and the tourism sector also contributes towards job provision.

The population of Bintan District in 2000 was just over 110,000, then grew slightly to 116,000 in 2005, around 142,000 in 2010, and finally grew to 153,000 in 2015. The highest annual growth rate (4 per cent) was recorded during the period between 2005 and 2010. It was the second highest annual growth rate in that period, after

Batam (8.9 per cent). The highest concentration of population is in the East Bintan subdistrict. From the built-up area analysis in the previous section, we can see how urban development is actually occurring near the airport of Tanjungpinang - towards Kijang town, in the southeast of the island. Another concentration of population is in the North Bintan subdistrict, site of the Bintan resort development.

One of the development issues that Bintan District currently faces is land disputes. Several development proposals have been halted due to disputes between landowners and developers. One example is the proposal for a major resort development in Trikora Beach area. The resort developer claimed that they had secured all permits to build the resort, only later to find out that some portion of the land was claimed by an individual landowner (*Lintas Kepri*, 6 July 2017). There is a possibility that multiple land titles were issued by the local land agency, which may have involved counterfeit transactions (*Batam Today*, 3 February 2017). A similar issue in the past sparked a major demonstrations and occupation of a power station on the island, which frightened hoteliers and investors (Borsuk 2000).

Another related issue is the boundary dispute between Bintan District and Tanjungpinang City. Tanjungpinang used to be part of Riau Islands District, which has now been renamed as Bintan District. When Tanjungpinang was created, there was no clear boundary between the two local governments. When Tanjungpinang government drew its map, the Bintan District government complained that one of its villages had been taken by Tanjungpinang. The matter has now been brought to the provincial government, at the request of the mayor of Bintan District. The mayor of Tanjungpinang thought that the matter was settled by the province, but the mayor of Bintan District was not informed about the settlement (*Batam Pos*, 3 February 2017). A lack of coordination between the neighbouring governments seems to be the underlying issue, which cannot be resolved easily.

The spatial plan of Bintan District (RTRW Kabupaten Bintan 2011–2031) reveals the structure of the district's urban system. There are three urban centres developed in Bintan, i.e., Bandar Seri Bentan in the centre of the island, where the new district government centre has been built: Tanjung Uban, which is a port on the west side of the island, located around 10 kilometres from the industrial estate in Lobam; and Kijang on the southeast of the island, located around 20 kilometres east of Tanjungpinang City. Additionally, Bintan District also plans to develop an industrial zone in Galang Batang and maritime activities in East Bintan, in addition to Lobam industrial estate. The district also plans to develop several tourist spots around the island, including Lagoi, Sebong Pereh, Sebong Lagoi, Trikora Beach and Kuala Sempang. With the international resort in Lagoi in the north, urban development will cover all sides of the island. All the above-mentioned areas are designated as district strategic areas in the RTRW (Pemerintah Kabupaten Bintan 2012).

CONCLUSION

Urbanization in the Province of Riau Islands has been analysed using three different approaches: population growth and distribution; urban area growth; and urban status. The population growth analysis shows that more than half of the province population and two-thirds of the urban population reside in Batam. Batam is the newest metropolitan city in Indonesia with 1.2 million people. However, concentration of urban population is not only in Batam and Tanjungpinang, but also in Karimun and Bintan Districts. In terms of population growth rate, if Batam posted the fastest annual growth rate in the country for the 1990–2000 (15.1 per cent) and 2000–10 (8.1 per cent) periods, for the later period of 2008–14, it was Lingga District that recorded the fastest annual growth rate of 8.1 per cent, after its secession from the Riau Islands District. For the same period, Batam had an annual growth rate of 5.9 per cent, while that of Tanjungpinang was slightly slower at 5.6 per cent.

Analysis of the growth of built-up areas shows that Batam also has the highest built-up area in the province, followed by Bintan District and Tanjungpinang. However, the highest growth of built-up areas between 2009 and 2015 is seen in Bintan District and Tanjungpinang, followed by Lingga District and then Batam. Its spatial analysis shows that the development of built-up areas is visible in and around Tanjungpinang City towards the east. It is also visible along the coast of Karimun Besar Island in Karimun District. Lastly, the urban status analysis suggests that several subdistricts in some districts of PRI, including Karimun, Bintan and Lingga, can be considered as urban subdistricts. We can expect those subdistricts to become urban centres in the future.

The urbanization trends that have occurred in the newly created PRI over the past ten years reflect the dual processes of urbanization and decentralization (Salim 2016): urbanized decentralization and decentralized urbanization. The former refers to a process in which urban centres are getting more independent, and then become autonomous local governments. In PRI, this process is seen by the creation of Batam and Tanjungpinang as municipalities. Meanwhile, decentralized urbanization refers to a process in which the establishment of new provinces by local governments creates new urban centres, either as the capital, or a new growth centre, which then increases the rate of urbanization. This process is observed in the urbanization trends in Bintan, Karimun and Lingga Districts.

The growth potential of urban areas in Riau Islands Province can be predicted from these trends. Batam's population will grow in the future, but its urban development will be limited by land and water availability. Thus, we will see vertical development for housing and commercial purposes in Batam. As for Tanjungpinang, it will grow further in terms of population and urban areas, especially as the result of provincial capital development in Dompak Island, as well as due to the relocation of the city government centre to Senggarang, in the north of Tanjungpinang. In the meantime, Bintan Island—which has seen major resort development in Lagoi area in the north, and the development of industrial parks in Lobam area in the west—will see more development in Teluk Bintan as a result of new district capital development in Bandar Seri Bentan and the ribbon development along the road from Tanjungpinang to Kijang. As for Karimun District, we will see increasing development in Kundur Island and Tebing on Karimun Besar Island, accompanying existing development in Karimun and Meral subdistricts. Lastly, Lingga District will witness more development in Lingga Island following the district capital development in Daik, which is the former capital of Riau-Lingga Sultanate in the nineteenth century, instead of Singkep Island that is more developed in the past few decades.

Another driving force for further urbanization in PRI is the designation of some parts of Batam, Tanjungpinang, Bintan, and Karimun districts as free ports and free trade zones by the central government. This area has been considered as one of the national strategic areas due to its proximity to Singapore and Malaysia, and the former status of Batam. The government expected that an additional 30,000 workers would be absorbed by activities brought by the free port and free trade zone status (*Hukum Online* 2007). But this time, they are to be distributed between other districts/islands, and not just in Batam. The central government has prepared a spatial planning document (RTRW Kawasan BBK) to coordinate development in the area (Presiden Republik Indonesia 2011). The provision in this document would need to be accommodated by each local government (Batam City, Tanjungpinang City, Bintan District and Karimun District) to align it with local development plans.

Notes

1. I would like to thank Francis Hutchinson and Siwage Dharma Negara for the invitation to carry out and present this study as well as for feedback on an earlier draft. I also would like to thank Dr Samsul Bahrum and Dedy Hamidy (Kepulauan Riau Province), Irfan Syakir (BP Batam), Azril Apriansyah (Batam City), Heni Ariputranti and Renna Lestyono (Tanjungpinang City), and Erie Sadewo (Karimun District) for providing data and information during the fieldwork in 2017. Lastly, I would like to thank Uly Faoziyah for creating all maps in the paper.
2. In Indonesia, the Central Bureau of Statistics classifies each village into two categories: urban and rural. This status is used in the census or other surveys conducted by the agency. The status of urbanity used in this study is based on the Village Potential (PODES) data of 2014. As the unit of analysis in this study is at the subdistrict- and not the village-level, data of urban status at village level from PODES was first compiled by aggregating them into subdistricts. The rule for aggregation is that, if the majority of the villages in a subdistrict has urban status, that subdistrict is considered urban.
3. For detailed discussion about the confusion between the two authorities at the beginning of decentralization and the current status, see Amri (2016).
4. Interview with Wan Darussalam, Head of the Batam Development Planning Agency Batam, 26 January 2015.
5. The total number of immigrants coming to the Riau Islands Province from 2005 to 2010 was estimated at 210,000; around 82 per cent came to Batam City, around 5.9 per cent came to Bintan District, 5.8 per cent came to Tanjungpinang City, and the rest came to other districts (Badan Pusat Statistik Indonesia 2011). The approximate annual figure of immigrants who came to Tanjungpinang is derived from these statistics.

References

Amri, Mulya. 2016. "A Periphery Serving Three Cores: Balancing Local, National, and Cross-Border Interests in the Riau Islands". In *The SIJORI Cross-Border Region: Transnational Politics, Economics, and Culture*, edited by Francis E. Hutchinson and Terence Chong, pp. 154–80. Singapore: ISEAS – Yusof Ishak Institute.

Ananta, Aris. 2016. "The Population of the SIJORI Cross-Border Region". In *The SIJORI Cross-Border Region: Transnational Politics, Economics, and Culture*, edited by Francis E. Hutchinson and Terence Chong, pp. 41–65. Singapore: ISEAS – Yusof Ishak Institute.

Andaya, Barbara, and Leonard Andaya. 2001. *A History of Malaysia*. Honolulu: University of Hawaii Press.

Badan Pusat Statistik. 2011. "Sensus Penduduk 2010". Jakarta.

Badan Pusat Statistik Batam. 2016. "Batam City in Figures 2016". Batam.

Badan Pusat Statistik Tanjungpinang. 2013. "Tanjungpinang Dalam Angka". Tanjungpinang.

Badan Pusat Statistik Kabupaten Bintan. 2015. "Bintan in Figures 2015".

Batam Pos. 2015. "Pendatang ke Batam akan Dibatasi, Pemko Siap Aktifkan Perdaduk". 21 September 2015. http://batampos.co.id/2015/09/21/pendatang-ke-batam-akan-dibatasi-pemko-siap-aktifkan-perdaduk/ (accessed 13 November 2017).

———. 2017. "Serobot Lahan Pemko Tanjungpinang Digugat Pemko Bintan". 3 February 2017. http://batampos.co.id/2017/02/03/serobot-lahan-pemko-tanjungpinang-digugat-pemko-bintan/

Batam Today. 2017. "Polemik Lahan Pembangunan Resort di-Trikora, Ini Tanggapan Bupati Bintan". 19 July 2017. http://batamtoday.com/home/read/94226/Polemik-Lahan-Pembangunan-Resort-di-Trikora-Ini-Tanggapan-Bupati-Bintan

BIFZA. 2015. "Forthcoming Project: Transportation Development in Batam 2015". Batam: Batam Indonesia Free Zone Authority.

———. 2016. "Investment Opportunities and Prospects in Batam Free Trade Zone". Batam: Batam Indonesia Free Zone Authority.

Borsuk, Richard. 2000. *Wall Street Journal*. 1 March 2000. https://www.wsj.com/articles/SB951851406368233113

BP Batam. 2011. *Batam Economic Outlook 2011–2014*. Batam.

BPS Kepulauan Riau. 2006. *Kepulauan Riau in Figures 2005*. Tanjungpinang: Central Board of Statistics of Kepulauan Riau Province.

———. 2016. "Kepulauan Riau in Figures 2015". Tanjungpinang.

Bunnell, Tim, Carl Grundy-Warr, James Sidaway, and Matthew Sparke. 2012. "Geographies of Power in the Indonesia-Malaysia-Singapore Growth Triangle". In *International Handbook of Globalization and World Cities*, by Ben Derudder, Michael Hoyler, Peter Taylor and Frank Witlox, pp. 465–75. Edward Elgar.

Chang, C.T. 2001. "Configuring New Tourism Space: Exploring Singapore's Regional Tourism Forays". *Environment and Planning A* 33: 1597–619.

Firman, Tommy. 2004. "Demographic and Spatial Patterns of Indonesia's Recent Urbanisation". *Population, Space and Place* 10: 421–34.

———. 2009. "Decentralization Reform and Local Government Proliferation: Towards a Fragmentation of Regional Development". *Review of Urban and Regional Development Studies* 21, no. 2: 144–57.

Fitriani, Fitria, Bert Hofman, and Kai Kaiser. 2005. "Unity in Diversity? The Creation of New

Local Governments in a Decentralising Indonesia". *Bulletin of Indonesian Economic Studies* 41, no. 1: 57–79.

Friedmann, John. 2013. "Planning for Sustainable Regional Development". *UNCRD Expert Group Meeting on Integrated Regional Development Planning*.

Gorlinski, Virginia. 2016. "Riau Islands". *Encyclopaedia Britannica*. 27 May 2016. https://www.britannica.com/place/Riau-Islands (accessed June 2017).

Grundy-Warr, Carl, Karen Peachey, and Martin Perry. 1999. "Fragmented Integration in the Singapore–Indonesian Border Zone: Southeast Asia's 'Growth Triangle' Against the Global Economy". *International Journal of Urban and Regional Research* 23, no. 2: 304–28.

Haluan Kepri. 2017. 13 April 2017. http://haluankepri.com/tanjungpinang/101495-cek-reklamasi-tanjung-unggat.html

Hukum Online. 22 August 2007. http://www.hukumonline.com/berita/baca/hol17423/selamat-datang-di-batam-bintan-karimun.

Hutchinson, Francis E., and Terence Chong. 2016. "The SIJORI Cross-Border Region: More Than a Triangle". In *The SIJORI Cross-Border Region: Transnational Politics, Economics, and Culture*, edited by Francis E. Hutchinson and Terence Chong, pp. 9–29. Singapore: ISEAS – Yusof Ishak Institute.

Kimura, Ehito. 2007. "Provincial Proliferation: Territorial Politics in Post-Suharto Indonesia". University of Wisconsin-Madison.

Lintas Kepri. 2017. "PT GWS Diduga Serobot Tanah Milik Dahnoer Yoesoef di Bintan". 6 July 2017. http://lintaskepri.com/pt-gws-diduga-serobot-tanah-milik-dahnoer-yoesoef-di-bintan.html

Lith, P.A. van der. 1893. *Nederlansch Oost-Indie*. Leiden: Brill.

Massy-Beresford, Helen. 2015. "Where Is the Fastest Growing City in the World?". *The Guardian*, 18 November 2015. https://www.theguardian.com/cities/2015/nov/18/where-is-the-worlds-fastest-growing-city-batam-niamey-xiamen

Miksic, John N. 1989. "Urbanization and Social Change: The Case of Sumatera". *Archipel* 37: 3–29.

Ministry of Public Works. 2008. "Free Trade Zon Batam-Bintan-Karimun Study".

Pemerintah Kota Batam. 2004. "Peraturan Daerah Kota Batam Nomor 2 Tahun 2004". *Rencana Tata Ruang Wilayah Kota Batam Tahun 2004–2014*. Batam.

Pemerintah Kabupaten Bintan. 2012. "Peraturan Daerah Nomor 2 Tahun 2012". *Rencana Tata Ruang Wilayah Kabupaten Bintan 2011–2031*. Kijang: Pemerintah Kabupaten Bintan.

Presiden Republik Indonesia. 2006. "Peraturan Pemerintah Nomor 5 Tahun 2006". *Perubahan Nama Kabupaten Kepulauan Riau Menjadi Kabupaten Bintan Provinsi Kepulauan Riau*. Jakarta, 23 February 2006.

―――. 2011. "Peraturan Presiden Republik Indonesia Nomor 87 Tahun 2011". *Rencana Tata Ruang Kawasan Batam, Bintan dan Karimun*. Jakarta, 2 December 2011.

Salim, Wilmar. 2016. "Decentralization, Urbanization, Proliferation and the Achievements of Sustainable Development Goals". Visby.

Toh Mun Heng. 2006. "Development in the Indonesia-Malaysia-Singapore Growth Triangle". Working Paper, Economics, National University of Singapore, SCAPE.

―――, and L. Low. 1993. *Regional Cooperation and Growth Triangles in ASEAN*. Singapore: Times Academic Press.

Tribun Batam. "Masalah Perbatasan Dengan Tanjungpinang. Bupati Bintan Serahkan Masalahnya ke Pemprov Kepri". 15 January 2017. http://batam.tribunnews.com/2017/01/15/

masalah-perbatasan-dengan-tanjungpinang-bupati-bintan-serahkan-masalahnya-ke-pemprov-kepri

Wee, Vivienne. 2016. "The Significance of Riau in SIJORI". In *The SIJORI Cross-Border Region: Transnational Politics, Economics, and Culture*, edited by Francis E. Hutchinson and Terence Chong, pp. 241–66. Singapore: ISEAS – Yusof Ishak Institute.

12

THE TRADITIONALIST RESPONSE TO WAHHABI-SALAFISM IN BATAM[1]

Norshahril Saat

INTRODUCTION

Existing research on Batam-Singapore relations has focused more on economic and trade ties as opposed to social issues. The ties between the two cities, which are 20 kilometres apart, are always discussed within the framework of SIJORI, a joint development and business venture between Singapore, Malaysia, and Indonesia.[2] To be sure, links between the three states transcend economic, trade and security matters to also include religion and cultural exchanges. It only takes a 45-minute ferry ride from Singapore to Batam and the number of Singaporeans crossing over to Indonesia via Batam is high—comparable to the number that travels to Jakarta.

Batam is a highly industrialized city, attracting immigration from other parts of Indonesia, especially Java. According to the 2010 census, Batam has a population of 1.2 million people. 77 per cent of them are Muslims, 17 per cent Christians, and 6 per cent Buddhists (Effendy 2014, p. 149). In terms of ethnicity, 27 per cent are Javanese, and the other major ethnic communities include: Malays (17.6 per cent); Bataks (15.0 per cent); Minangkabau (14.9 per cent); and Chinese (6.3 per cent) (Effendy 2014, p. 150). Even though the proportion of Malays is smaller than the Javanese, yet as part of the Riau Islands, Batam strongly upholds its Malay character. It also has a sizeable minority Bugis community, which has strong trade networks (Firdaus 2016). Historically, Riau was part of the Johor-Riau Kingdom, and the name Riau appeared at least three times in seventeenth- and eighteenth-century sources (Wee 2016, p. 243).

Lately, there have been security concerns between the two cities. In August 2016, Batam authorities foiled a plot by a terrorist group called Cell Gonggong Rebus (GR) which planned to launch a rocket from the island towards Marina Bay in Singapore. The police arrested five Indonesians for the failed attempt. The militants were believed to have links with ISIS (Islamic State in Iraq and Syria), and separatist groups in Xinjiang, China (Wahyudi 2017). The leader of GR, Gigih Rahmat Dewa, travelled to Singapore several times before he was detained. He was married to a Batam resident and has a house in the city. Gigih also made several contacts with Bahrun Naim, another Indonesian radical linked to ISIS and the alleged mastermind of the Jakarta attacks in 2016 (Arlina 2016a).

Within a matter of days after the Cell GR discovery, the Singapore Ministry of Home Affairs revealed that it had detained two Singaporeans under the Internal Security Act and another two were given restriction orders. They were detained for either being ISIS sympathizers, or for considering flying to the Middle East to fight in Syria. Although the arrests involved Singaporeans, there was a link with Batam. The two ISA detainees—Rosli Hamzah and Mohamed Omar Mahadi—were self-radicalized and avid listeners of Batam's Islamic radio station, Radio Hang FM or Radio Dakwah Sunnah (Arlina 2016b). The station is easily accessible via radio or online. Security analysts have alleged that the station is disseminating exclusivist, anti-pluralist and Wahhabi-Salafi ideas.

These two separate incidents indirectly support the narrative that Batam Muslims are becoming more radical and puritan. This chapter discusses whether the nexus between Batam and terrorism is a fair assessment of Muslims on the island. Do these episodes manifest a changing character of Islam in Batam, a city known for its tolerance, pluralist values, and Sufism?

This chapter argues that Batam Muslims condemn terrorism and are largely traditionalists. In other words, they are generally anti-Wahhabi-Salafi. Being anti-Wahhabi-Salafi, or Sufi-oriented traditionalists, however, does not make them less exclusive. For example, we still hear Batam Muslims desiring to see Muslim leadership in the city and country rather than a non-Muslim President or Governor.[3] Thus, Batam Muslims may be religiously traditionalist, but politically exclusivist.

This chapter serves as a preliminary study of Batam Muslims and does not seek to advance definitive conclusions. To begin, there is little literature that discusses Islam in Batam. This chapter is based on the author's participatory observation and personal interactions with local Muslims on the island. This included: visits to some of the boarding schools and welfare homes in the city; and a focus group discussion (FGD) with the city's religious elites, who are also key actors representing Muslims in the city. The FGD gave insights into their organizations' activities as well as the mode of thinking towards terrorism and wider societal issues.

TRADITIONALISM, MODERNISM AND SALAFI-WAHHABISM

In terms of religious orientation, Indonesian Muslims can be characterized into two dominant categories: traditionalists and modernists. These are ideal-type categories which academics apply in their study of Muslim societies, and Muslims in general would not consider themselves to be part of those camps. There are also many overlaps between the two groups in terms of political affiliation, class identity, and location.

Very broadly, traditionalists are more appreciative of Islam being infused with local culture. They believe that Muslims should follow one of the four classical jurists: Hanafi, Maliki, Hanbali or Shafie. Indonesians generally follow the Shafie School of law. Traditionalists contend that in today's context, religious texts can be reinterpreted to meet modern needs. However, a majority of traditionalists argue that the gates of independent judgement (*ijtihad*) are discouraged, thus Muslims need to obtain guidance from the four jurists who lived within the first three generations after the Prophet's death in formulating religious rulings. It is in the event that the writings of the four jurists are not helpful that they can come up with independent reasonings.[4]

The traditionalists are represented by an organization called Nahdlatul Ulama (NU, Revival of the Ulama), which was formed in 1926. In terms of membership, it is the largest religious organization in Indonesia. It oversees many Islamic boarding schools across the country, and has networks in many parts of the world. So powerful was NU that, in 1999, its chairman, Abdurrahman Wahid became the Republic's fourth president. Even though NU started off as a religious organization, for a period in its history, it functioned as a political party. In 1984, NU leaders decided to withdraw the organization from party politics for two reasons: on the one hand, they were pressured by then President Soeharto to be apolitical; on the other, the organization's leader then, Abdurrahman Wahid, felt that NU should not bow to government pressure.[5]

Apart from NU, there are other organizations that are inclined to the traditionalist outlook. They are Nahdlatul Wathan and Al-Washliyah, which are smaller organizations compared to NU.

In contrast, modernists believe that there exists a normative Islam, defined by the religion's holy texts of the Quran and hadith (sayings of the Prophet Muhammad), and local cultures have to be amended to suit Islamic traditions. In Indonesia, modernists are critical of those practising rituals such as visiting graves of pious Muslims (*ziarah kubur*); celebrating Prophet Muhammad's birthday (*maulid Nabi*); organizing communal feasting (*kenduri*); and joining Sufi *tariqah* networks which continue the practices mentioned. These rituals are widely practised by the traditionalists and within NU circles. Modernists believe that the gates of *ijtihad* are not closed and can be interpreted and reinterpreted to meet modern needs. The modernists are influenced by the reformist movement that began in Egypt at the turn of the twentieth century.

In Indonesia, the organization closely associated with the modernist movement is the Muhammadiyah. It was founded in 1912 by Kyai Haji Ahmad Dahlan, a Muslim reformer. For promoting modernist ideas, Muhammadiyah is seen as NU's ideological rival. Unlike NU, Muhammadiyah as an organization has never been a formal political party. This, however, does not prevent them from having members participating in politics. Its former chairman, Amien Rais, became a prominent politician; and between 1999 and 2004, he was the chairman of People's Consultative

Assembly (MPR). On the social front, Muhammadiyah is interested in welfare, charity work, and education.

There has been some confusion about what constitutes Wahhabi-Salafi ideology, as it shares many views with the modernists as opposed to the traditionalists. On rituals, Wahhabi-Salafis also frown upon practices such as *maulid, ziarah kubur* and *tariqah*. Nevertheless, in this chapter, Wahhabi-Salafis are distinguished from Indonesian modernists because, over time, the latter have become more tolerant of local cultures. In Indonesia today, it has come to a stage whereby the traditionalists and modernists have agreed to disagree, and focus their efforts on tackling common challenges. The modernists in Indonesia have also distanced themselves from the Wahhabi-Salafi orientation and have condemned the group.

Wahhabi-Salafism was founded in eighteenth century Arabia by Muhammad Ibn Abdul Al-Wahab (Delong-Bas 2004). Followers of the ideology have sought to cleanse Islamic beliefs of "innovations". Wahhabi-Salafism believes that Muslims should adhere to the Quran and Sunnah, and not strictly follow the four legal schools of thought, though in reality, they promote the Hanbali perspective. A majority of Indonesian Muslims consider this school of thought to be divisive.

Wahhabi-Salafism first came to Southeast Asia through students who studied in Saudi Arabia. This is not a recent phenomenon. Traces of the ideology found in the region date from the nineteenth century. The Islamic resurgence period of the 1970s also led to greater penetration of Wahhabi-Salafism into Southeast Asia. Scholars have shown how the Saudi Arabian government exported the ideology accompanied by "petro-dollars" in the form of donations to mosques and religious institutions. According to Leila (2011),

> The soaring oil prices after the war of 1973 [Yom Kippur War between Arabs and Israel] and the enormous wealth the Arab oil states commanded thereafter would give rise to other conditions—aside from vastly increased resources for funding Islamist outreach—that would further contribute to the spread of Islamism and that would promote the spread of Saudi Arabian and Gulf forms of religious practice to Egyptians and other Arabs and Muslims (Leila 2011, p. 101).

A majority of Indonesian Muslims are traditionalists, though there are provinces in which modernists dominate. The majority of Muslims in Java are traditionalists, except for Yogyakarta, the province in which Muhammadiyah was founded. On the other hand, the modernists are dominant in Sumatra, particularly in towns such as Padang. The same generalization cannot be made for other communities such as the Malays and Bugis, because they can either be traditionalists or modernists, depending on where they reside.

Today, NU and Muhammadiyah have converged on many aspects of their religious outlook. In fact, members of both organizations participated in the state-formed Indonesian Ulama Council (Majelis Ulama Indonesia, or MUI). MUI members consider their organization as an umbrella body overseeing other Islamic organizations in the country. In 1975, President Soeharto formed the MUI, a national-level *ulama* organization that seeks to represent all religious elites in Indonesia. The main task of the organization is to issue religious rulings or *fatwa* (non-binding legal opinions), at the national level. The first chairman of the organization was Hamka, a modernist-oriented scholar. Subsequent chairmanships of the organization have rotated between traditionalists and modernists (most of them were either from NU or Muhammadiyah).

In recent times, scholars have condemned MUI for being conservative and exclusive. One religious ruling made by the organization that was widely condemned was the SIPILIS *fatwa* in 2005, an acronym coined to mean secularism, pluralism, and liberalism. MUI has also declared minority sects such as Shias and Ahmadiyyahs as deviant. Although MUI is a largely conservative organization, the leaders are not Wahhabi-Salafis oriented, and this is reflected in their public conduct. Some have joined public rituals and prayers associated with the traditionalist school and NU. In fact, the majority of MUI leaders are affiliated with NU, including its current chairman, Kyai Ma'ruf Amin.

ISLAMIC ORGANIZATIONS IN BATAM

In Batam, there are about forty-three Islamic organizations (Effendy 2014). Most of them are branches of societal organizations (*ormas*) headquartered in Jakarta. The number of Islamic organizations in Batam has grown exponentially in the last two decades, corresponding to the rise in religious piety of Batam Muslims. In 1995, there were 110 mosques and 96 prayer spaces (*musollahs*) in the city. By 2014, the number had increased to 612 mosques and 411 prayer spaces in all (Effendy 2014). There have been rumours that some of these prayer spaces receive funds from foreign donors, especially from the Middle East. However, most of them are funded through donations from Muslims residing in Batam. Indonesian Islamic organizations have also funded these prayer spaces.

The most influential Islamic organization in Batam is the MUI, which is a chapter of the organization based in Jakarta. As mentioned, MUI serves as an umbrella organization for all Islamic organizations in the country. MUI issues religious rulings (*fatwas*) which are non-binding on Muslims, though they are generally followed.

According to Khairuddin, the Head of the Assessment Institute for Food, Drugs, and Cosmetics of MUI (LPPOM-MUI), Muslim organizations in Batam and Indonesia more widely regard MUI as the umbrella for all Islamic organizations.[6] Nonetheless, the national MUI has little control over chapters in the provinces and the districts, even though their leaders are in regular contact (Norsharil 2016). Some of the branch leaders are invited to MUI national congresses held once every five years. The truth is that many of the MUI chapters are small and run by less than ten members.[7]

MUI Batam is headed by Kyai Haji Usman Ahmad.[8] Its main office is located in the basement of the Masjid Raya in the city centre. To date, there is no *fatwa* compilation published by the Batam MUI, unlike the central MUI, which has published all *fatwas* issued since 1975. Just like the national MUI, the Batam chapter has a halal-certification arm, LPPOM-MUI, which is active in promoting shariah-based consumption, and issuing halal certificates to food outlets and slaughterhouses in the city. LPPOM-MUI has a team of officials to determine whether food outlets selling halal products meet Islamic requirements. Batam's halal industry is supported by the local government because it contributes to the city's tourism industry. Many Singaporean and Malaysian tourists visit the city, and the majority of them opt for a one- or two-day stay to purchase halal cakes and delicacies and patronize halal-certified restaurants. Muslim tourists expect Batam hotels to meet their dietary requirements (Jannatun 2013).[9] Restaurants owned by non-Muslims also carry the halal label issued by LPPOM-MUI.

Apart from its involvement in halal-certification, MUI also conducts raids on houses or shops it suspects to be promoting deviant Islamic teachings. In 2006, MUI declared seventy Gafatar (Gerakan Fajar Nusantara) members deviant and urged its followers to return to true Islam. Later, it realized that the organization remained active underground despite MUI's warning. Some MUI Batam leaders urged the relevant local government agency to be stricter in issuing any permit for such religious groups (*Jawa Pos*, 15 January 2016). This behaviour sums up MUI Batam's powers, in which it has no authority to ban any groups except to lobby the local authorities to do so.[10]

NU and Muhammadiyah also have branches in Batam. These organizations also issue *fatwas* to their members. In terms of membership, NU is the biggest organization in Batam, just as it is in the whole country. Currently, the chairman of the organization in Batam is Kyai Haji Hairul Saleh. Hairul claimed that in today's context, his organization (NU) and Muhammadiyah share similar views in condemning terrorism and what they consider deviations from mainstream Islam.[11] They also run boarding schools on the island, although NU's far outnumber Muhammadiyah's.

BATAM MUSLIMS AND TRADITIONALISTS

Analysts, scholars, and religious teachers in Singapore are concerned that Muslims in Batam are influenced by Wahhabi-Salafi ideas. In September 2016, the *Jakarta Post* published an article on the rise of the Salafi movement in Batam, where it indicates that there are about 100 radio stations across the country promoting Salafism, and one of them is located in Batam (Haeril and Fadli 2016). In March 2017, the Voice of America ran an article claiming the Wahhabi-Salafi movement is on the rise in Batam (Varagur 2017). The article states that Batam has become a crossroad for Salafis in the region, including Singapore and Malaysia. It also pointed out the existence of Wahhabi-Salafi-oriented boarding schools, such as Pesantren Anshur al-Sunnah, located in the Cendana district. These schools were started in 2004 by an Acehnese, who was a graduate of the Medina University in Saudi Arabia.

However, as many observers will attest, it is difficult to pinpoint which schools are Wahhabi-Salafi-oriented and which promote traditionalism. The difficulty in doing so raises doubt about how some scholars are able to claim that Wahhabi-Salafism is on the rise in the city. To begin, it is difficult for analysts to determine whether a group or a religious leader is pro-Wahhabi-Salafi because these have never claimed to be such. Their refusal to use the label is not because they fear being ostracized or condemned by fellow Indonesian Muslims. Rather, they hold that their beliefs and practices represent "true" Islam—in line with the teachings of the Prophet Muhammad—and they do not consider themselves a "sect". Thus, it is impossible to ascertain if particular schools are Wahhabi-Salafi-inclined, because the label is not indicated in their names, logos, and official statements. However, there may be clues nevertheless, as when followers tend to use terms like "the Prophet's actions" (*Sunnah*) or "followers of the pious generations of the Prophet and his companions" (*Salaf*) to describe themselves; it is however premature to conclude that all madrasahs employing those terms are Wahhabi-Salafi.

One indication that Batam could be becoming exclusivist in its orientations is the discourse promoted by Radio Hang FM106. The station first started as an entertainment channel but was transformed into a *dakwah* (spreading the message of Islam) station in 2004, promoting Wahhabi-Salafi ideas. A businessman by the name of Zein Alatas owned the station, and he was allegedly a strong proponent of Wahhabism-Salafism (Varagur 2017). The content of the sermons of the station range from spirituality to Islamic jurisprudence. In the 1990s, Radio Hang FM featured ideas from a Wahhabi-Salafi scholar from Indonesia, Abdull Hakim Abdat (Lee 2016). To this day, the station plays very little music, and instead features sermons and Quranic recitation.

In early 2011, prominent Singaporean preacher Ustaz Rasul Dahri urged his followers to donate to and support Radio Hang FM. In a sermon uploaded on YouTube, he implied that his followers are supporting Salafism (the way of the Prophet and his companions) through their donations, and promised that God would reward all of them. Rasul claimed that it was through Radio Hang FM that his followers had access to his teachings. The use of the Batam radio station by a Singaporean preacher here is interesting. Wahhabi-Salafi ideas do not gain much support in Singapore and Johor, where the majority of the Muslim population is traditionalist in outlook (Norsharil 2017). The Johor religious authorities have banned Rasul from preaching in the state, and he was later arrested for preaching without permit. On 10 January 2017, *Berita Harian* (Malay daily in Singapore) ran a story claiming that a prominent terrorist, Mas Selamat Kastari, attended Rasul's classes in Johor (until he was banned) before joining Jemaah Islamiah (JI) (*Berita Harian*, 10 January 2017). In June 2017, the Ministry of Communications and Information (MCI) of Singapore banned nine books that Rasul authored, for extremist content.

The perception that Radio Hang FM preaches Wahhabi-Salafism has raised concerns among Batam residents. Some traditionalist *ulama* have come out in the open to engage the station's scholars. In December 2013, the Head of Ministry of Religion for Batam approved a public debate between preachers from Radio Hang FM (the so-called supporters of Wahhabism-Salafism) and the traditionalists (Aswaja, Sunni). The debate was held at Masjid Raya Baitulrahman, Sekupang. It showcased civil and cordial relations between the two camps, despite their differing views. The full debate was recorded and made available on YouTube.[12] Representing the traditionalists were Muhammad Idrus Romli and Muhammad Thobary Shadizly; and Radio Hang FM was represented by Zainal Abidin Shamsudin and Firanda Andirja. Both camps were allowed to speak for the same amount of time on issues pertaining to texts and rituals.

Judging from the debate, the traditionalists in Batam do not see Wahhabi-Salafism as a threat and are willing to engage them openly. The debate also shows that the disagreement between the two camps mainly rests on rituals associated with prayers and death. There was no indication that any camp condones terrorism. Interestingly, preacher Zainal Abidin, who raised many points that could see him accused as a Wahhabi-Salafi, indicated that he is also NU-inclined (meaning he has traditionalist roots). Zainal's case demonstrates the difficulty in pointing out whether a person is a Wahhabi-Salafi or otherwise.

Undeniably, Wahhabi-Salafi followers exist in Batam, but their reach is not as extensive when compared to the traditionalists. While Radio Hang FM is still under operation there are altogether seventeen radio stations in Batam, including Radio Salam FM102.7 which is also a *dakwah* station (Effendy 2014, p. 155). In fact, according to NU members, they also run other radio stations in Batam that support Sufi and traditionalist practices. Also, the station is closely scrutinized by the Indonesian Broadcasting Corporation. Radio Hang spokespersons have denied the link between the station and terrorism, indicating that the station is against any form of radicalism (Soezean 2016).

The popularity of traditionalist rituals provides clues that the NU-style of thinking is alive in Batam (Larno 2013). For example, in 2014, the Batam municipal government invited the famous Indonesian Sufi, Habib Syech Bin Abdul Qodir Assegaf, to lead a Sufi chanting session organized to commemorate the 185th year of the city's founding (*Tribun Batam*, 19 December 2014). The session involved the use of music and the reciting of praises to the Prophet Muhammad, and thousands came to join the session. These practices are in fact frowned upon by Wahhabi-Salafi scholars.

In the same vein, on 12 December 2016, 3,000 congregants gathered at the Masjid Raya Batam, the biggest mosque in the city, to celebrate the Prophet Muhammad's birthday. The organizers claim that the event did not require any funding from the state government, as funds were collected from attendees (*Batam Pos,* 12 December 2016).

Islamic NGOs also seek to prevent Wahhabi-Salafi ideas from penetrating into the island state. In 2014, NU, The Forum of the Prophet Muhammad (Majelis Rasulullah), and Forum of Mosque Managers and Prayer Spaces in Batam (Forum Pengurus Masjid dan Mushollah Kota Batam) organized a protest demanding that the local authorities disband Radio Hang FM. The station was allowed to continue, nevertheless, despite these protests.

Kyai Usman also argued that MUI, NU and Muhammadiyah were constantly in dialogue with Radio Hang, urging them not to preach divisive ideas in the community.[13] Once, he cited that the Wahhabi-Salafis were against them reading the special prayers commonly read by traditionalists (*Hizib*), but MUI argued that the practice has always been part of mainstream Islam. Thus, there are constant attempts by key religious leaders in Batam to ensure that Wahhabi-Salafism remains marginal.[14]

The NU Batam Chairman also confirms that Batam remains a traditionalist city owing to his organization's efforts in preserving the boarding schools (*pesantrens*). It also organizes the Majlis Zikir Al-Khidir every year, which is normally attended by 20,000 people. In another example, the Jamaah Al Khidmah Batam, a traditionalist group, also organizes a special congregation that conducts Sufi rituals (Jamaah Al Khidmah Batam n.d.). This event was attended by 30,000 people. This group mainly preaches the teachings of KH Romly Tamim, who was a leader of the Sufi order Tariqah Qodariah Wa Naqsyabandiah. This is yet another sign that NU's influence remains strong in Batam.

Often, analysts argue that Batam is turning to Wahhabi-Salafism because its religious schools receive donations from Saudi Arabia or Kuwait. While there are personal anecdotes that some prayer spaces receive funds from Middle East donors, there is, nevertheless, very little evidence to suggest that mosques that receive Saudi funding have shifted towards Wahhabi-Salafism. On the contrary, some mosques that receive money from such sources continue to be run the way traditionalist schools are normally run. For example, these schools continue to practise Sufi rituals such as mass chanting after their five daily prayers.

THE SINGAPORE DIMENSION

There have been rumours that Saudi Arabia is funding some of the mosques and prayer spaces in Batam. While there may be some truth to this, Batam boarding schools and mosques also welcome donations from the region, especially from Muslims in Singapore and Malaysia. Singaporeans frequently visit these boarding schools and make donations directly to them, mainly for mosque building or orphanages. One mosque supported by Singaporeans is Masjid Muttaqin, located in the rural area of Batu Besar. Every year, the mosque receives donations, and in 2017, it received about SGD 6,000 from Singaporean donors. A tour group organizes a visit to the mosque, with about 100 Singapore Muslim participants. The imams of the mosque will organize series of talks and *maulids* (celebration of the Prophet's birthday) for their Singaporean guests. Some of the participants I spoke to during the tour shared that they followed such programmes every year.

In addition, there are some Singaporeans who come to Batam to conduct their ritual sacrifice of a goat or cow (*Qurban*) held during the Festival of Sacrifice (*Eidul Adha*). Several agencies have arranged for packages, targeting Singapore Muslims, to witness animal slaughtering ceremonies in Batam's boarding schools. More Singaporeans are coming forward to participate in these Qurban rituals, and donating to the boarding schools in Batam. The reason why Singaporeans choose to conduct their Qurban in Batam is because they feel they can donate the meat to the Muslim community in the city. Comparing the Muslim community in Singapore and Batam, the Singaporean participants feel that their countrymen are better off, and the meat would serve the Batam's underclass in a better way.

CONCLUSION: EXCLUSIVISM AND TRADITIONALISM

There are fears, especially in neighbouring Singapore, that Batam is becoming religiously intolerant. The fears of Singapore leaders and security agencies are understandable, given the historically close ties between the Muslim communities of both countries. The recent arrests of a potential terror attack aimed at Singapore has exacerbated this fear. This has had an impact on Batam Muslims crossing over to Singapore, as some of them complain about the additional security checks placed on them by the Singapore immigration authorities. Nonetheless, the fear that Muslims in Batam are becoming fundamentalists is unfounded. Discussions with Batam religious elites show that they are largely traditionalists and are seeking to combat the spread of fundamentalism.

As it is, the battle between moderates and terrorists remain within the domain of civil society. Dominant religious organizations—the MUI, NU, and Muhammadiyah—along with other *tariqah* groups and boarding schools have been strong in mitigating terrorism and fundamentalism, despite their internal differences. Batam has a self-checking mechanism that can monitor the rise of intolerance, including Wahhabi-Salafism, without any interference from Batam authorities.

However, concerns about Batam becoming the bastion of Wahhabi-Salafism and terrorism sidestep the question of exclusivist attitudes that Muslims may have towards non-Muslims. This chapter contends that, for future research, analysts of Islam in Batam have to pose the right questions. While the Muslim leaders consulted condemn terrorism and radicalism and they are traditionalists when it comes to religious rituals, they have also raised concerns about the possibility of having non-Muslims as their political leaders. They feel that Muslims are being marginalized in Batam. One plausible reason for this feeling is rapid urbanization, which has changed the demographic characteristics of the island significantly. The Malays complain that they are outnumbered by the Javanese, and they are still grappling with what they imagine to be a significant rise in the number of Chinese. This demographic change resulted from immigration from other parts of Indonesia (particularly from Java) to Batam. The city has also become a tourist spot, and is famous for its massage parlours, golf courses, and duty-free liquor shops, the last of which causes discomfort among Muslims (Haeril and Fadli 2016).

The religious elites' exclusivist attitudes towards non-Muslims is a reflection that, while traditionalists may be open to differences regarding rituals, they may not be as open when it comes to political leadership and inter-ethnic relations. This was reflected in conversations with Batam Muslims who followed events in Jakarta, such as the 2017 Jakarta gubernatorial elections. The incumbent Jakarta governor, Basuki Tjahaja Purnama (Ahok) was running for re-election, but was accused of contravening the city's blasphemy laws after he quoted a verse from the Quran during one of his speeches. Some Muslims took offence at his speech and launched two massive protests in November and December 2016. The Muslim leaders interviewed for this chapter were concerned that their leaders in Central MUI were not treated with sufficient respect. In the end, Ahok lost the election.

Batam Muslims dispel the simplistic view of analysts and observers who conclude that traditionalist Muslims are moderates, while Wahhabi-Salafists are extreme. In reality, one has to closely examine the issues on which they are extreme or moderate. In addition, it is important to note that while Batam influences Singapore, there are also dynamics that operate in the opposite direction.

Notes

1. This chapter was first published as *The Traditionalist Response to Wahhabi-Salafism in Batam*, Trends in Southeast Asia, no. 7/2017 (Singapore: ISEAS – Yusof Ishak Institute, 2017).
2. SIJORI is an acronym which stands for Singapore, Johor, and Riau. See Hutchinson and Chong (2016).
3. This chapter does not make the claim that traditionalists equates to moderation or progressivism. Recent race and religious in tensions in Jakarta spearheaded by traditionalists Habib Rizieq Shihab demonstrates that traditionalists, or someone who practices traditional rituals, can also be exclusivist.
4. Increasingly, traditionalists have become open to independent reasoning. Today, the progressives in NU are creative and innovative in coming up with religious rulings, applying local and modern context to their reading of classical texts.
5. For more on this episode, see Fealy (2007).
6. Interview with Khairuddin Nasution, Head of LPPOM-MUI, Batam, 15 February 2017.
7. Olle studied the MUI chapter in East Java and pointed out the impactful nature of the fatwas to the extent of promoted violence on "heretics". Similarly, Nur Ichwan conducted a study of the MUI chapter in Banten, and concluded the organization's role in promoting violence (Olle 2009; Moch Nur 2012).
8. Interview with Kyai Usman Ahmad, Batam, 15 February 2017.
9. LPPOM-Batam's office is located on the same floor as the MUI Batam. LPPOM-MUI Batam feels that existing regulations should be strengthened in order to improve the capability of the organization to conduct spot checks on any abuses of halal certificates. See also *Antara Kepri*, "Pengawasan Produk Halal di Kepri Masih Lemah", 30 September 2015.
10. Badan Kesatuan Bangsa, Politik dan Perlindungan Masyarakat is a body which oversees all societal organizations in the city, and addresses issues seen as divisive. See Badan Kesatuan Bangsa politik dan Perlindungan Masyarakat Kota Batam (n.d.).
11. Interview with Hairul Saleh, Chairman of Nahdlatul Ulama, Batam, 15 February 2017.
12. See Bareng (2016).
13. Interview with Kyai Usman Ahmad, 15 February 2017.
14. Interview with Hairul Saleh, 15 February 2017.

References

Antarakepri. 2015. "Pengawasan Produk Halal di Kepri Masih Lemah". 30 September 2015.
Arlina, A. 2016a. "IT Guy Who Plotted Terror from Batam". *Straits Times*, 14 August 2016.
———. 2016b. "ISA arrests: Batam Radio Station Draws Strong Opposition for Extreme Leanings". *Straits Times*, 20 August 2016.

Badan Kesatuan Bangsa Politik dan Perlindungan Masyarakat Kota Batam. N.d. "Struktur Organisasi". https://arsipskpd.batam.go.id/batamkota/skpd.batamkota.go.id/kesbang/profil/struktur-organisasi/ (accessed 13 April 2017).

Bareng, N. 2016. "Debat Wahabi vs Aswaja di Batam". YouTube, 18 November 2016. https://www.youtube.com/watch?v=DSkouYNtpOU (accessed 29 May 2017).

Batam Guide. N.d. Batam Indonesia Free Zone Authority. PB Batam, http://www.bpbatam.go.id/eng/batamGuide/customs.jsp (accessed 20 October 2016).

Batam Pos. 2016. "3000 Umat Islam Bersholawat di Peringatan Maulid Nabi Muhammad". 12 December 2016.

Berita Harian. 2017. "Mas Selamat Pernah Ikut Kelas Rasul Dahri di Johor Sebelum Sertai JI". 10 January 2017.

DeLong-Bas, N.J. 2004. Wahhabi Islam: From Revival and reform to Global Jihad. New York: Oxford University Press.

Effendy, A. 2014. Peta Dakwah Kota Batam. Batam: Majelis Ulama Indonesia Kota Batam.

Firdaus, H. 2016. "Membangun KEPRI Lewat Pendekatan Historis". Opini 1, no. 2.

Fealy, G. 2007. "The Political Contingency of Reform-mindedness in Indonesia's Nahdlatul Ulama: Interest Politics and the Khittah". In Islamic Legitimacy in a Plural Asia, edited by A. Reid and M. Gilesenan, pp. 154–66. London: Routledge.

Haeril, H. and Fadli. 2016. "Salafi Movement Gains Ground in Public Sphere". Jakarta Post, 2 September 2016. http://www.thejakartapost.com/news/2016/09/02/salafi-movement-gains-ground-in-public-sphere.html (accessed 18 April 2017).

Hutchinson, F. and T. Chong, eds. 2016. The SIJORI Cross-Border Region: Transnational Politics, Economics, and Culture. Singapore: ISEAS – Yusof Ishak Institute.

Jamaah Al Khidmah Batam. N.d. https://alkhidmah-batam.blogspot.sg/search/label/Haul%20Akbar%20Batam (accessed 5 April 2017).

Jannatun, N. 2013. "Pemkot Batam gesa sertifikasi halal restoran". Antara, 17 October 2013.

Jawa Pos. 2016. "MUI: Kami Kecolongan, Ini Kelemaham Kami". 15 January 2016.

Larno. 2013. "Pesantren Cetak Generasi Intelektual dan Spiritual". Antara, 20 July 2013.

Lee, A. 2016. "Extremist Ideology a Staple Item on Batam's Radio Hang". Today, 19 August 2016.

Leila, A. 2011. A Quiet Revolution: The Veil's Resurgence, from the Middle East to America. New Haven & London: Yale University Press.

Moch Nur, I. 2012. "The Local Politics of Orthodoxy: The Majelis Ulama Indonesia in the Post-New Order Banten". Journal of Indonesian Islam 6, no. 1: 166–94.

Norshahril Saat. 2016. "Theologians 'Moralising' Indonesia?". Asian Journal of Social Science 44, nos. 4–5: 546–70.

———. 2017. Johor Remains The Bastion of Kaum Tua. Trends in Southeast Asia, no. 1/2017. Singapore: ISEAS – Yusof Ishak Institute.

Olle, J. 2009. "The Majelis Ulama Indonesia Versus 'Heresy': The Resurgence of Authoritarian Islam". In State of Authority: The State in Society in Indonesia, edited by G. van Klinken and J. Barker, pp. 95–116. Ithaca: Cornell Southeast Asian Program Publications.

Soezean, M. 2016. "Radio Hang in Batam Denies Airing Extremist Sermons as Claimed by MHA". The Online Citizen, 23 August 2016. https://www.theonlinecitizen.com/2016/08/23/radio-hang-in-batam-denies-airing-extremist-sermons-as-claimed-by-mha/ (accessed 11 April 2017).

Tribun Batam. 2014. "Besok Acara Batam Berselawat Bersama Habib Syech bin Abdul Qodir Assegaf". 19 December 2014.

Varagur, K. 2017. "Salafi Movement Grows on Indonesia's Batam Island". 14 March 2017. http://
www.voanews.com/a/salafi-movement-grows-on-indonesias-batam-island/3764858.html
(accessed 18 April 2017).

Wahyudi, S. 2017. "Batam Cell Leader 'Helped' 2 Uighurs Flee from Malaysia". *Straits Times*,
10 April 2017.

Wee, V. 2016. "The Significance of Riau in SIJORI". In *The SIJORI Cross-Border Region:
Transnational Politics, Economics, and Culture*, edited by F. Hutchinson and T. Chong,
pp. 241–66. Singapore: ISEAS – Yusof Ishak Institute.

13

RECONCILING ECONOMIC AND ENVIRONMENTAL IMPERATIVES IN BATAM[1]

Lee Poh Onn[2]

INTRODUCTION

Batam's economic growth has been nothing short of spectacular. In the 1990s, it experienced an investment boom fuelled by investments from Singapore. This lasted for two decades and transformed the economy and landscape of what was an outpost into a place with a major industrial city of over 1 million inhabitants.

This impressive pace of development has often been accompanied by a marked degradation of the natural environment. Mangrove areas have rapidly disappeared, floods have occurred around the city because of erosion caused by land clearing; illegal squatter settlements have intruded into protected forests, and toxic substances from the offshore cleaning of ships have affected the quality of Batam's coastal waters.

But all is not lost. Economic and environmental imperatives can be reconciled if Batam's development trajectory takes into account the impact of economic growth on the environment. Sustainable development is not impossible (Hezri and Dovers 2012, p. 277).

Negative environmental impacts have to be controlled by regulations and by proper enforcement. The institutional framework (regulations and property rights) plays a central role to ensure that negative environmental impacts are accounted for and minimized. Problems generally arise from either an absence of regulations or property rights to regulate the environment or from the absence or lack of enforcement by the relevant authorities.

The Riau Islands Province (PRI) is made up of five rural regencies (*kabupaten*) and two cities or urban municipalities (*kota*). Batam and Tanjungpinang are the two cities within PRI, while Bintan, Karimun, Lingga, Anambas and Natuna form the five regencies (Amri 2016, p. 155). Batam Island's land area totals 415 km^2 (41,500 hectares).

This chapter will examine the various manifestations and causes of environmental degradation against the backdrop of economic transformation, population growth and enforcement (or lack thereof). It also provides a comprehensive update where possible of the present state of environmental affairs in the municipality, and the challenges involved in maintaining the carrying capacity of the environment to cope with development.

Following a discussion of the methodology used in this study, the next section will examine the impact of government policies on economic transformation, and of migration on population growth. Regulations and enforcement measures are then discussed in general, followed by an examination of Batam's environmental management challenges across many fronts. These include industrial pollution (electronics industry); shipyards and pollution; cut and fill and land reclamation; general wastes; water pollution in reservoirs; wastewater and sewage treatment; mangroves and conservation; and air pollution emissions.

METHODOLOGY

The methodology for this study includes site visits, gathering of key informant materials from four interviews, and extracting of information from published primary and secondary sources.

Two site visits were conducted in March 2017 and April 2017 primarily to observe and update environmental conditions existing throughout the municipality. This also involved trips to various parts of the island including the fringes of forest areas and reservoirs, and to industrial sites. The first site visit also included discussion with officials at Badan Pengusahaan Batam (BP Batam) to understand the present state of economic development and existing challenges faced by development planners.[3] The second visit included an informal interview with an academic/activist with deep knowledge of environmental issues in Batam, including locations where the environmental impact of projects and urbanization processes are visible.

Besides the two site visits, this study involved a selection of key informants in November 2016, including: an academic in the law faculty, two environmental NGOs, and an official from the Government of Indonesia's Environmental Impact Agency (Badan Pengendalian Dampak Lingkungan, or BAPEDAL). The interviewing was conducted by a fellow Riau resident to ensure that the respondents felt at ease answering the set of prepared interview questions. These in-depth interviews focused on: identifying major environmental challenges facing Batam; the existence or non-existence of environmental regulations to manage pollution; investigating reasons behind weak enforcement; identifying the various manifestations of environmental degradation and its impacts on communities; and challenges faced by those in charge of managing the environment and natural resources.

Relevant information found in public policy documents, statistical sources, online resources, and also numerous secondary published sources, and newspaper articles were also examined.

STATE POLICIES, ECONOMIC TRANSFORMATION, AND POPULATION GROWTH

State Policies and Economic Transformation

Batam's rapid economic growth can be traced back to 1971 when the central government designated it as an industrial zone by presidential decree (Farole 2013). The Batam Industrial Development Authority (BIDA) was established that same year to facilitate the island's industrial development. Batam was thereafter designated by Pertamina, the state-owned oil and natural gas corporation based in Jakarta, as a logistics and operational base for the oil and gas industry (Sari 1998, p. 8).[4]

Policy planners had not anticipated for Batam to achieve rapid transformation in such a short period of time, as has happened. Initially, Batam was set up with the intention to compete with Singapore, with the period 1971–75 being documented as the preparation phase during which major infrastructure and institutions in the urban municipality were established. Ibnu Sutowo was the chief of BIDA during this period (Amri 2016, p. 160).

In 1976, Batam was transformed by J.B. Sumarlin, Sutowo's successor, from being Pertamina's gas and oil outpost into an export-oriented industrial zone with manufacturing as its mainstay (Amri 2016, p. 160). This change paled somewhat when compared to the next period of transformation, which was led by Dr B.J. Habibie in 1978.

Under Habibie, Batam was not seen as a competitor of Singapore but as a complementary location to "capture the spillover effects of Singapore's growth" (Amri 2016, p. 161). In a presidential decree issued in 1978, Batam was declared a "bonded zone" exempted from a range of taxes (value added tax, luxury tax, and import taxes) and was reoriented as a duty-free zone to take advantage of Singapore's development.

Habibie also envisioned Batam as "a site for environmentally-friendly industries" (Sari 1998, p. 13). A Negative Industries List was drawn up then to ensure that polluting industries would not be allowed to set up shop in Batam; however, the list did not provide clear definitions or standards of what constituted a polluting industry (Sari 1998, pp. 12–13).

The late 1980s and early 1990s marked the turning point when Singapore started playing a more active role and began investing in Batam. In December 1989, the then First Deputy Prime Minister of Singapore, Mr Goh Chok Tong, mooted the concept of the "Growth Triangle", involving Singapore, Johor in Malaysia, and

Riau in Indonesia (Wong and Ng 2009, p. 3). Investments from Singapore started flowing in, especially after the Riau Agreement was signed on 28 August 1990 between Singapore and Indonesia (Sari 1998, p. 5), which lifted restrictions on foreign ownership. The rapid industrialization of Batam therefore "began in earnest with the involvement of Singapore government-linked companies" (Phelps 2004, p. 211) and the establishment of the Batamindo industrial estate in 1990.

By 1990, the scope and geographical coverage was extended beyond Batam to include neighbouring islands where a Bonded Zone was now declared. After Soeharto stepped down in 1998, Indonesia's centralized structure was replaced by a policy of local autonomy and decentralization, where much of the power was devolved straight to the local government (cities and regencies).

The new laws that declared Batam an autonomous city did not involve BIDA initially. These laws later identified the city government as the main authority in Batam but with it involving BIDA in its activities after some "calls were made by some congress members" (Amri 2016, p. 164). Functional and jurisdictional overlaps between both authorities have created problems and confusion. This has impacted, for example, land use rights and also the enforcement of regulations. At present, this overlap has "complicated the local regulatory environment for firms and dampened consumer confidence" (Hutchinson 2017, p. 32). It has also resulted in inertia and unclear lines of authority and action.

In July 2005, the status of the Batam Industrial Bonded Zone together with Bintan Industrial Estate and Karimun Industrial Cooperation Zone were upgraded to "Bonded Zone Plus". In 2007, Batam was granted Free Trade Zone (FTZ) status while Bintan and Karimun were granted enclave status (Farole 2013, p. 219). In 2017, the central government began planning to rescind the status of Batam as an FTZ and turn the municipality into a Special Economic Zone (SEZ) (Negara and Hutchinson 2017). It remains to be seen what the exact implications of this move will be on Batam's development prospects.

Population Growth through Migration

Batam enjoyed impressive double-digit economic growth rates in the 1990s up till the 1998 financial crisis. In recent years, growth has only averaged just above 6 per cent (see Table 13.1).

However, the municipality remains attractive, and the movement of labour to the island has led to far-reaching demographic and environmental changes (Hutchinson 2017, p. 18). Migrant labourers have come from other areas in Indonesia such as West Sumatra, North Sumatra, and Flores Island in East Nusa Tenggara (Amri 2016, p. 168). Even in recent years, Batam has been the fastest-growing municipality in Indonesia, with its population increasing at 11 per cent per year (Asian Development Bank 2016, p. 6).

In just forty-five years, Batam's population grew from 6,000 people in 1971 to 1.05 million in 2016 (Batam Indonesia Free Zone Authority 2017, p. 39),[5] representing a 200-fold increase (5.7 times per year). Batam's population is expected to increase

TABLE 13.1
Batam Economic and Population Indicators, 2012–16

	Remarks	2012	2013	2014	2015	2016
Gross Domestic Regional Product (Current Price)	Trillion Rupiah	83.75	99.66	107.21	121.13	121.13
Economic Growth	Per cent	7.40	7.18	7.20	6.75	6.75
Population	People	1,235,651	1,135,412	1,030,528	1,037,187	1,055,040
Water	Litre/second	2,720.53	2,903.25	2,771.90	3,147.16	3,132.50

Source: BIFZA (2016).

further to 2.5 million by 2025 (Asian Development Bank 2016, p. 11). As the ensuing discussion will show, population increase has exerted great pressure on the infrastructure and housing and also on the city's environment and its natural resources.

ENVIRONMENTAL REGULATIONS AND ENFORCEMENT

In Indonesia, BAPEDAL, established by a presidential decree in 1990, is responsible for implementing environmental pollution control measures as well as monitoring the environment and enforcing laws and regulations formulated by the Ministry of Environment. BAPEDAL consists of the Department of Water and Marine Pollution Control, the Department of Air Pollution Control, and the Department of Hazardous and Toxic Wastes Management. There is also the Department of EIA Implementation, which promotes the implementation of environmental impact assessments (EIAs).

Decentralization and Environmental Management

In 1999, the Indonesian government embarked on a decentralization endeavour that affected almost every policy sector including the environment. A considerable amount of autonomy was granted to districts and municipalities (Niessen 2006, p. 143). In 2002, BAPEDAL's responsibilities and powers were transferred to regional governments. Districts and municipality authorities known as local BAPEDAL or BAPEDALDA (in Batam, it was sometimes referred to as the Batam BAPEDAL) are now directly in charge of enforcement. The Batam section of BAPEDAL directly manages and enforces environmental regulations formulated by the Ministry of Environment. Decentralization was expected to give local governments more empowerment and autonomy to manage environmental resources. Local governments are also supposed to be armed with a better understanding of the areas that they come into contact with. Be that as it may, environmental degradation has however continued to recur.

Perhaps the limited administrative, technical and legal capacity of local governments on environmental issues hampered management. Not only was there a lack of legal and technical expertise, but most district and municipal governments used their expanded autonomy to "increase their regional incomes, with negative consequences for the environment within their territories" (Niessen 2006, p. 166). Vested interests were at play. Provincial and regency leaders "whose status and prestige have been elevated by the decentralization movement" have been increasingly observed to engage in rent-seeking behaviour.[6]

A higher degree of local autonomy combined with direct local elections has "shaped the attitude of most local governments to become more revenue oriented" (Widianarko 2009, p. 4). This focus towards local revenue generation resulted in and continues to result in exploitation of natural resources, pollution, and degradation of ecosystems because each local/municipal government considered the generating of income as a top priority (Widianarko 2009). It is therefore not surprising to observe that environmental degradation continued unabated post-decentralization in Indonesia and in Batam itself.

Environmental Regulations

Regulations have existed for a myriad of environmental issues ranging from sanitation to air, water and marine pollution; including the requirement of Environmental Impact Assessments (EIAs) for construction activities. Coverage in terms of regulations has been generally comprehensive. However, enforcement is absent or inadequate in most instances as the ensuing sections will show.

Indonesia's first environmental legislation involved the formulation of Law No. 4 in 1982 on Environmental Management. This was pushed by Dr Emil Salim, the then State Minister for Population and the Environment, who was very influential in shaping environmental policies, and who was a member of the so-called "Berkeley Mafia",[7] and a close aide to President Soeharto. Government Regulation No. 29 in 1986 on Environmental Impact Assessments supplemented this overarching environmental law. The latter required all new industrial plants to undertake EIAs (Analisis Mengenai Dampak Lingkungan, or AMDAL) (Sari 1998, p. 17). The committee of each EIA is to include NGOs (who are on the ground and can monitor infringements), and the affected communities. As Sari pointed out, although AMDAL was strong as a legislation, it was hardly enforced in practice (Sari 1998, p. 18).

Non-enforcement in the 1990s was particularly severe in Batam. Only a handful of companies in Batam actually conducted a full AMDAL process; "the vast majority conducted none" (Sari 1998). Regulations relating to air pollution have existed since 1999, and there have also been regulations regarding the management of hazardous wastes since 1999 and which were revised in 2008. In 2009, Law No. 32 in 2009 on the Protection of the Environment and Management was implemented, covering a range of issues including sustainable development, conservation, protecting and regulating environmental effects through EIAs, the management and disposal of wastes (including toxic waste substances), water quality standards, protection of the marine environment, and climate change, among other concerns.

The lack of supervision however has made it difficult to control or limit the extent of environmental degradation. Reportedly, there are only about eighteen officers on the entire Batam Island who have been tasked with supervisory/enforcement duties for all environmental matters.[8] Of these, fourteen are inspectors (enforcement officers) and four are investigators. This would amount to one officer to 2,305 hectares of land. This ratio is however much better than in other instances in Indonesia, where one forester is allocated for every 100,000 to 300,000 hectares of forests (Poffenberger 1998, p. 42).

BATAM'S ENVIRONMENTAL MANAGEMENT RECORD

Batam's economic structure is dominated by manufacturing (56.3 per cent); construction (19.1 per cent); wholesale and retail (cars and motorcycle) (5.9 per cent); transportation and stowage (3.3 per cent); financial services and insurance (3.6 per cent); provision of accommodation, food and beverages (2.2 per cent); and information and communication (2.1 per cent). Where manufacturing is concerned, the electrical and electronic industry, and shipyards easily pose threats to the environment if not carefully managed, notably through the polluting of surrounding water areas and the atmosphere. A direct consequence is the expansion of construction activities which affects surrounding soils and forested areas. Rapid population growth has a huge impact on water usage and leads to an urgent need for proper management of water disposal and sewage. The following sections will cover all of these aspects, and a useful starting point is to discuss a study undertaken in 2000 on how managers perceived Batam's environment and environmental scorecard.

Environmental Scorecard in 2000

In the early 2000s, after development had already taken off, Batam's natural environment scorecard was perceived to be better relative to Indonesia as a whole (Broadfoot 2003). A survey was conducted at that time with three groups of business people to collect their views on the environment. These were: managers residing in Singapore and Hong Kong with first-hand experience dealing with their Batam operations; managers with foreign direct investments residing on the island; and managers based in Jakarta who were familiar with Batam.

Batam's natural environment was ranked better than Indonesia's in general: the overall grade was 5.27 compared to 9.12 for Indonesia (0 being the best grade and 10 the worst). The quality of the government's environmental protection/enhancement policies was graded 5.61 compared to 9.41 for Jakarta (Broadfoot 2003, section 3.8) (Table 13.2).

Batam's grades, though considerably better than most other countries (except for Singapore's which had a better overall grade of 2.32), still warranted attention. Managers complained about the water quality in particular, as well as its cost. What

TABLE 13.2
Quality of Natural Environment, Early 2000

Variable in Batam Survey	Batam	Variable in Regionwide Survey	CH	India	INDO	MA	PH	SI	TH	VN
Quality of the government's environmental protection/ enhancement policies	5.61	Quality of the government's environmental protection/ enhancement policies	7.67	8.08	9.42	5.71	8.17	3.3	7.56	6.14
Air quality	5.01	Air quality	8.67	8.7	9	4.86	8.92	2	8.22	7.29
Water quality	4.96	Water quality	8.33	8.18	9	5.14	7	1.4	6.22	7.71
Noise pollution	4.84	Noise pollution	7.67	8.37	8.67	3.86	7.33	2.6	7.89	7.71
Traffic congestion	5.92	Traffic congestion	7.33	8.83	9.5	3.86	8.92	2.3	7.67	6
Average Grade	5.27	Average Grade	7.93	8.43	9.12	4.69	8.07	2.32	7.51	6.97

Notes: Grades range from 0 to 10, with 0 being the best grade possible and 10 the worst.
(CH=China, INDO=Indonesia, MA=Malaysia, PH=Philippines, SI=Singapore, TH=Thailand, VN=Vietnam)
Source: Broadfoot (2003).

also contributed to degradation in the quality of the environment was the rapid influx of new immigrants, which affected Batam's existing housing infrastructure and utilities. Such facilities had not developed fast enough to deal with the growing population. These issues have more or less persisted to this day.

Industrial Pollution Management (Electronics Industry)

The electronics industry was surprisingly perceived as "clean" by state planners even when it was known that it produced many toxic and hazardous substances. Batam was not well equipped for disposing of such substances up till the late 1990s. In 1996, BIDA facilitated the formation of Bina Lingkungan Hidup Batam (BILIK), a "semi-formal roundtable in Batam for the industrial community to learn about environmental regulation[s] in Batam" (Sari 1998, p. 15). This body was established as an information clearing house and a mediator for environmental conflicts.

But were regulations enforced? Anecdotal evidence suggests that enforcement did take place, but only after an official had first filed a complaint with BILIK. This was a reported incident of accumulated municipal wastes at the Bukit Samyong landfill, which was emitting smoke and noxious fumes and wastes were being burned at the landfill without proper toxic and hazardous waste treatment. Facilities that could handle that function were unavailable in the 1990s. The health hazard of the smoke also severely affected workers in neighbouring factories. Bukit Samyong Landfill is located in the Bukit Ampar Industrial Zone in Kecamatan Batamkota (see Figure 13.1). In this instance, the overlap in responsibilities between BIDA and the local government hindered immediate action. Eventually, the official filed a complaint to BIDA and the issue was raised there. BILIK members then put pressure on BIDA to take action. Consequently, BIDA accelerated its plan to build a permanent waste management facility at Telaga Punggur, a remote area southeast of Batam (Sari 1998, p. 16).

Electronics industries were sometimes located in close proximity to reservoirs and toxic substances would seep into and contaminate drinking water. There was also no toxic and hazardous waste management system back then in Batamindo Industrial Park, where most of the electronic industries are located. These wastes were either dumped into ordinary municipal waste facilities or piled up in proximity to these industries. When it rained, carcinogenic substances were washed into neighbouring reservoirs.

It was only in 1998 that regulations prohibiting toxic wastes were passed. The illegal disposal of toxic wastes has been deemed a criminal activity since 2008 carrying a maximum penalty of IDR5 billion for an infringement against Law No. 18 in 2008 on Waste Management (Article 40).

Toxic industrial wastes are managed and collected by a private entity (PT Prasadha Pamunah Limbah Indonesia) and transported to Cileungsi in the district of Bogor in West Java Province for treatment (Asian Development Bank 2016, p. 11). It has been stipulated that industries should not be built in zones allocated for housing; however, the issue is with industrial sites that border on housing zones and has

FIGURE 13.1
Districts, Shipyards and Industrial Areas in Batam

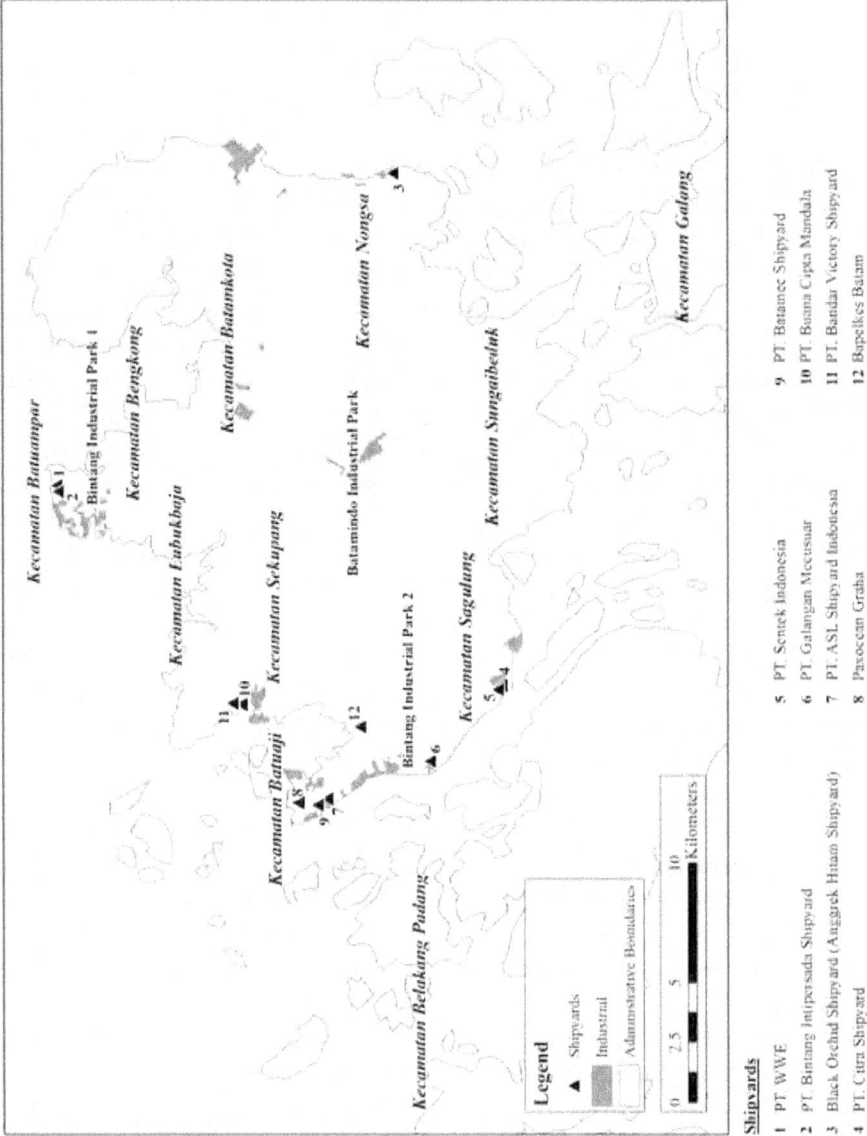

Shipyards

1 PT WWE
2 PT Bintang Intipersada Shipyard
3 Black Orchid Shipyard (Anggrek Hitam Shipyard)
4 PT Citra Shipyard

5 PT Semek Indonesia
6 PT Galangan Mecussar
7 PT ASL Shipyard and Indonesia
8 Paroccean Graha

9 PT Batamec Shipyard
10 PT Buana Cipta Mandala
11 PT Bandar Victory Shipyard
12 Bapelkes Batam

Source: Map provided by ISEAS – Yusof Ishak Institute. © 2017 ISEAS – Yusof Ishak Institute.

spillover impact on residential areas. In terms of zoning, the government has yet to make requirements with regards to the siting of pollutive industries. EIAs are however required for the setting up of manufacturing industries.[9] However, as noted earlier, only a few companies actually conduct a full EIA.

Interviews conducted reveal that enforcement is still spotty; the lack of staffing and funding constrains effective enforcement.[10] As the BAPEDAL respondent has indicated, whenever superiors choose to be "lenient", subordinates find it difficult to enforce regulations. However, criminal charges have been laid for serious offences, such as the indiscriminate dumping of toxic wastes.

With the electronics industry on the decline in recent years (van Grunsven and Hutchinson 2017), it may appear that pollution levels should be falling. However, measures must still be in place to ensure that regulations are enforced and that wastes are disposed of carefully. In 2016, there were four such cases that came to light.[11] The good news is that that same year, 19.7 hectares of land were allocated for the treatment of industrial toxic and hazardous wastes (Batam Indonesia Free Zone Authority 2017, p. 30).

Shipyards and Pollution

Presently, of the 198 shipyards in Indonesia, 110 are located in the Batam FTZ (*Jakarta Post*, 12 November 2014). An EIA is needed before a shipyard can be constructed.[12] The approval comes from BAPEDAL. Figure 13.1 shows the location of the various shipyards in Batam. They are concentrated in Tanjung Uncang (Nanindah, Batamec, ASL), Kabil (Anggrek Hitam, Labroy), Sekupang (Bandar Victory, Cahaya Samudera), Batu Ampar (McDermott, Bintang Intipersada), and Sagulung (Sentek, Citra, Patria Maritim) (Negara 2017, p. 4). Relocated shipyard companies from Singapore have in recent years been blamed for negative impacts on the marine environment and public health (*Jakarta Post*, 15 March 2012). Indeed, one of the biggest sources of pollution are shipyards, as confirmed in the interview with the BAPEDAL official.[13]

Ships have also been disposing toxic wastes generated from offshore ship cleaning (*AntaraNews.Com*, 26 December 2012). These wastes are not easily soluble and have eventually reached the northern coasts causing pollution and damaging the Putri Island mangrove ecosystem.[14] Not only were the mangroves destroyed, the floating seaweed and beaches around the island were also tainted by these wastes. It was reported that around 365,000 tonnes of waste were disposed off the Riau Islands in 2010, calculated on the assumption that 10,000 ships pass by these islands and dispose of about 10 kg per ship per year.

As an interviewed member of an environmental NGO stated, pollution from the shipyards is as yet not very evident as its levels are still under the threshold, and is not always easily visible. However, sandblasting (with silica) from the shipbuilding industry has visibly caused pollution. Rust from sandblasting has also been disposed in the sea. Rust is a toxic and hazardous waste, classified as B3 waste and potentially dangerous to marine life. A member of another environmental NGO that was interviewed commented that seafood from Tanjung Uncang should be avoided because of the high arsenic content found in the water, caused by sandblasting.[16] The media has reported that the seas around Batam have indeed been polluted with arsenic.[17] Marine pollution is most evident in Batu Ampar, Tanjung Uncang, Tanjung Sekupang and Sagulung where shipyards are located.[18] Pollution from shipyards has also affected fishing activities.[19] It has been difficult to fully enforce environmental regulations in relation to shipyards because of a lack of personnel and funding. Only the bigger operators are supervised on a case-by-case basis by BAPEDAL.[20] Again, although the penalties are severe, regulations are not widely enforced.[21] About twenty sanctions are given out for breaches in quality standards or breaches concerning permits every year.[22] The NGO respondent suggests that funding be provided to increase the size of BAPEDAL's enforcement.[23]

Land Clearance, Construction, Cut and Fill, and Land Reclamation

Construction in Batam has had an extensive impact on soil erosion, after forested areas are cleared. In this instance, regulations have skewed behaviour towards activities that are environmentally destructive and generally unproductive. In Batam, land is leased from the government for an initial thirty-year term, subsequently extendable to fifty and eighty years. BIDA stipulates that such leased lands have to be developed immediately. This was to discourage the acquisition of land for speculation. However, this rule was not accompanied by clear stipulations, which has allowed for transgressions to occur. In order to demonstrate that efforts are being made to develop the land, lessees sometimes simply clear the land, and keep it cleared upon receipt of the concession with no further follow-up activity (Sari 1998, p. 13).

To measure the magnitude of this problem, an audit of lease arrangements was conducted to free up unused land including an estimated 7,000 hectares that had been allocated but had reportedly not been built upon (Hutchinson 2017, p. 31). All in all, 300 cases of unused land were uncovered. Such cleared lands were prone to soil erosion, and cause deterioration of soil fertility, sedimentation of coastal waters and in reservoirs. Also, such eroded soils made areas "almost impossible to regreen" because of its loose texture (Sari 1998, p. 13). This has not only affected soils but caused sedimentation which destroys many coral reefs, fish habitats, and mangrove areas. The destruction of mangrove areas has been particularly evident to this author during his two field trips to Batam. Mangroves were destroyed by construction works, and some mangrove areas have now been completely wiped out.[24]

Rapid population growth leads immediately to a hugely increased need for housing. If this need for housing was met early, environmental impacts may have been better regulated. However, housing needs are met merely through the building of squatter settlements known as *rumah liar* or *ruli* (Amri 2016, p. 169). Based on 2000 values, building a *ruli* costs IDR3 million in Batam, compared to IDR185 million for constructing a proper house in the city and IDR80 million in the suburbs. There were 50,000 *ruli* in Batam in 2000 spread across sixty areas (Amri 2016).

In January 2017, it was reported that the municipal government had begun compiling a record of illegal squatter housing in Batam. This represented a first step for understanding the extent of the problem and will hopefully lead to the construction of formal housing for these squatters (*Tribun Batam*, 10 January 2017). To date, 147 households in Lubok Baja alone are classified as squatters.[25] Squatters have not only destroyed and decreased protected forests and Batam's water catchment areas, they have also created problems for investors who have leased land from BIDA. These investors have to pay financial compensation to these illegal settlers if they wish to "reclaim" the leased land for investment purposes. In such instances, as the division of authority between BIDA and the municipal government is unclear, each side has had to be "nudged" to take action against squatters, and this has caused delays to the investment process (Amri 2016, p. 170).

Unlawful construction has also placed strains on water supplies. Batam does not have many hills and natural water springs to generate supplies. Areas that serve as water catchments for reservoirs are also encroached upon by squatter constructions. The Batam land use plan classifies about 60 per cent of its 415 km² land area as water catchment areas and protected forests, while the remaining 40 per cent is zoned for development purposes. Presently, perhaps just over 33 per cent of land in Batam is covered in forest.[26] Another more optimistic estimate places forest coverage at about 50 per cent.[27] In 2000 alone, squatters illegally damaged about 20.57 km² of protected forests, and the government had to allocate IDR3 billion in 2001 to replant trees in these areas (Amri 2016, p. 170).

Cut and fill is a widespread activity that occurs in Batam (*BatamNews*, 5 December 2016). Land is cut not only for shipyard building but also for real estate projects like housing and the construction of hotels or for new streets. Huge areas of lands have been reclaimed along the coastlines of Batam for such developments. This has had "enormous impact on the environment and has influenced the landscapes appearance enormously. When driving around the island, you will see half erased hills all over the place" (Topalovic et.al. 2012, p. 52). This phenomenon was also clearly visible on a recent field trip made by this author in 2017.[28]

Batam's land belongs to BIDA, which decides where soil can be removed (or cut) from, and the investor is thereafter responsible for the filling process. BIDA also decides on spatial planning, where the best sites are reserved for industrial purposes while the municipal government is left with commercially less attractive and with areas and slopes that are harder to develop (Asian Development Bank 2016, p. 7).

The overlap in responsibilities between BIDA and the municipal government of Batam creates confusion for potential investors. It happens that investors who have purchased land from BIDA are subsequently informed by the municipal government that the land they just purchased is actually part of a forestry reserve. Such disputes have affected up to 22,000 land titles in Batam (Hutchinson 2017, p. 17). Such discrepancies show that a greater level of coordination will need to take place.

In 2004, the local government of Batam approved a reclamation project in Bengkong District for the development of an integrated area of housing, public facilities, and services (Priyandes and Majid 2009, p. 2).[29] Reclamation activities along the coast of subdistricts Bengkong Laut, Sadai and Tanjung Buntung triggered slope deformation, river sedimentation, and soil erosion, and destroyed mangroves while reducing the fishery caught (Priyandes and Majid 2009, p. 4). The size of the mangrove forest in these subdistricts dwindled from 24,000 m^2 to 2,500 m^2 (Priyandes and Majid 2009). About 90 per cent of the mangrove disappeared. The loss of mangroves affected the communities relying on them for their day-to-day living. Mangrove wood is used as charcoal, firewood, building material and also for traditional medicine (Priyandes and Majid 2009, p. 6). Flooding frequencies have also increased. Coral reefs which play an important role as spawning, feeding, and nursery ground for coastal organisms including fish were also badly affected.

In this case, development plans had not seriously considered conserving the mangroves in this area. The coastal areas, which had 23.24 per cent of reef coverage saw all the reefs eradicated. Fish catch was reportedly reduced by 55 per cent after reclamation. The catch of mullet fish (*belanak*), a species that thrives in mangrove areas, was reduced by 70 per cent.

Incomes for the fishers were also reduced. Previously, a fisher's earnings ranged from IDR2 million to IDR2.5 million. Post reclamation, this stood at between IDR1 million to IDR1.5 million per month. Fishers who were able to catch 15 kg of seafood before the reclamation were only able to catch 5 kg after the reclamation. Some have had to diversify their income sources by working as labourers, and others as small-time traders (Priyandes and Majid 2009, p. 10). Developers obtained their backfill materials from the surrounding hills (districts of Bengkong and Batu Ampar), and it was reported that there was severe erosion and sedimentation as well as an increase in flooding, around the Bengkong District (Priyandes and Majid 2009, p. 7). Elsewhere, sea water reportedly turned brownish red after reclamation.[30]

In December 2016, "cut and fill" activities were stopped by Batam City Government and considered a cause of flooding. In most cases, permission was not obtained in the first place. Separately, in March 2017, cut and fill was again causing flooding in Batam City and again, developers were not following regulations fully (*Tribun Batam*, 21 March 2017). In addition, garbage in the drainage system was compounding the flooding problem. Cut and fill was also increasing sedimentation.

Land reclamation for ports comes under BP Batam, and BAPEDAL enforces the law to the extent it can.[31] However, enforcement activities are sometimes frustrated by companies using their "backing"—political or otherwise—to circumvent regulations.

The impact of the growing tourism sector in Batam on the environment needs to be carefully watched in the years to come. Batam is still viewed as an industrial/ business zone rather than a tourist destination, though pockets of tourist activities exist. It is also difficult to isolate the impact of tourism on the environment due to a dearth of information. Also, the construction of hotels is often lumped under general construction activities. Construction has indeed seen reasonably healthy growth rates averaging 7.55 per cent (estimated) over the period 2010–14 (*Batam Economic Outlook 2011*, p. 37).

There is however increasing recognition of the tourism potential in Batam, and companies continue to invest and construct apartments and hotels. Sinarmas Land, for example, is involved in a S$400 million five-year project consisting of a high-end residential development with premium serviced apartments, commercial and retail outlets, and a wide range of hotels and condotels in Nuvasa Bay in Nongsa, Batam (*Business Times*, 15 December 2015). For Bintan, the potential of the tourism sector is great, and the eco-tourism and spa sector has been burgeoning in the past decade.

General Waste

Currently, general wastes are disposed of in a controlled and managed landfill site of about 40 hectares in Telaga Punggur by the City Sanitation Department (Asian Development Bank 2016, p. 10). About 12 hectares have already been utilized.[32] Industries have to deposit their wastes in a special site (Kabil) owned by BIDA and managed by a private operator.

It is estimated that within five years, there will be no landfill space left for Batam City to dump its wastes. Currently, the municipal sanitation agency collects about 750 tonnes of household waste, 140 tonnes of non-toxic industrial wastes, and 50 tonnes of yard and street wastes daily (Asian Development Bank 2016). Given the limited land resource for landfills, the cost of investment and operations of a landfill site and the need to recover material waste as a useful resource, the government is looking into converting municipal waste to energy (WTE) using the appropriate and scientifically approved technology (ibid., p. 41). Batam is also considering the establishment of a General Municipal Public Service Body following the example of other cities. A WTE plant is planned, with a capacity of 700 tonnes per day expected to generate 15 MW of power that will be sold to the national electric company.

However, the authorities have to increase fees and identify ways to improve fee collection and reduce operating expenditures. There is also a need to ensure that collection regulations are effectively enforced and monitored. According to 2015 reports, the collection of solid wastes was insufficient, causing overspills and public health hazards.[33]

Pollution in Reservoirs

Batam's reservoirs can reportedly meet the demand of 1 million people.[34] However, reservoir capacity is already being strained, and the unofficial population now actually stands at more than 1.2 million. To make matters worse, space and catchment area constraints limit the construction of new reservoirs.[35]

Water supplies operate under a concession granted by BP Batam (BIFZA) to PT Adhya Tirta Batam for twenty-five years from 1995 to 2020. The company serves 99.5 per cent of Batam's population, accounting for 260,000 connections (Figure 13.2).

Batam depends solely on rainfall collected in dams for water, which makes production, distribution and water conservation a huge challenge. The concessionaire

FIGURE 13.2
Reservoirs and Forested Areas in Batam

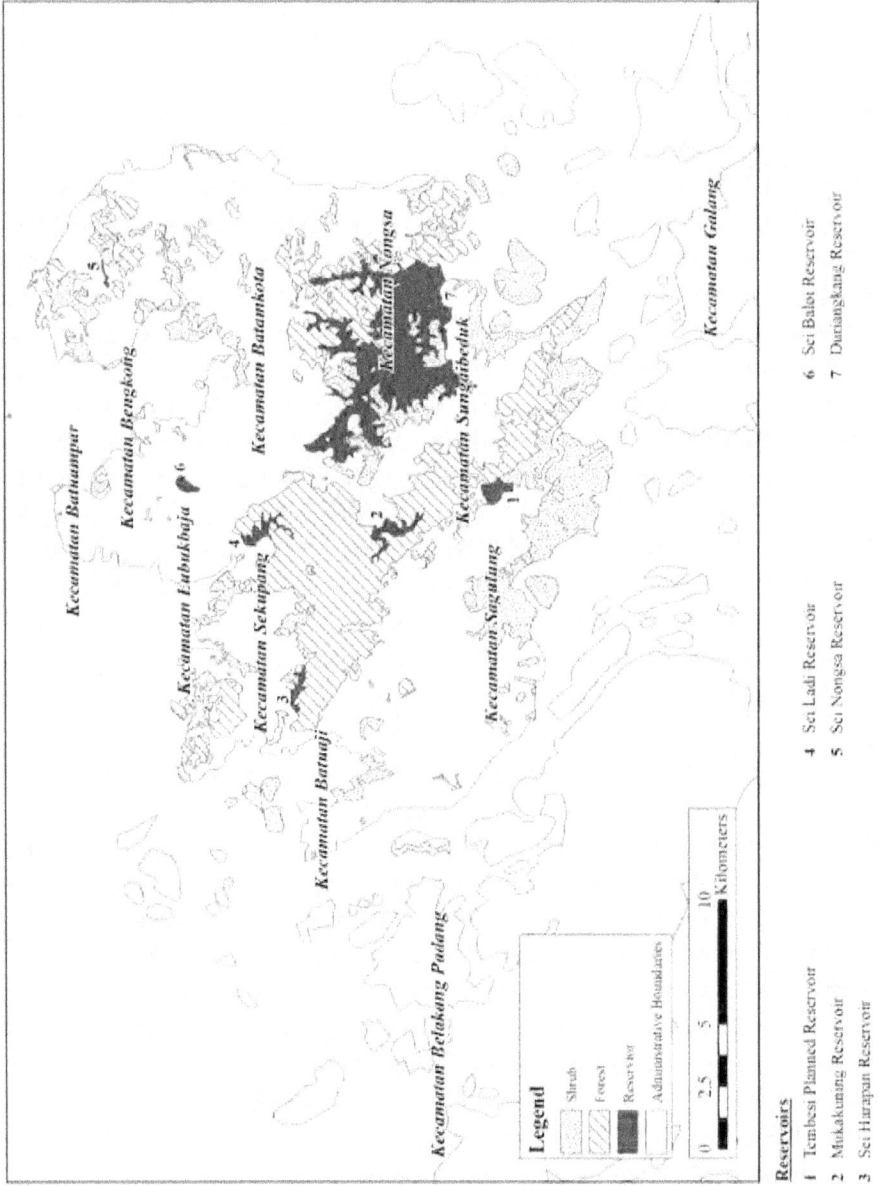

Source: Map provided by ISEAS – Yusof Ishak Institute. © 2017 ISEAS – Yusof Ishak Institute.

expects Batam to be in a water crisis after 2020. As the population continues to grow, there will be additional strains on supplies, and it is critical that the government plan for an increase in future supplies, or shortages in water supplies will be inevitable.

What is more worrisome is the pollution of the Duriangkang reservoir (in operation since 2001), which is the island's main source of water, supplying 75 per cent of Batam's freshwater (Table 13.3). The area of the reservoir is about 23.4 km^2. Pollution sources include industrial and human activities in the catchment. Storage capacity has also been affected by silting of the reservoir due to land clearance and construction near the catchment. The lack of enforcement has resulted in the illegal construction of housing and fishponds in the water catchment protected area, which has in turn impacted its water quality. Construction within the drainage catchments of the reservoir (linked to the sanitation programme) and poorly constructed and managed off-site sanitation facilities located within the catchment area has also affected water quality severely. The current average quality is rated poor: COD is 134.61 mg/l; BOD5, 58.22 mg/l, and ammonia, 10.5 mg/l (Asian Development Bank 2016, p. 27).[36] The BOD levels in the reservoir has been known to exceed the acceptable standard by fifty times. BP Batam is responsible for managing the area surrounding the reservoir and has been facing constant problems with unauthorized intrusions, unregulated disposal of household and livestock waste (pig rearing), and illegal logging (*Batam Pos*, 9 January 2017). There is the case of the Baloi Reservoir where water sources there became so polluted that it had in effect become a "septic tank" (Asian Development Bank 2016).

TABLE 13.3
Reservoirs in Batam

Reservoir	Volume	Design Capacity	Capacity Installed	Production Capacity
Sei Harapan Reservoir	3,600,000 m^3	210 L/sec	210 L/sec	202.23 L/sec
Sei Ladi Reservoir	9,490,000 m^3	240 L/sec	270 L/sec	217.84 L/sec
Mukakuning Reservoir	12,270,000 m^3	310 L/sec	310 L/sec	300.83 L/sec
Sei Nongsa Reservoir	720,000 m^3	60 L/sec	110 L/sec	30.34 L/sec
Tanjung Piayu	Water from Duriangkang	375 L/sec	375 L/sec	290.30 L/sec
Duriangkang Reservoir	78,180,000 m^3	3,000 L/sec	2,200 L/sec	2,090.95 L/sec
Baloi Reservoir	270,000 m^3	30 L/sec	60 L/sec	—
Tembesi Planned Reservoir	41,876,080 m^3	600 L/sec	—	—
Rempang Reservoir	5,166,400 m^3	232 L/sec	—	—
Sei Gong Reservoir	—	20 L/sec	—	—
Total	151,572,480 m^3	4,682 L/sec	3,535 L/sec	3,132.50 L/sec

Source: BIFZA 2016.

Wastewater and Sewerage Treatment

Presently, Batam has an existing sewerage system at Batam Centre, which however is run down and does not operate efficiently (Asian Development Bank 2016, p. 33). More than 50 per cent of the city's domestic wastes also enters the Duriangkang reservoir which has drastically reduced the water quality and now require a greater treatment intensity. Many parts of the city have basic onsite systems like septic tanks and pit latrines. About 75 per cent of unconnected households use private septic tanks. The total waste management capacity at Batam stood at only 12 per cent of the required capacity in 2015 (Asian Development Bank 2016, p. 10).[37] To date, effective regulation does not exist to ensure that "sludge (or septage) is removed (pumped) at regular intervals, and the operation of tankers for septage pumping is not well managed" (Asian Development Bank 2016). About 70 per cent of the septic tanks has contaminated the ground water. Assuming the population to be about 1.2 million, there are in effect about 300,000 homes pumping out wastes.[38]

In 2012, the Directorate General of Human Settlements in the Ministry of Public Works and Housing provided technical assistance through Indii (AusAid) to prepare a master plan and feasibility study for the city's sewerage system. Four locations for a wastewater treatment plant have been identified, including one in the Batam Centre (Kecamatan Batamkota) and another in Bengkong. The government plans to provide a citywide central sewerage system by 2020. The 2020 target also includes increasing sewage pipeline to 81 km from 2 km in 2015, providing sewer house connections to 11,000 households from the present zero households in 2015 (which would then serve 16 per cent of the total population), and providing regular septage customers to 5,000 household from 1,500 families in 2015 (Asian Development Bank 2016, p. 35). Current human waste management capacity is 33 litres per second, and is only connected to 2.3 per cent of the population. By law, industries are required to build their own human waste management facilities, but again, controls have not been stringently applied (Asian Development Bank 2016, p. 10).

Actions are in place for the implementation of the preparatory stage for the sanitation programme which will take place from 2016 to 2018 (Asian Development Bank 2016, p. 36),[39] and the establishment of the regular septage pumping (desludging system) and management system from 2016 to 2017. Septic tanks will remain the principal form of urban sanitation as the sewer network is not extensive (Asian Development Bank 2016, p. 38). Septic tanks also require regular removal, hence a coordinated septage management system is required or this may not result in improved sanitation, health and environmental protection. Private companies will also be considered to provide septage collection and transport services. Communal septic tanks will be provided in the Cagar-Budaya area where an older village exists.

In 2016, BP Batam was reported to be completing a Waste Water Treatment Plant at Batam Centre.[40] To date, the Batam Wastewater Investment Master Plan, Stage 1 project, has been completed in Batam Centre, Bengkong and Sei Beduk and will continue to Stage 2. The Stage 2 Wastewater Treatment Plants are located at Batu Ampar, Sagulung, Sekupang and Batam Centre (expansion of current facility) (*Jakarta*

Post, 12 December 2016). These will take four years to complete, with an estimated investment of US$157 million.

Mangroves and Conservation

Forested mangrove areas in Batam have been reduced from 24 per cent of the total island size in 1970 to about 4.2 per cent in 2015 (*Tempo.co,* 15 June 2015). Activities like construction, piling for the development of tourism, sand mining (cut and fill), logging, and dam building have been identified as culprits. In 2015 alone, Batam's Environmental Agency, BAPEDAL, reported that the island had lost about 800 hectares of its forests. Over 620 hectares have been lost from Tembesi in Sagulung itself because of constructions and where a dam was built. The Head of BAPEDAL, Dendi Purnomo, however reiterated that BAPEDAL took strict action against violators, though such violations have continued to recur.

To be fair, efforts have been made by the Batam authorities to conserve its natural areas wherever possible. In a Clean Development Mechanism (CDM)[41] project, the Ministry of Forestry (MoF) of Batam City (local government support), and YL Invest Co. Ltd. Japan (the funder) implemented a conservation and mangrove reforestation project on three Indonesian islands.

PT Yamamoto Asri was then established by YL Invest Co., to implement this particular project in Batam. PT Yamamoto Asri collaborated with the community in implementing this project. The total area covers 115 hectares, with the boundaries decided with Batam City officials and the local community involving three islands, Sekenah, Teraling and Tenggau in Batam City.[42] Mangrove reforestation was carried out where such trees have never existed. There is no further documentation on this CDM project; however, the first stage of the project was completed successfully where healthy trees of up to 1.3 metres were recorded, covering an area of 29 hectares. There are also conservation efforts in Bintan, a regency in Riau Islands Province to increase its mangrove forests.[43]

Air Pollution Emissions

Batam has been facing growing traffic congestion and air pollution. This has been caused by an increase in motorized vehicles (currently over 1 million, and fivefold in comparison to 2000). The Green City Action plan noted that the "[c]ontinued reliance on, and uncontrolled growth, of private motorized transport is deemed unsustainable" (Asian Development Bank 2016, p. 59).

A study on air pollutant emissions in Batam (Triwinarko et al. 2015) published in 2015 (based on data collected in 2012) however identified the major sources of pollution in the municipality to be industries and power plants.

In this study, emissions were identified at their source: point source for individual source with large emission, area source for individual sources with small emissions, and mobile sources for emitters that move from one place to another (Triwinarko et al. 2015, p. 73). The pollutants that were inventoried included nitrogen oxides

(NO$_x$) sulphur oxides (SO$_x$) volatile organic compounds (VOC), 10 mm particulates (PM10), carbon monoxide (CO) and carbon dioxide (CO$_2$).[44]

In terms of pollutants, industries and power plants produced 99 per cent of pollutant emissions (NO$_x$, SO$_x$, VOC, PM10, and CO) and 99 per cent of greenhouse gas (CO$_2$) (Table 13.4).

For emissions from mobile sources, 64 per cent of emissions of NO$_x$ emissions came from roads (cars, buses, and heavy-duty vehicles) while 30 per cent came from the ports (marine transportation).

In terms of SO$_x$, 83 per cent came from road sources, 13.8 per cent from port sources; for HC, 99 per cent came from road sources; for PM10, 77 per cent came from road sources, and 22 per cent from port sources; for CO, 98 per cent came from road sources, and for CO$_2$, 30 per cent came from road sources and 68 per cent from port sources.[45]

It is important that the government identifies and then focuses on the main sources of pollution. However, as supervision is lacking for enforcement of violations in air pollution, this will remain a challenging task.[46]

CONCLUSION

Batam's spectacular growth in the 1990s has been accompanied by significant population increases, with negative impacts on the environment. The transformation of the island's economy has not come without its costs, the most visible of these across all fronts is in the form of environmental degradation.

It has been challenging for Batam to reconcile environmental concerns with economic development. Rapid population increases due to the economic opportunities available in Batam created strains on the carrying capacity of the environment, notably on water supplies, sewage and waste treatment and illegal land clearance.

TABLE 13.4
Sources of Air Pollutants

Point Source	Industries and Power Plants	Other Sources (Hospital, University, Bank, Shopping Mall)	Total Emission Rates (ton/year)
Air Pollutant Emissions: Nitrogen oxides (NO$_x$), carbon monoxide (CO), 10mm particulates (PM10), Sulfur oxides (SO$_x$) hydro carbons (HC)	99% (for all chemicals and particulates)	1% (for all chemicals and particulates)	NO$_x$: 6,623.03 CO: 992.28 PM10: 203.62 SO$_x$: 4,376.51 HC: 2,506.63
Greenhouse Gas Emissions: Carbon Dioxide (CO$_2$)	99% (for all chemicals and particulates)	1% (for all chemicals and particulates)	CO$_2$: 3,453,688.43

Construction activities increased in tandem with growth, with land clearance and cut and fill activities creating soil erosion and floods in the city. Mangrove forests have also been massively cleared from 24 per cent of the total land area to just 4.2 per cent in 2015.

The situation was exacerbated not only by increases in population but by the number of squatters who illegally occupied land and polluted waterways and cleared forested areas illegally in order to build their homes. Coupled with the inadequate wastewater treatment plants, with domestic wastes polluting the reservoirs, the problem remains unresolved.

Regulations that only encouraged land clearing without follow up created problems when lands were left exposed without any further construction activity. Soil erosion and sedimentation in turn affected waterways and destroyed coral and fish habitats.

In Batam, it was interesting to note that enforcement was weak or non-existent in many instances. For environmental degradation to be regulated, and for development to be sustainable, the Indonesian government will have to devote more resources towards supervision and enforcement.

Also, the carrying capacity of Batam's public amenities like waste and water treatment plants was incapable of meeting present demand. With population expected to increase to 2.5 million by 2025, there is even greater urgency to ensure that not only enforcement is in place but that additional amenities are constructed in time to ensure that population pressures do not affect environmental amenities. Also, the issue of squatters will need to be resolved.

Notes

1. This chapter was first published as *Reconciling Economic and Environmental Imperatives in Batam*, Trends in Southeast Asia, no. 6/2018 (Singapore: ISEAS – Yusof Ishak Institute, 2018).

2. The author would like to thank Ulla Fionna, Francis E. Hutchinson and Siwage Dharma Negara for their guidance, and Jason Salim and Amoz Hor for translating text gathered from his interview questionnaires in Batam. Appreciation is also expressed to the following: Francis E. Hutchinson and Serina Rahman for very useful feedback on an earlier version of this paper; Ooi Kee Beng for editing; and Benjamin Hu for producing the maps on Batam.

3. Visit on 8 March 2017 to BP Batam with Francis E. Hutchinson and Siwage Dharma Negara.

4. See also Hutchinson (2017), p. 3.

5. Batam Indonesia Free Zone Authority (BIFZA) is also known as BIDA or BP Batam.

6. See Tan (2004), p. 179.

7. This was the term given to a group of US-educated Indonesian economists who had great influence on the government of the day.

8. Questionnaire Answer from BAPEDAL Respondent, December 2016 and also Interview with Academic/Activist, 3 April 2017.

9. Questionnaire Answer from Academic Respondent, December 2016.

10. Questionnaire Answer from BAPEDAL Respondent, December 2016.
11. Questionnaire Answer from BAPEDAL Respondent, December 2016.
12. Questionnaire Answer from BAPEDAL Respondent, November 2016.
13. Questionnaire Answer from BAPEDAL Respondent, November 2016.
14. Mangrove consists of trees or shrubs growing in tidal flats of tropical and subtropical coastal regions that become inundated at high tides. Indonesia has about 25 per cent of the total distribution of mangroves in the world (4.5 million hectares of mangrove forests).
15. Questionnaire Answer from NGO Respondent 2, December 2016. While travelling and observing seas at the coastal areas during my Batam fieldwork on 8 March 2017 and 3 April 2017, pollution was not visible to the naked eye.
16. Questionnaire Answer from NGO Respondent 1, December 2016.
17. Questionnaire Answer from Academic Respondent, December 2016.
18. Questionnaire Answer from NGO Respondent 1 and Academic Respondent, December 2016.
19. Questionnaire Answer from NGO Respondent 2, December 2016.
20. Questionnaire Answer from Academic Respondent and BAPEDAL Respondent, December 2016.
21. Questionnaire Answer from NGO Respondent 2, December 2016.
22. Questionnaire Answer from BAPEDAL Respondent, December 2016.
23. Questionnaire Answer from NGO Respondent 2, December 2016.
24. Interview with Academic/Activist, 3 April 2017.
25. Single Data Rumah Liar, Pemerintah Kota Batam, http://perakimtan.batam.go.id/ruli/index.php?page=home (accessed 16 January 2018).
26. Questionnaire Answer from BAPEDAL Respondent, November 2016.
27. Personal conversation with Informant in Batam who obtained information from official in the Ministry of Forestry in Batam, 10 April 2017.
28. Fieldwork travels to Batam on 8 March 2017 and 3 April 2017.
29. Data collection was undertaken through field observation, questionnaires, and in-depth interviews.
30. Questionnaire Answer from NGO Respondent 2, December 2016.
31. Questionnaire Answer from BAPEDAL Respondent, November 2016.
32. Questionnaire Answer from NGO Respondent 1 and Academic Respondent, December 2016.
33. Fieldwork travels to Batam on 8 March 2017 and 3 April 2017 confirmed that such wastes are still left uncollected around parts of the city; and Asian Development Bank (2016), p. 46.
34. The construction of these reservoirs have been enabled with cooperation between the Batam Industrial Development Authority (BIDA) now known as the Batam Indonesia Free Zone Authority (BIFZA), and local and international companies. See Batam Center (n.d.).
35. Interview with Academic/Activist, 3 April 2017.
36. The current average quality has been rated as poor: COD: 134.61 mg/l, BOD5: 58.22 mg/l, and ammonia: 10.5 mg/l. BOD refers to Biochemical Oxygen Demand, while COD refers to Chemical Oxygen Demand.
37. This is based on a population of 1,030,528 and water consumption of 150 litres per capita daily, and assuming that 80 per cent of the water is converted into waste. The daily human waste production will be about 123,000 m^3, while total waste management capacity stands at 14,720 m^3 per day or 12 per cent of the total capacity.

38. Questionnaire Answer from BAPEDAL Respondent, December 2016.
39. This includes a review of the current sanitation master plan and feasibility study, establishment of a City Sanitation Committee, creation of a sanitation baseline, and the undertaking of a public campaign and socialization programme.
40. Questionnaire Answer from Bapaedal Respondent, December 2016.
41. CDM is designed to promote projects that reduce greenhouse gas emissions. An example of a CDM would be a replanting activity where bare areas are replanted with trees.
42. Clean Development Mechanism Project Design Document Form for Small-Scale Afforestation and Reforestation Project Activities (CDM-SSC-AR-PDD) (Version 02), "Small Scale and Low-Income Community-Based Mangrove Afforestation project on Tidal Flats of Three Islands Around Batam City, Riau Islands Province, Republic of Indonesia" (Version 05, 15 April 2010), pp. 3–4.
43. See Siregar (2013).
44. Results were also obtained from the local environmental agency the Badan Pengedalian Dampak Lingkungan (BAPEDAL) of Batam Municipality.
45. Total emissions for NO_x, SO_x, VOC, PM10, CO and CO_2 were 2,263.76 tonnes/year, 78.92 tonnes/year, 13,296.65 tonnes/year, 201.60 tonnes/year, 25,453.09 tonnes/year and 1,571,544.77 tonnes/year, ibid., p. 74.
46. Questionnaire Answer from NGO Respondent 2, December 2016.

References

Amri, Mulya, 2016. "A Periphery Serving Three Cores: Balancing Local, National, and Cross-Border Interests in the Riau Islands". In *The SIJORI Cross-Border Regions: Transnational Politics, Economics, and Culture*, edited by Francis E. Hutchinson and Terence Chong. Singapore: ISEAS – Yusof Ishak Institute.

AntaraNews.Com. 2012. "Toxic Wastes Polluted Waters off Northern Cost of Batam". 26 December 2012. http://www.antaranews.com/en/news/86404/toxic-waste-pollutes-waters-off-northern-coast-of-batam (accessed 19 October 2017).

Asian Development Bank. 2016. "Green City Action Plan 2035: City of Batam". Manila: Asian Development Bank. https://www.adb.org/sites/default/files/related/72276/green-city-action-plan-gcap-batam.pdf (accessed 24 August 2017).

Batam Center. N.d. "Infrastructure and Facilities". http://www.batam-center.web.id/geninfo_facilities.html (accessed 15 April 2017).

Batam Economic Outlook: 2011–2014. 2011. Tim Batam Outlook PPDSI, BP Batam.

Batam Indonesia Free Zone Authority (BIFZA). 2016. *Development Progress of Batam.* Edisi II Vol. XXX 2016 (Draft Mei 2017) (accessed 21 July 2017).

BatamNews. 2016. "Kegiatan Cut and Fill 12 Perusahaan di Batam Juga Disetop, Ini Daftarnya". 5 December 2016. http://batamnews.co.id/berita-18282-kegiatan-cut-and-fill-12-perusahaan-di-batam-juga-disetop-ini-daftarnya-.html (accessed 16 April 2017).

Batam Pos. 2017. "ATB Berkewajiban Mengolah Air Baku, Pemeliharaan Waduk dan Sekitarnya Tanggungjawab Pemerintah". 9 January 2017. https://batampos.co.id/2017/01/09/atb-berkewajiban-mengolah-air-baku-pemeliharaan-waduk-dan-sekitarnya-tanggungjawab-pemerintah/ (accessed 15 January 2018).

Broadfoot, Robert C. 2003. "Batam: A Formula for Growth". Summary Paper of the Executive Investment Forum in Batam. Political and Economic Risk Consultancy (PERC) Ltd, June 2003.

Business Times. 2015. "Sinarmas Land to Invest at Least 4 Trillion Rupiah in Batam Project". 15 December 2015. http://www.businesstimes.com.sg/real-estate/sinarmas-land-to-invest-at-least-4-trillion-rupiah-in-batam-project (accessed 17 January 2017).

Clean Development Mechanism Project Design Document Form for Small-Scale Afforestation and Reforestation Project Activities (CDM-SSC-AR-PDD) (Version 02). 2010. "Small Scale and Low-Income Community-Based Mangrove Afforestation Project on Tidal Flats of Three Islands Around Batam City, Riau Islands Province, Republic of Indonesia". Version 05, 15 April 2010.

Farole, Thomas. 2013. *The Internal Geography of Trade: Lagging Regions and Global Markets*, pp. 218–19. Washington, DC: World Bank. http://documents.worldbank.org/curated/en/435791468147845613/The-internal-geography-of-trade-lagging-regions-and-global-markets (accessed 16 November 2017).

Hezri, A.A., and S.R. Dovers. 2012. "Shifting the Policy Goal from Environment to Sustainable Development". In *Malaysia's Development Challenges: Graduating from the Middle*, edited by Hal Hill, Tham Siew Yean and Ragayah Mat Zin. London and New York: Routledge.

Hutchinson, Francis E. 2017. *Rowing Against the Tide? Batam's Economic Fortunes in Today's Indonesia*. Trends in Southeast Asia, no. 8/2017. Singapore: ISEAS – Yusof Ishak Institute.

———, and Terence Chong, eds. 2016. *The SIJORI Cross-Border Regions: Transnational Politics, Economics, and Culture*. Singapore: ISEAS – Yusof Ishak Institute.

Jakarta Post. 2012. "Shipyard Industry in Batam Faces Restrictions". 15 March 2012. http://www.thejakartapost.com/news/2012/03/15/shipyard-industry-batam-faces-restrictions.html (accessed 19 April 2017).

———. 2014. "Govt Plans Incentives for Shipbuilders". 12 November 2014. http://www.thejakartapost.com/news/2014/11/12/govt-plans-incentives-shipbuilders.html (accessed 18 July 2017).

———. 2016. "BP Batam Invests in Water, Waste Water Management". 12 December 2016. http://www.thejakartapost.com/adv/2016/12/12/bp-batam-invests-in-water-waste-water-management.htm> (accessed 12 December 2016).

MacAndrews, Colin. 1994. "The Indonesian Environmental Impact Management Agency (Bapedal): Its Role, Development and Future". *Bulletin of Indonesian Economic Studies* 30, no. 1.

Negara, Siwage Dharma. 2017. "Can the Decline of Batam's Shipbuilding Industry be Reversed?". *ISEAS Perspective*, no. 2017/4, 16 February 2017.

——— and Francis E. Hutchinson. 2017. "Will Batam Shake-up Bear Fruit?". *Straits Times*, 2 November 2017. http://www.straitstimes.com/opinion/will-batam-shake-up-bear-fruit (accessed 3 November 2017).

Niessen, Nicole. 2006. "Decentralized Environmental Management". In *Environmental Law in Development: Lessons from the Indonesian Experience*, edited by Michael Faure and Nicole Niessen. Cheltenham: Edward Elgar Publishing.

Phelps, N.A. 2004. "Archetype for an Archipelago? Batam as Anti-Model and Model of Industrialization in *Reformasi* Indonesia". *Progress in Development Studies* 4, no. 3.

Poffenberger, Mark, ed. 1998. *Communities and Forest Management in Southeast Asia*. Berkeley: World Conservation Union (IUCN).

Priyandes, Alpano, and M. Rafee Majid. 2009. "Impact of Reclamation Activities on the Environment Study Area: Northern Coast of Batam, Indonesia". *Jurnal Alam Bina* X, no. 1.

Sari, Agus P. 1998. "Environmental and Human Right Impacts of Trade Liberalization:

A Case Study in Batam Island, Indonesia". A Project of the Earth Council, San Jose, Costa Rica, March 1998.

Single Data Rumah Liar. Pemerintah Kota Batam. http://perakimtan.batam.go.id/ruli/index. php?page=home (accessed 16 January 2018).

Siregar, Ahmad Faisal. 2013. "Activity Report: Review and Policy Analysis of Community-Based Mangrove Ecosystem Management in Bintan District". MoF-ITTO PROJECT RED PD 064/11 Rev. 2 (F) (accessed 17 October 2016).

Tan, Alan Khee-Jin. 2004. "Environmental Laws and Institutions in Southeast Asia: A Review of Recent Developments". *Singapore Year Book of International Law*. Singapore: Faculty of Law, National University of Singapore.

Tempo.Co. 2015. "Batam Loses 800 Hectares of Its Mangrove Forests", 15 June 2015. https:// en.tempo.co/read/news/2015/06/15/206675016/Batam-Loses-800-Hectares-of-Its-Mangrove-Forest (accessed 19 October 2016).

Topalovic, Milica, Marcel Jaeggi, Martin Knuesel, Livio de Maria, Martin Garcia, Guila Luraschi, Magnus Nickl, Staphanie Schenk, and Karl Wruck. 2012. "Singapore, Indonesia and Malaysia Project 1". ETH Zurich, Spring 2012.

Tribun Batam. 2017a. "Rumah Liar di Kota Batam Akan Ditata Tahun 2017. Ini Target ke Depan". 10 January 2017. http://batam.tribunnews.com/2017/01/10/rumah-liar-di-kota-batam-akan-ditata-tahun-2017-ini-target-ke-depan (accessed 2 September 2017).

———. 2017b. "Titik Banjir di Kota Batam Terus Bertambah. BP dan Pemko Akan Lakukan Ini". 21 March 2017. http://batam.tribunnews.com/2017/03/21/titik-banjir-di-kota-batam-terus-bertambah-bp-dan-pemko-akan-lakukan-ini (accessed 16 April 2017).

Triwinarko, Andy, Dwi Kartikasari, Didi Intardi, Syafei Ghozali and Dian Mulyaningtyas, 2015. "Air Pollutant Emissions in Batam: An Overview". *Jurnal Teknologi* 77, no. 23: 71–76.

van Grunsven, Leo, and Francis E. Hutchinson. 2017. "The Evolution of the Electronics Industry on Batam Island (Riau Islands Province, Indonesia): An Evolutionary Trajectory Contributing to Regional Resilience?". *GeoJournal* 82, issue 3: 475–92.

Widianarko, Budi. 2009. "Democratization, Decentralization and Environmental Conservation in Indonesia". Plenary Presentation at the 9th Asia-Pacific NGO Environmental Conference (APNEC9) and 30th Anniversary of Japan Environmental Conference (JEC), Kyoto, 20–21 November 2009.

Wong, Poh Kam, and Ng Kwan Kee. 2009. "Batam, Bintan and Karimun: Past History and Current Development Towards being a SEZ". Asia Competitiveness Institute, Lee Kuan Yew School of Public Policy, National University of Singapore.

14

LIVING ON THE EDGE
Being Malay (and Bugis) in the Riau Islands[1]

Andrew M. Carruthers[2]

EPIGRAPHS

Ayuhai segala anak cucunya,
hendaklah ingatkan datuk neneknya,
serta fikirkan fiil lakunya,
hendaklah ikut sebarang dapatnya.

Hear ye, all children and grandchildren,
you should remember your ancestors,
and think upon their behaviour,
you should trace back whatever they did.

Barangsiapa sungguh anak cucunya,
hendak ikut tingkah lakunya,
sama ada aib malunya,
atau pada teguh setianya.

Whoever is truly child or grandchild,
you should trace back their behaviour,
whether it be horrible and shameful,
or thoroughly firm and loyal.

Jika diperbuat demikian itu,
sahlah kamu anak cucunya tentu,

If this should be done,
You will be true children and grandchildren indeed,

bolehlah disebut bangsa ratu,
di negeri Bugis keturunan datu.
— Raja Ali Haji, *Silsilah Melayu dan Bugis*, 1865.

You may be called nobles,
in the land of the Bugis descended from kings.

Narekko sompe'ko,
aja' muahcaji ana'guru,
ancaji punggawako.
— Bugis proverb.

If you wander to a foreign land,
do not become a subordinate,
but become a leader.

INTRODUCTION: "LIKE BLACK AND WHITE PARTS
OF THE EYE"

In April 2008, and only six years following the legal formation and secession of Indonesia's Riau Islands Province (Provinsi Kepulauan Riau, or Kepri) from adjacent Riau Province, then Governor of Riau H.M. Rusli Zainal (2003–13) attended a meeting of the South Sulawesi Family Association (*Kerukunan Keluarga Sulawesi Selatan*, or KKSS) in Riau's provincial capital of Pekanbaru.[3] The South Sulawesi Family Association is one of Indonesia's largest and most active ethno-regional associations, with members hailing from or tracing their roots to South Sulawesi, an east Indonesian province widely known as the ancestral homeland of Indonesia's Bugis people.[4] Outnumbering that province's indigenous Makassarese, Mandar and Torajan peoples, South Sulawesi's Bugis people are historically renowned as much for their seafaring prowess as they are for the wanderlust that fuels their travels throughout Indonesia, Malaysia, and beyond in "search of good fortune" (Bugis: *massappa' dallê*).

The Riau Governor, a "Malay of Bugis ancestry" (Malay: *Melayu keturunan Bugis*), had been previously honoured by the ethno-regional association with the honorary "title" (*gelar*) of *Daeng Magguna*. Roughly translatable to "he who is useful", the title bestowed upon the Riau Governor by the association featured the Bugis-Makassar honorific "Daeng", commonly given to Bugis-Makassar people of noble birth. *Daeng* is also a title whose meaning reverberates in the historical imaginary of Riau and Riau Islands Provinces, two places whose contemporary borders closely align with those of the once-sprawling Malay Sultanate that stretched from what we today call Indonesia, through Singapore, to Malaysia. Among Riau Islanders and their neighbours in Riau Province, the noble honorific *Daeng* is iconically associated with five legendary Bugis brothers—Daeng Parani, Daeng Marewah, Daeng Menambun, Daeng Celak, and Daeng Kemasi—whose involvement in the region changed the course of history across the Malay world in the early eighteenth century.

Riau Governor H.M. Rusli Zainal (alias Daeng Magguna) used his April meeting with the South Sulawesi Family Association to thank them for their continuing support and involvement in Riau's everyday life, but also to ruminate on the ethno-historical linkages between the Bugis people and the region's indigenous, ethnically Malay community. "Both of these people since the beginning cannot be separated",[5] the Governor said. Continuing, he explained that "[t]he Malays and the Bugis are like the black and white parts of the eye, both are fused together and have worked together in various ways, and this has been the case since a long time ago."[6] The Governor's words tacitly gestured towards a conventionally understood history of Bugis-Malay kinship and collaborative exchange dating back almost 300 years to the arrival of the five Bugis brothers.

Six years after the Governor's meeting with Riau's South Sulawesi Family Association, and amidst a whirlwind of national political drama leading up to the impending 2014 Indonesian Presidential Election, former vice-president of Indonesia and then vice-presidential candidate Jusuf Kalla found himself campaigning in Riau. During his campaign stop, Kalla—a Bugis hailing from South Sulawesi's

Bone regency who, alongside his presidential running mate Joko Widodo would later win the hotly contested election—noted the enduring legacy of the region's "Malay language" (*bahasa Melayu*) to the nation. "It is so great that this nation chose the Malay language to be used ... it means that our foundational language is Malay",[7] he said.

Alluding to Raja Ali Haji (1808–73)—a Bugis-Malay aristocrat, historian and lexicographer who, from his home on Penyengat Island in today's Riau Islands Province developed the first monolingual Malay dictionary—the vice-presidential candidate spoke of the historical role played by the Bugis in codifying a standard Malay variety that would later be renamed *Bahasa Indonesia* by Indonesian proto-nationalists in the 1928 "Youth Pledge" (*Sumpah Pemudah*): "As a Bugis person I'm also very proud because the structure of the Malay language was also built up from the Bugis",[8] Kalla noted. Then, echoing the aforementioned words of Riau Governor Rusli Zainal Daeng Magguna, the vice-presidential candidate "romanticized" the Bugis-Malay relationship, explaining, "So, between the Bugis and Malays, it's like the relationship between white and black parts of the eye. So that we're so romantic and cherish one another." (*DetikNews*, 7 June 2014).

This chapter—the first of several centred on different ethnic collectivities and inter-ethnic dynamics in Indonesia's Riau Islands Province—examines the putative "inseparability" of Kepri's Bugis and Malay people.[9] Framed less obtusely, and drawing upon ethnographic field data collected in February and March 2017 alongside secondary source material, the chapter highlights one segment of Kepri society which has played a disproportionately central role in the governance, politics, history, and historiography or "history-telling" in Riau Islands society: self-identified "Malays of Bugis descent" (*Melayu keturunan Bugis*).

Aims and Structure of the Chapter

This chapter's primary objective is to offer readers a broad overview of this particular segment of Riau Islands society, and to highlight how contemporary perceptions of a shared, Bugis-Malay history inflect contemporary life in Riau Islands Province. In turn, the chapter has a number of secondary objectives, listed below in order of their exposition.

1. To provide readers unfamiliar with anthropological or ethno-historical approaches to "Malayness" with a synopsis of how the concept has been defined or evaluated, and the ways in which the meaning of Malayness shifts across contemporary geopolitical borders.
2. To show how conceptions of Malayness and Malay ethno-history in the Riau Islands have been "authoritatively defined" (Shamsul 2001)[10] by Malays of Bugis ancestry and shape contemporary senses of belonging and outsidership.
3. To examine how perceptions of the past animate current provincial government policy priorities surrounding the "preservation" (*pelestarian*) of

"Malay cultural values" (*nilai-nilai budaya Melayu*) or in the multiethnic Riau Islands.

4. To explore how these government efforts may be read as a reflex or reaction to ongoing issues associated with the islands' rapid sociodemographic shift.

5. To examine how the effects of these shifts have led to feelings of "marginalization" (*peminggiran*) among certain members of the islands' Malay, Bugis, and Malay/Bugis inhabitants, some of whom envision themselves as having been pushed to the figurative and literal "edge" (*pinggiran*) of Riau Islands society.

6. To examine how the islands' Bugis/Malays are positioning themselves vis-à-vis other "native" Indonesian (*pribumi*) immigrants, whom they increasingly characterize as a marginalizing presence that is rapidly transforming everyday life in Riau Islands Province.

7. To bring these developments to bear on current issues in Indonesia surrounding inter-ethnic cleavages and conflict.

I explore these issues in three expository sections: (i) Authority-Defined Meanings of *Melayu* in the Riau Islands; (ii) The Politics of Ethno-Historical Commemoration and Demographic Shift; and (iii) Conclusion: Ethnicity on Edge. Throughout, frequent reference will be made to various sites in the Riau islands—sites relevant for the description of Bugis-Malay involvement in local history, or places where I conducted ethnographic fieldwork and interviews in February and March 2017. I suggest readers consult Figure 14.1, which lists various sites of interest in Batam, Tanjungpinang in Bintan island, and Penyengat Island that will be referred to throughout the piece, and Figure 14.2, which illustrates the relative distribution of the Malay community throughout the island province.

AUTHORITY-DEFINED MEANINGS OF MELAYU
IN THE RIAU ISLANDS

Some readers might assume that Malays are Malays are Malays. For those readers, a preliminary question regarding the topical scope of this chapter might immediately present itself. Why the conceptual focus on Malays of Bugis extraction, rather than simply attending to Malay or *Melayu* proper as the predominant ethnic category in Riau Islands province—a place envisioned as a *Provinsi Melayu* or a distinctly "Malay Province" prior to its legal formation in 2002? Brief reference to the ethno-historical literature on Malayness will help clarify this issue.

In his important 2001 article, "A History of an Identity, an Identity of a History: The Idea and Practice of 'Malayness' in Malaysia Reconsidered", Shamsul A.B. critiques ethnic theories of *Melayu* and "Malayness" that presuppose a kind of ethnic primordialism or essentialism—"the idea that ethnic traits are innate (essences) both in the individual and the 'ethnie' as a social group". In so doing, he takes to task those historians "in mainstream Malaysian historiography" who, he argues, have "wittingly or unwittingly" adopted ethnic theories of essentialism "in their effort

FIGURE 14.1
Map of Research Sites in Riau Islands Province

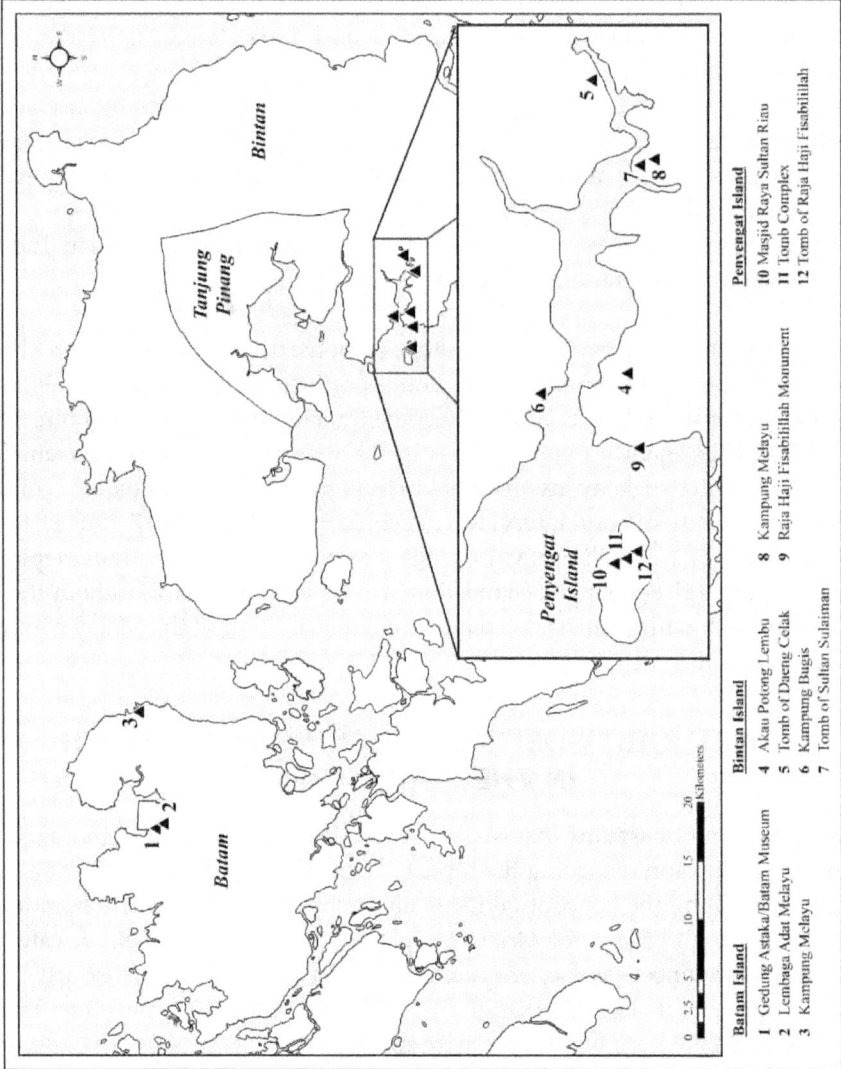

Source: Map courtesy of the ISEAS – Yusof Ishak Institute GIS Project.

FIGURE 14.2
Relative Concentration of Malay Population across Kepri Province

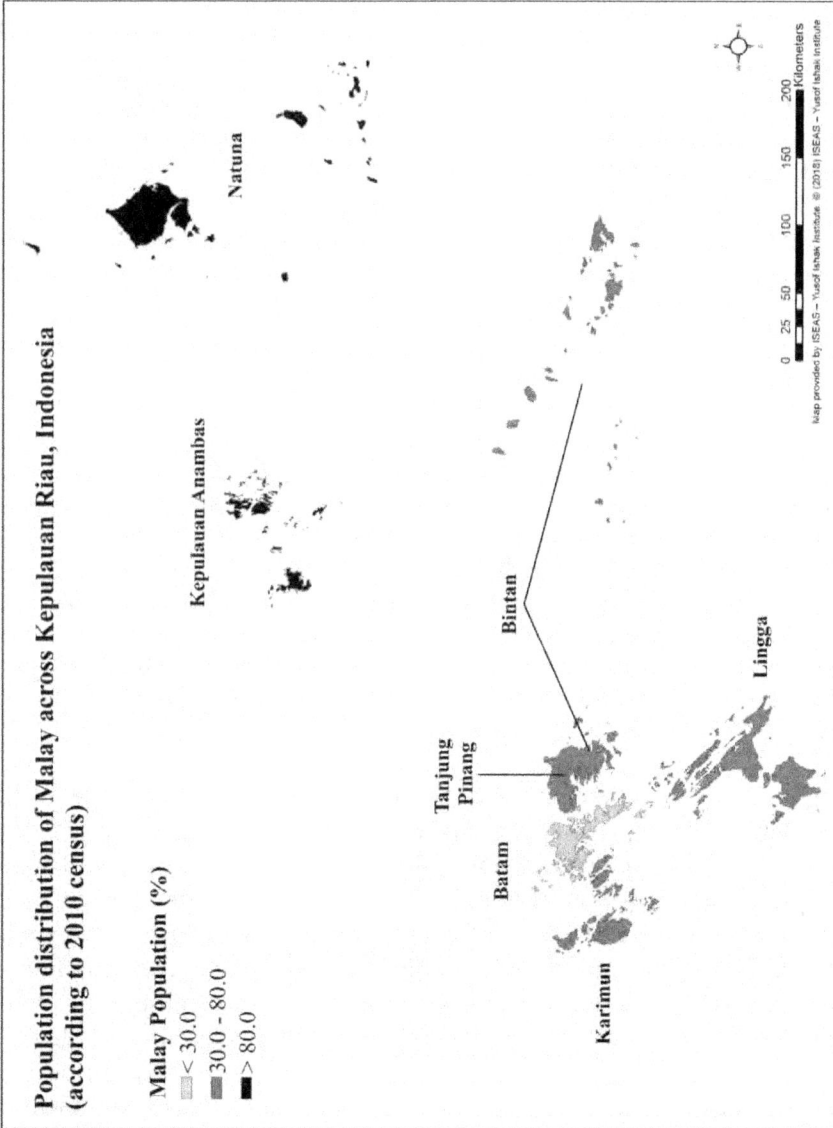

Population distribution of Malay across Kepulauan Riau, Indonesia
(according to 2010 census)

Malay Population (%)
< 30.0
30.0 - 80.0
> 80.0

Source: Map courtesy of the ISEAS – Yusof Ishak Institute GIS Project.

to explain the formation of 'Malay-Malayness' as a social identity" (Shamsul 2001, p. 355).

Engaging in a genealogy of "Malayness", and inspired by approaches developed by anthropologist Bernard Cohn's (1996) *Colonialism and Its Forms of Knowledge: The British in India*, Shamsul argues that "the history of hotly debated concepts such as 'Malay identity' and 'Malayness' is largely based on an Orientalist-colonial construction as reflected in the history of Malaya and, later, Malaysia" (Shamsul 2001, p. 357). Shamsul examines British colonial "investigative modalities" (2001, p. 357; c.f. Cohn 1996), namely, those techniques and technologies like the census that the British used to extend their authority and gather information about their colony. He argues that these colonial era practices—by which the British sought to authoritatively define the nature of ethnicity and belonging in the Malayan colony—came to shape and continue to shape understandings of Malay identity. He concludes his piece by discussing how the meaning of Malayness is constructed, meaning different things in different places among different people, and is shaped across space and time by a variety of authoritative discourses and configurations of power. This is worth quoting at length:

> Like most societal phenomena, identity formation takes place within two social realities at once: the "authority-defined" reality—the reality that is authoritatively defined by people who are part of the dominant power structure—and the "everyday-defined" reality experienced by people in their daily life. These two realities exist side by side at any given time. Although intricately linked and constantly shaping each other by way of contestation, they are certainly not identical: "everyday-defined" social reality is experienced whereas "authority-defined" social reality is primarily observed and interpreted, and possibly imposed. Both are mediated through the social position of those who interpret social reality and those who experience it. Woven into the ever-tense relationship between these two social realities is social power (2001, p. 365).

Shamsul focuses his attention on those "authority-defined" meanings of Melayu in colonial Malaya and contemporary Malaysia. Following suit, I examine here certain authority-defined and authority-defining notions and histories of Malayness in the Riau Islands. In the process, I choose to focus on one segment of Kepri's Malay society—Malays of Bugis descent (*Melayu keturunan Bugis*), who, while self-identifying as steadfastly "Malay", readily acknowledge the enduring importance of their non-Malay ethnically Bugis roots. This group's disproportionate level of influence (or authority) in ideologically arbitrating what it means to be "Malay" in the islands may be seen in a number of ways: in the widely circulating works of Malay literature or history produced by its members (e.g., Raja Ali Haji);[11] in the historical roles accorded to its members by the Riau Islands provincial government and the Indonesian state; in provincial government urban planning projects commemorating its more famous members; or in the incorporation of these figures' mausoleums into the state's tourism sector.[12]

I will turn to these authority-defined discourses of Malayness momentarily, but first, and following Shamsul's (2001) example, I sketch a variety of ways in which Malayness is labile—its meaning shifting across contexts and geopolitical borders.

Labile Labels and Shifting Settings

Melayu means different things, to different people, across different contexts, and its various meanings have changed across shifting geopolitical and historical settings. By way of example, consider a segment of Malaysian national laureate Usman Awang's (1929–2001) well-known and oft-cited poem, *Melayu*:

Jawa itu Melayu, Bugis itu Melayu,	The Javanese are Malay, the Bugis are Malay
Banjar juga disebut Melayu,	The Banjarese are also called Malay
Minangkabau memang Melayu,	The Minangkabau are indeed Malay
Keturunan Aceh adalah Melayu,	The Acehnese are Malay
Jakun dan Sakai asli Melayu ...	The Jakun and Sakai are original Malays...[13]

The Malaysian national laureate's poem was recited by then Malaysian Prime Minister Najib Razak during the 61st General Assembly of the United Malays National Organization (UMNO) in 2010 (and has been widely circulated since then). From a more critical angle of vision, it reflects the decidedly labile and enveloping nature of *Melayu* in the contemporary Malaysian context, one where "Malays" are constitutionally defined as Malay-speaking Muslims who are locally born and habitually practise "Malay custom" or *Adat Melayu*. Contemporary Malaysian (and, by extension, Singaporean) notions of Malayness, however, are inextricably linked to British colonial efforts to evaluate and enumerate ethnicity in colonial Malaya—a domain which, from the eighteenth century up to 1946, encompassed contemporary Singapore and peninsular Malaysia.

In "The Meaning and Measurement of Ethnicity in Malaysia", Charles Hirschman (1987) examines how early British projects of census-taking—a key colonial investigative modality (Cohn 1996; Shamsul 2001)—came to shape contemporary notions of Malayness (Hirschmann 1987). Drawing on historical census data, Hirschman explores how a British colonial typology of ethnic difference gradually narrowed, until only three racial categories—the three primary racial categories that continue to operate in contemporary Malaysia—remained: Malay, Chinese, and Indian. Initial British censuses conducted in 1871 and 1881 divided "Malays" from ethnic groups like "Bugis" or "Javanese" hailing from the Dutch East Indies. A subsequent census conducted in 1901 would—for pragmatic purposes—unify these different ethnic collectivities under the rubric of "Malays and other Natives of the Archipelago". Later censuses would continue this trend. A 1911 census would unify these groups under the label "Malays and Allied Races", a 1921 census under "The Malay Population", and the 1931 census deployed the ever-more general rubric of "Malaysians". The categorical and enumerative logic that underpinned the definition of what it means to be "Malay" continues to operate today both in Malaysia and Singapore, where Malay-speaking Muslims might generally self-identify as members of the so-called "Malay race" (*bangsa Melayu*). And yet, if asked to identify their ethnic roots or affiliations, Malaysians and Singaporeans who—on the surface—self-identify as "Malay", might readily acknowledge or reveal their Javanese, Bugis, Minangkabau, Acehnese, or other roots, all of which are encompassed by the superordinate racial category of "Malayness" that coalesced, to some extent, because of colonial-era projects of census-taking.

In Indonesia, the story about *Melayu*'s meaning is starkly different. Returning once more to the example of Usman Awang's poem, consider a video uploaded to YouTube by an (ostensibly) Malaysian user of the video-sharing platform. Entitled, "Jawa, Bugis, Banjar, Minang, Aceh adalah MELAYU!!!" [The Javanese, Bugis, Banjar, Minang, Aceh are MALAY!] the video features former Prime Minister Najib Razak reciting the aforementioned verses from Usman Awang's poem at the 2010 61st UMNO General Assembly.[14] Comments on the video made by self-identified Indonesian YouTube users offer a window into Indonesian assumptions about Malaysian (and, by extension Singaporean) notions of Malayness. Consider a few examples:

1. YouTube user Adi Prasetiyo writes, "I'm Javanese not Malay."[15]
2. YouTube user A. Zulkifli Pasinringi comments, "BUGIS are not Malay."[16]
3. YouTube user Ridha Kcg notes, "The Minang people are not Malays."[17]
4. Tongue firmly in cheek, and tacitly critiquing the broadly inclusive notion of Malayness put forth in Usman Awang's poem and articulated by Najib, YouTube user Hj. Misai writes, "Mexicans are Malay, Hispanics are Malay, Latin Americans are Malay, people from the Czech Republic are Malay."[18]
5. Identifying and explicating for his fellow commentators the contrast between Malaysian and Indonesian definitions of Malayness, YouTube user Ivan P. writes a longer response: "Actually, this is about the different versions of each country. The Malaysian government version suggests that Malays are from all the islands in the archipelago and peninsular Malaya ... including Javanese, Bugis, Dayak, and others. While in the Indonesian government version, the Malays are only from Sumatra and the Riau Islands, yeah."[19]

The last of these comments succinctly summarizes the different institutionally operating (or authority-defined) assumptions that distinguish Malaysian Malays from those in Indonesia. In Malaysia, a Malay is defined in Article 160 of the Constitution of Malaysia as: "a person who professes the religion of Islam, habitually speaks the Malay language, conforms to Malay custom and—(a) was before Merdeka Day born in the Federation or in Singapore or born of parents one of whom was born in the Federation or in Singapore, or (b) is the issue of such a person."[20] And in Indonesia, while they are not constitutionally defined "ethnic Malays" (*suku Melayu*) are widely characterized as being indigenous to Riau and the Riau Islands.

These different ontologies or sets of assumptions about what it means to be "Malay" in Indonesia versus Malaysia[21] are thrown into stark relief in YouTube comments one through four. Over my seven years of extended ethnographic fieldwork conducted in the Bugis homeland of South Sulawesi, I often encountered similar assumptions about what "Malay" means or who counts as "Malay" among my Bugis interlocutors. During one conversation with a Bugis friend hailing from the province's Bone regency, and with Usman Awang's poem and Malaysian notions of Malayness in the back of my mind, I asked him if he "considered himself Malay", anticipating the kind of reaction such a question would likely elicit. Laughing at the ignorance of such a misguided question, my friend quickly replied, "I'm Bugis! The Malays live in the Riau Islands."[22] All of the friends I asked replied in a similar manner. And yet, responses solicited from self-identified Bugis, Malay, or Malay-Bugis individuals living in the Riau Islands paint a different picture worthy of additional analysis.

The Malay-Bugis Nexus and Ethnic In- and Out-Groups

On 14 October 2017, then former (and re-elected) Malaysian Prime Minister Tun Dr Mahathir Mohamad courted controversy due to comments he allegedly made at an opposition-led "anti-kleptocracy rally" in Selangor. Accounts of the rally allege that Mahathir took aim at then Prime Minister Najib—his erstwhile mentee turned political adversary whom he ousted—reportedly saying, "Maybe he can trace his ancestry to Bugis pirates. Somehow, he lost his way and came to Malaysia. Go home to Bugis [Sulawesi]!" (*Malaysiakini*, 16 October 2017). These alleged comments gestured towards Najib's well-documented ancestral roots in the Bugis homeland of South Sulawesi.[23] Mahathir's purported comments were widely panned in the Malaysian and Indonesian media, leading not only to a police report filed against him, but also to calls from Indonesia's Bugis Youth Assembly of Makassar, Indonesia (PPBMI) for him to apologize. In a prepared statement, PPBMI members allegedly reminded Dr Mahathir that "the Bugis was an ethnic group that had played an important role in the formation of the Malay government and Sultanate", and that "the insult had hurt the feelings of everyone of Bugis descent throughout the world, especially in Indonesia" (*Malay Mail*, 20 October 2017). Mahathir's comments are useful for our purposes here, insofar as the reactions they elicited—reactions that foregrounded the "important role" played by the Bugis in the formation of the Malay sultanate—apply to our discussion of the meaning of Malayness in Riau Islands history.

Widespread notions about Bugis roles in the formation of the Malay sultanate may be read with an eye to anthropologist Nicholas Long's (2013) analysis of so-called "poisoned histories" in the Riau Islands. In his book, *Being Malay in Indonesia* (Long 2013)—whose title this chapter echoes, albeit with a Bugis twist—Long draws attention to the contested, negotiated nature of historiography and historical description in the Riau Islands, arguing that Malays of Bugis descent are characterized by some Riau Island Malays as having wielded disproportionate control over the writing of "Malay history" (*sejarah Melayu*). Long draws particular and important attention to efforts to "redefine the focus of Malay history" (2013, p. 70), efforts that reflect a frustration among certain Riau Island Malays that "Malay history", as one of his interlocutors noted, is "much more Bugis than Malay". Long connects these efforts to "anti-Bugis sentiment among the Malays of the Riau Archipelago" (2013, p. 71) and allegedly widespread notions of "Bugis colonialism" and definitions of "Malayness" which hold that "Bugis identity" is "irreconcilable with Malay identity" (2013, p. 73).

Curiously, during the course of my fieldwork in Kepri I encountered no such statements regarding the irreconcilability of "Bugis" and "Malay" in a distinctly "Malay" province. Instead, and across conversations with a variety of Malay and Bugis-identifying Riau Islanders, I encountered just the opposite. I began this chapter by discussing how the relation between Malays and Bugis has been characterized as something "like the black and white parts of the eye", insofar as both groups "cannot be separated". During the course of my time in Kepri, this phrase recurred—almost as if read from a conventionally shared ethno-historical script—in interviews conducted with a cross-section of Kepri society, ranging from government servants from the Department of Culture and Tourism, to tour guides describing the history of Penyengat, to self-described "Bugis gangsters" hailing from South Sulawesi, to taxi drivers, to policemen. Self-identified "Pure Malays", "Malays of Bugis descent", "Bugis immigrants" from Sulawesi, and Bugis born in Riau Islands province all testified, in one way or another, to an alleged unity established between their peoples in the eighteenth and nineteenth centuries, and its lasting importance in contemporary Kepri. These observed allegations of steadfast unity or affiliation do not necessarily conflict with Long's (2013) account of "poisoned histories". Indeed, they may be read diagnostically, serving as evidence of a distinctly (and authority-defining) Bugis reformulation or adjudication of "Malay history" in the Riau Islands, and of the ideological power such a history has on many Riau Islanders' (mis)rememberings of the past.[24] We might consider some examples of how such a history—however contested or distorted—inflects contemporary definitions of the boundaries between groups.

One individual, a government servant associated with Batam's Institute for Malay Customs and a self-identified "pure Malay", explained that even before the five legendary Bugis brothers arrived in Riau in the 1700s, the Bugis were already present, and indeed, welcomed by the Malays because "they mixed with Malay society",[25] a practice that Bugis immigrants from Sulawesi continue to this day. "The process kept moving",[26] he told me. Another self-identifying "pure Malay" working as a guide in the mausoleums of Penyengat explained the contemporary closeness between Bugis and Malays by way of historical reference to the Oath of Malay Bugis Loyalty (*Sumpah Setia Melayu Bugis*) explaining, "The Malays married the Bugis, occasioning an oath of loyalty, that's why the Bugis and Malays are considered one, they cannot be separated."[27] A Malay of Bugis extraction descended from the legendary Bugis brothers used himself as an example of the lasting legacy of Bugis-Malay interaction and intermarriage in the Riau Islands, explaining to me at the Grand Mosque of the Sultan of Riau that "I am Malay-Bugis, that [connection] cannot be erased, and the Malay-Bugis promise cannot be forgotten."[28] An elderly man in Tanjungpinang who, while born in Bintan, identifies as pure Bugis with no "Malay blood" (*darah Melayu*) explained that "Bugis who migrate here, can become Malay" due to the historical closeness forged between the two over the course of centuries. "The Bugis are Malay and the Malays are Bugis,"[29] he told me, laughing.

In these various ways, while Malays of Bugis ancestry may self-identify as Malay, they readily acknowledge the special, historical importance of their Bugis roots. So too, self-identifying Bugis members of contemporary Kepri society—even those who may have migrated there from the Bugis homeland of South Sulawesi—acknowledge the ethno-historical commonality between themselves and their Malay counterparts. In this crucial respect, while Malays, Malays of Bugis ancestry, and Bugis members of contemporary Kepri society may acknowledge the definitional "edges" between "Bugis" and "Malay" qua ethnic categories—and here, think of the hyphens in the phrases "Melayu-Bugis", "Bugis-Melayu", or "Sumpah Setia Melayu-Bugis" as a kind of iconic representation of this "edge"—they are, to a certain extent, members of the same ethno-historically defined "in-group." The same cannot be said for other ethnic collectivities in Kepri's shifting demographic terrain.

While many members of Kepri's Malay majority might count the Bugis as honorary members of a shrinking in-group, the lines between themselves and other "non-Malay" members of the province are more starkly drawn. This is particularly true of Javanese, Batak, and Minang or Padang migrants who, in the words of a Malay taxi driver in Batam, do not have the right to "take control of [his] place of birth".[30] A government servant working in Batam offered a similar, but more delicately stated opinion, explaining that "The Bugis and Malays can't be separated, but the Javanese ... that's a different case. As are the Minang. And the Batak are clearly different. That's the reality of the situation."[31]

Putative (or authority-defined) histories of arrival, interaction, and assimilation were often deployed by my informants as evidence for in- and outgroup status. "Why weren't Minang people welcomed [in the Malay empire]?", one historically minded Malay informant working in Batam rhetorically asked me. "Because Minang had their 'pride'",[32] he answered, adding that they "were unable to get power". "Furthermore", he added, "there's still an historical wound", alluding to a legacy of Minangkabau-led threats to the Sultanate in the eighteenth century. "Why weren't the Javanese welcomed into the Malay community?", he continued, answering "The Javanese never 'played around' in Malay sultanate territories. They have only recently come as labourers. And they were never given the space to become Malay. The Bugis were given the space."[33]

Referring to the ethnic Chinese community (a group whose members have long been approached as prototypical "others" by analysts), this informant continued his inter-ethnic exposition, noting that—unlike the Javanese or Batak, for example—"the Chinese have long played a role in the Riau Islands", noting their historically important role as economic mediators for the Malay sultanate (*Kapitan Cina*). In stark contrast to national-level anti-Chinese discourses—while tacitly counterpoising members of this community with those of the Minangkabau and other ethnic communities in the Riau Islands—he noted, "there has never been conflict between the Chinese and the Malays"[34] in the Riau Islands. Concluding his evaluation of in-group and out-groups in the Riau Islands, he returned to the position of the Bugis, and in so doing re-emphasized an imagined history of interaction, assimilation, and alliance building as evidence for Bugis in-group belonging: "The Bugis were welcomed"[35] into the Malay community, he said, explaining that "the reason is, first, the ones who came here already came in waves. Before the Daengs came here",[36] referring to the famous five Bugis brothers, "the Bugis were already here … they already mixed with Malay society. Automatically, they were proud to become Malay."[37]

These observations about in- and out-groups may once again be viewed with a critical eye toward authority-defined discourses about ethnic belonging and history in the Riau Islands. This issue aside, however, what does this authority-defined history—however "poisoned" (Long 2013), distorted, or contested—look like? In what follows, I offer an outline of a Bugis-centric history of Malay ethno-locality in the Riau Islands, one that illustrates a particular framing of Bugis and Malays of Bugis descent as an ascendant force in Riau Islands history. This is a rough, if not distorted history, necessarily truncated and missing alternative narratives or much of the empirical richness (or historiographic "objectivity") that readers are encouraged to pursue elsewhere.[38] And yet, I offer it here insofar as this was the history repeatedly recounted to me by a number of Riau Islanders—from officials working at the Institute of Malay Customs, to tour guides, to amateur historians—over the course of my fieldwork. I highlight the rough edges of this orally transmitted history (interlineated with relevant references to the historical literature), to ground a subsequent discussion of how historical consciousness or (mis)rememberings of the past may be viewed as having shaped a Malay ethno-nationalism that inflects the Riau Islands Province's sociocultural and political climate today.

A (Bugis-Centric) History of Malay Ethno-Locality

In 1699, the young ninth Sultan of the Johor-Pahang-Lingga Sultanate, Mahmud Shah II (1675–99), was assassinated in Johor by one of his admirals hailing from Bintan, due to his propensity towards impulsiveness and brutality. With no apparent heirs, the Sultan's Viceroy [Bendahara], Abdul Jalil IV assumed the throne with the nominal approval of Johor's royal court. Despite initial controversy surrounding the newly throned Sultan's alleged lack of "legitimate" royal roots, Abdul Jalil IV ruled for almost two decades, amidst his empire's ever-increasing instability. In 1718, Abdul Jalil IV was overthrown by an individual claiming to be the late Mahmud Shah II's posthumous heir, Raja Kecik. Emerging from Siak in present-day Riau Province, Raja Kecik's coup d'état was assisted by ethnically Minangkabau or "Minang" troops (a fact, we will later see, has not been forgotten by today's Riau Island Bugis-Malays). In response, Abdul Jalil IV's son, Raja Sulaiman, enlisted the help of five Bugis warrior-prince brothers—Daeng Parani, Daeng Marewah, Daeng Celak, Daeng Menambun, and Daeng Kamasi (recall the reference to these figures in this chapter's introduction). The ousted sultan's son promised the hand of his daughter, Tengku Tengah, to Daeng Parani in exchange for assistance in reconsolidating his family's power as custodians of the Malay world. Agreeing, the five brothers spearheaded a Bugis assault on Johor that drove Raja Kecik and his court to Riau. After additional skirmishes, Bugis forces effectively drove Raja Kecik from the expanse of the empire, and ousted Abdul Jalil IV's son Raja Sulaiman was installed as Sultan of Johor-Riau-Pahang-Lingga on the island of Bintan in 1722.

As per their arrangement, the new Sultan's daughter, Tengku Tengah, married Daeng Parani, whose brother Daeng Marewah was then named "Viceroy" (*Yang Dipertuan Muda*) of Riau by Sultan Sulaiman, pragmatically transforming the Bugis from a peripheral, "outsider" presence in "domestic" royal Malay affairs to powerful political stakeholders in a Malay world stretching from present-day Indonesia, to Singapore, to Malaysia. This began a long process of intermarriage between Bugis "interlopers" and Malay royalty, and forged the *Sumpah Setia Melayu Bugis* or "Malay-Bugis Oath of Loyalty". This oath of allegiance between the Bugis and Malays contained the following pledge: "If you are a friend of the Bugis, then you are a friend of the Malays, and if you are a friend of the Malays, then you are a friend of the Bugis" (*Jikalau tuan kepada Bugis, tuanlah kepada Melayu, dan jikalau tuan kepada Melayu, tuanlah kepada Bugis*).[39]

The agreement between the Bugis and Malays stipulated that only relatives of Riau's legendary Bugis brothers or their descendants could inhabit the role of the *Yang Dipertuan Muda* position. After Daeng Marewah—the first viceroy—died in 1728, his brother Daeng Celak took over as the second viceroy (1728–45), followed by Daeng Kamboja (1745–77), the son of Daeng Parani. After Daeng Kamboja's tenure, subsequent *Yang Dipertuan Muda* possessed "Malay-Bugis blood" (*darah Melayu Bugis*) due to ongoing practices of intermarriage, and all lineal descendants of the five legendary Bugis brothers received (and continue to receive) the first name, "Raja".[40]

Amidst these ongoing "domestic" or internal developments—whereby the role and status of the Malay sultan became, as Barnard (2009, p. 68) puts it, "increasingly irrelevant"—a storm was brewing. The Dutch presence in Melaka led to tensions between colonial interlopers and Bugis-Malay armadas renowned for their "military prowess" (Barnard 2009, p. 68) on land and at sea. *Yang Dipertuan Muda* II Daeng Celak's son, Raja Haji Fisabilillah ibni Daeng Celak, followed in his father's footsteps as the fourth *Yang Dipertuan* of the sultanate, serving from 1777 to 1784. While overseeing the restoration of the empire to its "former prominence" (Barnard 2009, p. 68), Raja Haji Fisabilillah began leading a series of raids attacking the Dutch presence over the course of 1783 to 1784, ultimately dying in battle in present-day Teluk Ketapang in Riau Province. This led to a brief period of uncertainty.[41]

However, Barnard, notes, "the nadir of Bugis rule in the Riau Archipelago ended around 1800, when Sultan Mahmud III invited Raja Ali back to Riau and reinstalled him as the Yang Dipertuan Muda" (Barnard 2009, p. 68). In a symbolic re-embodiment of the *Sumpah Setia Melayu Bugis*, the reinstalled *Yang Dipertuan Muda*'s daughter, Engku Puteri Raja Hamidah, was married to the Malay sultan. The Sultan gifted his new wife and the family of Raja Haji Fisabilillah with Penyengat Island adjacent to Tanjungpinang, effectively "split[ting]", Barnard (2009) notes, the "kingdom into two distinctive halves. The Bugis would rule Riau from Penyengat, while the Malay elite would rule Lingga from the island of the same name" (Barnard 2009, p. 68).

In the ensuing years, colonial control over the empire increased. The British created the state of Johor, whose first Chief Official (*Temenggong*) (Daeng Ibrahim) was also of mixed Bugis-Malay descent (Trocki 2007).[42] In 1818, the Dutch signed a treaty with the kingdom's Bugis-Malays that gave Dutch ships freedom of movement in the area, and established Dutch control over the selection of future Sultans. Adding insult to injury, the subsequent 1824 Treaty of London between the British and Dutch divided the geographical expanse of the Johor-Pahang-Riau-Lingga Sultanate between the two vying colonial powers. Singapore and Johor was ceded to the British, while Riau and Lingga was ceded to the Dutch. Almost 100 years later, the Dutch dissolution of Riau-Lingga's institutional infrastructure was complete, when in 1911 they deposed the Sultan of Riau-Lingga Abdulrahman Muazam Shah (*Singapore Free Press and Mercantile Advertiser*, 13 February 1911, p. 5).

One might assume that this rapid series of events radically transformed senses of belonging in a divided Malay empire. And yet, a sense of transregional ethno-nationalism would continue to incubate and endure well into the twentieth century. After Indonesia's proclamation of independence on 17 August 1945, a selection of agents who identified as descendants from Riau-Lingga sought to re-establish relations with the Dutch, such that they might lobby for the re-establishment of the sultanate over and against their incorporation into an Indonesian "nation". On 11 December 1947, the *Straits Times* (p. 6) offered a synopsis of these affairs:

> The people of Rhio formed a committee called Jawatan Kuasa Penguros Rakyat Rhio (the Rhio People's Committee) consisting of 24 members with Raja Haji Abdullah bin Osmar as president ... The Principal objectives of this committee were (1) the restoration of the Sultanate of Rhio-Lingga and (2) the establishment of a "Rhio Raad," or council of state ... [I]f the N.E.I. [Netherlands East Indies] Government approved the restoration of the Sultanate, the person who should be elected as Sultan should be one of the lawful descendants of the last Sultan of Rhio-Lingga ... The senior surviving lawful descendant of the late Sultan living in Singapore is Yang Amat Mulia Tengku Ibrahim bin Tengku Omar ... a grandson of the late Sultan.

Aside from Raja Haji Abdullah's involvement in the movement for the Sultanate's re-establishment, another Malay of Bugis descent—Raja Muhammad Yunus—who held the military rank of Major and once engaged with Japanese forces during the interregnum was also involved in separatist efforts. A descendant of Raja Haji Fisabilillah, Raja Muhammad Yunus spearheaded a five-year military conflict between Riau royalist and Indonesian nationalist forces that, as Wee (2016, p. 249) notes, has been "omitted in dominant versions of Indonesian historiography". Ongoing attempts to reassert Riau's independence from the Indonesian state ultimately failed when Riau was incorporated as a province in 1957, leading Raja Muhammad Yunus to flee to nearby Johor, where he was given sanctuary by the Sultan.

Several decades later, and following the formation of the 1989 SIJORI growth triangle—a tripartite economic initiative that forged logistical and investment transactions between Indonesian Riau, Singapore, and Malaysian Johor (three places roughly corresponding to the once sprawling Johor-Riau-Lingga Sultanate sketched above)—Malay ethno-nationalism reared its head again, albeit in a new context of competing interests associated with Indonesian decentralization. Nicholas Long (2013) writes that "Riau Islanders' interest in regional autonomy was couched in terms of returning to a state of affairs they had once enjoyed but which had been cruelly and senselessly wrested from them" (Long 2013, p. 46). "This sentiment", Long writes, had "hardened" in part because of the experienced effects of transregional economic development: "The growing disparity between the Riau Islands and Singapore, perceived to have been equals as recently as the 1970s, fostered resentment towards the political systems that were preventing the archipelago from developing at a similar pace" (Long 2013, p. 46).

Long notes that—in contrast to "earlier efforts to break away from the newly independent Indonesia [that] had failed to garner popular support in either Insular or Mainland Riau" (see Long 2013)—regional sentiments taking aim at centralized rule became increasingly popular among Indonesian citizens living in what we today call Riau Islands Province (Long 2013, p. 47). This rising regionalism was inadvertently enabled by Suharto-era cultural policy, whereby the socio-culture of Indonesian provinces became distinctly defined with reference to particular ethnic groups. This New Order policy effectively reaffirmed everyday assumptions about "ethno-locality"—"a spatial scale where 'ethnicity' and 'locality' [or place] presume each other to such a degree that they become, in essence, a single concept" (Boellstorff 2005, p. 18; see Long 2013, p. 47). Informed and shaped by Dutch colonial-era administrative practices and Leiden school scholarship on *adat* or "custom", New Order ideologies of ethno-locality forged linkages between people and place, whereby ethnicities were defined by provincial regions and provincial regions by ethnicity: e.g., South Sulawesi with "Bugis" or "Bugis-Makassar", Bali with "Balinese", Riau with "Malay", and so on. Long suggests that "Malayness" became a principle idiom for regional political participation and contestation for Riau Islanders.

More covert forms of regional secessionist ideology became more overtly articulated following the fall of Suharto. In Pekanbaru in Riau Province, a "Free Riau" (*Riau Merdeka*) movement called for the formation of an independent Federal Republic of Riau (Long 2013, p. 48). And yet, in the adjacent Riau Islands, similarly regional sentiments were developing, although they were taking aim not at Jakarta, but at "centralized" control in Riau's provincial capital of Pekanbaru. Long (2013) writes that "Led by the regent of the Riau Islands, Hoezrin Hood, a cross-party consensus grew that of the two power centres, Jakarta and Pekanbaru, it was the latter that was the more insidious" (2013, p. 48). Again, Riau Islanders' aversions to mainland Riau were articulated through an ethno-localized idiom of Malayness: "Pekanbaru was dominated by Minangkabau and Bataks and had long behaved in a "colonial" way towards the archipelagic heartlands, resulting in the complete marginalization of island populations, especially Malays" (2013, p. 48). So too, the establishment of a new Riau Islands province would allow the Islands to "better exploit its natural gas reserves, realise its strategic potential from being located near the border with Singapore, and improve its human resource base if it became an autonomous province and ensured that profits from its resources were directed towards archipelagic needs rather than welfare and development projects on the mainland" (2013, p. 48).

Hood's efforts gained momentum with the support of the Islands' Bugis-Malay aristocrats—descendants of the five brothers and the *Yang Dipertuan Mudas*—whose involvement, my informants told me, was crucial for Hood's efforts. Long (2013) describes how Hood convinced this segment of Island society by appealing to the accomplishment of their ancestors, contraposing these with the current state of affairs in which Malays found themselves, "trapped in coastal villages, living on the brink of poverty in the world they had once considered to be their oyster" (2013, p. 50). Hood lobbied the central government for the formation of Riau Islands province, and in 2002 then President Megawati Sukarnoputri agreed.[43] In 2004, Riau Islands began formally operating as a province.

Markers of Malayness

Today, signs of the ethno-localized Malayness that so centrally figured in calls for the new province continue to circulate widely in the Riau Islands. These signs or markers of Malayness are, at the same time, deeply imbued with a transregional sense or perception of Malay history, reflecting certain conceptions of the past, while shaping the ways history lives on in the present. These signs are, of course, explicitly displayed during exemplary "traditional Malay ceremonies" (*upacara adat Melayu*) when male participants assemble wearing the traditional *baju Melayu* (Figure 14.3). And yet, signs or markers of Malayness are also readily evinced in more banal, everyday interactions. Consider, for example, the mediating role of language in everyday life.

During the course of my fieldwork, multiple Malay informants of Bugis descent identified the language they spoke not as Indonesian (Bahasa Indonesia), but Malay (Bahasa Melayu), a language, they told me, descended from courtly Malay spoken by their ancestors in the Riau-Lingga-Johor sultanate, and one later codified by Raja Ali Haji—that Bugis-Malay aristocrat who, from his home on Penyengat Island, developed the first monolingual Malay dictionary (recall Vice-President Jusuf Kalla's comments noted in the introduction). Interestingly, the Malay variety spoken by Riau Islanders is also an object of attention among their "co-ethnic" relatives living in the contemporary Malaysian state of Johor, who view it as an emblem of transregional and cross-border Malayness. Upon learning of my forthcoming travels to Kepri in February 2017, one informant from Johor suggested that the language spoken there figures as a kind of "legacy" (*warisan*) from a Malay sultanate that cut across contemporary transnational lines of difference. Another put it more simply still, excitedly telling me that I would "hear the original Malay language there!"[44]

It is beyond the scope and aims of this chapter to socio-linguistically situate this ideologically "pure" Malay variant and its speakers within broader debates surrounding Riau Malay and other Malay varieties across the Malay-speaking world. What matters most to our conversation here, rather, is its ideological salience as a kind of ethno-linguistic code, one shared within the Riau Islands' Malay community

FIGURE 14.3
Showing Signs of Malayness at the Institute of Malay Customs

Source: Photograph by the author.

that distinguishes true "Malays" from outsiders who speak the "national" language of Indonesian. Allow me briefly, however, to identify one of its more iconic features—one that distinguishes it from the national language, and brings it (and its speakers) into alignment with their imagined, co-ethnic "Malays" living elsewhere in the Malay world: schwa [ə] in word-final position. In the Malay variety spoken by my Malay informants of Bugis descent, standard Indonesian words *saya* ("I"), *kita* (first-person plural inclusive "we"), *apa* ("what"), or any word featuring the final letter "-a" would not be pronounced as it would in standard Indonesian. Rather, in this variety, /a/ transforms to /ə/. This sound is salient enough as an in-group identity marker that, from text-messages to graffiti in the Riau Islands, the final letter -a in words like "kita" or "apa" is frequently orthographically rendered as "-e" to capture the "uh" sound of the schwa. By way of example, consider a graffiti image on a wall directly outside the ferry terminal that shuttles travellers back and forth between Tanjungpinang and nearby Penyengat Island—a frequent destination for local and transnational Malay tourists and pilgrims (Figure 14.4). The painted image features an anthropomorphic edible sea snail (*gonggong*) (itself a kind of icon in Kepri society), announcing "Tanjungpinang Kampung Kite!" Note how the -a ordinarily occurring in Indonesian first-person plural inclusive *kita* or "we" is replaced with -e, and consider the ideological importance of this replacement, insofar as it serves as a

FIGURE 14.4
A Sign of Exclusionary Inclusion? "Tanjung Pinang Kampong Kite!"
(Tanjung Pinang is Our Home!)

Source: Photograph by the author.

marker of in-group Malay identity in the (inclusive yet simultaneously exclusionary) declaration that "Tanjungpinang Kampung *Kite!*" (Tanjungpinang is *Our* Home!).

Aside from Malay language, we might also consider the names of its speakers as salient markers of a certain kind of Malayness in contemporary Kepri society. Recall the special role played by and afforded to those descendants of the five Bugis brothers. Recall, too, how descendants of these five brothers—decidedly Bugis figures who intermarried with the Malay royal line—received the first name Raja, several of whom would go on to serve as "Viceroys" (*Yang Dipertuan Muda*) of the Malay sultanate.[45] Today, the name *Raja* continues to serve as an easily identifiable marker of those Malay-Bugis men and women of noble birth, some of whom staff provincial government positions.

During my fieldwork, I met one such Raja based in Batam's Department of Culture and Tourism (*Dinas Kebudayaan dan Pariwisata*) housed in the island's Institute of Malay Customs (*Lembaga Adat Melayu*) Nong Isa Building. One of Raja's previous charges was to join government efforts to commemorate and promote other signs of Malayness in Kepri. He was part of a "naming team" that was tasked by former Batam Mayor Ahmad Dahlan (2006–16)—a part-time Malay historian whose administration worked to promote the history of Batam and the greater Riau Islands Province—to develop a list of "names of Malay-Bugis figures" (Malay: *nama-nama tokoh Melayu Bugis*). These figures' perceived (or authority-*defined*) influence in Riau Islands' history was to be commemorated in the form of street and building names.

I turn to examples of political acts of government-sponsored commemoration in the next section, explaining how these are part of a broader government mission, and are seen to a certain extent as a reflex of ongoing processes of transregional migration and demographic shift.

THE POLITICS OF ETHNO-HISTORICAL COMMEMORATION AND DEMOGRAPHIC SHIFT

Visions and Missions of the Kepri Government (2016–21)

In advance of the 2016 year, Kepri's regional government released a draft report of its "Regional Medium-Term Development Plan" (Rencana Pembangunan Jangka Menengah Daerah, or RPJMD), or, a plan that articulates the "vision" (*visi*), "mission" (*misi*), and programmes projected over a five-year period. Projected from 2016 to 2021, the Kepri RPJMD report detailed a number of visions, missions, and programmes that may be glossed over as broadly centring on:

- improving the quality of infrastructure, education, and health and health care;
- developing a maritime, tourist, and agricultural economy conducive to investment;
- strengthening small businesses and large-scale industries; and
- developing a clean, accountable and disciplined government system with a higher work ethic for government servants.

With respect to these goals, Kepri's RPJMD might not be that different from those of other regional governments. However, and relevant for our discussion here, one of its articulated goals readily distinguishes Kepri's RPJMD from those of other provinces elsewhere in Indonesia. This particular programme and vision is: "To develop a society life that is religious, democratic, just, orderly, harmonious and safe under the umbrella of Malay culture."[46] This particular programme is geared towards the "Embodiment of Kepri Province as the Mother of the Malay Land".[47]

This broader "mission" (*misi*) of developing a society under "the umbrella of Malay culture" is accompanied by a goal (*tujuan*), namely:

Preserve the values and art of Malay culture in order to realize a Riau Islands society
with personality and noble character.[48]

This goal is accompanied by an additional "target" (*sasaran*):

Increase the preservation of Malay cultural values and arts as part of the cultural
richness of the region.[49]

The enunciated "strategy" to reach these goals is to:

Empower Malay figures and institutions in Kepri Province to preserve cultural values
in the lives of the people.[50]

The "policies" (*kebijakan*) that will be undertaken aspire towards:

The increased understanding and practice of Malay cultural values, cultural promotion,
fostering of local arts and traditions, the preservation of objects, sites, and cultural
heritage areas (tangible), and the preservation of intangible cultural heritage.[51]

Finally, these goals, targets, strategies, and policies have the "mission focus" (*fokus
misi*) of:

The embodiment of Kepri Province as the Mother of the Malay Land.[52]

In what follows, I evaluate how these visions, missions, and goals are playing out
on the ground, and I highlight some of Kepri's important Malay sites and cultural
heritage areas which double as "tourist objects" (*obyek wisata*). Then, and turning to
demographic data, I consider how intensifying government interest in these visions,
missions and goals may be read as a kind of reflex or response to issues of ongoing
demographic shift.

Street Names, Monuments, Mausoleums and Museums

In Batam, the drive from the international ferry terminal to Kepri's Lembaga Adat
Melayu, or the Institute of Malay Customs, is a short one. Disembarking travellers
headed to the Lembaga Adat Melayu from Batam Centre International Terminal
need only turn left on Daeng Kamboja Street, turn right on Raja Isa Street, and—
after passing by the Engku Putri Street intersection—will have reached the institute,
housed in a three-story structure known as the Nong Isa Building. These street
names and others in the vicinity of the Institute of Malay Customs—names like
Raja H. Fisabilillah, Raja Husin or Raja M. Tahir—elicit ostensibly little attention
from tourists arriving from nearby Singapore, whose immediate goal is often to
find "cheap sex, food and shopping" (Chong 2016, p. 310). And why would such
tourists care about the names of the streets they traverse while on holiday? Street
names are, after all, just street names: "quintessentially mundane and seemingly
obvious" (Azaryahu 1996, p. 311).

However, and as geographer Maoz Azaryahu (ibid.) puts it, "The use of street
names for commemorative purposes is instrumental in transforming the urban
environment into a virtual political setting". In Batam, this is certainly true of

those streets named after local Bugis and Malay/Bugis historical figures like Daeng Kambodja, Raja Isa, Engku Putri and so on—names which reflect the enduring and everyday ideological salience of the Bugis influence on "Malay history" (*sejarah Melayu*) in contemporary political life in the Riau Islands. Indeed, "'Historical' street names", Azaryahu notes, "are a distinctive *lieux de memoire* of modernity. From the perspective of those in charge of moulding the symbolic infrastructure of society, the main merit of commemorative street names is that they introduce an authorized version of history into ordinary settings of everyday life" (1996, p. 312).

In Batam, the commemorative naming of these streets after Bugis figures and Malays of Bugis extraction—people like Daeng Kambodja, Raja Isa, Engku Putri and so on—reflects an authorized or authority-defined version of "Malay history" as it is understood in the contemporary Riau Islands. The commemorative naming of these streets highlights the Batam and Kepri government's political mission in action, as it seeks to authorize a certain ethno-historical vision and infuse that vision into settings of everyday life.

The commemoration of these historical figures—ones detailed in the foregoing section—is not limited to street names, of course, but is also performed in other kinds of projects. Consider Raja Haji Fisabilillah International Airport in Tanjungpinang. Originally named Kijang Airport, the name change ceremoniously occurred in 2008, and was officiated by Provincial Governor Ismeth Abdullah, Deputy Governor H.M. Sani and Indonesian Transportation Minister Jusman Syafii Djamal. Raja Haji Fisabilillah—declared an Indonesian "national hero" (*pahlawan nasional*) by Suharto's government in 1997—is not only commemorated on street signs or airports. After his declaration as a national hero, then-*bupati* of Riau Islands regency Abdul Manan Saiman (1990–2000) constructed the Raja Haji Fisabilillah monument. Depicting images of Raja Haji's battles against the Dutch, the monument continues to attract tourists and local people today (Figure 14.5).

Other "sights and cultural heritage areas"[53] also double as tourist objects (*obyek wisata*) or religious destinations (*destinasi religi*) especially the mausoleums of those Bugis and Bugis-descended aristocrats so legendary within Riau Islands history. Attracting transregional and local tourists and pilgrims, the mausoleums on Bintan island include the tombs of Malay Sultan Sulaiman, and two of the Bugis brothers—Daeng Celak and Daeng Marewah (Figure 14.6). On Penyengat Island, tourists may visit the tombs of Raja Hamidah Engku Puteri, Raja Ahmad, Raja Ali Haji, Raja Abdullah, Raja Aisyah, and Raja Haji Fisabilillah (Figure 14.7). Penyengat Island—itself branded as a location of "historical heritage"—is a tourist destination in its own right, where visitors can visit the Grand Mosque of the Sultan of Riau, among other sites (Figure 14.8).

Government-driven revitalization efforts do not only centre on the creation of monuments or the preservation of historical, cultural, or religious sites such as these (Hutchinson 2017). They also focus on disseminating "new" kinds of knowledge about "old" things. Consider a meeting that occurred over the course of two days at the Institute of Malay Customs, when an international cohort of Malay anthropologists, historians and cultural critics gathered at the Nong Isa building from 29 through

FIGURE 14.5
Raja Haji Fisabilillah Monument, Tanjung Pinang. Top image: The monument proper;
Bottom image: depiction of Raja Haji at battle

FIGURE 14.6
Tomb of Daeng Celak, Second Yang Dipertuan Muda of Riau

Source: Photograph by the author.

FIGURE 14.7
Penyengat Tombs. Top image: Tomb complex including Enku Puteri and Raja Ali Haji;
Bottom image: Tomb of Raja Haji Fisabilillah

Source: Photographs by the author.

FIGURE 14.8
Penyengat's Historical Heritage. Top image: Location Map of Penyengat Island's
Historical Heritage; Bottom image: Grand Mosque of the Sultan of Riau

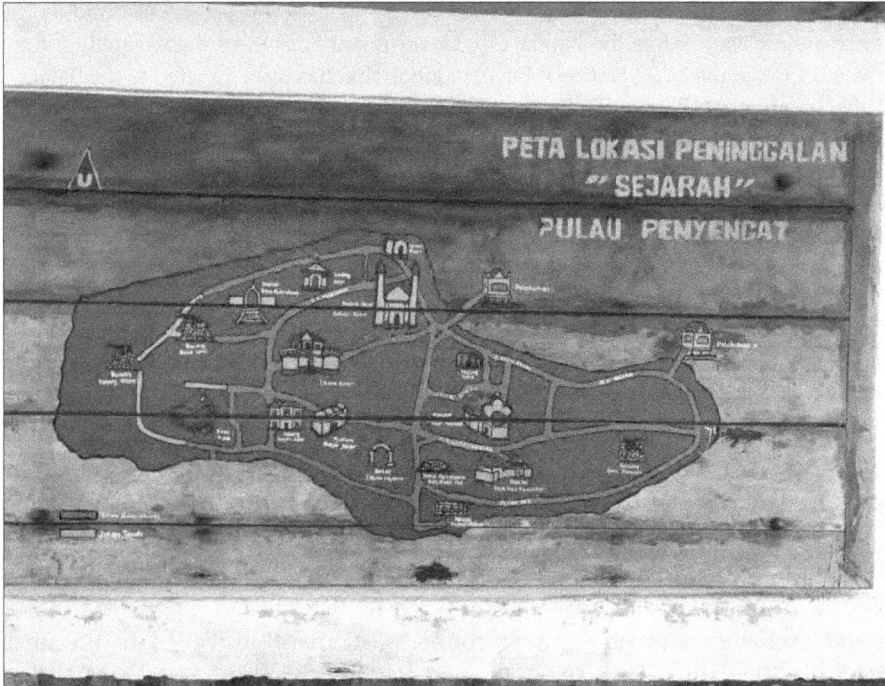

Source: Photographs by the author.

30 March 2017. The purpose of their meeting was clearly stipulated in the formal invitation that each received from the Batam government's Department of Culture and Tourism:

> We may inform you that the Batam City Government has built a display gallery for the museum at the MTQ National Level pavilion that has been donated to the Batam City Government. Batam's Department of Culture and Tourism, via Preservation of Heritage, History, and Museum activities, will hold a Focus Group Discussion (FGD) to finalize the concept and materials of the museum. The FGD on Achieving the Full Potential of Museum Materials and Concepts aims to get input and suggestions from FGD participants, so that the museum concept and materials that have already been arranged may be made more perfect.[54]

Participants assembled at the Institute of Malay Customs Nong Isa building. Reflecting another kind of commemoration, the three-story building is named after Raja Isa (alias Nong Isa), a Malay/Bugis aristocrat, great-grandson of Daeng Parani, and representative of the Riau-Lingga sultanate credited with pioneering Batam's governance and development in the mid-nineteenth century. The building—currently under renovation, or so I was told—not only houses the Institute for Malay Customs, but is also home to Batam's Department of Culture and Tourism, reflecting the close and mutualistic relationship between two entities jointly working towards the advancement of Malay cultural values (Figure 14.9).

After exchanging greetings over coffee, participants travelled to the nearby Musabaqah Tilawatil Quran XXV National Pavilion (Gedung Astaka Musabaqah Tilawatil Quran Nasional XXV), which was completed in 2014 and inaugurated by then Governor of the Riau Islands, H. Muhammad Sani, in advance of the twenty-fifth Musabaqah Tilawatil Quran—a national Islamic festival that took place in Batam in June of that year (Figure 14.10).

Participants then entered the multi-purpose building, whose halls were newly outfitted with a series of empty museum display galleries that periodized Riau Islands history and highlighted the enduring value of Malayness in contemporary Riau Islands society. Focus Group Discussion participants moved through the series of galleries in sequence: (1) Riau-Lingga Period,[55] (2) Dutch Period,[56] (3) Japanese Period,[57] (4) Independence Period,[58] (5) The Formation of Riau Islands Province,[59] (6) The Batam Economy,[60] (7) Malay Treasures,[61] (8) The History of the Pavilion and the Implementation of the National MTQ.[62]

Focus group participants were led past the empty display cases by an official from Batam's Department of Culture and Tourism, who pointed to empty displays, suggesting what content or "material" might fill them, and soliciting feedback and constructive critiques in the process. "The floor layout needs improvement", noted one participant. "What icon or symbol might best represent Batam? A gonggong?", asked another, referring to the ubiquitous sea snail popularly consumed throughout the Riau Islands. "We should have a life-size replica of a traditional Malay house, we can place it outside adjacent to the museum", suggested one participant. "What about language? Will there be any materials on Malay language and literature?",

FIGURE 14.9
Nong Isa Building, Institute of Malay Customs, Batam

inquired another, noting the Riau Islands' special role in the development of "pure" Malay language and literature. Government officials recorded these and other observations, and before heading back to the Institute of Malay Customs for an extended discussion, participants assembled on the pavilion steps for a commemorative group photo.

I attended the museum tour and ensuing Focus Group Discussion as a participant observer, accompanied by a Malay friend and Batam native. Sometime after the tour, I took the opportunity to ask my companion what he thought of the focus group and the proposed museum. "For me, their intention is just to remind the people of Batam",[63] he said, "so they just know about the history of Batam from the beginning".[64] And yet, he had his reservations. "But it's a bit late",[65] he said. "Right? Malay culture and customs have already been marginalized at this point of time … Because Batam already has many other ethnic groups coming in",[66] he added. His comments echoed an earlier comment made by a mutual and ethnically Bugis friend, one that explicitly referred to ongoing dynamics of perceived "marginalization" (*peminggiran*) in macro-sociological terms. "It's called a majority becoming a minority",[67] he told me, as we sat in Tanjungpinang's Akau Potong Lembu night market, surrounded

FIGURE 14.10
MTQ XXV National Pavilion and Museum Tour

by ethnically Minang, Javanese, and Chinese vendors. "Before, all of these vendors were Bugis and Malay",[68] he told me, gesturing around us.

Epocholist formulations such as these regarding the imagined end of a Malay majority in Kepri must, however, be objectively evaluated with respect to the demographic data at hand.

Demographic Dynamics and Uncertain Majorities

The available demographic data suggests that, while notions of "majorities becoming minorities" may seem overstated or dramatic, Kepri's Malay community is indeed declining in population. The opening of the Riau Islands to transnational logistical and investment linkages associated with the formation of the SIJORI growth triangle led to the development of new formal sector jobs in Batam. These developments brought demographic changes in their wake, eliciting large-scale migration flows from throughout the Indonesian archipelago. Statistics Indonesia data shows that from 2000 to 2015, the total population of the Riau Islands grew by nearly 400 per cent, from over the course of fifteen years from around 500,000 to 1.9 million. In Batam specifically, these shifts were particularly dramatic, with a 1990 population of 100,000 people in 1990 expanding by twelve times to 1.2 million in 2015. Hutchinson (2017) has usefully charted these dynamics (see Figure 14.11).

These shifting dynamics have, as my respondents alluded to in the previous section, had a marked impact on the islands' ethnic composition. In 2000, the Malay population was 354,853, constituting 35.59 per cent of a total population of 997,075 (Ananta 2016). The Javanese community was a distant second, with a population of 221,756, constituting 22.24 per cent of the total population. Only ten years later, census data show that although they still outnumbered the islands' other ethnic groups, the Malay community had shrunk by 5.3 per cent. The 2010 Malay population numbered 505,391 people, or 30.23 per cent of a total population of 1,671,891. In

FIGURE 14.11
Total Population in Batam and Kepri, 1990–2015

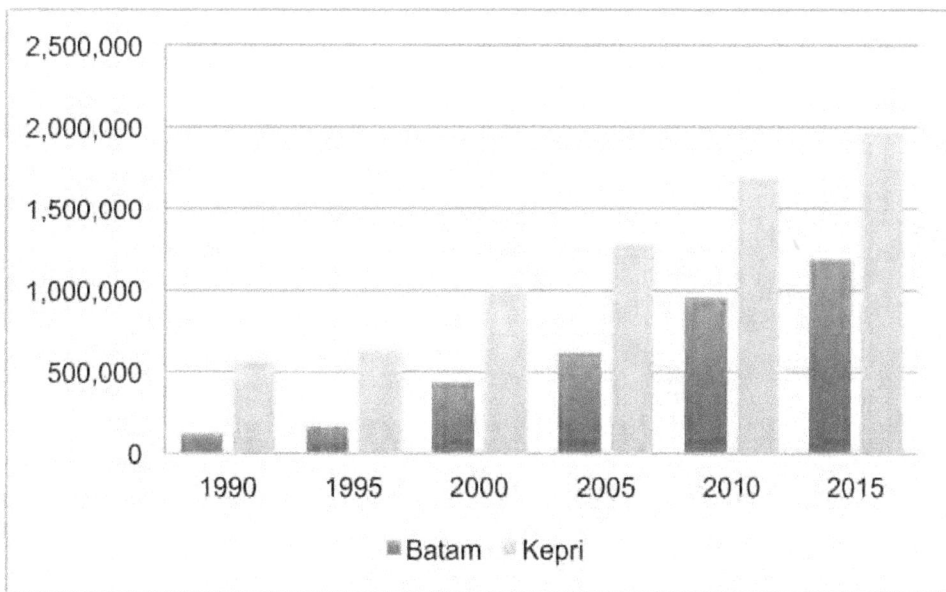

Source: Hutchinson (2017, p. 19) drawing from BPS Data.

contrast, the province's Javanese community grew, expanding to 410,428 in number, or 24.55 per cent of the islands' total population (Ananta 2016, p. 61). The Riau Islands' shifting ethnic composition is laid out in Figure 14.12. Although a 2030 population projection is unavailable for Riau Islands province, Ananta (2016) notes that—assuming these trends continue—the Javanese may very well overtake the islands' Malay community by 2030.

These population trends lend a certain degree of ballast not only to Malay/Bugis folk-assumptions about ethno-demographic shift, but also their senses of being spatially "edged out" (*dipinggirkan*) of the putative centres of economic life in Kepri, such as Batam. As one disgruntled member of Batam's Malay community told me, "If you want to find the original Malays or original Malay places here in Batam, all that's left are the memories ... The original Malays have left for the Islands ... the peripheral people are the Malays."[69] Statements such as these may be viewed with an eye to the relative spatial distribution of the province's Malays vis-à-vis other ethnic groups (see Figure 14.13).

Ongoing processes of such spatial and ethno-demographic marginalization (peminggiran) may, as Ananta (2006, p. 60) crucially notes, serve as "an early warning signal" of potential ethnic conflict. Here, Ananta draws upon the history of religious conflict in Maluku province as a precedent for forecasting this potential in the Riau Islands. Maluku once had equivalent numbers of Christians and Muslims, but this changed after the 1970s when an influx of Muslim migrants threw this into flux, effectively tipping the scale on behalf of the province's Muslim community and

FIGURE 14.12
Shifting Ethnic Populations in Kepri, 2000 and 2010

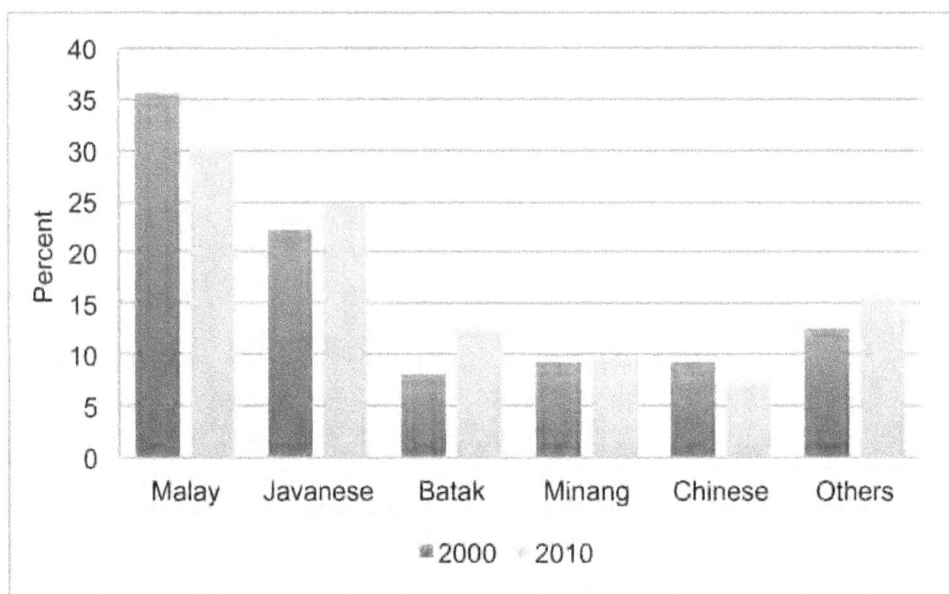

Source: Hutchinson (2017, p. 20).

FIGURE 14.13
Relative Population Distribution of Major Ethnic Groups across Kepri

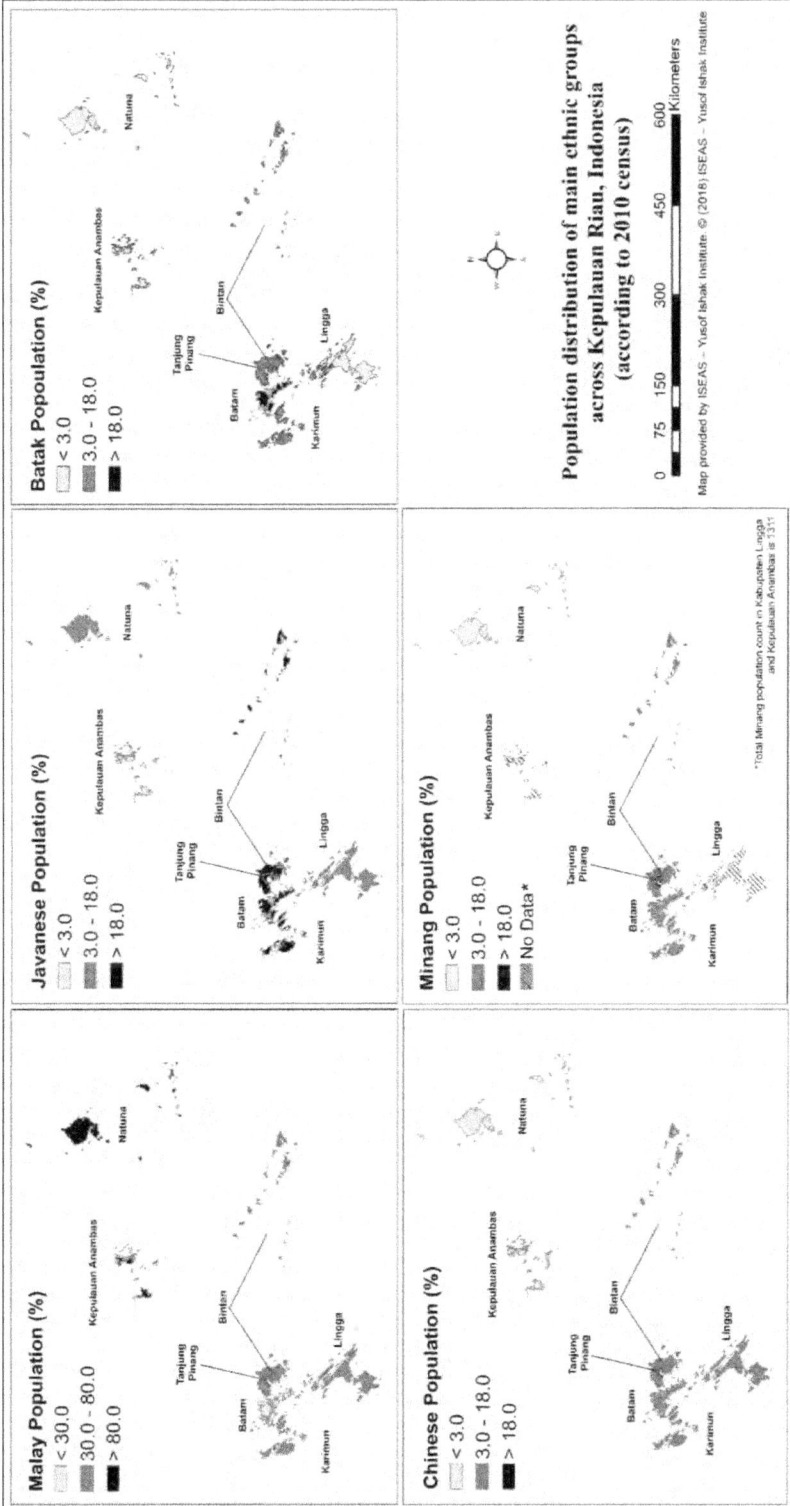

Source: Map courtesy of the ISEAS – Yusof Ishak Institute GIS Project.

sparking inter-religious conflict in 1999. Turning to the Riau islands, Ananta notes
that an "inflow of migrants, mostly from other provinces, was the main source of
population growth in the historically Malay-Muslim province" (2006, p. 59), effectively
transforming the "Malay land" (*tanah Melayu*) into a multiethnic and religious
province of non-Malay interlopers. Recall that one of the reasons the province's
Malays chose to secede from their mainland Riau counterparts was due to issues
they had with other ethnic collectivities—Batak and Minangkabau— who were
perceived as having a countervailing effect on Malay socio-economic and political
supremacy in Riau (Faucher 2005). Amidst increasing senses of ethno-demographic
marginalization that shape Malay senses of being pushed to literal and figurative
edge of life in Kepri, these developments may, as Ananta (2006) notes, be read as a
harbinger of potential conflict.

These developments may also shed light on the Kepri government's prioritization
of policies intended to strengthen the islands' ethno-cultural institutions, rather than
focusing on formal sector motors of the provincial economy (see *RPJMD for Riau
Islands Province 2016–2021*; Hutchinson 2017). That is to say, they help explain the
emphasis placed on the aforementioned government-driven efforts to "preserve" and
"protect" the province's "Malay cultural values" (*nilai-nilai budaya Melayu*) and Malay
historical heritage sites like those described above. Such efforts may be interpreted
as the attempts of an unstable or uncertain majority to recentre themselves as the
ethnic and cultural overlords of the Riau Islands, and to "remind" (*mengingatkan*)
(as my informant above noted) Kepri's ethnic "others" that they are living beneath
an "umbrella of Malay culture".[70]

CONCLUSION: ETHNICITY ON EDGE

In October 2017, in Kepri's adjacent province of Riau, a Chinese Mooncake Festival
was subject to formal protest by Riau's Institute of Malay Customs (Tanjung 2017).
Governor of Riau Arsyadjuliandi 'Andi' Rachman had attended the event, and had
allegedly spoken in support of the traditions of Pekanbaru's Chinese community.
In a letter addressed to the Governor, the Institute of Malay Customs reminded
the governor of the province's Riau 2020 Vision to "make Riau a centre of Malay
Culture",[71] to position Riau as "The Homeland of Malay [*sic*]", and to "build Riau
on the basis of Malay culture".[72] These "visions" for Riau as a "Malay centre" bear a
striking family resemblance to those of Riau Islands province, and as such, we might
view Riau's Mooncake Festival protest with an eye to ongoing ethnic dynamics in
the adjacent Riau Islands.

After Indonesia's Ahok saga—something that captivated the attention of
Indonesian and international audiences alike[73]—this event might be taken as evidence
in an (ongoing) argument that Chinese Indonesians are prototypical others, or people
who fundamentally do not "belong" in contemporary Indonesian society. Readers of
this chapter, however, might already have a sense that this assumption does not fully
capture the nature of inter-ethnic cleavages in the Riau Islands. In Kepri, the division
is not rhetorically cast as "Native" versus "Chinese" (*pribumi* versus *Tionghoa*), but

as Malays (and their Bugis interlocutors) versus the unwanted interlopers (*pribumi* and Chinese alike) whom Malays (or Bugis-Malays) perceive as having pushed them to the literal and figurative edges of society.

This chapter has troped on the idea of the "edge"—an English gloss for the Indonesian/Malay item *pinggiran*—in a number of different ways. Riau Islands Province, once an exemplary centre of the Riau-Lingga-Johor-Pahang Sultanate and Malay world, now lies on the geographical *edges* of a sprawling archipelagic nation state and the trilateral SIJORI "growth triangle". The Bugis—once dwelling on the *edges* of the Malay empire in their homeland of what we today call South Sulawesi province—asserted themselves militarily and socio-politically in the eighteenth to nineteenth centuries in the Riau sultanate, situating themselves in the literal and figurative *centre* of the Malay world. Over time, the definitional *edges* of what it meant to be Bugis and Malay in the Riau Islands became ideologically blurred. Amidst increasing colonial intervention—especially following the Anglo-Dutch treaty of 1824—Riau's Malay royals and the Malay/Bugis viceroys found their dominion divided and themselves pushed to the political and administrative *edges* of life in a once powerful Malay empire. In turn, and following Indonesian independence, these same groups found themselves at the *edge* of a nascent nation-state to which they felt they did not belong. And almost sixty years later, these same groups supported the formation of a distinctly Malay Riau Islands province due to enduring concerns about being *edged out* of sociocultural, political, and economic life in a Riau province that had its administrative centre in mainland Pekanbaru.

In March 2017, and communicating with a self-identified member of Batam's indigenous Malay community, after passing by billboards advertising various "associations" (*persatuan*) for non-Chinese *pribumi* outsiders in Batam, the notion of "edginess" recurred once more. As we passed by the proposed museum put together by the island's Institute of Malay Customs, I asked my driver about recent efforts by the Kepri government to "preserve" Malay culture. "Malay culture and customs have already been marginalized [or *edged out*] today",[74] he stated, using a grammatical derivation of the Malay item "edge" (*pinggir*)."But we as Malay people would agree if the programme [to revitalize Kepri's Malay heritage] becomes reality."[75] When I asked if his notion of "Malay people" included the Bugis, he responded by saying "Yeah ... including the original Batam people",[76] where "original Batam people" are understood as those who lived there prior to the arrival of "newcomers" (*pendatang*).[77]

When asked about issues of ethno-demographic shift in Kepri, one informant working at Batam's Department of Culture and Tourism simply told me *di mana bumi dipijak di situ langit dijunjung*. This oft-repeated phrase loosely translates to "wherever one goes, one must observe local custom", and may be idiomatically glossed in English with "When in Rome, do as the Romans do." In other words, when you find yourself in a foreign land, take your cues from those who are authoritatively defined as belonging to that land.

When he visited Kepri once again in November 2017, three years after declaring that the relationship between the Bugis and the Malays is "like the relationship between white and black parts of the eye", Vice-President Jusuf Kalla did as the

Bugis-Malays do. Joining Indonesia's Minister of Administrative and Bureaucratic Reform Asman Abnur, Governor of Kepri Nurdin Basirun, Regent of Lingga Alias Wello, Head of Kepri's Institute for Malay Customs Abdul Razak, and Head of Kepri's South Sulawesi Family Association Daeng M. Yatir, Vice-President Kalla read from a historically authoritative text, one that came to define and continues to define the parameters of a certain authoritative in-group in Riau Islands society: the Malay-Bugis Oath of Loyalty (Gunawan 2017). Accompanied by the foregoing individuals, Vice-President Kalla recited the following:

> *Jikalau tuan kepada Bugis, tuanlah kepada Melayu, dan jikalau tuan kepada Melayu, tuanlah kepada Bugis.*
> If you are a friend of the Bugis, then you are a friend of the Malays, and if you are a friend of the Malays, then you are a friend of the Bugis.

Notes

1. This chapter was first published as *Living on the Edge: Being Malay (and Bugis) in the Riau Islands*, Trends in Southeast Asia, no. 12/2018 (Singapore: ISEAS – Yusof Ishak Institute, 2018).
2. I thank Francis E. Hutchinson, Barbara Watson Andaya and James T. Collins for their helpful comments and suggestions. Any and all errors are my own.
3. *Nota Bene*: Riau Islands Province was legally declared Indonesia's thirty-second province by way of Law No. 25/2002, but did not begin formally operating as such until 2004.
4. See van Klinken (2008) for a case analysis of the KKSS as it relates to ethnic clientelism in Indonesia.
5. *"Kedua kaum ini sejak dulu memang tidak bisa dipisahkan."*
6. *"Orang Melayu dan Orang Bugis itu bagaikan mata hitam dan mata putih, keduanya saling menyatu dan bekerjasama dalam berbagai hal dan ini terjadi sudah sejak lama."*; Riau Post, "Melayu-Bugis Bagai Mata Hitam dan Putih", 19 April 2008.
7. *"Begitu hebatnya bangsa ini sampai memilih bahasa Melayu yang dipakai ... berartinya bahasa dasar kita Melayu."*
8. *"Sebagai orang Bugis juga saya bangga sekali karena struktur bahasa Melayu dibangun juga dari Bugis."*
9. Future Trends in Southeast Asia articles will potentially centre on Batak, Chinese, Javanese, and other ethnic communities in contemporary Riau Islands Province.
10. See also Wee (1985).
11. Raja Ali Haji (1808–73), a Malay noble of Bugis descent, was a prolific writer whose historical work situated (and sought to justify) the Bugis role in Riau's Malay history. See Ahmad, Hooker and Andaya (1982).
12. To be sure, and as I shall touch upon later, these authority-defined, Bugis-centric discourses of Malayness are by no means uncontested among Riau Islands Malays. See Long (2013).
13. Usman Awang's poem continues, noting *"Arab dan Pakistani semua Melayu, Mamak dan Malbari serap ke Melayu, Malah mualaf bertakrif Melayu, setelah disunat anunya itu"* [Arabs and Pakistanis are all Malay, the Mamak and Malbari have been absorbed into the Malays, even converts define themselves as Malay, if that "thing" is circumcized]. For a lengthier analysis of the poem as it reflects notions of "Malayness", see Carruthers (2016).

14. [budakpoli], "*Jawa, Bugis, Banjar, Minang, Aceh adalah MELAYU!!!*" [The Javanese, Bugis, Banjar, Minang, Aceh are MALAY!]. [Video File], hack3line (2010).
15. "*Aku jawa bukan melayu.*"
16. "*BUGIS bukan Melayu.*"
17. "*[O]rang minang bukan orang melayu*".
18. "*[M]exican itu melayu, hispanic itu melayu, america latin itu melayu, czech republic itu melayu.*"
19. "*[S]ebenarnya ini adalah tentang perbedaan versi dari masingnegara. Versi pemerintah malaysia, mengemukakan melayu itu adalah kepulauan yang ada di nusantara dan semenanjung malaya … termasuk juga jawa, bugis, dayak dan lain. Sedangkan versi pemerintah indonesia, melayu itu hanya di pulau sumatra dan kepulauan riau, ya.*"
20. See "Malaysian Federal Constitution, Reprint, as at 1 November 2010", Article 160, Clause 2.
21. Or Singapore, for that matter, with an historical eye to the city-state's inclusion in the Federal Territory of Malaysia prior to 1965. For a recent overview regarding the "expansive" nature of "Malay-ness" in Singapore with respect to the country's recent presidential election, see Hussain (2017).
22. "*Saya orang Bugis! Melayu itu tinggal di kepulauan Riau.*"
23. See Carruthers (2016).
24. Notwithstanding Riau Islanders' allegations of unity and alliance between the Bugis and Malays, there exists a history of hostility between these groups. See Andaya (1975).
25. "*[K]arena membaur dengan masyarakat.*"
26. "*[P]roses itu bergerak terus.*"
27. "*Suku Melayu menikah dengan suku Bugis, dan terjadi sumpah setia, itu lah sebabnya Bugis dan Melayu dianggap satu, tak bisa dipisahkan.*"
28. "*Saya Melayu Bugis, itu tidak bisa dihilangkan, dan perjanjian antara Melayu Bugis tidak bisa dilupakan.*"
29. "*Bugis itu Melayu dan Melayu itu Bugis.*"
30. "*[B]erkuasa ditempat tana lahir saya.*"
31. "*Orang Bugis dan Melayu nda' bisa dipisahkan, tapi Jawa … itu beda. Orang Minang beda. Orang Batak jelas beda. Realitasnya memang begitu.*"
32. "*[K]arena Minang sudah punya 'pride'.*"
33. "*Jawa itu dia tidak bermain di wilayah-wilayah istana. Dia baru datang sebagai tenaga kerja. Mereka nda' pernah diberikan ruang untuk menjadi Melayu. Bugis dikasih ruang.*"
34. "*[B]elum pernah ada konflik antara Cina dengan Melayu.*"
35. "*Bugis ini diterima.*"
36. "*[A]lasannya ada, pertama, yang datang ke sini sudah bergelombang. Sebelum para Daeng datang ke sini.*"
37. "*Mereka sudah membaur dengan Masyarakat Melayu. Automatis, dia bangga jadi Melayu.*"
38. In addition to important histories of the region (e.g., Andaya and Andaya 2017), readers might pursue the following: Andaya (1997); Andaya (1975); Andaya (2001); Andaya (2008); Derks (1997); Faucher (2005); Wee (2004).
39. A pledge repeated, as we will see, by Vice-President Jusuf Kalla when he visited Kepri in November 2017. See Gunawan (2017).
40. Multiple times during the course of my fieldwork I was reminded by men bearing the first name "Raja" (a couple of whom I encountered at the Institute of Malay Customs) that Raja is not a title or *gelar*, but a name or *nama*.
41. Barnard (2009) concisely describes the impact on Bugis power in and around Riau and

Lingga: "The death of Raja Haji brought an end to much of the Bugis military presence in Riau. The decline in their martial prowess was further emphasized when the fifth Yang Dipertuan Muda, Raja Ali [ibni Daeng Kamboja], fled to Borneo in November 1784 to escape a Dutch military offensive against Riau. The role of Yang Dipertuan Muda fell into disuse for the next sixteen years due to the destruction of any legitimacy the Bugis may have had in a military sense" (Barnard 2009, p. 68).

42. See Trocki (2007).

43. Although, and as Long notes (2013, p. 51), this may have been a strategic decision on the President's part to derail the "Free Riau" movement that was gaining momentum on the mainland.

44. *"Dengar bahasa Melayu yang asli."*

45. See note 40.

46. *"Mengembangkan perikehidupan masyarakat yang agamis, demokratis, berkeadilah, tertib, rukun dan aman di bawa payung budaya Melayu"*, in *RPJMD Provinsi Kepulauan Riau* [RPJMD for Riau Islands Province] 2016–2021, Chapter VII, p. 1.

47. *"Perwujudan provinsi Kepri sebagai Bunda Tanah Melayu."*

48. *"Melestarikan nilai-nilai dan Seni Budaya Melayu guna Mewujudkan Masyarakat Kepulauan Riau yang berkepribadian dan Berakhlak Mulia."*

49. *"Meningkatnya kelestarian nilai-nilai dan seni budaya Melayu sebagai kekayaan budaya daerah."*

50. *"Memberdayakan tokoh-tokoh dan lembaga-lembaga adat Melayu di Provinsi Kepri untuk melestarikan nilai-nilai budaya dalam kehidupan masyarakat."*

51. *"Peningkatan pemahaman dan pengamalan nilai-nilai budaya Melayu, promosi budaya, pembinaan kesenian dan tradisi lokal, pelestarian Benda, Situs, dan Kawasan Cagar Budaya [tangible], dan pelestarian warisan budaya tak benda [intangible]."*

52. *"Perwujudan provinsi Kepri sebagai Bunda Tanah Melayu."*

53. *"Situs dan Kawasan Cagar Budaya."*

54. *"Dapat kami informasikan bahwa Pemerintah Kota Batam telah membangun display gallery untuk museum di purna astaka MTQ Tingkat Nasional yang telah dihibahkan kepada Pemerintah Kota Batam. Dinas Kebudayaan dan Pariwisata Kota Batam melalui kegiatan Pelestarian Cagar Budaya, Sejarah dan Permuseuman, akan mengadakan Focus Group Discussion (FGD) guna mematangkan konsep dan materi museum tersebut. Adapun FGD Pematangan Konsep dan Materi Museum bertujuan untuk mendapatkan masukan dan saran para peserta FGD, sehingga konsep dan materi museum yang telah dususun dapat lebih sempurna."*; Pebrialin, SE, M. Si., *"FGD Pematangan Materi Museum Kota Batam"* [Focus Group on Achieving the Full Potential of Batam City Museum Materials], Letter to the Author, 23 March 2017, MS. N.p.

55. Masa Riau-Lingga.

56. Masa Belanda.

57. Masa Jepang.

58. Masa Kemerdekaan.

59. Kepulauan Riau.

60. Ekonomi Kota Batam.

61. Hasannah Melayu.

62. Sejarah Astaka dan Pelaksanaan MTQ Nasional.

63. *"Kalau saya itu hanya niat ingin mengingatkan sama warga Batam saja, bang."*

64. *"Supaya tahu tentang sejarah Batam dari awal."*

65. *"Tapi terlambat juga."*

66. *"Budaya adat Melayu udah terpinggir pada saat ini … karena Batam udah ada banyak suku-suku lain yang masuk."*

67. *"Itu namanya mayoritas menjadi minoritas."*
68. *"Dulu, semua orang ini Bugis Melayu."*
69. *"Kalau mau cari orang asli Melayu dan tempat asli orang Melayu Batam ini, udah tinggal kenangan aja ... penduduk aslinya udah pergi ke pulau-pulau ... orang pinggiran itu Melayu asli lagi."*
70. *Payung budaya Melayu.*
71. *"Visi Riau 2020 yang menjadikan Riau sebagai pusat budaya Melayu."*
72. *"Membangun Riau berbasis kebudayaan Melayu."*
73. For a review of the saga, see Setijadi (2017).
74. *"Budaya adat Melayu udah terpinggir saat ini bang."*
75. *"Kita sebagai orang Melayu merasa setuju kalau programnya jadi bang."*
76. *"Termasuk orang asli batam."*
77. Where "newcomers" could also, ironically, and depending on one's temporal frame of reference, refer to those "original" Bugis migrants so heralded in authority-defined Kepri histories.

References

Ananta, Aris. 2006. "Changing Ethnic Composition and Potential Violent Conflict in Riau Archipelago, Indonesia: An Early Warning Signal". *Population Review* 45, no. 1: 48–68.

Andaya, Barbara Watson. 1997. "Recreating a Vision; Daratan and Kepulauan in Historical Context". *Bijdragen Tot De Taal-, Land- En Volkenkunde/Journal of the Humanities and Social Sciences of Southeast Asia and Oceania* 153, no. 4: 483–508.

———, and Leonard Y. Andaya. 2017. *A History of Malaysia*. London: Palgrave Macmillan.

Andaya, Leonard Y. 1975. *The Kingdom of Johor, 1641–1728*. Oxford: Oxford University Press.

———. 2001. "The Search for the 'Origins of Melayu'". *Journal of Southeast Asian Studies* 32, no. 3: 315–30.

———. 2008. *Leaves of the Same Tree: Trade and Ethnicity in the Straits of Melaka*. Hawaii: University of Hawaii Press.

Ahmad, Raja Ali Haji ibn, Virginia Matheson Hooker, and Barbara Watson Andaya. 1982. *The Precious Gift (Tuhfat Al-Nafis)*. Oxford: Oxford University Press.

Azaryahu, Maoz. 1996. "The Power of Commemorative Street Names". *Environment and Planning D: Society and Space* 14, no. 3: 311–30.

Barnard, Timothy P. 2009. "The Hajj, Islam, and Power among the Bugis in Early Colonial Riau". In *Southeast Asia and the Middle East: Islam, Movement, and the Longue Durée*, edited by Eric Tagliacozzo, pp. 83–110. Singapore: NUS Press.

Carruthers, Andrew. 2016. "Specters of Affinity: Clandestine Movement and Commensurate Values in the Indonesia-Malaysia Borderlands". PhD dissertation. Yale University.

Chong, Terence. 2016. "Imaginary Frontiers and Deferred Masculinity: Singapore Working-Class Men in Batam". In *The SIJORI Cross-Border Region: Transnational Politics, Economics, and Culture*, edited by F. Hutchinson and T. Chong, pp. 310–28. Singapore: ISEAS – Yusof Ishak Institute.

Cohn, Bernard S. 1996. *Colonialism and Its Forms of Knowledge the British in India*. Princeton, NJ: Princeton University Press.

Derks, Will. 1997. "Malay Identity Work". *Bijdragen Tot De Taal-, Land- En Volkenkunde/Journal of the Humanities and Social Sciences of Southeast Asia and Oceania* 153, no. 4: 699–716.

DetikNews. 2014. "Temui Tokoh Adat Riau, JK: Hubungan Melayu Dan Bugis Itu Romantis".

7 June 2014. https://news.detik.com/berita/2601969/temui-tokoh-adat-riau-jk-hubungan-melayu-dan-bugis-itu-romantis

Faucher, Carole. 2005. "Regional Autonomy, Malayness and Power Hierarchy in the Riau Archipelago". In *Regionalism in Post-Suharto Indonesia*, edited by M. Erb, P. Sulistiyanto and C. Faucher, pp. 125–40. London: RoutledgeCurzon,

Gunawan, Hendra. 2017. "JK Ingatkan Sumpah Setia Melayu – Bugis". *Tribunnews.com*, 22 November 2017. http://www.tribunnews.com/regional/2017/11/22/jk-ingatkan-sumpah-setia-melayu-bugis

hack3line. 2010. "PM Malaysia : Jawa di Indonesia adalah MELAYU!". YouTube video, 2:15. 23 October 2010. https://www.youtube.com/watch?v=bgZvN5NaDCE

Hirschman, Charles. 1987. "The Meaning and Measurement of Ethnicity in Malaysia: An Analysis of Census Classifications". *Journal of Asian Studies* 46, no. 3: 555–82.

Hussain, Zakir. 2017. "Doubts about Presidential Hopefuls Not Being Malay Enough Are Off Track". *Straits Times*, 2 September 2017. http://www.straitstimes.com/opinion/doubts-about-presidential-hopefuls-not-being-malay-enough-are-off-track

Hutchinson, Francis E. 2017. *Rowing Against the Tide? Batam's Economic Fortunes in Today's Indonesia*. Trends in Southeast Asia, no. 8/2017. Singapore: ISEAS – Yusof Ishak Institute.

Long, Nicholas J. 2013. *Being Malay in Indonesia: Histories, Hopes and Citizenship in the Riau Archipelago*. Singapore: NUS Press.

Malay Mail. 2017. "Dr M Urged to Apologise to Indonesian Bugis Community over Insult". *Malay Mail* (Malaysia), 20 October 2017. http://www.themalaymailonline.com/malaysia/article/dr-m-urged-to-apologise-to-indonesian-bugis-community-over-insult#TRBlYs15Vg6b9pzD.97

Malaysiakini. 2017. "PAS Man Slams Dr M over Remark on Najib's 'Ancestry'". 16 October 2017. https://www.malaysiakini.com/news/398487

Riau Post. 2008. "Melayu-Bugis Bagai Mata Hitam dan Putih", 19 April 2008.

Setijadi, Charlotte. 2017. "Ahok's Downfall and the Rise of Islamist Populism in Indonesia". *ISEAS Perspective*, no. 38/2017, 8 June 2017, pp. 1–9.

Shamsul, A.B. 2001. "A History of an Identity, an Identity of a History: The Idea and Practice of 'Malayness' in Malaysia Reconsidered". *Journal of Southeast Asian Studies* 32, no. 3: 355–66.

Singapore Free Press and Mercantile Advertiser. 1911. "Sultan of Rhio. Deposed by Dutch Government. Allegations of Hostility". 13 February 1911, p. 5.

Straits Times. 1947. "The Singapore Heir to the Rhio Islands", 11 December 1947, p. 6.

Tanjung, Chaidir Anwar. 2017. "Tradisi Kue Bulan Di Pekanbaru Diprotes Lembaga Adat Melayu, Kenapa?". *DetikNews*, 12 October 2017. https://news.detik.com/berita/d-3680897/tradisi-kue-bulan-di-pekanbaru-diprotes-lembaga-adat-melayu-kenapa?utm_source=facebook

Trocki, Carl A. 2007. *Prince of Pirates: The Temenggongs and the Development of Johor and Singapore, 1784–1885*. Singapore: NUS Press.

van Klinken, Gerry. 2008. "The Limits of Ethnic Clientelism in Indonesia". *Review of Indonesian and Malaysian Affairs (RIMA)* 42, no. 2: 35–65.

Wee, Vivienne. 1985. "*Melayu: Hierarchies of Being in Riau*". PhD thesis. Australian National University.

———. 2004. "Ethno-Nationalism in Process: Ethnicity, Atavism and Indigenism in Riau, Indonesia". *Pacific Island Review* 15, no. 4: 497–516.

———. 2016. "The Significance of Riau in SIJORI". In *The SIJORI Cross-Border Region: Transnational Politics, Economics, and Culture*, edited by F. Hutchinson and T. Chong, pp. 241–66. Singapore: ISEAS – Yusof Ishak Institute.

15

THE JAVANESE IN THE RIAU ISLANDS PROVINCE

Sita Rohana

INTRODUCTION

With its territory consisting of some 2,000 islands scattered from the Malacca Strait to the Natuna Sea, and its claim to be "The Mother of the Malay Land",[1] the Riau Islands Province is proud of its maritime and Malay heritage. Yet, while it specifically refers to its "Malayness", the Riau Islands also has a tradition of openness to outside influences and has acted as a melting pot by welcoming different communities over the centuries. This tradition continues to this day as, with the rapid economic development of the Riau Islands—particularly Batam and Bintan—many workers from across the country have migrated there in search of economic opportunities.

The largest such community of migrants is the Javanese, which has come to outnumber the number of Malays in several urban centres. The presence of this particular ethnicity in the Riau Islands raises a number of important questions. The Javanese living in the province are mostly permanent migrants who have resided there for two or more generations. Many of them have married members of other communities, including Malays. Thus, the issue of ethnic identity—of being Javanese or Malay and about Javaneseness or Malayness—is complex, especially in how it is presented and represented in social, economic and political relations.

This chapter will focus on the Javanese community in the Riau Islands. This will be done by exploring: how their identity is defined in relation to local people; to what degree they are assimilated; how they are depicted in political discourse in the province; and in what fashion they participate in its political life. In order to do so, this chapter will draw on data from various sources, including: historical texts; statistics; media reports; and unstructured key informant interviews carried out in the provincial capital, Tanjungpinang.

This chapter is comprised of six sections. Following this introduction, the second section will provide the historical background to the formation of the Province of the Riau Islands. The subsequent section will look at Malay and Javanese conceptions of identity. The fourth will look at available information regarding Javanese migration to the Riau Islands. The following section will look at Javanese expressions of political identity through focusing on the 2015 provincial elections. The sixth and final section will conclude.

HISTORICAL BACKGROUND

Since the thirteenth century, the Riau Islands, along with the Malayan peninsula and the east coast of Sumatra were under the sovereignty of various Malay sultanates, including those of Temasik (now Singapore), Malacca, Johor, Johore-Riau and then Riau-Lingga.

From the 1600s until the Anglo-Dutch Treaty of 1824, the Riau Islands were under the aegis of the Malay sultanate of Johore-Riau. This agreement, signed by the British and Dutch, carved the territory into two. The northern part encompassing Singapore and the Malay Peninsula was ruled by the United Kingdom; and the southern part, including the Riau Islands, was ruled by the Netherlands. This line subsequently became the foundation of the geopolitical border between Indonesia, Malaysia and Singapore.

After Indonesia's independence, the Riau Islands became one small part of the sprawling Province of Central Sumatra. In 1958, the province was divided and the new province of Riau, comprising the regions of the Riau Islands, Kampar, Bengkalis, and Inderagiri was established. Its capital was initially located on the island of Bintan in the Riau Islands.[2] Later that year, the capital was moved to Pekanbaru in Sumatra.

Thus, in just a few decades, the Riau Islands and its inhabitants went from being at the centre of a sultanate to being a peripheral region within a province remote from the national centre of power. However, despite its distance from the centre of political power, the Riau Island's proximity to Singapore was an asset. Malays in the Riau Islands considered Singapore and Malaysia as "the states across the ditch".[3] People and commodities floated freely as the Singapore dollar became the currency in the region and Tanjungpinang was referred to as "dollar heaven"[4] (Liamsi 1997, p. 29).

This period ended with *Konfrontasi*[5] in 1963, with a hardening of Indonesia's border and the *dedolarisasi* campaign to gradually replace the Singapore dollar with the Indonesian rupiah. *Konfrontasi* finally ended in 1966, and Malaysia reopened its borders to people from the Riau Islands two years later (Gafnesia 2005, p. 13).[6] In the 1970s, the Indonesian government chose one of the Riau Islands, Batam, to be a centre for the oil and gas industry. Over the subsequent decades, Batam and its neighbour Bintan came to host other industries, including the electrical and electronics as well as ship-building sectors.

Beyond Batam and Bintan's growing industrial sectors, there were other drivers drawing people to the islands. Hugo's study on Indonesian labour migration to Malaysia in the 1990s shows the majority of clandestine migration to Malaysia used illegal ports in the Riau Islands as a point of departure (1993, pp. 45–47). Gafnesia (2005, p. 13) contends that there were approximately a hundred migration "agents" in Bintan, Batam, Karimun, and elsewhere which regularly sent migrant workers to Malaysia, legally or illegally (Hugo 1993, pp. 45–47). The flood of migrants—whether to stay or transit—became a characteristic of the Riau Islands.

As workers from other parts of the country migrated to the Riau Islands in search of opportunities, they became a melting pot. This influx of people made the Malays feel "pushed to the margin" (Al Azhar 1997, p. 765). And, as more people arrived, this sentiment grew. The marginalization the Malays in the Riau Islands was "a deep-seated grievance" held against the provincial government based in Pekanbaru, which was accused of neglecting the Islands and the indigeneous Malays (Long 2013, p. 7).

This feeling underpinned the creation of the Province of the Riau Islands, which separated from the larger Riau Province in 2004. The push for secession as well as its aftermath increased the awareness of ethnic identity and brought the notion of "sons of the soil" (*putra daerah*)[7] associated with Malayness rooted in the Riau Islands to the fore. This notion sought a return to the centrality of the Riau-Lingga polity with local Malays as leading actors. Following its creation as an autonomous province, the Riau Islands has sought to promote Malay custom (*adat*) in many dimensions, and the notion of "sons of the soil" is present in public discourse regarding cultural, economic, and political issues. It is within this context that the Javanese community in the Riau Islands has sought to define itself and advance its interests.

MALAY-MALAYNESS AND JAVANESE-JAVANESENESS

Malay narratives such as *Hikayat Hang Tuah* describe the hybridity of Malayness in the Malacca sultanate—which can be interpreted as a result of its openness to the "Other". One of these relationships is the link between Malays and the Javanese kingdom and people.

> And the singer said: "Good, my lord. What kind of melody shall we play because the melodies of the people of Indrapura are not Malay? Really, we may be Malays, but we are hybrid, not like the real Malays of Malacca." The *Laksamana* [Hang Tuah] smiled and said: "Maybe the people of Malacca are hybrid as well, mixed as they are with the Javanese of Majapahit, that is. You act like one, as though you want to put me to the test." … And the Laksamana said: "Do not try to put me to the test because the lord of this man from Malacca is mixed with Majapahit Java, he does not know how to dance." Answered Tun Jenal: "What words are you saying, sir? We are playing relatives. You should not have distrust in your heart." (Maier 1997, pp. 673–74).[8]

Maier (1997, pp. 673–76) took the above passage from the historic Malay text *Hikayat Hang Tuah* to interpret the question of Malayness, highlighting the word "hybridity" (*kacukan*) and the phrases "playing at being siblings" (*bermain adik-beradik*) and "not having distrust in the heart" (*jangan menaruh syak di hati*) as what Malayness is all about—flexibility and the willingness to include others. As Tun Jenal in the passage explicitly said, there is a desire to create a feeling of communality and kinship with mutual trust. Thus, being a Malay, speaking Malay and acting Malay is a willingness to adapt and assimilate. The explanation of the term "hybridity" as an opposite of the term "real" (*sungguh*) pervades the discussion of the Malay language and, in a wider sense, Malay behaviour and value every time there is contact with outsiders.[9]

Another historic Malay manuscript, *Sulalatussalatin* (Ahmad 2015), provides an illustration about the Javanese-Malay relationship during the post-Majapahit and pre-Malacca period. The six passages in the first half of the manuscript show the changing relationship between Javanese and Malays in terms of power negotiation and positioning (conquest vs. defeat; superordinate vs. subordinate) by using martial arts and language (Ahmad 2015, pp. 69–128). As with the previous example, this manuscript refers to the notion of hybridity, in arguing that the Javanese Majapahit Empire is also hybrid as it is mixed with Malayness. This manuscript includes examples of Malays and Javanese playing at being siblings as they negotiate their respective positions in relation to one another.

Andaya (2008, p. 80) provides another interpretation of both manuscripts, highlighting the definition of "Malay" which is only used when confronted by a distinct "Other", such as the Javanese, Siamese or the Portuguese. Yet, Andaya's reading confirms Maier's conclusion of Malayness as containing an "all-pervasive" flexibility. Indeed, the very flexibility of the definition of Malayness has captivated the attention of many scholars, including Wee (1985), Reid (2001), Milner (2003), Andaya (2008) and Long (2013).

The two manuscripts cited above depict the Javanese from a Malay standpoint. However, it is important to note that this perspective has also changed over time and in different contexts. The Javanese have been considered to be Malay at times. One example is in Malaysia, where Javanese people are legally defined as Malay—even while they retain their ethnic awareness and customs (Sekimoto 1994, p. 174).[10] Yet, the general Southeast Asian perception is that Javanese are ethnically different from Malays. Thus, in the Riau Islands and elsewhere in Indonesia, where ethnicity is a cultural marker, they are regarded as distinct—even though this is not legally or explicitly stated on official documents.

Let us now examine the definition of "Javaneseness" from a Javanese perspective. Magnis-Suseno provides an ethnic definition, which describes the Javanese as "indigenous people from Central and East Java who share the real Javanese language" (1991, p. 11).[11] While illuminating, this definition immediately raises questions in the present context, not least because Javanese have moved to all regions in Indonesia as well as overseas, and their offspring—Java-born or not—still call themselves Javanese. Nonetheless, this genealogical definition is the basic foundation for defining Javanese ethnic identity.

The second definition is ethical, based on the argument that being Javanese is not merely about inheriting Javanese blood, but rather refers to how someone understands the meaning and the importance of Javanese ethics (Damami in Sutarto 2006, p. 41). Being Javanese means becoming someone who is wise and continually striving to do good and to be good in behaviour and attitude (Sutarto 2006, pp. 38–41).[12] The references of Javanese cultural values are the written documents of past Javanese kings from different dynasties from the royal cities of Surakarta and Yogyakarta (Bratawijaya in Irawanto, Ramsey and Ryan 2011, p. 127).[13]

In practice, both definitions are important in defining Javanese people and Javaneseness. This chapter will use both definitions as conceptual tools for understanding Javaneseness as defined by the Javanese living in the Province of the Riau Islands.

Among other aspects of culture, Javanese values are embedded in language. One important marker of politeness within Javanese culture involves showing respect by using the appropriate degree of formality when addressing others (Poedjosoedarmo 1968, p. 54). There are three levels of speech: coarse (*ngoko*); middle (*madya*); and refined (*kromo*). These are defined by the degree of politeness, principally by means of the selection of vocabulary and choice of affixes (Poedjosudarmo 1968, p. 57). The three levels of speech may be seen as two opposite categories with an additional one in the middle. This can be seen as reflective of the social hierarchy in Javanese feudal society, with: commoners (*wong cilik*); the middle class (*priyayi*); and aristocrats (*ndara*) (Magnis-Suseno 1991, p. 12).

These three categories pervade other cultural values, which tend to put the "in-between" category of these three as the preference instead of choosing one of the other two oppositional categories. A fundamental Javanese value is to preserve peace, thus symbolic language is used in order not to insult others (Sutarto 2006, p. 45). Indeed, "the 'yes' term in Javanese does not mean absolute 'yes'" (Irawanto, Ramsey and Ryan 2011, p. 135). Yet, people from other cultural contexts may find it hard to understand Javanese people, for they never show their real emotions or intentions.[14]

Another Javanese cultural concept is the unity of subject and lord (*manunggaling kawulo-Gusti*) as either the unity between people and the Creator or the unity between people and their king. The superordinate is expected to take responsibility for the world, to enforce laws and maintain authority, to have a noble character and to treat their subordinates justly and equally. For their part, the subordinate is expected to be obedient (see Sutarto 2006, p. 50). This dichotomy is the basic foundation of many relationships, including those between a leader and their people, those between higher and lower ranks, as well as those between elders and the young.[15]

With regard to themselves and others, there are four categories for the Javanese. This includes: Javanese (*Jawa*); not yet Javanese (*durung Jawa*); unlike the Javanese (*ora Jawa*); and not Javanese at all (*dudu Jawa*) (Sutarto 2006, p. 41). Someone is said to be *Jawa* when his/her behaviour reflects a noble character based on "guidance" (*pituduh*) and "prohibition" (*wewaler*). The opposite is being unlike the Javanese through ignoring "guidance". The category of "not yet Javanese" is used to refer to children still in their formative years. Albeit in differing degrees, these first three terms refer to some "degree" of Javaneseness. The fourth category is used to refer to non-Javanese. However, it can be used to highlight the line between a Javanese and a non-Javanese "Other", or for referring to how "Others" do not conform to Javanese expectations of behaviour.

JAVANESE MIGRATION TO THE RIAU ISLANDS

"Unity in diversity" is the Indonesian slogan to capture the plurality of its population living in archipelago of more than 16,000 islands. Since Independence, this ideal has always been given a high priority by the country's ruling elite (Tirtosudarmo 1997, p. 302). Despite successfully promoting economic development, its highest priority was to regulate political activities and especially to submerge any potentially divisive issues between classes, ideology, etnicity, race and religion. This was particularly the case under President Soeharto's New Order.

Beyond the country's heterogeneous composition, successive Indonesian administrations have also had to deal with high levels of population density in Java.[16] This issue dates back to the colonial period, when population growth in the island began to soar.[17] Within Indonesia itself, the Dutch began a large-scale resettlement programme in 1905 which, by the 1930s, had sent more than 600,000 Javanese to Sumatra as estate labourers (Repetto 1986, p. 14).

Resettlement continued in the post-independence era, particularly under the New Order. The so-called Transmigration Programme aimed to increase agricultural production as well as promote development and political stability on sparsely settled outer islands (Repetto 1986, p. 15). Others contend that the initiative was essentially geared at accelerating the process of national integration (Tirtosudarmo 1997, pp. 302–3).[18]

The Transmigration Programme and the variable rates of economic growth within Indonesia produced complex and extensive social changes, including increasing migration from rural to urban areas and between provinces (Tirtosudarmo 1997, p. 294). The programme was gradually phased out in the mid-1980s, when oil prices fell, affecting government revenue. Since this period, levels of voluntary migration have begun to climb as people gravitate towards new economic sites. This process has also been accelerated by the rapid improvement of inter-island transportation in the 1970s.

While high rates of internal migration are an inevitable part of economic transformation, this process is not without its risks. Tirtosudarmo contends that, more than the archipelagic nature of Indonesia or its diversity, population mobility has the strongest probability of generating conflict (1997, p. 305). Among other reasons, this is because higher numbers of incoming people increase competition for economic opportunities, with locals often feeling displaced.

High rates of migration have drastically changed the demographic size and composition of the Riau Islands, whose population surged from 500,000 in 1990 to 1.9 million in 2015. Batam was at the centre of this demographic shift, with its population increasing twelvefold over the same period, from 100,000 to 1.2 million (Hutchinson 2017, p. 19).

From a predominantly Malay area, the province's composition has become more heterogeneous. In 2000, 36 per cent of the province's population was ethnically Malay, followed by 21 per cent Javanese, 9 per cent Minangkabau and 9 per cent Chinese. By 2010, the proportion of the Malay population had contracted to 30 per cent. Conversely, the Javanese were almost 25 per cent, followed by the Bataks, Minangkabau, and Chinese at 13, 10, and 8 per cent respectively (Hutchinson 2017, pp. 19–20; Table 15.1).

The inflows of people have affected the various parts of the province differently. Indeed, in the more urban parts of the province, the Javanese are already the largest community. In Batam, the province's demographic heartland, they are 25 per cent of the population, followed by the Bataks who account for 19 per cent of the population, and then the Malays at 15 per cent (Table 15.2). Similarly, in the Bintan regency, the Javanese are slightly ahead of the Malay population, accounting for 32 per cent for the former as opposed to 31 per cent for the latter (Tables 15.3 and 15.4). In contrast, Malays remain the majority in the more isolated and rural island groups of Karimun, Natuna, Lingga, and Anambas (Carruthers 2018, p. 49).

As the Javanese have migrated to other locations, they have established "Kampung Jawa" or majority-Javanese neighbourhoods. Beyond concentrations of people with a specific identity, these agglomerations also perform important functions. Javanese kampongs serve as a new home village, where Javanese people gather, talking in Javanese, conducting ceremonies (selametan),[19] and attending self-help meetings (arisan). In addition, social relations are not limited to the specific kampong, as "Kampung Jawa" also serve as the locus where Javanese maintain their connection to their home village.

There are several such communities in the Riau Islands. One notable example is the eponymous "Kampung Jawa"[20] in Tanjungpinang, considered to the first such

TABLE 15.1
Population by Ethnicity: Riau Islands Province, Indonesia, 2010

No.	Rank	Ethnic Group	Population	Percentage
1.	1	Malay	505,391	30.32
2.	2	Javanese	410,428	24.62
3.	3	Batak	208,678	12.52
4.	4	Minangkabau	161,141	9.67
5.	5	Chinese	128,704	7.72
6.	6	Sundanese	44,544	2.67
7.	7	Madurese	3,050	0.18
8.	8	Sekak/Lom/Mapur/Ameng Sewang/Sakai/ Anak Laut/Laut/Orang Sampan	2,826	0.17
9.	13	Buginese	1,861	0.11
10.		Others	200,373	12.02
		Total	1,666,996	100.00

Source: Arifin et al. (2014).

TABLE 15.2
Population by Ethnicity: Municipality of Batam, Riau Islands Province, Indonesia, 2010

No.	Rank	Ethnic Group	Population	Per cent
1.	1	Javanese	263,984	25.10
2.	2	Batak	177,677	18.91
3.	3	Malay	136,745	14.56
4.	4	Minangkabau	124,533	13.26
5.	5	Chinese	61,883	6.59
6.	6	Sundanese	34,496	3.67
7.	13	Madurese	1,484	0.16
8.		Others	138,587	14.75
		Total	939,389	100.00

Source: Arifin et al. (2014).

TABLE 15.3
Population by Ethnicity: Municipality of Tanjungpinang, Riau Islands Province, Indonesia, 2010

No.	Rank	Ethnic Group	Population	Per cent
1.	1	Malay	57,121	30.63
2.	2	Javanese	51,125	27.42
3.	3	Chinese	26,516	14.22
4.	4	Minangkabau	17,456	9.36
5.	5	Batak	12,121	6.50
6.	6	Sundanese	5,408	2.90
7.	13	Madurese	655	0.35
8.		Others	16,061	8.61
		Total	186,463	100.00

Source: Arifin et al. (2014).

TABLE 15.4
Population by Ethnicity: Regency of Bintan, Riau Islands Province, Indonesia, 2010

No.	Rank	Ethnic Group	Population	Per cent
1.	1	Javanese	44,816	31.65
2.	2	Malay	44,041	31.10
3.	3	Batak	9,361	6.61
4.	4	Chinese	8,755	6.18
5.	5	Minangkabau	8,179	5.78
6.	6	Sundanese	4,895	3.46
7.	13	Madurese	538	0.38
8.		Others	21,035	14.85
		Total	141,620	100.00

Source: Arifin et al. (2014).

settlement in the Riau Islands (Wijaya 2002; Harsono 1999). The kampong is located in the city centre, behind the Dutch jail which was built in 1857. It is very likely that this "kampung" was the first such neighbourhood, since only the first Javanese kampong in each area is given that specific name, with other areas established later acquiring other names—frequently the name of the home village in Java.

There are at least two versions of the story behind the settlement. The first is that the neighbourhood was founded by Javanese who came to the town in the 1930s, after fleeing indentured labour on plantations in North Sumatra (Harsono 1999, p. 202; Rohana 2004, p. 216). The second is that the first Javanese to the area were former domestic workers who had been in the houses of Dutch officials, given that they often accompanied them when posted to new locations (Wijaya 2002, pp. 111–15). Most of these workers were from Central and East Java. In 1950s, Kampung Jawa was already overcrowded, so some inhabitants moved south to an area near the Dutch military area, Sekip, which was renamed Yudowinangun in 1963 (Wijaya 2002, p. 120).

These versions are not contradictory. Stories about former indentured workers fleeing from North Sumatra to the Riau Islands were very common among the Javanese, not only in Tanjungpinang but also in other islands such as Karimun, Moro and Tanjungbatu.[21]

Javanese settlements also grew as the result of a second group of arrivals, who were white-collar workers posted to Tanjungpinang in the 1950s when it was the provincial capital. These newer arrivals lived in areas such as Kampung Kolam and Teluk Keriting, which were located near the former Dutch military post and housing area for Dutch officials that became the Indonesian naval base after independence.

The population of Tanjungpinang has continued to grow as people from across the country have come to the city. Consequently, the ethnic composition of kampongs has also become more heterogeneous. Some Javanese have moved to Kampung Bukit, which was originally a Malay kampong, even though other Javanese kampongs such as Sukorejo, Purwodadi, Karangrejo, and Sukajadi have emerged in the area. Conversely, the existence of Javanese-named kampongs does not mean that their inhabitants are all Javanese, as other ethnicities can be found among them. And, even within majority-Javanese kampongs there can be considerable diversity in terms of where people originate from. Thus, the Javanese from Pacitan are considered to be the most numerous among those present in Tanjungpinang, followed by those from Solo and other regions.

There are other "Kampung Jawa" in the northern part of Bintan Island. In contrast to those in Tanjungpinang, these were established in the 1950s. Indeed, the Javanese came after substantial numbers of ethnic Chinese established gambier plantations in the eighteenth century under the Riau-Lingga sultanate. And, unlike the area around Tanjungpinang, this area has many kampongs with Chinese names such as Ekang, Anculai and Kangboi. However, some of these villages have substantial numbers of Javanese from Pacitan in Central Java, who have continued their way of life as farmers.[22] Elsewhere in Bintan, Javanese communities can be found in Kijang, which is linked to bauxite mining and Air Raja that used to be a transmigration destination from Kendal, Central Java (Purwaningsih 2000, p. 204).

While the Javanese in Tanjungpinang and Bintan established their kampongs in the 1950s or even earlier, Batam is characterized by much newer communities. Indeed, the majority of the Javanese on the island today arrived from the 1970s onwards. As with Bintan, Batam also has its own Kampung Jawa, which is comprised of mostly Pacitan Javanese (see Lindquist 2002).[23]

JAVANESE ASSOCIATIONS (*PAGUYUBAN*) AS VESSELS FOR PRESERVING JAVANESE IDENTITY

As the Javanese population continued to increase in Tanjungpinang, a group of Javanese government officials established the first Javanese association (*paguyuban*) called Paguyuban Among Mitro in the 1980s (Rohana 2004, p. 231). However, the association had limited success in attracting many Javanese from the island's working class, who felt shy (*isin*) in a predominantly middle-class context.

However, inspired by the Among Mitro, other Javanese associations were set up in Tanjungpinang. More than generic associations, these groupings were based on regions such as Pakumas (Banyumas), Paguyuban Warga Pacitan, Arema (Malang), Paguyuban Purbolinggo (Purbolinggo), Kendal Asri (Kendal), and Paguyuban Warga Cilacap (Cilacap). These associations were then complemented by other professional groupings for Javanese, such as Batik-Solo which is for batik traders from that city. Other examples include associations of diverse origins such as Paguyuban Perantau Jawa Mandiri, Manunggaling Sadulur, Jogoboyo, and Punggowo; and numbers of *reog* (traditional dance from Ponorogo) and *kuda lumping* (hobbyhorse dance) troupes from East and Central Java.

All of these social associations have monthly gatherings to meet and greet, sometimes with self-help meetings (*arisan*), or yearly festivals (*mudik*).[24] In every *paguyuban* there is always a prominent individual or elder (*sesepuh*), that in Javanese culture is someone to turn to, to ask for advice, help or protection. Due to Javanese values, the members of *paguyuban* usually obey their elders as part of the obligation of being the member of the given association and in line with Javanese values.

The increasing number of associations pushed some leaders in the Among Mitro Paguyuban to open the associations to incorporate a wider spectrum of members. As a result, there are Among Mitro branches at the provincial level, as well all regions and almost district in the Riau Islands Province. That said, the number of *paguyubans* continues to increase, and other notable larger associations include one for the Javanese on Batam Island, and also Punggawa and Manunggaling in Tanjungpinang. The total number of Javanese associations in the Riau Islands cannot be calculated, since not all of them have been registered yet. In addition, some associations are only for informal gatherings. However, the estimation is that there are more than one hundred.[25]

However, not all of the members of these associations are Javanese. Indeed, all associations allow non-Javanese spouses to join. And, others allow people of any ethnicity to join if they have an interest in Javanese traditions or have a link with the island. Some smaller associations do have specific limitations on who can join, but the bigger associations do not. There are also other means of being linked to such associations. For example, some honour prominent leaders from other communities by inviting them to sit on advisory boards. This is a strategic step to cultivate broader support for the *paguyuban* to achieve its goals.

Thus, such associations become means to gather all Javanese and supportive members from other communities under the flag of Javanese identity. The cultural or "play" element is seen in the way that such associations perform Javanese traditions such a *kuda lumping* from Central Java, lion-peacock trance-dance (*reog*) from East Java, and puppet performances (*wayang kulit*) on many occasions.

Figure 15.1 shows a public advertisement of a puppet performance to celebrate New Year's Eve organized by the Bintan local government or regency. Although the Mayor or Regent of the area is not Javanese, this ethnicity is the most numerous in his constituency. Thus, these performances are traditionally organized at public events—usually with the help of local Javanese associations. Famous puppeteers (*dalang*) are invited from Surakarta or Yogyakarta, and the performances are attended by both Javanese and non-Javanese.

From this perspective, these social and cultural associations serve, not only as vessels for preserving identity, but also as a means for political mobilization.

FIGURE 15.1
Wayang Kulit for New Year's Eve Celebration in Bintan, 2016

Source: Bintan Regency.

THE 2015 PROVINCIAL ELECTIONS: ETHNICITY AND IDENTITY AT PLAY

Ethnicity also has political ramifications, both in terms of how specific groups are appealed to in the political realm, as well as what cultural symbols and mechanisms are used to articulate this.

The 2015 provincial elections in the Province of the Riau Islands offer a means of analysing this. One of the candidates for Governor was Surya Respationo (see Figure 15.2). A Javanese from Semarang, he served as Vice-Governor from 2010 to 2015. Over the years, he had become known for his consistent encouragement for Javanese people in the province to express their identity and maintain their culture.[26] For the Javanese in the Riau Islands, he is the father (*romo*)[27] of the community. Surya chose Ansar Ahmad, a Malay and former Regent of Bintan, as his running mate and candidate for Vice-Governor.

Appeals to Javanese tradition and culture were a central aspect of Surya's campaign platform. This can be seen in the large *reog* festival organized by one of the local Javanese associations, Manunggaling Sedulur. The main supporter of the festival was Surya Respationo, who was also a member of the association's advisory board. At the event, he stated that the festival's aim was to enable the Javanese community to always remember their ancestors' traditions. However, he also sought to reach out to other communities, especially the Malays. He stated

FIGURE 15.2
Reog Festival in Tanjungpinang, 2015

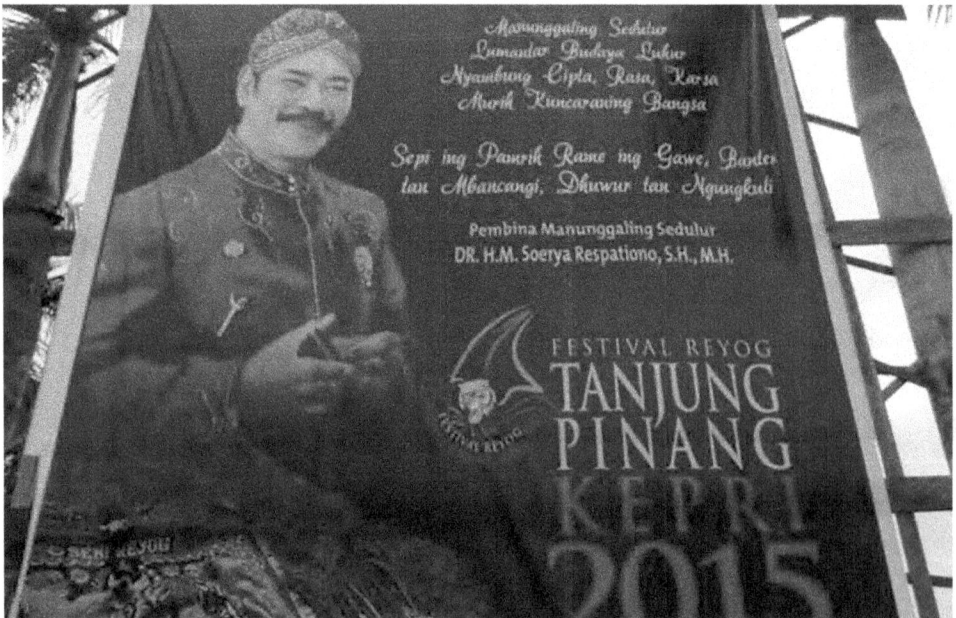

Source: Ministry of Education and Culture, Riau Islands Province.

that the Javanese should also adapt to the local context, and to illustrate his point quoted a Malay expression "the land we step on it, the sky we should uphold" (*Haluan Kepri*, 24 May 2015).

The opposing team, comprised of incumbent Governor Muhammad Sani and Nurdin Basirun, the former Regent of Karimun, was entirely Malay. Sani was an established figure in the province, having served first as Vice-Governor (2005–10) and then as Governor (2010–15). Very popular among the Malays, he was referred to as the father (*ayah*) of his community (Fionna 2017, p. 18).

Despite both candidates being Malay, Sani's team also sought to appeal to Javanese voters. One method was through religion, by stressing the piety of both candidates. Another way was to present Sani also as Javanese, highlighting an ancestral connection to the island. This did not negate his Malayness, as he was able to demonstrate his "hybridity" and "openness" to other influences.

Furthermore, for many older Javanese, Surya, despite his ethnicity, did not behave in public according to Javanese mores. One interviewee, Noto[28] stated that some older Javanese thought that he was "not like the Javanese" (*ora Jawa*) in his lack of manners and way of disrespecting elders and community leaders. In addition, Javanese mores posit that one must act in accordance with one's position. Being a Javanese leader in Malay land is considered inappropriate in some ways as, in the social hierarchy in the Riau Islands, the Malays as the original inhabitants should occupy a higher rank. This, thus, enabled Sani's team to reach out to more Javanese voters.

In the run-up to the election, Sani was able to attract the support of a number of important ethnically based associations including Javanese organizations such as Perpat (Riau Islands Malay), Ikabsu (North Sumatra), IKSB (West Sumatra), KBB (Banjarese), Paguyuban Pacitan (Pacitan, Central Java), Paguyuban Pasundan (Sundanese), Paguyuban Bawean (Bawean, East Java), PKBSS (South Sumatra), Keluarga Besar Demak (Demak, Central Java), Perkit (East Indonesia), and Pemuda Pasundan Viking (Sundanese) (*Republika*, 29 July 2015).

An analysis of the 2015 results shows that despite his ethnicity, Surya was unable to capture all of the Javanese vote. His team captured 66.3 per cent of the vote in Bintan regency, where Javanese are the largest community. However, the track record of his running mate, Ansar Ahmad, former Regent of the area, may also have been a contributing factor. In contrast, Surya's team only garnered 48 per cent of the vote in Batam, the other Javanese-majority area in the province (Fionna 2017).

Consequently, this case shows that ethnicity is an important factor in electoral contests in the Riau Islands. However, the notion of Javaneseness is not monolithic, nor is it the only mobilizing factor. Furthermore, both Javanese and Malay culture offer cultural concepts such as hybridity and mores such as demonstrating appropriate forms of behaviour that allow appeals to voters from the other community.

CONCLUSION

Over the years, and as a result of several waves of migration, the Javanese have come to be the second-largest community in the Riau Islands. In their new home, they have come to mobilize culturally and politically through establishing a variety of ethnically based associations. These associations seek to preserve traditions and culture, as well as provide a means of reaffirming identity and helping members. They have also emerged in the province in response to growing political mobilization among Malays, who position themselves as the original "sons of the soil".

Nonetheless, Javanese identity is not monolithic, nor is it impervious to other influences. This porosity will only increase over time as more Javanese inter-marry with members of other communities and the ability of successive generations to speak Javanese decreases with time. Consequently, many of these associations are flexible, allowing non-Javanese to join through a variety of mechanisms.

While both Javanese and Malay communities are self-aware and have sought to assert themselves, neither identity is impervious to the other. Furthermore, there are means of dialogue and negotiation between the two communities, both in terms of history and historical associations, as well as cultural concepts that continue today, such as playing at being siblings, making virtue of hybridity, or using language as a means of joining a specific community.

Notes

1. *Bunda Tanah Melayu* was first used in Lingga region of Riau Islands Province, but the late governor Muhammad Sani appropriated it for the whole province (*Antara Kepri*, 11 December 2011). This appeal sought to unite all of the province's regions through appealing to their "Malayness" and was done with the support of the Malay Heritage Institution (Lembaga Adat Melayu) (*Riau Telivisi*, 27 April 2016).
2. The name "Riau" originally came from the name of a river and main port on Bintan Island in the Johore-Riau era (Wee 1985).
3. *Negeri seberang parit.*
4. "Surga dollar", as the currency in Riau Archipelago was mainly in Singapore dollars—even the salary of the government officials was paid in that currency.
5. *Konfrontasi* was Indonesian President Sukarno's opposition to the creation of Malaysia in 1963, comprised of Malaya, Singapore, North Borneo and Sarawak.
6. In 1968, people from the Riau Islands entered Malaysia using *Pas Lintas Batas* (Cross Border Pass) to work in plantations and construction sites.
7. A Malay association, the Local Youth Union (Persatuan Pemuda Tempatan, or Perpat) was established in Batam in 2003. Now this association has grown bigger and covers all regions in the Riau Islands.
8. "*Maka kata biduan itu: baiklah tuanku; ragam apa diperhamba palu ini karena ragam orang Indrapura bukan Melayu? Sungguh beta Melayu, kacukan juga bukan seperti Melayu Melaka sungguh.*" *Maka Laksamana pun tersenyum seraya berkata: "Orang Melaka gerangan Melayu kacukan, bercampur dengan Jawa Majapahit! Dayang pun satu sebagai hendak mengajuk beta pula." (...) Maka kata Laksamana: "Jangan sahaja diajuk, karena orang Malaka dan tuannya bercampur, Jawa Majapahit. Tiada tahu menari," Maka kata Tun Jenal: "kata apa Tuan katakan itu? Kita bermain adik-beradik; hendaklah jangan menaruh syak di hati."*
9. Malay "language" (*bahasa*), refers not just to the network of words (spoken or written), but also to the set of good and relevant manners—or culture—that keep a community together in peace and harmony (Maier 1997, p. 676).

10. This definition used by both the British colonial authority and the present Malaysian government.

11. The Indonesian phrase is *"bahasa Jawa yang sebenarnya"* (Magnis-Suseno 1991, p. 11).

12. The original Javanese expression is *"berbudi bawa leksana lan ngudi sejatining becik"*.

13. Surakarta was ruled by two dynasties: Surakarta Hadiningrat (headed by Sunan Pakubuwono) and Puro Mangkunegaran (headed by Mangkunegoro); Yogyakarta was also ruled by two dynasties: Ngayogyakarta Hadiningrat (headed by Sultan Hamengku Buwono) and Puro Pakualaman (headed by Pakualam).

14. By way of illustration, the famous Javanese nod of the late President Soeharto did not always mean an agreement (Sutarto 2006, p. 40).

15. *Pareng rikat, nanging ora pareng ndisiki* (allowed to be quick, but not to overtake), *pareng pinter, nanging ora pareng nggurui* (allowed to be smart, but not to teach), *pareng kuwat, nanging ora pareng maneni* (allowed to be strong, but not to act defiantly) (Sutarto 2006, p. 50).

16. Java's population increased impressively, from 5 million at the end of eighteenth century to 25 million at the end of nineteenth century to more than 95 million in 1980s (Repetto 1986, p. 14), and in 2012 reached 141 million.

17. There were several studies about Javanese migration to Malaya and Singapore from the end of nineteenth century to the 1920s (see Bahrin 1967a, 1967b; Kaur 2004; Hugo 1993; Sekimoto 1994; Spaan, van Naerssen, and Kohl 2001; Spaan 1994). Those studies present at least three commonalities that echo the present reality. First, the development of an export-oriented economy required huge recruits of labour in Malaya (now Malaysia) and Singapore (Hugo 1994, p. 95; Kaur 2004, pp. 6–8). Second, the Javanese as the major population in this migration (Bahrin 1967b, p. 238). Third, the rising Javanese population and settlement in Malaysia and Singapore.

18. This may be rooted in the idea of "harmony" among Javanese, as President Soeharto of the New Order was known for the influence of Javanese philosophy in his political strategy (see Sutarto 2006).

19. *Selametan* can be compared to a thanksgiving ceremony to bless and pray for somebody who enters a new phase of life or who will be going somewhere. It is also a feast where people gather and eat together.

20. Liamsi (1997, p. 18) mentioned Kampung Jawa in Tanjungpinang along with Kampung Tambak and Kampung Bukit in the 1820s but there is no further detailed information. The area was formerly called Kampung Jawa Paya, with *paya* meaning swamp.

21. Interview with Noto (pseudonym) on 24 November 2017.

22. Interview with Karti (pseudonym) on 20 November 2017. Karti said when she first came in 1970s, she lived with her aunt who owned several hectares of rubber plantation in Cikolek. She said Cikolek was a Javanese kampong populated mainly by people from Pacitan. Only one Chinese family lived by the main road to Tanjunguban.

23. Karti said that many people from Pacitan travel in search of work (*merantau*) to seek out a better life.

24. *Mudik* means going back to their home village usually during the Hari Raya festival.

25. On 29 August 2017, Punggowo celebrated its ninth anniversary and managed to gather 150,000 people from more than 100 Javanese *paguyubans* (cnnindonesia.com, 29 August 2017).

26. On 26 January 2014, his daughter's wedding ceremony included an all-Javanese procession, imitating the Javanese royal wedding with Javanese food and an art festival.

27. Title used in *kromo*, the highest rank of the Javanese language.
28. Interview with Noto on 25 November 2017.

References

Ahmad, S.A. 2015. *Sulalatussalatin: Sejarah Melayu Edisi Pelajar*. Kuala Lumpur: Dewan Bahasa dan Pustaka.

Al Azhar. 1997. "Malayness in Riau: The Study and Revitalization of Identity". *Bijdragen tot de Taal-, Land- en Volkenkunde* 153, no. 4: 764–73.

Ananta, A. 2006. "Changing Ethnic Composition and Potential Violent Conflict in Riau Archipelago, Indonesia: An Early Warning Signal". *Population Review* 45, no. 1: 48–67.

Andaya, L.Y. 2008. *Leaves of the Same Tree: Trade and Ethnicity in the Straits of Melaka*. Honolulu: University of Hawai'i Press.

Antara Kepri. 2011. "Budayawan Serumpun Deklarasikan Lingga Bunda Tanah Melayu". 11 December 2011, https://kepri.antaranews.com/berita/19228/budayawan-serumpun-deklarasikan-lingga-bunda-tanah-melayu

Arifin, E. N., A. Ananta, D.R.W.W. Utami, N.B. Handayani, A. Pramono, and A. Purbowati. 2014. "Statistics on Ethnicity in Indonesia's Districts: Based on Indonesia's 2010 Population Census". BPS-Statistics Indonesia and ISEAS Singapore.

Bahrin, T.S. 1967a. "The Pattern of Indonesian Migration and Settlement in Malaya". *Asian Studies* 5, no. 2: 233–58.

———. 1967b. "The Growth and Distribution of the Indonesian Population in Malaya". *Bijdragen tot de Taal-, Land- en Volkenkunde* 123, no. 2: 267–86.

Bintan Regency. 2016. "Pagelaran Wayang Kulit Semalam Suntuk Menyambut Tahun Baru 2017". 27 December 2016. http://bintankab.go.id/master/pagelaran-wayang-kulit-semalam-suntuk-menyambut-tahun-baru-2017

Carruthers, A. 2018. *Living on the Edge: Being Malay (and Bugis) in the Riau Islands*. Trends in Southeast Asia, no. 12/2018. Singapore: ISEAS – Yusof Ishak Institute.

Chou, C. 1997. "Contesting the Tenure of Territoriality The Orang Suku Laut". *Bijdragen Tot De Taal-, Land- en Volkenkunde* 153, no. 4: 605–29.

———, and V. Wee. 2002. "Tribality and Globalization: The Orang Suku Laut and the 'Growth Triangle' in a Contested Environment". In *Tribal Communities in the Malay World: Historical, Cultural and Social Perspectives*, edited by G. Benjamin and C. Chou. Singapore: Institute of Southeast Asian Studies; Leiden: IIAS.

CNN Indonesia. 2017 "Halal Bihalal Punggowo Pecahkan Rekor MURI". 29 August 2017 https://m.cnnindonesia.com/gaya-hidup/20170829151442-307-238108/halabihalal-punggowo-pecahkan-rekor-muri

Fionna, Ulla. 2017. *Parties in the Periphery: Organizational Dilemmas in Indonesia's Kepri Province*. Trends in Southeast Asia, no. 21/2017. Singapore: ISEAS – Yusof Ishak Institute.

Gafnesia, D. 2002 "Smokkel: Jaringan Perdagangan Unik di Daerah Riau Kepulauan". *Seri Penerbitan Balai Kajian Jarahnitra Tanjungpinang* No. 19: 76–101.

———. 2005."Riau Kepulauan: Sejarah persinggahan TKI di Indonesia Bagian Barat". *Seri Penerbitan Balai Kajian Jarahnitra Tanjungpinang* No. 21: 1–28.

Haluan Kepri. 2015. "Festival Reog Event Perdana di Kepri". 24 May 2015. https://www.haluankepri.com/news/detail/77720/festival-reog-event-perdana-di-kepri

Harsono, T.D. 1999. "Pola Interaksi Antarsuku Bangsa di Kota Tanjungpinang". *Seri Penerbitan Balai Kajian Jarahnitra Tanjungpinang* No. 15: 183–253.

Hugo, G. 1993. "Indonesian Migration to Malaysia: Trends and Policy Implications". *Southeast Asian Journal of Social Science* 21, no. 1: 36–70.

Hutchinson, F.E. 2017. *Rowing Against the Tide? Batam's Economic Fortunes in Today's Indonesia*. Trends in Southeast Asia, no. 8/2017. Singapore: ISEAS – Yusof Ishak Institute.

Irawanto, D.W., P.L. Ramsey, and J.C. Ryan. 2011. "Challenge of Leading in Javanese Culture". *Asian Ethnicity* 12, no. 2 (June): 125–39.

Kaur, A. 2004. "Mobility, Labour Mobilisation and Border Controls: Indonesian Labour Migration to Malaysia since 1990". Paper presented to the 15th Biennial Conference of the Asian Studies Association of Australia in Canberra, 29 June – 2 July 2004.

Lapian, A.B. 1979. "Le rôle des Orang Laut dans l'histoire de Riau". *Archipel* 18: 215–22.

Lenhart, L. 2003. "Orang Suku Laut Identity: The Construction of Ethnic Realities". In *Tribal Communities in the Malay World: Historical, Cultural and Social Perspectives*, edited by G. Benjamin and C. Chou. Singapore: Institute of Southeast Asian Studies; Leiden: IIAS.

Liamsi, R.K. 1997. *Tanjungpinang Kota Bestari*. Tanjungpinang: Pemda Kota Administratif Tanjungpinang.

Linquist, J. 2002. "The Anxiety of Mobility: Development, Migration, and Tourism in Indonesian Borderland". A thesis for Department of Social Anthropology, Stockholm University.

Long, N.J. 2013. *Being Malay in Indonesia: Histories, Hopes, Citizenship in the Riau Archipelago*. Singapora: NUS Press.

Magnis-Suseno, F. 1991. *Etika Jawa*. Jakarta: Gramedia Pustaka Utama.

Maier, H. 1997. "'We Are Playing Relatives': Riau, the Craddle of Reality and Hybridity". *Bijdragen tot de Taal-, Land- en Volkenkunde, Bijdragen tot de Taal-, Land- en Volkenkunde* 153, no. 4: 672–98.

Milner, A. 2008. *The Malays: The Peoples of South-East Asia and the Pacific*. Oxford: Wiley-Blackwell.

Ministry of Education and Culture of the Riau Islands Province. 2015. "Festival Reog Tanjungpinang Kepri". 25 May 2015. http://kebudayaan.kemdikbud.go.id/bpnbkepri/2015/05/25/festival-reog-tanjungpinang-kepri-2015/

Poedjosoedarmo, S. 1968. "Javanese Speech Level". *Indonesia*, no. 6 (October): 54–81

Purwaningsih, E. 2000. "Pemukiman Masyarakat Transmigran di Air Raja, Kecamatan Bintan Utara". *Seri Penerbitan Balai Kajian Jarahnitra Tanjungpinang*, no. 16: 191–222.

Reid, A. 2001. "Understanding *Melayu* (Malay) as a Source of Diverse Modern Identities". *Journal of Southeast Asian Studies* 32, no. 3: 295–313.

Repetto, R. 1986. "Soil Loss and Population Pressure on Java". *Ambio* 15, no. 1: 14–18.

Republika. 2015. "Pasangan Sani-Nurdin Resmi Daftar ke KPUD". 29 July 2015. https://m.republika.co.id/amp/ns93df282

Riau Telivisi. 2016. "Kepri Adalah Bunda Tanah Melayu". 27 April 2016. https://www.riautelevisi.com/berita-kepri-adalah-bunda-tanah-melayu.html

Rohana, S. 2004. "Orang Jawa di Tengah Masyarakat Melayu". *Seri Penerbitan Balai Kajian Jarahnitra Tanjungpinang*, no. 21: 208–39.

Sekimoto, T. 1994. "Pioneer Settlers and State Control: A Javanese Migrant Community in Selangor, Malaysia". *Southeast Asian Studies* 32, no. 2 (September): 173–96.

Spaan, E. 1994. "Taikongs and Calos: The Role of Middlemen and Brokers in Javanese International Migration". *International Migration Revies* 28, no. 1 (Spring): 93–113.

———, T. van Naerssen, and G. Kohl. 2001. "Re-imagining Borders: Malay Identity and Indonesian Migrants in Malaysia". *Royal Dutch Geographical Society KNAG* 2, no. 2: 160–72.

Sutarto, A. 2006. "Becoming a True Javanese: A Javanese View of Attempts at Javanisation". *Indonesia and the Malay World* 34, no. 96 (March): 39–53.

Swastiwi, A.W. 2004. "Sejarah Penambangan Bauksit di Pulau Bintan". *Seri Penerbitan Balai Kajian Jarahnitra Tanjungpinang*, no. 21: 91–115.

Tirtosudarmo, R. 1997. "Economic Development, Migration and Ethnic Conflict in Indonesia: A Preliminary Observation". *SOJOURN: Journal of Social Issues in Southeast Asia* 12, no. 2: 293–328.

Wee, V. 1985. "Melayu: Hierarchies of Being in Riau". PhD thesis, Australian National University, Canberra.

White, B. 1973. "Demand for Labour and Population Growth in Colonial Java". *Human Ecology* 1, no. 3: 217–36.

Wijaya, A. 2002. "Sejarah Kampung Yudowinangun". *Seri Penerbitan Balai Kajian Jarahnitra Tanjungpinang*, no. 19: 102–35.

16

HASANGAPON
Understanding the Political Aspirations
of Batak Migrants in the Riau Islands

Deasy Simandjuntak

INTRODUCTION

According to the 2010 population census, Bataks comprise 12.5 per cent (209,000) of the total population of the Riau Islands. They are the third-largest ethnic group after the "host" ethnic group, the Malay, and then the Javanese, which account for 31 per cent and 25 per cent of the population, respectively. As a sizeable migrant community in the Riau Islands, the Bataks play a role in both the economic and political life of the province. This chapter deals with the migration of Bataks to the Riau Islands and their political aspirations in their new home.

Traditionally, the Batak is one of the Indonesian ethnic groups most prone to voluntary migration. There are many motives for Batak migration, however, traditional understandings of social and economic capital articulate several forms of success, which individuals should strive for. They include: progress (*hamajuon*); higher education (*hagabeon*); wealth and the capacity to be generous (*hamoraon*); and glory (*hasangapon*), which refers to securing a high position in the government or the military.

Many male Bataks have played a role in Indonesia's political history. Indonesians generally would remember Mr Adam Malik Batubara, former Vice-President of Indonesia under Soeharto, and prominent generals such as A.H. Nasution, T.B. Simatupang, Feisal Tanjung, and Luhut Binsar Pandjaitan (currently Coordinating Minister for Maritime and Investment Affairs).

On an individual level, these names have become an inspiration for many Bataks. This can be seen in how Batak migrants aspire to gain political positions in the places where they reside. In Riau Islands, for example, several Batak migrants have succeeded in attaining elected positions, the most prominent of whom is Jumaga Nadeak, the current Speaker of the provincial parliament.

This chapter aims to answer the following questions: First, how does tradition shape the political aspirations of Batak migrants to the Riau Islands? Second, how do Batak migrants in Riau Islands play a role in the province's political life? Third, how do Bataks, as politicians, interact with other ethno-religious groups in the Riau Islands?

To answer these questions, the chapter starts with a brief note on Batak political history. It then highlights the traditional motives of migration among the Bataks and their movement to Riau and the Riau Islands. Following this, it discusses the current political role of Bataks in the Riau Islands, through analyzing cases of individual politicians as well as the largest clan association. The final section relates these findings back to the research questions.

A BRIEF POLITICAL HISTORY OF THE BATAK OF NORTH SUMATRA

The Batak ethnic group's ancestral land is in what is today known as North Sumatra province, specifically the areas around the Lake Toba, the highlands and the western coast. The Bataks comprised of six subethnic groups, namely Toba (the largest), Angkola, Mandailing, Simalungun, Karo and Pakpak. According to the 2010 census, the last which identified respondents' ethnic group, there were almost 8.5 million Bataks, which constituted 3.6 per cent of Indonesia's total population. This made it the third-largest ethnic group in Indonesia, after the Javanese (95 million, 40.2 per cent) and Sundanese (37 million, 15.5 per cent), as well as the largest non-Java-based group in the country.

Due to regular voluntary migration out of North Sumatra since the nineteenth century, the Batak can now be found everywhere in Indonesia. The majority, or 55.6 per cent, of the Batak is Christian (Protestant and Catholic). The Batak ethnic church, Congregation of Protestant Christian Batak (Huria Kristen Batak Protestan, or HKBP) is the largest Protestant denomination in Indonesia, with 4.5 million members. Other than Christians, 44.2 per cent of the Batak are Muslim, and a smaller proportion adheres to traditional religions.

Despite North Sumatra's significant role in plantation and trading activities in the colonial era, the Batak people in the highlands lived relatively isolated up until the intensification of the Dutch authority in the later part of the nineteenth century (Andaya 2008, pp. 146–72). The Dutch East Indian Company, the VOC, which had started trade relations around 1694, only had limited contacts via couriers who went to the coasts (Rodenburgh 1993, p. 21). Europeans did not enter the interior of Sumatra until 1824, when British missionaries reached the populated region of Silindung in

Simalungun area. In 1842, the central Batak land around Balige came formally under Dutch rule. In 1861, the German Rheinische Mission, with Pastor Nommensen as its leader, began their work in the Tapanuli area. This was followed by the arrival of Dutch government officials in the 1870s, although complete administrative control was not achieved until 1907. The Rheinische Mission in North Sumatra itself became the progenitor of today's HKBP.

Traditionally for Toba-Batak society, everyday life revolved around the observance of the customary law (*adat*) which found its centrality in a marriage. The Batak social system is patrilineal and patrilocal, with exogamous (outside own clan) and asymmetrical cross-cousin marriage. The first important feature of *adat* is the relations between the clans of wife-givers and the wife-receivers, which forms the social hierarchy of the Batak, and constitutes the foundation of the groups' "politics". Consequently, the tripartite relationship between the wife-giver clan, the wife-receiver clan, and one's own clan, dubbed "the three-legged stove" (*dalihan na tolu*) became the foundation of the Batak's social structure—an individual's position in the hierarchy is adaptable, depending on who he is interacting with. These relations continue to play a significant role.

The second important feature is the emphasis on the individual's forms of "capital". Similar to Bourdieuan economic, cultural and social forms of capital (Bourdieu 1986), for the Batak, forms of capital consist of: *hasangapon*, or glory, whose pursuit became the fundamental duty of every male especially those who chose to participate in the struggle for the chief's position; *hagabeon*, or "completeness" (traditionally attributed to having many male heirs); and *hamoraon*, or wealth and generosity. In modern times, the three forms of capital still play a role as an aspiration for Batak males, with *hasangapon* referring to having a high position in the military or the government, and *hagabeon*, which, in addition to having sons, also refers to having high education and good reputation (Simandjuntak 2012).

The third feature is the special quality of a person's spirit (*sahala*). Powerful individuals, such as chiefs, were said to have the spirit of leadership (*sahala harajaon*), the measurement of which was his worldly success and the attainment of the above capitals. Similarly, when a chief lost a battle, it was said that his *sahala* had left him. This belief persisted even after the intensification of the Dutch authority in the Toba lands, when chiefly positions were absorbed into the government structure and some chiefs began to receive salaries. Moreover, when some leaders were also exempted from mandatory labours and taxes, the leadership position generated both native and "foreign" prestige. The Toba people's inclination towards education was attributed to the attempt to achieve white-collar employment in which a person received salary and was exempted from physical labour.

The Batak's first encounter with elections was attributed to the Dutch attempt at managing the Batak lands (Castles 1972). In order to regulate the succession of village chiefs, Resident Vorstman, who governed the area in the early 1900s, attempted to abolish the hereditary system of chieftainship by establishing elections for village chiefs. Voting rights were given only to the male heads of the families, and the right to be elected was confined to members of the founding clans. Resident Ypes, who replaced Vorstman in 1921, carefully redrew boundaries of the district so as to be congruent with the boundaries of clan territories, hoping that the new territories would develop into *adat*-based communities. However, elections brought problems of bribery and those chiefs whose sons could no longer inherit the chieftainship then refused to carry out their duties. The election system was abolished in 1934 and was replaced by a new system of "consultation", in which the candidates for chiefly positions would speak in front of the Dutch subdistrict officer (*controleur*) and an assembly stressing their suitability, much like today's open rallies (Simandjuntak 2010).

THE BATAK MIGRATION

Purba and Purba (1997) recorded several motives for migration traditionally recognized among the Bataks: opening new agricultural lands (*manombang*); moving due to reasons outside of farming, as civil servants or to gain education (*mangaranto*); mostly unmarried men seeking any kind of employment (*marjalang*); to be involved in thuggery (*marlompong*); mostly whole families settling in with relatives in new areas in order to get better living (*mangalului jampalan na lomak*); seasonal workers and sojourners staying temporarily in a certain area for work (*mangombo*); or a temporary relocation for trading (*marjajo* (men) or *marengge-rengge* (women)). In modern times, most Batak migrants would refer to *mangaranto*, even when the reason for relocation was to look for any job or when a whole family settles with relatives in a new area.

In his 1958 book, Cunningham wrote that during the latter part of the nineteenth century, much of the east coast of Sumatra was developed by foreign planters who had gotten licences from the rulers of petty states or sultanates (Cunningham 1958). Jungle lands were cleared, roads and railways were established, and Javanese labourers were brought in in large numbers. The region became an important producer of export commodities. Yet the use of lands was changed in the aftermath of the Japanese occupation, as Dutch and other plantation administrators were put in concentration camps. Post-war attempts to re-establish plantations failed while a large number of Batak from the highlands continued flocking to the coastal areas in search for fertile lands to cultivate. Cunningham estimated that by 1956 at least 250,000 Toba Batak had left the highlands. Castles estimated that by 1961 there were already 29,000 Batak residing in Jakarta, out of a total of 40,000–50,000 residing in Java (Castles 1967).

Such massive migration was triggered by the lack of development in the highlands, while there were other opportunities elsewhere. Farming was still the main production activity in the highlands, however, even when there were lands available, they would prefer to migrate elsewhere to assume non-farming occupations, as these were considered providing a greater opportunity to gain riches (*hamoraon*) and prestige (*hasangapon*). Another contributing factor was education. The Rheinische Mission which have converted hundreds of thousands of the Batak had opened schools offering Western education in the hinterlands. Thus, in the early 1940s, many Batak had Western education, which was rare elsewhere during the Dutch times. Educated Batak who aspired to gain white-collar jobs then left in large numbers to cities and towns across Indonesia. Bruner (1972) recorded that although in the 1930 census the number of Batak in Medan, the capital city of North Sumatra, was less than 5 per cent of the total Medan population of 76,000, this number rapidly increased to 10–20 per cent in the 1950s and possibly a quarter of the total in 1970s. Medan then increasingly became a Batak town by the end of 1970s (Brunner 1959).

In modern times, Batak migration still focuses largely on seeking a better life. Some quantitative studies carried out by migration scholars present reliable findings. Borualogo and van de Vijver (2016) compared the migration motives of three ethnic groups, namely the Batak, Minangkabau and Sundanese. The first two are known to be traditionally prone to migration. Like the Batak, the Minangkabau leave their hometowns voluntarily in search for work or other life experiences such as studies. However, unlike the Batak, according to Naim, the Minangkabau mostly had the intention to come back to their places of origin in West Sumatra (Naim 1984). The Sundanese, on the other hand, are not avid migrants and tend to stay in their hometowns. Table 16.1 shows Indonesia's main ethnicities' propensity to migrate.

The 1961 census did not actually indicate ethnic groups, thus Naim (1984) provided an estimation of the extent of migration for each ethnic group based on each group's average population growth. Ethnic groups were indicated in the later censuses in 2000 and 2010. Based on the 2010 census, seven ethnic groups are categorized as having a high propensity of migration, with six of them having had a high propensity since 1930, namely Minangkabau, Batak, Banjar, Bugis, Manado and

TABLE 16.1
The Propensity to Migrate by Ethnic Group

Migration Intensity	Ethnic Groups	Proportion		
		1930	1961	2010
High	Minangkabau	11.0	31.6	34.7
	Batak	15.3	19.5	31.7
	Banjarese	14.2	12.2	34.9
	Buginese	10.5	6.6	43.3
	Manadonese	9.5	n.a.	17.6
	Ambonese	9.1	11.5	17.7
Low	Javanese	3.4	3.4	31.8
	Sundanese	3.4	3.4	9.3
	Madurese	3.4	3.4	9.2
	Balinese	0.1	1.4	15.5
	Acehnese	1.1	2.6	6.6
	Malay	3.4	3.3	15.8

Source: Naim (1984); Abdurrahman et al. (2013).

Ambon. The propensity for Javanese to migrate increased sharply to 31.8 per cent from only 3.4 per cent in 1930 owing largely to the "transmigration" programme, or the involuntary relocation programme of people from Java to elsewhere in the archipelago during the Soeharto era.

Table 16.2 shows the size of Batak populations in some Indonesian regions according to the 2010 census. These are the provinces to which most Batak migrants have relocated over the years.

The table shows that despite their high propensity to migrate a majority of the Batak—almost 6 million or 68.3 per cent of the total Batak population—still resides in the homelands in North Sumatra province, where they comprise 45 per cent of the province's total population. The second-highest Batak concentration is in Riau, with almost 700,000 Batak, or 8.2 per cent of the total Batak population and 12.6 per cent of Riau's total population. Early Batak migration to Riau owed to the economic opportunities the province had offered, for example by the opening of agricultural lands and employment in the oil sector. The third-largest concentration of Batak is in the Riau Islands, with around 207,000 people or 12.5 per cent of the province's total population. Although not as many as in West Java or Jakarta, the Bataks are the third-largest ethnic group in the Riau Islands. Despite the city being the capital, Jakarta's Batak population only constitutes 3.4 per cent of the greater city's total population.

BATAK MIGRATION TO THE RIAU ISLANDS[1]

According to the record written by Purba and Purba (1997), in 1928 there were only three Batak households (consisting of an employee at subdistrict (*controleur*) office, a policeman, and a forest guard) in Tanjungpinang. They were relocated by the government from North Sumatra. There were also some young Batak job-seekers, and one person involved in thuggery at the harbour. There were more Bataks in towns such as Pekanbaru, Siak, Selat Panjang, Bagan Siapiapi and Bengkalis in mainland Riau due to the greater range of economic activities. According to the 1930 census—the only one recording ethnicity prior to the 2000 census—there were 262 Bataks in the Riau regency (which included the Riau Islands). In Pekanbaru,

TABLE 16.2
Five Provinces with the Largest Batak Populations

Province	Total	Distribution	Concentration
North Sumatra	5,785,716	68.3	44.8
Riau	691,399	8.2	12.6
West Java	467,438	5.5	1.1
Jakarta	326,645	3.9	3.4
Riau Islands	206,678	2.5	12.5

Source: Ananta et al. (2015), p. 154.

in 1940, there were seventeen Batak households, of which ten were Christians and seven Muslims. Most of them worked as officials or at government-run plantations.

In 1942, as the Japanese invaded, Batak officials evacuated their families back to North Sumatra. Some young male Bataks were taken from Tapanuli, North Sumatra, as forced labourers to build railways from Pekanbaru to Sijunjung in West Sumatra, while some escaped to the hinterlands. Yet those showing potential were sent by the Japanese to the military school in Malaka to become *heiho* (auxiliary troops) or *giyugun* (voluntary troops). After the proclamation of independence, these men became nationalist leaders in their own regions. Among them was D.I. Pandjaitan, who became a military commander in Pekanbaru during the first Dutch Aggression in 1947.[2]

In 1949, a Batak pastor who transited in Tanjungpinang on his way to Singapore reported that there were fifty Christian Bataks living in the town. They were members of the Indische Kerk, a non-ethnic church, because there was no Batak church (HKBP) yet. However, these Christian Bataks still regularly donated money to the HKBP church in Singapore, showing their ethnic affinity. There were also Bataks in other islands, such as Karimun and Natuna, who worked as government officials.

In 1954, the first HKBP church of the oil regions was established in the new town of Minas. In 1958, a Batak official became the chief of the harbour in Dumai. Most of the Batak in the oil regions were government officials or employees of the oil companies. Those who could not find a job were sponsored by the Christian Bataks to teach the Sakai community in the forests of Kandis. The lessons included reading, hygiene, basic agriculture and Christianity. Their activities were followed by missionaries in 1962, who also taught the community to plant rubber, coffee and rice.

In the 1960s, the Riau province became an attractive destination for the Bataks, due to increasing employment opportunities. In 1960, the provincial capital was moved from Tanjungpinang to Pekanbaru, when Riau was upgraded from a regency to a province. Due to their educational qualifications, many Bataks and Minangs became officials in the new local government. In 1964, the government of North Sumatra began sending Batak teachers to Riau. Meanwhile, the development of the oil industry also attracted young Bataks to Riau and the archipelago. In the 1970s, a growing number of civil servants, teachers and nurses were sent from North Sumatra to Tanjungpinang.

Due to the development of Tanjungpinang and its proximity to Singapore, some Bataks from Medan, especially older women, were involved in smuggling, creating a triangle of network between Medan, Tanjungpinang and Jakarta. A very rare study done by Ng Chin-keong (1976) from Nanyang University in Singapore recorded that,

> Chinese merchants in Tanjungpinang ordered cargoes from Singapore and distributed them to Java and Sumatra through Batak women called *inang* ("mother" in Batak, author's note) or Chinese vendors from Medan, both were also called *shui-k'e* or

"vendors who travelled by the sea" in Chinese. They travelled on a state-owned two-thousand-ton ship sailing to and from weekly between Jakarta, Bangka, Tanjungpinang and Medan. There were about two or three hundred Batak *inang-inang* travelling between Medan, Tanjungpinang and Jakarta. Each of them possessed a capital ranging from a few thousand to even ten or twenty thousand Singapore dollars. They preferred carrying with them delicate but expensive items such as perfumes and high-quality textiles to sell in Jakarta.

No one could precisely estimate the unrecorded trade flowing between Tanjungpinang and Singapore. One estimate in 1968 states that "smuggling cost the country at least US$200 million a year". Another report says that "smuggling has been publicly estimated at US$100 million or more annually and has by all accounts increased dramatically since the ending of confrontation with Malaysia and Singapore.... In 1974, there was a smuggling case investigated by the authorities in Tanjungpinang. It involved an attempt to smuggle in goods from Singapore, consisting of textiles, household utensils and other goods totalling 1,000 bales with a value of IDR60 million. It was just a single case thwarted by the authorities." (Ng 1976, pp. 59–70)

It was clear that the smuggling business between Singapore, Tanjungpinang, Medan and Jakarta was booming in 1970s. A historian at the Tanjungpinang-based Culture Preservation Center (BNPB) confirmed that many older Batak women were still involved in an activity called "smokkel", deriving from the Dutch word "smokkelen", meaning smuggling, even until early 1980s. This activity benefitted from the trajectory of the large Tampomas ship from Tanjung Priok-Belawan-Tanjungpinang.[3]

With regard to intergroup relations, generally, the Batak lived in peace with other ethnic groups in the province. There were only a few instances in Batam Island in which members of the Batak community were involved in communal riots with other migrants, such as from Flores island, East Nusa Tenggara. One such incident took place in 1999, when unrest involving the Bataks and the Flores ended with a written peace agreement between the two groups (*Tribunnews*, 19 June 2012). A similar incident occurred in 2012. What began as a land dispute between two companies soon became "ethnicized" as each company engaged security personnel with a specific ethnic background. Eleven people were victims of this communal clash (*JPNN*, 19 June 2012).

Other than these incidents, the Bataks have coexisted peacefully with other ethnic groups. Especially in Tanjungpinang, where Malays are still the largest group, members of the Batak community understand the need to maintain harmony, which includes adapting to Malay values and "knowing one's place as 'newcomers' (*pendatang*) in the province". Interviews with parliamentarians, presented in the next section, reveal the adoption of such adaptation strategy while still maintaining Batak identity and culture. In May 2018, the Bataks of Tanjungpinang held a large cultural festival, attended by thousands of city inhabitants from various ethnic groups. City parliamentarian P.M. Sitohang, who was one of the organizers, mentioned that they "would like to show that the Bataks are respectful people, upholding our principle of *dalihan na tolu* which showcases our ability to adapt to different circumstances".[4]

FIGURE 16.1
A Batak Cultural Festival in Tanjungpinang, 2018

Vice-Speaker of Tanjungpinang parliament A.D. Pasaribu (fourth from left) and city parliamentarian P.M. Sitohang (fifth from left) traditionally greeting the chiefs of Batak clans and guests.
Photo by Deasy Simandjuntak, May 2018.

Raja Ariza, Tanjungpinang's acting mayor who is Malay, similarly reiterated the need for "sons of the soil" and "newcomers" to live in harmony.

Table 16.3 shows the proportion of the main ethnic groups across the districts of Riau Island according to the 2010 census. Most Bataks live on Batam Island (178,000, where they comprise 18.9 per cent of Batam's population). Here, the Javanese are the largest group (264,000 or 28.1 per cent) and the Malays the second largest (137,000 or 14.6 per cent). Many Bataks also reside in and around Tanjungpinang (12,000 or 6.5 per cent), where the Malays are the largest group (57,000 or 30.6 per cent) followed by the Javanese (51,000 or 27.4 per cent). In Bintan, the Bataks comprise 6.6 per cent (9,400) whereas the Javanese are the largest group and comprise 31.7 per cent (45,000), and the Malays are the second-largest group, as they make up 31.1 per cent (44,000) of Bintan's total population (see Figure 16.2). Compared to other groups, however, the Bataks have grown more rapidly between 2000 and 2010, most likely drawn by the economic opportunities that Batam has offered.

Thus, as with the Javanese, the Batak in the Riau Islands mostly live in Batam and Bintan (including Tanjungpinang)—the two largest and most urbanized islands of the province (see Figure 16.3). This is likely due to the Batak's preference for higher education and white-collar or urban jobs. Aside from the Batak's own aspirations

TABLE 16.3
Population of Main Ethnic Groups by District in the Riau Islands

No.	District/City	Malay	Javanese	Batak	Minang	Chinese	Others	Total
1	Batam	136,745 (14.6%)	263,984 (28.1%)	177,677 (18.9%)	124,533 (13.3%)	61,883 (6.6%)	174,567 (18.6%)	939,389
2	Tanjung Pinang	57,121 (30.6%)	51,125 (27.4%)	12,121 (6.5%)	17,456 (9.4%)	26,516 (14.2%)	22,124 (11.9%)	186,463
3	Bintan	44,041 (31.1%)	44,816 (31.7%)	9,361 (6.6%)	8,179 (5.8%)	8,755 (6.2%)	33,768 (18.7%)	141,620
4	Karimun	110,506 (52.1%)	39,224 (18.5%)	7,674 (3.6%)	10,096 (4.8%)	23,426 (11%)	21,210 (10%)	212,136
5	Natuna	56,695 (82.5%)	6,723 (9.8%)	880 (1.3%)	877 (1.3%)	1,346 (2%)	2,200 (3.2%)	68,721
6	Lingga	67,667 (78.5%)	3,645 (4.2%)	777 (0.9%)	*incl. in "Others"	5,863 (6.8%)	**8,207 (9.5%)	86,159
7	Anambas	32,616 (87.2%)	911 (2.4%)	188 (0.5%)	*incl. in "Others"	915 (2.5%)	**2,773 (7.4%)	37,403
	Total	505,391	410,428	208,678	162,452	128,704	264,850	1,671,891
	Percentage	30.2%	24.6%	12.5%	9.%	7.7%	15.4%	100%

Notes:
*The Minang figures for Lingga and Anambas are included in "Others" in the abovementioned source.
**Including the Minang figures.
Source: Data processed from Arifin et al. (2014).

FIGURE 16.2
The Ethnic Composition of the Riau Islands

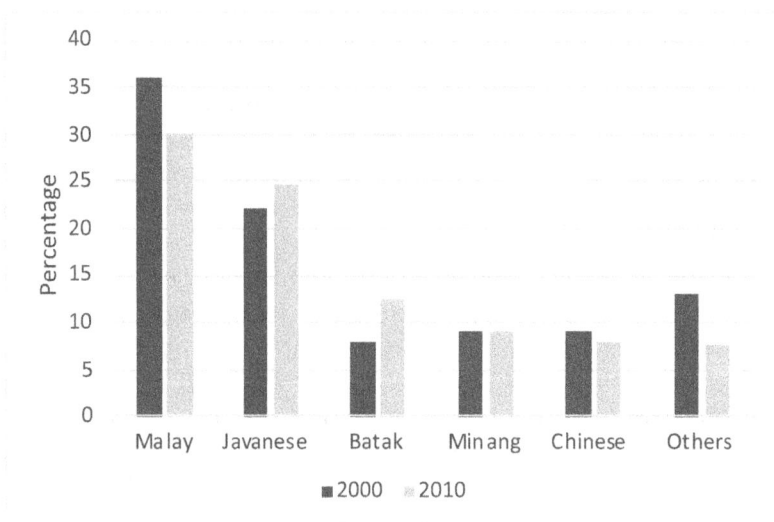

Source: Ananta (2006); Arifin et al. (2014).

FIGURE 16.3
The Proportion of Batak by District in the Riau Islands

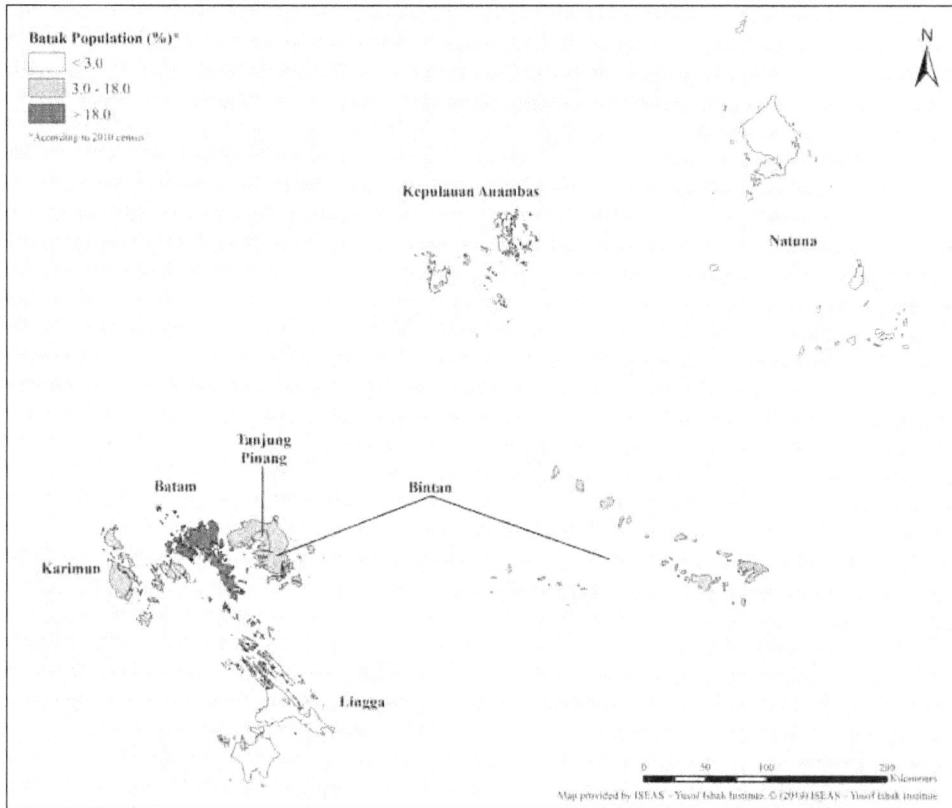

Source: Arifin et al. (2014).

and drive for progress, being the third-largest group in these two islands has also been accompanied by a desire to seek political representation in local parliaments.

POLITICAL ASPIRATIONS OF BATAKS IN THE RIAU ISLANDS

In modern times, Batak migrants no longer only focus on the betterment of their economic condition. Once economic stability is attained, some begin aspiring for political office. Due to their good educational background and ability to attract votes from their own community as well as other groups, some Batak migrants have succeeded in securing seats. In the provincial parliament, seven out of forty-five members are Batak, including the Speaker who is a Christian Batak. In the provincial capital Tanjung Pinang, there were five Bataks out of thirty parliament members. The following sections deal with the life stories of three Batak parliamentarians and the role of the United Batak Clans Association (Rumpun Batak Bersatu, or RBB) in helping them secure seats in the provincial parliament.

J. Nadeak, Speaker of the Riau Islands Provincial Parliament[5]

In 2014, Mr Nadeak, a Christian lawyer, became the Speaker of the Riau Islands provincial parliament. Nadeak had studied and practised law starting in the 1980s in Pekanbaru, the capital city of Riau Province. His father was a farmer in Samosir Island, North Sumatra, and his mother was illiterate—yet both aspired for their son to become successful. The young Nadeak had quickly rejected a scholarship to study at an Agricultural Institute in Bogor, because he did not want to be a farmer like his father. Instead, he went to Padang, West Sumatra, to study medicine, yet soon realized he could not handle the study load. Trying his luck in Pekanbaru, he enrolled in a faculty of law of an Islamic university.

His rector was interested in his academic achievement and trained him to become a lawyer. From then on, Nadeak gradually became well known in Riau and had networks among politicians. In 1997, the provincial branch of the then Indonesian Democratic Party invited him to join the party.[6] In 1999, he ran as candidate for the Indonesian Democratic Party for Struggle (PDI-P) in Riau Islands—which was then still a district within the province of Riau—and won a seat. He then regularly visited the Riau Islands, as the official district representative from PDI-P.

In 2004, the Riau Islands became a province in its own right. Megawati, PDI-P chairperson, asked Nadeak to lead the Riau Islands branch of the party. In the same year, he ran to be parliament member from Riau Islands Province and won. The victory was repeated in the 2009 and 2014 elections. In 2014 he officially became Speaker of the Riau Islands provincial parliament. He now feels the Riau Islands is his home. He claimed that many Batak clan associations in Batam supported his candidacy, although he was not specifically close to the RBB in Tanjungpinang.

There was some tension when Nadeak was inaugurated, as some people preferred a "son of the soil"—a Malay-Muslim born in Riau Islands—to be the head of the parliament, however the protests were short-lived (*Sijorikepri*, 29 October 2014). As the only Christian Speaker of Parliament in any Muslim-dominated province in Indonesia, he feels that he has a special duty to safeguard religious harmony. Nadeak states that he had helped build both churches and mosques to show that he was being fair. He believes that the majority of his voters were Muslims and that it was important to pay attention to people's needs regardless of their religion. Instead, Nadeak criticized churches which did not show enough attention to social issues.

Nadeak also feels that, unlike in Jakarta, the interaction between political parties in the Riau Islands is still harmonious, due to "local wisdom". However, he admitted that social tension could get aggravated by fake news, referring to the past tension between ethnic groups in Batam. "Batam has many migrants who have failed in other cities", and they have had a hard life, thus it was not difficult to aggravate the tensions he said. Migrants had flocked to Batam due to the promise of a better life, especially during the Batam Industrial Development Authority (BIDA) era under Soeharto. Yet, many have also been affected during the province's periodic downturns.

P.M. Sitohang, Tanjungpinang City Parliamentarian from PDI-P[7]

Mr Sitohang, a Catholic accountant, finished his study in economics in Brawijaya University, Malang, East Java in 1991, and worked in a private company in Jakarta. In 1995, he moved to Tanjungpinang when he secured a job in an Indonesian-Singaporean joint-venture company developing the Bintan Lagoi resort. In 2006, he became a financial consultant to the district parliament of Tanjungpinang. By 2013 he was already familiar with the workings of the Tanjungpinang city parliament. The local branch of the Indonesian Democratic Party for Struggle (PDI-P) invited him to join the party. He sees PDI-P as a nationalist party suitable for the Bataks and Christians. In 2013, he ran as parliament member for the PDI-P and won.

When asked why he wanted to run, Sitohang stated he would not dare to run in a Batak area in North Sumatra, as the constituents would be "culturally and sociologically homogeneous". By this, he meant to say that it would be difficult to compete in a region where many candidates are also Batak. This is understandable as his strategy in Tanjungpinang was to attain at least half of the Batak and Christian votes, which collectively totalled some 3,000 votes in his constituency of East Tanjungpinang. In the end, he only obtained around 1,200 votes, but this was enough for him to win the parliamentary seat.

Ideally, Sitohang wanted to help the Batak and Christian communities in Tanjungpinang. In Tanjungpinang, the Bataks constitute only 6.5 per cent, and Christians 8 per cent of the total population. Whereas the Malays are the majority with 30.7 per cent and Muslims are 78.6 per cent of the whole. While the interaction between ethnic and religious groups is in general harmonious, Sitohang admitted that there were a few areas of discrimination against minorities. For example, while not as grave as in Jakarta, there was discrimination in the job market. Moreover, in parliament itself, it was also quite openly suggested by some members that some positions in the commissions and budget department should be reserved for Muslims. There were also some challenges against policies targeted to assist Christians, for example, the assigning of Christian religious teachers at public elementary schools.

However, he also lamented the fact that some of his constituents seem to not yet understand the function of parliament members. Some, at times, came up to him directly to ask for financial assistance for their communities, clan associations, church and private events. Sitohang would first ask them to write proposals to the city government. However, as the government usually needs some time to process the proposals, impatient constituents would urge him to give from his own purse.

Still, he had praises for Malay culture in Tanjungpinang, whose "politeness" helped to keep harmony among the different ethnic and religious groups. Even in Batam, a city in which the Malays are no longer the majority, the Malay culture still dominates and mediates between different migrant groups. There were tensions between groups in the past, yet they were short-lived because the groups quickly "realized that they were only newcomers". As a "member of the diaspora", he maintained, a Batak should follow the proverb which states the need to be kind to our neighbours, or the people that we meet, no matter which ethnic group they are from (*jonok dongan partubu, jonokan dongan parhundul*).

A.D. Pasaribu, Vice-Speaker of the Tanjungpinang City Parliament[8]

Mr Pasaribu is an interesting case of a Batak immigrant politician, as he comes from a humble background and is one of the few Muslim-Batak parliamentarians. His father was a rubber-tapper from a small community in North Sumatra, and had twelve children. In 2000 Pasaribu migrated to Tanjungpinang to look for a job. He had finished a three-year diploma programme on tourism and hoped to find work at the Lagoi tourism area. However, as he could not speak Mandarin, he failed to get a job. Too embarrassed to return to his parents' home, he took on odd jobs in Tanjungpinang.

To survive, he became a security guard, with a meagre salary of IDR200,000 (US$14) per month, and later became a motorbike taxi rider. In 2005, he and his wife, a local Malay woman whom he married in 2001, opened a small billiards centre in the city, and befriended many city politicians in the process. In 2008, the local branch of the then Nationhood Democratic Party (PDK) invited him to run in the city election as one of their candidates. At first, he was apprehensive as he did not have enough money to run his own campaign. Yet, on his birthday in January 2009, he decided to use his own savings to invite 600 people whom he knew in the city to have a meal at his home. As it turned out, 5,000 people attended the occasion. He became convinced of his popularity and that he could possibly win a seat in parliament.

Pasaribu stated that his purpose of being a parliament member is to help the Bataks. Despite his religion, Pasaribu has close relations with both Christian and Muslim Batak communities in Tanjungpinang and was the chairman of the RBB in 2011. When PDK could not run in the election in 2013, Pasaribu changed allegiance to a nationalist party, the People's Conscience Party (Hanura). He preferred a nationalist, and not an Islamic party, as Indonesian nationalism is crucial in heterogeneous areas such as Tanjungpinang. According to him, the interaction between different religions and ethnic groups is harmonious because, "we migrants know our place as newcomers here". Despite emphasizing that migrants need to behave in accordance to local culture, Pasaribu is against the notion of "sons of the soil". After direct elections were established in 2004, voters across the Riau Islands seem to prioritize candidates who were born in the regions where they run. Pasaribu believed, instead, that migrants could also be qualified individuals to lead the regions where they reside, as long as they are allowed to compete fairly.

He personally feels that the Bataks must stay united no matter which religion they adhere to. They should realize that, despite the Christian majority, there are also Muslim members, and that they are not "Malayanized". As a former Islamic boarding school student, and follower of the Muhammadiyah tradition, Pasaribu believes that religion is a private matter. Despite being a Muslim, he refused to be called "Malay", maintaining that he still observes Batak rituals on important events such as marriages. His Malay wife was also officially adopted into the Batak community and now has a Batak clan name—Sianipar—which is Pasaribu's mother's clan.

THE UNITED BATAK CLANS OF TANJUNGPINANG, A "POLITICALLY ACTIVE" SOCIAL ORGANIZATION

There are many Batak clan associations in the Riau Islands, especially in Batam and Bintan. However, the RBB, established in 2012, was one which recently adopted a "political" function. It is an amalgamation of two older Batak organizations which started in the 1980s, namely: Bond of Batak Families (Ikatan Keluarga Batak); and the Bond of Bintan Tapanuli Families (Ikatan Keluarga Tapanuli Bintan, or IKTB). The second organization changed its name to the Bond of Riau Islands Tapanuli Families (Ikatan Keluarga Tapanuli Kepri, or IKTK) to include all Bataks in the new province, when the Riau Islands separated from Riau. Like other ethnic organizations, such as those of the Javanese, RBB organizes gatherings and other social activities, which aim to "improve the welfare of its members and facilitate interactions with other ethnicities".[9]

According to several sources, RBB has around 8,000 members from 57 Batak clans (*marga*) or clan clusters (*puak*).[10] In many Indonesian regions, Batak organizations are generally associated with Christianity because the majority of this community is Christian. However, despite being dominated by Christians, RBB is religiously inclusive in its membership which is likely due to its adaptation to a Malay-Muslim majority environment. In fact, RBB's vice-chairman, A.D. Pasaribu, is a devout Muslim. When asked how he could get support from Christian members, Pasaribu, who is also the Vice-Speaker of Tanjungpinang City Parliament (DPRD Tanjungpinang) from the Hanura party, claimed, "We (Bataks) have to be united. We must accept that not all Bataks are Christians. My parents said everyone is responsible for their own religious preference. Anyone can convert to any religion they want, but a Batak will always be Batak. I'll give you an example: wherever I go, even to other countries, I would still belong to the Pasaribu clan. I can never change clan because it is in my blood, but I could still change my religion if I have to."[11]

In addition to being religiously inclusive, RBB has been influential in the political life of the Bataks in Tanjungpinang. In the 2014 municipal election, the organization succeeded in mobilizing the community to vote for Batak candidates from different political parties. This not only involved an appeal for members to vote for Batak candidates, but was an intricate process, which included designating which candidates to endorse and managing the votes so as to maximize the chance for Batak candidates to win seats in the local council.

B. Sirait, former Chairman of RBB and member of Tanjungpinang parliament, and P.M. Sitohang, member of Tanjungpinang parliament, revealed the process as follows.[12] In the 2009 election there were eighteen Batak candidates coming from various political parties, who sought to win some of the thirty seats in parliament. However, only two Bataks managed to secure seats. Seeing this aspiration among Bataks as well as the rather large membership of RBB, the leaders of the organization realized that it could be used to consolidate the Batak vote to improve their chances of victory.

Thus, in 2013, RBB began a "convention" which aimed at gathering all members who aspired to run for parliamentary seats in the 2014 election. Seven prominent members of RBB oversaw this convention. They were considered experts in the areas of bureaucracy/local government, education, finance, association, tradition (*adat*), and "decorum". Meanwhile, twenty-two members coming from three electoral districts (*dapil*) in Tanjungpinang registered for the convention. Knowing that an aspiring candidate would need at least around 2,000 votes to win a seat in parliament, the RBB leaders realized that having twenty-two candidates would split the 8,000 Batak votes (as well as, they estimated, 12,000 Christian votes, which would be inclined to vote for a Christian-Batak candidate) reducing the probability of Bataks securing the seats. Thus, over a three-month period, RBB tested the twenty-two aspiring candidates. RBB envisaged that each electoral district in Tanjungpinang should have two Batak representatives.

In the aftermath of the process, six people were chosen: P.M. Sitohang and Saragi representing East Tanjungpinang electoral district. During the process, Saragi moved to Bandung, and H. Silitonga took his place in East Tanjungpinang. For West Tanjungpinang, RBB endorsed B. Sirait and A.D. Pasaribu, a Muslim candidate. The late L. Siahaan and Panjaitan represented Tanjungpinang Bestari electoral district. The six became the "official" candidates approved by the RBB. The association then called for its members residing in the three electoral districts to vote for the six members, which they overwhelmingly did. This convention strategy turned out to be useful, as five RBB candidates managed to secure seats in parliament. Out of the 30 parliament members from Tanjungpinang, there were five representatives of the Batak community.

CONCLUSION

This chapter has elaborated on the underlying factors which contribute to the motives for Batak migration. Traditionally, the Bataks aspire to attain various forms of "capital", including the aspiration to gain wealth, "completeness", as well as personal glory. The drive for social, economic, and political progress among the Batak is due to this worldview.

This has also underpinned the drive for many Bataks to migrate. The early migration of Bataks out of the highlands of North Sumatra was largely due to the aspiration to attain better living standards in the eastern coastal areas including obtaining non-farming, white-collar jobs. In modern times, this perspective is still pervasive, as seen in the life stories of the three members of parliament, who migrated in search of higher education and formal employment.

However, this does not stop at merely gaining formal employment, as some Batak migrants then seek to attain political office. Yet, their personal experience as migrants informs their political strategies, as they emphasized their position as migrants in the Riau Islands vis-à-vis the "host" ethnic and religious group.

Frequently, the notion of "knowing one's place" surfaced in the discussion with the Batak politicians. This is due to the fact that the host group, like some other ethnic groups in Indonesia, adheres to the concept of "sons of the soil", or the inclination to prioritize the interests of their own ethnic group. However, the Malays also have the tradition of being accepting of others, hence the migrants need to navigate between these two polarizing attributes.

Especially on religion, unlike the Malays or the Javanese which are predominantly Muslim, the Bataks are split between Christians and Muslims. Of the three largest communities in Riau Islands, the Batak is the only one with a significant Christian community. Thus, to maintain group cohesion, they emphasize their ethnic, and not religious, identity. Such need to maintain cohesion, and the Batak's own traditionally rigid clan system, make the Batak associations more closed to outsiders than the Javanese ones. This also influences political participation, which is traditionally valued. Gaining political position is considered an achievement, yet due to the Batak's multireligious composition, their political drive is mediated by religious tolerance. Emphasizing the need to maintain ethno-religious harmony, all Batak politicians prefer nationalist parties such as the PDI-P, instead of religious parties.

In Tanjungpinang, the RBB has successfully played a role in political mediation. They carefully carried out a filtering process in which potential members were chosen and groomed to be candidates. They also calculated the chance for these members to win based on the estimation of the number of Batak and Christian voters in the area. In short, the political aspirations of the Batak could successfully be channelled through this association, whose initial aim had only been to organize social gatherings and activities, but gradually evolved to include political objectives.

Notes

1. Data from this section largely derives from a seminal work by O.H.S. Purba and Elvis F. Purba. *Migrasi Spontan Batak Toba (Marserak): Sebab, Motip, dan Akibat Perpindahan Penduduk dari Dataran Tinggi Toba*, Monora, 1997.
2. In 1965, Pandjaitan was among the top military generals who were murdered during the failed communist coup.
3. Interview with Parasian Simamora, historian at the Culture Preservation Centre, Tanjungpinang, 10 November 2017.
4. Interview with P.M. Sitohang, Tanjungpinang member of parliament, 5 May 2018.
5. Interview with J. Nadeak, Speaker of Riau Islands provincial parliament, 16 November 2017.
6. PDI, which was the progenitor of the existing Indonesian Democratic Party for Struggle (PDI-P).
7. Interview with P.M. Sitohang, Tanjungpinang member of parliament, 10 November 2017 and 5 May 2018.
8. Interview with A.D. Pasaribu, Vice-Speaker of Tanjungpinang parliament, 17 November 2017.
9. Rumpun Batak Bersatu Tanjungpinang (Tanjungpinang's United Batak Clans

Association) http://www.petrusmarulaksitohang.com/2013/02/rumpun-batak-bersatu-tanjungpinang.html (accessed 27 April 2018).
10. Interview with B. Sirait, former chairman of RBB and member of Tanjungpinang city parliament, 17 November 2017.
11. Interview with A.D. Pasaribu, Vice-Chairman of RBB and Vice-Speaker of Tanjungpinang city parliament, 17 November 2017.
12. Interview with B. Sirait and P.M. Sitohang, both are members of Tanjungpinang city parliament from PDI-P, 16 and 17 November 2017.

References

Abdurrahman et al. 2013. "Migrasi Suku-Suku dan Asimilasi Budaya di Indonesia". Program Magister Kajian Kependudukan dan Ketenagakerjaan, Program Pasca Sarjana, Universitas Indonesia.

Ananta, Aris. 2006. "Changing Ethnic Composition and Potential Violent Conflict in Riau Archipelago, Indonesia: An Early Warning Signal". *Population Review* 45, no. 1.

———, et al. 2015. *Demography of Indonesia's Ethnicity*. Singapore: Institute of Southeast Asian Studies.

Andaya, Leonard Y. 2008. *Leaves of the Same Tree: Trade and Ethnicity in the Straits of Melaka*. Hawai'i: University of Hawaii Press.

Arifin, Evi Nurvidya, et al. 2014. "Statistics of Ethnicity in Indonesia's Districts: Based on 2010 Indonesia's Population Census". BPS-Statistics Indonesia and Institute of Southeast Asian Studies, Singapore, December 2014.

Bourdieu, Pierre. 1986. "The Forms of Capital (1986)". In *Cultural Theory: An Anthology* 1, (2011): 81–93.

Borualogo, Ihsana Sabriani, and Fons JR Van de Vijver. 2016. "Values and Migration Motives in Three Ethnic Groups in Indonesia". In *Unity, Diversity and Culture*, edited by C. Roland-Lévy, P. Denoux, B. Voyer, P. Boski, and W.K. Gabrenya Jr. Proceedings from the 22nd Congress of the International Association for Cross-Cultural Psychology. https://scholarworks.gvsu.edu/iaccp_papers/191

Bruner, Edward M. 1959. "Division of Anthropology: Kinship Organization among the Urban Batak of Sumatra". *Transactions of the New York Academy of Sciences* 22, no. 2, Series II: 118–25.

———. 1972. "Batak Ethnic Associations in Three Indonesian Cities". *Southwestern Journal of Anthropology* 28, no. 3: 207–29.

Castles, Lance. 1967. "The Ethnic Profile of Djakarta". *Indonesia* 3: 153–204.

———. 1972. "The Political Life of a Sumatran Residency: Tapanuli 1915–1940". Unpublished PhD Diss. thesis, Yale University.

Cunningham, Clark E. 1958. *The Postwar Migration of the Toba-Bataks to East Sumatra*. No. 5. Yale University, Southeast Asia Studies.

JPNN. "Dua Kubu Bentrok, Batam Mencekam" [Two Groups Clashed, Batam in a Tense Situation]. 19 June 2012. https://www.jpnn.com/news/dua-kubu-bentrok-batam-mencekam (accessed 14 March 2019).

Naim, Mochtar. 1984. *Merantau: Pola Migrasi Suku Minangkabau*. Yogyakarta: Gadjah Mada University Press.

Ng Chin-keong. 1976. "The Chinese in Riau: A Community on an Unstable and Restrictive Frontier". Institute of Humanities and Social Sciences College of Graduate Studies Nanyang University, Research Project Series No. 2, December 1976, pp. 59–70.

Purba, O.H.S., and Elvis F. Purba. 1997. *Migrasi Spontan Batak Toba (Marserak): Sebab, Motip, dan Akibat Perpindahan Penduduk dari Dataran Tinggi Toba*. Monora.

Rodenburgh, Adriana N. 1993. "'Staying Behind': Rural Women and Migration in North Tapanuli, Indonesia". PhD Thesis, University of Amsterdam, Amsterdam.

Sihombing, Batara. 2004. "Batak and Wealth: A Critical Study of Materialism in the Batak Churches in Indonesia". *Mission Studies* 21, no. 1: 9–37.

Sijorikepri.com. 2014. "Jumaga Nadeak nahkodai DPRD Kepri" [Jumaga Nadeak Pilots Riau Islands Parliament]. 29 October 2014, http://sijorikepri.com/jumaga-nadeak-nahkodai-dprd-kepri/ (accessed 24 January 2019).

Simandjuntak, Deasy. 2010. "Who Shall Be Raja? Patronage Democracy in North Sumatra, Indonesia". PhD thesis, University of Amsterdam, Amsterdam.

———. 2012. "Gifts and Promises: Patronage Democracy in a Decentralised Indonesia". *European Journal of East Asian Studies* 11, no. 1: 99–126.

———. 2017. "Faced with a Troubling Blasphemy Verdict, Ahok at Least Left Jakarta a Legacy of Reform". Channel News Asia commentary, 11 May 2017, https://www.channelnewsasia.com/news/asia/commentary-ahok-left-jakarta-legacy-of-reform-8836708

Sitohang, Petrus Marulak. 2013. "Rumpun Batak Bersatu Tanjungpinang" ("Tanjungpinang's United Batak Clans Association") http://www.petrusmarulaksitohang.com/2013/02/rumpun-batak-bersatu-tanjungpinang.html (accessed 27 April 2018).

Tribunnews.com. 2012. "Dua Kelompok Berdamai di Novotel" [Two Groups Make Peace at Novotel]. 19 June 2012. https://www.tribunnews.com/regional/2012/06/19/dua-kelompok-berdamai-di-novotel (accessed 14 March 2019).

17

THE ETHNIC CHINESE IN THE RIAU ISLANDS
A Community with a Frontier Spirit at the Edge of Indonesia

Leo Suryadinata[1]

INTRODUCTION

Situated at an important trading crossroads in the precolonial and colonial periods, the Riau Islands have long been open to external influences. People of various ethnicities came to the region to trade, barter, and grow a variety of crops for export. This diversity has further increased in recent decades as, following the turn towards export-oriented industrialization in the 1990s, people from all over the country came to the Riau Islands in search of formal sector jobs—driving up the area's population and further increasing its heterogeneity.

While many different communities trace their arrival and establishment in the province to the post-1990 period, it is also home to a significant Chinese population. Playing a significant role in the Riau Islands' cultural, political, and economic life, this community has long been an integral part of the region, with a presence dating back to the seventeenth and eighteenth centuries.

This chapter will explore how the Chinese community arrived in the Riau Islands and how it has negotiated its place within it. To this end, it is comprised of six sections. Following this introduction, the next section will trace the history of the Chinese community in the Riau Islands. The subsequent part will set out what aspects of Chinese culture are expressed in daily life in the province. The fourth will look at the role played by ethnic Chinese politicians in the province. The fifth will explore the trajectories of prominent Chinese businessmen. The sixth and final section will conclude.

THE HISTORY OF THE CHINESE COMMUNITY IN THE RIAU ISLANDS

Available records indicate that the arrival of the Chinese community in the Riau Islands began in the seventeenth century, due to the archipelago's location on the Chinese maritime Silk Road. Junks travelling to and from China are reputed to have stopped at Bintan for supplies, as well as to trade tea, ceramics and silks in exchange for opium from India, in addition to tin and pepper from the Riau Islands (Trocki 2007, p. 36; Shi and Xu 2017, pp. 82–83).

Over time, Chinese traders spread to other nearby locations such as Singapore and Johor. At that point in time, these three territories and a small part of Sumatra were part of the Johor-Riau Kingdom, a well-established political entity and maritime trading power located at the intersection of two important trading routes, the first between India and China, and the second between Java and northern Sumatra (Wee 2016, p. 242).

In addition to trading activities, from the eighteenth century onwards gambier was produced on a large scale in the Riau Islands for export to Java as well as China. This was initially grown on plantations owned by Malay and Bugis notables, who employed large numbers of Chinese workers. Due to this, the Chinese community was recognized by the traditional rulers as an important component of the area's economic dynamism (Raja Ali Haji 1982 in Wee 2016). Indeed, in 1784, there were an estimated 10,000 ethnic Chinese living in Bintan (Colombijn 1997; Trocki 2007, pp. 34–35).

During the nineteenth century, Chinese entrepreneurs took over the cultivation of gambier from the Malay and Bugis notables.[2] The Chinese lived in specific locations, usually at river mouths or estuaries and were under the authority of headmen, called *kangchus* (港主) (Trocki 2007). The principal groups in the archipelago at that time were Teochiu (Chaozhou), who mainly resided in Senggarang, and Hokkien, who largely resided in Tanjungpinang (Shi and Xu 2017).[3]

However, in 1824, the Dutch and the British reached an agreement to divide the Malay archipelago into two spheres of influence. The northern part of Malacca Straits encompassing Singapore and Johor belonged to the British, while the southern part encompassing the Riau Islands belonged to the Dutch. Thus, the Johor-Riau Kingdom was effectively split into two (Andaya and Andaya 2017).

Despite this arbitrary division, due to cultural links and geographical proximity, the interactions between Riau and Singapore and Johor continued to be intensive. Indeed, different economic policies implemented by the British and Dutch boosted formal and informal trading links between Johor and Singapore on one hand, and between Singapore and the Riau Islands on the other. Consequently, the border region became an area of intense economic interaction driven by ample arbitrage opportunities, further enabled by the extensive maritime border between the two colonies (Tagliacozzo 2005).

In the early twentieth century, following changing trends in farming technology as well as demand, the main export crops produced in the Riau Islands, Johor and Singapore changed from gambier to rubber and coconut. Leveraging on their possession of land, access to labour, and agricultural expertise, Chinese farmers were able to move into these new areas (Ng 1976).

Despite the Dutch claiming formal sovereignty over the Riau Islands in 1824, their presence on the ground in the archipelago was relatively light until the early twentieth century. In 1911, the Dutch established a Residency (*Residentie*), with a capital in Tanjungpinang on Bintan Island. The Residency consisted of two aspects, namely the Indragiri Division which encompassed a swathe of the island of Sumatra, and the Tanjungpinang Division, which spanned the Riau Islands. For its part, the Tanjungpinang Division was subdivided into four areas: Lingga, Karimun, Tanjungpinang and Pulau Tujuh.

With regard to the Tanjungpinang Division as a whole, in 1930, the Chinese numbered some 34,000 and accounted for a quarter of the total population. Within the division, Tanjungpinang harboured the largest number of Chinese, who comprised more than one third of the population based on the 1930 Population Census (Table 17.1).

While the Teochiu and Hokkien were the numerically most important communities in the Riau Residency, they were supplemented by the arrival of other groups, notably significant numbers of Hailamese and Hakkas (Table 17.2). However, it is important to note that these figures refer to both the divisions of Riau, namely the Riau Islands as well as the mainland, or Sumatra, aspect. Given the nature of migration flows at that time, principally focused on trade as well as hard agricultural labour, the number of men significantly outnumbered women.

It should be noted that, after the 1930 population census which provided detailed ethnic information, the population censuses carried out following independence did not include questions on ethnicity, which was considered a sensitive issue. In the

TABLE 17.1
Number of Chinese in the Tanjungpinang Division of Riau, 1930

Subdivision	Natives	Chinese	Others	Total	Chinese as a Proportion of Total Population
Tanjungpinang	26,339	14,788	718	41,845	35.3
Karimun	23,200	11,888	216	35,304	33.7
Lingga	24,490	5,630	404	30,524	18.4
Pulau Tujuh	25,207	1,942	54	27,203	7.1
Total	99,236	34,248	1,392	134,876	25.4

Source: Adapted from Ng (1976), p. 19.

TABLE 17.2
Dialect Groups in the Riau Residency, 1930

	Male	Female	Total	Proportion of Total
Teochiu	11,540	4,765	16,305	41.7
Hokkien	5,247	2,820	8,067	20.6
Others	4,685	1,281	5,966	15.3
Hailam	4,142	561	4,703	12.3
Hakka	3,083	850	3,943	10.1
Cantonese	89	11	100	0.0
Total	26,796	10,288	39,084	100

Source: Adapted from Ng (1976), p. 21.

1961, 1971, 1980 and 1990 population censuses, only questions pertaining to religion and languages spoken on a daily basis were included. Although we can use this data to estimate the number of ethnic Chinese in Riau Province, the numbers are educated guesses. This difficulty is compounded after 1971, when Confucianism was not included as an option in the questionnaires.[4]

According to the 1971 population census, that year there were 154,229 adherents of Confucianism and 67,507 Buddhists in the Riau Province.[5] Using this as a means of estimating the overall Chinese population yields the calculation that ethnic Chinese constituted at least 13.5 per cent of the province's population—which at that time included both the Riau Islands and part of Sumatra. This calculation is conservative, as it does not include Chinese Christians or Catholics. The 1971 population census also shows that, of the province's population of 221,736, 56.6 per cent were citizens of China.[6] This meant that, at that time, Riau was the Indonesian province with the highest number of Chinese who were foreign citizens.

During the New Order, and particularly the move towards export-oriented industrialization in the Riau Islands, the area's ethnic composition changed dramatically. Following the islands' adoption of a manufacturing-for-export economic model, considerable quantities of foreign direct investment flowed in. The ensuing generation of formal sector employment drew in aspiring workers from across the country. Consequently, the Riau Island's population grew in size and became more diverse. In 1990, there were 500,000 inhabitants in the Riau Islands, a number which had swollen to 1.9 million in 2015, and 2.2 million in 2019 (Hutchinson 2017; BPS 2019).

This has been on the back of significant migration from other parts of the country, particularly Java and Sumatra. Thus, the Chinese population, while still substantial, has declined in importance over time. In 2010, the most recent year for which data on ethnicity is available, the Chinese population comprised 7.7 per cent of the province's total population (Table 17.3). This contrasts to the year 2000, when the Chinese were the province's third largest population and constituted almost 10 per cent of the total.

In spite of its decline in relative terms, the Chinese population in the Riau Islands is one of the most significant within Indonesia. At a national level, ethnic Chinese

TABLE 17.3
Ethnic Composition of the Riau Islands, 2010

	Ethnicity	Number	Percentage
1.	Malay	505,391	30.23
2.	Javanese	410,426	24.55
3.	Batak	208,678	12.48
4.	Minangkabau	162,452	9.72
5.	Chinese	128,704	7.70
6.	Sundanese	49,439	2.96
7.	Buginese	37,145	2.22
8.	Flores	29,852	1.79
9.	Palembang	29,374	1.78
10.	Banjarese	11,811	0.71
11.	Others	98,617	5.90
	Total	1,671,891	100

Source: Adapted from Ananta et al. (2015), p. 110.

TABLE 17.4
The Largest Concentration of Ethnic Chinese by Province, 2010

	Province	Number	Percentage
1.	Jakarta	632,372	6.62
2.	West Kalimantan	358,451	8.17
3.	North Sumatra	340,320	2.63
4.	Banten	183,689	1.73
5.	Riau Islands	128,704	7.70
6.	Riau	101,864	1.85
7.	Bangka-Belitung	99,624	8.17
8.	Jambi	37,246	1.21

Source: Adapted from Ananta et al. (2015), p. 215.

TABLE 17.5
Distribution of Ethnic Chinese Population in Kepri by Regency, 2010

Regency/Municipality	No. of Chinese	Proportion of Total Population
Batam	61,883	6.6
Karimun	39,224	11.0
Tanjungpinang	25,516	14.2
Bintan	8,755	6.2
Lingga	5,863	6.8
Natuna	1,346	2.0
Anambas	915	2.5
Total	143,502	7.7

Source: Adapted from Ananta et al. (2015), p. 215.

constitute 1.2 per cent of the Indonesian population.[7] The largest concentration of Chinese is found in Jakarta, with other large communities found in West Kalimantan, North Sumatra and Banten. The Riau Islands comes in fifth in absolute terms, and third in relative terms.

Within the Riau Islands, the Chinese population is concentrated in the larger and more urbanized islands of Batam, Karimun, and Bintan, which have been more exposed to international trade and commerce. On Bintan, reflecting its historical presence on the island, the Chinese community is largely found in Tanjungpinang, rather than in rural areas.

Having set out the development of the Chinese community in the Riau Islands and its demographic importance, the next sections will look at which aspects of Chinese culture are manifested today.

KEY ASPECTS OF CHINESE CULTURE IN THE RIAU ISLANDS

When speaking of Chinese culture outside China, analysis tends to focus on specific manifestations of culture, particularly: religion; Chinese-medium schools; and civic organizations and associations. The paragraphs ahead will deal with each of these in turn.

Religion

According to the 2000 population census, the majority of Chinese in the Riau Islands are Buddhist (84.8 per cent), with significant numbers of Muslims (4.4 per cent), Protestants (3.9 per cent), Catholics (3.2 per cent) and Hindus (2.6 per cent).[8]

There are many Buddhist or traditional Chinese temples in the Riau Islands, with fifty-two temples on Bintan Island alone (Shi and Xu 2017, p. 87). One of the newest temples is known as Vihara Ksitigarbha Bodhisattva or Ling Shan Jiyu Si (灵山济玉寺). It is popularly known as 500 Lo Han Temple (500 罗汉) as the Vihara consists of 500 life-sized Lohan (Arhats, Buddha Disciples) (Zheng 2015).[9] This project was begun by an influential local Chinese businessman, Bobby Jayanto, who is also a member of the Riau Islands provincial parliament. Jayanto succeeded in collecting

TABLE 17.6
Religion by Ethnic Group in the Riau Islands, 2000 (in percentage)

Ethnic Group	Buddhist	Muslim	Protestant	Catholic	Hindu	Others	Total
Chinese	84.8	4.4	3.9	3.2	2.6	1.1	100
Malay	0.6	98.3	0.6	0.5	0.1	0	100
Javanese	0.2	97	1.5	1.3	0.1	0	100
Minang	0.1	99.4	0.4	0.1	0	0	100
Batak	0.3	26.9	64.1	8.6	0	0.1	100
Total	8.9	80.7	7.4	2.5	0.4	0.2	100

Source: Ananta et al. (2008), p. 40.

donations from ethnic Chinese Buddhists in Indonesia, Singapore and Malaysia. The project took thirteen years to complete and was open to the public in 2017, with the official launch attended by the Governor of the Riau Islands, Nurdin Basirun. Since then, the Vihara has become one of Bintan's tourist attractions, visited by many mainland Chinese as well as local tourists.

Another large temple is located in Batam and known as Maha Vihara Duta Maitreya (or Meitreya Buddist Temple), also known as Tianen Mile Foyuan (天恩弥勒佛院). Occupying 4.5 hectares, it is claimed to be the largest Meitreya temple in Southeast Asia. The temple took seven years to build and was officially opened in January 1999, about eight months after the fall of Soeharto. When opened, it was reported that 10,000 Buddhists attended the opening ceremony.

Unlike the 500 Lohan temple which relied on mainland Chinese craftsmen, and is indirectly linked to mainland Chinese, the Meitreya temple is linked to the Yiguandao (I Kuan Tao, 一贯道), a Chinese salvationist sect based in Taiwan (Liao 2002, pp. 77–78). In the initial period, the temple conducted Mandarin classes for children, using textbooks imported from Taiwan (ibid.).

According to the data, in 2000 about 4.4 per cent of the Chinese population in the Riau Islands was Muslim, forming the second largest religious group.[10] It is likely that many Chinese converted into Christianity and Islam after the 30 September 1965 movement during which the Indonesian Communist Party (Partai Komunis Indonesia) was banned and eliminated.

The presence of Chinese Muslims in the Riau Islands should not be a surprise, as the majority of the population is Muslim and converts are welcomed. However, in the past, many Chinese converts to Islam were absorbed and assimilated. However, in post New Order Indonesia, some Chinese Muslims have chosen to retain their ethnic identity. This group has even revived their own Chinese Muslim association, called the Chinese Muslim Union (Persatuan Islam Tionghoa Indonesia, or PITI).

In Indonesia, the PITI branches in Java and Sumatra are quite active. These branches have even established their own mosques, often called Cheng Ho mosques, after the famous Chinese-Muslim navigator. However, these mosques are open to all ethnic groups who are Muslim.

While PITI has established branches in the Riau Islands, there are no Cheng Ho mosques in the province, meaning that Chinese Muslims there attend other mosques. However, there are several well-known Chinese Muslim public figures in the Riau Islands, which will be discussed below.

Interestingly, some Chinese Muslims are still able to speak Chinese. Those who can still speak Mandarin or a Chinese dialect can be said to have been able to retain their Chineseness, although they have been converted into Islam and partially integrated into the indigenous Muslim community.

Chinese-Medium Education

Before 1966, there were Chinese schools in the Riau Islands catering to ethnic Chinese children. One of the well-known schools was Toan Hwa (端华), in Tanjungpinang.[11]

The school is said to have been established about 100 years ago (Fu 2014). However, Toan Hwa was closed down during the Soeharto era, in its drive to assimilate Chinese Indonesians. After the end of the New Order, the school was re-established by its alumni. However, the new school is in fact an Indonesian national "plus" school, which uses the national curriculum but teaches Mandarin as a foreign language (Fu 2014). This is in contrast to the Chinese-medium school that existed during the pre-Soeharto era.

There are several other Chinese-run schools in Batam and Karimun that are also national "plus" schools. In Karimun, there was a Chinese school called Yu Min Xuexiao (育民学校) which was also closed down during the New Order. After the fall of Soeharto, the school was reopened and renamed Sekolah Bina Bangsa (Karimun Fisherman Reports 2016).

In the capital of Karimun, Tanjung Balai, there is a large secondary school named SMA Maha Bodhi, which was established by the local Vihara Buddha Diepa (同心善社), which is a foundation established in 1965 and appears to be linked to the Tzu Chi Buddhist Association in Taiwan (Vihara Buddha Diepa 2015a, 2015b). This is an Indonesian school that follows the national curriculum. Not all of the students are Buddhists, but most are ethnic Chinese from the Riau Islands. Despite the composition of the students, it is worth noting that many of the schoolteachers are Muslim.

Despite the absence of Chinese-medium schools and a Chinese-language daily newspaper published in the province, a substantial number of Chinese in the Riau Islands speak Mandarin or a Chinese dialect, particularly the elite. This is an anomaly in Indonesia, given the banning of Chinese-language education and much Chinese-medium content in Indonesia during the New Order. There are two reasons for this. First, over the years, a substantial proportion of Chinese from the Riau Islands have gone to Singapore for their education, which is predominantly in English and Mandarin. Second, due to the proximity with Singapore, Mandarin radio and TV channels have been continuously available even during the New Order period.[12]

Chinese Civic Organizations

Following the fall of Soeharto and the end of the New Order, there was a resurgence of ethnic Chinese organizations in Jakarta such as: Indonesian Chinese Clan Association (Paguyuban Sosial Marga Tionghoa Indonesia, or PSMTI), which was established by retired Brigadier General Tedy Jusuf Cs.; and Chinese-Indonesian Association (Perhimpunan Indonesia-Tionghoa, or Perhimpunan INTI) founded by Eddie Lembong Cs.[13] These two ethnic Chinese social organizations aim to unite fellow Chinese Indonesians, and promote good relations with other ethnic Indonesians to achieve national unity. Benefiting from a resurgence in cultural awareness, they have been able to set up branches in many provinces in Indonesia within a short period of time.

Both organizations have branches in the Riau Islands, and have had an influence on the province's society and culture. In particular, leadership positions within these two organizations are linked with political activity, with many current or former chairmen going on to be active in politics.

The current chairman of PSMTI is Ed Hussy, the president of an Indonesian real estate association (*Batam Pos*, 22 October 2017). Past chairmen of PSMTI include local politicians such as Bobby Jayanto and Asmin Patros.[14] It is noteworthy that two of the national PSMTI congresses have been held in Batam, attesting to the influence of the local community within the national Indonesian-Chinese community. The local chapter of PSMTI also played a foundational role in establishing one of Batam's leading higher education institutions, Batam International University.[15] Perhimpunan INTI is currently led by Benny Suwandi, a lawyer (*Batam Pos*, 25 April 2016). In addition to his role in PSMTI, Bobby Jayanto is also made the Honorary Chairman of the Advisory Committee of the Perhimpunan INTI in the Riau Islands.

CHINESE PARTICIPATION IN POLITICS

During the Soeharto era, ethnic Chinese were discouraged from participating in the formal political process. Much of the energy aspiring Chinese Indonesians was thus channelled into business, partially explaining the strong economic position of the community. The late Indonesia economist Thee Kian Wie noted that "the Soeharto government … gave the ethnic Chinese wide opportunity in the economic field, it severely limited their activities in other fields, notably in politics." (Thee 2006, p. 97). Indeed, the New Order was associated with the rise of a small number of very well-connected Chinese-owned conglomerates (*konglomerat*), who tacitly supported the Soeharto regime, and partnered with politically well-connected "indigenous" (*pribumi*) elites (Pepinsky 2009).

Following the end of the New Order, anti-Chinese riots occurred in urban centres such as Jakarta, Solo, Surabaya, Lampung and Palembang. These disturbances are thought to have been linked to elite-level conflicts over how to tackle the emerging fiscal crisis (Crouch 2010; Pepinsky 2009). However, civil disturbance of this nature was conspicuously absent in the Riau Islands.

Following the end of the New Order and the move towards greater democratization, Chinese Indonesians began to formally participate in politics. Although ethnic Chinese in the Riau Islands have been running for seats for more than two decades, none has yet been elected to the National Parliament (Dewan Perwakilan Rakyat, or DPR), nor has one run for the Provincial Governorship. Nevertheless, there is a Chinese member in the Regional Representative Assembly (Dewan Perwakilan Daerah, or DPD) representing the Riau Islands, four members in the Provincial Representative Assembly (DPRD I) and about seven or eight at the municipal level (DPRD II), representing Tanjungpinang City and Batam City.[16]

At the beginning of the Reform era, Nurdin Purnomo (alias Go Nen Pin 吴能彬) established an ethnic Chinese-dominated political party called the Unity in Diversity Party (Partai Bhinneka Tunggal Ika, or PBI) and formed a chapter in the Riau Islands.

A few local Chinese joined the party and ran in the 1999 elections, when the Riau Islands were still part of Riau Province. In 2004, following the secession of the Riau

Islands and the creation of the new province, two ethnic Chinese Indonesians were elected to the Provincial Representative Assembly, namely: Rudy Chua (Chinese surname: 蔡), representing Tanjungpinang; and H. Saptono Mustaqim (Chinese name: Dai Yunliang 戴运良), representing the Lingga regency. However, Saptono resigned soon after as he was appointed the deputy regent (*bupati*) of Lingga, becoming the first ethnic Chinese Indonesia to hold the post.

Rudy Chua was born in 1970 in Tanjungpinang, and is a Buddhist from a middle-class family. He received an Indonesian-medium education and obtained a Bachelor's Degree in Economics and Master of Management. He worked in the travel industry before joining politics, as a member of the Hanura Party.

Saptono was born in 1954 in Singkep in Lingga regency. As Chinese schools were closed down in 1966, it is likely that he completed his primary education in a Chinese-medium school before moving into an Indonesian-medium secondary school. Saptono came from a poor family, but later became a businessman and converted to Islam before joining politics. Initially, he joined the PBI, but subsequently joined the NasDem Party.

Saptono has a younger brother, Asmin Patros (Dai Yingming, 戴运明), who is also active in local politics. Born in 1962, Asmin obtained a law degree and an MM degree, and is a long-standing member of Golkar. Asmin was elected to the Riau Islands Provincial Representative Assembly on the Golkar ticket (2009–14) and subsequently became its Chairman. In 2019 he was re-elected as a DPRD member for another five-year term.

Apart from the two brothers and Rudy Chua, there are two other ethnic Chinese who became members of the Riau Islands Provincial Representative Assembly, namely: Harlianto (known as A Leng, from Bintan); and Haripinto Tanuwijaya (also known as Chen Hanping 陈涵平). Haripinto was formerly a member of the Batam Municipal Council (2009–14) in Batam, but became a member of Regional Representative Assembly (DPD) representing the Riau Islands in 2014. He was re-elected in 2019 and represents the New Indonesia Struggle Party (PPIB).

One of the most active Indo-Chinese politicians is Bobby Jayanto (a.k.a. Jauw Bu Hui 姚武辉). Born in 1953, he was from a local poor Hakka family in Tanjungpinang. He joined the Pemuda Pancasila, a youth organization linked to Golkar, and became an active politician in Tanjungpinang. In 2004 he joined the Partai Patriot and was elected as a member of the Provincial Representative Assembly for Tanjungpinang, and subsequently Chair of the Council, a position which he held until 2009.

After 2009, Jayanto left politics and became chairman of the Indonesian Chamber of Commerce (KADIN) for Tanjungpinang as well as Mentor of the Indonesia-China Business Council (2010–15). He later returned to politics and served as the chairman of the NasDem party for Tanjungpinang and was re-elected in 2019 as a member of the Tanjungpinang Municipal Council. A Buddhist, Jayanto has long been active in promoting Buddhism, including playing a foundational role in the Vihara temple in Tanjungpinang.

In addition to the above-mentioned members of the Regional Provincial Assembly, there are also several Chinese politicians who have successfully contested elections at the municipal level, including in Tanjungpinang and Batam City. This includes four members in the Tanjungpinang Municipal Assembly: Fengky Fesinto (NasDem Party), Reni (Hanura Party), Agus Chandra Wijaya (NasDem Party) and Asman (PDI-P) (DPRD Kota Tanjung Pinang, n.d.). There are also two Chinese Indonesian members in the Batam Municipal Assembly, Lik Khai (NasDem Party) and Tan A Tie (PSI) (Hasrullah 2019).

Even though the number of Chinese politicians in the Riau Islands is still small, they have been able to attain seats in the provincial parliament as well as the municipal assemblies of the Riau Islands' two largest cities. That said, they have yet to run for apex positions, such as the governorship, which historically have been held by Javanese or Malay politicians. With the exception of the short-lived ethnic Chinese political party, PBI, the Chinese politicians in the Riau Islands have joined a variety of multi-ethnic political parties. There appears to be no particular pattern to their partisan allegiance, although there is a marked preference for nationalist as opposed to Islamic parties. In addition, despite the end of the New Order and the suppression of ethnic identity, it is worth noting that most of the politicians surveyed here have chosen to retain their Indonesianized names.[17]

THE ROLE OF ETHNIC CHINESE IN LOCAL BUSINESS

The Chinese community is well represented in business circles, and some politicians are also businessmen. Thus, Bobby Jayanto is active in several sectors, including cable TV, plantations, and tourism, including a resort in Bintan.[18] Asmin Patros is said to be active in the tourism industry, owning the Patros Harbour Bay Hotel, and Rudy Chua owns the Pelangi Hotel in Tanjungpinang.[19]

Many big businessmen in the Riau Islands, however, are not directly involved in politics. One of them is Santoni, a Chinese Muslim who established the alumina company known as PT BAI (Bintan Alumina Indonesia), based in Bintan.[20] He speaks Mandarin and cooperates closely with a major Chinese alumina corporation, the Nanshan Group (*Sohu.com*, 18 December 2018).

Another big businessman is Abidin Hasibuan (Chinese surname Fan (范)), who began in the electronics sector and then moved into mobile phones. His firm, Sat Nusapersada, is a company that "supplies printed circuit boards (PCB's) and mechanical parts assembly for supply multinational industries in Batam" (Bloomberg 2019). He also introduced Xiaomi mobiles to the Riau Islands.[21]

Another prominent Chinese Indonesian businessman is Kris Taenar Wiluan, president of the Citramas Group in Batam, a well-known oil and gas, real estate, and media services conglomerate. He was listed as the fortieth richest person in Indonesian in 2009 according to Forbes (2009). Initially, Wiluan began supplying to oil companies, later set up oilfield equipment plants in Malaysia, Thailand and Vietnam, and eventually started fabricating oil rigs. Unlike the other Chinese entrepreneurs discussed, Kris Wiluan is not from the Riau Islands, having moved to Batam in 1976.

Sunny Sukardi (also known as Guo Shaoxing 郭绍兴), is another ethnic Chinese businessman who is active in Tanjungpinang. After working in construction in Singapore, he later became a representative of an Indonesian furniture association in China. Following this, he moved into tourism and real estate and became the CEO of the TH (Tai Ho Group) in the Riau Islands.

In the last several years, Sukardi has developed close ties with China-based business associations. In 2012, China's Trading Association awarded him the "Most respected entrepreneur in the Asia Pacific Region" in Beijing (Taihe Group 2018). Sukardi was also invited to speak (in Mandarin) by the ethnic Chinese Businessman Think Tank (Huashang Zhiku 华商智库), linked to the Department of Economics, Peking University, as an example of a successful Indonesian-Chinese entrepreneur in 2016 (Peking University Business Intelligence 2016). He has also been at the forefront of establishing a university in Bintan with links to Peking University, albeit without much success (*Surya Kepri*, 22 November 2019; *Seputar Kepri*, 22 November 2019).

When we look at the background of Chinese-Indonesian businessmen in the Riau Islands, many of the most successful are actually from the region itself. They are also quite broad-based, choosing to be active in a range of sectors, including real estate, construction, and natural resources. Another frequent theme is links with China either in terms of technology or investment. In many cases, the ability to speak Mandarin is key for establishing contacts and developing networks.

Looking forward, networks with China-based operations as well as linguistic skills are likely to pay dividends in future. The volume of mainland China investment in the Riau Islands has increased remarkably since 2015, amounting to US$52.8 million (Setijadi 2018, p. 5). These investments have spanned a number of sectors, including mineral processing, electronics, construction of industrial estates, fisheries, transportation and tourism.

In recent years, the number of firms, businessmen and workers from China has increased. A group of mainland Chinese entrepreneurs has established an association known as the Riau Islands – China's Businessmen Association (Asosiasi Pengusaha Tiongkok Kepri Indonesia) (Setijadi 2018, p. 6).[22] There are also reported cases of substantial numbers of Chinese workers active in the Riau Islands. This could pose problems, as while skilled workers for specific projects are welcome, unskilled workers from overseas are not allowed under current legislation.[23]

CONCLUSION

The Chinese community has had a long-established presence in the Riau Islands dating back to the seventeenth century. Initially focused on trading, the Chinese then moved into plantation labour, before moving into the production of crops for export. Over time, the community has come to occupy a central role in the economy of the Riau Islands, which was recognized by the rulers of the Johor-Riau Kingdom.

Initially based in and around Tanjungpinang, the Chinese moved to other parts of the kingdom, and also became more heterogeneous as the initial core of Teochiu and Hokkiens were supplemented by members of other dialect groups. While recent flows of migrants from Java and Sumatra have meant that the Chinese community has decreased in relative terms, it is still one of the five largest communities, largely concentrated in the urban parts of the province, particularly Batam and Tanjungpinang.

In contrast to other parts of Indonesia, where the Chinese community has been assimilated to a large degree, in the Riau Islands there are many markers of Chinese culture in daily life. Many Chinese Riau Islanders speak Mandarin, and there is a tradition of Chinese-medium education that is re-emerging. Reasons for this include: the relatively large Chinese population; distance from Jakarta; and proximity to Singapore and Chinese-medium education and media content produced there.

While the Chinese community has always played a central role in the province's commercial and business life, the community is now in a pivotal position to help the province engage with China. However, in contrast to the New Order period, when political participation was discouraged, Indonesian-Chinese leaders are entering politics.

Notes

1. The author would like to thank Francis Hutchinson and Siwage Dharma Negara for their comments and assistance.
2. For further details on this process, consult Trocki (2007), Ch. 1.
3. But Teochiu remains as the largest dialect group in Riau Islands, followed by Hokkien and others. See the footnote in Table 3 in Shi and Xu (2017).
4. It was only after the end of the New Order that the authorities reintroduced questions pertaining to ethnicity. This explains the dearth of estimates following 1930 and before 2000.
5. See Badan Pusat Statistik (1974, p. 46).
6. It is important to note that in the 1980s, the Soeharto government encouraged Indonesian Chinese with foreign citizenship to apply for the Indonesian citizenship and many of them were naturalized and became Indonesian citizens.
7. As the population census is based on self-identity, it is possible that some ethnic Chinese no longer consider themselves as ethnic Chinese, therefore the percentage of the ethnic Chinese in Indonesia is likely lower in the census than the actual number. Nevertheless, it is unlikely that it would exceed 2 per cent as the Chinese birth rate is low and there is no significant number of new Chinese immigrants.
8. As the census did not list Confucianism, which was the sixth recognized religion in Indonesia, it is likely that many Confucianists or believers of the Three-Religions (Sam Kauw, also known as Tridharma in Indonesian) have been included in the category of Buddhists.
9. This temple is also miscalled as 1,000 Patung Buddha, although the number of actual statues is only 500.
10. If the Chinese Protestants and Catholics were put together as Christians, Chinese Christians form 7.1 per cent of the provincial Chinese population and they become no. 2, and the Muslims become no. 3.
11. The full name: Toan Pen Chung Hwa School 端本中华学校, abbreviated as Toan Hwa 端华).

12. In 1976, Dr Ng Chin Keong made a similar observation. See Ng (1976, p. 73). In recent years, Singapore and Malaysian Chinese programmes are still popular among the Riau Islands Chinese. My own observation and interviews with a group of Batam Chinese, Vivo City, Singapore, 23 December 2019.

13. Tedy Jusuf is one of the few Chinese Indonesians who was promoted to Brigadier General. His Chinese identity was only known by the public after the fall of Soeharto in 1998. His original Chinese name is Him Tek Ji (Xiong Deyi), see Suryadinata (2015, p. 84); Eddie Lembong was known as Ong Joe San (Wang Youshan, 1936–2018), a leading pharmacist and a social activist. See ibid., pp. 124–26).

14. Based on written information provided by Bapak Bobby Jayanto, received on 10 December 2019; interestingly he is currently holding the position of chairman of the advisory council for both PSMTI and of Perhimpunan INTI.

15. Ibid. Wawancara Bersama Bapak Asmin Patros Anggota DPRD Batam, see EL JOHN TV (2016).

16. DPD stands for Dewan Perwakilan Daerah or Regional Representative Assembly, which is equivalent to the Senate. The Dewan Perwakilan Rakyat (DPR) or People's Representative Assembly is the Indonesian parliament. Both are at the national level. DPRD stands for Dewan Perwakilan Rakyat Daerah or regional parliament at the provincial level (DPRD I) and municipal level (DPRD II).

17. The name-changing regulation was introduced in late 1966 during the Soeharto era and began to be implemented in 1967. Many Chinese Indonesians began to change their Chinese names to Indonesian sounding names. Foreigners are not allowed to change their names to Indonesian names. I suspect that many foreign Chinese in the Riau Islands changed their names into Indonesian names after they were naturalized to become Indonesian citizens in the mid-1980s.

18. Based on written information provided by Bobby Jayanto, received 10 December 2019.

19. "Daftar Pengusaha Keturunan Tionghoa di Kepulauan Riau", provided by researchers from the Universitas Maritim Raja Ali Haji at Kepri.

20. I would like to thank Dr Siwage Dharma Negara for alerting me on the background of Santoni.

21. Information provided by Dr Siwage Dharma Negara.

22. Note that this is the mainland Chinese businessmen association, different from the local Chinese businessmen association.

23. Interview with Drs Naharuddin of Kepri Planning Unit in Singapore, 10 December 2020.

References

Ananta, Aris, et al. 2008. "Chinese Indonesians in Indonesia and the Province of Riau Archipelago: A Demographic Analysis". In *Ethnic Chinese in Contemporary Indonesia*, edited by Leo Suryadinata. Singapore: Institute of Southeast Asian Studies.

———, et al. 2015. *Demography of Indonesia's Ethnicity*. Singapore: Institute of Southeast Asian Studies.

Andaya, Barbara Watson, and Leonard Y. Andaya. 2017. *A History of Malaysia*. 3rd ed. Basingstoke and London: Macmillan Palgrave.

Badan Pusat Statistik. 1974. Penduduk Riau (Sensus Penduduk 1971, Seri E. no. 04). Jakarta.

BPS (Badan Pusat Statistik). 2019. *Statistik Indonesia 2019*. Jakarta: BPS.

Batam Pos. 2016. "Benny Kembali Terpilih Jadi Ketua Inti Provinsi Kepri". *batampos.co.id*,

25 April 2016. https://batampos.co.id/2016/04/25/benny-kembali-terpilih-jadi-ketua-inti-provinsi-kepri/

———. 2017. "Edy Hussy Kembali Pimpin PSMTI Kepri." *batampos.co.id*, 22 October 2017. https://batampos.co.id/2017/10/22/edy-hussy-kembali-pimpin-psmti-kepri/

Bloomberg. 2019. "Sat Nusapersada Tbk PT". *Bloomberg.com*. https://www.bloomberg.com/profile/company/PTSN:IJ (accessed 14 December 2019).

Colombijn, Freek. 1997. "The Ecological Sustainability of Frontier Societies in Eastern Sumatra". See *Paper Landscapes: Explorations in the Environmental History of Indonesia*, edited by Peter Boomgaard, Freek Colombijn and David Henley. Leiden: KITLV Press.

DPRD Kota Tanjung Pinang. 2019. "Fengky Fesinto, SH. MH." DPRD Kota Tanjung Pinang: Profil Anggota". https://dprd-tanjungpinangkota.go.id/index.php/profil-anggota/609-fengky-fesinto-sh-mh (accessed 13 December 2019).

EL JOHN TV. 2016. "Wawancara Bersama Bapak Asmin Patros Anggota Dprd Batam dalam Acara Konfrensi Paguyuban Sosial Marga Tionghoa Indonesia atau Biasa di Sebut PSMTI yang Berlokasi di Batam dari Tanggal 19–22 Oktober 2016". *Youtube* Video, 4:27, 21 October 2016. https://www.youtube.com/watch?v=hwA5ixMiTYY

Forbes. 2009. "Indonesia's 40 Richest #40 Kris Wiluan". *Forbes.com*, 12 September 2009. https://www.forbes.com/lists/2009/80/indonesia-billionaires-09_Kris-Wiluan_KIAQ.html

Fu Huiping (符慧平). 2014. "Dān róng bīnláng shì huáwén jiàoyù gàikuàng gàikuàng 丹戎槟榔市华文教育概况". *International Daily News* (国际日报), 13 September 2014. http://www.guojiribao.com/shtml/gjrb/20140913/164255.shtml

Hasrullah. 2019. "Ini 50 Nama DPRD Kota Batam Terpilih Periode 2019–2024", edited by JK Wak. kumparan. *Kepripedia*, 12 August 2019. https://kumparan.com/kepripedia/ini-50-nama-dprd-kota-batam-terpilih-periode-2019-2024-1reJx69YDC0

Hutchinson, Francis E. 2017. *Rowing Against the Tide? Batam's Economic Fortunes in Today's Indonesia*. Trends in Southeast Asia, no. 8/2017. Singapore: ISEAS – Yusof Ishak Institute.

Karimun Fisherman Reports (吉里汶 渔夫报道). 2016. "Liào qúndǎo jílǐ wèn xiàn yù mín xuéxiào 廖群岛吉里汶县育民学校". *International Daily News* (国际日报), 28 May 2016. http://www.guojiribao.com/shtml/gjrb/20160528/270351.shtml

Liao Jianyu (廖建裕). 2002. *Ethnic Chinese in Indonesia at This Stage (现阶段的印尼华人族群)*. Singapore: NUS Chinese Department and Global Publishing.

Ng, Chin Keong. 1976. *The Chinese in Riau: A Community on an Unstable and Restrictive Frontier*. Research Project Series No. 2. Singapore: Institute of Humanities and Social Sciences, College of Graduate Studies, Nanyang University.

Peking University Business Intelligence (北大华商智库). 2016. "Huáshāng zhìkù jīngdiǎn ànlì zǒu jìn běidà kètáng--guō shàoxīng xiānshēng 华商智库经典案例走进北大课堂--郭绍兴先生". Peking University (北京大学), 27 August 2016. http://cs.xinyisheji.com/sxj/index.php?m=content&c=index&a=show&catid=116&id=203

Pepinsky, Thomas B. 2009. *Economic Crises and the Breakdown of Authoritarian Regimes: Indonesia and Malaysia in Comparative Perspective*. Cambridge and New York, NY: Cambridge University Press.

Seputar Kepri. 2019. "School of Economics, Peking University Bertaraf Internasional Akan Hadir di Bintan". 22 November 2019. https://seputarkepri.co.id/2019/11/22/school-of-ekonomics-peking-university-bertaraf-internasional-akan-hadir-di-bintan/

Setijadi, Charlotte. 2018. "Chinese Investment and Presence in the Riau Islands". *ISEAS Perspective*, no. 28/2018, 10 May 2018.

Shi, Xueqin (施雪琴), and Tingting Xu (徐婷婷). 2017. "Maritime Silk Road and the Chinese

Folk Religion in Bintan, Indonesia (海上丝绸之路与民丹岛华人民间信仰的传播)". *Journal of Maritime History Studies* 1.

Sohu.com (搜狐). 2018. "Shǒu gè hǎiwài yǎnghuà lǚ xiàngmù! Yìnní bīn tǎn nánshān yǎnghuà lǚ xiàngmù jǔxíng kāigōng yíshì 首个海外氧化铝项目! 印尼宾坦南山氧化铝项目举行开工仪式". 18 December 2018. http://www.sohu.com/a/282871258_697331

Surya Kepri. "Kampus Peking University Beijing Akan Hadir di Batu Licin Bintan". 22 November 2019. https://suryakepri.com/2019/11/22/kampus-peking-university-beijing-akan-hadir-di-batu-lincin-bintan/

Suryadinata, Leo. 2015. *Prominent Indonesian Chinese: Biographical Sketches*. 4th ed. Singapore: ISEAS – Yusof Ishak Institute.

Tagliacozzo, Eric. 2005. *Secret Trades, Porous Borders: Smuggling and States Along a Southeast Asian Frontier, 1865–1915*. New Haven and London: Yale University Press.

Taihe Group (太河集团). 2018. "Tài hé jítuán CEO guō shàoxīng huò 'yàtài dìqū zuì shòu zūnjìng huárén qǐyè jiā 太河集团CEO郭绍兴获'亚太地区最受尊敬华人企业家". 25 April 2018. http://taihegp.com/shownews.asp?m_id=31&newtype=0&t=1575038740768

Thee, Kian Wie. 2006. "The Indonesian Government's Economic Policies Towards the Ethnic Chinese: Beyond Economic Nationalism?". In *Southeast Asia's Chinese Businesses in an Era of Globalization: Coping with the Rise of China*, edited by Leo Suryadinata, pp. 76–101. Singapore: Institute of Southeast Asian Studies.

Trocki, Carl A. 2007. *Prince of Pirates: The Temenggongs and the Development of Johor and Singapore, 1784–1885*. Singapore: NUS Press.

Vihara Buddha Diepa. 2015a. "Yayasan Vihara Buddha Diepa Maha Bodhi Karimun TK, SD, SMP, SMA". 3 May 2015. https://zh-cn.facebook.com/679177638765884/photos/yayasan-vihara-buddha-diepamaha-bodhi-karimuntk-sd-smp-smamenerima-pendaftaran-s/1090371967646447/

———. 2015b. "Yìndùníxīyà jílǐ wèn xiàn bā lái pō tóngxīn shàn shè chénglì wǔshí zhōunián jìnián zhàopiàn 印度尼西亚吉里汶县峇来坡 同心善社成立五十周年纪念照片". 3 July 2015. https://www.facebook.com/679177638765884/videos/印度尼西亚吉里汶县峇来坡同心善社成立五十周年纪念照片歌曲-朋友/1131659283517715/

Wee, V. 2016. "The Significance of Riau in SIJORI". In *The SIJORI Cross-Border Region: Transnational Politics, Economics, and Culture*, edited by F.E. Hutchinson and T. Chong, pp. 241–66. Singapore: ISEAS – Yusof Ishak Institute.

Zheng Jinliang (鄭金亮). 2015. "Zuò luò mín dān dǎo·shànxìn hélì jiàn·500 luóhàn dàochǎng niándǐ kāifàng 座落民丹岛·善信合力建·500羅漢道場年底開放." *Sin Chew Daily* (印尼星洲日報), 6 May 2015. https://indonesia.sinchew.com.my/node/54222

Conclusion

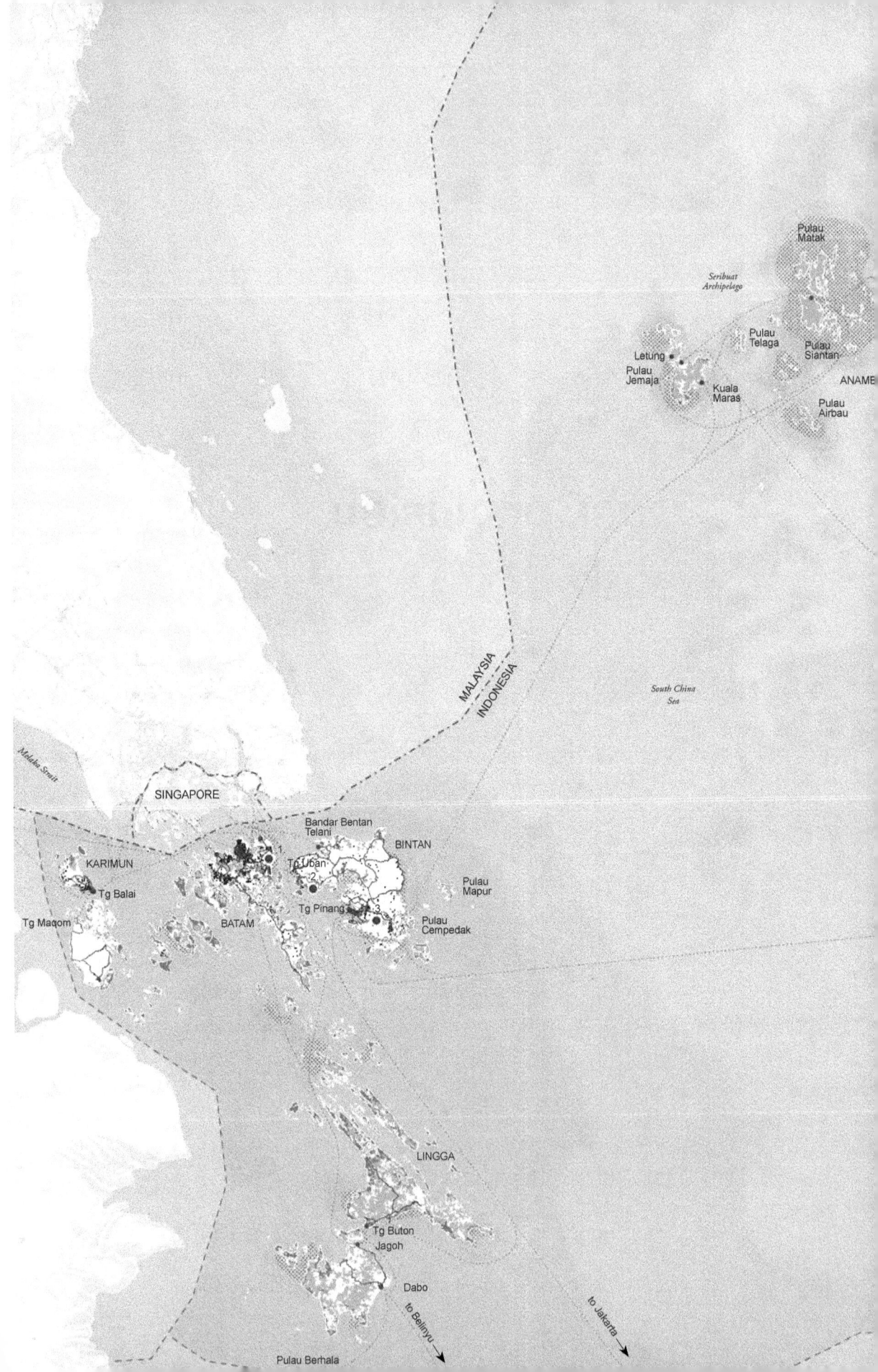

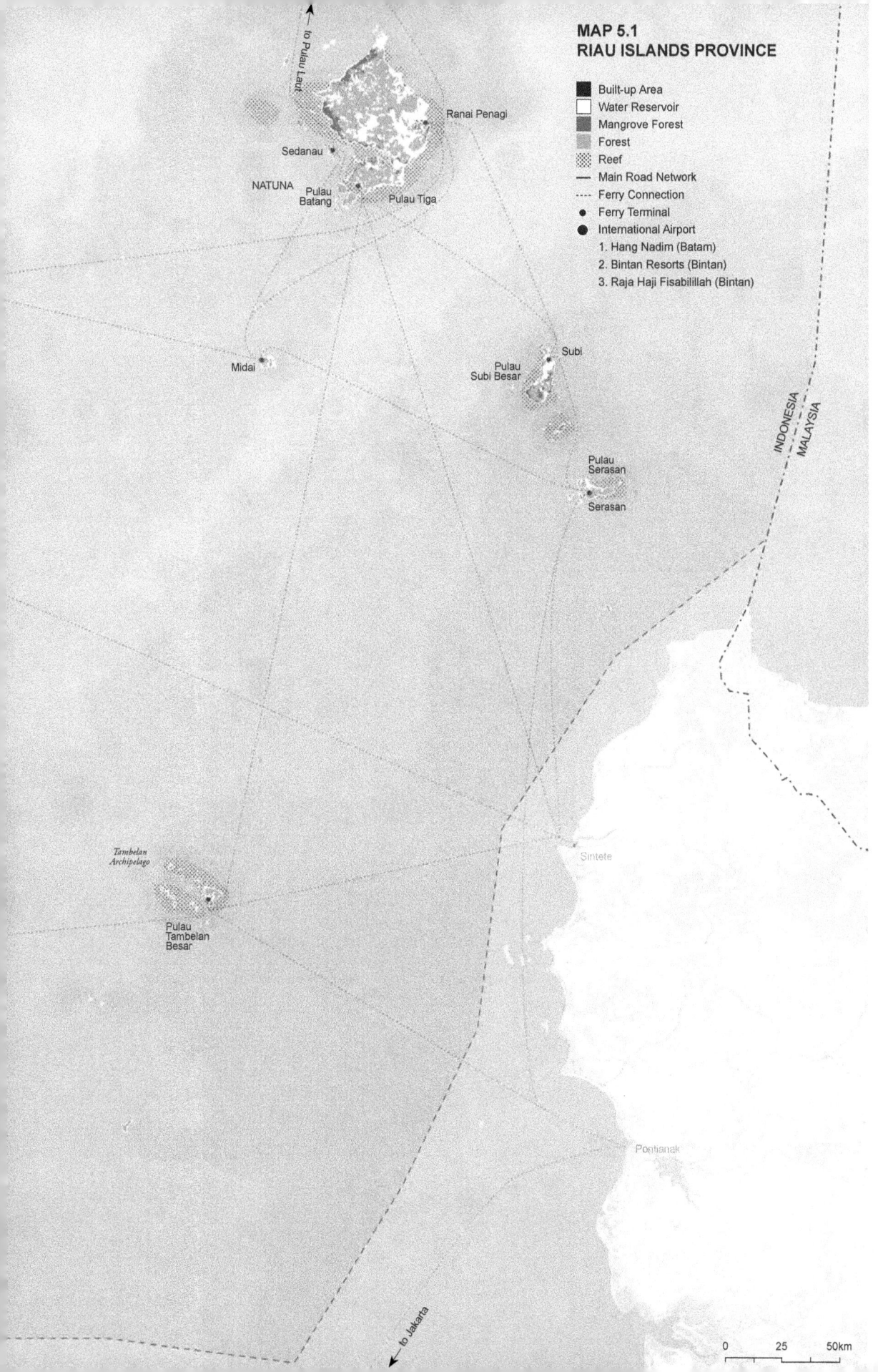

MAP 5.1
RIAU ISLANDS PROVINCE

- ■ Built-up Area
- □ Water Reservoir
- ▨ Mangrove Forest
- ▨ Forest
- ▨ Reef
- — Main Road Network
- ⋯ Ferry Connection
- ● Ferry Terminal
- ⬤ International Airport
  1. Hang Nadim (Batam)
  2. Bintan Resorts (Bintan)
  3. Raja Haji Fisabilillah (Bintan)

to Pulau Laut

Ranai Penagi

Sedanau

NATUNA Pulau Batang
Pulau Tiga

Midai

Subi
Pulau Subi Besar

Pulau Serasan
Serasan

INDONESIA MALAYSIA

Tambelan Archipelago

Sintete

Pulau Tambelan Besar

Pontianak

to Jakarta

0   25   50km

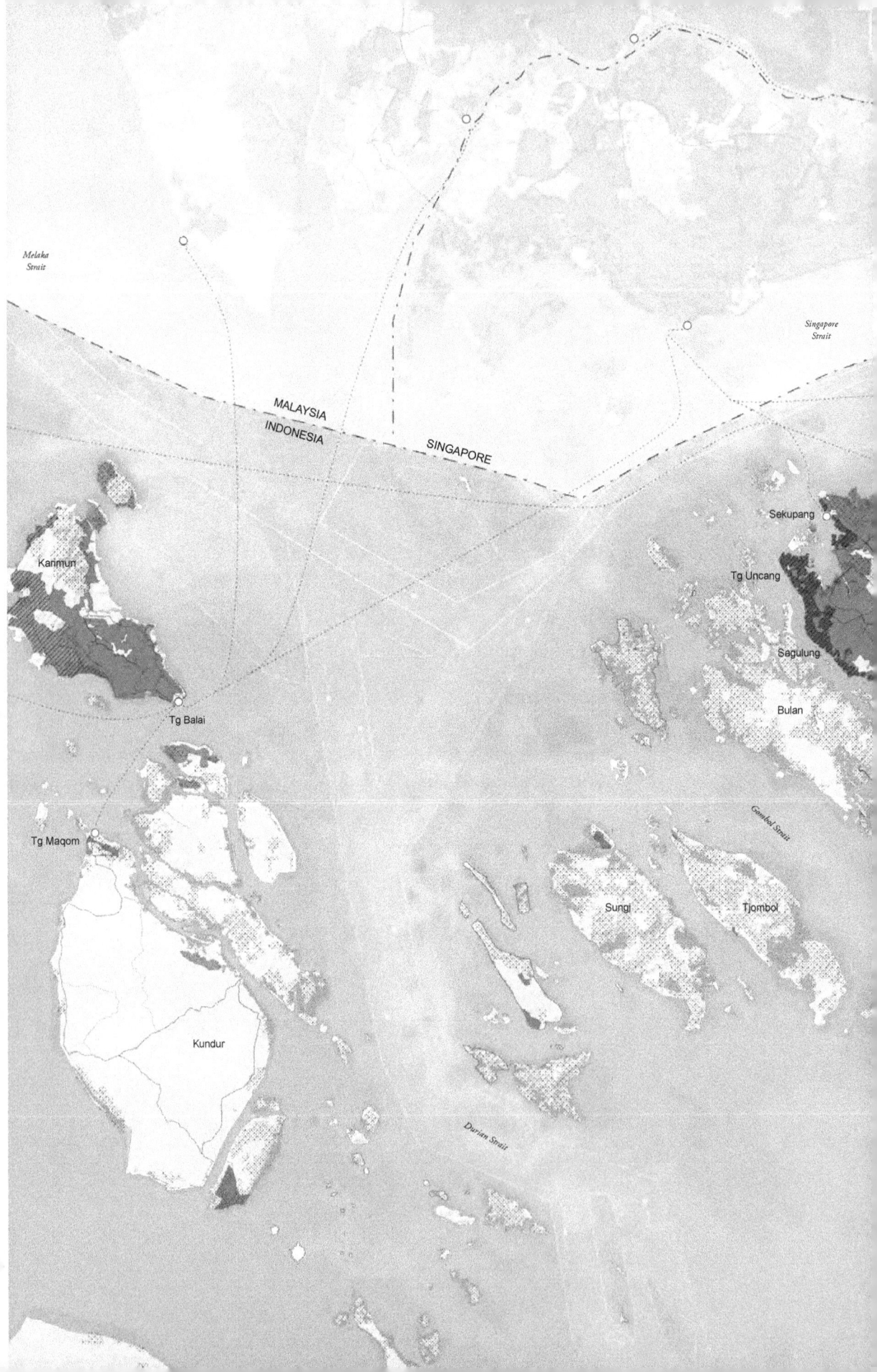

Melaka Strait

Singapore Strait

MALAYSIA

INDONESIA

SINGAPORE

Karimun

Sekupang

Tg Uncang

Sagulung

Bulan

Tg Balai

Gombol Strait

Tg Maqom

Sungi

Tjombol

Kundur

Durian Strait

MAP 5.2
BATAM, BINTAN AND KARIMUN

○ Ferry Terminal
- - - Ferry Connection
—— Main Road Network
Fairway
Built-up Area
Industry and Logistic
Shipbuilding Industry
Water Reservoir
Mangrove Forest
Forest

*South China
Sea*

MALAYSIA

INDONESIA

Nongsa

Batam
Center

Hang Nadim
Airport

Batamindo

Kabil

Punggur

Tg Ubin

Bandar Bentan
Telani

Bintan Beach
International Resort

Trikora
Beach

Bintan

Bintan Resorts
Airport

Riau Strait

Rempang

Tg Pinang

Raja Haji
Fisabilillah
Airport

Pulau Dompak

Kijang

Galang

0   5   10km

18

THE RIAU ISLANDS
Setting Sail?

Siwage Dharma Negara and Francis E. Hutchinson

INTRODUCTION

This publication is the third in a trilogy that focuses on the Singapore-Johor-Riau Islands or SIJORI Cross-Border Region (CBR). The first of the series, *The SIJORI Cross-Border Region: Transnational Politics, Economics, and Culture*, takes Singapore as the anchor-point for the composite entity. In contrast, this volume on the Riau Islands and its predecessor on Johor focus on the other two territories in the Cross-Border Region. They explore how these are influenced by their belonging to a larger political entity—Indonesia and Malaysia, respectively—yet are also shaped by their connections to their neighbours.

This volume takes 1990 as a point of departure. Seeking to capitalize on flows of foreign direct investment (FDI) in the manufacturing sector, policymakers in Indonesia reduced the regulatory burden on business and liberalized ownership restrictions. Propelled by the influx of capital from leading economies in Northeast Asia and elsewhere, the Riau Islands' economy grew in size and complexity. In a very short period of time, Batam, and to a lesser extent Bintan, were drawn into a range of global production networks in the electrical and electronics sectors.

Driven by this investment, the Riau Islands' economy grew at break-neck speed and very rapidly became a major site for manufacturing within Indonesia. Attracted by formal sector jobs, people from across the country came to the islands, increasing its population and ethnic diversity. Increased per capita income, connections to world markets, and a unique sense of identity led to a campaign to secede from the larger Riau province, and establish a new province, with Tanjungpinang as the capital.

Thirty years on, it is timely to revisit this developmental trajectory, explore the lessons learned, and then look forward. With this as a backdrop, the guiding questions for this volume are:

- What can be said about the sustainability of the Riau Island's manufacture-for-export economic model, as well as measures implemented to catalyse the development of new sectors?
- What have been the political, social and environmental effects on the Riau Islands of the rapid economic development seen since 1990?
- How is the province influenced by developments within Indonesia as a whole, as well as dynamics within the SIJORI Cross-Border Region?

The structure of this book seeks to explore these questions in the same order. Thus, the first section looks at the workings of the state's economy, through analysing the performance and prospects of key sectors as well as policy measures to develop existing or new activities. The second and third sections proceed to explore the Riau Islands' political context and current social and environmental challenges, many of them directly linked to the province's economic model. The three sections collectively examine the Riau Islands' place within Indonesia, particularly as it is influenced by policies implemented in Jakarta, as well as the manner within which the province is influenced by its proximity to Singapore and southern Malaysia within the SIJORI Cross-Border Region.

This final chapter will briefly review each of the three sections of the book to: draw out key themes and findings; identify areas for continuing and future research; and then conclude by relating the themes back to the Cross-Border Region.

ECONOMICS

In line with the first research question, Chapter 2 focuses on the manufacturing sector and attempts to understand the challenges facing it, and whether Batam's export-oriented model is still viable (Maps 2.6, 2.7, 2.13 and 4.10). Using data from Indonesia's largest and most comprehensive data source on manufacturing, the chapter shows that, while relatively small in number, firms in Batam in the electrical goods, electronics, and shipbuilding and repair sectors employ more workers per capita and have higher levels of output, as well as a greater proportion of exports and imports relative to their counterparts in Java and Sumatra. Compared to firms in Java and Sumatra, in general firms in Batam show considerably higher levels of productivity measured by output per worker. The increase in workers' productivity seems to outweigh the growth of nominal wage levels. This indicates that, despite rapid wage growth on the island, overall it still remains a competitive location for manufacturing.

The chapter also shows that despite more firms being established in Batam of late, the proportion of firms exporting has been declining and the proportion of firms importing has been increasing. This indicates that, over time, the domestic economy is more important for firms based in Batam. Moreover, firms in the electronics and electrical goods industries in Batam produce higher output per worker than their counterparts in Java and Sumatra. Consequently, the island still has a strong comparative advantage in these two sectors. In contrast, indicators pertaining to the shipbuilding sector paint a less positive story. Looking forward, these results indicate that the first two sectors should remain central to strategies for the island, but that further promotion of investment into the shipbuilding and repair sector may need to be re-evaluated.

In contrast to the manufacturing sector which has struggled of late, the tourism sector has become increasingly important for PRI. Beyond its proximity to Singapore and southern Malaysia, which account for a significant proportion of visitors, the Riau Islands has considerable assets for attracting tourists, such as natural landscapes and rich cultural heritage. Chapter 3 explores the potential and challenges facing this sunrise sector (Map 2.8, 2.9 and 4.11). Despite a considerable number of operators and a growing range of events geared at international markets, the sector is hindered by a complex policy environment. The provincial government has faced difficulties in reconciling its development plan with local governments, who have developed their own strategies without consulting others. One of the biggest issues is that unclear or conflicting spatial plans trigger conflicts over land ownership and use. Given Indonesia's current governance structure, it is likely that these coordination problems will continue to hinder the sector's development.

Chapter 4 looks at the emergence, development, and comparative advantage of another sunrise sector—Batam's digital economy (Map 2.10). As this chapter argues, the digital economy sector offers considerable potential for attracting investment and job creation, much as the manufacturing sector did in the 1990s and 2000s. Crucially for Batam, this new sector can generate demand for skilled workers, in contrast to the more labour-intensive electronics and shipbuilding sectors. However, it should not be forgotten that much of the infrastructure and policy frameworks underpinning the digital economy were laid by these less glamorous activities. The chapter foresees that the limited pool of Batam's skill base may hinder the sector's growth. Indeed, sourcing labour is a perennial issue for digital economy companies, not only in Batam but also in Indonesia generally. Finally, this chapter argues that the digital economy needs to generate tangible benefits for local residents.

The subsequent chapter examines the legal and regulatory framework in Batam, Bintan, and Karimun (BBK). Due to their proximity to Singapore as well as international shipping lanes, these three islands have enjoyed a range of special regulatory regimes. In 2007, parts of BBK were made into FTZs (set out in Maps 2.11 and 2.12). However, in recent years, SEZs, which enjoy a slightly different range of tax incentives and benefits, have been established across the country. Consequently, policymakers in the central government have sought to change Batam's status from an FTZ to an SEZ. However, Chapter 5 argues that an altered regulatory status will not be effective in addressing the island's economic issues, which have little, if anything, to do with nomenclature. In addition to overlooking dire infrastructure shortages hindering the operation of the island's main port, the change in status may entail the physical relocation of many firms and industrial parks to comply with new zoning requirements. Furthermore, the change will create uncertainty among investors, as the original FTZ regime was meant to last for seventy years. The chapter proposes, instead, that consideration be given to reducing the economic "firewall" between the BBK FTZ and the domestic market, which would allow firms operating in Batam to be able to sell part of their output in Indonesia. At present, this is precluded by the current regulatory structure.

In 2018, the Riau Islands' Gross Regional Domestic Product (GRDP) was about IDR249 trillion (US$16.9 billion). In that year, provincial per capita income was about US$7,932—almost double the national average of US$3,945. This is testament to the fruits of the Riau Islands' outward-oriented development model put in place in 1990.

However, one theme that emerges is the degree to which the province's economy depends on Batam's performance. Indeed, the island generates 61 per cent of the province's GRDP. Thus, the final chapter in this section proceeds to explore what options there are for maximizing spillover between Batam and other parts of the province, as well as catalysing growth on other islands (Maps 2.2–2.5 cartographically display some aspects of this relationship). As explored in the subsequent sections of this book, inclusive growth is a vital aspect of the sustainability of any economic model.

POLITICS

The second section of the book sets out the key aspects of the PRI's political context. Chapter 7 revisits the history of the Riau Islands in the light of developments over the last twenty years, taking as its point of departure the maxim that "the sea is the glue of the Indonesian archipelago". Rarely questioned, this widely accepted assumption is open to debate when one considers the recent history of the Riau Islands. Even at the national level, where the connections between land (*tanah*) and water (*air*) have provided the terminology for "our homeland" (*tanah air kita*) that is so entrenched in nationalistic rhetoric, the seas have only recently moved to the forefront of the government's agenda.

Chapter 7 discusses the role of the sea in the formation of Indonesia and the particular position of the Riau Islands, where sections of the provincial maritime boundaries are national boundaries as well. It then considers the relationship between land and water in PRI's predecessor, the Johor-Riau Kingdom, and how this relationship changed during the colonial period (Map 3.1). The chapter also reviews the creation of PRI in 2004 in the light of post-1997 research and turns to the contemporary issues facing this archipelagic province where 96 per cent of its surface area is water (Map 2.1). Notwithstanding the historical connections between the Kepri heartland in the Riau-Lingga archipelagos and the many islands of the

South China Sea, the realities of distance, economic disparities and cultural diversity pose a significant challenge for provincial cohesion. Despite calls for unity, these challenges will persist unless greater resources are invested to draw the disparate parts of the province together and share the benefits of development.

With this as a backdrop, Chapter 8 looks at the establishment of the Province of the Riau Islands in 2002/4 (Maps 3.2–3.3). This was part of a broader national trend called "blossoming" (*pemekaran*), which saw the creation of seven new provinces and more than 100 new districts in the country, following the fall of the New Order in 1998. The chapter argues that the main motivation for these subnational movements was a combination of rational interests and cultural sentiments. In the case of PRI, rational interests involved struggles over the unfair distribution of power and resources, including the way development under the control of (mainland) Riau Province had been detrimental to the Riau Islands. In addition, cultural sentiments also played an important role, as the people of the Riau Islands considered themselves as "archipelagic Malays" and heirs of the great Malay-maritime empires of the past, as opposed to "mainland Malays" who were mostly farmers.

This chapter argues that since becoming its own province, PRI has performed well and surpassed Riau, its "parent" province, in multiple aspects including human development, poverty alleviation, and economic growth. Ultimately, the formation of the Province of the Riau Islands is argued to be a natural process in a large, diverse, and decentralizing country like Indonesia, where cultural identities are being reasserted and local autonomies renegotiated. Despite the usual hiccups such as capacity gaps and corruption, the formation of the province has been positive in achieving a balance between keeping the country intact while allowing local stakeholders a substantial level of autonomy.

Chapter 9, for its part, moves away from state structures to look at how political parties operate in the province. The Riau Islands Province is characterized by two attributes: its relatively small size and distance from major population centres, particularly the national capital (Map 1.1); and the fact that its economic heartland, Batam, is separate from its political capital, Tanjungpinang. These characteristics have important implications for the organizational capacities of political parties. Upon examining the attributes of branch offices of major political parties, the chapter argues that: the infrastructure of the offices is very basic, with cadres and volunteers acting as the main administrators; while activities, funding and recruitment remain erratic, insufficient and disorganized. This is further accentuated by the need to maintain facilities in two locations to satisfy legal requirements and increase membership. The overall low level of capacity is seen in the low level of political education activities, which has accentuated the personalistic nature of campaigns—which centre on candidates rather than issues.

Chapter 10 looks at the development of industrial relations in Batam. It argues that over the past two decades, trade union activity on the island has been heavily influenced by regional demographics, employment conditions, and the prevailing political scenario. Following the end of the New Order era, the single state-authorized union was fragmented, giving rise to many new enterprise unions. Batam's young and diverse immigrant population with no pre-existing loyalties to particular trade unions, and expanding ranks of large factories and workers, made it a hotspot for industrial relations activities.

Low wages for workers throughout Indonesia and an outbreak of social unrest resulted in the formation of three strong national-level unions. By the mid-2000s, these unions were also active in Batam. Unsettled ethnic relations resulted in escalation of labour mobilizations from 2011 to 2013. One union in particular spearheaded several intense demonstrations throughout Indonesia, including Batam, during this time. The 2012 mobilization was particularly effective, and the union bodies were able to successfully negotiate for significantly higher minimum wages for workers. After intervention by the Widodo government, there has been a change in the unions' approach in demanding wages and the improvement of working conditions. Instead of addressing employment concerns through national-level campaigns, matters are now to be resolved at the enterprise level. While there are no visible signs of confrontational mobilization in Batam in the near future, a number of key issues remain unsettled.

SOCIAL AND ENVIRONMENTAL ISSUES

One of the key changes wrought upon the Riau Islands by its rapid economic development is the influx of many people into the province from across the country. This demographic shift has also been accompanied by a substantial increase in the province's religious, ethnic, and cultural diversity.

Chapter 12 examines the relationship between different strands of Islam in the province (Maps 4.4 and 4.5), in particular between the local, traditionalist school and Wahhabi-Salafism. This issue rose to the fore due to several events, including: broadcasts by a radio station, Hang FM; a plan by several people to launch a missile at Singapore from the island; and the arrest of individuals linked to ISIS (Islamic State in Iraq and Syria). The chapter argues that key religious leaders from the province have come out against Wahhabi-Salafi's anti-pluralist ideas. Contrary to expectations, key traditionalist practices like mass prayers (*zikr*) and praises to the Prophet Muhammad (*selawat*)—which Wahhabi-Salafis frown upon—continue to attract a huge following in Batam. And, against the prevailing wisdom that religious influences only travel from Batam to Singapore, the chapter argues city-state also exerts influence on its neighbour, with visits from Singapore Muslims to attend ceremonies and fund traditionalist activities.

The preceding chapter provides an overview of urbanization trends in the Riau Islands since the establishment of the new province. Thus, Chapter 11 focuses on the demographic, physical, and territorial aspects of urbanization in the Riau Islands and attempts to forecast future potential urbanization trends in the different parts of the province (Map 4.3). One key takeaway is that Batam's population will grow in the future, but its urban development will be limited by land and water availability. Thus, it foresees there will be more vertical development for housing and commercial purposes on the island. The other key urban agglomeration, Tanjungpinang, will grow further in terms of population and urban areas, especially as the result of the development of the provincial capital on Dompak Island (Map 3.2), as well as due to the relocation of the city government centre to Senggarang—in the north of Tanjungpinang.

As Batam's population has grown and its economy has developed, the island's environment has come under considerable pressure (Maps 4.1 and 4.2). Chapter 13 explores the drivers behind much of the island's environmental degradation. Beyond population growth, one key driver is the profusion of informal settlements, which has been accompanied by the clearance of primary forests, as well as the pollution of waterways. This is exacerbated by a lack of wastewater treatment plans. Another key driver is the lack of enforcement of environmental regulations. Conversely, one key finding is that the stipulation that land must be cleared when it is acquired has actually accelerated deforestation, with new landowners are keen to show their commitment to development. The chapter also argues that the government needs to devote more resources towards supervision and enforcement.

The last four chapters in this section analyse different ethnic communities in the province, exploring key aspects such as their: size and composition; historical association with the Riau Islands; key cultural and political activities; and relationship with other groups (Maps 4.6–4.9).

Chapter 14 looks at the Malay/Bugis community in the Riau Islands. In the province—envisioned as a distinctly "Malay Province" upon its establishment— ethnic Malays are the proud heirs and custodians of a rich legacy associated with a once-sprawling empire that stretched across the present-day borders of Indonesia, Singapore, and Malaysia.

Malays of Bugis descent have long played a disproportionately central role in the history and historiography of the region. While "Malay", members of this community readily acknowledge that their ethnically Bugis roots maintain salient in their everyday lives. However, economic trends and rapid socio-demographic shifts shaped by ongoing migration flows have led to feelings of "marginalization" (*peminggiran*) among the Malay-Bugis. This has led them to claim that they are being gradually pushed to the literal and figurative "edges" of social life in the Riau Islands Province. Fears that a one-time ethnic "majority is becoming a minority" (*mayoritas menjadi minoritas*) have fuelled feelings of inter-ethnic resentment, and have shaped provincial government policies geared toward the "preservation" of Malay custom. While much research continues to centre on the relations between Indonesia's *pribumi* and Chinese communities as an indicator of wider inter-ethnic and religious relations, a grounded assessment of ethnicity in the Riau islands offers an alternative perspective on these important issues.

Chapter 15 then explores the Javanese community in the Riau Islands, the province's largest community of migrants, which has come to outnumber Malays in several urban centres. The chapter examines: how their identity is defined in relation to local people; to what degree they are assimilated; how they are depicted in political discourse in the province; and in what fashion they participate in its political life. The chapter explains that the Javanese living in the province are mostly permanent migrants who have resided there for two or more generations. Many of them have married members of other communities, including Malays. Thus, the issue of ethnic identity—of being Javanese or Malay and about Javaneseness or Malayness—is complex, especially in how it is presented and represented in social, economic and political relations.

In their new home, the Javanese have come to mobilize culturally and politically through establishing a variety of ethnically based associations. These associations seek to preserve traditions and culture, as well as provide a means of reaffirming identity and helping members. They have also emerged in the province in response to growing political mobilization among Malays, who position themselves as the original "sons of the soil". The chapter argues that Javanese identity is not monolithic, nor is it impervious to other influences. This porosity will only increase over time as more Javanese inter-marry with members of other communities and the ability of successive generations to speak Javanese decreases with time. Consequently, many of these associations are flexible, allowing non-Javanese to join through a variety of mechanisms.

The subsequent chapter examines the Batak community in the Riau Islands Province. The Batak is the third-largest ethnic group after the Malay and Javanese. As a relatively large community, the Batak play a role both in the province's economic and political life. Thus, Chapter 16 examines how tradition shapes the political aspirations of the Batak migrants. It then looks at how Batak migrants play a role in the political life of the province and how politicians from this group interact with those from other ethno-religious communities in the Riau Islands.

Chapter 17 looks at the development of the Chinese community in the Riau Islands. Despite recent flows of migrants from Java and Sumatra, the Chinese community is still one of the five largest communities, concentrated in the urban parts of the province, particularly Batam and Tanjungpinang (Map 4.8). The chapter explores: how the first Chinese arrived in the area; the trajectories of prominent Chinese businessmen; and the role played by ethnic Chinese politicians in the province. Several themes emerge from the chapter. One is that the Chinese community has been in the Riau Islands for generations, with the first arriving in the days of the Johor-Riau Kingdom. Another is that, in contrast to other parts of Indonesia where the Chinese community has been assimilated to a large degree; in the Riau Islands, there are many markers of Chinese culture in daily life. Many Chinese Riau Islanders are still able to speak Mandarin, and there is a tradition of Chinese-medium education that is re-emerging. This is because of combination of factors, such as the relatively large Chinese population; distance from Jakarta; and proximity to Singapore and Chinese-medium education and media content produced there.

AREAS FOR CONTINUING AND FUTURE RESEARCH

In addressing the guiding questions set out above, this volume has sought to be as comprehensive as possible. Nonetheless, many topics have been omitted, and the rapid pace of change in PRI means that even those subjects covered will require consistent updating. The following paragraphs will briefly set out some of the gaps in knowledge and will highlight key trends to follow in the coming years.

Concerning the province's economy, the industrial sector will continue to be a key motor of the province's economy and an employer of note. While the future of the shipbuilding sector looks uncertain unless key regulatory changes are addressed to allow sale on the local market, the electrical and electronics sector continues to hold potential. However, despite this sector's promise, simple proximity to Singapore is not enough, and sufficient policy attention needs to be placed on developing capabilities to attract and retain activities across the value chain. Future research might be directed towards understanding the institutional prerequisites for attracting investment and creating a conducive economic environment for businesses to flourish. Looking forward, mineral processing may emerge as a sunrise sector leveraging on the province's abundance of bauxite and other metals.

In addition, the services sector is likely to continue to grow and diversify. Turning to services, Batam and Bintan have been successful in catalysing the development of tourism sectors. The two islands now aspire to attract new investment in the education sector, as well as moving the tourism sector more upmarket and hosting visitors for longer stays. Looking forward, the government will need to ensure constant attention to these sectors as they grow, as requirements for follow-up and facilitation increase, requiring agility and responsiveness. There may also be interesting synergies between sectors, such as higher education and the digital economy.

Logistics, in particular, is a key sector for the PRI's future development. Despite access to world markets via Singapore, the Riau Islands is poorly connected within Indonesia. The costs of sending goods from Batu Ampar Port in Batam to Singapore is more expensive than sending the same volume of goods from Singapore to Jakarta. Furthermore, connectivity within the province itself remains lacking. There is a lack of reliable transportation connecting the province's many islands (Map 2.1). With its large sea area and dispersed island chains, reliable sea transportation is critical. The PRI government has plans to develop and to expand Batu Ampar port's infrastructure—which is a crucial "backbone" sector for the province's wider economy. However, implementation challenges abound.

Looking forward, the planned development of several SEZs in the province may have significant impact. Many businesses located to BBK with the understanding that the overall regulatory framework would be valid for seventy years. Yet, the transition to the new status implies a range of important changes, and thus should be approached with caution. A whole-scale move to an SEZ may leave many existing manufacturing firms outside established zones and their associated benefits. In addition, the current SEZ framework does little to attract the skill-heavy but asset-light activities that characterize the digital economy.

Also crucial for the Riau Islands, and BBK in particular, is how the "economic firewall" separating the province from Indonesia's growing domestic economy can be dealt with in a fair manner. While areas with FTZ status do enjoy tariff-free imports and associated benefits, residents of the Riau Islands do pay more for staples procured from other parts of the country. In addition, growing numbers of investors are requesting permission to be able to sell at least part of their output on the local market. Unless this is dealt with, the Riau Islands will find it hard to catalyse the development of new sectors or even retain their manufacturing base.

Also, on the economic front, it will be important to monitor how archipelagic provinces are treated by the central government. At present, a group of such provinces including the Riau Islands, is lobbying the central government for a different formula for revenue-sharing. The argument is that these provinces face specific logistical issues that other provinces in the country do not. Consequently, they deserve a greater amount of resources from the central government. However, this same argument is also brewing within the Riau Islands, as Natuna and Anambas frequently argue that they face even greater logistical and connectivity issues than the relatively accessible BBK islands.

With regard to politics, several dynamics warrant monitoring. In 2020, there will be elections for the Governor of the Riau Islands, as well the Mayor of Batam. These elections will certainly be influenced by the economic situation, as well as the degree to which the various communities feel included in the province's daily life. Looking back at the last elections, there is a high risk of populist policies which may hinder investment. Interestingly, despite Batam's large and heterogeneous population, voting turnout rates are low among the island's recent migrants. Should these voters be effectively targeted in campaigns and mobilized to vote, this could dramatically alter the province's political complexion.

Much has been made of eliminating the overlap in authority and responsibility between the Batam municipal government and the Batam Investment Authority (BP Batam). The most recent policy change was to place BP Batam under the authority of the Batam Mayor. It remains unclear how the transfer of all the responsibilities for managing Batam's economic development to the municipal government will be implemented. In addition, for the first time, the island's asset base in the form of the airport and seaport will be placed under a politically elected government official, rather than technocrats answerable to the central government. The degree of responsible stewardship of these resources will be a key aspect to monitor in the years to come.

With regard to PRI's social, cultural and environmental context, the province's growing population and the scale of many construction projects have put pressure on the environment, as highlighted by this volume. This pressure will continue to augment, requiring innovative policies to deal with growing urban centres, pressure on the environment, and the province's increasingly diverse population. Looking forward, some of PRI's priorities may clash, such as the push to develop the manufacturing industry and the drive to increase tourism revenues.

PRI WITHIN THE SIJORI CROSS-BORDER REGION

Due to its proximity, long-standing ties, comparative factor endowments, and hospitable investment framework, the Riau Islands continues to have a deep, multi-levelled, and vital relationship with Singapore. Looking at the components of this deep economic relationship, the pillars of the relationship centre on manufactures, such as shipbuilding and repair, as well as electrical and electronics. While the province's manufacturing base may well shrink, there are a number of positive signs regarding tourism, as well as the digital economy. In the case of the tourism sector, the province benefits from its domestic market as well as visitors from Singapore as well as a considerable number from Malaysia. With regard to the digital economy, the city-state is the main client. As it stands, the ecosystem that is emerging is rooted in the Singapore market, and is, as of yet, operating independently from the domestic market.

However, the relationship is not only one way. Indeed, at present the Riau Islands export virtually all of the live pigs consumed in Singapore, and are a vital source of fresh fish and vegetables (Hutchinson 2020). Looking forward, the province's population will grow in size and per capita income, constituting a vital source of labour-power and room for growth for the increasingly land- and labour-constrained city-state.

Despite the deep linkages, trends towards greater and deeper integration are not always constant. The political situation can and does change, with ensuing alterations in policy mix and investment in modern sector activities in the Riau Islands, as opposed to traditional occupations such as fishing and farming. Notwithstanding this, the proximity between PRI and Singapore, and their symbiotic existence across several key axes acts as a strong incentive to pursue continued engagement.

However, the relationship between the Riau Islands and Singapore is not the only one in the Cross-Border Region. Johor and the Riau Islands also have a relationship that is independent of Singapore and growing in size and complexity. As with Riau Islands and the city-state, deep cultural ties rooted in the precolonial period link the two territories. For example, for many Johor Malays, the Riau Islands are the site of "genuine" Malay culture, as they house heritage sites from the Johor-Riau Sultanate and were the home of pioneers of the Malay language (Hutchinson 2020; Carruthers, this volume).

Furthermore, porous maritime borders and a tradition of sea-based commerce have long given rise to cross-border movement of goods between Malaysia and Indonesia (Tagliacozzo 2005). Based on the same factors, this trade still exists today and encompasses medicine, cigarettes, drugs, and small ships. It is also used to ferry workers between the two territories (Hutchinson 2020).

Recent policy frameworks have deepened these connections, as Johor has sought to develop its services sector, and the Riau Islands focuses on manufacturing and tourism. For example, Johor has sought to develop its private healthcare and higher education sectors. With regard to the former, the Malaysian state explicitly targets customers in the Riau Islands and is able to leverage transport infrastructure developed for the tourism sector. With regard to education, inhabitants from the Riau Islands have increasingly sought to study engineering and education in the state's public universities, many of which have scholarships from the Riau Islands provincial government (Hutchinson 2020).

In addition, there are considerable labour flows from the Riau Islands and Indonesia more widely. Proximity, linguistic affinity, and a welcoming visa regime allow Indonesians to stay up to thirty days in Malaysia. This has given rise to a lively cross-border movement of people travelling from Batam, Bintan and Karimun north into Johor. These flows of labour are drawn in by opportunities offered by Johor's plantations, port operations, as well as well-developed retail sector. To cater to the many thousands of its citizens in Johor and southern Malaysia, the Indonesian government has established a consulate that offers: health services; three shelters; and primary, secondary, and tertiary education (Hutchinson 2020).

One of the themes of the book is the province's distance from Jakarta as well as major population centres in Java and Sumatra, and its proximity to Singapore and southern Malaysia (Map 1.1). While President Joko Widodo has pledged to develop Indonesia's maritime sector as well as to boost connectivity within the country, proximity to Singapore and, through it, world markets will continue to exert a very powerful force on the Riau Islands.

While the Riau Islands certainly will be affected by decisions taken at the central level, the many and deep linkages it shares with not just Singapore, but also Johor will continue to exert influence on this strategically located archipelagic province.

References

Antaranews.com. 2019. "BP Batam Tingkatkan Kapasitas Pelabuhan Batuampar Jadi Lima Juta TEUs". 10 October 2019. https://www.antaranews.com/berita/1105990/bp-batam-tingkatkan-kapasitas-pelabuhan-batuampar-jadi-lima-juta-teus

Carruthers, A.M. 2021. "Living on the Edge: Being Malay (and Bugis) in the Riau Islands". In *The Riau Islands: Setting Sail*, edited by Francis E. Hutchinson and Siwage Dharma Negara. Singapore: ISEAS – Yusof Ishak Institute.

Hutchinson, Francis E. 2015. *Mirror Images in Different Frames? Johor, the Riau Islands, and Competition for Investment from Singapore*. Singapore: ISEAS – Yusof Ishak Institute.

———. 2020. "In the Gateway's Shadow: Interactions between Singapore's Hinterlands". *Growth and Change*: 1–17.

———, and Terence Chong. 2016. *The SIJORI Cross-Border Region: Transnational Politics, Economics, and Culture*. Singapore: ISEAS – Yusof Ishak Institute.

Pangestu, Mari. 1991. 'The Growth Triangle: An Indonesian Perspective". In *Growth Triangle: The Johor–Singapore–Riau Experience*, edited by Lee Tsao Yuan. Singapore: Institute of Southeast Asian Studies.

Tagliacozzo, Eric. 2005. *Secret Trades, Porous Borders: Smuggling and States Along a Southeast Asian Frontier, 1865–1915*. New Haven and London: Yale University Press.

Tempo.co. 2019. "Menhub: Kapasitas Bongkar Muat Pelabuhan Priok Bisa 12 Juta TEUs". 6 October 2019. https://bisnis.tempo.co/read/1256418/menhub-kapasitas-bongkar-muat-pelabuhan-priok-bisa-12-juta-teus/full&view=ok

Appendix

SOURCES FOR THE RIAU ISLAND MAPS

Hans Hortig and Karoline Kostka

The maps presented in this book are based on site-specific field studies, official datasets and online resources compiled by Karoline Kostka and Hans Hortig between July 2019 and April 2020. They are uniquely produced for this publication.

The authors gathered additional insights into the Singapore-Johor-Riau region during their work at the Chair of Architecture of Territory at the Singapore ETH-Centre, Future Cities Laboratory (FCL), from 2013 to 2015. Further discussions and feedback from the editors Francis Hutchinson and Siwage Dharma Negara helped to shape the final version of the map sections.

The most significant sources for creating a base map in all sections are:

- Open Street Map (OSM), Open source geo-referenced information, data retrieved in the period of July 2019 to April 2020.
- Natural Earth, free vector and raster map data, https://www.naturalearthdata.com/downloads/ (accessed December 2019).
- Badan Informasi Geospasial (BIG), Indonesia Geospasial Portal, http://portal.ina-sdi.or.id (accessed between July 2019 and February 2020).

Additional information for the specific map sections are derived from the following sources:

Introduction
Indonesia and Riau Islands Province
Global Administrative Areas. "GADM dataset of Global Administrative Areas". https://gadm.org/index.html (accessed November 2019).

BIG. 2017. "Peta Negara Kesatuan Republik Indonesia (NKRI)". https://www.big.go.id/artikel/show/peta-negara-kesatuan-republik-indonesia (accessed October 2019).

Section 1: Economics
Mobility and Transport

Rusdi, S. 2019. "Shipping and Logistics Challenges in Kepulauan Riau". Workshop on Economic Update for the Riau Islands, ISEAS – Yusof Ishak Institute, November 2019.

PELNI. 2006. "Pelayaran Nasional Indonesia". https://www.wikiwand.com/id/Pelayaran_Nasional_Indonesia (accessed December 2019).

BIG. "Sistem Informasi Batimetri Nasional". http://portal.ina-sdi.or.id/batimetri/ (accessed October 2019).

Kostka, K., and H. Hortig. 2019. Mapping via Google Maps, Wikimapia, Bing Maps, October 2019.

Topalovic, M., H. Hortig, and K. Kostka. 2016. "Sources for the SIJORI Maps". In *The SIJORI Cross-Border Region: Transnational Politics, Economics, and Culture*, edited by F. Hutchinson and T. Chong, pp. 465–70. Singapore: ISEAS – Yusof Ishak Institute.

GINI Ratio, 2017; Human Development Index, 2018; Population Growth Rate, 2017–18; Unemployment, 2018

Badan Pusat Statistik (BPS). 2019. "Indikator Utama Provinsi Kepulauan Riau", Semester I 2019. https://kepri.bps.go.id/publication/download.html (accessed January 2020).

The Manufacturing Sector in Batam, Bintan and Karimun

Topalovic, M., H. Hortig, and K. Kostka. 2016. "Sources for the SIJORI Maps". In *The SIJORI Cross-Border Region: Transnational Politics, Economics, and Culture*, edited by F. Hutchinson and T. Chong, pp. 465–70. Singapore: ISEAS – Yusof Ishak Institute.

Kostka, K., and H. Hortig. 2019. Mapping via Google Maps, Wikimapia, Bing Maps, November 2019.

Shipbuilding Facilities and Shipyards in Batam, Bintan and Karimun

Negara, Siwage Dharma. 2017. "Can the Decline of Batam's Shipbuilding Industry be Reversed?". *ISEAS Perspective* No. 2017/10, 16 February 2017.

Kostka, K., and H. Hortig. 2019. Mapping via Google Maps, Wikimapia, Bing Maps, January 2019.

Tourism

Kostka, K., and H. Hortig. Mapping via Google Maps, Wikimapia, Google Earth, AirBnb, October 2019 to February 2020.

Topalovic, M., H. Hortig, and K. Kostka. 2016. "Sources for the SIJORI Maps". In *The SIJORI Cross-Border Region: Transnational Politics, Economics, and Culture*, edited by F. Hutchinson and T. Chong, pp. 465–70. Singapore: ISEAS – Yusof Ishak Institute.

KEPRI Travel. "Wonderful Riau Island", Tourism Portal. http://kepri-travel.kepriprov.go.id (accessed January 2020).

Rusdi, S. 2019. "Shipping and Logistics Challenges in Kepulauan Riau". Workshop on Economic Update for the Riau Islands, ISEAS – Yusof Ishak Institute, November 2019.

Tourism in Batam, Bintan and Karimun

Dinas Kebudayaan dan Pariwisata, Pemerintah Kota Batam. https://disbudpar.batam. go.id (accessed January 2020).

Kostka, K., and H. Hortig. Mapping via Google Maps, Wikimapia, Google Earth, AirBnb, October 2019 to February 2020.

Topalovic, M., H. Hortig, and K. Kostka. 2016. "Sources for the SIJORI Maps". In *The SIJORI Cross-Border Region: Transnational Politics, Economics, and Culture*, edited by F. Hutchinson and T. Chong, pp. 465–70. Singapore: ISEAS – Yusof Ishak Institute.

Digital Connectivity

TeleGeography. "Submarine Cable Map". https://github.com/telegeography/www. submarinecablemap.com (accessed February 2020).

United Nations International Telecommunication Union (ITU). "Interactive Transmission Map". https://www.itu.int/itu-d/tnd-map-public/ (accessed January 2020).

Zones and Trade Regimes

Kostka, K., and H. Hortig. Mapping via Google Maps, Wikimapia, Google Earth, AirBnb, October 2019 to March 2020.

ESDM OneMap. Minyak dan Gas. https://geoportal.esdm.go.id/migas/ (accessed December 2019).

Malaysian Investment Development Authority. "Infrastructure Support". http://www. mida.gov.my/home/infrastructure-support/posts/?lg=EN (accessed November 2018).

Zones and Trade Regimes in Batam, Bintan and Karimun

Kostka, K., and H. Hortig. Mapping via Google Maps, Wikimapia, Google Earth, AirBnb, October 2019 to March 2020.

ESDM OneMap. Minyak dan Gas. https://geoportal.esdm.go.id/migas/ (accessed December 2019).

BatamIndo Industrial Park, Batam

Open Street Map (OSM). Open source geo-referenced information, data retrieved in November 2019.

Kostka, K., and H. Hortig. Mapping via Google Maps, Wikimapia, Google Earth, November 2019.

Bintan Beach International Resort, Bintan

Open Street Map (OSM). Open source geo-referenced information, data retrieved in February 2020.

Kostka, K., and H. Hortig. Mapping via Google Maps, Wikimapia, Google Earth, February 2020.

Section 2: Politics

Straat Riouw, 1840

Straat Riouw met plan: Binnen-Reede van Riouw. 1840. Nationaal Archief, Den Haag,

Dienst der Hydrografie: Groen Archief Oost-Indische Archipel, nummer toegang 4.HYDRO122, inventarisnummer 11.31.

Pulau Dompak, Capital of Riau Islands Province
Open Street Map (OSM). Open source geo-referenced information, data retrieved in January 2020.

Program Studi ilmu Administrasi Negara Fakultas ilmu Sosial dan Ilmu Politik Universitas Maritim Raja Ali Haji Tanjungpinang. "Implementasi Kebijakan Pemerintah Dalam Meningkatkan Pulau Dompak Sebagai Pusat Pemerintahan Provinsi Kepulauan Riau". http://repository.umrah.ac.id/505/1/JURNAL%20ridwan%20pdf.pdf (accessed February 2020).

Kostka, K., and H. Hortig. Mapping via Google Maps, Wikimapia, Google Earth, December to February 2020.

Regencies and Cities of Riau Islands Province
Global Administrative Areas. "GADM Dataset of Global Administrative Areas". https://gadm.org/index.html (accessed November 2019).

Parliamentary Constituency Boundaries in Riau Islands Province
Komisi Pemilihan Umum (KPU). "Parliamentary Constituency Boundaries Riau Islands Province, General Election of 2019". https://mkri.id/public/content/pemilu/KKPU/SK%20273%20THN%202018.pdf (accessed November 2019).

Legislative Elections in Riau Islands Province, 2019
KPU. "Hasil Hitung Suara Pemilu Presiden & Wakil Presiden RI 2019". https://infopemilu.kpu.go.id/pemiludpd2019 (accessed January 2019).

Presidential Elections in Riau Islands Province, 2019
KPU. "Rekapitulasi Hasil Pemilu Legislatif DPR RI 2019". https://pemilu2019.kpu.go.id/#/ppwp/hitung-suara/ (accessed January 2019).

Section III: Social and Environmental Issues
Natural Landscape Elements
Atlas Nasional Indonesia. Atlas SDA Nasional Dan Pembangunan Berkelanjutan. https://atlas.big.go.id/eatlas1/Ebook/pilih/12 (accessed November 2019).

Global Forest Watch. "Malaysian Peat Land". http://data.globalforestwatch.org/datasets/8d8462fca7b74b298598490b85d3bd44_9?geometry=85.922%2C0.353%2C133.427%2C8.018 (accessed November 2019).

UN Environment World Conservation Monitoring Centre. 2010. "Global Mangroves Watch". http://data.unep-wcmc.org/datasets/45 (accessed December 2019).

———. 2018. "Global Distribution of Seagrasses". http://data.unep-wcmc.org/datasets/7 (accessed November 2019).

Protected Nature
Asian Development Bank. "Coral Reef Rehabilitation and Management Program: Coral

Triangle Initiative Project (RRP INO 46421)". https://www.adb.org/sites/default/files/linked-documents/46421-001-sd-01.pdf (accessed November 2019).

Kementerian Kelautan dan Perikanan. "Peta Kawasan Konservasi Perairan, Pesisir dan Pulau-Pulau Kecil". http://bpsplpadang.kkp.go.id/pubs/uploads/files/PETA%20KKPD1(1).jpg (accessed October 2019).

Konservasi dan Keanekaragaman Hayati Laut. "Marine Protected Area Data". http://kkji.kp3k.kkp.go.id/index.php/en/marine-protected-area-data?group_by=mstmpabasic_en___Province (accessed November 2019).

Protected Planet. "World Database on Protected Areas (WDPA)". https://www.protectedplanet.net (accessed November 2019).

Transformation of Batam

Longman Atlas. 2005. *Singapore and the World*. Singapore: Pearson Education Asia Pte. Ltd.

Rencana Pola Ruang Kabupaten Kota Tanjungpinang (RTRW TP). 2008. Bappada Kabupaten Bintan.

Spatial Planning for 2010–2030 Batam-Bintan-Karimun. 2011. Rencana Tata Ruang Kawasan Batam, Bintan dan Karimun (RTR Kawasan BBK), Bappada Kota Batam.

Mosques

Kostka, K., and H. Hortig. Mapping via Google Maps, Wikimapia, Google Earth, March 2019.

Direktorat Urusan Agama Islam dan Pembinaan Syariah. "Sistem Informasi Masjid". http://simas.kemenag.go.id/index.php/profil/masjid/287329/ (accessed December 2019).

Mosques in Batam, Bintan and Karimun

Kostka, K., and H. Hortig. Mapping via Google Maps, Wikimapia, Google Earth, March 2019.

Topalovic, M., H. Hortig, and K. Kostka. 2016. "Sources for the SIJORI Maps". In *The SIJORI Cross-Border Region: Transnational Politics, Economics, and Culture*, edited by F. Hutchinson and T. Chong, pp. 465–70. Singapore: ISEAS – Yusof Ishak Institute.

Ethnic Communities

BPS. 2010. Indonesia's Population Census. "Statistics on Ethnicity in Indonesia's Districts". https://sp2010.bps.go.id (accessed October 2019).

Batam West Coast, Shipping Industry

Open Street Map (OSM). Open source geo-referenced information, data retrieved in December 2019.

Kostka, K., and H. Hortig. Mapping via Google Maps, Wikimapia, Google Earth, December to January 2020.

Bintan East Coast, Trikora Beach

Open Street Map (OSM). Open source geo-referenced information, data retrieved in December 2019.

Kostka, K., and H. Hortig. Mapping via Google Maps, Wikimapia, Google Earth, February 2020.

Conclusion
Riau Islands Province and Batam, Bintan and Karimun
For source description, see the previous chapters.

INDEX

www.ingramcontent.com/pod-product-compliance
Lightning Source LLC
Chambersburg PA
CBHW080123220326
41598CB00032B/4939